System Programming

Vol. I

Revised Edition

Jin-Jwei Chen

Chen Publishing LLC

System Programming

June 2024 – Revised edition (240606)

December 2020 – First printing

ISBN: 978-1-7361930-0-6

Dedication

To my loving parents, SoonDer Chen and BauUyi Gor Chen, my grandpa, JonSern Chen, and my grandpa-in-law, WounSwu Gor, for their loves, sacrifices and encouragements. To my very handsome and wonderful twin sons, Stephen and Jason, and my beautiful granddaughter Olivia for the joy they bring. To my ex-wife, JinRwei Lai, for her support.

Preface

This book is meant to be a first course in system programming for students of computer science or engineering major at undergraduate or graduate level (either a one-year System Programming course or a one-semester System Programming followed by another semester of Network Programming). It is also meant to be a reference or self-study guide for computer professionals already working in the computer software industry.

This book aims at providing a systematic education to readers in cross-platforms software development at the system level using POSIX APIs. It covers fundamental concepts, knowledge, issues, technologies, techniques, skills and solutions in system programming space. It discusses basic operating system APIs required in developing various system software products including database systems, networking and distributed systems, operating systems and tools, cluster systems, client-server applications and many others.

APIs from the POSIX Standard (2018 edition) are used whenever applicable. Example programs included in the book are meant to be portable across most, if not all, platforms. Almost all example programs are tested in RedHat Linux, IBM AIX, Oracle/Sun Solaris, HP HP-UX, and Apple Darwin except those in the network security (OpenSSL) chapter which are tested in Linux and Apple Darwin only. The networking programs are also tested in Windows platform as well so long as Windows support is available.

POSIX APIs introduced in the book include file operations, signals, process management, interprocess communications, multithreading, concurrency control, shared memory, network socket programming, socket options and performance tuning of network applications.

For extremely high-performance concurrency control, designing and implementing your own locking routines in assembly language is introduced. Performance gains of up to 80+% are observed. Program examples in Intel x86, IBM Power PC, Oracle/Sun SPARC, HP PARISC, and HP/DEC Alpha processors are provided.

Advanced security using OpenSSL is also discussed. Example programs doing message digest, HMAC, encryption, decryption, PKI, digital signature and SSL/TLS are presented. How to create self-signed X.509 certificates, how to create, use and verify certificate chains in doing SSL/TLS, and how to require client authentication in SSL/TLS are also covered.

Many common real-world problems in system software, distributed systems and cross-platform development are presented and very simple, elegant, and once-for-all solutions are provided. Update loss, cross-endian, alignment, versioning, backward compatibility, reentrance, mutual exclusion, performance comparisons of various mutual exclusion technologies, producer-consumer problem, thread-local storage, fixing dangling mutex, avoiding deadlocks, asynchronous connect, automatic reconnect, multicast, using fixed or dynamic ports, shared memory, system tuning, and design of error codes and error handling, just to name a few. These examples illustrate programming is an art of knowing how to do the minimum and achieve the maximum.

In addition, software design principles and programming tips for developing first-class computer software are discussed.

Why do I write this book?

Working in the computer software industry in the U.S. for over three decades, I have had the opportunities and privileges to work on a very wide range of system software products, including development of AT&T UNIX System V Release 3 and 4 for multiprocessor computers, development of multiple database systems, clustered systems, network management, Web Server, Web services and application server products. I have learned a lot from these experiences. I have seen excellent quality system software like AT&T Unix System V R3 and R4. Yet I have also worked on the worst system software products I have ever seen.

Throughout my career, my frustrations built up over the years after seeing countless unnecessary complexities in the software products that I had to work on during the late stage of my career. I have seen enormous unnecessary complexities in some of the world-famous system software products used around the world. The extraordinary inefficiencies and problems within the products, the excessive time and resources wasted in supporting, maintaining and improving the products, and the so many unpleasant disruptions to the customers' operations are just unimaginable!

I saw so many problems that can be solved in much simpler ways with very substantially less lines of code having top-notch quality. So many things can be simplified by 50 to 100 times. It made me feel so strongly that I need to share what I learned and know.

There are just too many very basic problems that did not get solved the right way which creates incredible amount of completely unnecessary complexities and work, resulting in way too many bugs, lowering product quality, wasting too much time and resources, unnecessarily reducing the productivity and customer satisfaction, and very significantly increasing the product development and maintenance costs.

I saw too many software engineers working in the computer software industry today are so inadequately educated and trained that many of the basics are not even done right or practiced. Yes, thanks to the fast expansions of computer applications and creation of so many jobs. But the computer software industry as a whole can be and needs to be a lot more efficient and productive. Many software products need to be much leaner, simpler, less buggy, easier to use, and less costly to maintain and support. The developers need to be better trained and more knowledgeable, the software products need to be much better designed and have much higher quality, and the end users deserve a much more productive and pleasant experience.

Besides, I see a software quality crisis from two other places. First, from the poor quality of many world-famous system software products produced by world-leading companies and the huge blunders these companies made in recent years in immediately cancelling new releases whose mistakes are so obvious to me. I see a lack of expert software engineers, architects and managers. Second, going through the computer courses taught at hundreds of top universities, I see lots of more colleges are teaching object-oriented programming in Java/C++ than system programming in C while we all know that although object-oriented paradigm is conceptually very neat, its hierarchical nature just does not model most real-world problems very well except a very small number of high-level applications. A huge number of objected-oriented database systems were born in 1980s and all of them faded away is just an example of object-orientation is not really a best choice for system software.

This is why I decided to write this book. I hope through reading a book like this, computer software engineers all become very well prepared for their jobs, knowing what technologies, basic building blocks and tools are available and how to solve many of the basic problems the right way, build extremely lean and solid foundations and robust infrastructures at the core of every software product they develop.

Most importantly, after reading this book, I believe readers will not stray into a wrong direction while trying to figure out how to solve a problem in the very first place, which is where all of the unnecessary complexities start. Readers will know enough to not go into a wrong direction in formulating the solution to a problem and avoid all the unnecessary complexities.

I also hope that when people read the software code you develop, they will say, "Wow, this was developed by some real expert!", "It's very easy to read and understand this code. It's a real treat!", "This software is very easy to maintain because it simply has no bugs."

I have always believed that the purpose of a person's life is to provide a better environment for the future generations. And part of that is to pass on what our generation has learned as a payback to what our ancestors have passed on to us so that we could build upon. This is my intended paying back. Writing this book is my way of fulfilling that responsibility.

Finishing this book completes the biggest dream of my life; I have always had the dream of wanting to help out others and the young. Hopefully, this book will make a tiny contribution to the world's computer education, computer software industry, and to better the quality of software products developed around the world. I'll be very happy if it does.

English is my third language. I really wish my English is better than this. However, I have tried my best. So if you find any errors, mistakes or imperfectness, please pardon me. Thank you very much for your support. I hope you will find what I share here useful. Happy reading!

Sincerely,

Jin-Jwei Chen

Table of Contents

Volume I

System Programming

11 More on Interprocess Communication Mechanisms 639

Volume II

16 Software Design Principles and Programming Tips......................................1343

System Programming

1 Basic Computer Concepts

This chapter introduces to you some of the very basic concepts about computers. It discusses the basic makeup of a computer, in both hardware and software.

1-1 Two Necessary Parts -- Hardware and Software

Computers are problem-solving tools for human being.
In some way, a computer is like a person. It carries out tasks and it can memorize things.

Just like a live person always has the physical body and spiritual soul, a computer in operation always has two components: **hardware** and **software**. Hardware is the circuitry and devices that actually do computations and perform tasks. But tasks are accomplished by hardware executing the software. In other words, computers are driven by software. Computer hardware alone is like a dead person. The software makes a computer come alive. It determines what a computer does. That is, software defines tasks a computer executes. A computer in operation always has both hardware and software working together. Either one alone won't accomplish anything. Computer hardware is like a person's physical body whereas computer software is like a person's spirit and thinking.

Software is the logic. It embodies the complex logic of how to accomplish tasks in a language the computer understands. The term software generally refers to any and all programs that a computer executes.

A **program** is a sequence of instructions that tell the computer how to accomplish a task step by step. Computer software engineers develop programs to solve different problems using computers. We human being use computers to solve problems and have them do work for us. When a computer does work, its hardware is executing some software program(s).

A program in execution is called a process. In other words, a **process** is an instance of a software program in execution. The same software program can have multiple instances in execution at the same time on a given computer. In this case, multiple processes exist in the computer system that is executing the same program, but usually with different data. For example, one may start multiple web browsers on his or her computer where each browser is visiting a different web site, viewing different web pages. In this case, multiple instances of the web browser program are in execution at the same time while they are computing on different data.

In other words, a computer does work by executing software programs on the computer hardware. The software program being executed may be the operating system or some application programs, or both.

```
---------------------
| Computer software |
---------------------
          |
---------------------
| Computer hardware |
---------------------
```

Figure 1-1 Two necessary components of a computer

1-2 Overview of Computer Hardware

```
------------
|   CPU    |/------------------------------------------\
|          |            Control Bus                    /
| -------  |\------------------------------------------
| | ALU |  |
| -------  |-------------------------------------------\
|          |            Address Bus                    /
| -------- |-------------------------------------------
| |Control| |                              | I/O Controller
| |Unit   | |       |              |        ---------
| -------- |    ---------    -------------  | ------ |
|----------| |   |         |  |    DMA    | | |      | |
||Registers|| | Memory |  |Controller|  | |      | |<-> I/O Devices
|----------| |   |         |  |           | | ------ |
|          |    ---------    -------------  ---------
| -------  |        |              |            |
| | MMU |  |        |              |
| -------  |/------------------------------------------\
| -------  |            Data Bus                       /
| |Cache|  |\------------------------------------------
| -------  |
------------
```

Figure 1-2 Computer Hardware Organization

As shown in Figure 1-2, in a simplified view, a computer is comprised of a processor (the so-called CPU, which stands for Central Processing Unit), some memory, some Input/Output controllers, and some peripheral devices such as keyboard, mouse, monitor, speaker, disks, and network interface/ adapter cards.

We will describe each of these components in the section below.

1-2-1 Functions of Various Computer Hardware Components

Now let's look a bit deeper into each hardware component shown in Figure 1-2.

1-2-1-1 Processor

The central processing unit (CPU, for short) is the brain of the computer. It is the unit that does the actual computations and control of operations

2

in the computer. Typically, a CPU consists of one arithmetic and logical unit (ALU), one control unit, a number of registers, a memory management unit (MMU) and optionally a processor cache.

Many modern computers may also have an additional floating-point or math processor that is separate from the regular processor for speeding up massive floating-point operations often seen in graphics or games applications. It is called a co-processor because its role is to assist CPU. Originally, it is called an FPU (Floating-point Processing Unit). Now it's often called a GPU (Graphics Processing Unit) because it's specially designed to accelerate graphics and video rendering. The so-called AI computer is one equipped with one or more very powerful GPUs from companies like NVIDIA with AI application software. Contrary to NVIDIA CEO's claim, programming is still needed. And despite Tesla CEO's claim, AI computers won't take away all human being's jobs!

Be aware that in a high-end computer, a computer may have multiple processors instead of just one. Some may even have dozens or hundreds. These are called multiprocessor computers. It's slightly more complicated but much more powerful because it can perform multiple operations in parallel.

1. ALU

Every computer processor has an arithmetic and logical unit (ALU).
ALU consists of digital electronic circuits that carry out various arithmetic operations such as addition, subtraction, multiplication and division, as well as logical operations such as AND, OR, NOT, etc.
When a computer computes, most of the time it is performing some arithmetic or logical operations, comparing or moving data, or making decisions.
Note that nowadays many processors may also have multiple ALUs.

A computer processor's ALU usually consists of an integer execution unit which performs arithmetic operations on integer numbers and a floating-point execution unit which carries out arithmetic operations on floating-point numbers (or the so-called real numbers).

2. Control Unit

A CPU also contains a control unit which controls the overall operations and synchronization of the entire computer. The control unit is like the cop who directs traffic at the intersection of streets. This unit is similar to the central nerve system of a human being. Therefore, the processor is like the brain and the entire neural system of a person.

The sub-functional units in the control unit include instruction fetching unit that is responsible for fetching instructions from the memory into CPU for execution, instruction decoding unit which decodes each assembly language instruction into microcode that actually controls the execution of the instruction, cache control unit, memory segmentation control, and others.

In short, the control unit interprets machine/assembly language instructions, decodes them into microcode that generates control signals to control the operations of various computer hardware components.

3. Registers

In addition to the ALU and control unit, a computer processor normally contains a number of registers in it for temporarily storing data used in various computations. CPU registers are for storing operands and intermediate results of various arithmetic, logical, data movement and control operations.

Note that it's much faster to access a register than a memory location because registers are located inside the CPU itself. Therefore, frequently used or currently needed operands and data items are typically stored in CPU registers rather than in memory to improve performance.

Each register has a name which is often an English letter or two, or a number.

There are at least two types of CPU registers: general-purpose and special-purpose. As its name implies, general-purpose registers are for general use. They can be used in many different types of instructions and operations. They are available for programmers to use. Special-purpose registers have designated functions. They assist program executions and are generally not directly available for use by programmers. Special-purpose registers include the program counter, status register, stack pointer, index registers, the accumulator and others.

Remember that general-purpose registers are very small amount of memory storage located within the processor itself. They are usually used to store operands and partial results of the operations that the processor is currently executing.

A. General-Purpose Registers

Each processor usually has a number of general-purpose CPU registers. They can be used as temporary storage within the CPU by all programs. Storing frequently used data, operands and intermediate results in these registers inside the CPU is faster than storing them in memory.

Remember these general-purpose registers are shared by all programs running on the computer. Therefore, to use any of them, a program must save its current contents before using it and restore it after use. Generally, programs push the register's contents onto the stack to save it and pop it from the stack to restore. If you program in assembly language, you actually do this yourself at the top of your routine to save register contents and at the bottom to restore them. If you program in high-level languages such as C, C++, C# or Java, the compiler does it for you.

This is necessary because you don't know who was using these registers before you (i.e. right before your program or routine starts executing) and that user (actually program) could be in the middle of some computation when it gets interrupted or context-switched to your program.

B. Special-Purpose Registers

Stack Pointer

Every computer has a stack. A **stack** is special memory area (the so-called stack segment) that implements a Last In First Out (LIFO) data structure.

A stack supports two operations: **PUSH** and **POP**. Pushing some data into stack means storing or saving the data in stack and popping it means retrieving it back. The unique characteristic of a stack is it is a sequential ordered list. The last data item pushed into stack is stored at the top of the stack and is the item you get back if you perform a POP operation.

The **stack pointer** register holds the memory address of the top of the stack. It tracks where the stack grows and shrinks to. The value of the stack pointer is automatically increased and decreased as PUSH and POP operations are performed.

Stack is used for temporarily saving aside some data and parameter passing during subroutine or function calls. It is also used to store local variables declared and used in subroutines/functions.

Stack is available to programmers. As a C programmer, the local variables you declare within a function are normally allocated on stack. Function parameters are often passed via the stack from the caller function to the callee function as well during the invocation. The space allocation is done by the C compiler.

Note that programmers don't use the stack pointer directly. They use stack which will cause the value inside the stack pointer to be changed automatically because it is used to track the top of stack.

As an assembly language programmer, stack is available to you for use via the PUSH and POP instructions. And you have to know how to use it. Note that a computer executes multiple programs all the time. In a time-shared computer, the processor is shared by all users and all programs. In order to serve multiple users and programs, a processor interleaves these programs by executing each of them a very small fraction of time. Because of this, a processor can leave the program it is executing at any time and switch to another, due to reasons such as context-switching or hardware interrupts. Therefore, when a processor comes to execute your program or any program, it may be (and most likely) that it was just in the middle of some other totally unrelated program computation and leaving some intermediate results in some of the CPU registers. Therefore, your program has a responsibility to preserve and not mess up the previous computation.

For this reason, **the unwritten rule in assembly language programming is that every assembly language routine MUST save aside the contents of all CPU registers that it will use onto stack and restore them when it finishes using them**. The convention is at the very beginning of every assembly language routine, you push the contents of all the registers your routine will use into stack. And at end of your routine, right before return, you pop them up from stack to restore them. By doing so, it guarantees that your program's use of the CPU registers, which are shared between all programs, won't interfere with any other programs. It ensures programs do not step on one another's toes.

Note that as with any other resources, stack has a limited size. It's extremely important that you know what the maximum size of the stack is on the machine you program so that you don't exceed it. **'Stack overflow'** is a frequent source of program errors. This error means your program tries to use more stack memory than is allowed by the system. Perhaps, for instance, it allocates huge arrays locally. A program usually dies when it encounters the 'stack overflow' error condition. Be aware that most systems let you tune or adjust the maximum stack size. As a programmer of a high-level language such as C and Java, one needs to be concerned with this issue.

Program Counter (PC)

1 Basic Computer Concepts

Every CPU has a special register for keeping track of which instruction within the current program it is executing so that it won't miss any. That register is called **Program Counter (PC)** or **Instruction Pointer (IP)**. The Program Counter register always points to the assembly language instruction in memory that is to be fetched and executed next. This means its contents is the memory address of the next instruction to be fetched and executed.

As CPU fetches an instruction from memory, the contents of the Program Counter is automatically incremented by one to point to the next instruction. This results in a sequential execution through the program instructions. In case of executing a jump or branch instruction which alters the execution order, the target memory address of the jump/branch is calculated and that value is loaded into the Program Counter such that the next instruction fetched and executed will come from the new memory location. The control flow of the program is thus changed as a result of executing such a jump or branch instruction.

Each instruction of a program being executed is stored at a certain memory location and it has a memory address. For instance, when you write the following statement in C:

```
goto label1;
```

or

```
if (x == 1)
    x = x + y;
else
    x = x * y;
```

The code will get translated into an unconditional jump or branch instruction in the former and a sequence of instructions including a conditional jump or branch instruction in the latter. The operand of the jump/branch instruction will be the memory address (often in an offset or relative form) of the instruction to be executed after the jump/branch. In executing such an instruction, the absolute address of this destination will be computed and loaded in the Program Counter such that the next instruction to be fetched and executed comes from this new location, rather the one following the current instruction.

The Program Counter or Instruction Pointer register is not available to programmers.

Accumulator

In addition to the program counter, accumulator is another typical example of a special-purpose register. However, the difference is that accumulator is for programmers to use whereas programmers have no access to program counter at all.

Accumulator is mainly for use in performing an addition operation which is one of the very common operations a computer performs. Accumulator is used to hold one of the source operands and the result (i.e. the sum) of an add operation.

Status (or Flag) Register

Every processor always has a status register too. A **status register** is used to record the status of the current operation. This register is a collection of status bits, or the so-called flags. Each bit records a different status. Most common examples of status bits include whether the current operation generates carry, overflow, or zero result. Others include whether interrupt is currently enabled/allowed.

Index Register

Index registers provide indexed addressing method/mode. It is used to hold the base address in an array processing so that programs can easily loop through all array elements by simply incrementing the index value by one in each iteration.

Wrap-up on Registers

For those who program in the C language, if you ever use the keyword 'register' in your C program, it is telling the compiler to keep the data in one of the general-purpose registers inside the CPU for fast accesses.

For those who program in low-level assembly language, you will need to know how many registers a CPU has, what their names are, what they are for, what restrictions each one has, and use them properly in your LOAD, STORE, and arithmetic and logical instructions.

For example, once author was programming in assembly language on IBM Power processor in 2002. I noticed if I used one of the CPU registers in an assembly language routine, the entire computer would crash immediately. It seems a security hole and CPU design flaw to me because that gives hackers a very easy way to take down a computer. I have to say that I never had any similar experience with the rest of many other processors that I have programmed.

```
                              CPU
      -----------------------------------------------------------
     |    ------------------                                      |
     |   | General-Purpose  |                                     |
     |   | Registers        |        . . .                        |
     |    ------------------                                       |
     |                                                            |
     |    ------------------          ------------------          |
     |   | Program Counter  |        |   Accumulator    |         |
     |    ------------------          ------------------          |
     |                                                            |
     |    ------------------          ------------------          |
     |   | Stack Pointer    |        | Status Register  |         |
     |    ------------------          ------------------          |
     |                                                            |
     |    ------------------                                      |
     |   | Index Register   |                                     |
     |    ------------------                                      |
     |           :                                                |
      -----------------------------------------------------------
```

Figure 1-3 CPU Registers

4. Processor Cache

It's very important to mention that modern computer processors all have some processor cache (on-chip memory). A processor cache is a very small amount of very fast memory that exists inside each processor for improving performance. The idea is that getting information from inside the processor itself is faster than having to get it from the memory outside the processor. As semiconductor technology advances, CPU designers find that they can put more and more processor cache into each processor to aid performance. Processors with 8+ MB of processor cache are not uncommon. Normally, the bigger the processor cache, the better the performance.

5. MMU and Others

Besides the major units mentioned above, a processor often also has the memory management unit (MMU) which supports virtual memory with address translation via **segmentation** and/or **paging**. There are some other functional units, too.

MMU is the hardware circuitry that manages the computer memory, by dividing it into segments and/or pages, such that the entire memory can be shared among all programs running concurrently or simultaneously on a computer. Through the memory management software in the operating system kernel, MMU makes it possible for a computer to be able to execute multiple programs at the same time and without mixing it up. It also makes it possible for a program to run no matter where it is placed in memory, and only part of the entire program needs to be resident in memory.

We will discuss shared memory in chapter 10 later in this book. That software technology is made possible by the MMU hardware component. MMU provides translation of virtual memory addresses into physical addresses which on one hand provides the isolation and protection between different processes and on the other enables the shared memory technology.

6. Multiprocessors

Be aware that many computers, especially those at high end, are often equipped with multiple processors. In that case, the processors often share the memory, buses and I/O devices. Additional arbitration or control circuitry is needed to allow multiple processors to share the same set of memory and I/O devices without stepping on each other's foot. In addition, cache coherency is also a typical problem to solve in these computers to ensure data integrity when these processors cache the same piece of data in each of their own processor cache.

7. Multi-core Processors

Most modern processors are also multi-core CPUs, meaning within each processor there is more than one processing core or ALU that allows the processor to execute multiple computations or instruction streams at the same time. For instance, a 4-core CPU will be capable of executing four distinct arithmetic/logical operations at the same time.

This multiplicity is embedded inside each processor, in contrast to the multiprocessors mentioned in the preceding paragraph where the multiplicity exists outside each processor. As you can imagine, a modern computer could have multiple processors where each of them is a multi-core processor. It would be very interesting to program this type of computers such that they deliver optimal performance.

8. Word Size

One very important attribute of each computer processor is its **word size.**
This is the amount of information a computer processor can compute or
operate on in a typical operation. For instance, most computer processors
today can operate on (e.g. add) 64-bit of information in a typical
instruction. Such processors are therefore called 64-bit processors.
Normally, with everything else being equal, the bigger a processor's word
size is, the more information a computer can process in each instruction,
the faster it is.

Note that although most instructions of a processor operate on its word size,
there are always instructions which operate on smaller amount of data
(for instance, one byte or 32 bits) as well.

9. Clock Frequency

Nowadays, the central processing unit is almost always made on a single
silicon chip delivered in a single package, the so-called microprocessor.
It usually contains billions of transistors, which is the most basic active
element making up many of the computer circuitries. It also typically runs
a clock between two to six giga-hertz (GHz) or beyond, at which speed it
operates. The higher clock frequency a computer runs at, the faster it does
things and at the same time the more heat it generates. Cooling off a
high-frequency processor is often a challenge. Overheating could cause a
computer to automatically shut down itself.

Computer clock frequency has advanced dramatically in the past. It has
increased 1000 times from 1 MHz in mid-1980s to 1 GHz in March of 2000.
It has relatively slowed down a little bit in recent years because it may
be approaching the absolute limit of physics. Clock frequencies of computer
processors between 3 to 6 GHz are common these days.

1-2-1-2 Memory (ROM and RAM)

The computer memory is sometimes also called main memory.

Computers do things for human being by executing programs.
The programs currently being executed by the computer are stored in the
memory, at least partially. Each program is a (long) sequence of instructions.
A single-processor computer with a single-core processor can execute
only one instruction at a time. The instruction the computer is currently
executing must reside inside the processor itself. This means, before
a program instruction can be executed, it must be fetched from the main
memory and brought into the processor.

Since the processor has all the complex circuitry for doing computations
and control, it just doesn't have enough room for storing all program
instructions. Therefore, there is a need of the main memory to store the
programs that the processor currently executes and the data they use.

In the very old days, computer main memory was made of magnetic cores.
Nowadays, it is made of semiconductor. There are two types of semiconductor
memories: **ROM** (stands for Read-Only Memory) and **RAM** (Random Access Memory).
ROM usually constitutes only a very small portion of the computer memory.
Its contents, once written or burned into, are readable only.

One nice feature with ROM is its contents remain after power is off.

RAM is readable and writeable and ROM is read-only, not writeable.
RAM is used to store programs the computer is currently executing and
the data the programs are operating on. When power goes off, information
stored in RAM disappears. Therefore, to persist computation results,
information must be written from memory to some permanent storage media
such as disks before power goes off.

The bulk of the computer memory is RAM.

ROM typically has a small capacity and is used to store the small program
that a computer must execute immediately after it is powered on.
This program is stored at a fixed address so that the computer always knows
where to start. The program usually does the initialization of the
computer hardware, especially the input and output subsystems and devices.
This program is sometimes called the **BIOS** (Basic Input Output System).
In many cases, it is also called the 'firmware'. A firmware is a little piece
of software used to control some specific hardware and it is typically stored
in an EPROM or flash ROM because it seldom changes.

Through reading the bootstrap program stored in ROM and executing it,
the computer gets its own feet on the ground. After initializing the
basic hardware input/output devices, it will proceed to find the image of
the operating system software on hard disk, load the operating system
into the main memory (RAM), and start executing the operating system.
And then the whole computer is open for business.

Each time you power on your computer after you power it off, it still boots
up. That's because, as we said, computer's small bootstrap code is stored
in ROM and the bigger operating system code is stored in storage media such
as hard disks, both of which are persistent.

Modern computers often make the program in the ROM updateable by using a
special type of ROM named **EPROM** (Erasable ROM). If you ever update the
firmware on your computer, this is exactly it. You erase the current version
of the firmware and overwrite it with a newer version.

Most of the time, when we say computer memory we are referring to the
read-writeable portion of it. That is, we are talking about the RAM.
As mentioned above, the ROM portion of the computer memory has a very
specific function. Today's computers usually have 4-32 GB of RAM or more.

1-2-1-3 Bus

Buses are communication paths inside a computer. Each bus is a bunch of
parallel wires carrying information between hardware components of the
computer.

Functionally, there are at least three types of buses in a computer:
address bus, data bus and control bus.

Address Bus

The **address bus**, which carries address information, allows the processor
to send an address to select a memory or I/O register location that it

wants to communicate with, namely, to read data from or write data into.

The address bus is uni-directional. It goes only from the processor to the memory and I/O devices because it's always the processor that determines which memory or I/O location it needs to read from or write into.

Each wire/bit in the address bus has a corresponding pin on the processor.

The size (or width) of the address bus of a computer processor determines the absolute maximum amount of physical memory that a computer using the processor can have. A computer can have a less amount of physical memory installed, but the total amount of memory installed can never exceed this absolute number. For instance, if the address bus of a computer processor is 32 bits wide, then a computer using this processor can have up to 2^{32} bytes, which is 4 gigabytes (GB), of memory.

Sizes of the address buses of today's computers all exceed 32 bits. This means they can all address up to more than 4 GB of main memory.

Data Bus

The **data bus** carries the actual data currently being read or written by the computer processor. The data bus is bi-directional.
It allows data to flow in and out between the hardware components.
In general, a computer processor can read data from and write data into memory and I/O devices except those input-only (e.g. keyboard and ROM) and output-only (e.g. display) devices.

Each wire/bit in the data bus has a corresponding pin on the processor.

The size or width of the data bus is the computer processor's word size. It represents the maximum size of the actual data that the processor can operate on at a time in normal cases. It does not necessarily mean that the computer always operates at that amount of data all the time.
For example, in a 64-bit processor, its data bus is 64-bit wide, meaning it can move 64-bit of information in parallel in or out of the CPU at one operation or instruction. It also means it can add up two 64-bit numbers in one instruction. However, there may exist some instructions that operate on less than 64 bits of information.

Control Bus

In addition to the address bus and data bus, there are a number of other control signals that go between the processor and other components. Collectively, these control signals form the so-called 'control bus'. These signals coordinate the operations of the hardware components of a computer. For example, there is the clock signal that goes to almost all of the computer hardware components to synchronize the operations among all of them. In some way it's like the drum in a musical band.

As another example, there is one (or more) pin on the processor that carries the Interrupt signal, which allows an I/O device to interrupt the processor and tell the processor that it is ready for I/O.

Most control signals are uni-directional. Some go from the CPU to other components. Some go in the opposite direction. That is, some control signals are input to the CPU and some are output.

The control signals are very important. However, as a software developer, you normally do not even need to know they exist.

Sizes of Address Bus and Data Bus

It seems that many people often are confused by two numbers with computer -- the size (or width) of the address bus and that of the data bus.

Please notice that for a given computer processor (and thus computers built with such a processor) the size of the data bus is completely independent of the size of its address bus. They are usually different, too.

For example, in the old days, during the 1990s, for quite a long time, most computers were 32-bit computers. Their data buses were all 32-bit wide. Coincidentally, some of their address buses were 32-bit wide as well for some time. However, some of these computers were updated to have a 36-bit address bus for demand of more memory.

Nowadays, most computer processors are 64-bit processors. They certainly all have a 64-bit data bus. However, their address bus is usually less than 64-bit. Some have, for instance, a 48-bit address bus.

```
         Memory bus
                                    _____    _____
 _____     _____    _____  | I/O        |   |         |
|       |   |         |   |       | |            |   |         |
| CPU   |<--->| Memory |  | I/O   | |Controllers|<-->|Devices|
|       |   |         |   |Devices| |            |   |         |
|       |   |         |   |       | |_____|   |_____|
 _____     _____    _____
   ^             ^           ^            ^
   |             |           |            |
   |             |           |            |
   v             v           v            v
  ------------------------------------------------
              I/O bus
```

Figure 1-4 Computer buses

1-2-1-4 Input/Output Controllers

Input/output controllers are also called peripheral controllers. They control the input and/or output devices that are attached to the computer. Examples include the hard disk controller that controls the input/output operations to and from the disk drives and the network adapter that handles the network packets sent to and received from the network.

Input/output controllers enable input and/or output devices, which operate at varying speeds typically much slower than the processor, to be connected to the processor. They handle the communications and data exchanges between the processor and the input/output devices, bridging the speed gap.

Normally, the processor is busy executing various programs. When an input or output device is ready for data communication, the device typically sends an interrupt signal via one of the control bus pins to let the processor know. The processor will then temporarily put whatever it is doing aside and go executing a special device interrupt service routine (ISR, for short) to take care of the device. After the ISR, the processor will resume what it was doing before the interrupt.

1-2-1-5 DMA Controllers

Notice that there is the **DMA** (Direct memory Access) controller in the computer organization diagram in Figure 1-2.

The **DMA controller** allows the computer to do large amount of information transfer between an input or output device and the memory without the CPU's intervention. Normally, an input or output device is much slower than the CPU. If the CPU has to be involved in every byte of information transferred to and from an I/O device, then the computer will be slowed down a lot. To improve I/O performance, DMA is used where the CPU sets up an I/O operation by allocating needed memory buffer and setting up the beginning addresses and the number of bytes to be transferred and then just kicks off the transfer and lets the DMA controller take care of the actual transfer. When the I/O transfer is done, the DMA controller or the I/O device will notify the CPU by sending it an interrupt signal. This frees up the CPU during the actual I/O operation.

An I/O using DMA via a DMA controller is also called direct I/O because the I/O (i.e. the actual data transfer) happens directly in-between the memory and the I/O device without CPU handling it. (Note that later in the file I/O chapter we will discuss another file system feature that is also named direct I/O. Be aware that these two are not related. For this reason, we call DMA I/O as DMA transfer. Direct here means bypassing CPU.)

1-2-1-6 Basic Input/Output Devices

Just like a human has mouth, eyes and ears, a computer has a number of different input and/or output devices to communicate with human being and its outside world.

The most typical computer input devices include keyboard and mouse. They allow computer users to enter data and commands into the computer. Computers often take orders from human operators via these input devices. Of course, there are many other computer input devices. Examples include Game joystick, microphone and others.

The most typical computer output devices include display monitor and printers. They allow users to see the computation results, some of the computation processes, and information stored in the computer.

Basic input and output devices such as keyboard, mouse and display monitor enable human interaction with computers. Other input and output devices described below serve other slightly different purposes.

1-2-1-7 Storage Devices

Storage devices are part of the input and output devices. They provide massive permanent storage of information.

Computers not only do complex computations but store a lot of information. As you already know, information stored in computer memory (except that in ROM) disappears once the power gets turned off. Therefore, in order to store and remember things for users, computers need permanent storage.

The most common computer persistent storage device is the hard disk drives. They sometimes are simply called hard disks or disks. Disks give the computer ability to remember things for us because information stored on disks remains after the power goes off.

A computer hard disk is an electro-magnetic device. It is controlled by electrical circuits. It usually has a number of magnetic plates (or discs) that can record information permanently stacked together on an axis. The stack of plates rotates at a speed of around 5400 to 7200 RPM (Round Per Minute), or even faster. Because the media is magnetic, once recorded, the information stored in it persists even after the power goes off.

Disks have much higher capacity than memory and are usually much cheaper, too. However, it's also much slower than memory. With semiconductor getting cheaper and cheaper, solid-state disks, which are faster, are getting popular.

Each hard disk drive usually comes with two connectors on it -- the power connector and the interface (or device bus) connector. Some disk drives also have jumper pins on them for Master/slave selection or SCSI id setting. The interface connector is hardware interface protocol specific. The interface connector is connected to the disk controller via an interface cable so that the disk controller can send control signals and data to and from the disk drive.

Different hard drive interfaces have existed. They include IDE (Intelligent Drive Electronics or Integrated Drive Electronics), EIDE (Enhanced IDE), ATA (Advanced Technology Attachment), SATA (Serial ATA), PATA (Parallel ATA), SCSI (Small Computer Systems Interface), Fibre Channel and others.

The capacity of hard disk drives just keeps increasing while their prices and sizes keep falling. A typical hard disk drive in the late 1980s had a 5 and 1/4 inch form factor, could store about 300 MB of information and costed more than US$1,000. Nowadays, a 3.5-inch hard drive can store 4 TB (terabytes) or more and costs only about US$100 or less.

Many companies use computers for database applications. These computers usually keep very important information such as personal data of all employees in the company, customer order data, inventory data and so on. The information is very critical to a company's business. Losing it would mean a disaster. Therefore, typical database processing would not consider job done until after the information is correctly and safely saved on some hard disk drive. For those who develop database management software and database applications, redundancy and fault tolerance are usually also required.

Note that there are other types of storage devices, including CD and DVD. DVDs can be read-only or read-writeable. Many computers at big companies' data centers may also have tape drives for backing up data for off-line and/or off-site storage, too.

1-2-1-8 Network Adapters

In the early days, most computers were stand-alone. They are seldom so today.

Instead, most computers are connected to some internal network or the Internet -- the world-wide public computer network that speaks the TCP/IP protocol.

A computer that is connected to a network can communicate with other computers that are also on the network.

Hardware-wise, a computer is physically connected to a computer network via a piece of hardware called the **network adapter card** or **network interface card** (NIC), which in turn is connected to the wire that forms the local network to your computer. This local network may in turn connect to the global Internet via a network router device. For computers at home, the network router needs to go through yet another device called modem to get to the outside Internet via the analog telephone line or cable TV wire that comes to your home. The modem device performs the necessary analog-to-digital signal conversion and vice versa. Nowadays the modem and router at home are combined into a single device.

The network adapter used to be a separate add-on interface card you need to plug into one of the expansion slots on the motherboard of your computer, although many motherboards have an integrated network adapter on it now. Note that a computer can have multiple network adapter cards installed, either for connecting to multiple different networks or as a redundancy.

Today, all laptop computers and cell phones use wireless network interfaces and the WI-FI protocol to connect to network.

1-3 Basic Operations of a Computer

When a computer works, it's always hardware and software working together. Both hardware and software are always needed in order for a computer to function.

Normally computer software products you purchase or download are installed on the hard disks of your computer, usually from software distribution media like CD or DVD or via the network in the case of downloading. This includes the operating system software.

For a software program, including the computer's operating system, to be executed by a computer, it must be loaded from disks into the computer main memory first. Today's computers all use **virtual memory**. Therefore, a program can be only partially loaded into memory when it is being executed.

When executing a program, the computer central processor (CPU) fetches the program instructions from memory into the CPU one at a time and then executes them. The execution of the instruction may involve loading data from memory into some CPU registers (e.g. the LOAD instruction), storing some data from a CPU register into some memory location (e.g. the STORE instruction), or simply adds two numbers that are already in CPU registers (e.g. the ADD instruction).

In addition, the CPU may execute some I/O instruction that actually reads data from some input device (such as keyboard and disks) or writes some data out to some output devices (such as display and disks). The input or output operation can also be to or from a network adapter card when a computer sends a packet to or receives one from network.

Figure 1-5 shows some of the typical basic operations on a computer.

```
                                                          Disk
                                                          Controller
CPU                             Memory                    ------
-----                           -------   -------
|   | fetch program            |     |   |     |  |<------------------|    |
|   | instruction              |     |   |     |  | read program/data |    |
|   |<--------------------|     |     |   |     |  | file              |    |-disks
|   |read data from memory |    |<->|  |     |  |------------------->|    |
|   |<--------------------|     |     |   | DMA |                    |    |
|   |write data to memory  |    |     |   |     |  | write program/data|    |
|   |-------------------->|     |     |   |     |  | file              | ------
|ADD|                     |     |     |   |Ctrlr|                     ------
|SUB|                           |     |   |     |                    |    |
|AND|                           |<->|  |     |  |<------------------|    |
|OR |                           |     |   |     |  | receive net packet |    |-network
|   |                           |     |   |     |  |------------------->|    | wire
|   |                           |     |   |     | ------- send network packet|    |
-----                           -------       ^        ------
  ^                               ^           |                     Network
  |                               |           |                     Adapter
  ----------------------------------------------
```

CPU performs various arithmetic and logical operations
all the times when it executes software programs.

Figure 1-5 Basic Computer operations

1-4 Computer Software

A computer with only hardware and without any software is like a dead
human being. It cannot do anything and is thus useless.

Computer software is a bunch of computer programs. A computer program is
a sequence of instructions or statements that direct the computer to do
certain computations or tasks.

The way that a computer does work for human being is via computer hardware
executing computer software, carrying out the instructions given in the
computer programs it is executing.

Normally, there are many different software products that a computer executes.
Just to boot up and start basic operations, every computer must have an
operating system software installed on it.

The operating system software is the most important one. It's essentially
the first piece of software each computer executes. It is also the software
that a computer executes most of the time. It controls the basic operations
of the entire computer. It makes the computer "open for business".
After a computer starts and boots up with the operating system software,
it is ready for users to login and run any application programs the user
chooses. Running application programs (e.g. text editor software, web
browser) actually gets something done for users.

This section gives a quick overview of computer software in general and
the next section will provide a very brief overview of the operating system
software in particular.

1-4-1 Programming Languages at Different Levels

Every computer software product is written in a computer programming language. There have been a large number of computer programming languages designed for human being to program computers. This section gives a very brief overview in this area.

Machine Language

At the very bottom layer, computer hardware is made up of transistors. A transistor is like a switch. It turns on by getting an input signal and it turns off by getting no input signal. In other words, it operates in binary mode, either on or off. That is why today's computers are not only digital but also binary computers.

This means intrinsically, at the lowest level, a computer operates on having signal and no signal, on and off, or 1 and 0. We therefore say the computer understands only the machine language -- a sequence of 0's and 1's. Because of this, any computer software program must be translated into machine language before they can be understood and executed by a computer. Indeed, the very first computers were programmed in machine languages.

The machine language is what computers understand. But it's not friendly to human being at all. It's also error-prone. As a result, computer scientists soon developed more human-friendly computer programming languages.

Assembly Language

As we explained earlier, one level up from transistors at the very bottom, computers are a bunch of digital electronic circuits that can carry out arithmetic (such as add, subtract, multiple, and divide) and logical (such as AND, OR, NOT) operations. Computers can be programmed at this level, too. The computer language that expresses program instructions at this basic arithmetic and logical operation level is called the assembly language. As a matter of fact, this was the language that many computer scientists used after they realized that programming in machine language is just too 'hard' and not productive enough. Assembly language uses a mnemonic name to represent each machine instruction, for instance, ADD for addition, SUB for subtraction, DIV for division, AND for logical and operation, OR for logical or operation, and NOT for negation, and so on.

Programming in assembly language requires you to have some understanding of computer hardware and how computer operates, what CPU registers the processor has, what they are for, and how I/O is done at the lowest level, etc. It gives you a taste of how computer works at the near bottom level.

Programming in assembly language gives programmers a lot of freedom and flexibility. It allows programmers to write most efficient programs because they directly manipulate computer hardware resources to get the job done.

High Level Programming Languages

Assembly language is certainly an improvement over the machine language. But still, it is very low level. It's still too close to the way computer thinks as opposed to how human thinks. After all, how many people care about using this and that registers. What most of us care about is to solve the problem we have at hand. So there came the high-level programming languages such as C, FORTRAN, COBOL, PASCAL, etc. which make computer programming a bit easier. Programs written in these high-level programming languages must be translated by another program called compiler into machine languages first so that they can be understood and executed by the computer.

This means if you want to program in the C language, then you have got to have a C compiler first. You need the compiler to translate your program such that it can be understood and executed by the computer.

Compiled versus Interpreted Languages

There are actually two types of programming languages: compiled languages and interpreted languages. With a compiled language, you write your program in a language and then you invoke the compiler to translate your program into the machine code and store the compiled program in an executable file. At run time you invoke the executable file to run your program.
In other words, your program is compiled and translated first before it can be executed.

In contrast, with an interpreted language, you write your program and then you run it without first compiling it. Normally you invoke an interpreter to execute your program. The interpreter will translate your program on the fly as it executes it. In other words, your program is translated at run time as it's being executed.

In general, compiled languages have run-time performance advantages over the interpreted languages. This is mainly because compiled programs need no translation at run time and they can be optimized before run time.

Examples of compiled programming languages include C, C++, FORTRAN, COBOL, PASCAL and many others.

Examples of interpreted programming languages include BASIC, Perl, Python, and others.

4GL Languages

The high-level programming languages such as C, C++, FORTRAN, COBOL and PASCAL are considered the third-generation languages.

The 4th generation languages (4GLs), which were very popular back in the 1980's, attempted to bring the high-level programming languages one step even closer to natural languages. These languages use an English-like constructs to program a computer. It reduces the number of lines of code one has to write. It had some degree of success.

Examples of 4th generation languages include PowerBuilder, Foxpro, Ingres 4GL, Progress 4GL, Informix 4GL and many others.

Natural Languages

After so many years of research, natural language computer interfaces have made some good progress. Some robots, special devices and smart phones take natural language instructions from human being. No need to program to use them. Of course, they run some operating system and application software inside.

For those who have used smart phones, you know there exist applications that enable you to talk to your phone and it talks back to you, too. Certainly, there is a long way to go in natural language interfaces with computers. However, it's exciting to see certain progress has been made so far.

Scripting Languages

I think it is incomplete to touch upon the computer programming languages without mentioning the scripting languages. There have been many scripting languages developed and in use for decades. Unix shell script languages are among some of the most popular ones. These languages allow you to assemble a sequence of operating system commands and user programs in a file and execute it to accomplish your task. They are very useful in automating jobs that need to be repeatedly executed.

Note that these scripting languages are almost all interpreted languages.

Summary

Obviously, the higher level the language one can use to program the computer, the easier it is for human. In general, the natural language interfaces will continue to advance and penetrate into more applications. But at the lower system level, most, if not all, of the system programs have been written in C. These include the operating systems, the database management systems, and various networking software products. That will continue for a long time to come because of the extreme high efficiency, performance, power, precision, rigor and simplicity of the C language.

1-5 Operating System

It's very hard to talk about computer software without mentioning arguably the most important piece of computer software -- the operating system.

An operating system is a piece of very complex and sophisticated computer software that controls the basic day-to-day operations of a computer. Without the operating system, a computer won't come alive.

The first and most important computer software that every computer needs is an operating system. The operating system controls the operations of all hardware devices on the computer. For example, when you type in the name of a command or program you want to execute, the operating system software will read that from the computer keyboard, go find that program, load it into computer memory, and start executing it.

When the program or command runs and generates screen output, the operating system will put the output on the screen. If the program opens and reads a file, the file system code of the operating system will locate the file on disk and read in the requested data.

As you can see, the operating system is there to serve users and application programs. It carries out what applications or users want to do and get it done. It makes it easier for users to use the computer and it helps application programs get their jobs done.

A computer usually comes with a hard disk drive with an operating system installed on the hard drive. It also comes with a startup bootstrap program (called BIOS or firmware) stored in the ROM portion of the computer memory. When you first power on a computer, it will load and execute the startup bootstrap little program from the ROM, which will then automatically load the operating system software into the RAM portion of the computer memory and start executing the operating system. With the operating system up and running, a computer is in business. It allows users to login to the computer, start using the computer, and launch their application programs such as web browsers, text editors, email, database applications, and so on.

When a computer goes to work, it first loads the software program(s), be it an operating system or application program, from hard disk into computer main memory. Then the CPU fetches instructions in the program one at a time from memory into the CPU and executes it.

1-5-1 Time-sharing and Multitasking

In this section we discuss two very important features made possible by the operating system software (with support from hardware).

Modern computers are all **time-sharing**, **multi-tasking** computers. This means a computer can execute multiple programs to serve multiple users at the same time. You may remember we said that a single processor computer can execute only one instruction at a time. Given so, how could it execute multiple programs and serve multiple users at the same time? Well, to be exact, a computer executes multiple programs **concurrently**. Illusion is the trick! And difference in speed between computers and human being makes it possible.

Since computers operate at a very high speed, typically at 2 GHz or higher, it takes only about 1 ns (nano-second, 0.000000001 second) or even less for a computer to execute one instruction.

Assuming there are five users using a computer at the same time, each is running his or her own program. We then have five programs loaded into and stored in the computer memory. The way today's computer works is the operating system will schedule the computer processor to execute each of these programs for a very small slice of time (called **time quantum** or time slice), say 1 ms (milli-second, 0.001 second), one after another, and do so repeatedly. As a result, each of these five users will feel like his or her program is being executed by the computer all the time. In other words, due to the computer operating at a much higher speed than human being, by interleaving between multiple programs belonging to multiple users, the computer creates an illusion that all of the users are being fully served at the same time. In other words, the computer executes multiple programs concurrently. However, remember that on a multiprocessor computer, multiple programs are literally being executed in parallel **simultaneously** at exactly the same time.

Another concept worth mentioning is that modern computer operating systems all implement **virtual memory** and **demand paging**. This feature enables computers to execute programs that are only partially resident in the computer memory. In other words, a program does not need to be 100% loaded into the main memory before it can get executed by the processor. This allows a computer to execute programs that are actually bigger than the physical memory in size. It also makes it possible for the computer to concurrently execute multiple programs, where each is only partially resident in memory, at the same time.

1-5-2 Functional Components of the Operating System

As we said, an operating system is a piece of very complex software. It manages the entire computer. Functionally, an operating system has the following components:

- Virtual memory
- File system
- Networking
- Hardware support and device drivers
- Process scheduling
- Security
- Others

The virtual memory component of an operating system kernel implements the virtual memory concept, which essentially gives every program a virtual address space that is normally divided into relocatable segments and/or pages. These segments or pages can be individually loaded into arbitrary location in the main memory on demand. Mapping of a segment or page from the virtual logical space to the physical space is done at load time. Address translation at instruction level is done at run time to translate each virtual memory address into a physical memory address.

The techniques of dividing the entire program address space into segments and/or pages and using mapping and address translation to separate the user's logical address space from the machine's physical memory address space enable the computer to execute a program that is only partially resident in memory. It hence allows a program to be bigger than the physical memory in size. As a software developer, you need to be aware that **translation of a virtual memory address into physical memory address** happens all the time when a program is executed and the memory addresses you see most of the time are virtual, not physical. This address translation is done by the memory management unit (MMU) of the computer processor. It also protects each program from others.

The file system component implements a file system such that users can create, read, write and update files. Each file opened by users is represented by some data structures in the kernel.

The file system component usually has three layers. At top is an abstraction layer named virtual file system that extracts the commonalities of all file systems and makes it easier to support multiple physical file system types in a system. In the middle is the implementation of the actual file system. At the bottom is the disk device driver(s) that performs the actual data input/output to and from various disk devices.

Typical physical file systems include the S5 file system from original AT&T System V Unix, the UFS file system from Berkeley (BSD) Unix, ext3 and ext4 file systems on Linux, and FAT and NTFS on Windows. These are all local file systems that manage files residing on disks connected directly to the local computer. For managing files on disks that are on a remote computer which is connected to the local computer via a network, Oracle/Sun's Network

File System (NFS) is a very popular choice.

The networking component of an operating system implements the transport, network and Data Link layers in the ISO model. It allows processes running on a computer to be able to communicate with programs running on other computers on the network. The most typical implementation implements and supports the TCP and UDP protocols at the transport layer, the IP protocol at the network layer, and the Ethernet protocol at the Data Link layer. The TCP/IP protocol is the backbone of the Internet.

Device Drivers

Most components in an operating system kernel are generic and hardware independent. For example, scheduling, concurrency control, thread management, virtual file system, security, networking transport (TCP/UDP) and network (IP) layers. Others are more hardware specific.

Program code inside an operating system kernel that is hardware specific and is used to directly interface with and control each specific hardware is generally called 'device drivers'. Device driver code is viewed as sitting at the very bottom of the operating system kernel because it is closest to the hardware. Examples of device drivers include keyboard driver, mouse driver, Ethernet driver (which implements the Data Link layer protocol in the network stack), hard disk driver, DVD driver, etc. These drivers have knowledge about the specific hardware peripheral devices they are controlling and implement the protocols required to communicate with them.

Just like other kernel components, device drivers run in the privileged kernel mode because they control hardware. For security sake, only the super or root user has the privilege to directly manipulate hardware components.

Device drivers can be pre-built and linked into the operating system kernel. In fact, most of them are. Some of them are installed and loaded into the operating system kernel when the devices are added to the system. Some operating systems also support dynamically loadable device drivers where drivers are loaded into the operating system kernel address space on demand at run time when devices are first used or detected. Doing so eliminates the need to relink the operating system kernel and reboot the system in order to add, delete or update a device driver.

Other operating system components include job scheduling, security, and real-time support, hardware support and others. You could consult books on operating systems if you are interested.

In later chapters we will talk about how to program using the application programming interfaces (APIs) an operating system provides in various areas including file system, process management, interprocess communication, networking, security and others, as they are essential to development of system and application software. These APIs interact directly with the operating system components described here.

1-5-3 Two Spaces of the Operating System

Some of you may have the privilege to work on developing various components of an operating system, though most are probably or will be developing some system or application software that uses the services provided by the operating system. Regardless, having a basic understanding of the makeup of an operating system is certainly very helpful.

This section talks about some of the basic concepts of an operating system that are useful to system and application software developers.

The first concept about an operating system software is that it has components in two spaces: kernel and user spaces.

The first and most important component of an operating system software is the operating system kernel itself.

An **operating system kernel** is the core of an operating system software. It is a huge, complex and sophisticated software program by itself. It consists of code that directly communicates and controls various hardware components of a computer, including managing the use of the computer main memory, manipulations of disk files, network packets transmission and receiving, keyboard inputs, output to display monitor, process scheduling and so on.

It exists as an executable file residing in some directory of a computer's boot drive (hard disk). When the computer gets powered on, the bootstrap program residing in the ROM gets loaded into the computer main memory and executed first. It then loads the operating system kernel software into the memory and transfers control to it so that it starts executing. When the computer processor runs the operating system kernel code, it switches itself into the privileged kernel mode (there is a special assembly language instruction does so) which has special privileges to access all of the hardware components on the computer.

An operating system kernel consists of all of the most important code that manages all processes, file systems, memory, networking, hardware devices and I/Os. As we just said, when executing the operating system kernel code, the processor is in privileged mode. It has permissions to essentially do anything.

Besides the operating system kernel, an operating system software typically also consists of many utilities, tools, libraries, configuration files and scripts that exist in the **user space** outside the O.S. kernel.

Examples of the operating system user space stuff include the most useful Standard C library (libc.a or libc.so) that almost every C program must link with, and many other very useful libraries in areas like networking, multithreading, and so on. They also include many utilities and tools in areas such as file system (for instance, the list directory command, the change directory command, etc.), networking (for example, the ping and netstat commands), memory management, security, process management (the list processes command), etc. The list goes on.

The operating system kernel is to run the computer, keep the computer up and running, and service its users, whereas the user space tools and libraries are to assist users in use of the computer and developers in developing software.

1-5-4 APIs of the Operating System

To a software developer, perhaps the most interesting thing about an
operating system is what application programming interfaces (APIs)
it provides. One of the major roles of an operating system is to provide
services to all software that runs on top of the operating system. Although
the operating system user space tools and utilities do provide some services,
most of the services provided by an operating system come from the set of
APIs made available by the operating system.

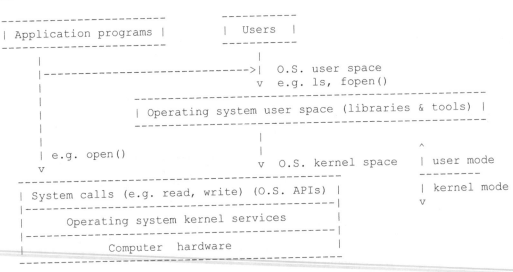

Figure 1-6 Dual spaces and modes of operating system

Just as operating system software exists in both user and kernel spaces,
an operating system's APIs exist in both spaces, too. That is, some of
the operating system's APIs exist as **library functions** in the user space
libraries while others exist as system calls inside the operating system
kernel itself. In other words, **system calls** are operating system APIs
that are implemented inside the operating system kernel.
Please note that some of the operating system user space library functions
eventually make system calls as well to get their jobs done, so do many
operating system tools and utilities. Figure 1-6 shows this.

Note that except the operating system itself, almost all computer software
runs on top of or above the operating system and thus relies on the services
provided by the operating system. Therefore, they are all called
applications to the operating system. We will use the terms applications
and application programs interchangeably.

Be aware that there are applications to applications. For instance, there
exist many relational database management system (RDBMS) products today:
Oracle RDBMS, DB2, SQL Server, SYBASE, MYSQL, etc. These RDBMS software
products are applications to the operating system. They run on top of an
operating system and rely on the services provided by the operating system.
However, most end users do not use these RDBMSes directly. Instead, they
use applications of the RDBMSes, such as order entry system, accounting
software, personnel software, etc. These database applications run on top of

the underlying RDBMS.

Here you see the multiple layers of computers. Database applications run on top of database management systems (DBMSes), which in turn run on top of the operating system, which runs on top of computer hardware.

Programs running in the user space have no privilege to directly access any hardware or resources (such as files) that exist on the hardware. Those tasks must be done via making system calls into the operating system kernel. Examples include commands like ls and C library functions like fopen().

Applications make system calls into the operating system kernel to obtain system services such as reading files, writing files, synchronizing between processes, and communicating with other processes on the same system or across network. The system calls are at the very bottom layer to applications (although they are at the very top of the operating system kernel). Therefore, they need to be very efficient and very high performance.

For instance, the open(), read() and write() API functions in Unix and Linux are examples of system calls. They allow application programs to open, read and write a file, respectively. These APIs are very efficient because they are implemented as system calls. They call right into the operating system kernel code. We will talk about how to use these system calls in your programs in later chapters.

Kernel Callout to User Space

Note that although it's not standard, nor often being done, it's possible to reverse the direction and call user space commands from an OS kernel. Author designed and implemented Unix kernel callouts to user commands and used it to implement dynamically loading device drivers on demand into Unix kernel in 1990s. It works beautifully. It should have been patented.

When the system boots into single user mode, a user-space daemon is started. This daemon spawns multiple threads which call into kernel, sleeping there and waiting for requests to come. When a new hardware device is added or first used, kernel detects that. This event will wake up one of these kernel threads which will return to use space, execute the necessary commands (e.g. execute a kernel load command to load that device's driver code into kernel space) and then bring the results back into kernel.

1-5-5 Two Modes of a Process

The user and kernel modes apply to a process as well.

When you start running your program, normally your program runs in the so-called **'user mode'** because it is just normal code (say, it adds two numbers). From time to time, your program may make some system calls to invoke operating system services such as performing some file system or network operations. As soon as the execution of your program hits some system call, your process transitions from user mode to the **'kernel mode'** because it (your process) is executing some operating system kernel code. Each system call is implemented in the operating system kernel. The kernel mode gives your process the privilege to perform operations like creating a file, writing a file, sending a network packet or receiving a network packet which are only done in the operating system kernel.

In other words, in executing a system call made by your program, the computer processor transits from user mode into kernel mode because the code that actually implements the system call (e.g. creating a file) resides in the operating system kernel. And upon return from a system call, the CPU switches from kernel mode back to user mode. CPU remembers which mode it is in because the privileges are very different.

As you can imagine, during the entire course of executing an application program, the application process normally enters and exits the kernel mode many times.

Note that a process may enter the kernel mode for good reasons or bad. For example, if a program is running in user mode and it tries to access some memory location that either does not exist or is protected, then an error occurs and the execution will then trap into kernel mode which may terminate your program.

Obviously, for robustness and security reason, the operating system kernel code does all of the necessary checking and verifications to ensure the security and integrity of the system is not compromised by malicious or un-intentional applications. You certainly don't want a careless or malicious program making a system call by passing in some bad arguments to corrupt data in the operating system kernel or crash the kernel taking down the entire system with it.

1-5-6 Program to Standard OS APIs -- the POSIX Standard

This book is on system and application programming in C. It's about writing programs at the system and application levels that directly use standard-defined operating system services (i.e. APIs) in the form of system calls and library functions provided by the base operating system.

This approach to developing system and application software enjoys the highest efficiency and best performance via direct system calls. It also possesses the benefit of lowest cost through portability across platforms -- write once, recompile and run everywhere. In addition, the simplicity, robustness and stability provided by these standardized O.S. APIs are just priceless.

From this chapter on, the APIs we will introduce and use are all defined by industry standards (specifically, the POSIX standard) unless there is no industry standard covers them.

To date, the only broadest computer industry standard on operating system APIs is the POSIX standard. This is the standard that programs in this book conform to. Software developers are strongly encouraged to write to this standard because it makes your software application portable across different platforms. When you develop your software, if you write to the POSIX standard, then with simply a recompilation your software should be able to run on any operating systems that support and conform to the standard. It will save you a lot of time, effort and resources! Hence, write to the POSIX standard is the way to go to develop software that supports different platforms or wants to achieve best performance.

For this reason, before we start out, let's talk about this standard a little bit.

1-5-6-1 POSIX Standards (and Their Names)

In the old days, most computer operating systems were proprietary. Each operating system has its own implementation and its own APIs. It makes application development very costly. One has to write one version of his or her own application for each different operating system.

During the 1970's and 1980's, open operating systems like Unix became very popular, especially among minicomputers and workstations. Computer hardware vendors offering UNIX systems in that era include, but not limited to, IBM, DEC (digital), Data General, Sun, SGI, Apollo (later acquired by HP), Prime, Stratus and Tandem. That is, almost every major computer hardware vendor had a product based on Unix.

Originally, there were two major flavors of UNIX: the original AT&T System V (SVRn) developed at AT&T Bell Labs, and the Berkeley Software Distribution (BSD) UNIX developed by University of California at Berkeley based on source code of AT&T System V.

The thing is to differentiate themselves, hardware vendors always added their own enhancements, extensions and features. This led to many different flavors of Unix and a fragmentation of the Unix market. Applications were not portable from one vendor's UNIX to another. Writing a single version of an application to be able to run on all vendors' Unixes became almost impossible.

Because of this, the computer industry felt very strongly to have a standard on the Application Programming Interfaces (APIs) of the UNIX operating system. Out of this desire to standardize operating system interfaces and develop a common core set of APIs, the POSIX.1 standard was produced in 1988, which was based on the Unix operating system.

POSIX.1 defines the basic core services of an operating system, including process creation and control, signals, file and directory operations, standard C library, pipes, I/O port interface and control, and process triggers.

Later,
- the POSIX.2 standard, which defines shell (command interpreter) and utilities, was produced in 1992,
- the POSIX.1b standard, which defines real-time extensions such as priority scheduling, real-time signals, clocks and timers, semaphores, shared memory, message passing, synchronous and asynchronous I/O, and memory locking interface, was defined in 1993, and
- the POSIX.1c standard, which defines threads extensions, was also introduced in 1995.

In short, POSIX stands for **Portable Operating System Interface.**
It is a family of standards based on UNIX operating system.
These standards define a standard operating system interface and environment to support applications portability at the source code level.
They specify system calls, library functions and shell commands for application developers and operating system implementors to use for

portability across operating systems.

The standards include the following (the number in parentheses is the year
that the standard was published):

  POSIX.1 (1988) - core services (ANSI C, process creation, file I/O,
    signals, errors, etc.)
  POSIX.2 (1992) - Shell and utilities
  POSIX.1b (1993) - real-time extensions (System V IPC, sync and async I/O,
    real-time scheduling and signals)
  POSIX.1c (1995) - threads extensions (the so-called POSIX threads or
    pthreads)

In 2001, all these standards became POSIX.1-2001, which is also known
as IEEE Std 1003.1-2001. After that, many revisions have been published,
which include POSIX.1-2004, POSIX.1-2008, POSIX.1-2013, POSIX.1-2016
and POSIX.1-2017.

  IEEE Std 1003.1-2001 (POSIX.1-2001)
  IEEE Std 1003.1-2004 (POSIX.1-2004)
  IEEE Std 1003.1-2008 (POSIX.1-2008)
     This standard consists of:
     - the Base Definitions (XBD) volume, issue 7
     - the **System Interfaces** (XSH) volume (POSIX.1, POSIX.1b, POSIX.1c), issue 7
     - the Shell and Utilities (XCU) volume (POSIX.2), issue 7
     - the Rationale (XRAT) volume
  IEEE Std 1003.1-2017 (POSIX.1-2017)
     - Revision of IEEE Std 1003.1-2008

Incidentally, an industry consortium called "the Open Group" was formed.
It also publishes the Single UNIX Specification (SUS) Version 1 in 1995
and Version 2 in 1997. These are essentially tracking the POSIX standards
although it has more and also includes other services such as Networking
Services and X/Open Curses.

As of this writing, IEEE Std 1003.1-2017, a Revision of IEEE Std 1003.1-2008,
is the current standard. It is POSIX Base Specifications issue 7, available
from either IEEE or The Open Group. And that's what this book bases on.

In 1998, a joint technical working group named the Austin Group or the
Austin Common Standards Revision Group was formed to develop and maintain
a common revision of POSIX.1 and parts of the Single UNIX Specification.
The Austin Group published the Single UNIX Specification version 3 in 2001,
which essentially tracks POSIX.1-2001, and the Single UNIX Specification
version 4 in 2008, which tracks POSIX.1-2008.

  Single UNIX Specification version 1 (1995) - POSIX.1 and more
  Single UNIX Specification version 2 (1997) - POSIX.1 and more
  Single UNIX Specification version 3 (2001) - POSIX.1-2001 and more
  Single UNIX Specification version 4 (2008) - POSIX.1-2008 and more

The 1996 edition of IEEE Std 1003.1 standard was also approved as an
international standard, which is called ISO/IEC 9945-1:1996.
A more up-to-date version as of this writing is ISO/IEC 9945-1:2008,
which was actually published in September of 2009.

  International Standard ISO/IEC 9945-1:1996 - IEEE Std 1003.1-1996

International Standard ISO/IEC 9945-1:2003 - IEEE Std 1003.1-2003
    International Standard ISO/IEC 9945-1:2008 (published in 2009-9) - IEEE Std
1003.1-2008

As you can see from the above, the original POSIX standards have been
adopted by different standard organizations over time and thus have at
least four different sets of names.

Operating systems that have been certified to be POSIX compliant include
IBM AIX, Oracle/Sun Solaris, HP HP-UX, HP/DEC Tru64 UNIX, UnixWare,
Silicon Graphics IRIX, Apple macOS (since 10.5), INTEGRITY, and others.

Many operating systems have not officially been certified as POSIX compliant
but are mostly compatible. These include Linux, FreeBSD, NetBSD, OpenBSD,
Apple Darwin (core of macOS and iOS), Google Android, VxWorks, MINIX, Xenix
and others.

In general, being POSIX-compliant means these operating systems support the
APIs defined by the POSIX standards. To software developers, it means if you
develop POSIX-compliant software applications, they should be portable across
all these POSIX-compliant operating systems. That is, with just a simple
recompilation your software should run on all these POSIX-compliant
operating systems. Example programs provided in this book are POSIX standard
compliant except those in the security chapter (chapter 15), which the POSIX
standards do not cover.

In this book, we will introduce the most frequently used C-language APIs
at the operating system interface level defined in these POSIX standards
(in the System Interfaces volume).

The APIs we will discuss are defined in POSIX.1, POSIX.1b and POSIX.1c
in the original standard names or in POSIX.1-2017, IEEE Std 1003.1-2017
and ISO/IEC 9945-1:2009 in the more recent names. For simplicity, we will
refer to these standards as the POSIX.1 standard, or simply the POSIX
standard, in this book.

1-6 Program, Process and Thread

This section defines some terminologies that software engineers use every
day in discussing program execution.

A **'program'** is a sequence of statements or instructions that accomplishes
a specific task. A program exists as an executable file on some disk.
The program file contains the sequence of statements or instructions that
make up the program and some other information. Normally there is only one
copy of the program executable file on the whole system.

Example of a program: /bin/ls

A **'process'** is a program in execution. This is a dynamic representation
of the program. Note that multiple users may be running exactly the same
program on the same system at the same time. In that case, a program will
have multiple processes on the system. For instance, three users may be all
running the same 'ls' program on the same system at the same time.
In that case, there will be three 'ls' processes exist on the system.

A **'thread'** is a flow of control within a program. Typically, a program is single-threaded. That is, there is only one flow of control within the process at any given time. A single-threaded program can do only one thing (e.g. respond to only one event) at a time. Nowadays, programs are becoming more multitasking and can perform multiple tasks either at the same time or concurrently. This is accomplished by creating multiple threads within the same program. A thread is sometimes called a **'light-weight process'**. Multiple threads within the same program share the same address space, the same text and data segments, and the heap. But each thread has its own stack.

Special APIs (i.e. function calls) are used to create multiple threads within the same program. In POSIX-compliant systems, applications normally use the **pthreads library**, which is a POSIX standard, to create and manage multiple threads within the same program. Some operating system vendors (e.g. Sun) also provide their own proprietary implementation of thread packages as well.

(a) Single-threaded program   (b) Multithreaded program

Figure 1-7 single-threaded vs. multithreaded program

1-7 Layers in Computer

A computer is an extremely complex system. Just the hardware alone or the software itself is a very complex system. Let alone it's both hardware and software working together.

1-7-1 Layers in Computer Hardware

On the hardware side, a computer is composed of one or more central processors, memory, I/O controllers, I/O devices and others. The CPU consists of arithmetic and logical unit (for short, ALU), control unit, and a number of registers. Many of these components are made of logic gates such as AND, OR, NOT, NAND and NOR gates, which are in turn made of transistors. Transistors are the most basic devices that make up the computer hardware. A transistor is again made of three layers of silicon material, in the form of either PNP or NPN. A modern-age computer processor consists of millions, billions, or even hundreds of billions of transistors (e.g. in an AI GPU).

In hardware, an electronic computer, which is what today's computers are, is made up of silicon semiconductor material at the very bottom layer. There are N-type and P-type of silicon. Three layers of silicon material put together, in the form of either PNP or NPN, can form a transistor. A transistor is an active device. It functions like a switch. By supplying with appropriate electronic signal and voltage levels, a transistor can be made to either conduct or not-conduct, representing on and off, or 1 and 0. That's why today's computers are all binary computers. Transistors are the lowest level of active devices that make up an electronic computer. That's why many people say computers are made of transistors.

By connecting two transistors in a back-to-back feeding back manner, you get a device called flip-flop which can 'memorize' one bit of information, a one or zero. Hence, a flip-flop is a one-bit memory. It takes two transistors to make. This is how you get the semiconductor memory. Putting eight, sixteen, thirty-two or sixty-four of these together, you have a 8-bit, 16-bit, 32-bit, or 64-bit 'register', respectively, which can store a 8-bit, 16-bit, 32-bit, or 64-bit information (e.g. an integer number).

In addition, you can make digital electronic circuits that perform the very basic logical operations such as negate, and, and or operations from transistors too. These circuits are referred to as the NOT, AND, and OR gates in digital electronics. Going further, by combining the basic NOT, AND and OR gates in different ways, you can make circuits that can do not only the ADD, SUBTRACT, MULTIPLICATION AND DIVISION arithmetic operations but also the COMPARE operation. This is to say that you can build the ALU of a computer processor entirely from the silicon and transistors.

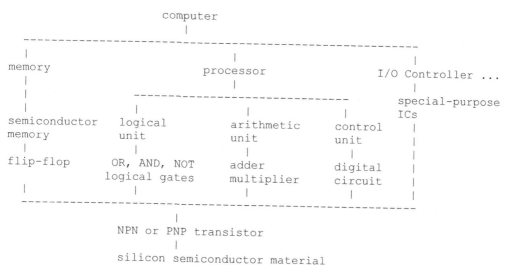

Figure 1-8 How a computer is built from silicon

Besides, using the transistors and the basic AND, OR and NOT gates, you can build almost any digital circuits that decode instructions and control the operations of a processor as well -- the control unit of the processor.

In summary, you can build a computer's processor, memory and I/O controllers by using transistors. It is really so amazing that human can build so complicated computers on and from the silicon semiconductor material. Figure 1-8 shows the layers inside the computer hardware.

1-7-2 Layers in Computer Software

On the software side, at the very minimum, each computer needs an operating system software to function. The operating system is the most fundamental software that a computer needs. It contains program code and logic that controls the operations of the various computer hardware components such as the keyboard, mouse, display, disk drives, network interface cards, etc. The operating system alone is very basic and generic. It allows users to start their computers and do some basic things with it. But to perform many other more advanced and interesting tasks, you need application software.

Application software is software that runs on top of the operating system and solves specific problems for users. For example, many companies use computer to do database processing. For that you need some database software such as Oracle RDBMS, IBM DB2, Microsoft SQLServer, MySQL, and so on. These database management software products are application programs to the operating system. And yet, very often they are the base where many companies build further higher-level database applications on. For instance, when bank tellers use computers every day, they are probably using some banking applications that build upon and rely on some relational database management system (RDBMS) products. Furthermore, there may be other applications that run on top of these applications' applications. As is evident, there exist many layers in the computer software domain.

Figures 1-9, 1-10 and 1-11 illustrate different layers inside a computer. It is very important that you have this layer concept in your mind because that will not only help you truly understand computers but enable you to design better software. In addition, it also helps you troubleshoot and debug , too, in isolating where the bug is in an extremely complex system.

In general, you want to build a software at a particular layer by leveraging the existing layers below it. In doing that, you also need to understand the layers the software you are building needs to depend on, collaborate with, and interface with, and what application programming interfaces (APIs) they have available for you to use.

```
software products
    |
programs
    |
source code modules/files
    |
statements
    |                                    ^
machine language instructions      |  software
    |                              -----------
CPU, memory, and peripherals       |  hardware
    |                               v
ALU, memory cells
    |
logical gates, registers
    |
AND, OR, NOT gates
    |
transistors
    |
silicon (P-layer or N-layer)
```

Figure 1-9 Layers of computers

In addition, you may also need to think about what application programming

interfaces your software needs to provide such that other software
(for instance, some other higher-layer applications) can use and build upon.

In a simplest scenario all of the layers mentioned above exist in a single
system. In many cases, the application could be a distributed one where
more than one system is involved in its execution. For example, the Web
application could be running on system A, the Web Server on system B, and
the DBMS on system C. In this distributed case, there is also the networking
software and hardware involved which handle the communications between
the multiple computers so that they can collaborate with one another.

Figure 1-9 shows one view of layers in computers. A computer typically runs
many software products at the same time. Each software product may contain
multiple programs which are built from multiple software source code modules
or files. Each software module has multiple subroutines each of which consists
of many statements. The software statements must be translated into machine
language instructions before they can be executed by the central processor
(CPU) of a computer. While being executed, machine code is stored in
computer memory. CPU fetches instructions from memory and executes them
using ALU and other hardware components. ALU, memory and other hardware
components are made up of digital logical gates and registers which are in
turn made up of most basic gates such as AND, OR and NOT gates, which in
turn are built from transistors that contain three-layer of silicon
at the very bottom (PNP or NPN transistors).

Figure 1-10 shows a second view of computer layers.
At the very top, computers run various application software products to
solve end user's problems. These application software products may run
on top of another application system software products such as database
management systems (e.g. ORACLE, DB2, SQL Server), which in turn run on
operating system. All software products run on top of the operating system,
directly or indirectly. So they may call O.S. APIs and other products' APIs.

```
-----------------------------------------------------------------
| Software | other higher-level applications                    |
|          |-------------------------------------------------   |
|          | database & network applications, web server, etc.| |
|          |-------------------------------------------------   |
|          | database system, network system, etc.              |
|          |-------------------------------------------------   |
|          | operating system                                   |
|          |               -----------------------------------  |
|          |    kernel      | device drivers                    |
|----------|-------------------------------------------------   |
|          | processor, memory, I/O controllers                 |
|          |-------------------------------------------------   |
|          | ALU, control unit, memory modules                  |
|          |-------------------------------------------------   |
|          | logical gates, memory cell (flip-flop)             |
|          |-------------------------------------------------   |
|          | transistor                                         |
|          |-------------------------------------------------   |
| Hardware | silicon semiconductor material                     |
-----------------------------------------------------------------
```

Figure 1-10 Another view of layers in computers

1 Basic Computer Concepts

Computer operating system software controls the operations of computer hardware which consists of CPU, memory, I/O controllers and I/O devices. These hardware units are mostly made up of digital logical gates and flip-flops (in the case of semiconductor memory), which are made up of transistors which are three-layer silicon.

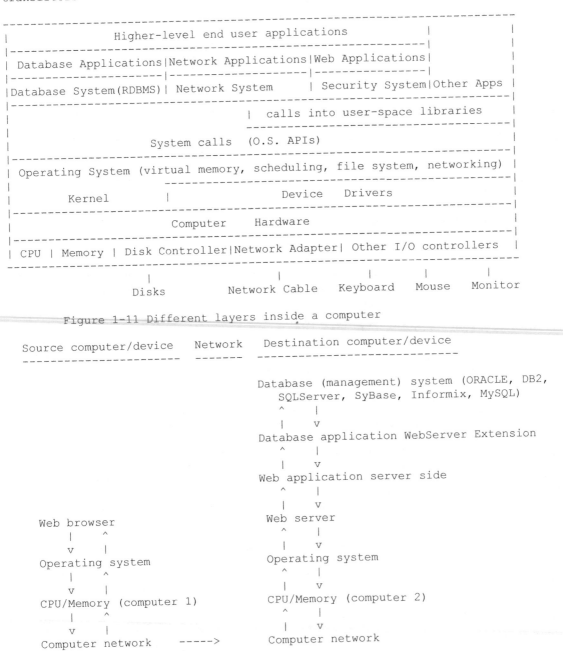

```
---------------------------------------------------------------------------
|                Higher-level end user applications          |           |
|-----------------------------------------------------------|           |
| Database Applications|Network Applications|Web Applications|           |
|----------------------|--------------------|---------------|           |
|Database System(RDBMS)| Network System     | Security System|Other Apps |
|----------------------------------------------------------------------|
|                               | calls into user-space libraries      |
|                               ----------------------------------------|
|              System calls   (O.S. APIs)                              |
|----------------------------------------------------------------------|
| Operating System (virtual memory, scheduling, file system, networking)|
|                   ---------------------------------------------------|
|       Kernel            |         Device   Drivers                    |
|----------------------------------------------------------------------|
|                 Computer    Hardware                                  |
|----------------------------------------------------------------------|
| CPU | Memory | Disk Controller|Network Adapter| Other I/O controllers |
---------------------------------------------------------------------------
          |                     |             |       |        |
        Disks          Network Cable  Keyboard  Mouse   Monitor
```

Figure 1-11 Different layers inside a computer

```
Source computer/device    Network    Destination computer/device
----------------------    -------    ----------------------------

                                     Database (management) system (ORACLE, DB2,
                                        SQLServer, SyBase, Informix, MySQL)
                                         ^      |
                                         |      v
                                     Database application WebServer Extension
                                         ^      |
                                         |      v
                                     Web application server side
                                         ^      |
                                         |      v
Web browser                          Web server
    |      ^                              ^      |
    v      |                              |      v
Operating system                     Operating system
    |      ^                              ^      |
    v      |                              |      v
CPU/Memory (computer 1)               CPU/Memory (computer 2)
    |      ^                              ^      |
    v      |                              |      v
Computer network     ----->           Computer network
                     <-----
```

Figure 1-12 How a web application uses layers of computer

Figure 1-11 is a third view of the computer layers which is similar but slightly different from Figure 1-10. It displays all software uses operating system services by either making direct system calls into the operating system kernel or calling into some user-space library functions which may eventually turn into system calls as well.
This book is all about these application programming interfaces (APIs) as defined by the industry standards.

Figure 1-12 gives an example of how the execution of an application travels through all these different layers in a computer and across network.
The example application is a user uses a web browser on a computer or mobile phone to browse a web site on the Internet.

The web browser is an application program that runs on the user's computer or mobile device. It runs on top of the operating system and hardware of that computer or device. When the application runs, messages are sent between the two or many computers or devices involved in the communication.
When a user clicks on a link in a browser, it sends a request message which travels from the source computer/device to the destination computer/device. When the corresponding application software (it's the web server in this case) on the destination computer gets the request message, it will perform some processing (e.g. retrieves the web page the user is accessing from a database) and then sends the computation result back to the source application on the source computer/device. As shown in the figure, these request and response messages travel through different layers of the computers/devices and the network equipment (e.g. network routers) connecting them.

The web server, Web application server side's code, usually is a generic HTTP server with extensibility which allows different web applications to plug in application-specific extension modules to extend the functionality of the generic web server and to serve the needs of different applications. These web server extension modules often access some backend databases to retrieve information the end user at web browser requests or may even update some data in the database.

This is a very typical client-server application. The web browser is the client and the web server is the server which serves the client.
The web server is often written in C or Java programming language. Very often it is a multithread application.

Exercises

1. What are the two necessary components required for a computer to function?

2. Describe the hardware organization of a computer and the names and functions of its major hardware components.

3. What are the basic units inside a computer processor? Describe the function of each.

4. What registers does a computer processor normally have? Describe the function of each of them.

5. What is a multiprocessor computer? And what are multi-core processors? What additional capabilities do they have?

6. What's the role of the computer main memory?
   What is the difference between ROM and RAM? What are they for?

7. Where the program being executed by the computer must be?
   Does it have to be all in?

8. What is a computer bus? What are the typical three buses in a computer?
   What characteristics do they have?

9. Is size of a computer's address bus related to size of its data bus?
   Why?

10. What is DMA transfer?

11. What is software? What is a program? What is a process?

12. What is assembly language?

13. Why are there high-level computer programming languages?
    What are the two major types of high-level programming languages?

14. What is a computer operating system?
    Name and describe the major components of an operating system.

15. Describe the two spaces/modes of an operating system.

16. Describe the layers within a computer, both hardware and software.

17. Describe how a single processor computer can execute
    multiple programs and service multiple users at the same time.
    Explain the techniques it uses.

18. Describe the differences between a compiled language and an interpretative
    language.

Projects

1. Research into and describe why and how a computer can execute a program
   that is only partially resident in the computer main memory.
   What hardware and operating system features and techniques does it use?
   You may have to consult some books on operating system.

2 Software Development and Engineering Processes

This chapter introduces the software development process and software engineering process that software developers live and breathe every day. These processes are designed to increase overall productivity and ensure software quality. Knowing these processes are essential for software developers and will certainly help boost their productivity and quality of their work.

2-1 Software Development Process

This subject is important because from time to time the companies I worked for would hire young software engineers recently graduated from colleges with BS, MS or PhD degrees in computer science. And this is one of the things that they sometimes struggle with.

Software engineers' daily job is to develop software components and products. This section gives an overview of the software development process that software engineers go through almost every day.

In general, software development involves the following steps and phases:

1. Given a problem to solve or a new feature to add.

2. Investigate the feasibility and estimate the amount of work required.

3. Develop a high-level **functional specification** and have it reviewed.

4. Develop a more detailed **design specification** and have it reviewed. Make a better estimate of the effort required.

5. Coding

6. Unit testing

7. Code review

8. Running **regression test suites**

9. Submit (or merge) the code changes

10. Integration testing, performance testing and stress testing

All software projects start with the idea of solving a problem for users or customers. This could be a big one that eventually leads to a brand new software product, or it could be adding a new component or feature to an existing product.

The project idea could originate from an entrepreneur's creative idea, a requirement from a customer as a result of talking to customers, a thinking of some engineer(s), or a result from a brainstorming meeting of a development team.

Once you have got a problem to solve at hand, it's very important that you have a very clear problem statement, know exactly what needs to be solved and what all of the requirements are. Thus, step 1 is to truly understand the problem at hand and derive a very clear and well-defined problem statement.

Step 2 is to look into the problem at hand and investigate its feasibility. Some research may be needed. This can sometimes be very expensive. In general, almost every software problem is solvable; it's just a matter of how much effort is involved and how long it's going to take. Some **prototyping** may be required to just prove the concept is feasible. A prototyping could also help the investigator(s) better understand the problem and what issues might need to be addressed. Depending on the scope and complexity of the given problem, this step may take days, weeks, months or sometimes even a year or more to finish.

After it is determined that the problem is solvable, the next step is to write down a high-level description of what the problem is and what functionalities the solution must provide. This is usually called the functional specification.

The function specification should stay at high level, at functional level, and state what the solution should provide and not provide. Its primary audience is the high-level executives and customers. The goal of the functional specification is for them to get a clear picture of what problem is being solved and what the solution will provide. Essentially, it states what the software product will do and not do. The functional specification needs to be reviewed and approved.

With a functional specification, the next step is to develop a design specification which drills deeper into each of the functions listed in the functional specification and describes technically how each function will be achieved. The goal is to describe how the problem will be technically solved to a certain detail level. It should discuss every technical aspect of the solution, including the data structures, layers in the solution, components involved, the routines that need to be implemented to deliver the functionalities, the set of application programming interfaces (APIs) required from other layers and components, the set of APIs that will be made available to other layers and components. Diagrams, data structures, APIs, technical design and implementation details usually make the bulk of a design specification.

For all the routines and APIs that need to be implemented, the design specification should provide the name of each routine, have a brief description of what each routine does, what parameters each routine has, what inputs it expects, what outputs it produces, and what errors and status it can possibly return.

The design specification could potentially break the solution down into multiple functional units. It could also provide some high-level pseudo code.

Besides describing technically how the problem will be solved, a typical design specification also often includes sections in other related areas such as security, performance, testing, documentation and potentially open issues. These sections describe how security and performance issues, if any, are to be addressed, what functionalities need to be tested, and what needs to be documented.

A design specification may also include resources needed and time to complete.

The design specification needs to be reviewed and approved, too.

After the design specification is approved, it's time to start coding the solution, compiling and building the software and unit testing it. These are the responsibilities of the developer(s). As a developer I always unit test the code I write.

Every software product requires a lot of testing, including integration, performance and stress testing and others. In parallel to or following the development of the design specification about how the product will be developed, a test plan about how the software will be tested must also be developed to ensure the software product is well-tested before it ships. The test plan must describe what tests, automatic and/or manual, will be done to verify that the product works and achieves its design goals. It will include resources needed and time to complete.

In some companies, the test plan is a separate document while in others it's a part of the design specification.

A test can be manual or automated. Ideally, it's a written test that can be automated and included in a regression suite which gets run nightly. In some companies, it's the developer's responsibility to also develop the unit test while in others quality assurance engineers write all tests.

Following the unit testing, there is usually a peer code review step to ensure the coder does not miss anything. The philosophy here is "Four or eight eyes are better than two eyes.".

After the code review process, usually there is a project lead approval. And then the code should be submitted into the source control system so that it's available to other developers and the nightly build. Integration tests by the quality assurance team can then be carried out after the submitted code builds successfully.

If automated regression tests have been developed and are available, it is very important that an engineer runs through those before the code is submitted/merged to ensure his/her changes have not introduced any regression.

For big projects, it's very typical that automated build and tests are done each night to ensure incremental changes do not cause major regressions and to catch them as early as possible if they do. Very occasionally, if regressions are introduced after a code change transaction is merged, the changes may have to be backed out to restore the stability of the project.

All of the tests developed for the unit and integration testing will become the regression test suites for the product features. Ideally, they should be run by every developer after they make changes and before they submit or merge in their changes to ensure their changes do not introduce any regression. The regression suites should also be run once every night to ensure no regression is introduced after combining together all developers' changes for the day.

Please note that in reality some iterations through some of the above steps may be needed. For instance, after you start coding, you may discover some of your design may need to be altered and thus you need to go back and change your original design or even the functional specification.

Also, during the testing you may find issues that require you to go back and update your design and/or change your implementation as well. It is not uncommon that one has to iterate through some of the steps in the process more than once. Very often it's the case that things only become clearer after you actually start implementing it. Very often problems and issues cannot be foreseen until you actually start coding. These are the reasons that necessitate iterating through some of the steps in the process.

Figure 2-1 Software Development Process

```
 _____   _____   _____   _____   _____   _____
|Given a|->|Investigate|->|Functional|->|Design|->|Coding|->|Unit    |->
|problem|  |feasibility|  |spec.     |  |spec. |  |      |  |testing|
 _____   _____   _____   _____   _____   _____


 _____    _____   _____     _____   _____
|Code   |->|Pre-submit|->|Submit/merge||->|Integration|->|Performance and|
|review|   |Regression|  |changes      |   |testing     |  |Stress testing |
 _____   |check      |   _____     _____   _____
            _____
```

In next section we will talk about some of the processes involved in the coding and unit testing phases of the software development process mentioned above.

2-1-1 A Word on Code Review Comments

Peer review of code changes is a very common practice in software development. It's based on the theory that two brains are better than one. This is especially important when new engineers come on board. Having the new engineer's changes reviewed by some old timers can often catch some of the obvious mistakes because perhaps the new guy may not be very familiar with the product yet. Not just that, every engineer has his/her own experience and expertise, having more eyes look over the changes can sometimes catch mistakes made. This especially true when the code reviewer is more familiar with the code area being changed. Many times an engineer has to make changes in other areas as well in order to implement what he/she wants. It is very critical that the changes are carefully reviewed by the owners of those components.

The caveat to avoid in the code review process is that the code reviewers should focus on correctness and technical merits, but not on styles or cosmetic. It is very important to always separate correctness and technical merits from styles, personal preferences and cosmetic! Try to comment on the former but not the latter.

Over the years working in the industry, I have seen many engineers who tend to always focus on styles and personal preferences. It's a bit like religion in these areas. Everyone seems to have their own views, opinions and preferences, and there is no absolute right or wrong. It's often counter-productive to engage in debates in these areas. The time and energy should instead be spent on getting the code and product to work correctly, deliver more and better functionalities, be more robust, high-performance, secure, user-friendly, and simple. Styles and cosmetic things often make no difference in whether the product will work correctly and robustly or not. Therefore, they should not be the focal point.

It's a waste of energy and a distraction to comment on style and cosmetic.

For example, some company insists on adding a pair of brackets to every if statement even if there is only a single statement to execute when the condition is true. Some company insists code indentation should be always 8 spaces instead of 2 or 4. Or each line can have at most 80 characters. These are all very trivial cosmetic. Either way has its pros and cons. Being consistent perhaps is the main reason to do it. But it's no big deal if it's not. I'm not sure it's really worth fighting over it or even have those in the **coding standard**. After all, there are always many other more important things to fight for. It's not worth letting the team being tied down with these very trivial little things that ultimately make no real difference in the ultimate quality of the product.

2-2 Source Control System and Process

In almost every software company, it's almost always the case that many software engineers are working on the same product or project simultaneously, doing developments parallel to one another, and potentially modifying the same set of source files at the same time. To coordinate the parallel or concurrent development activities and ensure the integrity of the source files, typically a **source control system** is used.

A source control system is a software. It performs many functions including recording each revision of each source file made by engineers, merging multiple changes to the same source file made by different engineers, maintaining the history of changes to each source file, making each engineer's changes invisible to others before submit and making them visible to others after submit, and so on.

There exist a large number of source control systems. Some of them cost a lot of money to license and some of them are open source and free. Some operating systems even come with a source control system too. For example, AT&T Unix has Source Code Control System (SCCS) and some flavors of Unix (e.g. BSD Unix) also has Revision Control System (RCS).

Licensed source control software products include IBM ClearCase, Microsoft SourceSafe, and others.

Open source free source control software products include CVS, Perforce, Subversion and others.

Many big companies also developed source control systems themselves for their own internal uses.

No matter which source control software product you use, as a developer, what you do is almost always very similar.

Note that there is no industry-wide standard on source control systems. Hence, all of these products differ to certain degree.
In this section, we will go over the common core functionalities of all source control systems.

There are multiple steps in using a source control system.
In general, as software developers working on a project whose source files are controlled and managed by a source control system, below is an example of very typical daily development activities:

1. Create a **view** or **sandbox** that backs to a certain snapshot (usually daily) of the entire source code tree. This step gives you an environment to see all of the current source files in the entire source tree structure that corresponds to the project you are working on. It gives you a private workspace where you can try to make changes to the product and rebuild it without affecting anyone else.

   The command for doing this is usually called mkview, createview or mksandbox. It is 'ct mkview' in Clearcase.

2. Create a source file in a particular directory in the source control system if it does not already exist. This operation creates a new file in the source control system.

   The command for doing this is usually called mkelem, create, ct mkelem (in Clearcase), cvs add (in CVS) or admin (in SCCS).

3. **Check out** a source file so that you can start modifying it.

   Before you can modify an existing file, you must first check it out.

   If you check out a file locked, then no one else will be able to check out the same file at the same time until you check it in. This essentially blocks out all other developers from modifying the same file as you are modifying it.

   You check out the file in shared (not locked) mode if you want to allow other engineers to work on the same file at the same time. Typically, this is what most engineers do.

   In this shared mode, if two or more engineers check out and modify the same file(s), whoever submits/merges first will encounter a simpler merge and the person who submits/merges in second (or even the third) will have to pick up and merge the changes made by other engineers that went in already.

   The command for checking out a file for modification is usually called co, checkout, ct co (in ClearCase), cvs checkout (in CVS), or get (in SCCS).

4. Use an editor to modify the source file(s) you have checked out or newly created. You can use your favorite editor to edit the file (e.g. vi, emacs, or whatever).

5. Compile and test your changes.

6. **Check in** the source file(s) you have modified.

   This will allow your changes to be recorded in the repository of the source control system. It also makes your changes visible to other developers. Note that until you do this step, the changes you made remain on a private branch of your own and they won't affect any other developers. Other developers do not see your changes at all until you check them in.

   Also, until you check them in successfully, your changes are not recorded in the source control system yet. Therefore, if you lose your files, your changes are gone unless you have saved a copy of your changes somewhere else. It's a very good habit to always save a copy of your changes somewhere else so that you could recover in case the system crashes or your working copy in the view/sandbox is somehow lost.

   The command for checking in your changes is usually called ci, checkin, ct ci (in ClearCase), cvs commit (in CVS), or delta (in SCCS).

7. Bring in other developer's changes and merge them with yours.
   You may not always perform this step.
   The command for merging in other's changes is 'cvs update'.

8. Officially submit/merge your changes. Some source control systems have this extra step while others don't. For those don't, checkin is the only step needed to make your changes visible to others.

   The command for doing this is usually called merge or submit.

9. Un-checkout or cancel checkout a file if you decide not to change a file afterwards.

   The command for doing this is usually called unco, uncheckout, ct unco (in Clearcase), or unget (in SCCS).

10. Often you will need to find out the differences between two revisions of a file. Cases include displaying the changes you have made so far against the backing tree or displaying the changes someone else made between, for example, revisions 1.3 and 1.4 of the file.

    The command for doing this operation is often called diff, ct diff (in ClearCase), cvs diff (in CVS), or sccsdiff or delta (in SCCS).

11. There are always many other commands. Examples include listing the change history of a file ('ct lshistory' in Clearcase and 'cvs history' in CVS), listing or printing the current configuration spec (called 'ct catcs' in Clearcase), and printing the configuration of your view ('cat catcs' in Clearcase).

In summary, typical source control operations include the following:

- Creating a view or sandbox backing to a snapshot version of the entire source tree.
- Creating a new file in the source tree. Typically, the create action includes a checkout as well by default.
- Checking out an existing source file so that you can start modifying it.
- Checking in your changes so that they are recorded in the source control system and become visible to other developers.
- Merge your changes with other engineers' changes to the same file(s) and resolve the conflicts if any.
- Submit your changes to end your source code change transaction.

Figure 2-2 displays some of the basic source control commands in ClearCase, SCCS, and CVS.

For more or a complete list of commands, please read the documentation of source control software you are using.

Figure 2-2 Basic source control commands

operation	Source control software		
	SCCS	ClearCase	CVS
Create a view		ct mkview	
Enter/use a view		ct setview	
List all views		ct lsview	
End a view		ct endview	
Create a file	admin	ct mkelem	cvs add
Remove a file		ct rmelem	
Check out a file	get	ct co	cvs checkout
Un-checkout a file	unget	ct unco	
List checked out files		ct lsco	
		ct lscheckout	
Check in changes	delta	ct ci	cvs commit
Find out differences	sccsdiff,delta	ct diff	cvs diff
Display file history		ct lshistory	cvs history
Print view spec		ct catcs	

2-3 Software Release Process

Once a software product is first shipped, it will live through many different releases over time; for instance, version 1, version 2, version 3, and so on.

Each **software release** has a target date and has a number of planned features and functionalities. When all features and functionalities of a release are in, a branch (split-off) usually takes place. At this point, a single source code tree forks and becomes two.

The **MAIN branch** continues to host the latest and greatest, accepting more drastic and usually less stable code changes for new functionalities and enhancements going into the next release. At the same time, the branch off source tree becomes the candidate for the current release and it will accept only bug fixes so that it can stabilize and reach a quality level that is suitable for shipping to customers.

Since there are at least two source trees, bug fixes that go into the current release-candidate source tree normally must also be submitted into the MAIN branch (the latest and greatest) as well. This is because the bugs being fixed probably exist in both source code streams.

Figure 2-3 Software releases and branches

```
   Date             Source tree branches
 ----------    -----------------------------------


                 MAIN (latest) branch
                   |
  2023-1-5         | branch off for V1
                   |\
                   | \
  2023-4-15        |  version 1.0 released
                   |
                 continue to develop for version 2.0
                   |
  2023-12-16       | branch off for V2
                   |\
                   | \
  2024-2-20        |  version 2.0 released
                   |
                 continue to develop for version 3.0
                   |
  2025-1-30        | branch off for V3
                   |\
                   | \
  2025-3-30        |  version 3.0 released
                   |
                 continue to develop for version 4.0
                   |
                   v
                   :
```

As time goes on, you see different releases get branched off the latest and greatest MAIN branch. And the branched off version will get stabilized and thoroughly tested until it reaches a satisfactory quality level. Then it is shipped.

2-4 Building the Product in Different Modes

Before a software can be delivered to customers, it must be built and tested. Hence, building a software is always part of the development activity.

To build a software, you need to compile all of the source modules and link them into libraries and executable programs. Each software product has its own components and build process. In a very small project, the number of source files can be very small and it may all reside in a single directory. It may take just a handful of commands and a few minutes to build. In this case, it's easy to build the software by hand.

However, in a big software project such as an operating system, a database management system, or a networking router software, there are typically tens of thousands source files spread over dozens or hundreds of directories. In addition, there are dependencies between different components and the build has to be done in a particular order to succeed. In such a complex software, normally the build is automated by using some build tools.

If you are a Release Engineer, you are probably responsible for building the whole product every day or night and troubleshooting all build errors and problems. If you are a developer, you are probably working on changing just one component and a very small number of files and debugging your code changes. In that case, depending on what components and/or files you change, sometimes you just need to rebuild the modules you change. Other times you may have to rebuild a number of components. In the most extreme case, you may be required to rebuild the entire product or the majority of it. Hence, how much of the entire product you have to rebuild after making your changes varies. As a developer, it is your responsibility to figure it out.

For instance, if you change a header file that is included in other components as well, you may have to rebuild some other components or the entire product.

Build for Debugging and Build for Release

Please note that depending on what you are building the product for, you may build it a bit differently.

During the development phase, source files are normally compiled with debugging on to facilitate debugging. This means compiling each source module with the -g option for most C compilers. By compiling the source files with debugging on, the binaries will contain symbol tables needed by the debugger. And the product is ready to be debugged using a debugger.

For instance, this is how you compile a C program with debugging turned on:

```
cc -g myprog.c
```

When the time gets close to shipping the product, the debugging option typically gets turned off and is replaced by the optimization option to build the software in the optimized mode. For instance,

```
cc -O2 myprog.c
```

Building the software in optimized mode results in smaller binary object files, libraries and executables. In addition, it also produces more efficient code.

2-5 Project Building Tools

Different operating systems provide different build tools. Many third-party software vendors also provide **Integrated Development Environments** (**IDE**s) which are usually GUI-based development environments and tools. Examples include IBM VisualAge on AIX, Sun Workbench on Solaris, Visual Studio on Windows. For Java developers, Java IDEs include Eclipse, NetBeans, IntelliJ IDEA and more. Of course, there are many others.

In this section, we introduce to you a very simple and popular program building tool that usually comes with POSIX-compliant operating systems. It is free. It is command-line based as opposed to an IDE. It is the make command.

The make command was available in Unix operating system back in 1970s. It is available now in so many other operating systems including Linux. The GNU make is also very popular too and is available in multiple platforms. Please note that there are many flavors of make. Although the make command is part of the POSIX Standard, not all make commands are created equal.

Here in this chapter, we try to discuss some of the basic common features of the make command. And we will try to point out any feature whose behavior differs between different makes. But remember the make command you use may differ slightly from what we describe here.

2-5-1 Make

In a POSIX-compliant operating system, the most common build automation tool is the make command or utility. Make is a utility program that can automatically walk down your source tree and build all of the libraries and programs in your product for you. The way make works is it reads and follows a specification file named **makefile** in each directory and knows what to do to build the libraries and/or programs in and below that directory. That is, the make command reads the makefile that exists in the current directory and does what is specified in that file. You as a developer create the source files and create the makefiles to automate the build.

Be aware that the make command reads and parses the entire makefile and determines what needs to be built and in what order first before it starts building anything.

To use make to build your entire software, you organize your source files into a tree structure and create a makefile in each directory. The makefile in each directory tells the make what to do to build the software in that directory and in the subdirectories below it.

If you do everything right in all of the makefiles by specifying the correct rules in building each target and correct dependencies between the targets, then all it takes to build the entire product or a particular component is just to change directory to the top of your source tree or that component and type

    make

at the operating system command prompt. That's it! It's that simple.

Based on rules and specifications in each makefile, the make utility will know how to walk down all the subdirectories, as you tell it to in the makefile, build the different components in the order you specify in the makefiles. The build may take hours. But all you need to do is enter one command. It's that simple and easy! Many operating systems, database systems, and network systems are built this way.

The advantages of using the make program to automate the build of your software product include the following:

1. It's very simple.

   To build the entire product, you change directory to the top level of the source tree and type make. To build an individual component, you change directory to the directory in the source tree corresponding to that individual component and type make. It is that simple.

2. It's automated.

   The magic is all coded in the makefiles. Once you have created the makefiles correctly, building the entire product happens automatically after you kick off the build.

3. It's smart.

   The make program has some intelligence. It has a very nice feature that compares the timestamps of files and knows to build only those files or components that are out-of-date and need to be re-built.
   In other words, if most of the source files have not changed since the last build, the make program is smart enough to know that it does not need to recompile them. It knows to rebuild only those files that have been changed since the last build and those that are affected by the updates. This often saves a lot of time. This intelligence resides in the make command and also in rules inside the makefile that developers create.

   For instance, if the timestamp of myfile.o is newer than that of myfile.c, that means the source file myfile.c has not changed since last build. The make command will know not to recompile that file, assuming you create the makefile correctly. In addition, if myfile.c has changed since last build, then the make command will rebuild myfile.o and all other libraries and programs that depend on myfile.o. Again, assume you crafted the makefile correctly.

4. It's easy.

   You will find it's in fact very easy to learn how to create your own makefiles and automate the build of your project. In the following sections , we will give a couple of examples and show you how to code your own build rules in the makefiles to automate the build of your own project.

So now you know the make utility is a very smart program. It knows to automatically walk down the entire source tree, figure out what has been changed and what needs to be rebuilt, and rebuild them. And this intelligence all comes from the rules you as a developer write in each makefile.

Hence, the magic is in the makefiles.

Typically, each directory or subdirectory has a makefile specifying to the make utility what needs to be built and how to build them and in what order. You need to build the dependents (e.g. the library) first before you can build a target (e.g. a program).

2-5-2 Makefile

By now you know the magic of using make is all in the makefile.

A makefile essentially contains a set of build rules where each rule has the following form:

```
target [target2 target3 ...]: dependent1 dependent2 ...
[TAB] command1
[TAB] command2
   :
```

Normally each rule has a single target, which is the name of the object that needs to be built or an alias for it. Note that a rule can have multiple targets which are separated by space (not comma).

The target is followed by the ':' and then optionally followed by the target's dependent(s), if any. The dependent(s) is the prerequisite(s) of the target. The make program will build the dependent(s) before it tries to build the target. This is how you tell the make utility in what order the components need to be built. Besides building the dependent(s) before the target(s), the make command builds the dependent(s) or target(s) in exactly the order they are listed.

Below the target line, you specify the commands that need to be executed in order to build the target.

Please note that **each command to build a target must start with a TAB character, not spaces, or it won't work.** The make program won't be able to recognize the command if it does not start with the TAB character. When a command in a rule does not start with the TAB character, you get a not so obvious error message like the following:

```
makefile:10: *** missing separator.  Stop.
```

The above build rule says that the target depends on 'dependent1', 'dependent2', and so on. This means to build the target, dependent1, dependent2, and so on must be built first and in the order listed. After the dependents are built, then execute command1, command2 and etc. to finish the build of the target. To build a dependent, the make command will follow the command(s) given under the dependent target.

You choose the name of each target. It should be descriptive. Common practice is to use the name of the file to be built and generated.

A makefile can define multiple rules where each rule builds a distinct target.

When you invoke the make command, you can specify the target(s) you want to

build on the command line. If you don't it will try to build the first
target found in the makefile.

A line that starts with the # character is considered a comment in a
makefile. The # character can be preceded by spaces.

Below are some examples of rules in a makefile:

1. Cleanup

```
clean:
   rm -fr *.o
```

The target named 'clean' typically cleans up the entire directory.
It removes all of the object (the *.o or *.obj) files, the libraries
and the executable programs that were or might have already been built
so that the build can start from scratch.

You do 'make clean' only when you want to clean up and rebuild everything
from scratch, or you want to free up disk space occupied by these binary
files. Normally you don't do this because you want to keep what have
already been built and not rebuilding them to save time.

To perform this build action, you type the following at the command prompt:

```
$ make clean
```

And it will execute the following command you specify

```
rm -fr *.o
```

The clean rule tells the make command what files to remove to clean up.

2. Create a *.o file from a *.c file

```
prog1.o : prog1.c
   cc -c prog1.c -o prog1.o
```

This rule says the target prog1.o depends on prog1.c.
To build prog1.o, execute this command:

```
cc -c prog1.c -o prog1.o
```

2-5-2-1 The Name of Makefile

The make program performs the build task by reading instructions given in
the rules in the makefile.

The makefile in each directory can be named Makefile or makefile.
Choose one of the two names and do not have both. If you have both makefile
and Makefile in the same directory, most make will read and follow the file
named makefile.

By default, the make program attempts to read the file named 'makefile' in
the current directory first. If such a file does not exist, then the make

program tries to read a file named 'Makefile'. If neither file exists, then the make program will output an error saying 'no makefile found'.

You can name a makefile something else too. For instance, you may have multiple versions of the same makefile, one for each OS, in the same directory and call them the following:

```
Makefile.linux
Makefile.mac
Makefile.aix
   :
```

When the makefile is not called makefile or Makefile, to use it you will have to specify the name of the makefile on the make command line.
For example, to use the makefile named Makefile.linux, instead of just typing make, you will issue the following command

```
make -f Makefile.linux
```

In other words, you issue the 'make -f name_of_makefile' command instead. Of course, alternatively, you can choose to write a single makefile that works for multiple different operating systems using makefile directives.

The advantage of naming your makefile as 'makefile' or 'Makefile' is you can just type 'make' to kick off your build without having to specify the name of your makefile.

2-5-2-2 Typical Makefile Targets

There are some makefile targets and build steps that are very common across all projects. Below are some examples:

- make clean
- make all
- make install

Note that these commands or build steps are typically run in the order listed.

As we have said, 'make clean' cleans up all of the object and executable files. The 'make all' command normally builds the entire product or component. The 'make install' step installs the product to a target directory on the current system. It extracts and copies all of the executables (and perhaps some other files such as libraries or configuration files) that are to be shipped to customers to a target install directory and place them in a directory structure that represents the product in the installed form.

2-5-3 Makefile Macros

Makefile macros are similar to macros or variables in C programs.

Just like you can define macros in a C program, you can define macros in a makefile and use them throughout the makefile. Using macros provides the advantage that if you ever need to change it, you only need to change it in one place. By convention, macros are in capital letters.

You pick the names of the makefile macros.

For example, it is very common to define the C compiler, the linker, the options for the compiler, the options for the linker, and the libraries in macros like the following:

```
CC = cc
LD = ld
CFLAGS = -g
LDFLAGS =
LIBS = -lnsl -lpthread
```

After a macro is defined, you need to wrap it with $() to use it. For instance, to use the CC macro, you write $(CC).

Note that don't use quotes or double quotes around the value of a macro.

Special Macros

Normally there are some predefined macros. They include the following:

- $@ is the name of the current target to be made.
- $< is the name of the file causing the action. For instance, the name of the current object file needing to be built, e.g. prog1.o.
- $? is the names of the changed dependents needing to be built. This is the list of prerequisites that are newer than the current target. For example, "prog1.o mylib.o" for target prog1.
- $* is the prefix shared by target and dependent files. The $* macro represents the current target name with its suffix deleted. For example, in the .c.a inference rule, $*.o represents the out-of-date .o file that corresponds to the prerequisite .c file.

For example, you could have the following rule telling make how to compile a *.c file into a *.o file:

```
.c.o:
    $(CC) -c $(CFLAGS) $<
```

or

```
.c.o:
    $(CC) -c $(CFLAGS) $< -o $@
```

This is a generic rule. It applies to all *.c files. It tells the make command how to build a xxx.o object file from a xxx.c source file.

The rules above assume the macro CFLAGS does not include -c in it. If it does, then the -c in front of it should be removed. The difference between the two rules above is the second one specifies the name of the output file by "-o $@". It's the default so it's optional.

Note that the target .c.o means "to make a *.o file from a *.c file". Hence, if the name of the C source file needing compilation is file1.c, then in this context $< is file1.c and $@ is file1.o.

Or if using the special macro $*, the same rule could be written as this:

```
.c.o:
    $(CC) -c $(CFLAGS) $*.c
```

All of the three .c.o rules listed above work.

If your source files are in C++ language, then the target would be .cpp.o instead of .c.o in the above examples.

By the way, the above rule is also an implicit rule for make. If you don't specify it, the make command still knows it.

Conventional Macros

There are also some other predefined makefile macros. Following are some of these:

```
CC - The C compiler command. Default value is cc.
AS - The assembler command. Default value is as.
AR - The archive command. Default value is ar.
```

You can get a list of these macros by running the "make -p" command.

Macros at Command Line

You can also define macros at the command line as shown below:

```
$ make CC=/usr/bin/cc
```

2-5-4 Some Special Characters for Commands

There are a small number of special characters that you can place in front of a command in a rule to change the default behavior.

Normally, the make program prints out the command it is about to execute on the screen (standard output). But if you place an at sign (@) in front of a command, then the make program will just execute it without printing the command, like running it in silent mode. This can be used to reduce the amount of output produced by the make utility.

By default, the make program outputs an error and stops if it encounters an error in executing a command. But if you place a minus (-) sign in front of a command, then the make program will ignore the error from executing that command and continue to execute the command after.

When you run 'make -n', it is supposed to print out all the commands it would execute and does not execute any of them. However, if you put a plus sign (+) in front of a command, then that command will get executed even in the 'make -n' ('no execute') mode.

Below is a simple example that shows the function of these special characters.

```
$ cat makefile

  special:
```

```
        @echo "  A command starts with @ sign"
        +echo "  A command starts with + sign"
        -echo "  A command starts with - sign"
        echo  "  A command after an error"

$ make -n special
echo "  A command starts with @ sign"
echo "  A command starts with + sign"
  A command starts with + sign
echo "  A command starts with - sign"
echo  "  A command after an error"

$ make special
  A command starts with @ sign
echo "  A command starts with + sign"
  A command starts with + sign
echo "  A command starts with - sign"
/bin/sh: -c: line 0: unexpected EOF while looking for matching `"'
/bin/sh: -c: line 1: syntax error: unexpected end of file
make: [special] Error 2 (ignored)
echo  "  A command after an error"
  A command after an error
```

Figure 2-4 display a Makefile that demonstrates these special characters.

Figure 2-4 Some special characters used in front of commands (makefile)

```
all:
        @echo "  A command starts with @ sign"
        +echo "  A command starts with + sign"
        -echo "  A command starts with - sign"
        echo  "  A command after an error"
```

2-5-5 Makefile Implicit Rules

Note that some of the very basic makefile target rules are implicit.
They exist in make and are used if you don't specify them.
The first one is to compile the source file into the object file.
That is, even if you don't specify the actual compilation command in your
makefile, the make command still knows an implicit rule of how to compile
a *.c or *.cpp source file into a *.o object file.

This implicit rule is as follows:

For C language:

```
.c.o:
    $(CC) -c $(CFLAGS) $*.c
```

   or

```
.c.o:
    $(CC) -c $(CFLAGS) $<
```

For C++ language:

```
      .cpp.o:
        $(CC) -c $(CFLAGS) $*.cpp
```

    or

```
      .cpp.o:
        $(CC) -c $(CFLAGS) $<
```

The second implicit rule that the make command has is how to produce the executable file from the source file. This implicit rule is below:

  For C language:

```
    .c:
      $(CC) $(CFLAGS) $@.c $(LDFLAGS) -o $@
```

  For C++ language:

```
    .cpp:
      $(CC) $(CFLAGS) $@.cpp $(LDFLAGS) -o $@
```

Note that in this case, since you want to build the actual executable, the CFLAGS must NOT have -c in it so that the linker will be invoked. The -c flag means compilation only, no linking.

Besides, if you have additional object files or libraries to link in, then you cannot use the implicit rule either because by default they are not included.

Make sure the rules do not contradict each other if you specify both rules for building the *.o and the executable.

2-5-6 Makefile Examples

There are different types of projects. For instance, most big projects build a small number of executable programs out of a huge number of object files (i.e. *.o files). Another type of projects builds many executable programs where each program consists of a very small number of object files. Some projects fall in between the two.

For each project, there are multiple ways of constructing a makefile. One way is the most straightforward one which is to explicitly list all of the rules for each target to build. This way one will be able to code exactly what you want the make to do, no more and no less. But it requires one to write a lot of rules in the makefile.

Another way is to be simple and write as few rules as possible. This requires least amount of makefile work but it may not lead to an optimal makefile where the make command does exactly what is necessary only. In other words, it will still build the targets you want but may be doing a bit of more than what's necessary. We will give one example on each of these approaches in this section.

The example project we will use is a very simple one. It builds two

programs which share a common library. There is one library module
and two programs to build. Figure 2-5a is an example makefile which
explicitly lists all of the rules one by one for each build target.
It requires a little bit of more work if the number of files is large.
If you like, you could even explicitly specify a rule for each *.o file
too, with whatever compilation flags needed. For instance:

```
 prog1.o: prog1.c
    cc -c prog1.c -o prog1.o
```

Note that in our example the following rule is optional because it's implicit:

```
 .c.o:
       $(CC) $(CFLAGS) $*.c
```

Note that building the example programs does not really need to link
in the pthreads library (-lpthread). We use it here just to illustrate
how to specify some system libraries to link with.

Figure 2-5b is another example which use multiple targets.
This makefile saves you from explicitly listing all of the rules.
All you need to do is to list all of the names of the program executables
under the variable PROGS and all of the names of the object files under the
variable OBJS. That's it. The only drawback of this version of makefile
is it is not optimal. Specifically, it relinks all programs even if just
one source file has changed. It does more work than necessary.
This is due to the multiple targets.

Figure 2-5a Example Makefile - explicit rules for each target (Makefile)

```
# Makefile for building multiple executables
# Authored by Mr. Jin-Jwei Chen.
# Copyright (c) 1991, 2012-2016, 2020 Mr. Jin-Jwei Chen. All rights reserved.
#

CFLAGS = -c
CC = cc
LD = cc

LDLIBS = -lpthread
MYLIBS  = mylib.o

all: prog1 prog2

# This rule builds *.o from *.c. This rule is optional because it is implicit.
# Both rules work.
.c.o:
#         $(CC) $(CFLAGS) $<
          $(CC) $(CFLAGS) $*.c

prog1: prog1.o $(MYLIBS)
          $(CC) -o $@ $(@).o $(MYLIBS) $(LDLIBS)

prog2: prog2.o $(MYLIBS)
          $(CC) -o $@ $(@).o $(MYLIBS) $(LDLIBS)
```

```
clean:
        rm -fr prog1 prog1.o prog2 prog2.o $(MYLIBS)
```

Figure 2-5b Example Makefile - use multiple targets (Makefile.ex2)

```
# Makefile for building multiple executables
# Authored by Mr. Jin-Jwei Chen.
# Copyright (c) 1991, 2012-2016, 2020 Mr. Jin-Jwei Chen. All rights reserved.
#

# List of executables to be built
PROGS = prog1 prog2
OBJS = prog1.o prog2.o

CFLAGS = -c
CC = cc
LD = cc
LDLIBS = -lpthread
MYLIBS  = mylib.o

all: $(MYLIBS) $(PROGS)

# This rule builds each executable target, single or multiple.
$(PROGS): $(OBJS) mylib.c
        $(CC) -o $@ $(@).o $(MYLIBS) $(LDLIBS)

# This rule builds *.o from *.c.
.c.o:
        $(CC) $(CFLAGS) $<

clean:
        rm -fr $(PROGS) $(OBJS) $(MYLIBS)
```

Figure 2-6 displays the three source files used in this example.

Figure 2-6 Program source files for the Makefile example

(a) prog1.c

```
#include <stdio.h>

int main(int argc, char *argv[])
{
    extern void sayHello();

    sayHello();

    return(0);
}
```

(b) prog2.c

```
#include <stdio.h>

int main(int argc, char *argv[])
{
```

```
        extern void sayHello2();

        sayHello2();

        return(0);
    }
```

(c) mylib.c

```
    #include <stdio.h>

    void sayHello()
    {
        fprintf(stdout, "Hello, there!\n");
    }

    void sayHello2()
    {
        fprintf(stdout, "Hello, there!!\n");
    }
```

2-5-7 Makefile Directives

2-5-7-1 The include Directive

In a big project, typically there are so many different components making up the entire product and the product also has to support many different operating systems. So even the makefiles themselves can get very complicated. Therefore, it is very common to split some of the common rules into different makefiles and have one makefile includes other makefiles, just as a header file can include other header files.

The makefile include directive enables the make command to suspend reading the current makefile and read one or more other makefiles before continuing. The syntax of the include directive is very simple, as shown below:

```
    include filenames...
```

For example:

my.mk

```
    MACRO1 = from my.mk
```

Makefile

```
    include my.mk

    test:
        @echo "Testing ..."
        @echo "MACRO1=" $(MACRO1)
```

```
    $ make test
    Testing ...
```

```
MACRO1= from my.mk
```

2-5-7-2 The ifdef and ifndef Directives

The ifdef and ifndef directives test if something is defined or not defined.

```
ifdef X -- means if X is defined
ifndef X -- means if X is not defined
```

This is very useful in creating a single Makefile for multiple platforms. For instance, you may have to do the build in a slightly different way between Linux and Windows. You use ifdef or ifndef to specify different rules for different platforms so that a single Makefile works for multiple platforms.

As an example, the following construct does the build one way on LINUX platform and the other on the rest of platforms.

```
ifdef LINUX
  ...
else
  ...
endif
```

For instance, for the given Makefile below:

```
Makefile

  ifdef LINUX
OS = Linux
  endif

  test:
      @echo "OS =" $(OS)
```

When you run make, this is what your get:

```
$ make
OS =

$ make LINUX=1
OS = Linux
```

2-5-7-3 The ifeq and ifneq Directives

The ifeq and ifneq directives test if two arguments are equal or not equal. The two arguments are separated by a comma and surrounded by parentheses. The lines following the directive in the makefile are executed if the condition is true. Otherwise, they are ignored.

If any of the arguments consists of variables, then variable substitution is performed before the comparison.

Below is the construct of the ifeq directive:

```
ifeq (…,…)
  ...
else
  ...
endif
```

Just replace ifeq with ifneq for the ifneq directive.

Below is an example of using the ifeq directive in a makefile.

Makefile

```
ifdef SOLARIS
CC = gcc
else
CC = cc
endif
ifeq ($(CC),gcc)
LDLIBS = -lnsl -lsocket -lpthread
else
LDLIBS = -lnsl -lpthread
endif

test:
    @echo "CC =" $(CC)
    @echo "LDLIBS =" $(LDLIBS)
```

```
$ make
CC = cc
LDLIBS = -lnsl -lpthread

$ make SOLARIS=1
CC = gcc
LDLIBS = -lnsl -lsocket -lpthread
```

2-5-8 Some Useful Make Command Switches

1. make -n (display what make would do)

   Sometimes you may want to find out what the make command would do
   without actually doing it.

   The "make -n" command displays what the make command would do.
   It prints the commands that would be executed, but does not actually
   execute them. If you pass in a target as the argument, it will print the
   commands it would execute in building just that target.

   For instance, in the example of two programs (prog1 and prog2) sharing
   one library module (mylib.c), below is the output of the 'make -n' command:

```
$ make -n
cc -c prog1.c
cc -c mylib.c
cc -o prog1 prog1.o mylib.o -lpthread
```

```
cc -c prog2.c
cc -o prog2 prog2.o mylib.o -lpthread

$ make -n prog1
cc -c prog1.c
cc -c mylib.c
cc -o prog1 prog1.o mylib.o -lpthread
```

2. make -k (Don't stop when encountering an error)

The make command terminates right away if any build step returns a failure status. Sometimes you may want the build to ignore errors and go as far and do as much as it possibly can. In that case, you run "make -k". Below is an example.

```
$ make clean
rm -fr prog1 prog1.o prog2 prog2.o mylib.o

$ make -k
cc -c prog1.c
prog1.c: In function 'main':
prog1.c:12: error: 'xxx' undeclared (first use in this function)
prog1.c:12: error: (Each undeclared identifier is reported only once
prog1.c:12: error: for each function it appears in.)
make: *** [prog1.o] Error 1
cc -c mylib.c
cc -c prog2.c
cc -o prog2 prog2.o mylib.o -lpthread
make: Target `all' not remade because of errors.
```

As you can see from the output of "make -k", the build encountered an error in compiling prog1.c. Normally the entire build would stop there. However, since we use the -k option, it did not stop at the first error. It actually went ahead and built prog2.

3. make -s (run make in silent mode)

If you want to run the make command in silent mode, do 'make -s'. This will execute all the commands to build the product without printing them.

Again, using the same example application:

```
$ make clean
rm -fr prog1 prog1.o prog2 prog2.o mylib.o
$ make -s
$ ./prog2
Hello, there!!
```

Run the 'man make' command to get all of the command line switches available to the make command.

2-5-9 Example of Building a Small Project Using Make

To demonstrate how to use make in building a product, here we give an example of a very small project and show you how to organize the source files and construct makefiles to automate the build of a very simple program using a very simple library containing two source files. Although the project is very small, it illustrates most of the ideas, concepts and techniques that apply to one with a very large number of directories and files. It also demonstrates how to construct makefiles to walk down a directory structure recursively.

The project is comprised of a library named mylib.a and an executable program named prog1. We organize the library under the lib subdirectory and the program under the prog1 subdirectory.

We also construct three makefiles. The top level makefile has two rules that build and clean the entire project. It has the knowledge to walk down to the two subdirectories and build the corresponding library and program in those directories in order. The makefile in the lib subdirectory has the rules to build and clean the library. The makefile in the prog1 subdirectory contains the rules to build the prog1 program and clean that directory.

Figure 2-7 Organization of files of the Example Project

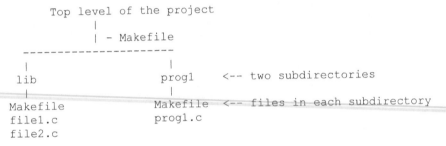

Figure 2-8 Makefiles of the example project

1. Top-level Makefile

```
# Top-level makefile to build all.

DEPEND1 = lib
DEPEND2 = prog1

all: $(DEPEND1) $(DEPEND2)
      (cd $(DEPEND1); make)
      (cd $(DEPEND2); make)

clean:
      (cd $(DEPEND1); make clean)
      (cd $(DEPEND2); make clean)
```

2. Makefile in the lib subdirectory

```
# Build the library from source files

OBJS = file1.o file2.o
LIB1 = mylib.a
```

```
CC = cc
CFLAGS = -c

all: $(OBJS)
      ar rv $(LIB1) $(OBJS)

.c.o:
      $(CC) $(CFLAGS) $< -o $@

clean:
      rm -fr $(OBJS) $(LIB1)
```

3. Makefile in the prog1 subdirectory

```
# Build the executable program named prog1.

PROG1 = prog1
PROG1OBJ = prog1.o
LIB1 = ../lib/mylib.a

CFLAGS = -c
CC = cc
LD = cc

$(PROG1): $(PROG1OBJ) $(LIB1)
      $(LD) $(LDFLAGS) -o $(PROG1) $(PROG1OBJ) $(LIB1)

.c.o:
      $(CC) $(CFLAGS) $< -o $@

clean:
      rm -fr $(PROG1) $(PROG1OBJ)
```

Figure 2-9 shows the source programs.

Figure 2-9   Source files for the example

(a) file1.c

```
#include <stdio.h>

void func1()
{
   printf("Function func1 was called.\n");
}
```

(b) file2.c

```
#include <stdio.h>

void func2()
{
   printf("Function func2 was called.\n");
}
```

(c) prog1.c

```
#include <stdio.h>

int main()
{
    func1();
    func2();
}
```

To see how the build works, just change directory to the top level and run

```
make clean
make
```

The output of cleaning all, building all, and running the program built is given in Figure 2-10.

Figure 2-10 Output of cleaning and building the example project

1. Linux

```
$ make -n
(cd lib; make)
(cd prog1; make)
```

```
$ make clean
(cd lib; make clean)
make[1]: Entering directory `/root/myprog/make/lib'
rm -fr file1.o file2.o mylib.a
make[1]: Leaving directory `/root/myprog/make/lib'
(cd prog1; make clean)
make[1]: Entering directory `/root/myprog/make/prog1'
rm -fr prog1 prog1.o
make[1]: Leaving directory `/root/myprog/make/prog1'
```

```
$ make
(cd lib; make)
make[1]: Entering directory `/root/myprog/make/lib'
cc -c file1.c -o file1.o
cc -c file2.c -o file2.o
ar rv mylib.a file1.o file2.o
  ar: creating mylib.a
  a - file1.o
  a - file2.o
make[1]: Leaving directory `/root/myprog/make/lib'
(cd prog1; make)
make[1]: Entering directory `/root/myprog/make/prog1'
cc -c prog1.c -o prog1.o
cc  -o prog1  prog1.o ../lib/mylib.a
make[1]: Leaving directory `/root/myprog/make/prog1'
```

```
$ ./prog1/prog1
Function func1 was called.
Function func2 was called.
```

2. AIX

```
$ make clean
(cd lib; make clean)
rm -fr file1.o file2.o mylib.a
(cd prog1; make clean)
rm -fr prog1 prog1.o
```

```
$ make
(cd lib; make)
cc -c file1.c -o file1.o
cc -c file2.c -o file2.o
ar rv mylib.a file1.o file2.o
  ar: Creating an archive file mylib.a.
  a - file1.o
  a - file2.o
(cd prog1; make)
cc -c prog1.c -o prog1.o
cc  -o prog1  prog1.o ../lib/mylib.a
```

```
$ ./prog1/prog1
Function func1 was called.
Function func2 was called.
```

Please be aware that the make utility actually varies somewhat from operating system to operating system, although most of the basic functionalities are supported by all. The basic functionalities of the make utility are included in the POSIX standard.

For further details and more advanced features, please consult the documentation of make and makefile in your operating system.

Throughout this book, we will try to provide a Makefile for the example programs we use in each chapter of this book on the Linux and Apple Darwin platforms. They will be named Makefile.lin and Makefile.mac, respectively. They can be copied and modified to use in other platforms.

As we said it earlier, there exist multiple ways to construct the Makefile(s) for a given project. Our approach here is trying to minimize the work one has to do. In fact, you will find the Makefile(s) we provide is very simple and easy to copy and modify, although it's not optimal. In many cases, all you need to do is to change the names of the list of programs you need to build, and that's it! It's the macro named PROGS in the Makefile.

2-6 Regression Suites

Most software projects develop code and tests at the same time.
As a result, there often exists a set of tests. It's very common and a very good idea that before you check in your code changes, you always run the entire test suites and ensure your changes do not cause any regression. Adding new code and new functionalities but breaking existing functionalities is always bad and needs to be caught as early as possible.

It's very important that whenever you develop and add some new functionalities, you always add more tests to the existing test suites so that if anyone breaks the functionalities you've added, it will get caught. One thing you don't want it happening is that someone breaks your code and it never gets caught because there is no test for it. Not just functionality, whenever you fix a bug, you may also want to add a test for it as well.

The idea is to discover the bugs before shipping the product to customers. You want your regression suites to cover every single core functionality of your product. You want to cover all the important features. You want to cover all of the normal cases. You want to cover all of the edge cases. You want to cover all bug fixes. You also want to do all of the negative testing. The number of tests that need to be written and run is almost open ended! The thing is, the more comprehensive and complete your test suites are, the better coverage you get. And that will translate into higher confidence you have in shipping the product and probably less bugs will be reported by customers.

It's always extremely important to ship a product without any regression! That is, whatever used to work in the old versions must continue to work when customers upgrade to a newer version. You rely on the regression suites to achieve that goal. Hence, regression suites is a necessary component of your project.

As software products get bigger and more complex, testing and quality assurance get more challenging. A very extensive and complete regression suites is a necessary and very important component of a product.

2-7 Compiled versus Interpretative Languages

2-7-1 Types of Program Languages and Execution

Computer programs can be written in many different languages. Examples of programming languages include C, C++, Java, C#, PASCAL, Basic, Perl, Python, shell scripting, FORTRAN, COBOL, ADA, Assembly and many more.

Not all programming languages are born equal. Some (e.g. C) are at a slightly lower level and thus more concise, rigorous and efficient than others (e.g. Java and Perl). Some are more generic (e.g. C, C++, Java, C#) while others are designed for a more specific industry (e.g. COBOL for business application and FORTRAN for scientific applications).

Some of the computer programming languages are **compiled** languages and others are **interpretative** languages. For example, C, C++, FORTRAN, COBOL and ADA are compiled languages. Perl, BASIC and shell scripting are interpretative languages. Java, C# and Python are in-between. They are both compiled and interpretative. Programs written in these languages are compiled into some intermediate language first and then being interpreted and executed.

Programs written in compiled languages must be compiled into machine languages or some intermediate languages before they can be executed. Programs written in interpretative languages can be executed directly without going through the compilation step. The interpreter, which usually is another program by itself, reads in the commands or statements from the source file one by one and interprets and executes them 'on the fly'.

Interpretative programming languages normally have the advantages of easier to debug, faster development turn-around time, and less number of lines of code. Their disadvantages usually are they tend to be at a higher level and, accordingly, have less and/or looser control, and less efficient in execution. Some of them appear to be cumbersome and/or not rigorous enough.

In contrast, compiled languages take more steps to get to the execution phase and often need debuggers to help debug. But some of them tend to be at a lower level, can make direct system calls into the kernel, and thus have tighter control and result in higher efficiency due to the intimacy to the operating system and compiler optimization. Some (e.g. C) also have the **rigor, power, efficiency, performance, precision, simplicity and control** that other languages at a higher level lack.

One thing to notice is that not all compiled languages are compiling source programs into the machine code of a target machine. Java and C# are examples. Java was designed with a goal of 'compile once and run on multiple platforms' in mind to save programmers from having to compile the same program for every single hardware platform they like to support and thus save development time and lower the development cost.

Toward that end the Java language compiles its source programs into some intermediate code named bytecode, which is platform independent, using the Java compiler (the 'javac' program) and then executes the intermediate code using another platform specific tool named 'java'.

Compiling using compiler

   - C programs (compiled into target machine code)
   - Java programs (compiled into intermediate code)

Interpreting using Interpreter

   - Shell scripts
   - Perl scripts
   - Java bytecode

In general, compiled languages are more efficient and powerful and at a slightly lower level. But interpretative languages are easier and quicker to learn and use. Many scripting languages (e.g. Perl) have to use a lot of library functions which may not be as efficient, robust, rigorous and portable as standard C library functions or system calls.

2-7-2 Process of Program Compilation

Most software engineers develop software using a compiled language. Figure 2-11 depicts the steps in compiling and building a program in this kind of development.

Figure 2-11 shows the process of building and executing a compiled language program and the system utilities involved (compiler, assembler, linker, loader). The example program is comprised of two source modules: one C source file named myprog.c and one assembly language source file called utils.s.

C source files are compiled by the C compiler, which is another program named cc in Unix and Linux systems and cl.exe in Windows.
Source files written in assembly language are compiled by the assembler program, named as in most systems. They both compile the source files into the machine language and output a xxx.o object file.

Figure 2-11 Process of building and executing programs using compiler

```
Source Program(myprog.c/myprog.cpp)    assembly language module(utils.s)
     |                                            |
     v                                            v
 -----------                               -----------
| Compiler |   cc in Unix (cl in Windows) |assembler|  as command
 -----------                               -----------
     |                                            |
     v                                            v
Object Files   (myprog.o)                 object file (utils.o)
     |                                            |
     |<-------------------------------------------
     v
 ----------
| Linker |   ld
 ----------
     |
     v
Executable program   (e.g. a.out or myprog.exe on disk)
     |
     v
 ----------
| Loader |   loader
 ----------
     |
     v
computer memory
     |
     v
execution (by CPU)
```

Most software projects have multiple source modules. These object modules (that is, all of the *.o files) must be linked together and also with some of the operating system libraries they reference, such as the standard C library (libc), to form an executable program. This linking step is performed by the **linker program**, which is usually named **'ld'**. You can think of the linker program as the final assembler that puts pieces of your program together into a final single piece. It does so by resolving all external references your program makes. Because of so you must specify all of the modules and libraries that are referenced by your program on the linker command line in order for the linking step to succeed. If not, you will get "unresolved symbols" error from the linker. If the linker runs successfully, it will produce an executable file on your hard disk.

Remember we said every program must be loaded into computer memory before it can be executed by the CPU. To execute a program, you generally type in the name of the program at a command prompt. When you do so, the system will invoke the loader to load your program from disk into memory and then transfer the control of the computer to it.

The program that the operating system invokes to transfer your program from disk into memory is called the **'loader'**. It is provided as part of the operating system by the operating system vendor and it usually lives in the /sbin directory.

Note that the loader program is different from the linker. They are two completely separate programs that perform different functions at different stages. Many software engineers, some with 20 or 30 years of experience, often cannot tell them apart. Many even wrongly think one as the other or they are one program.

The linker is the system utility that links multiple object files and libraries together to produce an executable program and stores it as an executable file on disk. The loader is another system utility that reads an executable program stored on disk into memory so that it is ready to be executed by the CPU.

2-8 Choosing Programming Languages

There have been many computer programming languages invented so far. Over time some have faded away while others live on.

For example, throughout my study and professional life, I have learned and programmed in assembly languages of at least seven different processors, FORTRAN, COBOL, BASIC, PASCAL, C, C++, Java, and C#. I have also programmed in scripting languages including shell and Perl.

Each programming language has its strength and weakness. As of today, the C language has proven to be the most powerful, efficient, highest-performance, rigorous, precise and concise in developing system software such as operating systems, database management systems, networking systems, application servers and many others. There has not been any close competitor. Therefore, it's probably safe to say that the C programming language is the no-brainer choice for system programming and will live on for hundreds of years to come.

At the application level, many software products still use C.
But in object-oriented programming space, Java has been very popular across platforms while C# is popular in Windows environment. Even so, many people find Java too cumbersome in many cases. Not to mention the object-oriented model is hierarchical which has its intrinsic limitation of not modelling the real world very well. Clearly, Java and C# are not for system software.

Perl and Python seem to be gaining popularity too in some applications. However, these languages tend to be loose, not as rigorous, inefficient and cumbersome for many projects. I have seen projects turned into disaster with terrible quality in multiple cases simply because people picked these languages to do software projects that really should have been done in C. For any program that needs to be robust, efficient, precise, high-performance, highly portable and tight control, it is wise to stay away from these languages.

They also rely upon huge number of library functions which are inefficient, cumbersome and not truly portable in many cases. For instance, although Perl was designed to be portable across operating systems and platforms, its implementations are just not. I was very surprised by the number of portability snags I hit in using Perl.

Going even higher at the Web programming space, there are multiple choices and competing frameworks and languages. And their turn-over rate seems to be higher compared to system and application programming languages. Every once a while, you see a new language and framework comes out, being touted as the future and promising to replace what are already in use, just to see that it again solves some problems but brings a set of new problems of its own.

In summary, **it's extremely important that you very carefully choose the programming language to use for your projects.** I have seen it first-hand that many teams chose Perl or Python for their projects and the resulting quality of their products is just terrible. It's so obvious because these languages are just so loose, not rigorous enough, not efficient and too high-level to undertake many serious tasks. If you want to produce very high-quality software products with tight control, extreme robustness, very high efficiency, very high-performance and very high portability, make sure you use a programming language that is rigorous, efficient, not too loose and not too high-level. In general, C language is a no-brainer choice for all projects at system level and many at application level.

The point is that choice of an appropriate programming language has a great impact on the success of your project! So, make sure you do it right.

The success of your project starts with choosing the right programming language to use!

Exercises

1. Describe all phases of software development process.

2. What is a functional specification? What is it supposed to contain?

3. What is a design specification? What is it supposed to contain?

4. Give the name of the source control system you are using in your development. List the commands that perform the following operations:

   - Creating a view or sandbox
   - Creating a new file in the source tree
   - Checking out an existing source file
   - Checking in a file with your changes
   - Merge your changes with others' changes
   - Submit your changes to make them appear in the release stream

5. What is a source tree branch off?

6. Describe the program compilation process.

7. Create a very small project consisting multiple source files. Create Makefiles to automate the project build using the make command.

8. Explain the differences between compiled and interpretative programming

languages and discuss their pros and cons.

References

1. https://www.tutorialspoint.com/makefile/index.htm

3 Building Programs and Libraries

It is very rare to develop software without using any libraries.
In this chapter, we provide an introduction to software libraries and
different ways of using and building them. We also touch upon different
ways of building a program.

3-1 What Is a Library?

A software library or just **library** is a file that contains a collection of
routines or functions compiled into object code and ready for use by programs.
The routines in a software library are usually common utility functions
that many programs will need.

A library is all about **code re-use**. Once someone writes a function, compiles
it and builds it into the form of a library, other people can use the
function in their programs without re-writing it as long as they have
a copy of the library. Hence, it's kind of write once and use it as many
times as you like.

A lot of software code has been re-used through the form of libraries.
In particular, when you purchase a computer, it normally comes with an
operating system software installed on the computer. And most of the time,
the operating system software includes a number of libraries that not only
the operating system itself uses them but also any software developers
can use them in developing their application programs. An example is
that many operating systems come with the standard C library. Another example
is almost all operating systems come with a network library that enables
developers to develop network applications.

Besides, when you purchase other software products (e.g. database management
systems such as Oracle RDBMS, DB2, SQLServer, etc.), they may also come
with some libraries of their own which allow you to develop applications
using the functions and APIs in those libraries.

In other words, there are at least two types of libraries in terms of
who provide them. One is provided by the operating system for general use
by any software applications including the operating system itself.
The other is provided by software vendors or developers like you.
These are for use by certain software products and related applications.
As software developers, you can certainly provide your own libraries, too.

It is very common that almost every software product extracts a set of
common functionalities, codes them into functions and builds them into
libraries.

In short, a software library is a file that contains software code compiled
into object format for re-use by other software (programs and libraries).

In C language, a function or subroutine you define is by default global
unless you restrict its scope to file local by adding a 'static' keyword
in front of it. After the source module gets compiled, as long as a program
links in that *.o file, it will get to use that function. Alternatively,
if that *.o file gets archived into a library, any program links in that
library will be able to call that function and reuse that code as well.

A library can contain both exported functions and un-exported functions.
Exported functions are meant for programs to call and use. Un-exported
functions are used internally by the exported functions in the library.
In order for users to know how to use them, exported library functions are
usually documented. That is, they are documented APIs (Application
Programming Interfaces). The following are what must be published:

- the name of each library function
- the data type of the function's return value (void if no return value)
- the names, data types and order of all parameters of the function
All of the above constitutes the **'signature'** of the function.
- whether a parameter is INPUT only, OUTPUT only, or both INPUT and OUTPUT
- all potential return values, including errors, of the function

Besides, a description of what each function does, how to use it, and a
description of what each parameter is, are always very helpful to developers.
Some example program code demonstrating the use of it helps a lot too.

Below is an example of the minimum information that a developer needs to
know in order to be able to use the library function strcpy():

```
char *strcpy(char *dest, const char *src);
```

On Unix and Linux systems, documentation of library functions is available
via the man pages. Library functions are documented in the third section
of the man pages. For instance, to look up the documentation of the standard
C library function that does a string copying, on most systems you do:

```
$ man strcpy
```

or on some systems you do:

```
$ man 3 strcpy
```

where 3 means the library function strcpy() is documented in the third
section of man pages. For Windows search the function name on Microsoft MSDN.

3-1-1 Always Re-use Code

It is extremely important that you always reuse as much code as you can.

Whenever you are writing some code you need to think about if a piece
of code could be used more than once in the entire product.
If yes, then you should write it into a subroutine (called function in C)
so that others and/or other components can reuse that same code.

Also, always make the code that performs a specific task a subroutine.

The worst thing that can happen in a software project is that there exist multiple versions of doing one thing in multiple places.

Author has worked on a very big project in a very big company where I experienced these two terrible things:

(1) Every time when I found I needed to do something very basic and common and I was looking for an existing subroutine that does that for me, I couldn't find it.

(2) There are so many times that when I expected to change code at a single place in order to add an enhancement or fix a bug, I found I had to change it in multiple places. In one case, I had to make the same change at 13 different source modules instead of one.

I found it's just no code reuse at all! It is software development nightmare. It shows no software engineering at all!

Software programming rule #1 is to make code that could potentially appear more than once in the entire product a subroutine so that the code is re-used and there is no repetition of the same code in multiple places in the entire product.

Making common code a subroutine not only simplifies and improves the entire product but also makes code maintenance much easier and simpler.
It saves a lot of time and effort. If the code has a bug or needs to be changed for an enhancement or any other reason, there is a single place to change, instead of multiple! It's just wrong that one has to make the exactly same change at so many different places in the code! There should be just one.

There is something wrong if you find you have to make the same changes at more than one location. It means the code is not modularized and not reusing code.

It's really sad to see such computer programming basics not even being practiced in the computer software industry, especially on a team where so many software engineers have a B.S. or M.S. degree in computers! This is part of the reasons why there are so many bloated and buggy software products on the market today.

It cannot be emphasized enough that one should always try to make code into subroutines or functions so that code is reused and you don't end up with doing the same or similar thing in different ways at multiple places or duplicate the code. **Re-use code and modularize your code!**
This makes your code simpler, cleaner, modular and much easier to understand and maintain.

A neat code should look like this:

```
main()
{
  ret = func1(...):
```

```
      ret = func2(...);
       :
      ret = funcn(...);
    }
```

And this applies to all functions, not just the main() function.
This says the program or function is performing n tasks, each is done in
a function or subroutine. Of course, each of the functions may further call
into other functions.

3-2 Archive Library and Shared Library

There are two types of software libraries. In other words, a software
library can exist in one of the following two forms or both:

  - an archive library
  - a shared library

An **archive library** is also called a **static library** and a **shared library** is
called a **dynamic library**.

In the very early days, only archive libraries were used. Shared libraries
came later and have been getting very popular nowadays.

The main difference between an archived library and a shared library is how
they are used. Functions in an archived library are meant to be copied into
your program when it is built. In this sense, they are just like some of
the compiled source modules of your own code in a multiple source file
program. In other words, each program will have a private copy of the code
of the functions it uses from an archived library.

In contrast, functions in a shared library are not physically copied into
the executable file of a program. Instead, the shared library will be
loaded into a shared global area in computer memory when your program runs
and it will be shared by all programs using it.

In most POSIX-compliant systems, archive libraries are named as libxyz.a
where xyz is some string uniquely identifying the library.
Note that the file name has the .a as its extension or suffix, meaning it
is an archive library -- just a collection of the object files.
In contrast, shared libraries are generally named as libxyz.so. Its file
name extension/suffix is .so on most systems, meaning it's a shared object.
Shared libraries have a .sl file name extension on HP's HP-UX and .dll
on Windows.

For example, below are some of the libraries that we will program with in
this book and their names on most systems.

    Standard C library: libc.a, libc.so (msvcrt.lib and msvcrt.dll in Windows)
    Standard C++ library: libstdc++.a, libstdc++.so
    Network library: libnsl.a, libnsl.so
    Pthread library: libpthread.a, libpthread.so

In most POSIX-compliant systems, the software libraries are generally
installed into the /lib and /usr/lib directories.

Some systems install the shared libraries separately into a directory such as /shlib while others mix them in the same directories with static ones.

On Windows, static libraries have the .lib file name extension and shared libraries have the .dll file name extension. They usually exist in the C:\Windows\System32 directory. Microsoft Visual C/C++ installs into a separate directory like C:\Program Files\Microsoft Visual Studio 10.0 and the libraries are usually installed beneath the VC\ subdirectory.

Later in this chapter, we will talk about how to build and use these two types of software libraries. Before that, let us look at how a program is normally built first.

3-3 Two Phases of Building a Program or Library

There are at least two phases in compiling and building an executable program or a library:

- compiling
- linking

Compiling involves translating individual program source files, whether they are written in C, C++, Java, Assembly, FORTRAN, PASCAL, or other languages, into object code. Linking involves connecting or assembling together multiple object files already translated by the compiler to form an executable program or a library.

There are two separate operating system commands to perform these tasks: the compiler command and the link-editor or linker command.
On most systems, if you just invoke the compiler command, unless you specify the compiling only (-c) option, it will automatically invoke the linker too after the compiling succeeds.

The name of the compiler command varies with language and from system to system. For the compiler program/command of the C language, most operating systems (especially traditional Unix systems) name it cc, which stands for C compiler. However, many vendors use different names for their compilers. For example, the open source C compiler from GNU, which is available in multiple platforms, is named gcc. Intel C compiler is called icc. And the C compiler on many IBM AIX systems is called xlc.
You may also see a C compiler command like c89 or c99, which means a C compiler that implements the ANSI C89 Standard and ISO 99 Standard, respectively.

The name of the linker command is more uniform. Most systems name it ld.

Sometimes it is a little hard just to find out what C compiler command you can use on a system.

When you are on a system that you are not familiar with and are trying to find out the name of the C compiler on that system, you may want to try to type all these different names on the operating system command prompt and see what you get. I would try them in this order: cc, gcc, ...
If you still have no luck, then you might want to snoop around some of

the standard places for installing software programs, such as the /bin,
/use/bin and /usr/ccs/bin directories on most systems to see if a
compiler program exists there. Be aware that many software products
install to their own private directories outside these standard places.
For instance, some Sun compiler may get installed into a directory like
    /opt/products/sun/c/
and an IBM AIX compiler may get installed in
    /usr/local/ibm/compiler/c/
These directories are just exemplary.

If you still couldn't find it, try to Google it, ask the system administrator
or someone who may know, or read the documentation.

As a developer, you have a choice of building your program in one step or
two steps. Typically, if you invoke the compiler command, by default it
will do the two phases in order. That is, it will invoke the compiler to
compile the source file(s) first and then if the compilation succeeds it
will automatically invoke the linker to produce an executable file.
For example, assuming you save the code into a file called myprog.c,
to compile and build the following simplest C program into an executable
program:

```
#include <stdio.h>
int main(int argc, char *argv[])
{
  printf("Hello, world!\n");
}
```

you do one of the following. You can either do both steps in one command:

```
cc -o myprog myprog.c
```

or do each of the two steps separately:

```
cc -c myprog.c
ld -o myprog myprog.o
```

In the latter case, the 'cc -c' tells it to do the compilation only and
not to invoke the linker as it would do by default, and the 'ld' invokes
the linker only.

If the C compiler on your system has a different name, then replace 'cc'
in the above examples with whatever compiler name you get. Do the same
for the linker.

If a C compiler is installed on the system you are using, typically the
standard C library is installed, too.

When linking an executable C program, the linker always automatically
searches the standard C library and links in those standard C library
functions referenced in your C program. Note that if your program uses
functions from libraries other than the standard C library, then you must
explicitly specify those libraries on the linker command line (or the
compiler command line if you are doing two phases in one step).
If you don't, the linking step will fail with an error stating those
library functions are 'undefined symbols'. As a developer, it's your job

to know the names of the libraries that have the functions your program is using and provide them to the linker command.

For instance, if you write a distributed application program sending and receiving messages over the network using the socket interfaces, then you must know the socket library functions typically exist in the libnsl.a or libnsl.so and supply that library on the linker command line.

Please notice that the way you specify a library to the linker command is to use the '-l' option and then give the short name of the library without the leading 'lib'. For instance, to tell the linker to search for functions in the library libnsl.a, you specify

```
-lnsl
```

on the linker command line.

If your program uses functions in the libnsl.a or libnsl.so library, then to build your program, you would do:

```
cc -o myprog myprog.c -lnsl
```

or
```
cc -c myprog.c
ld -o myprog myprog.o -lnsl
```

Note that as far as the two steps or phases is concerned, building a library is similar to building an executable program. The only real difference is the name of the output file that you specify with the linker's -o option. In building a library, you give a name with something like '-o libxyz.a' or '-o libxyz.so' instead of '-o myprog'.

3-4 Static Linking versus Dynamic Linking -- Two Ways of Building a Program

Just as a library can exist in two different forms, you have two ways of building, more specifically linking, a program you are trying to build. When you are trying to build a program, normally you can elect to link with the libraries it references either statically or dynamically. They are called static linking and dynamic linking, respectively.

Figure 3-1 Linker command options for static and dynamic linking

Operating System	Static linking	Dynamic linking
Linux	-static	-dynamic
Solaris	-Bstatic	-Bdynamic
AIX	(give static library)	(give dynamic library)
HPUX	(give static library)	(give dynamic library)
Apple Darwin	(give static library)	(give dynamic library)
Windows	(give static library)	(give dynamic library)

You do so by specifying the linker option of your choice. The names of these linker options vary from system to system. But on most systems, you specify the '-static' or '-non_shared' to link statically and '-dynamic' or '-shared' to link dynamically.

Figure 3-1 shows the linker options for static linking and dynamic linking on some of the systems.

With **static linking**, a copy of all of the library functions that are directly and indirectly referenced/used by your program is placed into your program. Therefore, your program has a copy of the code of these library functions. This means, with static linking, each program gets a private copy of the library functions it uses within the executable file of the program.

With **dynamic linking**, the code of the library functions directly or indirectly referenced by your program is not physically placed into your program. Instead, they are loaded into computer memory at run time. Therefore, all programs on a system share a single copy of the shared library at run time. No program holds a private copy of the shared library code.

There are advantages and disadvantages of using static linking or dynamic linking. Below is a list of them.

1. Static Linking

Pros

- A statically linked program is self-contained and self-sufficient. Once you build the program, it can be copied or installed to any system of that platform and it will run without requiring any of the libraries it linked with to be present. In other words, a statically linked program can always stand alone.

- Once you build the program with static linking and test it, the test results remain valid until the program is rebuilt again. In other words, since the program no longer changes after it is built, your test results remain valid.

- A statically linked program can always start because all of its dependencies are already resolved at build time. There is no dependency issues that could arise at run time to prevent the program from starting or hang the program. Hence, there won't be the so-called "DLL Hell" issues as described in the dynamic linking part of this section below.

Cons

- Since all of the library functions a program uses and links with are physically copied into the program executable file, the size of a statically linked program is actually much bigger than the dynamic linking one. Therefore, a statically linked program uses more disk space and memory. Nowadays disks and memory are much cheaper and abundant. As a result, this may not be a real issue any more.

- Statically linked programs can not automatically get bug fixes or updates in the newer versions of the libraries they statically link with unless they are relinked again with the new versions of the libraries.

2. Dynamic Linking

Pros

- Since the dynamic library functions a program uses and links with are not
  physically present in the program, the size of a dynamically linked program
  executable file is much smaller. It saves disk space and memory.

- Only one copy of the shared library code is loaded into the memory and
  shared by all programs. Hence, it saves memory.

- Programs automatically get bug fixes and updates in the libraries
  when newer versions of the libraries are installed. There is no need to
  rebuild or relink them.

Cons

- Under certain circumstances, a dynamically linked program may not even run.
  A dynamically linked program is not self-contained and doesn't stand alone.
  All of the library functions it dynamically links with are missing;
  they are not physically placed in the program's executable file.
  Consequently, the program won't run unless all of the dynamic library
  functions it depends on are all present on the system at the time of
  program execution.

- Because the library functions a program dynamically links with get loaded
  at run time from the system where the program is running, when you test
  a dynamically linked program, you test it with one particular combination
  of these libraries physically installed on your test system at the time
  of the testing. When the program gets delivered to the customer and gets
  installed there, it may run with a slightly different version of the
  libraries or a different combination of them. In other words, the
  environment and setting that you tested the program in may not be exactly
  what the program gets at run time. Therefore, there is some risk of
  unexpected issues or bugs that could occur at customer sites.

- While a dynamically linked program can automatically get bug fixes from
  a newer version of the shared libraries it links with, it can get new
  bugs from them, too. So it cuts both ways.

- The "DLL Hell"

  Those who have worked in Windows may be familiar with the "DLL Hell" issues.
  In short, using shared libraries (DLLs) in Windows can cause deadlock and
  hang in some cases. This is true at least in the Windows 95 or 2000 era.

  There is a lot of complexity, restrictions and in some cases dead ends
  in using DLLs in Windows .NET environment, especially when you mix C++ and
  C# code. If you build a DLL library or .EXE program that contains some
  compiled native code and some managed code in MSIL (Microsoft Intermediate
  Language), the interaction between the operating system (which does not
  understand managed code) and the .NET CLR runtime (which does not
  understand the native code) could be a source of troubles.

  In addition, when DllMain runs, the process holds a lock on the OS loader.
  Any attempt to call the LoadLibrary() function to load anything may

result in a circular dependency and lead to deadlock (i.e. hang).
This problem is independent of managed code (MSIL).

Besides, there is also the issue of redistributed Microsoft libraries
from different vendors overwriting each other.
For instance, many software vendors developing applications in Windows
re-distribute the Microsoft C run time library. By default, this library
is installed into a fixed directory. As a result, if you install multiple
software products from multiple vendors, the library will get overwritten
each time, possibly with a different version of the library.
This may cause some software product(s) installed earlier to malfunction.

Although Microsoft tried to solve the DLL overwriting problem
in .NET using Strong Naming, the strong naming itself is complex and
somewhat messy to use.

3-5 How Does the Linker Find the Static and Dynamic Libraries

When you build a program, the link editor or linker tries to assemble
together the object files you specify in the command line and all of the
library functions referenced in those object files to form an executable
program. To complete this task, the linker needs to search through some
directories, find the libraries you specify, search through those libraries,
and find all of the functions referenced by the program.

How does the linker find all the libraries referenced by a program
at link time?

Well, there are different ways that you can make the linker find the static
and dynamic libraries that your program attempts to link with. How this
actually works varies from operating system to operating system. Below are
the three most common methods. Some operating systems may use only one of
them while others may use two or even all three of them.

1. Specifying the directories for the linker to search for the libraries
   by using an **environment variable.**
2. Specifying the library name using the -llibname linker command line option
   preceded with the -L/directory_of_lib option.
3. Specifying the full pathname of the library on the linker command line.

Be careful when you decide to specify the library by providing its full
pathname on the linker command line. If it's a static library, it is OK
because once the linking succeeds at build time, there is no more need to
locate that library again at run time. Hence, using a full or even absolute
pathname for an archive library is not an issue. However, if it's a dynamic
library, then at run time when the program attempts to start, it will have to
locate that library again and if the library does not exist in that same
location, the program won't even run. In other words, using the full name
of a library, whether it's absolute or relative, is in general a bad idea
for shared libraries because it makes the library not relocatable -- it will
always have to exist at that exactly same location at run time on every
machine.

In general, you want to build a program such that it can always run even
if the libraries it links with are moved to a different directory.

This is true especially when you build software that will sell
and ship to different customers and get installed on different machines.

Some operating system (e.g. AIX) allows you to specify a full pathname of
a library on the linker command line and if you specify another linker
option, then it will record only the **base name** instead of the full pathname
of the library. That way, at the program run time, the library can be
present in a different location. For instance, in AIX, the library can
then be placed in any directories listed in the LIBPATH environment variable
at run time.

This pathname issue generally is not an issue when you link with shared
libraries provided by the operating system because they usually are
installed at exactly the same place on all machines for a given platform.
It's an issue when you link a program with your own libraries or libraries
from third-party vendors. Remember that the right way to do it is **never
specifying a shared library with a full or absolute pathname on the linker
command line.**

3-5-1 The ldd Command

To double check and ensure you link the program with your own shared
library the right way, use a command to list all the shared
libraries that a program depends on and make sure you see only the base
name of the library, not one with a full or absolute pathname.
For example, if your program links with libtst1.so, then you should see

    libtst1.so

instead of something like:

    /myproj/lib/libtst1/libtst1.so

This utility program is the ldd command in most systems including Linux,
Solaris, AIX and HP-UX. Use "otool -L" in Apple Mac Darwin.

The ldd command lists the shared library dependencies of a program or
shared library. It tells you where it expects to find all dependent
shared libraries when the program runs.

Here is an example of using the ldd command:

    $ ldd uselink
        linux-vdso.so.1 =>   (0x00007fffd79ff000)
        libtst1.so => not found
        libc.so.6 => /lib64/libc.so.6 (0x0000003b89a00000)
        /lib64/ld-linux-x86-64.so.2 (0x0000003b89600000)

3-5-2 How to Make the Linker Find the Libraries

The ways of making the linker find the **static (archive) libraries** it needs
on some popular operating systems are listed below:

    Linux: -L/directory_of_my_lib linker option

(Neither LIBPATH nor LD_LIBRARY_PATH works here.)
  For example:
    cc -static -o uselink uselink.o -L/myproj/lib/libtst1 -ltst1

Solaris:
  Simply give the full pathname of an archived library on the
  linker command line.

AIX: Either use '-L/directory_of_my_archive_lib -lmylib' on the linker
    command line or simply give the full path name of the archive library.
  For example:
    xlc -o uselink uselink.o -L/myproj/lib/libtst1 -ltst1

HP-UX: Just give the pathname of the archived library on the linker
  command.

Apple Darwin: Just give the pathname of the archived library on the linker
  command, either relative or absolute.

WINDOWS: Use LIB environment variable

The ways of making the linker find the **dynamic (shared) libraries** it needs
are listed below:

Linux: Use the '-L/directory_of_my_lib' linker option
    (Neither LIBPATH nor LD_LIBRARY_PATH works here.)
  For example:
    cc -dynamic -o uselink uselink.o -L/myproj/lib/libtst1 -ltst1

Solaris:

  Use the '-Wl,-Bdynamic -llibname' linker command line option and set up
  the environment variable LD_LIBRARY_PATH so that the linker can find
  the shared library.

AIX: Give full pathname of the shared library on the linker command
    line. But always specify the -bnoipath linker option as well so
    that only the base file name of the shared library is recorded.
    This allows the shared library to exist in any directory at run time
    and allows users to use the LIBPATH environment variable to make the
    loader find the shared library when the program runs.
    (Neither LIBPATH nor LD_LIBRARY_PATH works here.)
  For example:
    xlc -bnoipath -o uselink uselink.o ../../libtst1/libtst1.so

HP-UX: Just give the pathname of the shared library on the linker
  command.

Apple Darwin: Just give the pathname of the shared library on the linker
  command, either relative or absolute.

WINDOWS: Use linker option: /LIBPATH:\directory_of_my_lib
    For example: link /LIBPATH:C:\mylib
    In Windows, the linker does not use LIB nor PATH environment variable
    to locate a shared library.

3-6 How Does an Application Find Shared Libraries at Run Time

When you link a program statically against some libraries,
as long as the linker finds those libraries and links successfully then
you are all set. There is no business to take care of at run time.
In other words, with static linking there is no need for an application
program to find a library at run time.

However, when you try to run a program, whether it's built by you or someone
else, that is dynamically linked, you always have a responsibility to
correctly set up some environment variable such that the program can find
all of the shared libraries it references. Otherwise, the program won't
even start. This is true for running programs written in different languages,
including C and Java.

Be aware that a program may reference functions in many different libraries.
Some of these libraries may be part of the operating system. Some may be
your own. And some may come from third-party software vendors.
You need to make sure when you set up the environment variable for
search path of dynamic libraries, it includes directories of all of these.
For instance, on Linux and Unix systems, you must include both /lib and
/usr/lib in the search path because these are where the operating system
shared libraries reside.

In most systems, the system administrator may have a system-wide setup
such that the default value of the environment variable includes all of
the standard directory locations. In that case, you may only need to append
the locations of your own libraries or third-party vendor libraries to
the existing value.

The environment variable that you must set so that programs can find
the shared libraries they use at run time is listed below for some of
the most popular operating systems.

```
Linux:     LD_LIBRARY_PATH=/lib:/usr/lib:/shlib_dir1:/shlib_dir2
Solaris:   LD_LIBRARY_PATH=/lib:/usr/lib:/shlib_dir1:/shlib_dir2
Aix:       LIBPATH=/lib:/usr/lib:/shlib_dir1:/shlib_dir2
HP-UX:     SHLIB_PATH=/lib:/usr/lib:/shlib_dir1:/shlib_dir2
Apple Darwin:
    (a) To run a dynamically linked program
       DYLD_LIBRARY_PATH=/lib:/usr/lib:/shlib_dir1:/shlib_dir2
    (b) To run a program that loads a shared library at run-time
       LD_LIBRARY_PATH=/lib:/usr/lib:/shlib_dir1:/shlib_dir2
Windows:   PATH=C:\Program Files\Microsoft Visual Studio
10.0\Common7\Tools;\shlib_dir1;\shlib_dir2
```

Note that the separator between directory names is ';' (semicolon) on
Windows and ':' (colon) on almost all of the other platforms.
The values shown above are just examples. /shlib_dirn is not real.

Keep in mind that correctly setting the value of this environment variable
is how you make your C or Java application programs find all of the shared
libraries they use when they run.

For instance, below is an example of the value of this LD_LIBRARY_PATH environment variable on a Linux system. It includes the standard operating system shared library locations /lib and /usr/lib, the directory for all of my own shared libraries /myproj/lib, the directory for shared libraries of Oracle Database client software, and the directories for the Java software.

```
LD_LIBRARY_PATH=/lib:/usr/lib:/myproj/lib:/app/oracle/client/12.0.1/lib:
    /java/j2sdk1.6.2_06/jre/lib/i386:
    /java/j2sdk1.6.2_06/jre/lib/i386/native_threads:
```

If you are running Oracle Database system (the server) software, then your dynamic library search path should also include the $ORACLE_HOME/lib directory. For instance, /oracle/product/12.1/lib.

Note that in Linux and Unix systems, depending on which shell you are using, setting up an environment variable differs a little bit.
For example,

C shell (csh):

```
$ setenv LD_LIBRARY_PATH ${LD_LIBRARY_PATH}:/myproj/lib:/oracle/product/12.2/lib
```

Bourne shell (sh), Korn shell (ksh) and bash shell:

```
$ export LD_LIBRARY_PATH=$LD_LIBRARY_PATH:/myproj/lib:/oracle/product/12.1/lib
```

3-7 Dynamic Loading -- No Linking

Up to this point in this chapter we have said that there are two ways to use a library. That is, you can either statically or dynamically link your program with the libraries it references. In fact, we lied. There is indeed a third way. Here we introduce this third way of using a library. It is without linking. It's also called 'dynamic loading'.

Yes, your program can use a library without even linking with it at the build time.

The way **dynamic loading** works is that to use functions in a library, you don't link your program with it. Instead, within the program, at run time, your program opens and loads the library, then looks up the address of the library function it wants to use, saves that address in a pointer to function variable, and then de-references that pointer to invoke the function. No linkage needed since there is no direct invocation of the function.

With dynamic loading, no presence of the shared library is needed at all at the program's build time. The program only needs to know the names of the library, and functions and global variables it references at coding time. It will then load the shared library at run time, look up the addresses of those symbols, and then use them.

Dynamic loading is one step even further in the direction of dynamic linking. With dynamic loading, you get all advantages of dynamic linking, such as smaller program size and automatically getting bug fixes and updates of the library. In addition, you don't even need the presence of the library to build the application program.

The advantage of using dynamic loading could mean saving money from license fees in your development. For example, you may be developing some application software for the Oracle Database system by using the client library provided by Oracle. If you use static or dynamic linking, then you will need to purchase and install a copy of the Oracle client library on every development machine where you build your application. By using dynamic loading, you only need to license and install the Oracle client library on your test machine(s), not on development machines. That could lead to saving substantial amount of money. Using dynamic loading, all you need to know at development time is the specifications of the APIs that your application uses, namely, the names of functions and the names and data types of their parameters.

3-7-1 How to Program Dynamic Loading

To use a library via dynamic loading, your program needs to do the following basic steps:

- Load the library
- Look up symbols (e.g. function names) in the library
- Use the functions just looked up
- Close the library

The API function your program uses to load and open a shared library is named dlopen() in Unix and Linux and LoadLibrary() in Windows.
The dlopen() or LoadLibrary() function loads a library or object module into the address space of the calling program and returns a handle to the loaded library or module. The handle is needed in later processing.
If the library is loaded for the first time, its initialization function is called.

With the library loaded, your program can then call the dlsym() function in Unix and Linux, or the GetProcAddress() function in Windows, to look up the address of a symbol such as a function name. This function takes the handle of the loaded library and the symbol's name as input and returns the symbol's address. With the function's address, your program can then call that function as if it's a function from a regular library.

When your program is done with using the dynamically loaded library, it must call the dlcose() function in Unix and Linux, or the FreeLibrary() function in Windows, to unload the library. This function takes the handle of the library as input. Failing to unload the library could lead to memory leak.

In case of errors, an application program calls the dlerror() function to get the error message of the last error in Unix and Linux.
The dlerror() function takes no argument. It returns a pointer to a null-terminated string describing the last error that occurred in a dynamic loading function.

In a Java application, your application could load a shared library at run time using System.loadLibrary("xx") where xx is the name of the library. You could also use the ClassLoader object to dynamically load a Java class.

Please read the documentation (e.g. the man page in Unix and Linux) of these functions on your system to get further details. We will give a real example in Section 3-10-6.

3-8 Compile Time, Load Time and Run Time

I believe it is very helpful to get a certain understanding of what actually happens in the entire process from building to running a program.
In this section we take a closer look at this entire process.

Figure 3-2 Entire process of program building and execution

```
cc         ld       myprog    O.S.      system loader       main() of     dlopen()
                               kernel                        myprog
|---------|-------|--------|---------|---------|---------|------------|------>
compile   link     run      create    load      load shared  execute    load dynamic
                   program   process   program   libraries    program    library


      static/dynamic
          linking    |                    |<--- load time --->|    dynamic loading
<- compile time ->|<---------- run time ------------------------------------>
```

Figure 3-2 shows the entire process of program building and execution.
The bottom line of the figure shows the compile time and run-time phases.
The middle line of the figure shows the different actions and tasks that are actually carried out throughout the entire process.
And the top line in the figure shows the programs or code that are actually run at different points in time.

As you can see from the diagram, a program goes through many stages from building to execution. The very first phase is the so-called compile time or build time in which two steps are performed: compile and link.
The compile step invokes the compiler (typically, named cc) to translate all of the source files of the program into object code. The link step invokes the linker command (typically named ld) to assemble together the object code modules and the library code referenced by them into an executable program. This step generates the executable file of the program.
Symbol resolution is done at the link time. All functions and global variables referenced in the program must be located and resolved at this time or the program linking would fail.

Once the program is built, if you type in the program name at the operating system command prompt or do it any other way to start to run the program, it officially kicks off the "run time" stage of the program.

The very first step of a program's run time is the creation of a process by the operating system kernel. In Unix and Unix-like operating systems, the operating system basically does a fork() and exec() to create the process.
It first forks a child process from the current parent process that tries start the program. The parent process is the shell program if you try to run the program from the operating system command prompt.
This fork step creates a new process which is essentially a copy of the current parent. Then the operating system kernel does an exec to replace the new child process with the image of the program you try to run, giving the newly created process its own real identity.

Before the program can be executed, it must be first loaded from disk into memory. This begins the so-called "load time".

During the load time, the operating system typically invokes the system loader program to load your program into the memory. If shared libraries are used, then they are loaded too, again by the loader or on some systems by a separate program called the dynamic linker. Some relocation processing is also finished up at this point. (For instance, the real addresses of the symbols from the shared libraries are filled into the program.) The load step ends when the program and all needed shared libraries are loaded into memory. Then the control is transferred to the main() function -- the real beginning -- of the program and the program starts running.

As you can see, the so-called "run-time" that many people grossly refer to includes, in fact, a process creation time and a load time. These are times before the first line of code in the program actually gets to run. Then there is the time to actually execute the code in your program, which is what most people perceive as the run time which may include dynamic loading.

3-9 Mixed Mode Linking

A program usually links with multiple software libraries. Typically, you uniformly link a program with the static version of all libraries or the dynamic version of them.

However, it is important to know that on many systems, you as a developer can elect to have a mixed-mode linking. That is, you can choose to link your program statically with some libraries and dynamically with others at the same time within a single program.

These systems normally have a linker option or switch that you can use in front of the library specification to indicate whether you want to link that library statically or dynamically. On many systems, the option is a toggle switch. Once the switch is turned on in a certain mode, it remains in that mode for all libraries follow until it is flipped to the other.

For example, in Oracle/Sun Solaris, the -Bstatic and -Bdynamic linker options do exactly this. They set the preference for a library binding to the archive or shared library, respectively, if both static and dynamic versions of a library are available. During the linking, the linker uses archive libraries first after it sees the -Bstatic option and it uses the shared libraries first after it sees the -Bdynamic option. Of course, -Bdynamic is only valid in building dynamic mode programs or libraries.

In AIX, the -bstatic and -bdynamic work in similar way, too. These linker options act like toggle switches. You can use each of them multiple times on a single linker command. When -bdynamic is in effect, shared libraries are used as shared libraries. When -bstatic is in effect, shared libraries as treated as regular object files. That is, they are linked in statically.

For instance, in executing the following command

```
xlc -o myprog myprog.o -bstatic -L/myproj/lib/libtst1 -ltst1 -bdynamic
```

the libtst1.a will be used because of -bstatic option. However,

libc.so will be used because of the -bdynamic at end. If your system only
has libc.a, it will be processed as a shared library.

In Linux, the mixed-mode link command is like the following:

```
$ cc -o uselink uselink.c -static  -L../../../libtst1  -ltst1 -dynamic
$ cc -o uselink uselink.c -dynamic -L../../../libtst1  -ltst1 -static
```

3-10 Example of Building and Using Your Own Library

In this section we give an example of developing your own library and
then developing an application to use functions in your own library.
We also demonstrate all the three different ways of using your own library
-- static linking, dynamic linking, and dynamic loading.
Note that dynamic loading loads and uses the dynamic/shared version of
our own library.

The library we will be building contains three library functions in two
source files. Below are the names of the source files and the functions
defined in them:

```
tripleIt.c:
  int tripleIt(int x);

echoMsg.c:
  int echoMsg(char *msg);
  int echoMsg2(char *msg);
```

The source files are shown in Figure 3-3.

The tripleIt() function takes an integer as input, computes its triple and
returns the result. The echoMsg() function is meant to just echo the message
you pass in. To illustrate the idea that one library function can call
another, we make it calls the echoMsg2() function to actually print the
message, compute the length of the input message and return the length.
For demonstration purposes we add a printf() statement in each of
the two functions so that you can see the functions are actually called
and the order they are invoked.

Now we will build this library in static and dynamic formats. Then we will
develop applications to use it in the three different ways we discussed.

Figure 3-3 Source code of functions in our own library (tripleIt.c, echoMsg.c)

(a) tripleIt.c

```
/*
 * Library functions - source file #1.
 * Authored by Mr. Jin-Jwei Chen
 * Copyright (c) 1991-2013 Mr. Jin-Jwei Chen  All rights reserved.
 */

#include <stdio.h>

/*
```

```
 * Compute and return the triple of the input integer value.
 */

#if WINDOWS
__declspec(dllexport) int __cdecl  tripleIt(int x)
#else
int tripleIt(int x)
#endif
{
  printf("The library function tripleIt() was called.\n");
  return (3*x);
}
```

(b) echoMsg.c

```
/*
 * Library functions - source file #2.
 * These functions demonstrate that one library function can call another
 * library function and a library function can take input arguments and
 * return a value.
 * Authored by Mr. Jin-Jwei Chen
 * Copyright (c) 1991-2013 Mr. Jin-Jwei Chen  All rights reserved.
 */

#include <stdio.h>
#include <string.h>

/*
 * Call another library function to echo the input message.
 * Return the length of the input message.
 */

#if WINDOWS
__declspec(dllexport) int __cdecl  echoMsg(char *msg)
#else
int echoMsg(char *msg)
#endif
{
  int echoMsg2(char *msg);

  printf("The library function echoMsg() was called.\n");
  return(echoMsg2(msg));
}

/*
 * Echo the input message and return its length.
 */

int echoMsg2(char *msg)
{
  int  len = 0;

  printf("The library function echoMsg2() was called.\n");
  if (msg != NULL) {
    len = strlen(msg);
    printf("*** Your message is: %s\n", msg);
```

```
    }
    return(len);
}
```

3-10-1 Build Your Own Static Library (libtst1.a/libtst1.lib)

Building your own library is easy. There are two steps. First, you compile.
Then you create the library.

To build your own library as an archive/static library, you perform the
following two steps:

1. Compile all of the library source files into object code. (cc -c)
2. Put all of the library object files into a single archive library.

Below are how you build your own archive library on various platforms.

Linux

```
    cc -c tripleIt.c echoMsg.c
    ar rv libtst1.a tripleIt.o echoMsg.o
```

Solaris

```
    gcc -c -fPIC -m64 tripleIt.c -o tripleIt.o
    gcc -c -fPIC -m64 echoMsg.c -o echoMsg.o
    ar rv -S libtst1.a  tripleIt.o echoMsg.o
```

AIX

```
    xlc -c tripleIt.c echoMsg.c
    ar -rv libtst1.a tripleIt.o echoMsg.o
```

HP-UX

```
    cc -c  tripleIt.c -o tripleIt.o
    cc -c  echoMsg.c -o echoMsg.o
    ar rv libtst1.a  tripleIt.o echoMsg.o
```

Apple Darwin

```
    cc -c -fPIC tripleIt.c -o tripleIt.o
    cc -c -fPIC echoMsg.c -o echoMsg.o
    ar rv libtst1.a tripleIt.o echoMsg.o
```

Windows

```
    cl -c -DWINDOWS tripleIt.c echoMsg.c
    lib tripleIt.obj echoMsg.obj -out:libtst1.lib
```

In Windows you use the lib.exe command to create a static library.
Note that the compiler command includes '-DWINDOWS' because the source
files use the '#if WINDOWS'. You may not need that in compiling other
source files.

3-10-2 Build Your Own Dynamic Library (libtst1.so/libtst1.dll)

To build your own library as a shared/dynamic library, you perform the
following two steps:

1. Compile all of the library source files into object code. (cc -c)
2. Put all of the library object files into a single shared library.

Please remember what we talked about earlier that when you link a program
dynamically, you must make sure only the base names of dynamically linked
libraries are recorded in the program's executable file. Or the program
may fail to start.

Below are how you build your own shared library on various platforms.

Note:
  1. The +Z flag in HPUX is required, so is the -fPIC flag in Linux.
  2. Each exported function needs a special declaration in Windows.
     Or the library builds and loads OK but the symbol lookup will fail
     in getting each function's address with errno=0.

Linux

```
cc -fPIC -c tripleIt.c echoMsg.c
ld -shared -o libtst1.so tripleIt.o echoMsg.o
```

   (The -shared linker option produces a shared library. Whether you
   specify the -fPIC on the ld command or not does not seem to matter.)

   or

```
gcc -fPIC -c tripleIt.c echoMsg.c
gcc -shared -Wl,-soname,libtst1.so -o libtst1.so tripleIt.o echoMsg.o -lc
```

Solaris

```
gcc -c -fPIC -m64 tripleIt.c -o tripleIt.o
gcc -c -fPIC -m64 echoMsg.c -o echoMsg.o
gcc -G -m64 -o libtst1.so tripleIt.o echoMsg.o -lc
```

AIX

   Use a text editor to create an export file for the library: libtst1.exp.
   Figure 3-4 shows this export file.

```
xlc -c tripleIt.c echoMsg.c
xlc -o libtst1.so tripleIt.o echoMsg.o -bE:libtst1.exp -bM:SRE -bnoentry
```

   Figure 3-4 Library export file for AIX (libtst1.exp)

```
#! /myproj/lib/libtst1/libtst1.so
*
* Above is the full pathname to the shared library object file.
* Below is the list of symbols to be exported in the library:
*
```

```
        tripleIt
        echoMsg
```

```
HP-UX

   cc -c +Z tripleIt.c
   cc -c +Z echoMsg.c
   ld -b -o libtst1.so tripleIt.o echoMsg.o -lc
```

```
Apple Darwin on MacBook

   cc -c -fPIC tripleIt.c -o tripleIt.o
   cc -c -fPIC echoMsg.c -o echoMsg.o
   ld -dylib -o libtst1.so tripleIt.o echoMsg.o -lc
```

```
Windows

   cl -c -DWINDOWS tripleIt.c echoMsg.c
   link.exe -dll -out:libtst1.dll -nologo -map:libtst1.map tripleIt.obj echoMsg.obj
```

In Windows you use the link.exe command to create a dynamic library.
Note that the compiler command includes '-DWINDOWS' because the source
files use the '#if WINDOWS'. You may not need that in compiling other
source files.

Note that when you build a dynamic library in Windows, it creates a *.lib
file. When you try to build your application, you link your application
with the *.lib file, rather than the *.dll file. In our example, you
link the application with libtst1.lib.

In addition, the dynamic library is linked in without an absolute path.
Hence, you can move the dynamic library to a different directory after
building the application and it will still work as long as you set the
PATH environment variable to include the new location.

3-10-3 Develop an Application Using Your Own Library

Here we write a very simple program that invokes two of the functions in our
own library. There is nothing special. Calling functions in our own library
is exactly the same as calling functions in any other libraries.
The goal is just to show how you build your application with your
own library and to prove the whole thing works.

Figure 3-5 shows the very simple application C program that we will use to
demonstrate how to deploy static and dynamic libraries of our own.

Figure 3-5 Application program using static or dynamic linking (uselink.c)

```
/*
 * This program demonstrates calling functions in libraries of our own
 * via static or dynamic linking.
 * Authored by Mr. Jin-Jwei Chen
 * Copyright (c) 1991-2013 Mr. Jin-Jwei Chen. All rights reserved.
 */
```

94

```
#include <stdio.h>
#include <errno.h>

int main(int argc, char **argv)
{
  int  ret;
  int  x = 22;
  char *mymsg = "Hello, there!";

  /* Pass in an integer and get back another */
  ret = tripleIt(x);
  printf("Triple of %d is %d.\n", x, ret);

  /* Pass in a string and get back an integer */
  ret = echoMsg(mymsg);
  printf("There are %d characters in the string '%s'.\n", ret, mymsg);

  return(0);
}
```

3-10-4 Build an Application That Links with Your Own Static Library

To use a static library, whether it's provided by the operating system or yourself, you just simply add the library to the linker command line that links and builds the application.

For instance, to use the static version of our own library libtst1.a, we add "-ltst1" to the linker command line.

Besides, to tell the linker command you would like to link the program with the libraries statically, you also specify the "-static" linker option.

To tell the linker where to find your own library, use the "-Lpath_of_my_lib" right in front of -ltst1.

By default, the linker looks for libraries in the /usr/lib and /lib directories.

Following is the output from running the example application uselink:

```
$ uselink
The library function tripleIt() was called.
Triple of 22 is 66
The library function echoMsg() was called.
The library function echoMsg2() was called.
*** Your message is: Hello, there!
There are 13 characters in the string 'Hello, there!'.
```

Below are how you build your application by statically linking it with our own library libtst1.a.

Linux

```
cc -c uselink.c -o uselink.o
cc -static -o uselink uselink.o -L/myproj/lib/libtst1 -ltst1
```

or

```
gcc -static -o uselink uselink.c -L/myproj/lib/libtst1 -ltst1
```

(Note: The -static linker option prevents the program from linking with
 shared libraries on systems that support dynamic linking.)

Solaris

```
gcc -c uselink.c -o uselink.o
gcc -m64 -Bstatic -o uselink uselink.o ../../libtst1/libtst1.a
```

(Specifying -Bstatic or not does not seem to matter.)

AIX

Build A Program Using Static Linking

```
xlc -c  uselink.c -o uselink.o
xlc -o uselink uselink.o -L/myproj/lib/libtst1 -ltst1
```
or
```
xlc -o uselink uselink.o -bstatic -L/myproj/lib/libtst1 -ltst1 -bdynamic
```

(This links with libtst1.a statically and with other libraries
 dynamically. Make sure if you use -bstatic you always end the linker
 command with a -bdynamic unless you want all libraries to link
 statically.)

HP-UX

```
cc -c +Z uselink.c -o uselink.o
cc  -o uselink uselink.o   ../libtst1/libtst1.a
```

Apple Darwin

```
cc -c uselink.c
cc -o uselink uselink.o  ../../libtst1/libtst1.a
```

Windows

The linker in Windows uses the LIB environment variable to find static
libraries. To use a static library of your own, make sure you add the
name of the directory containing that static library to the LIB environment
variable. For example,

```
C:\> set LIB=C:\myproj\lib\libtst1;%LIB%
```

This assumes the path to our own library is
C:\myproj\lib\libtst1\static\win\libtst1.lib.

Then use the following command to build the application program by
statically linking with our own static library on Windows:

```
C:\> cl -DWINDOWS uselink.c libtst1.lib
```

3-10-5 Build an Application That Links with Your Own Dynamic Library

Following are how to build our application program and link it with the dynamic library of our own.

To build the program you use the linker option for dynamic linking for the platform. For example, in Linux you can use the '-L/directory_of_lib -lxyz' linker option to specify your own library libxyz.so.
After the program is built, to run it you must remember to add the directory where your own dynamic library resides to the environment variable specifying the search path of dynamic libraries on that platform.

Note that the biggest mistake one might make in linking a program dynamically with a shared library is linking with an absolute or fixed pathname of the shared library. In other words, the linking is done in a way such that the pathname of the shared library is 'hardwired' in the loader section of the application program. The problem with this is when the software is delivered to customers, the shared library may get installed at a different directory and that will prevent the program from running because the loader won't be able to find the shared library at the location that was hardwired in at the time when the program was linked.

Therefore, it's extremely important that you do this right. The right thing to do is to always ensure that you link application programs such that no full or absolute pathname of the shared libraries is recorded.
Rather, only the base names of the shared libraries should be recorded in the loader section of the programs. This way, the shared libraries can exist in any directory and as long as the user sets the dynamic library search path environment variable correctly, the loader will be able to find the shared libraries when the program runs.

To achieve this goal, for example, in AIX, you must use the -bnoipath option of the xlc linker command to link the program.

Below are how to link our own application with our own dynamic library libtst1.so.

Linux

```
cc -fPIC -c uselink.c
cc -dynamic -o uselink uselink.o -L/myproj/lib/libtst1 -ltst1
```

or

```
gcc -dynamic -o uselink uselink.c -L/myproj/lib/libtst1 -ltst1
```

Solaris

```
gcc -c -fPIC -m64 uselink.c -o uselink.o
gcc -m64 -Bdynamic -o uselink uselink.o -Wl,-Bdynamic -ltst1
```

Set up environment variable LD_LIBRARY_PATH so that the linker can find our own shared library libtst1.so during the linking.

AIX

Build a Program Using Dynamic Linking

```
xlc -c uselink.c -o uselink.o
xlc -o uselink uselink.o -bnoipath /myproj/lib/libtst1/libtst1.so
```

(Don't use '-L/myproj/lib/libtst1 -ltst1' here.)

HP-UX

```
cc -c +Z uselink.c -o uselink.o
cc -dynamic -o uselink uselink.o   -L../libtst1/  -ltst1
```

Apple Darwin on Mac

```
cc -c uselink.c
cc -o uselink uselink.o  ../../libtst1/libtst1.so
```

Windows

```
cc -c -DWINDOWS uselink.c
link uselink.obj /LIBPATH:C:\myproj\lib\libtst1  libtst1.lib
```

3-10-6 Develop and Build an Application That Dynamically Loads Your Own Library

Invoking library functions via dynamic loading involves a bit of more work than via static or dynamic linking. This is because your application program is not linked with the library at build time. In fact, you don't mention anything about the library at all when you build the application program. When the program is built, it absolutely requires no presence of the library on the system.

This means your program has to do some more work than usual.
First, your program has to know the name of the library it wants to use.
Second, your program has to physically load that library from disk into memory and open it. Third, your program needs to look up the address of each function it wants to call and use that address to actually invoke it.

Figure 3-6 Application program using dynamic loading (useload.c)

```
/*
 * This program demonstrates how to dynamically load a shared library.
 * This same program works on all of these platforms: Windows XP,
 * Solaris 9, AIX 5.2, HP-UX 11.11, Linux 2.6.9 and Apple darwin 19.3 and on.
 * Use "cc -DWINDOWS" when you compile this program on Windows.
 * Authored by Jin-Jwei Chen.
 * Copyright (C) 2007, 2013 by Jin-Jwei Chen. All rights reserved.
 */

#include <stdio.h>
#include <stdlib.h>
#include <errno.h>

#if WINDOWS
#include <windows.h>
```

```
#else
#include <dlfcn.h>
#endif

#if WINDOWS
#define   FUNCPTR    FARPROC
#define   SHLIBHDL   HMODULE
#else
typedef int (*FUNCPTR)();      /* define FUNCPTR as type of ptr-to-function */
#define   SHLIBHDL  void *
#endif

struct funcPtrEle {
    FUNCPTR *funcPtr;      /* pointer to (i.e. address of) the ptr-to-function */
    char     *funcName;    /* Name of the function */
};

typedef struct funcPtrEle FUNCPTRELE;

/* Declare the variables that will hold pointer to the functions. */
int (*FPechoMsg)();
int (*FPtripleIt)();

/* Set it up for symbol address lookup after loading the library.
 * First column gives address of the ptr-to-func variable. Second column
 * gives the name of the corresponding function.
 * The lookup will use the string value (the function name) in the second
 * column as input and fill in the pointer value in the first column.
 */
FUNCPTRELE funcPtrTbl[] = {
  /* FPechoMsg is a variable holding the ptr to the echoMsg() function */
   (FUNCPTR *)&FPechoMsg,   "echoMsg",
   (FUNCPTR *)&FPtripleIt,  "tripleIt",
   (FUNCPTR *)NULL,          (char *)NULL
};

SHLIBHDL load_shlib(char *libname, FUNCPTRELE *fptbl);

/*
 * Name of the shared library to load. Assuming most platforms use the .so
 * file name extension. Change the name accordingly to suit your system.
 */
#if WINDOWS
char SHLIBNAME[64] = "libtst1.dll";
#elif HPUX
char SHLIBNAME[64] = "libtst1.sl";
#else
char SHLIBNAME[64] = "libtst1.so";
#endif

/*
 * Start of main() function.
 */

int main(int argc, char **argv)
{
```

```
 int   ret;
 int   x = 22;
 char *mymsg = "Hello, there!";

 SHLIBHDL  hdl;

 /* Dynamically load the library and look up address of each function. */
 hdl = load_shlib(SHLIBNAME, funcPtrTbl);
 if (hdl == NULL) {
    fprintf(stderr, "Failed to load the library %s\n", SHLIBNAME);
    return(1);
 }

 /* Use the pointer-to-function to call each function. */

 /* Pass in an integer and get back another */
 ret = FPtripleIt(x);
 printf("Triple of %d is %d.\n", x, ret);

 /* Pass in a string and get back an integer */
 ret = FPechoMsg(mymsg);
 printf("There are %d characters in the string '%s'.\n", ret, mymsg);

 return(0);
}

/*
 * This function loads the shared library whose name specified by the
 * libname parameter. It then looks up the address of each function
 * whose name is specified by the second field of each element in the
 * array given in the fptbl parameter. The address obtained is returned
 * to the caller in the first field of each element in the array given
 * in the fptbl parameter.
 *
 * INPUT parameter: libname - name of the library to load
 * INPUT and OUTPUT parameter: fptbl - array of function pointers and
 *    function names.
 */

SHLIBHDL load_shlib(char *libname, FUNCPTRELE *fptbl)
{

    SHLIBHDL  hdl = NULL;

    if (libname == NULL || fptbl == NULL)
      return(NULL);

    /* Load the library */
#if WINDOWS
    hdl = LoadLibrary(libname);
#else
    hdl = dlopen(libname, RTLD_NOW | RTLD_GLOBAL);
#endif
    if (hdl == NULL) {
      fprintf(stderr, "Loading library %s failed.\n", libname);
#ifndef WINDOWS
```

```
            fprintf(stderr, "%s\n", dlerror());
#endif
        return(hdl);
    }


#ifndef WINDOWS
    /* Clear any existing error */
    dlerror();
#endif
    /* Look up symbols */
    while (fptbl->funcName != (char *)NULL)
    {
#if WINDOWS
        if ((*(fptbl->funcPtr) = GetProcAddress(hdl,
                            fptbl->funcName)) == (FARPROC)NULL)
        {
        fprintf(stderr, "Looking up symbol %s failed\n", fptbl->funcName);
        FreeLibrary(hdl);
        return (SHLIBHDL) NULL;
        }
#else
        if ((*(fptbl->funcPtr) = (FUNCPTR)dlsym(hdl, fptbl->funcName)) == NULL)
        {
        fprintf(stderr, "Looking up symbol %s failed\n", fptbl->funcName);
        dlclose(hdl);
        return (SHLIBHDL) NULL;
        }

#endif
        fptbl++;
    }
    return (hdl);
}
```

Figure 3-6 shows the program that uses dynamic loading to invoke the same two functions in the library of our own. Functionally, it is equivalent to the uselink.c shown above. Structurally you can see it is quite different.

The program in Figure 3-6 uses the following four functions in Unix and Linux to get its job done. These dynamic loading functions exist in the libdl.so shared library on these platforms. This means you must link your program doing dynamic loading by specifying the -ldl on the linker command in Linux, AIX, Solaris and Apple Darwin. But no need to specify -ldl or anything else in HPUX.

```
    dlopen()
    dlsym()
    dlclose()
    dlerror()
```

The dlopen() function loads a library from disk into memory and opens it. The dlsym() function looks up the address of a symbol such as a function name from the loaded library so that your program can then access it. The dlcose() function closes and unloads the library after use. The dlerror() function obtains the last error message.

On a Windows platform, the following three functions are used:

```
LoadLibrary() - loads the library
GetProcAddress() - looks up address of a symbol
FreeLibrary() - unloads the library
```

Note that building an application that uses dynamic loading to access a library has absolutely no need to mention that library at build time. The build just works without even knowing whether that library exists at all.

However, at run time, in order for the program to run successfully, you must set up the shared library search path environment variable to include the directory containing the shared library to be dynamically loaded. This ensures the operating system can find the library when the application runs. This setting in general is the same as that of making a dynamically linked program being able to find the shared libraries it references. The only exception is Apple Darwin which uses different environment variables for the two cases.

Following is the output from running the example application useload:

```
$ useload
The library function tripleIt() was called.
Triple of 22 is 66
The library function echoMsg() was called.
The library function echoMsg2() was called.
*** Your message is: Hello, there!
There are 13 characters in the string 'Hello, there!'.
```

Below are the commands for building and running the example application using dynamic loading on various platforms.

Linux

Note that in Linux when you use the ld command, the order you specify the libraries on the ld command line matters.
It's a bit tricky to use ld in Linux. Using cc and gcc is much easier.

```
cc -c -fPIC -g useload.c -o useload.o
cc -o useload useload.o -lc -ldl
```

or

```
gcc -c useload.c
gcc -rdynamic -o useload useload.o -ldl
```

To run the application, first set LD_LIBRARY_PATH:
    export LD_LIBRARY_PATH=$LD_LIBRARY_PATH:/myproj/lib/libtst1
This assumes libtst1.so exists in the /myproj/lib/libtst1 directory.

Solaris

```
gcc -c fPIC -m64 useload.c -o useload.o
gcc -m64 -o useload useload.o
```

To run the useload program, set up LD_LIBRARY_PATH environment variable to include the directory in which the shared library to be loaded resides.

AIX

```
xlc -c useload.c -o useload.o
xlc -o useload useload.o
```

To run the useload program, set up the LIBPATH environment variable to include the directory in which the shared library to be loaded resides.

HP-UX

```
cc -c +Z useload.c -o useload.o
cc -dynamic -o useload useload.o   -L../libtst1/  -ltst1
```

To run the useload program, set up the SHLIB_PATH environment variable to include the directory in which the shared library to be loaded resides.

Apple Darwin

Just build the program as usual without reference to the library.
```
cc -m64 -o useload useload.c
```

Set up environment variable LD_LIBRARY_PATH to include the directory where the dynamic library to be loaded resides. Assuming libtst1.so is in /myproj/lib/libtst1/ directory:

```
export LD_LIBRARY_PATH=$LD_LIBRARY_PATH:/myproj/lib/libtst1
```

Windows

Build the application using dynamic loading

```
C:\> cl -DWINDOWS useload.c
```

Run the application

```
C:\> PATH=C:\myproj\mybk1\lib\libtst1;%PATH%
C:\> useload.exe
```

3-11 Quick Reference of the Commands

This section provides a quick reference to the commands used in building libraries and programs in various ways on the most popular operating systems.

Linux

Build an Archive Library

```
cc -fPIC -c tripleIt.c -o tripleIt.o
cc -fPIC -c echoMsg.c -o echoMsg.o
ar rv libtst1.a tripleIt.o echoMsg.o
```

Build a Shared Library

```
cc -fPIC -c tripleIt.c -o tripleIt.o
cc -fPIC -c echoMsg.c -o echoMsg.o
ld -shared -o libtst1.so tripleIt.o echoMsg.o
```

Build a Program Using Static Linking

```
cc -c uselink.c -o uselink.o
cc -static -o uselink uselink.o -L/myproj/lib/libtst1 -ltst1
```

Build a Program Using Dynamic Linking

```
cc -c -fPIC uselink.c -o uselink.o
cc -dynamic -o uselink uselink.o -L/myproj/lib/libtst1 -ltst1
```

Build a Program Using Dynamic Loading

```
cc -o useload useload.o -lc -ldl
```

Set Up to Run a Dynamically Linked or Dynamically Loading Program

```
export LD_LIBRARY_PATH=$LD_LIBRARY_PATH:/myproj/lib/libtst1
```

Build a 32-bit Program

```
cc -m32 -o myprog myprog.c
```

Build a 64-bit Program

```
cc -m64 -o myprog myprog.c
```

Solaris

Build an Archive Library

```
gcc -c -fPIC -m64 tripleIt.c -o tripleIt.o
gcc -c -fPIC -m64 echoMsg.c -o echoMsg.o
ar rv -S libtst1.a tripleIt.o echoMsg.o
```

Build a Shared Library

```
gcc -c -fPIC -m64 tripleIt.c -o tripleIt.o
gcc -c -fPIC -m64 echoMsg.c -o echoMsg.o
gcc -G -m64 -o libtst1.so tripleIt.o echoMsg.o -lc
```

Build a Program Using Static Linking

```
gcc -c -fPIC -m64 uselink.c -o uselink.o
gcc -m64 -Bstatic -o uselink uselink.o ../../libtst1/libtst1.a
```

The -Bstatic linker option instructs the linker to use only static
libraries.

Build a Program Using Dynamic Linking

```
gcc -c -fPIC -m64 uselink.c -o uselink.o
gcc -m64 -Bdynamic -o uselink uselink.o -Wl,-Bdynamic -ltst1
```

The -Bdynamic linker option tells the linker to link with shared libraries whenever possible.

Setting up LD_LIBRARY_PATH environment variable before linking of your program so that the linker can find your own shared library.

Build a Program Using Dynamic Loading

```
cc -c fPIC -m64 useload.c -o useload.o
cc -m64 -o useload useload.o
```

Set Up to Run a Dynamically Linked or Dynamically Loading Program

```
export LD_LIBRARY_PATH=$LD_LIBRARY_PATH:/myproj/lib/libtst1
```

Build a 32-bit Program

```
gcc -m32 -o myprog myprog.c
```

Build a 64-bit Program

```
gcc -m64 -o myprog myprog.c
```

Note: The old 64-bit option -xarch=v9 is retired on some systems.

AIX

Build an Archive Library

```
xlc -c tripleIt.c -o tripleIt.o
xlc -c echoMsg.c -o echoMsg.o
ar rv libtst1.a  tripleIt.o echoMsg.o
```

Build a Shared Library

Create the export file libtst1.exp with exported function names in it:

```
#! /myproj/lib/libtst1/libtst1.so
*
* Above is the full pathname to the shared library object file.
* Below is the list of symbols to be exported in the library:
*
tripleIt
echoMsg
```

```
xlc -c tripleIt.c -o tripleIt.o
xlc -c echoMsg.c -o echoMsg.o
xlc -bE:libtst1.exp -bM:SRE -bnoentry -o libtst1.so tripleIt.o echoMsg.o
```

Build a Program Using Static Linking

```
xlc -c uselink.c -o uselink.o
xlc -o uselink uselink.o -L/myproj/lib/libtst1 -ltst1
```
or
```
xlc -o uselink uselink.o -bstatic -L/myproj/lib/libtst1 -ltst1 -bdynamic
```

```
(This links with libtst1.a statically and with other libraries
dynamically. Make sure if you use -bstatic you always end the linker
command with a -bdynamic.)
```

Build a Program Using Dynamic Linking

```
xlc -c uselink.c -o uselink.o
xlc -o uselink uselink.o -bnoipath /myproj/lib/libtst1/libtst1.so
```

```
(Don't use '-L/myproj/lib/libtst1 -ltst1' here.)
```

Build a Program Using Dynamic Loading

```
xlc -c useload.c -o useload.o
xlc -o useload useload.o
```

Set Up to Run a Dynamically Linked or Dynamically Loading Program

```
LIBPATH=/lib:/usr/lib:/myproj/lib/libtst1; export LIBPATH
```

Build a 32-bit Program

```
cc -q32 -o myprog myprog.c
```

Build a 64-bit Program

```
cc -q64 -o myprog myprog.c
```

HPUX

Build an Archive Library

```
cc -c tripleIt.c -o tripleIt.o
cc -c echoMsg.c -o echoMsg.o
ar rv libtst1.a  tripleIt.o echoMsg.o
```

Build a Shared Library

```
cc -c tripleIt.c -o tripleIt.o
cc -c echoMsg.c -o echoMsg.o
ld -dynamic  -o libtst1.so tripleIt.o echoMsg.o -lc
```

```
or
    cc -c +Z file1.c; cc -c +Z file2.c; cc -c +Z file3.c
    cc -b -o libtst1.sl file1.o file2.o file3.o
```

Build a Program Using Static Linking

```
cc -c +Z uselink.c -o uselink.o
cc -o uselink uselink.o   ../libtst1/libtst1.a
```

Build a Program Using Dynamic Linking

```
cc -c +Z uselink.c -o uselink.o
cc -dynamic -o uselink uselink.o   -L../libtst1/  -ltst1
```

Build a Program Using Dynamic Loading

```
cc -dynamic -o useload useload.o
```

Set Up to Run a Dynamically Linked or Dynamically Loading Program

```
SHLIB_PATH=/lib:/usr/lib:/myproj/lib/libtst1; export SHLIB_PATH
```

Build a 32-bit Program

```
cc +DD32 -o myprog myprog.c
```

Build a 64-bit Program

```
cc +DD64 -o myprog myprog.c
```

Apple Darwin (MacBook)

Build an Archive Library

```
cc -c -fPIC tripleIt.c -o tripleIt.o
cc -c -fPIC echoMsg.c -o echoMsg.o
ar rv libtst1.a tripleIt.o echoMsg.o
```

Build a Shared Library

```
cc -c -fPIC tripleIt.c -o tripleIt.o
cc -c -fPIC echoMsg.c -o echoMsg.o
ld -dylib -o libtst1.so tripleIt.o echoMsg.o -lc
```

Build a Program Using Static Linking

```
cc -c uselink.c
cc -o uselink uselink.o  ../../libtst1/libtst1.a
```

Build a Program Using Dynamic Linking

```
cc -c uselink.c
cc -o uselink uselink.o  ../../libtst1/libtst1.so
```

Build a Program Using Dynamic Loading

Simply build the program normally without any reference to the shared library to be loaded at run-time.

Set Up to Run a Dynamically Linked Program

```
export DYLD_LIBRARY_PATH=$DYLD_LIBRARY_PATH:/myproj/lib/libtst1
```

Set Up to Run a Program Dynamically Loading a Shared Library

```
export LD_LIBRARY_PATH=$LD_LIBRARY_PATH:/myproj/lib/libtst1
```

Build a 32-bit Program

```
cc -m32 -o myprog myprog.c
```

Build a 64-bit Program

```
cc -m64 -o myprog myprog.c
```

Windows

Build an Archive Library

```
cl -c -DWINDOWS tripleIt.c echoMsg.c
lib tripleIt.obj echoMsg.obj -out:libtst1.lib
```

Build a Shared Library

```
cl -c -DWINDOWS tripleIt.c echoMsg.c
link.exe -dll -out:libtst1.dll -nologo -map:libtst1.map tripleIt.obj
echoMsg.obj
```

Build a Program Using Static Linking

```
set LIB=C:\myproj\lib\libtst1;%LIB%
cl -DWINDOWS uselink.c libtst1.lib
```

Build a Program Using Dynamic Linking

```
cc -c -DWINDOWS uselink.c
link uselink.obj /LIBPATH:C:\myproj\lib\libtst1  libtst1.lib
```

Build A Program Using Dynamic Loading

```
cl -DWINDOWS useload.c
```

Set Up to Run a Dynamically Linked Program

```
set PATH=C:\myproj\lib\libtst1;%PATH%
```

Build a 32-bit Program

```
cl -DWINDOWS -DWIN32 useload.c
```

Build a 64-bit Program

```
cl -DWINDOWS -DWIN64 useload.c
```

Exercises

1. (a) What is a software library?
    (b) What is the purpose of a library? Why use it?
    (c) What are the two types of software libraries in terms of providers?
    (d) What are the two types of software libraries in terms of linking?
        What are the file name extensions (i.e. suffixes) of these library
        types on your system?
    (e) In what directory do software libraries reside on your system?

(f) Explain why code reuse is very important.

2. What are the two phases in building an executable program or a library? What are the names of the commands that perform these tasks on your system?

3. What is static linking? What is dynamic linking?

4.
  (a) What is the difference between dynamic linking and dynamic loading?
  (b) Describe the advantages and disadvantages of static linking, dynamic linking, and dynamic loading.

5. Describe the time that external references are first resolved with static linking, dynamic linking, and dynamic loading.

6. What is the difference between a loader and a linker?

7. How would you build a static library of your own on the system you use? And how would you do the same for a dynamic library?

8. What command(s) would you use to build a statically linked program on your system? And what command(s) would you use to build a dynamically linked program on your system?

9. What command(s) would you use to build a 32-bit application on your system? And what command(s) would you use to build a 64-bit program?

10. What is the so-called "DLL Hell"?

11. Describe what happens during the various phases in building and running a program on the system you use.

Projects

Design a software library of your own. Build a static and a dynamic versions of it.

Then develop an application program calling functions in this library. Build the application program in both static and dynamic linking with your own library.

Lastly, develop a program that calls functions in your own library using dynamic loading.

4 File I/O

When you develop a software, very often you will find you need to read and/or write files. For example, if you develop database management systems, you will find you deal with files all the time. Many databases are actually stored in disk files. Even if you develop other applications, chances are there is a need to read and/or write data files, configuration files, temporary files, etc. from a program.

This chapter discusses how to operate a file from within a C program, including open, create, read and write files. It also talks about different ways of manipulating a file, including sequential I/O, random I/O, synchronous I/O, asynchronous I/O, vectored I/O, buffered I/O and direct I/O.

There are many other standard APIs defined for working with permission, name, directory and other attributes of files. We will introduce those in the next chapter.

When working at a very big company, author saw other engineers try to reinvent the wheel and create a lot of very basic file manipulation functions for the product to use. It's completely redundant and in fact silly. Those operations such as creating a file, writing a file, reading a file and changing the permission of files are very rudimentary and have long been in the POSIX Standard. Almost all the operating systems I know support these for decades. So, just get familiar with the file I/O APIs introduced in this and next chapters. Try to use them in your programs. And remember that you don't need to recreate any of these yourself. Just use these standard APIs, they are efficient, robust, portable, simple and very easy to use.

4-1 Structure of a Disk

4-1-1 Physical Structure of a Disk

Computers store files on disks most of the time for a number of reasons. First, it is persistent. Information stored on disks remains even after the power is off. In contrast, information stored in computer memory disappears when the power goes off. Second, disk is a mass storage. Its capacity is much larger than memory. Third, it is affordable and cost effective.

Since when programs do file I/O, they do file I/O to and from disks most of the time. It would be very useful to get some understanding of what a disk is before we dig into various ways of operating on a file.

111

Modern computers are almost always equipped with some disks for permanent storage of information. Usually information is stored in files on disk. It is very common that software engineers develop programs that deal with files. Having a basic understanding of the physical structure of a disk is very important and helpful in developing and understanding programs that manipulate files. This section provides a very brief description of the physical structure of a disk.

Figure 4-1 shows the physical structure of a disk.

A hard disk, disk drive, or simply disk is composed of a number of flat, magnetically coated platters that are stacked together on a spindle. The spindle rotates at a high speed, usually 5400 RPM (Rotation Per Minute) or higher.

Each platter can have two surfaces. Each surface consists of a number of concentric rings. Each of these concentric rings is called a **'track'**. The width of a track allows storage of one bit of information. Each track is divided into a number of sectors. A **sector** is also called a **physical block** or a disk block. Each sector normally stores 512 bytes of information. We will use the two terms, sectors and physical blocks, interchangeably in this book.

Vertically, the group of tracks that are at the same distance from the center of the disk form a **'cylinder'**.

The disk arm containing **read/write heads** moves side way. It moves in and out to locate the track and then the read/write head touches the platter surface to actually read or write information.

In a nutshell, a hard disk drive is electric-mechanical. It consists of both electronic circuits and mechanical parts. The electronic circuit controls the operation of the disk and acts as the interface between the computer processor and the disk device. The mechanical portion includes two major parts. The **spindle** has a stack of platters with magnetic surfaces rotating at high speed, with information recorded on the magnetic surfaces. And the disk arms with read/write heads move in and out, seeking the desired surface/cylinder/track/sector, touching the surface and reading/writing information under the control of the electronic circuit.

It is worth pointing out that on a given disk platter, tracks are of different length. The inner tracks are shorter than the outer ones. Therefore, the number of sectors per track varies with the radius of the track. Apparently, the outer tracks have more sectors than the inner ones. Since it takes exactly the same amount of time for the innermost and the outermost tracks to make one rotation, the outermost track has to turn faster than the innermost one. In addition, if you store the information on the outermost track, you can read or write more information than if you do on an inner track in each disk rotation. As a result, for performance sake, the file system should store the most frequently accessed information in the outer tracks rather than in the inner ones.

Figure 4-1 Physical structure of a disk

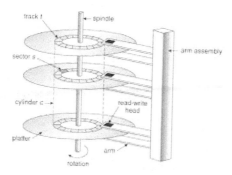

4-1-2 Partitions and File Systems

Normally, a computer is equipped with at least one hard disk drive on which the operating system software that controls the operations of the computer is installed. (When you power on a computer, the operating system software is read from disk into physical memory so that the computer can execute it and control the operations of the computer.) Very often you will see a computer has multiple disk drives and the rest of the disks are used to store other software and data.

On the disk where the operating system resides (this is sometimes called the "root" or system disk), a disk is often divided into multiple divisions where each is called a **partition** and is used for a different purpose.

For example, traditionally, a root disk has a partition to hold the operating system software (this partition is often called the "root" partition) and another partition to hold users' home directories. And it may also have a third partition to hold some application software.

Figure 4-2 Disk partitions and layout of a file system

```
          ----------------------------------------------------------------
A disk |    partition 1   |    partition 2    |    partition 3    |
          ----------------------------------------------------------------
         / file system       /home file system    /app file system

       holds O.S. software   holds users home dirs   holds applications

    (a) An example of disk partitioning


          ----------------------------------------------------------------
A file |boot |super|  inode list    |      data blocks           |
system |block|block|                |                            |
          ----------------------------------------------------------------

    (b) Layout of an example file system
```

Before a disk partition can be used, it must be formatted and a file system must be created. **Formatting** a disk partition erases all data on the partition.

Making a file system on a partition is to create some structure and management information on the partition, prepare it and make it ready to be used (for instance, letting applications to start creating files on it).

After a file system is created, it also needs to be mounted so that it is online. Each file system is mounted on its unique mount point, which is some directory in the root file system.

Although each disk partition usually has a file system residing on it, some disk partition may be used as a raw device and thus has no file system on it.

There are different types of file systems developed by different organizations and vendors at different times. In Unix, traditionally AT&T System V uses UNIX System V file system (S5). Berkeley UNIX has Unified File System (UFS). AT&T UNIX later supports both S5 and UFS file systems. Linux supports ext2, ext3, ext4. Windows supports FAT and NTFS.

File System Layout

Different **file system types** have different layout on the disk space it occupies. Each may also use a different logical block size.

As we said it earlier, a disk can be viewed as consisting of a sequence of **physical blocks** or sectors which are usually 512 bytes in size. When a file system is created on a partition, a **logical block** size is used, which is typically a multiple of 512. When the operating system reads/writes data to/from a file system, it does it in size of logical blocks. That is, the operating system kernel reads/writes a file system one or more logical blocks at a time.

Using bigger logical disk block size may improve the data transfer rate between disk and memory and thus improve performance because it is reading/writing more data at a time. However, it may waste more disk space because not all files are of that size and the unused gap at end gets larger too.

Figure 4-2(b) shows a typical layout of a file system. As you can see, each file system usually has a 'boot block' at the beginning, which is followed by a 'super block', then the 'inode list' (which we will discuss soon in section 4-4. For now, just remember the **inode** is a data structure that the operating system kernel creates to manage each file in the file system), and then the data blocks that contain actual data of the files.

The **boot block** typically contains the bootstrap code that is read into memory and executed when the computer boots. Note that even with a single disk on a computer, one may partition the disk into multiple partitions, install different operating systems into different partitions, boot and run different operating systems at different times on the same computer.

For instance, many computer engineers have personal computers with both Linux and Windows installed. In this case, the boot block of one partition contains Windows bootstrap code and the boot block of another partition contains the bootstrap code of the Linux operating system. It's best to have different operating systems reside on different partitions.

The **super block** contains the overall state and information of the file system. It stores the highest-level information about the file system, such as the file system type, the size of the file system, how many files it can store, and how much free space is left, etc.

Since the super block stores the most basic and important information about a file system, it is very critical to the integrity of the file system. If information in the super block is corrupt, it's possible one has to re-make the file system and thus lose all the data in the entire file system. Because of this, there is usually more than one copy of the super block stored on disk for redundancy sake.

The super block and the inode list are the so-called file system's **metadata**.

4-2 Some Concepts About Files

4-2-1 Two Different Views of a File

There are two different views of a file.

Logically, a file is just a sequence of contiguous bytes or blocks. This is the view of an application that uses files. Applications read, write and update bytes of data in a file.

Physically, a file consists of a number of physical disk sectors, which may or may not be physically contiguous. The operating system software actually manages the file on disk and reads, writes and updates one or more sectors each time.

Figure 4-3 Logical and Physical Views of a file

```
-----------------------------------------------------------
|AbCh28fYeKKp091GHmcXvJqrt;+-@e%hjbnYr4052:=XF1M .... |
-----------------------------------------------------------
```

(a) Logical view of a file (application's view)

```
-----------------  ---------  ---------  ---------  ---------
|sector1|sector2|  |sector6|  |sector3|  |sector4|  |sector5|
-----------------  ---------  ---------  ---------  ---------
```

(b) Physical view of a file (file system software's view)

In summary, to a program, a file is just a contiguous sequence of bytes. To the file system of an operating system, which actually manages the file on the disk device, a file is a set of sectors scattered around on a disk. Programs read/write bytes from/to files while the operating system reads/writes disk sectors (i.e. blocks).

4-2-2 Steps to Manipulate a File

There is a sequence of steps to follow in manipulating a file. In the simplest scenario, they include the following three steps:

1. Open the file (for reading, writing, or reading and writing)
2. Read and/or write the file.
3. Close the file.

Note that a program must open a file first before reading from or writing to it. If opening the file fails, then it cannot read from or write to it. Once the file is opened, a program can then read from or write to it.

Normally, a program opens a file for read only or write only. However, programs often open a file for read and write. Database management system software is a typical example. They read some contents from a file, modify them, and then write them back. This is the three steps of a typical database update operation.

Symmetric to the concept of opening a file, there is a concept of closing the file. After finishing using a file, a program must close the file. In a given process, each open operation should be matched with a close operation for each file.

There are many reasons for closing a file after use. First, file I/Os are often buffered or cached. This caching may be implemented at the program level, at the operating system level, or both. Updates may stay in memory until the file is closed. In that case, not closing the file may result in loss of data if the system were to crash or lose power right after. Second, if multiple programs are sharing the same file, without closing a file, updates made by that program might not be made available to others. Third, certain resources, for instance, locks, may still be held by the program. Without closing the file, the resources may not be released and it may lead to other programs not being able to access the same file or the file system cannot cleanly shut down.

On most operating systems, when a process terminates, either exits normally or dies unexpectedly, the operating system usually automatically closes the file(s) it has opened. But a good program should not rely on that. It is very important and always a good practice that a program always closes all of the files it has opened before terminating. Of course, a program might not be able to do so when it dies unexpectedly due to an unanticipated bug or an unexpected power outage. This is why on every boot-up, the operating system always checks the integrity of file systems (e.g. by running fsck or CHKDSK command) before mounting them online.

4-2-3 The Current File Offset

Remember, with file I/O, your process always has an implicit 'current file offset' associated with each open file. You may not even be aware of it. But it exists and the operating system keeps track of it.

The **current file offset**, sometimes also called the **current file pointer**, or simply file offset or file pointer, is the byte position in the file where your program will be reading from or writing into. That is, it is where the next I/O begins. Note that it's a byte position, a byte offset into the file from the beginning of the file. When a program opens a file, the current file offset always automatically points to the beginning of the file. In other words, immediately after a program opens a file, by default, the first read or write operation is always from or to the beginning of the file.

The file offset increases, i.e. the file pointer moves forward, automatically each time a program does a read or write operation. And it increases by exactly the number of bytes the program reads or writes each time.

Conceptually, you can think of the file offset as an integer variable with a non-negative value. That value is automatically set to 0 every time when a program opens a file. The value automatically increases each time when the program reads from or writes to the file, by exactly the number of bytes read or written at that time.

For example, after a program opens a file of size 4096 bytes, the current file offset is 0, pointing to the beginning of the file. If it reads 512 bytes, the current file offset will increase to 512. Then if it reads another 60 bytes, the current file offset will become 572.

The file offset keeps track of where a program reads from or writes into within a given file at any instant of time. Note that the current file offset is per process and per file specific. In other words, if multiple processes share the same file, each process will have its own independent current file offset on the file, reading and/or writing at different locations of the file. Also, if a given process opens multiple files, it will have a separate independent current file offset for each of them.

4-3 Two Programming Interfaces

When you program in the C language, there are two separate file I/O interfaces available for use. One is using the standard C library functions, which is part of the ANSI C standard and independent of any operating system. These APIs are part of the C language implementation. Programs using these **standard C APIs** run on any operating system supporting the ANSI C language.

The other is using **operating system APIs**, which are defined in the POSIX (Portable Operating System Interface) standard and are typically implemented as direct system calls into the operating system kernel. Programs using the file I/O APIs defined in the POSIX standard can run on POSIX-compliant operating systems only.

The standard C APIs are implemented as user-space library functions which usually call into the operating system APIs. Hence, it is at a higher level.

Apparently, programs using the standard C library functions for file I/Os are more portable because it's operating system independent in that it does not make use of the operating system calls directly. However, it may be less efficient. It also lacks some of the advanced features. In contrast, programs using the operating system interfaces for file I/Os are not as portable but are more efficient and yield better performance. In addition, using the operating system interfaces for file I/Os has other advantages including being versatile, tighter and more sophisticated control, and many advanced features such as vectored I/O, asynchronous I/O and direct I/O are available.

Because of this, most system software uses operating system interfaces, which is what this chapter will discuss. Since these APIs are defined in the POSIX standard, they are portable across all POSIX-compliant operating systems if you use only the standard features.

Please be aware that a program doing I/O using the operating system interfaces only compiles (links successfully, to be exact) and runs on an operating system that supports these APIs.

The POSIX standard is widely implemented across most popular operating systems including almost all flavors of Unix and Linux. Specifically, these operating systems include AIX, Solaris, HPUX, Tru64 Unix, Unixware, all Linuxes including RedHat Linux, and Apple Darwin. Some other operating systems outside the Unix and Linux domain also support POSIX standard.

Here we will give a very brief overview of the two file I/O interfaces.

Although it is perfectly OK for a C program to use both file I/O interfaces at the same time, it's very rare that people do so.

To allow co-existence, these two interfaces use different function names. For example, the names of most file I/O functions defined in the standard C library start with the letter f while those in the operating system interface don't. For instance, the names of the functions for opening, reading and writing a file are fopen, fread, and fwrite, respectively, in the standard C library interface and open, read, and write, respectively, in the operating system level interface.

Another example of difference is the file handle. A **'file handle'** is a representation of an opened file in a program. After a program opens a file, it gets a 'file handle' back and then uses that file handle to manipulate the file. A file handle is a pointer to the FILE structure in the standard C library file I/O interface:

```
FILE *fp;
```

In contrast, the operating system interface uses a file descriptor, which is an integer, to represent an opened file:

```
int fd;
```

Figure 4-4 A first glimpse of the two file I/O interfaces

File I/O Interface	Example Function Names		File Handle
C library interface	fopen fread fwrite		FILE *fp
OS interface	open read write		int fd

Figure 4-5 lists some of the most frequently used file I/O functions defined in the two interfaces.

It is worth pointing out that most of the file I/O functions defined in the POSIX Part 1 standard are implemented as system calls into the operating system, meaning that they are implemented inside the operating system kernel rather than as user space library functions. Therefore, they are very efficient. This is especially true in all of the Unix and Linux operating systems.

Figure 4-5 Sample file I/O functions in both file I/O interfaces

```
-------------------------------------------------------------------
O.S. interface          Standard C library interface
---------------         -------------------------------------------
open                    fopen

read                    fread  fgetc fgets fgetw fscanf

write                   fwrite  fputc fputs fputw fprintf

close                   fclose

fsync                   fflush

lseek                   fseek  ftell  fsetpos  fgetpos

readv                   N/A

writev                  N/A

aio_read                N/A

aio_write               N/A

fcntl                   N/A

ioctl                   N/A

pwrite                  N/A

select                  N/A

direct I/O              N/A
-------------------------------------------------------------------
N/A: Not Available
```

The man pages (online documentation) of Unix and Linux system calls are listed in the section 2 whereas the man pages for library functions are in section 3. For example, assuming the man pages are installed on your system, to get the online documentation on how to open a file, you do the following at the command prompt of a Unix and Linux operating system:

```
$ man open
```
or
```
$ man 2 open
```

```
$ man fopen
```
or
```
$ man 3 fopen
```

In the subsequent sections of this chapter, we will introduce the various operating system level interface functions for performing file I/Os.

4-4 File Descriptor and Associated Kernel Data Structures

4-4-1 Inodes

A file system typically stores tens of thousands of files or even more. To manage this large number of files, a file system creates and uses certain management data structures which are also stored in the file system, typically, in front of the actual file data.

We briefly describe the core of these data structures in this section.

Internally in the operating system, a file is represented by a data structure called **inode**, which stands for index node. An inode contains management information about a file such as owner, permissions, access times of the file, and so on. Note that a directory is also a file.

Each file has one inode, although it may have multiple different names referring to it. Each inode has an **inode number** which is unique within the file system. In other words, each file in a file system is described by an inode data structure and is identified by a unique inode number inside the operating system kernel. The kernel maintains one inode for each file, regardless of multiple pathnames may reach to that same file.

When a file is first created, the operating system kernel creates an inode for it in kernel memory. Inodes are also persisted in the file system on disk. Normally when an existing file is opened, the operating system kernel reads its inode from disk into an inode table in kernel memory. After that all file accessing operations (including reading, writing or updating the file and others) all use and perhaps update the information in the file's inode. Note that the operating system kernel (in particular, the file system component) is responsible for keeping the inode information consistent with the actual file contents.

While users and application programs refer to a file by its pathname, operating system kernel (i.e. the file system component) accesses it via the inode for efficiency. The kernel internally translates the pathname of a file into its inode number, done by the namei() routine in UNIX source code.

Note that the inode information exists both in memory and on disk. The actual contents of all files in a file system are stored in the file data blocks of the file system. All of the inode information of these files is stored in the disk blocks allocated for the **'inode list'**. The inodes of those files that are currently opened by some processes are read into memory from disk. We call the in-memory inodes **'inode table'** and on-disk inodes 'inode list'.

As you can probably tell, the inodes are extra management information besides the actual file data. It is management data and is sometimes called **metadata**. It is there for managing the files' actual data. Therefore, in a sense it is overhead, but necessary. The inode list takes disk space too, as shown in Figure 4-2b. The disk space for the on-disk inodes is normally reserved at the time when a file system is created.

Note that some operating systems attempt to generalize file system design. So they have the so-called virtual file system which is an abstraction of file systems. On these systems, they usually have the so-called **vnode** data structure which encompasses the inode.

4-4-2 Inode Table

As we have just said, the inodes of the files currently opened are read from disk into memory and put in the inode table so that the O.S. file system code can quickly access them. Information in the inode table is used and updated when the files they represent are accessed by processes.
Managing the inode table is always a key part of any file system's operations.

4-4-3 System Open File Table

The operating system kernel also maintains another system-wide table called **'open file descriptor table'**.

When a user process opens a file, the kernel also allocates an entry in the system-wide open file table for it. This entry contains a pointer to the inode entry in the inode table corresponding to this file.
If a process opens the same file twice or two processes open the same file, two separate entries in the system open file table will be allocated and both of these entries will point to the same entry in the inode table because they are the same file. Two separate open file table entries are allocated and maintained because the two may perform completely different operations on the same file. For instance, one may open the file as read only and the other as write only. In addition, the two will certainly have different values for the current file offset -- the current byte position of the file that the process is currently reading from or writing into.

In the example shown in Figure 4-6, the user process opens the same file /home/jc/myfile twice. Hence, there are two open file table entries allocated and they point to the same entry in the inode table.

4-4-4 User File Descriptor Table

Conceptually, when a program opens a file, it gets a 'file handle' back such that the program can then use it to identify the file and perform various operations to it. Actual representation of the file handle is interface dependent. As we pointed it out in the previous section, a **file handle** is represented as a pointer to the FILE structure in the standard C library interface whereas it is represented by an integer in the POSIX standard operating system level interface. Since we are going to discuss the operating system interface defined in the POSIX standard, here we explain the file handle representation in that interface.

In the file I/O interface defined in the POSIX standard, an open file is represented by a file descriptor within a program.
A **file descriptor** is a non-negative integer used by a process to uniquely identify an open file for the purpose of access within that process. File descriptors are process-specific. In fact, a file descriptor is just

an index into a per-process file descriptor table which the operating system creates to track all files opened by a process.

A system always has multiple processes running and each of them may open and access multiple files. To keep track the multiple files a given process opens, each process has a **'user file descriptor table'** where each entry tracks a file opened by the process. This table is private to each process. When a process opens a file, it gets a file descriptor back which is an integer. This integer indeed is an index into the open file descriptor table of the process. That's why the file descriptor is a non-negative integer, not a structure or pointer to a structure.

```
  per process
  user file       system open file       system inode table
  descriptor      descriptor table
  table
   --------       ---------------        ------------------
0 |stdin |       |              |       |                  |
  |------|       |--------------|       |------------------|
1 |stdout|       |              |   +-->|                  |
  |------|       |--------------|   |   |------------------|
2 |stderr|  +--->|              |   |---+                  |
  |------|  |    |--------------|       |------------------|
3 |      |  |--+ |              |       |                  |
  |------|     | |--------------|       |------------------|
4 |myfile|----->|              |  |------>|/home/jc/myfile  |
  |------|       |--------------|  +--->|------------------|
5 |myfile|--+    |              |  |  |  |                  |
  |------|  |    |--------------|  |  |  |------------------|
  |  :   |  +--->|              |  |--+  |                  |
            |--------------|       |------------------|
            |      :       |       |        :         |
```

Figure 4-6 Per-process file descriptor table and system-wide
            open file table and inode table

Note that when a C program starts, by default it always opens three standard text streams: the standard input, the standard output, and the standard error. They are associated with the user's terminal.
The standard input is associated with the keyboard device.
The standard output and the standard error are associated with the monitor display device or window. In a C program, these are represented by stdin, stdout and stderr, respectively. These three files always occupy the first three entries of the per-process user file descriptor table with index 0, 1 and 2. Because of this, the files a program opens usually has a file descriptor value of 3 or greater.

I/O Device or files	per-process File Descriptor
stdin	- file descriptor 0
stdout	- file descriptor 1
stderr	- file descriptor 2
first open file	- file descriptor 3
second open file	- file descriptor 4
third open file	- file descriptor 5
:	

When two or more processes open the same file, each of them gets an entry added to its own user open file descriptor table which may have completely different index and file descriptor values. These user open file descriptors will then point to their own entries in the system-wide open file table which will then point to the same entry in the inode table. This is how the operating system manages sharing of the same file between different concurrent processes. Figure 4-7 shows this. These concepts help you understand the internal working of the O.S. file system.

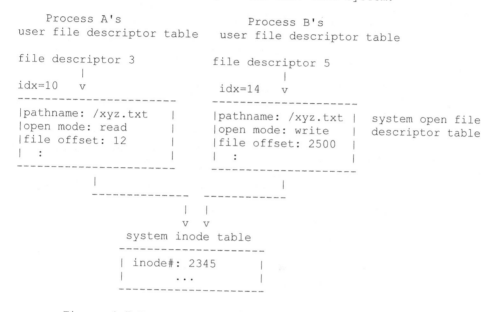

Figure 4-7 Two processes sharing a same file

In summary, the operating system maintains an inode table where each entry tracks an open file. It also maintains an open file table to manage the sharing of the same file between processes or multiple opens of the same file by the same process. These two tables are shared between the processes accessing the same file(s) on the same system.
In addition, each process has a private user open file descriptor table, which is not shared, where each entry tracks a file opened by the process. Entries in this table point to their own corresponding entries in the open file table, which in turn point to entries in the inode table. This is how typically an operating system manages files opened by processes.

4-5 Opening and Creating a File

There are multiple ways to create a file and there are at least two different functions for use. In POSIX, a program can use either the open() or the creat() function to create a file. The difference is creat() always creates/re-creates a new file while open() can also open an existing file. Their formats are below:

```
int open(const char *pathname, int flags, mode_t mode);
int open(const char *pathname, int flags);
int creat(const char *pathname, mode_t mode);
```

where pathname is the pathname of the file you want to create or open.
It can be an absolute or relative pathname. A pathname starting with the
'/' character is an absolute pathname. A relative pathname does not start
with the '/' character and it is relative to the process's current working
directory.

As you can see, the open() function has two flavors. One version has three
parameters and the other omits the third parameter. For the open() function,
the first parameter specifies the pathname of the file that you want to open.
The second parameter is a combination of flags where you must always specify
at least one of the following three: O_RDONLY, O_WRONLY, or O_RDWR.
These three flag values mean you want to open the file for read only, for
write only, or for read and write, respectively.

The third parameter to the open() function is optional. It specifies the
permissions that you want the file to have. For example, an octal value of
0644 means that you like to open the file with owner having read and write
permissions and group members and others having read only permission.

On success, the open() function returns a non-negative integer, the
so-called file descriptor, which will be the "handle" you use to access the
file later in your program. On error, the open() function returns -1 and
errno will be set to indicate the reason for failure to open. For instance,
an errno of ENOENT means the file specified in the pathname cannot be found.

Be aware that a few scenarios are possible in creating a file.
The file may not exist, which is typically what is expected, or it may
already exist. If the file already exists, you can choose to error out,
truncate the file (meaning erasing its current contents), or append to
the end of the file (meaning preserving its existing contents).

To handle these different possible scenarios, the open() function provides
a number of flags for programs to use. They include the following and
a few others:

O_WRONLY
  A program uses this flag to open or create a file for writing only.

O_RDONLY
  Open the file for reading only.

O_RDWR
  Open the file for reading and writing. The result is undefined if this
  flag is applied to a FIFO.

O_CREAT
  This flag means the program wants to create the file if it does not
  already exist. Without this flag, the open() function call will return
  an error without creating the file if the file does not already exist.
  The error number would be ENOENT, meaning "no such file or directory",
  in that case.

O_EXCL
  When used with O_CREAT, this flag means creating the file only if it does
  not exist. Return an error if it already exists. A call to the open()

function with a flags value of O_WRONLY|O_CREAT|O_EXCL would result in an error if the file already exists. The error number would be EEXIST, meaning "File already exists".

O_TRUNC

If the file is a regular file and already exists, then truncate its length to zero if the O_RDWR or O_WRONLY flag is specified and the open is successful. This effectively erases the existing file contents.

O_APPEND

Open the file in append mode, adding data to the end of the file.

O_SYNC

The file is open for synchronous I/O. Any writes on the resulting file descriptor will block the calling process until the data has been physically written to the underlying hardware (for example, disk).

O_NONBLOCK

For regular block special or character special files, specifying this flag tells the operating system that the open() function shall return without blocking and waiting for the device to become ready or available.

For a FIFO file, specifying this flag means an open() for reading-only shall return without delay. An open() for writing-only shall return an error if no process currently has the file open for reading.

Note that these are bit flags. To use more than one at once, you use the OR operator (|). For instance, a flag value of O_WRONLY|O_CREAT|O_TRUNC means the program wants to open the file for writing, to create the file if it does not exist, and to truncate the file and erase all of its existing contents if it already exists. That is, the program wants to create or re-create the file from scratch.

Obviously, if you try to open a file for read only, then you would not need most of the open flags we list here because they do not apply. To open a file for read only, O_RDONLY is all you need for the flags parameter of the open() function. If you like to open a file for both read and write, then you specify the O_RDWR flag instead.

When you try to create a file, the file may already exist. If the file already exists and you try to create it with the O_CREAT flag, the behavior depends on whether the O_EXCL flag is also present. If the O_EXCL flag is not specified, the open will succeed. But if O_CREAT and O_EXCL are both specified, then the open will fail if the file exists already.

The O_SYNC flag is used for synchronous I/O. Typically, file systems implement caching to improve performance. As a result, data written by applications may be kept in the file system cache in memory and not immediately written out to the actual hardware device. This could result in data loss if the system crashes or loses power soon after the write because the data is not persistent in the hardware device yet. Specifying this flag tells the operating system that a write() call to the file by this application should not return until the data is transferred to the actual hardware device. This is to avoid losing data from operating system caching in face of system crash or power outage.

There are more flags you can use with the open() function. Read its man page to get more details (by running the 'man open' or 'man 2 open' command at the O.S. command prompt).

Note that whenever your program uses the open() function, it must include the following header files. Or the program won't compile. The man page of each function tells you what header files are needed.

```
#include <sys/types.h>
#include <sys/stat.h>
#include <fcntl.h>
```

The creat() Function

If you choose to use creat() instead of open() function to create a file, then there is no need to have the flags parameter.

The two parameters for the creat() function are similar to those of the open() function. Most people use the open() function because it is more generic and covers more cases. You can use the open() function to open a file for read only, write only, read and write, create it if it does not exist, create it only if it does not exist, or create it even if it exists. The creat() function is a bit limited in comparison.

The following creat() call

```
creat(pathname, mode)
```

is equivalent to the following open() call:

```
open(pathname, O_WRONLY|O_CREAT|O_TRUNC, mode)
```

4-6 Writing a File

So far we know to create a file, a program needs to open the file using either the open() or creat() function. If that is all what it does, then the program would create an empty file if the file does not already exist. To put or add contents in a file, a program must write to it.

A program uses the write() function to write information into a file. The write() function has the following specification:

```
ssize_t write(int fd, const void *buf, size_t count);
```

The first parameter specifies the file descriptor, which is the integer value returned by the open()/creat() function, representing the file you want to write to. The second parameter specifies the starting address of the output buffer in memory containing the data to be written. The third parameter specifies how many bytes the output data is.

On error, the write() function returns -1 and the errno is set to indicate the error. On success, the write() function returns the number of bytes that are actually written.

Figure 4-8 shows a program that creates a file and writes data to it.

126

gendataf is a program that creates a file and writes a certain number of blocks to it. For ease of identification, it writes a block of all 0's, 1's, ..., a's, b's, ..., A's, B's, ... and so on. If the user asks to write more than 62 (10+26+26) blocks, then it repeats the same pattern. Note that it writes 512 bytes at a time but it does not have to be so. It can write 1024, 2048 or an arbitrary number of bytes each time. We use this program to create some input data files for testing programs introduced in this chapter.

Figure 4-8 gendataf.c

```c
/*
 * gendataf.c
 * This program opens a file and writes a number of 512-byte blocks to a file.
 * It can be used to create data files for testing.
 * Copyright (c) 2013, 2014, 2020 Mr. Jin-Jwei Chen.  All rights reserved.
 */

#include <stdio.h>
#include <errno.h>
#include <sys/types.h>
#include <sys/stat.h>
#include <fcntl.h>
#include <unistd.h>
#include <string.h>   /* memset() */
#include <stdlib.h>   /* atoi() */

#define   BUFSZ       512
#define   DEFBLKCNT    62

int main(int argc, char *argv[])
{
  char *fname;
  int   fd;
  ssize_t  bytes;
  size_t   count;
  char      buf[BUFSZ];
  int       blocks=DEFBLKCNT;   /* number of blocks to write */
  char      ch;                 /* byte content of each block */
  int       i, j, k;
  char      *bufadr;

  /* Expect to get the file name from user */
  if (argc > 1)
    fname = argv[1];
  else
  {
    fprintf(stderr, "Usage: %s filename [blocks]\n", argv[0]);
    return(-1);
  }
  if (argc > 2)
  {
    blocks = atoi(argv[2]);
    if (blocks <= 0)
      blocks = DEFBLKCNT;
  }
```

```c
    fprintf(stdout, "Writing %u blocks to file %s\n", blocks, fname);

    /* Open the output file. Create it if it does not exist.
     * Truncate the file to zero length if it already exists.
     */
    fd = open(fname, O_WRONLY|O_CREAT|O_TRUNC, 0644);
    if (fd == -1)
    {
        fprintf(stderr, "open() failed, errno=%d\n", errno);
        return(-2);
    }

    /* Write the number of blocks specified */
    for (k = 0; k < blocks; k++)
    {
        i = k % 62;   /* make i be 0-61 */
        if (i < 10)
            ch = '0' + i;
        else if (i < 36)
            ch = 'a' + (i - 10);
        else if (i >= 36)
            ch = 'A' + (i - 36);

        /* Fill the buffer with message to write */
        for (j = 0; j < BUFSZ; j++)
            buf[j] = ch;

        /* Write the contents of the buffer to the file. */
        count = BUFSZ;
        bufadr = buf;
        while (count > 0)
        {
            bytes = write(fd, bufadr, count);
            if (bytes == -1)
            {
                fprintf(stderr, "write() failed, errno=%d\n", errno);
                close(fd);
                return(-3);
            }
            count = count - bytes;
            bufadr = bufadr + bytes;
        }
    }

    /* Close the file */
    close(fd);
    return(0);
}
```

Note that writing text and binary data works the same way. You simply place the text or binary data that you want to write in the output buffer and then invoke the write() function. There is no difference as far as the write() function is concerned; the data is just a sequence of bytes in either case.

4-7 Write Robust Software Doing I/O

Be aware that every time your program makes a request to read or write
a certain amount of information, it may or may not actually transfer
exactly the amount of information you have requested. Many things could
cause that to happen. Some of the common causes include: disk is full and
no more space left for writing more data, it has reached the end of file
and no more data to read, your process gets interrupted in the middle
by a signal, hardware (such as disk or network) failure.
In some cases, an I/O operation can hang too.

We will discuss how to address the issue of dealing with possible hang
during an I/O operation later. Here we talk about how to address the rest of
potential error conditions.

Given so many "bad" things can happen during an I/O operation, to write very
robust software involved in any I/O operations -- be it file, network or
other types of I/O -- you must always keep this in mind and code your program
in such a way that it always performs correctly and properly in case of any
of these 'glitches'.

First, make sure your code always checks the return status of any I/O
function and properly handles each possible error condition.

To handle the case of end of file, your code must always check that
condition too. The read() function will return 0 if it reaches the end
of the input file.

To deal with the case where the amount of requested information may not be
100% fulfilled at a single read or write operation, the best way to do an I/O
is to always put the read or write operation in a loop and make sure that
all of the data you have requested are actually read or written.
Specifically, a read or write operation could transfer 100% of the data you
have requested, or only part of it. In the latter case you have to make a
second or even a third attempt to get the remaining amount of data done, or
until you know for sure there is no more data or there is an error.
The program gendataf in Figure 4-8 demonstrates this technique.

4-8 Reading a File

To read information from a file, a program must open the file first.
To open a file for read only, a program invokes the open() function passing
in the pathname of the file in the first argument and O_RDONLY in the
flags argument.

Once the input file is open, a program invokes the read() function to read
information from the file. The read() function has the following
synopsis:

```
#include <unistd.h>

ssize_t read(int fd, void *buf, size_t count);
```

This means to make a program that references the read() function compile,

the program must include the header file unistd.h.
And to use the read() function, the caller must supply the file descriptor
of the input file, the starting memory address of the buffer to receive the
input data (i.e. the data to be read from the file), and the length in bytes
of the input buffer (i.e. the number of bytes to be read). Note that the
caller must have already allocated the memory for the input buffer and
it must be big enough to hold the input data.

On success, the read() function returns the number of bytes that are actually
read. On error, the read() function returns -1 and the errno is set to
indicate the error. The read() function returns 0 if it has reached the
end of file (EOF).

Note that reading text and binary data works the same way. You simply
specify how many bytes you want to read and the read() function will
read it and place the input data in the buffer you specify.
There is no difference as far as the read() function is concerned; it simply
reads bytes. After the read, the program may process it in a slightly
different way depending on whether it's text or binary data. For instance,
if it's text data and you want to print it, then you will have to null
terminate it first by placing a zero byte ('\0') at the end of the data.

Figure 4-9 shows a program that reads the first 30 bytes from a file.

Figure 4-9 Reading data from a file -- read.c

```
/*
 * This program opens a file and reads the first few bytes from it.
 * Copyright (c) 2013, 2014, 2020 Mr. Jin-Jwei Chen.  All rights reserved.
 */

#include <stdio.h>
#include <errno.h>
#include <sys/types.h>
#include <sys/stat.h>
#include <fcntl.h>
#include <unistd.h>
#include <string.h>   /* memset() */

#define  BUFSZ              30
#define  READER_WAIT_TIME   1
#define  LOOPCNT            5

int main(int argc, char *argv[])
{
  char *fname;
  int  fd;
  ssize_t  bytes;
  char     buf[BUFSZ+1];
  size_t   i, j;

  /* Expect to get the file name from user */
  if (argc > 1)
    fname = argv[1];
  else
  {
```

```
      fprintf(stderr, "Usage: %s filename\n", argv[0]);
      return(-1);
   }

   /* Open the file for read only. */
   fd = open(fname, O_RDONLY);
   if (fd == -1)
   {
      fprintf(stderr, "open() failed, errno=%d\n", errno);
      return(-2);
   }

   /* Read some data from the file */
   bytes = read(fd, buf, BUFSZ);
   if (bytes == -1)
   {
      fprintf(stderr, "read() failed, errno=%d\n", errno);
      close(fd);
      return(-3);
   }
   buf[bytes] = '\0';
   fprintf(stdout, "Just read the following %ld bytes from the file %s:\n%s\n",
      bytes, fname, buf);

   /* Close the file */
   close(fd);
   return(0);
}
```

4-9 Sequential I/O

There are many operations a program can perform on a file.
Two of the very common and simple file operations are sequentially reading
a file and sequentially writing it.

In this section, we give an example that does just that -- making a copy
of an existing file. To copy a file, we open the source file for read only
and open the destination file for write only with O_CREATE and O_TRUNC
flags on. If both opens are successful, we then sequentially read from the
source file and sequentially write what is read to the destination file
until the end of the source file. At end we close both files.
It is that simple!

In our example, we arbitrarily choose to use a buffer of 2048 bytes.
You can use a smaller or bigger buffer. Different buffer sizes may have a
slight impact on performance. But performance is not a concern here for the
demonstration purpose.

Here in this example we put the write() function in a loop to
make sure we always write out everything we have read each time.
We do not place the read() function in a loop because we are just
copying the file and we don't have to read exactly 2048 bytes each time.
As long as we loop until we read to end of the file, we are covered.
When it reaches the end of the input file, the read() call will return 0.
The read loop will terminate when the whole file is read or when it gets

an error. If it hits an error, we close the files and exit.
Therefore, we cover all bases.

1. We ensure the read operation will read the entire file (until read()
   returns 0) unless it gets an error.

2. We ensure we write out everything we read each time unless it gets
   an error.

3. These two conditions together ensure the entire source file will be
   copied unless there is an error.

Figure 4-10 is an example program that does sequential read and write file
I/O. The program makes a copy of an existing file by sequentially reading
through the source file and sequentially writing it into the destination file.

Figure 4-10 Copying a file -- copy.c

```c
/*
 * This program makes a copy of an existing file.
 * It demonstrates sequential read and sequential write of files.
 * Copyright (c) 2013, 2014, 2020 Mr. Jin-Jwei Chen.  All rights reserved.
 */

#include <stdio.h>
#include <errno.h>
#include <sys/types.h>
#include <sys/stat.h>
#include <fcntl.h>
#include <unistd.h>
#include <string.h>   /* memset() */

#define  BUFSZ        2048

int main(int argc, char *argv[])
{
  char *infname, *outfname;  /* names of input and output files */
  int   infd, outfd;  /* input and output file descriptors */
  int   ret = 0;         /* return code of this program */
  ssize_t  bytes_rd, bytes_wr;  /* number of bytes read or written */
  size_t    count;
  int       done = 0;
  char      buf[BUFSZ];  /* input and output buffer */
  char      *bufadr;

  /* Expect to get the file names from user */
  if (argc > 2)
  {
    infname = argv[1];
    outfname = argv[2];
  }
  else
  {
    fprintf(stderr, "Usage: %s input_file output_file\n", argv[0]);
    return(-1);
  }
```

```c
/* Open the input file for read only. */
infd = open(infname, O_RDONLY);
if (infd == -1)
{
    fprintf(stderr, "opening input file failed, errno=%d\n", errno);
    return(-2);
}

/* Open the output file for write only. Create it if it does not already
 * exist. Truncate the file (erase old contents) if it already exists.
 */
outfd = open(outfname, O_WRONLY|O_CREAT|O_TRUNC, 0644);
if (outfd == -1)
{
    fprintf(stderr, "opening output file failed, errno=%d\n", errno);
    close(infd);
    return(-3);
}

/* Read from the input file and write to the output file. Loop until done. */
while (!done)
{
    /* Read the next chunk from the input file */
    bytes_rd = read(infd, buf, BUFSZ);
    if (bytes_rd == -1)
    {
        fprintf(stderr, "failed to read input file, errno=%d\n", errno);
        ret = (-4);
        break;
    }
    else if (bytes_rd == 0)   /* End Of File */
        break;

    /* Write the file contents we just read to the output file */
    count = bytes_rd;
    bufadr = buf;
    while (count > 0)
    {
        bytes_wr = write(outfd, bufadr, count);
        if (bytes_wr == -1)
        {
            fprintf(stderr, "failed to write output file, errno=%d\n", errno);
            ret = (-5);
            break;
        }
        count = count - bytes_wr;
        bufadr = bufadr + bytes_wr;
    }  /* inner while */
}  /* outer while */

/* Close the files */
close(infd);
close(outfd);
return(ret);
}
```

133

4-10 Sharing a File Between Concurrent Processes

Many real-life applications, not just database ones, involve sharing files between multiple processes running concurrently or simultaneously. For instance, one or more programs may create files while other programs try to read from them at the same time. Sharing files in a file system between programs is easy as long as you handle the concurrency properly, especially when two or more processes writing to the same file at the same time.

In this section, we give an example of sharing a file between two processes. We have a writer process, the writer program, opens and writes to the file one block at a time. And a reader process, the reader program, tries to read from the same file. To make it easier to understand and see the interaction, we make the writer pause after each write operation. We also make the reader and writer read and write the same size, one block at a time. It does not have to be so.

To run the demo programs, build them first and then issue the following two commands in the order shown from two separate windows:

    $ writer filename

    $ reader filename

Make sure you start the writer process first or the file won't exist when the reader process tries to open it.

As you can see from this example, as soon as a file is opened and written by a process, its contents are available to other processes as long as they know the pathname of the file and have permission to access it. In addition, the file does not have to be closed by the writer for the readers to see it. The beauty of this is the file can be shared in real time as it is opened and being written. Indeed, most of the time, the written file contents may be still in the file system's cache in memory without being flushed out to disk yet when the reader reads it.

Figure 4-11 shows the file writer and reader programs that demonstrate a file sharing.

    Figure 4-11 writer.c and reader.c

(a)   writer.c

```
/*
 * writer.c
 * This program creates a file and writes a block to it every few seconds.
 * It serves as the writer in the example of demonstrating
 * sharing a file between multiple concurrent processes.
 * Copyright (c) 2013, 2014, 2020 Mr. Jin-Jwei Chen.  All rights reserved.
 */

#include <stdio.h>
#include <errno.h>
```

134

```c
#include <sys/types.h>
#include <sys/stat.h>
#include <fcntl.h>
#include <unistd.h>
#include <string.h>   /* memset() */

#define  BUFSZ             512
#define  WRITER_WAIT_TIME  4
#define  LOOPCNT           5

int main(int argc, char *argv[])
{
  char *fname;
  int  fd;
  ssize_t  bytes;
  char     buf[BUFSZ];
  size_t   i, j;

  /* Expect to get the file name from user */
  if (argc > 1)
    fname = argv[1];
  else
  {
    fprintf(stderr, "Usage: %s filename\n", argv[0]);
    return(-1);
  }

  /* Open a file for write only. Create it if it does not already exist.
   * Truncate the file (erase old contents) if it already exists.
   */
  fd = open(fname, O_WRONLY|O_CREAT|O_TRUNC, 0644);
  if (fd == -1)
  {
    fprintf(stderr, "open() failed, errno=%d\n", errno);
    return(-2);
  }

  /* The write and wait loop. */
  for (i = 1; i < LOOPCNT; i++)
  {
    /* Fill the buffer with the block number */
    for (j = 0; j < BUFSZ; j++)
      buf[j] = i + '0';

    /* Write the contents of the buffer to the file. */
    bytes = write(fd, buf, BUFSZ);
    if (bytes == -1)
    {
      fprintf(stderr, "write() failed, errno=%d\n", errno);
      close(fd);
      return(-3);
    }
    fprintf(stdout, "%ld bytes were written into the file\n", bytes);

    /* Wait for a few seconds so the reader has a chance to read it */
    sleep(WRITER_WAIT_TIME);
```

135

```
     }

  /* Close the file */
  close(fd);
  return(0);
}
```

   (b)   reader.c

```
/*
 * This program opens a file and reads a block from it every time.
 * It serves as the reader in the example of demonstrating
 * sharing a file between multiple concurrent processes.
 * Copyright (c) 2013, 2014, 2020 Mr. Jin-Jwei Chen.  All rights reserved.
 */

#include <stdio.h>
#include <errno.h>
#include <sys/types.h>
#include <sys/stat.h>
#include <fcntl.h>
#include <unistd.h>
#include <string.h>   /* memset() */

#define   BUFSZ               512
#define   READER_WAIT_TIME    1
#define   LOOPCNT             5

int main(int argc, char *argv[])
{
  char *fname;
  int   fd;
  ssize_t  bytes;
  size_t   count;
  char     buf[BUFSZ+1];
  size_t   i, j;
  char     *bufadr;

  /* Expect to get the file name from user */
  if (argc > 1)
    fname = argv[1];
  else
  {
    fprintf(stderr, "Usage: %s filename\n", argv[0]);
    return(-1);
  }

  /* Open the file for read only. */
  fd = open(fname, O_RDONLY);
  if (fd == -1)
  {
    fprintf(stderr, "open() failed, errno=%d\n", errno);
    return(-2);
  }

  /* The read loop. */
```

```c
for (i = 1; i < LOOPCNT; i++)
{
  /* Read a block at each iteration */
  count = BUFSZ;
  bufadr = buf;
  while (count > 0)
  {
    bytes = read(fd, bufadr, count);
    if (bytes == -1)
    {
      fprintf(stderr, "read() failed, errno=%d\n", errno);
      close(fd);
      return(-3);
    }
    count = count - bytes;
    bufadr = bufadr + bytes;
  }
  buf[BUFSZ] = '\0';
  fprintf(stdout, "Just read the following block:\n%s\n", buf);
}

/* Close the file */
close(fd);
return(0);
}
```

4-11 Random I/O

In addition to sequentially reading or writing a file, a program can randomly read or write a file, too.

Remember we talked about the concept of the file pointer at the beginning of this chapter. The main difference between a sequential file operation and a random one is whether your code explicitly changes the file offset (i.e. moves the file pointer) or not before actually performing the operation.

In sequential read or write operations, your code does not explicitly change the file offset at all. It all changes implicitly. Your code simply does the next read or write and the data will be automatically from or to the next position. As an analogy, doing sequential write is like you are holding a painting brush and just slide it forward from left to right. The path your brush travels through is automatically painted. Therefore, with sequential read or write, you as a programmer are not even aware of there is a file pointer automatically moving along with as your program reads or writes. It all happens automatically behind the scene.

In contrast, random I/O means you don't automatically read from or write to the next file position. Instead, you know an exact file position where the data should be read from or written to next. You explicitly move the file pointer/offset to that position and then perform the read or write operation. So, the program changes the file offset to point to the new position and then does the read or write. Then it changes the file offset again and performs the next operation. The locations at which the file operations are performed change randomly. That's why it is called **random I/O**.

A program uses the **lseek**() function to move the file offset/pointer to the exact byte offset that it wants to read from or write into next. That is how a program does random I/O! This extra step is what mainly differentiates the random I/O from sequential I/O.

A database update application is a very typical example of random I/O. When a company has a database of some sort, whether it's the employee, inventory, order or other database, as time goes on and events happen, the next database record that needs to be updated or queried is sort of unpredictable; it can be located anywhere in the database, as opposed to the next adjacent one. In other words, the location distribution of the database query or update operations is typically random.

Figure 4-12 is an example program that does random I/O.

Figure 4-12 Doing random file I/O -- randomwr.c

```
/*
 * Random write.
 * This program opens an existing file, writes 5 bytes starting at offset 512,
 * and then writes another 5 bytes starting at offset 1024.
 * To test, use the output file from the writer program as the input file.
 * Copyright (c) 2013, 2014, 2020 Mr. Jin-Jwei Chen.  All rights reserved.
 */

#include <stdio.h>
#include <errno.h>
#include <sys/types.h>
#include <sys/stat.h>
#include <fcntl.h>
#include <unistd.h>
#include <string.h>   /* memset() */

#define  BUFSZ        512

int main(int argc, char *argv[])
{
  char *fname;
  int  fd;
  off_t  offset, offset_ret;
  ssize_t  bytes;
  size_t   count;
  char      buf[BUFSZ];

  /* Expect to get the file name from user */
  if (argc > 1)
    fname = argv[1];
  else
  {
    fprintf(stderr, "Usage: %s filename\n", argv[0]);
    return(-1);
  }

  /* Open a file for write only. This open() will fail with errno=2
     if the file does not exist. */
```

138

```
fd = open(fname, O_WRONLY, 0644);
if (fd == -1)
{
  fprintf(stderr, "open() failed, errno=%d\n", errno);
  return(-2);
}


/* Write 5 bytes starting at file offset 512 */
offset = 512;
offset_ret = lseek(fd, offset, SEEK_CUR);
if (offset_ret == -1)
{
  fprintf(stderr, "lseek() failed, errno=%d\n", errno);
  close(fd);
  return(-3);
}
fprintf(stdout, "offset_ret = %lld \n", offset_ret);

for (count=0; count < 5; count++)
  buf[count] = 'A';

bytes = write(fd, buf, 5);
if (bytes == -1)
{
  fprintf(stderr, "write() failed, errno=%d\n", errno);
  close(fd);
  return(-4);
}


/* Write another 5 bytes starting at file offset 1024 */
offset = 1024;
offset_ret = lseek(fd, offset, SEEK_SET);
if (offset_ret == -1)
{
  fprintf(stderr, "lseek() failed, errno=%d\n", errno);
  close(fd);
  return(-5);
}
fprintf(stdout, "offset_ret = %lld \n", offset_ret);

for (count=0; count < 5; count++)
  buf[count] = 'B';

bytes = write(fd, buf, 5);
if (bytes == -1)
{
  fprintf(stderr, "write() failed, errno=%d\n", errno);
  close(fd);
  return(-6);
}


/* Close the file */
close(fd);
return(0);
}
```

139

Note that before a program does a random read or write to a file, it moves
the file offset to a certain position in the file. The position is all
logical, relative to the beginning of the file.

When working with a file, application programs deal with only logical
structure and location of a file. It has no idea where the current block or
byte physically resides on disk. Only the file system component of the
operating system knows the physical structure and location of the file.
In other words, when an application program says that "I want to write this
data at this file location", it is actually saying that "I want to write this
data at the logical file location that is X bytes from the beginning of the
file." The operating system actually divides the whole logical file into
blocks of a certain size and places the logical blocks into physical sectors
on the disk. The file system figures out the mapping from logical file
blocks to physical disk sectors, maintains the mapping and actually maps
the logical position to the corresponding physical position during the
execution of the read/write operation.

In other words, when the file system component of the operating system
carries out an I/O request, it maps the logical file location of the request
to a physical one. For instance, when a program says "write this piece of
data to the position starting at byte offset 2078", the O.S. file system may
translate that into "write this data to the position starting at
byte number 30 in physical sector 2 on cylinder 10 of surface 3 on the disk".

```
Application Program                 Operating System (File System component)
-----------------------             ----------------------------------------
logical location of file            physical location of file
(e.g. at byte offset 2078           (e.g. at byte 30 of sector 2, cylinder
of the file)                        10, surface 3)
```

In addition to the logical versus physical difference, application programs
read/write bytes whereas the file system reads/writes sectors.
In other words, actual disk I/O operations are always done in unit of
physical disk sectors. The minimum amount of information transferred to and
from a disk is a physical disk sector. In fact, for performance reason,
actual disk I/Os are typically done in multiple sectors at a time.
That is, the file system writes out at least an entire sector a time.

In summary, unless you are doing operating system development and writing
file system code, most likely the program you are developing will be using
file system files and thus is an application program. In that case,
you are dealing with the logical structure and blocks of a file, rather
than the physical structure and physical sectors.

Only the file system code deals with the physical structure and sectors
of a file. The operating system physically places and maintains your file
on disk. It handles the allocation and deallocation of physical disk sectors
to a file and maintains the mapping between the logical file position used
by an application program and its corresponding physical position on disk.

Note that a program can do both random and sequential reads/writes,
or any combination of them to a file. For instance, a program could seek to
block 2, write some data, then seek to block 40, read some data, and then
seek to block 1000 and do a sequential write of 10 MB of data from there.
As long as it knows what it is doing, there is virtually no limitation;

it can do whatever it wants with the file.

The lseek() Function

We know that a program does random file I/O by using the lseek() function to set the file offset before actually performing the I/O operation. Here we explain the lseek() function in a bit more details.

The synopsis of the lseek() function is shown below:

```
#include <sys/types.h>
#include <unistd.h>

off_t lseek(int fd, off_t offset, int whence);
```

There are three different ways to re-position the file pointer of an open file. For any of the three, you always supply the file descriptor of the open file as the first argument to the lseek() function. You also supply an offset as the second argument. In the third argument, you specify how you want the offset you provide to be interpreted: specify SEEK_SET if you want the offset to be absolute, SEEK_CUR if you want the offset to be counted starting from the current file pointer position, and SEEK_END if you want the offset to be that many bytes beyond the current end of file.

Typically, programs use SEEK_SET to set the current file offset to an absolute byte position. From time to time, programs may use SEEK_CUR as well, to move the offset in relative to the current position. Occasionally, SEEK_END is used. Be aware that using SEEK_END essentially creates a "hole' at the end of the file. It does not change the file size. But reading from the "gap" will get null bytes until data is written into it. The read may even get EBADF error on some operating system's implementation.

Sequential I/O versus Random I/O

At this point, you already know that there are essentially two ways of doing file I/O: sequential read/write and random read/write.
With sequential I/O, you just read from or write into the next byte from where the current file offset is. With random I/O, you have a specific byte offset that you want to write into or read from. Therefore, you invoke the lseek() function to explicitly set the current file offset before performing the read/write operation.

So, which one do you use? Well, normally it is not up to you to decide. It's dictated by the application. Some applications (e.g. file copying) need sequential I/O and others (e.g. database updates) need random I/O.

However, performance could be different between the two given the same amount of data to read or write.

If free disk space is available and the operating system allocates consecutive physical disk blocks for consecutive logical file blocks, then doing sequential I/O could have a much better performance than random I/O because the disk drive does not need to move the read/write heads around as much to get to the blocks.

If your program needs to support both (for instance, if you are developing

a generic file system), then you probably need to build in tuning knobs
so that users can optimize it to their needs.

4-12 Vectored I/O

4-12-1 What Is Vectored I/O?

This section introduces you to a feature named vectored I/O that is part of
the POSIX standard.

What is vectored I/O? **Vectored I/O** allows programs to bundle multiple read
function calls into a single read function call and multiple write
function calls into a single write function call.

The primary reason for using vectored I/O is efficiency. With vectored I/O,
a program can bundle or consolidate potential multiple I/Os into one.

Vectored I/O is used in situations where a program either gets data from
multiple sources or distributes data to multiple destinations.
In a read application, the program would do a read operation and then break
the data so read into multiple segments, each in a separate buffer for
processing. It's like a 'scatter read' operation.
In a write application, the program would gather multiple pieces of data
from multiple sources and write them out in one function call.
This is like a "gather write" operation. Therefore, vectored I/O is also
called **"scatter/gather I/O"**.

Figure 4-13 scatter/gather I/O

On Read (scatter):

```
                    do one read from a file
                         |
                         v
    ---------------------------------------------
    |                    |                    |
    v                    v                    v
 worker thread 1    worker thread 2 .... worker thread n
```

perform a single read from a file, scatter the data read into
multiple separate buffers, one for each worker thread

On write (gather):

```
 worker thread 1    worker thread 2 .... worker thread n
    |                    |                    |
    ---------------------------------------------
                         |
                         v
```

gather data from multiple sources and write them out as one writev()
function call.

Note that vectored I/O works because either the order in which the multiple buffers are read into or written from does not matter or the application knows what the exact order is and lines them up correctly.

Note that vectored I/O is actually sequential I/O. It's actually doing a sequential write with data coming from multiple source buffers instead of one, or doing a sequential read with data being broken into multiple segments and distributed into multiple input buffers.

From a perspective, without the vectored I/O, a program would have to combine multiple separate buffers into a single contiguous one before issuing the read() or write() call. With vectored I/O, the operating system takes care of that chore behind the scene inside the readv()/writev() functions.

The actual performance benefit of vectored I/O can vary depending on applications. You should do performance measurements first to evaluate whether vectored I/O helps your application before using it.

In a web application, if the read/write involves reading/writing a HTTP document transferred by the HTTP protocol, vector I/O may help performance because it allows you to read/write the header with the contents at once.

4-12-2 How to Do Vectored I/O

To use vectored I/O, your program must include the header file sys/uio.h:

```
#include <sys/uio.h>
```

Once your program includes this header file, it can then invoke the following functions to do vectored reads or writes:

```
ssize_t readv(int fd, const struct iovec *vector, int count);
ssize_t writev(int fd, const struct iovec *vector, int count);
```

Notice that instead of calling the read() and write() functions, a program invokes the readv() and writev() for doing vectored I/O.

The first argument to the readv() and writev() functions specifies the file it wants to read from or write into. It should have been opened by the open() call.

The second argument to these two functions specifies a vector (or array) of buffers that you want to do I/O with. This argument provides the starting address of an array of iovec structures where each of these iovec structures is essentially a buffer descriptor. It tells the readv() or writev() function the starting memory address and size in bytes of each of your buffers. Specifically, the second argument is an array of the following structure:

```
struct iovec
{
   void *iov_base;      /* starting address of this buffer  */
   size_t iov_len;      /* size (in bytes) of this buffer  */
};
```

The iov_base specifies the starting address of the buffer and the iov_len field specifies the length of the buffer.

The third argument to readv()/writev() specifies how many buffers there
are in the I/O vector given in the second argument.

In other words, to perform vectored I/O, you provide a vector (i.e. array)
of iovec structures that you have already allocated and set up in the second
argument of the readv() or writev() function. You also specify the number
of iovec structures in that vector in the third argument of the readv()
or writev() function.

When the readv() or writev() function is executed, the operating system
will examine the value of the iov_len field in each iovec structure and
read or write exactly that amount of information into or from that particular
buffer whose starting address is specified by the iov_base field in that
iovec structure.

Note that the multiple buffers are processed in exactly the order they appear
in the iovec array/vector. That is, the first iovec in the array or vector
is processed first, then the second, the third, and so on.

For example, Figure 4-14 shows an example program, readv.c, that does
vectored reads. In the example, we have three input buffers: buf1, buf2 and
buf3. They are of different sizes. We allocate a vector, iov, that
contains an array of three iovec structures. We then set up the iovec
structures by putting the starting address and size of each buffer into
each of them. And then we call readv() with the third argument count=3.
As you can see, a single readv() call fills all three input buffers.

In executing the readv() call, the operating system will perform a sequential
read from the file from where the current file offset position is.
It will read a total of 1344 (=256+512+576) bytes from the file and
place the first 256 bytes into the first buffer, the next 512 bytes into
the second buffer, and the last 576 bytes into the third buffer.
It reads data into three buffers in one readv() call.

Figure 4-14 shows a program that does vectored I/O read (readv).
Figure 4-15 shows a program that does vectored I/O write (writev).

Figure 4-14 Vectored I/O read -- readv.c

```
/*
 * This program demonstrates vectored I/O. It uses the readv() function to
 * perform a read into multiple buffers from a file.
 * Copyright (c) 2013, 2014, 2020 Mr. Jin-Jwei Chen.  All rights reserved.
 */

#include <stdio.h>
#include <errno.h>
#include <sys/types.h>
#include <sys/stat.h>
#include <fcntl.h>
#include <unistd.h>
#include <string.h>    /* memset() */
#include <sys/uio.h>   /* readv()/writev() */
```

```c
#define  BUFSZ1  256
#define  BUFSZ2  512
#define  BUFSZ3  576

int main(int argc, char *argv[])
{
  char *fname;
  int   fd;
  ssize_t  bytes;
  struct   iovec  iov[3];   /* the I/O vector */
  char       buf1[BUFSZ1+1], buf2[BUFSZ2+1], buf3[BUFSZ3+1];

  /* Expect to get the file name from user */
  if (argc > 1)
    fname = argv[1];
  else
  {
    fprintf(stderr, "Usage: %s filename\n", argv[0]);
    return(-1);
  }

  /* Open the file for read only. */
  fd = open(fname, O_RDONLY);
  if (fd == -1)
  {
    fprintf(stderr, "open() failed, errno=%d\n", errno);
    return(-2);
  }

  /* Empty the input buffers */
  memset(buf1, 0, BUFSZ1);
  memset(buf2, 0, BUFSZ2);
  memset(buf3, 0, BUFSZ3);

  /* Set up the I/O vector */
  iov[0].iov_base = buf1;
  iov[0].iov_len = BUFSZ1;
  iov[1].iov_base = buf2;
  iov[1].iov_len = BUFSZ2;
  iov[2].iov_base = buf3;
  iov[2].iov_len = BUFSZ3;

  /* Perform the vectored I/O */
  bytes = readv(fd, iov, 3);
  if (bytes == -1)
  {
    fprintf(stderr, "readv() failed, errno=%d\n", errno);
    close(fd);
    return(-3);
  }
  fprintf(stdout, "%ld bytes were read\n", bytes);

  /* Null terminate the buffers so that we can print the strings */
  buf1[BUFSZ1] = '\0';
  buf2[BUFSZ2] = '\0';
  buf3[BUFSZ3] = '\0';
```

```
  /* Print the data read on screen */
  fprintf(stdout, "buf1:%s\n", buf1);
  fprintf(stdout, "buf2:%s\n", buf2);
  fprintf(stdout, "buf3:%s\n", buf3);

  /* Close the file */
  close(fd);
  return(0);
}
```

Figure 4-15 Vectored I/O write -- writev.c

```
/*
 * This program demonstrates vectored I/O. It uses the writev() function to
 * perform a write from multiple buffers into a file.
 * Copyright (c) 2013, 2014, 2020 Mr. Jin-Jwei Chen.  All rights reserved.
 */

#include <stdio.h>
#include <errno.h>
#include <sys/types.h>
#include <sys/stat.h>
#include <fcntl.h>
#include <unistd.h>
#include <string.h>      /* memset() */
#include <sys/uio.h>     /* readv()/writev() */

#define  BUFSZ1   256   /* size of buffer 1 */
#define  BUFSZ2   512   /* size of buffer 2 */
#define  BUFSZ3   128   /* size of buffer 3 */

int main(int argc, char *argv[])
{
  char *fname;
  int  fd;
  ssize_t  bytes;
  struct   iovec  iov[3];   /* the I/O vector */
  char     buf1[BUFSZ1], buf2[BUFSZ2], buf3[BUFSZ3];
  size_t   i;

  /* Expect to get the file name from user */
  if (argc > 1)
    fname = argv[1];
  else
  {
    fprintf(stderr, "Usage: %s filename\n", argv[0]);
    return(-1);
  }

  /* Open the output file. Create it if it does not exist. */
  fd = open(fname, O_WRONLY|O_CREAT|O_TRUNC, 0644);
  if (fd == -1)
  {
    fprintf(stderr, "open() failed, errno=%d\n", errno);
    return(-2);
```

```
    }

    /* Fill in the output buffers */
    for (i = 0; i < BUFSZ1; i++)
      buf1[i] = '1';
    for (i = 0; i < BUFSZ2; i++)
      buf2[i] = '2';
    for (i = 0; i < BUFSZ3; i++)
      buf3[i] = '3';

    /* Set up the I/O vector */
    iov[0].iov_base = buf1;
    iov[0].iov_len = BUFSZ1;
    iov[1].iov_base = buf2;
    iov[1].iov_len = BUFSZ2;
    iov[2].iov_base = buf3;
    iov[2].iov_len = BUFSZ3;

    /* Perform the vectored I/O */
    bytes = writev(fd, iov, 3);
    if (bytes == -1)
    {
      fprintf(stderr, "writev() failed, errno=%d\n", errno);
      close(fd);
      return(-3);
    }
    fprintf(stdout, "%ld bytes were written\n", bytes);

    /* Close the file */
    close(fd);
    return(0);
}
```

4-13 Asynchronous I/O

4-13-1 What Is Asynchronous I/O?

Up to this point, every I/O function we have used is synchronous in that when a program invokes an I/O function such as read() or write() to perform an I/O operation, the calling program blocks and waits until the I/O operation completes and the function returns before it can proceed. In this mode, the calling program cannot do anything else while the I/O operation is in progress. This **synchronous mode** is also known as the **'blocking mode'** because the calling process or thread actually blocks and waits during the I/O operation.

Since most I/O devices use some mechanical parts, an I/O operation can take several milliseconds or even longer. Therefore, I/O operations can be slow compared to regular data processing not involved in any I/O.

To improve performance, an alternative way of doing I/O is to use the so-called **asynchronous I/O** (**async I/O**, in short) or **non-blocking I/O**. In the async I/O or non-blocking mode, when a process or thread invokes the I/O function, it immediately gets the control back. Hence, it can then continue and do some other processing in parallel while the I/O operation is still being carried out. The price to pay is the calling process or thread must make another call later to check whether the I/O operation finishes or not.

An asynchronous I/O operation means the call to the asynchronous read or write function returns immediately as soon as the request is enqueued. The operation may not have completed yet (or it may) when the call returns. It gives your program an opportunity to do some other processing in parallel with the I/O operation itself. The key here is your program gets the control back right away while the actual I/O operation is still in progress, as opposed to being blocked.

Async I/O is a different programming paradigm than synchronous I/O. Different I/O functions are used and the way you structure your code is also different. The main difference is now your code needs to go back and check whether the I/O finishes or not. A simple read()/write() call in synchronous mode now becomes three different function calls in async I/O. So it is a bit harder to program than the synchronous I/O. But it does have the advantage of getting the control back right away. It not only allows you to do some parallel processing while the I/O is still progressing but also provides you with the flexibility of not being hung or at least can do something about it (for instance, cancel the operation) if the I/O operation appears to stall or hang.

4-13-2 How to do Asynchronous I/O

Async I/O has the following functions defined:

aio_read() - perform an asynchronous read operation
aio_write() - perform an asynchronous write operation
aio_return() - obtain return status of an asynchronous I/O operation
aio_error() - obtain error status of an asynchronous I/O operation
aio_cancel() - cancel outstanding asynchronous I/O requests for the
    specified file descriptor
aio_fsync() - does a sync on all outstanding asynchronous
    I/O operations associated with the specified file descriptor
aio_suspend() - suspend the calling process and wait for asynchronous I/O
    operation to complete or timeout

Note that in contrast to the synchronous I/O functions are normally implemented as system calls, the async I/O functions are usually implemented as user-mode library functions which apparently will end up with making system calls in the end. One of the reasons for this is that it needs to do something similar to what we did earlier in placing the I/O operation in a loop and making sure all data is read or written in the implementation. Therefore, the man pages for the aio_xxxx functions are in section 3 instead of 2. In addition, the aio_xxxx functions may reside in a separate library which you need to specify explicitly in order to make your program link successfully.

Note: On many systems including RedHat Enterprise Linux, the library containing the asynchronous I/O functions is /lib/librt.so.

We will introduce the various asynchronous I/O functions in some level of details below.

aio_write()

```
#include <aio.h>
int aio_write(struct aiocb *aiocbp);
```

Both aio_write() and aio_read() take a pointer to "struct aiocb" as an input argument. Shown below is an example of this structure:

```
/* Asynchronous I/O control block.  */
struct aiocb
{
  int aio_fildes;              /* File descriptor.  */
  int aio_lio_opcode;          /* Operation to be performed.  */
  int aio_reqprio;             /* Request priority offset.  */
  volatile void *aio_buf;      /* Location of buffer.  */
  size_t aio_nbytes;           /* Length of transfer.  */
  struct sigevent aio_sigevent; /* Signal number and value.  */
  __off_t aio_offset;          /* File offset.  */
  :
}
```

In terms of argument passing, the difference between using write() and aio_write() functions is that you pass the file descriptor, buffer pointer and the byte count as three separate arguments to the write() function whereas you set these values in the aio control block structure and pass the address of that structure to the aio_write() function in the case of aio_write().

One thing worth mentioning about async I/O is that inside the asynchronous I/O control block (struct aiocb), there is the **aio_offset** field which allows you to specify a file offset that you want the aio_write() to write to or aio_read() to read from. **Set this field only if you want to do random write or read. Leave it untouched if you want to do sequential write or read.** Setting this field is equivalent of using the lseek() to set the file offset before a read or write operation.

If O_APPEND flag is not set for the file descriptor aio_fildes, then the requested operation will take place at the absolute position in the file as given by aio_offset, as if lseek() were called immediately prior to the operation with an offset equal to aio_offset and a whence equal to SEEK_SET. If O_APPEND flag is set for the file descriptor, or if aio_fildes is associated with a device that is incapable of seeking, write operations append to the file in the same order as the calls were made.

If the asynchronous write request is successfully enqueued, aio_write() returns 0. If the request is not enqueued, aio_write() returns -1 and errno is set to indicate the error.

After aio_write() returns success (0), the calling process or thread is supposed to call aio_return() to get the actual result of the write. Normally, aio_return() returns the actual number of bytes written. If the write operation encounters an error, the aio_return() function returns -1. In that case, the calling process or thread should then call the aio_error() function to retrieve the error code, which would have

149

been the errno.

aio_error()

```
int aio_error(const struct aiocb *aiocbp);
```

The aio_error() function returns 0 if the I/O request associated with the
specified control block has completed successfully.
It returns EINPROGRESS if the request has not been completed yet.
It returns ECANCELED if the I/O request has been cancelled.
Otherwise, an error value is returned. This error value would be the errno
value in the case of synchronous I/O operation.

aio_return()

```
ssize_t aio_return(struct aiocb *aiocbp);
```

Note that the aio_return() function should be called only once for any
given asynchronous I/O request. And it should be called only after the
asynchronous I/O operation has actually completed.
To know whether an asynchronous I/O operation has actually completed or not,
a process or thread should call the aio_error() function and make sure it
returns something other than EINPROGRESS.

When it is called correctly, the aio_return() function returns the actual
number of bytes read or written. That is, it returns the value that
a synchronous read(), write() or fsync() function would have returned.

aio_read()

```
#include <aio.h>
int aio_read(struct aiocb *aiocbp);
```

A program using the aio_read() function is similar to one that is using
the aio_write(). The only major difference is you invoke aio_read()
instead of aio_write() and the direction of data movement is reverse.

Other fields in aiocb structure

The aiocb structure has a number of other fields which might also be
interesting to some of you. For instance, if _POSIX_PRIORITIZED_IO is
defined, then the aio_reqprio field allows you to set this field and
submit the asynchronous operation at a priority that is equal to that of
the calling process minus aiocbp->aio_reqprio.

Example Programs

Figure 4-16 shows an example program that does asynchronous write.
Figure 4-17 shows an example program that does asynchronous read.

Figure 4-16 Asynchronous write -- aiowrite.c

```
/*
 * This program opens a file and writes a number of KBs to it using
 * asynchronous I/O.
 * $ cc -o aiowrite aiowrite.c -lrtkaio -lrt
```

```
 * Copyright (c) 2013, 2014, 2020 Mr. Jin-Jwei Chen.  All rights reserved.
 */

#include <stdio.h>
#include <errno.h>
#include <sys/types.h>
#include <sys/stat.h>
#include <fcntl.h>
#include <unistd.h>
#include <string.h>   /* memset() */
#include <stdlib.h>   /* atoi() */
#include <aio.h>

#define  BUFSZ        (100*1024)
char      buf[BUFSZ];

int main(int argc, char *argv[])
{
  char *fname;
  int  fd;
  ssize_t  bytes;
  size_t   count;
  int       status;
  int       nkbs=20;
  struct aiocb  aiocb;
  size_t   i;

  /* Expect to get the file name from user */
  if (argc > 1)
    fname = argv[1];
  else
  {
    fprintf(stderr, "Usage: %s filename [KBs(1-100)]\n", argv[0]);
    return(-1);
  }
  if (argc > 2)
  {
    nkbs = atoi(argv[2]);
    if (nkbs <= 0 || nkbs > 100)
      nkbs = 1;
  }
  fprintf(stdout, "Writing %u KBs to file %s\n", nkbs, fname);

  /* Open a file for write only. */
  fd = open(fname, O_WRONLY|O_CREAT|O_TRUNC, 0644);
  if (fd == -1)
  {
    fprintf(stderr, "open() failed, errno=%d\n", errno);
    return(-2);
  }

  /* Initialize the entire buffer with letter 'A' */
  memset(buf, 65, BUFSZ);
  count = nkbs * 1024;

  /* Fill in the aio control block */
```

151

```
  memset((void *)&aiocb, 0, sizeof(aiocb));
  aiocb.aio_fildes = fd;
  aiocb.aio_buf = buf;
  aiocb.aio_nbytes = count;

  /* Write the amount specified to the file */
  status = aio_write(&aiocb);
  if (status == 0)
    fprintf(stdout, "The aio write request has been enqueued.\n");
  else if (status == -1)
  {
    fprintf(stderr, "aio_write() call failed, errno=%d\n", errno);
    close(fd);
    return(-3);
  }

  /* Do some other processing here. Otherwise, we wouldn't need async I/O. */

  /* Wait for the async I/O operation to complete */
  status = EINPROGRESS;
  while (status == EINPROGRESS)
    status = aio_error(&aiocb);
  fprintf(stdout, "The async I/O operation completed. aio_error returned %d\n",
    status);
  switch (status)
  {
    case 0:
      fprintf(stdout, "The async I/O operation completed successfully.\n");
    break;
    case ECANCELED:
      fprintf(stdout, "The async I/O operation was cancelled.\n");
    break;
    default:
      fprintf(stdout, "The async I/O operation encountered error %d\n", status);
    break;
  }

  /* Get the final return value of the async I/O call */
  bytes = aio_return(&aiocb);
  if (status == -1)
  {
    fprintf(stderr, "Async write operation failed, errno=%d\n", errno);
    close(fd);
    return(-4);
  }

  fprintf(stdout, "%ld bytes were written into the file.\n", bytes);

  /* Close the file */
  close(fd);
  return(0);
}
```

Figure 4-17 Asynchronous read -- aioread.c

```
/*
```

```
 * This program opens a file and reads a couple of blocks from it using
 * asynchronous I/O. The user can specify a starting offset to read from.
 * $ cc -o aioread aioread.c -lrtkaio -lrt
 * Copyright (c) 2013, 2014, 2020 Mr. Jin-Jwei Chen.  All rights reserved.
 */

#include <stdio.h>
#include <errno.h>
#include <sys/types.h>
#include <sys/stat.h>
#include <fcntl.h>
#include <unistd.h>
#include <string.h>   /* memset() */
#include <stdlib.h>   /* atoi() */
#include <aio.h>

#define  BUFSZ         (1024)

int main(int argc, char *argv[])
{
  char *fname;
  int    fd;
  ssize_t  bytes;
  size_t   count;
  int        status;
  int        offset=0;
  struct aiocb  aiocb;
  char        buf[BUFSZ+1];

  /* Expect to get the file name from user */
  if (argc > 1)
    fname = argv[1];
  else
  {
    fprintf(stderr, "Usage: %s filename [offset]\n", argv[0]);
    return(-1);
  }
  if (argc > 2)
  {
    offset = atoi(argv[2]);
    if (offset < 0)
      offset = 0;
  }

  /* Open a file for read only. */
  fd = open(fname, O_RDONLY);
  if (fd == -1)
  {
    fprintf(stderr, "open() failed, errno=%d\n", errno);
    return(-2);
  }

  /* Clear the entire buffer */
  memset(buf, 0, BUFSZ);
  count =  BUFSZ;
```

153

```c
  /* Fill in the aio control block */
  memset((void *)&aiocb, 0, sizeof(aiocb));
  aiocb.aio_fildes = fd;
  aiocb.aio_buf = buf;
  aiocb.aio_nbytes = count;
  if (offset > 0)
    aiocb.aio_offset = offset;

  /* Read the amount specified from the file */
  status = aio_read(&aiocb);
  if (status == 0)
    fprintf(stdout, "The aio read request has been enqueued.\n");
  else if (status == -1)
  {
    fprintf(stderr, "aio_read() call failed, errno=%d\n", errno);
    close(fd);
    return(-3);
  }

  /* Do some other processing here. Otherwise, we wouldn't need async I/O. */

  /* Wait for the async I/O operation to complete */
  status = EINPROGRESS;
  while (status == EINPROGRESS)
    status = aio_error(&aiocb);
  fprintf(stdout, "The async I/O operation completed. aio_error returned %d\n",
    status);
  switch (status)
  {
    case 0:
      fprintf(stdout, "The async I/O operation completed successfully.\n");
    break;
    case ECANCELED:
      fprintf(stdout, "The async I/O operation was cancelled.\n");
    break;
    default:
      fprintf(stdout, "The async I/O operation encountered error %d\n", status);
    break;
  }

  /* Get the final return value of the async I/O call */
  bytes = aio_return(&aiocb);
  if (status == -1)
  {
    fprintf(stderr, "Async read operation failed, errno=%d\n", errno);
    close(fd);
    return(-4);
  }
  buf[BUFSZ] = '\0';
  fprintf(stdout, "%ld bytes were read from the file.\n", bytes);
  fprintf(stdout, "%s\n", buf);

  /* Close the file */
  close(fd);
  return(0);
}
```

4-13-3 Different Programming Paradigm

As you can see from our examples, with async I/O, you no longer place the read() or write() function in a tight loop as you do in synchronous mode to make sure it always reads or writes all of the data you request. Instead, whatever size your request is, you just make the async I/O request and then wait for it to complete. Here you would put the big loop around all of the aio_read()/aio_write(), aio_error() and aio_return() to try to do the same. In case the aio_return() returns a size that is less than the size you have requested, you can try another request with the remaining unfinished data. This means you would have to adjust the starting buffer address and size in the aio control block and do the three aio function calls altogether.

Also note that with asynchronous I/O, you can do both sequential and random I/O too. The trick is this. To do sequential I/O with the async I/O functions, you leave the aiocb.aio_offset field in the aiocb structure untouched. To do random I/O with the async I/O functions, you set the aiocb.aio_offset field in the aiocb structure before you call aio_read() or aio_write(). This is equivalent to moving the file pointer/offset with the lseek() function prior to a read or write.

Notes

All the asynchronous I/O example programs compile and run fine on Linux, IBM AIX, Oracle/Sun SPARC Solaris, HP HP-UX IA64 and Apple Darwin.

Note that if you search all of the symbols in a program and you find none of these aio_xxxx function names at all, then you know for sure that particular program is not using asynchronous I/O at all.

The command to verify if a program is using async I/O or not is following:

```
$ nm myprogram | grep aio_
```

You should see aio_read or aio_write in the output if the program named myprogram is using async I/O.

4-13-4 Synchronous or Asynchronous I/O?

You may ask, should I use synchronous or asynchronous I/O?

Well, each has advantages and disadvantages.

First, with synchronous I/O, the calling process or thread is completely blocked during I/O. It cannot perform any other processing even if it wants to while the I/O operation is still in progress. Since I/O operations usually take time, the application would have a better performance if it could do some other processing in parallel with the I/O operations.

Second, occasionally an I/O operation may stall or hang due to various reasons such as hardware failures or network cable unplugged. If the program is not a threaded application (that is, it is single-threaded), then the entire program will stall or hang when an I/O operation stalls or hangs and there is nothing you can do about that but to kill the process. This is very undesirable. Async I/O enables the caller to do a graceful handling.

However, synchronous I/O offers simplicity. It is very easy to program. All a program needs to do is to invoke the I/O function. Each I/O operation is one function and one statement. That's it! And when the function returns, you have either the result or the error. There is no need to make additional function calls to get them as in async I/O.

A program doing synchronous I/O does one thing at a time. It finishes the current step before starting another. Pure and simple. No confusion. How often does a program really get some parallel processing to do anyway? If a simultaneous processing is really needed, one can always spawn another thread to do it.

In contrast, with asynchronous I/O, a program may have two activities going on at the same time: the I/O operation itself and whatever the other processing happening in parallel. It adds confusion.

Even the I/O operation itself is more complicated. The program needs to enqueue the asynchronous I/O request first. It then needs to go back and call aio_error() to check whether the I/O operation has completed or not. And if it does, then it needs to make another call to get the return result.

Therefore, if you opt for code simplicity, use synchronous I/O. If you like being able to more graciously deal with the hang situation and being able to squeeze out some more performance through parallelism, then choose asynchronous I/O.

Traditionally, synchronous I/O is what most programs do because it's simpler to program and that is what was available first. However, given that asynchronous I/O has been available for some time in most platforms and the advantages it provides, asynchronous I/O may offer some real benefits especially when multithreading is not available. However, with multithreading available, whatever activity that needs to happen at the same time with the I/O can be carried out using a separate thread. Therefore, one does not have to use async I/O that often anymore.

4-14 Direct I/O

4-14-1 What Is Direct I/O?

Note that when a program does I/O to or from a file, the I/Os are normally cached. This means the data written by the program to a file is usually stored in the file system cache in the memory and not actually written out to disk right away. The operating system's file system usually batches the actual disk writes and does it later. Because the writes are done to memory instead of disks, they are usually very fast. The only drawback of this caching is that should the system crash or power go out right after the writes and before the data is actually written out to the disk, the data can be lost. This is because computer memory is volatile and disk is persistent.

For the reads, especially sequential reads of a file, many file systems usually implement read ahead strategy as well so that when a program actually reads the data, it could be in the file system cache in memory already. This speeds up the read operations of file I/O. This kind of caching is very typical of any file systems.

Occasionally, the file system caching may not be desirable. An application may want to do I/Os directly to disks for different reasons. Performing I/O directly to disk without going through the file system cache is called **'direct I/O'**.

There are at least two occasions where a program may want to use direct I/O. First, some application, such as Oracle Relational Database System, implements its own caching already. Therefore, it doesn't need the double caching that is provided by the file system of the operating system. In fact, the double caching may end up with being an interference. With file system caching, data being written is first copied from application's memory buffer to the O.S. file system's cache memory. It is then copied from file system cache to disk. So there are two copy operations being done. On a read, data is copied from disk to file system cache first and then from there to application's buffer.

Second, some applications may want to measure the raw performance of disks without the effect of file system caching.

As the name implies, direct I/O actually does every read or write directly to disk. Therefore, the performance will be slower compared to going through the file system cache. Typically, reading or writing a block of data using direct I/O takes a few milliseconds, as opposed to microseconds in the case of file system caching.

On the other hand, since direct I/O eliminates the data copying from the operating system kernel buffer to the user's buffer and vice versa, it reduces the CPU overhead associated with the I/Os. It also saves some file system cache buffer space.

In short, direct I/O performs disk I/O from application buffers directly to disk, bypassing the file system buffer cache.

4-14-2 How to Do Direct I/O?

Direct I/O can be done at two different levels. First, some operating systems support a special option named -forcedirectio or the like in the operating system mount command that allows a system administrator to mount a file system with direct I/O on. Second, application programs can choose to use direct I/O on a per file basis.

Programming direct I/O is both operating system dependent and file system dependent. For example, in the early 2000's, HPUX and Linux did not even support direct I/O at all while AIX, Sun/Oracle Solaris and DEC/HP Tru64 Unix did. When Linux added support of direct I/O, some of the early file system types were not supported, either.

Besides, how a C program does direct I/O varies from operating system to operating system. AIX and Linux use the O_DIRECT flag of the open() system call to enable direct I/O. However, Sun/Oracle Solaris does not. Solaris started out with a separate library function named directio() to turn on and off direct I/O on a per file basis. Recently, it has implemented the O_DSYNC flag in the open() system call, which is similar to the O_DIRECT flag in Linux and AIX.

Also, on some Linux systems, such as Oracle Linux, direct I/O is not automatically available. To get the O_DIRECT flag for the open() function being defined, you have to add the following line in your program before you include any header files:

```
#define   _GNU_SOURCE
```

Figure 4-18 shows a program (directiowr.c) that writes a file using direct I/O. It writes a multiple of 4096-byte blocks into a file whose name is specified by the user in the first argument. The user can also specify the number of 4KB blocks to write using the second argument. The third argument allows the user to choose between direct I/O or not. A value of 0 means no direct I/O and a value 1 means using direct I/O.
The second and third arguments are optional.

As we mentioned earlier, if the application does not do additional caching, using direct I/O avoids or at least reduces the potential of losing data when the system crashes. However, it is slower. As this program demonstrates, on the system used for test, it takes roughly 0.3-1 ms to write twenty 4K-byte blocks to a file going through the file system cache while it usually takes 20-23 ms via direct I/O.

Figure 4-18 Writing to a file using direct I/O -- directiowr.c

```c
/*
 * This program opens a file and writes a number of 4096-byte blocks into it
 * using direct I/O.
 * Linux requires buffer address and write size be 512-byte aligned.
 * To compile:
 *    cc  -DLINUX -o directiowr directiowr.c
 *    gcc -DSOLARIS -o directiowr directiowr.c
 * Copyright (c) 2013-4, 2020 Mr. Jin-Jwei Chen.  All rights reserved.
 */

#ifndef SOLARIS
#define   _GNU_SOURCE     /* need this to get O_DIRECT on some Linux */
#endif

#include <stdio.h>
#include <errno.h>
#include <sys/types.h>
#include <sys/stat.h>
#include <fcntl.h>
#include <unistd.h>
#include <string.h>       /* memset() */
#include <stdlib.h>       /* atoi(), posix_memalign() */
#include <sys/time.h>     /* gettimeofday() */
#ifdef SOLARIS
#include <sys/fcntl.h>
#endif

#define  BUFSZ          (4*1024)
```

158

```c
#define   DEFBLKCNT     24

#ifdef LINUX
char       *buf=NULL;
#else
char       buf[BUFSZ];       /* the output buffer */
#endif

int main(int argc, char *argv[])
{
  char       *fname;
  int        fd;
  ssize_t    bytes;
  size_t     count;
  int        isdirectio = 1;    /* 1 - use direct I/O, 0 - no direct I/O */
  int        blocks=DEFBLKCNT;  /* number of blocks to write */
  int        oflags;            /* flags to the open() function */
  char       ch;                /* byte content of each block */
  int        i, j, k;
  struct timeval  tm1, tm2;
  int        ret;
  char       *bufadr;

  /* Expect to get the file name from user */
  if (argc > 1)
    fname = argv[1];
  else
  {
    fprintf(stderr, "Usage: %s filename [0|1 (direct I/O)] [blocks]\n", argv[0]);
    return(-1);
  }
  if (argc > 2)
  {
    isdirectio = atoi(argv[2]);
    if (isdirectio != 1)
      isdirectio = 0;
  }
  if (argc > 3)
  {
    blocks = atoi(argv[3]);
    if (blocks <= 0)
      blocks = DEFBLKCNT;
  }
  fprintf(stdout, "Writing %u %4u-byte blocks to file %s, directio=%d\n",
    blocks, BUFSZ, fname, isdirectio);

  /* If on Linux, allocate aligned memory for the buffer */
#ifdef LINUX
#define _XOPEN_SOURCE 600
  ret = posix_memalign((void **)&buf, 512, BUFSZ);
  if (ret != 0)
  {
    fprintf(stderr, "posix_memalign() failed, ret=%d\n", ret);
    return(-2);
  }
#endif
```

```
  /* Open the output file. Create it if it does not exist. */
#ifdef SOLARIS
  /* For Solaris */
  if (isdirectio)
    oflags = (O_WRONLY|O_CREAT|O_TRUNC|O_DSYNC);
  else
    oflags = (O_WRONLY|O_CREAT|O_TRUNC);
#else
#ifdef __APPLE__
    oflags = (O_WRONLY|O_CREAT|O_TRUNC);
#else
  /* For Linux, AIX and others */
  if (isdirectio)
    oflags = (O_WRONLY|O_CREAT|O_TRUNC|O_DIRECT);
  else
    oflags = (O_WRONLY|O_CREAT|O_TRUNC);
#endif
#endif

  fd = open(fname, oflags, 0644);
  if (fd == -1)
  {
    fprintf(stderr, "open() failed, errno=%d\n", errno);
    return(-3);
  }

#ifdef SOLARIS
  if (isdirectio)
    ret = directio(fd, DIRECTIO_ON);
  else
    ret = directio(fd, DIRECTIO_OFF);
  if (ret != 0)
  {
    fprintf(stderr, "directio() failed, errno=%d\n", errno);
    close(fd);
    return(-4);
  }
#endif
#ifdef __APPLE__
  if (isdirectio)
    ret = fcntl(fd, F_NOCACHE, 1);   /* turns data caching off */
  else
    ret = fcntl(fd, F_NOCACHE, 0);   /* turns data caching on */
  if (ret == -1)
  {
    fprintf(stderr, "fcntl() failed, errno=%d\n", errno);
    close(fd);
    return(-4);
  }
#endif

  ret = gettimeofday(&tm1, (void *)NULL);

  /* Write the number of blocks specified */
  for (k = 0; k < blocks; k++)
```

```
    {
        i = k % 26;   /* make i be 0-25 */
        ch = 'A' + i;

        /* Fill the buffer with message to write */
        for (j = 0; j < BUFSZ; j++)
            buf[j] = ch;

        /* Write the contents of the buffer to the file.
         * This will overwrite the beginning of the file if it already exists.
         */
        count = BUFSZ;
        bufadr = buf;
        while (count > 0)
        {
            errno = 0;
            bytes = write(fd, bufadr, count);
            if (bytes == -1)
            {
                fprintf(stderr, "write() failed, errno=%d\n", errno);
                close(fd);
                return(-5);
            }
            count = count - bytes;
            bufadr = bufadr + bytes;
        }
    }

    /* Report the time taken to write the file */
    ret = gettimeofday(&tm2, (void *)NULL);
    printf("Start time: %010ld:%010u\n", tm1.tv_sec, tm1.tv_usec);
    printf("End   time: %010ld:%010u\n", tm2.tv_sec, tm2.tv_usec);

    /* Close the file */
    close(fd);
    return(0);
}
```

As of this writing, the program directiowr works fine on AIX, SOLARIS and LINUX. Direct I/O does not seem to be supported in HP-UX IA64.
In Apple Darwin, direct I/O is done by calling the fcntl() function to turn data caching off as follows:

```
   ret = fcntl(fd, F_NOCACHE, 1);   /* turns data caching off */
```

It's worth mentioning that Linux's implementation of direct I/O has a very unique requirement which is the data buffer's starting address, write data size, and current file offset must be "suitably aligned". RedHat Linux's document also says it must be 512-byte aligned. That's why you see we invoke the posix_memalign() function to allocate the data buffer and make sure it is 512-byte aligned in directiowr.c. Without this step, the program may only succeed one out of 20 times. For the rest of time, it fails with following error:
    write() failed, errno=22
which is "invalid argument (EINVAL), which means alignment issue according to Linux documentation. After using the posix_memalign()

161

function to allocate the data buffer, this error disappears!

4-14-3 Notes on Direct I/O

Direct I/O is not included in the POSIX standard, although almost all operating systems support it. They include Linux, AIX, Solaris, HP-UX, Apple Darwin, HP/DEC Tru64 UNIX and SGI IRIX.

Most operating systems support direct I/O via the O_DIRECT flag of the open() function. However, some operating systems use a separate API for it. Besides, although most operating systems support direct I/O on a per file basis, some supports it on a per file system basis as well (for instance, via the mount command).

For instance, Oracle/Sun Solaris provides an API named directio() for applications to turn on or off direct I/O on a per-file basis. It also supports an "-o directio" option on the mount command to let system administrators enable or disable direct I/O on a per file system basis.

Linux kernel started to support direct I/O via the O_DIRECT flag in version 2.4.10. This flag was simply ignored in older versions of Linux kernels. For some file systems which do not support this, using the O_DIRECT flag in the open() call will fail with EINVAL error.

In some operating systems such as DEC/HP Tru64 Unix, direct I/O is not supported for files that are mmap-ed.

Some file systems may have special requirements for direct I/O. For example, Symantec VxFS requires starting and ending file offsets must be aligned to a 512-byte boundary and the file length must be a multiple of 512 bytes for direct I/O. And the memory buffer must also start at a 8-byte boundary. SGI IRIX operating system has alignment restrictions, too. And so does RedHat Linux, as we have mentioned.

In Red Hat Enterprise Linux 4, ext3 file system supports both Direct I/O and Asynchronous I/O at the same time.

As we briefly mentioned it earlier, Oracle Relational Database Management System (RDBMS) implements its own disk I/O cache system in a memory area named SGA (System Global Area). Hence, if you run Oracle RDBMS, make sure direct I/O is enabled both in the operating system and in Oracle to get optimal disk performance.

Oracle RDBMS controls direct I/O using a parameter in the init.ora parameter file. The parameter is called filesystemio_options. Oracle recommends setting this parameter to either "SetAll" or "DirectIO", with 'SetAll' meaning enabling both direct I/O and Async I/O. Using direct I/O with Oracle RDBMS allows data to be moved directly between disk and Oracle's own cache buffer (SGA), bypassing the redundant operating system file system buffer cache.

4-15 I/O Buffering

Be aware that buffering is done in Input/Output. This is called buffered I/O.

Notice that there are at least two levels of **buffered I/O**.
One is in user space when application programs use the I/O library functions
defined in the C Standard and the other happens in the operating system.

The first level of input/output data buffering could happen in user space
inside some standard C library functions. For instance, when a program
outputs data to a terminal screen, the stdout is buffered. The program may
write a character at a time, for instance, using the putc() or putchar()
function. You will find in some cases that the output data is not actually
written to the output device until a NEWLINE ('\n') character is seen.
That is, the output data is temporarily stored and held in buffer without
being actually sent to the output device. This is I/O buffering; output is
buffered. Another example is input buffering. Some people type very fast.
A user may have entered two or three commands in a row already at the
command prompt while the computer is still executing the first one.
In an input buffered system, the second and third commands the user has typed
will get stored somewhere in a buffer and then get executed after the
computer finishes executing the first command. In a non-buffered system,
the second and third commands would get lost and the user would have to
re-type again.

The second level of buffering occurs when a program does I/O through the
file system of the operating system. The buffering is file system caching,
as we have mentioned above. To improve performance, a file system usually
does the so-called **read ahead** and **delayed write**. Specifically, the file
system may predict what the application is going to need next and read blocks
of data from disk into memory and cache it there before your program
actually asks for it. Similarly, when your program does writes, the file
system may cache the output data in the file system cache in memory and
does not actually write it out to disk right away.

Read ahead does not actually cause any issues. However, delayed write may.
Since the computer memory is volatile, meaning it loses its contents if
the system loses power or goes down. If the entire system crashes right
after your program has written out some data to a file and before the file
system actually flushes the data out to disk, then there is a loss of data
-- your program has written the data to the file but it is not actually
recorded on disk by the file system yet. Your program thinks the data
has been persisted on disk while it actually has not -- still sitting in
memory in the file system cache.

Because the file system caching has a potential to result in data loss,
to ensure you never lose any data due to file system caching,
it's prudent to flush the data from the memory to disk after a write.
Of course, you may not want to do this after every write since that would
slow down the performance. Another option is to use direct I/O to
bypass the file system cache. But if you have to guarantee there is no data
loss in the event of system crash, then you need to do what you have to.

4-15-1 The sync(), fsync() and fdatasync() Functions

To flush the updated or written data from memory to disk, there are at least
three things a user or programmer can do. One is to issue a command like
sync in Unix and Linux to tell the operating system to flush written data
still sitting in the file system cache out to disk. I usually do it at least

twice in a row just to make sure. From within a program, if it uses the high level Standard C I/O interface, then the fflush(FILE *stream) function can be used to force a write of the buffered data to the specified I/O Stream. If the application uses the operating system interface, then, as shown below, a number of choices are available with different effects.

- fsync(int fd):

  The fsync() function flushes all modified contents of the file specified by the file descriptor argument and its associated meta data to the output device. This call is synchronized, meaning the function call does not return until the modified file and meta data have been transferred to the device.

  The fsync(fd) function is very useful for applications which know exactly changes to what file must be persisted to disk.
  When this function call returns successfully, it is guaranteed that changes to the file corresponding to the file descriptor fd have been written out to its storage device.

- sync(): This function takes no argument.

  The sync() function simply queues the writes of all modified file data and meta data in the file system cache to storage devices. The data include i-nodes, superblocks, indirect blocks and data blocks.
  This function call is more generic and broad range. It covers all file systems, not just one. Because of that, the sync() call returns when the write-outs are scheduled, not necessarily completed.
  This function does not return any value.

  The sync() function is typically used by operating system commands such as the fsck and df that examine a file system. These commands typically invoke sync() before they start doing their tasks.

- fdatasync(int fd):

  The fdatasync() function forces all currently queued I/O operations associated with the file represented by file descriptor fd to the synchronized I/O completion state.

  The functionality of fdatasync() is equivalent to fsync() with the symbol _POSIX_SYNCHRONIZED_IO defined, with the exception that all I/O operations shall be completed as defined for synchronized I/O data integrity completion. Note that even if the file descriptor is not open for writing, if there are any pending write requests on the underlying file, then that I/O will be completed prior to the return of fdatasync().

  On success, fdatasync() returns 0. Otherwise, it returns -1 and errno is set to indicate the error.

- Writing changes in a specified range of an open file to device.

  This feature is not very standard. Different operating systems use different function names. Below are some examples:
  -- In Linux, sync_file_range(fd, offset, bytes, flags) function
  -- In AIX, fsync_range(fd, how, start, length) function

These functions allow programs to flush changes in a certain range of a file. For details, please consult each operating system's documentation.

In summary, **I/O buffering improves performance but it may lead to data loss in the event of system crashes or power outage. As a programmer or user, you need to be aware of the risk and take appropriate actions to protect your data.**

Note that invoking the above functions to flush the cached data to disk may suffer some performance hit. But it's a tradeoff between reliability and performance. Hence, you've got to do what is necessary to ensure there is no data loss in the event of system crash.

4-16 Notes on Concurrent Updates of Files

When multiple processes or threads are updating a same file concurrently, it is paramount that they are synchronized such that they don't step on one another's toes overwriting one another and resulting in data loss or data corruption. Unless proper synchronization is performed between the concurrent writers, update loss will occur and the integrity of the file will be compromised.

There are at least two approaches to synchronizing multiple concurrent writers. One is to use file locking API (fcntl() function) to lock the region of file a process or thread intends to update. This ensures a file region is updated by only one process or thread at a time. In this way, if the file regions locked by the multiple processes or threads do not overlap, then the multiple updates will be able to be carried out simultaneously. Should the file regions locked overlap, the conflicting updates will be done one at a time so that they don't lead to data loss or corruption. We will discuss how to do this in the next chapter.

The other is to use generic, not file-specific, concurrency control mechanisms to ensure mutual exclusion between the multiple writer processes or threads trying to update the same piece of data. This ensures only one of them is executed at a time and it gets the exclusive access to the entire shared data.

This approach is widely used in database systems where multiple processes or threads try to update the same data item(s) at the same time. We will discuss this topic in the concurrency control chapter (9) later. One can either employ the concurrent control mechanisms, such as semaphores, provided by the operating systems, or, as we will demonstrate, design and implement your own locking functions yourself in assembly language which almost always delivers much better performance.

Questions

1. Describe the physical structure of a disk.

2. What are physical blocks and logical blocks?
   What is the size of the logical block on the file system(s) you are using?

3. What is the difference between a partition and a file system?

List the partitions and file systems on the root disk of the computer you are using.

4. What is the logical view of a file? Who uses that?
   What is the physical view of a file? Who uses that?

5. What are the three main steps in using a file?
   Name a function for performing each step.

6. Describe the concept of the current file offset (i.e. the so-called file pointer).

7. How many file I/O programming interfaces are available to a C program?
   Give an overview of each interface and compare them.

8. What is a file handle? And how is it implemented in each of the I/O programming interfaces?

9. What is a file descriptor? Is it private to a process or shared among processes?
   What is system open file table? Is it private to a process?

10. What is an inode? Where is it stored?
    What is an inode list? Where is it stored?
    What is an inode table? Where is it stored? Is it private to a process or shared among processes?

11. What is sequential I/O? What is random I/O? What are the differences between sequential and random file I/O?

12. What is vectored I/O? When is it used?
    What are scatter and gather I/O?
    How do you program vectored I/O?

13. What is synchronous I/O? What are its advantages and disadvantages?
    What is asynchronous I/O? What are its advantages and disadvantages?

14. What are the functions for synchronous read and write?
    What are the functions for asynchronous read and write?

15. How do you do sequential I/O with asynchronous I/O?
    And how do you do random I/O with asynchronous I/O?

16. What is direct I/O? Why would anyone want to use direct I/O?
    How do you do direct I/O in the platform you are using?

Programming Assignments

1. Write a program that exactly doubles the size of an existing file by duplicating its current entire contents at end of the file.

2. Write a program that copies an existing file but with the order of all of its current blocks reversed.

3. Write a program to create files of various sizes (e.g. 10 MB, 1 GB, 40 GB

and so on) and measure how long it takes.
Test two cases: one making the file size of that value without actually writing the data and the other actually writing that full amount of data.

4. Repeat the assignment in #3 but use direct I/O.

5. Write a program to create a file (say, 40 MB). Do it in two versions and compare their performance. The first one uses write() and the second one uses writev().

6. Write a program to read a big file (say, 40 MB). Do it in two versions and compare their performance. The first one uses read() and the second one uses readv().

7. Write a program to create a file (say, 40 MB). Do it in two versions and compare their performance. The first one uses write() and the second one uses fwrite().

8. Write a program to read a big file (say, 40 MB). Do it in two versions and compare their performance. The first one uses read() and the second one uses fread().

References

- The Open Group Base Specifications Issue 7, 2018 edition
  IEEE Std 1003.1-2017 (Revision of IEEE Std 1003.1-2008)
  http://pubs.opengroup.org/onlinepubs/9699919799/

- The Design of The UNIX Operating System, by Maurice J. Bach, Prentice-Hall

- Symantec Veritas VxFS documentation

https://sort.veritas.com/public/documents/sf/5.0/aix/html/fs_admin/ag_ch_interface_fs_4.html

- Oracle Direct I/O tips, Oracle Tips by Burleson Consulting
  http://www.dba-oracle.com/oracle_tips_direct_io.htm

- Advanced Programming in the UNIX Environment by W. Richard Stevens, Addison Wesley

- https://en.wikipedia.org/wiki/POSIX
- https://en.wikipedia.org/wiki/Single_UNIX_Specification
- http://pubs.opengroup.org/onlinepubs/9699919799/
- http://www.opengroup.org/austin/papers/posix_faq.html
- https://en.wikipedia.org/wiki/Austin_Group
- https://www.iso.org/standard/50516.html

5 Files and Directories

In chapter 4, we talked about the basic concepts of file I/O, what a file descriptor is, how to open a file, read data from a file and write data to a file. We also discussed various styles of doing file I/O, including sequential I/O, random I/O, synchronous I/O, asynchronous I/O, vectored I/O, buffered I/O and direct I/O.

In this chapter, we will go over various functions that programs can deploy to perform various operations on files and directories. These operations include renaming a file or directory, deleting a file or directory, changing owner, changing permission, duplicating a file descriptor, getting file/directory attributes, locking a file segment, performing file control operations and so on.

5-1 File Types and Permissions

Before we talk about various APIs and operations on files and directories, we need to introduce a couple of basic concepts.

5-1-1 Types of Files

As you may probably know already, in an operating system like UNIX or Linux, for simplicity everything is treated as or like a file. For example, a directory is a file and an I/O device is a file too. Nonetheless, they are also somewhat different. In this section, we talk about the different types of files.

According to POSIX Standard, the different types of files should be defined in the <sys/stat.h> header file. The symbolic constants defined for different types of files are listed in table 5-1.

```
       Table 5-1 Types of files
    ------------------------------------------------
    Symbolic constant        Type of file
    -----------------        ------------------
    S_IFBLK                  Block special
    S_IFCHR                  Character special
    S_IFIFO                  FIFO special
    S_IFREG                  Regular
    S_IFDIR                  Directory
    S_IFLNK                  Symbolic link
    S_IFSOCK                 Socket
    ------------------------------------------------
```

1. Regular File (S_IFREG)

   A regular file contains data. The data can be text or binary.
   Hence, data files, program source files, program object files and
   executable program files are all regular files in terms of file type.
   To the operating system or programs, a regular file is just a sequence
   of data bytes.

   A regular file is marked by a leading '-' character in the output of
   the 'ls -l' command. For example,

   ```
   -rw-r--r-- 1 jchen oinstall    87 May 19 14:51 readme
   ```

2. Directory (S_IFDIR)

   A directory contains files and/or other directories.

   A directory file is marked by a leading 'd' character in the output of
   the 'ls -l' command. For example,

   ```
   drwxr-xr-x 2 jchen oinstall  4096 Sep  6 10:24 sav
   ```

3. Symbolic Link (S_IFLNK)

   A symbolic link is a pointer to another file or directory.

   A symbolic link is marked by a leading 'l' character in the output of
   the 'ls -l' command. For instance,

   ```
   lrwxrwxrwx 1 jchen oinstall 16 Sep  4 15:50 mysymlink -> symlinktestfile1
   ```

4. FIFO (S_IFIFO)

   A FIFO file is marked by a leading 'p' character in the output of the
   'ls -l' command. For instance,

   ```
   prw-r--r-- 1 jchen oinstall    0 Sep  6 10:21 myfifo1
   ```

5. Character Device Special File (S_IFCHR)

   An I/O device which is read or written a character or one line at a time
   is normally represented as a character device special file. Examples
   include terminals and printers. Hardware device files are located in the
   /dev directory. For example, a terminal is usually represented by a
   character device file such as /dev/tty.

   Character device special files are marked by a leading 'c' character
   in the output of the 'ls -l' command. For instance,

   ```
   $ cd /dev
   $ ls -l tty*
   crw-rw-rw- 1 root tty      5,   0 Sep  7 09:56 tty
   crw-rw---- 1 root tty      4,   0 Sep  7 09:55 tty0
   crw------- 1 root root     4,   1 Sep  7 09:57 tty1
   ```

6. Block Device Special File (S_IFBLK)

Hardware devices which are read or written one block at a time are normally represented by block special files. Examples include disk and tape drives. Again, these files usually reside in the /dev directory or some subdirectory such as /dev/dsk or /dev/disk/. If it's a disk device, each partition has its own device special file.

Block device special files are marked by a leading 'b' character in the output of the 'ls -l' command. For example,

```
$ ls -l /dev/sd*
brw-r----- 1 root disk 8, 0 Sep  7 09:55 /dev/sda
brw-r----- 1 root disk 8, 1 Sep  7 09:56 /dev/sda1
brw-r----- 1 root disk 8, 2 Sep  7 09:56 /dev/sda2
brw-r----- 1 root disk 8, 3 Sep  7 09:55 /dev/sda3
```

7. Socket (S_IFSOCK)

Sockets are special files used in network communications. A socket represents a communication endpoint in a network communication. We will talk about network socket programming in chapter 12.

A socket file is marked by a leading 's' character in the output of the 'ls -l' command. For instance,

```
$ ls -l tmp/.udssrv_name
srwxr-xr-x 1 jchen oinstall 0 Apr  7  2018 tmp/.udssrv_name
```

Note that, a file entry can be a regular file, directory, link, symbolic link, socket file or any of the above seven types of files. Since they are all treated as a file programmatically, we will use file and file entry interchangeably in this book.

5-1-2 Permissions of Files

In UNIX/Linux and POSIX, each file or directory is owned by a specific user and a specific group. Accesses to a file entry are controlled by permission bits. When a file or directory is created, it is given a set of permission bits indicating who have what accesses to it.

Each user has a unique user name and belongs to one or more groups. Each group has a unique group name too.

Three types of accesses to a file entry are defined: read, write and execute.

Users are broken into three groups in terms of file access: owner, group and other.

Basically, the permission bits of a file specify whether the owner of the file entry has read, write and execute permission on the file entry, whether users in the group that owns the file entry have read, write and execute permission on the file entry, and whether the rest of users have read, write and execute permission on the file entry.

For instance, the following permissions of the file named myprog says that the owner of this file (i.e. the user named jchen) has read, write and execute permission on this file. This is indicated by the 'rwx' in the output of the 'ls -l' command. It also says that any user in the 'oinstall' group has read and execute permission on the file. It is indicated by the 'r-x' in the permission bits of the file. The '---' displayed at end of the permission bits of the file means that the rest of users have no read, write or execute permission on this file.

    -rwxr-x--- 1 jchen oinstall 62864 Jan 20 2010 myprog

Given three types of accesses are defined and all users are broken into three groups, there are 3x3=9 permission bits for each file entry. In fact, there are three more: set-user-ID bit (SUID), set-group-ID bit (SGID) and sticky bit, which we will introduce a bit later in this chapter. These twelve permission bits are usually displayed and written as four octal numbers. There is also a symbolic constant defined for each of these permission bits.

Table 5-2 lists the symbolic constants and their corresponding octal value bits.

Table 5-2 Permission bits (modes) of a file system entry

Symbolic constant	Octal Value	Meaning
S_ISUID	04000	set user ID on execution
S_ISGID	02000	set group ID on execution
S_ISVTX	01000	sticky bit
S_IRUSR	00400	readable by owner
S_IWUSR	00200	writable by owner
S_IXUSR	00100	execute/search by owner
S_IRGRP	00040	readable by group
S_IWGRP	00020	writable by group
S_IXGRP	00010	execute/search by group
S_IROTH	00004	readable by others
S_IWOTH	00002	writable by others
S_IXOTH	00001	execute/search by others

The first column in the table is the symbolic name to be used in a program. The second column is the actual value of the symbol in octal. A program can use these octal values in input as well in place of the symbols. The third column is the meaning of each mode.

Note that having execute permission on a directory means the user can search that directory. A user won't be able to change to a directory for which it does not have the execute permission on.

The execute permission on a file is normally given to executable programs and scripts to indicate who have the right to run it. For instance, it makes no sense to let a plain text file or document file have execute permissions for anyone, although it is not illegal. It just does not make sense.

For security sake, you **always give the least permission** and only the permission required. Toward that end, one should not set the execute permission bit on any file that is not a program or script or not supposed to be executed.

5-2 Create and Remove a Directory

Functions creating and removing a directory are introduced in this section.

5-2-1 The mkdir() and mkdirat() Functions

Two functions can create a new directory.

```
#include <sys/stat.h>

int mkdir(const char *newdirname, mode_t mode);
int mkdirat(int fd, const char *newdirname, mode_t mode);
```

The mkdir() function creates a new directory with the name specified in the newdirname parameter.

The permission of the new directory is set to the value of the mode parameter. The owner of the new directory is set to the process' effective user ID. The group id of the new directory is set to the group ID of the parent directory or otherwise to the effective group ID of the process.

The mkdirat() function is equivalent to the mkdir() function except in the case where newdirname specifies a relative path. In this case the new directory is created relative to the directory identified by the file descriptor fd instead of the current working directory.

Both mkdir() and mkdirat() return 0 on success and -1 on failure. If error, errno will be set to indicate the error and no directory is created.

5-2-2 The rmdir() Function

The following function removes a directory.

```
#include <unistd.h>

int rmdir(const char *path);
```

The rmdir() function removes the directory specified by the path argument. If path specifies the current working directory or its parent directory, the function will fail. If the directory being removed is not empty, the call will fail too.

If the directory's link count becomes 0 and no process has the directory open, the space occupied by the directory will be freed. The directory will become inaccessible.

The rmdir() function returns 0 on success and -1 on error. If error, errno will be set to indicate the error and the named directory is not changed.

5-3 Create Links

5-3-1 What Is a Link?

A **link** is a file with a different name of another file. It is like an alias of a file. A link is also called a **hard link** because a link is really tied to the file it is linked to. The link and the file are both referring to exactly the same disk file at the same time.
This means if one changes the contents of the file, it will reflect in the link right away. Similarly, if one changes the contents of the link, it will reflect in the file immediately as well. Hence, although the file and the link have different names they are exactly the same one file!
Note that creating a hard link for a directory is not allowed.

A **link count** is maintained for each file. When a file is created, its link count is 1. When a link is created for a file, the link count of the file is incremented by one. When a link is removed, the file's link count is decremented by one. When a file is deleted, the operating system will check its link count and actually delete the file only if its link count is 0 (and no process has the file open). So as long as there is at least one link exists the file continues to exist.

The command used to create a link is the ln command. The second column in the output of the "ls -l" command is a file's link count.
Figure 5-1 below shows the link count of the file named "file1" is incremented as links are created and decremented as links are removed.

```
Figure 5-1 Link count

$ ls -l file1
-rw-r--r-- 1 jchen oinstall 28 Sep  4 00:05 file1
$ ln file1 file1link1
$ ls -l file1*
-rw-r--r-- 2 jchen oinstall 28 Sep  4 00:05 file1
-rw-r--r-- 2 jchen oinstall 28 Sep  4 00:05 file1link1
$ ln file1 file1link2
$ ls -l file1*
-rw-r--r-- 3 jchen oinstall 28 Sep  4 00:05 file1
-rw-r--r-- 3 jchen oinstall 28 Sep  4 00:05 file1link1
-rw-r--r-- 3 jchen oinstall 28 Sep  4 00:05 file1link2
$ rm file1link1
$ ls -l file1*
-rw-r--r-- 2 jchen oinstall 28 Sep  4 00:05 file1
-rw-r--r-- 2 jchen oinstall 28 Sep  4 00:05 file1link2
```

5-3-2 The link() and linkat() Functions

From within a C program, one uses the link() function to create a link to a file.

```
#include <unistd.h>

int link(const char *path1, const char *path2);
```

174

```
int linkat(int fd1, const char *path1, int fd2,
        const char *path2, int flag);
```

The link() function creates a (hard) link for the existing file specified by the path1 argument. The name of the new link is given by the path2 argument. The link count of the file will be incremented by one.

If path1 names a symbolic link, the behavior is operating system implementation dependent. Some may follow the symbolic link while others may not.

The linkat() function is equivalent to the link() function except that symbolic links are handled as specified by the flag parameter and except in the case where either path1 or path2 or both are relative paths. In this case a relative path path1 is interpreted as relative to the directory represented by the file descriptor fd1 instead of the current working directory and similarly for path2 and the file descriptor fd2.

The flag parameter can specify a bitwise-inclusive OR of the following defined flags.

AT_SYMLINK_FOLLOW
    If path1 names a symbolic link and this bit flag is set, a new link for the target of the symbolic link is created.

Note that this flag is recently defined so it may not be implemented yet on some old versions of operating systems.

If fd1 or fd2 has the value AT_FDCWD, then the current working directory is used for the respective path argument.

If the AT_SYMLINK_FOLLOW flag is not set in the flag argument and the path1 argument names a symbolic link, a new link is created for the symbolic link path1 and not its target.

Both link() and linkat() functions return 0 on success and -1 otherwise. errno is set to indicate the error on failure.

Figure 5-2(a) lists a program named linkat.c which creates two links, one by calling the link() function and the other by calling the linkat() function. The AT_SYMLINK_FOLLOW flag is set when linkat() is called.

To show the differences, we create linkat2.c which is exactly the same as linkat.c except it clears the AT_SYMLINK_FOLLOW flag when linkat() is called. linkat2.c is not shown here but the only thing it differs from linkat.c is the following line:

```
int    flags = 0;
```

We also create a regular file named tt and a symlink named ttsymlink and run both linkat and linkat2 on these two files.

Figure 5-2(b) shows the output from our tests of running programs linkat and linkat2 on a regular file and a symlink.

As you can see for the test output, when using linkat() to create a link

175

on a given file, if the given file is a symbolic link and the linkat()
has the AT_SYMLINK_FOLLOW flag set, then it follows the symlink to the
target before it creates the new link. In other words, it actually creates
a new link to the target. In contrast, while with the AT_SYMLINK_FOLLOW flag
clear, it does not follow the symlink and it creates a new link to the
symlink itself.

Note that the linkat() function is not supported in some earlier version
of Unix/Linux, for instance, Linux 2.6, AIX 6.1 and HP-UX B.11.31.
But it is supported at later versions such as Linux 4.1.12 and AIX 7.1.

Figure 5-2a Using linkat() with AT_SYMLINK_FOLLOW flag set (linkat.c)

```
/*
 * link() and linkat() with AT_SYMLINK_FOLLOW flag
 * Pass in the name of an existing file when running this program.
 * Copyright (c) 2019 Mr. Jin-Jwei Chen. All rights reserved.
 */

#include <stdio.h>
#include <errno.h>
#include <sys/types.h>
#include <unistd.h>          /* link() */
#include <fcntl.h>           /* open(), AT_FDCWD */
#include <sys/stat.h>
#include <string.h>          /* strcat() */

int main(int argc, char *argv[])
{
  int     ret;
  int     fd;
  int     flags = AT_SYMLINK_FOLLOW;
  char    *fname = NULL;
  char    linkname[128];

  /* Get the names of the existing file */
  if (argc <= 1)
  {
    fprintf(stdout, "Usage: %s existing_file_name\n", argv[0]);
    return(-1);
  }
  fname = argv[1];
  fprintf(stdout, "Creating two links to the file %s...\n", fname);

  /* Open current directory */
  fd = open(".", 0);
  if (fd < 0)
  {
    fprintf(stderr, "open() failed, errno=%d\n", errno);
    return(-2);
  }

  /* Create the first link */
  strcpy(linkname, fname);
  strcat(linkname, "_link1");
  ret = link(fname, linkname);
```

```
if (ret < 0)
{
  fprintf(stderr, "First link() failed, errno=%d\n", errno);
  return(-3);
}

strcat(linkname, "_link2");
ret = linkat(fd, fname, fd, linkname, flags);
if (ret == -1)
{
  fprintf(stderr, "linkat() failed, errno=%d\n", errno);
  return(-4);
}

return(0);
}
```

Figure 5-2b Output from running linkat and linkat2 on a regular file and a symlink

```
$ uname -a
Linux jchenvm 4.1.12-124.27.1.el7.x86_64 #2 SMP Mon May 13 08:56:17 PDT 2019
x86_64 x86_64 x86_64 GNU/Linux
$ touch tt
$ ln -s tt ttsymlink
$ ls -l tt*
-rw-r--r--+ 1 jchen dba 0 Sep 15 11:10 tt
lrwxrwxrwx  1 jchen dba 2 Sep 15 11:10 ttsymlink -> tt
$ ./linkat2.lin64 tt
Creating two links to the file tt...
$ ls -l tt*
-rw-r--r--+ 3 jchen dba 0 Sep 15 11:10 tt
-rw-r--r--+ 3 jchen dba 0 Sep 15 11:10 tt_link1
-rw-r--r--+ 3 jchen dba 0 Sep 15 11:10 tt_link1_link2
lrwxrwxrwx  1 jchen dba 2 Sep 15 11:10 ttsymlink -> tt
$ ./linkat2.lin64 ttsymlink
Creating two links to the file ttsymlink...
$ ls -l tt*
-rw-r--r--+ 3 jchen dba 0 Sep 15 11:10 tt
-rw-r--r--+ 3 jchen dba 0 Sep 15 11:10 tt_link1
-rw-r--r--+ 3 jchen dba 0 Sep 15 11:10 tt_link1_link2
lrwxrwxrwx  3 jchen dba 2 Sep 15 11:10 ttsymlink -> tt
lrwxrwxrwx  3 jchen dba 2 Sep 15 11:10 ttsymlink_link1 -> tt
lrwxrwxrwx  3 jchen dba 2 Sep 15 11:10 ttsymlink_link1_link2 -> tt
$ rm tt_link1 tt_link1_link2 ttsymlink_link1 ttsymlink_link1_link2
$ ./linkat.lin64 tt
Creating two links to the file tt...
$ ls -l tt*
-rw-r--r--+ 3 jchen dba 0 Sep 15 11:10 tt
-rw-r--r--+ 3 jchen dba 0 Sep 15 11:10 tt_link1
-rw-r--r--+ 3 jchen dba 0 Sep 15 11:10 tt_link1_link2
lrwxrwxrwx  1 jchen dba 2 Sep 15 11:10 ttsymlink -> tt
$ ./linkat.lin64 ttsymlink
Creating two links to the file ttsymlink...
$  ls -l tt*
-rw-r--r--+ 4 jchen dba 0 Sep 15 11:10 tt
```

```
-rw-r--r--+  4 jchen dba 0 Sep 15 11:10 tt_link1
-rw-r--r--+  4 jchen dba 0 Sep 15 11:10 tt_link1_link2
lrwxrwxrwx   2 jchen dba 2 Sep 15 11:10 ttsymlink -> tt
lrwxrwxrwx   2 jchen dba 2 Sep 15 11:10 ttsymlink_link1 -> tt
-rw-r--r--+  4 jchen dba 0 Sep 15 11:10 ttsymlink_link1_link2
```

5-4 Create Symbolic Links

5-4-1 What Is a Symbolic Link

A **symbolic link**, or simply **symlink**, is a file that contains a reference to another file or directory. The contents of a symlink file is a text string that is automatically interpreted and followed by the operating system as a path to another file or directory. This other file or directory is called the "target".

A symlink is a separate file that exists independently of its target. When a symbolic link is deleted, its target remains unaffected. If a symlink's target is deleted, renamed or moved, the symlink itself is not affected either. It remains pointing to the old target, which may not exist anymore.

A symlink is also called a **soft link**. It is not really completely tied together with its target, like a hard link is. It just provides a different path to get to the target.

Below is an example of how one creates a symbolic link using the "ln -s" command:

```
$ ls -l symlinktestfile1 mysymlink
ls: mysymlink: No such file or directory
-rw-r--r-- 1 jchen oinstall 28 Sep  3 21:34 symlinktestfile1
$ ln -s symlinktestfile1 mysymlink
$ ls -l symlinktestfile1 mysymlink
lrwxrwxrwx 1 jchen oinstall 16 Sep  4 15:50 mysymlink -> symlinktestfile1
-rw-r--r-- 1 jchen oinstall 28 Sep  3 21:34 symlinktestfile1
```

Notice the size of the symbolic link, mysymlink, is 16.
That is because the name of the target "symlinktestfile1" has 16 characters.

There are three differences between a symlink and a hard link. First, a hard link cannot go beyond or across file systems while a symlink can reference a file or directory in another file system. Second, a symlink can reference a directory but a hard link can't. Third, a hard link always refers to an existing file whereas a symlink can refer to something that does not exist at all, being dangling.

5-4-2 The symlink() and symlinkat() Functions

```
#include <unistd.h>

int symlink(const char *path1, const char *path2);
int symlinkat(const char *path1, int fd, const char *path2);
```

178

The symlink() function creates a symbolic link. The second argument path2 specifies the symbolic link's name and the first argument path1 specifies the directory entry (file, directory or symbolic link) that the new symbolic link will point to. This effectively creates a file, whose name is specified by path2, that contains the string given by argument path1. The path1 argument specifies the target.

At runtime when a program references a symbolic link, the operating system will know it is a symlink and will automatically interpret the contents of the symlink as a pathname, do a pathname substitution and try to access the file or directory identified by that pathname.

Figure 5-3 lists a program using the symlink() function.

Figure 5-3 Create a symbolic link (symlink.c)

```
/*
 * symlink()
 * Copyright (c) 2019 Mr. Jin-Jwei Chen. All rights reserved.
 */

#include <stdio.h>
#include <errno.h>
#include <sys/types.h>
#include <unistd.h>          /* symlink() */

int main(int argc, char *argv[])
{
  int    ret;
  char   *filename, *symlinkname;

  /* Get the names of the two files */
  if (argc > 2)
  {
    filename = argv[1];
    symlinkname = argv[2];
  }
  else
  {
    fprintf(stderr, "Usage: %s filename symlinkname\n", argv[0]);
    return(-1);
  }

  /* Create the symlink */
  ret = symlink(filename, symlinkname);
  if (ret == -1)
  {
    fprintf(stderr, "symlink() failed, errno=%d\n", errno);
    return(-2);
  }

  return(0);
}
```

The symlinkat() function creates a symbolic link relative to a directory specified by a file descriptor.

The symlinkat() function is equivalent to the symlink() function except
in the case where path2 specifies a relative path. In this case the symbolic
link is created relative to the directory associated with the file
descriptor fd instead of the current working directory.

5-5 Remove and Rename a File or Directory

This section introduces the functions that delete a file system entry.

5-5-1 The unlink() and unlinkat() Functions

The unlink() and unlinkat() functions delete a directory entry, which
can be a file, symlink, hard link or even directory in some cases.
It needs operating system support to remove a directory using unlink().

```
#include <unistd.h>

int unlink(const char *pathname);
int unlinkat(int fd, const char *pathname, int flag);
```

The unlink() function removes the file, symlink or hard link whose pathname
is specified in the argument.

On success, the unlink() function returns 0. On error, it returns -1 and
errno is set to indicate the error.

The unlinkat() function is functionally equivalent to the unlink() or
rmdir() function except in the case where pathname specifies a relative path.
In this case the directory to be removed is determined relative to
the directory associated with the open file descriptor fd rather than
the current working directory. If the file descriptor was opened without
O_SEARCH, the function will check whether directory searches are permitted
using the current permissions of the directory underlying the file
descriptor. If the file descriptor was opened with O_SEARCH, then the
function does not perform the check.

Values of bit flags that can be passed in via the flag argument are
defined in fcntl.h. For instance, if the operating system supports it,
passing in the AT_REMOVEDIR flag will make the unlinkat() function
removes the directory entry specified by fd and pathname as a directory.

Upon success, unlink() and unlinkat() return 0. They return -1 on failure.
errno is set to indicate the error if failure. The named file is not
changed if the function returns -1.

Figure 5-4 lists an example program using unlink.

Figure 5-4 Remove a file, link or symlink (unlink.c)

```
/*
 * Remove a file, symlink or hard link using the unlink() function.
 * Copyright (c) 2013, 2014 Mr. Jin-Jwei Chen. All rights reserved.
```

```
*/

#include <stdio.h>
#include <errno.h>
#include <unistd.h>      /* unlink() */

int main(int argc, char *argv[])
{
    int       ret;

    /* Get the file or link name */
    if (argc <= 1)
    {
        fprintf(stdout, "Usage: %s pathname\n", argv[0]);
        return(-1);
    }

    /* Remove the file or link */
    ret = unlink(argv[1]);
    if (ret == -1)
    {
        fprintf(stderr, "unlink() failed, errno=%d\n", errno);
        return(-2);
    }

    return(0);
}
```

5-5-2 The remove() Function

The remove() function removes a file, symlink, hard link or directory. As you can see, the remove() function is the most generic function to delete a file or directory.

```
#include <stdio.h>

int remove(const char *pathname);
```

If the pathname argument of the remove() function names a directory, then the remove() function is equivalent to the rmdir() function. If the pathname argument names a file, symlink or hard link, the remove() function is equivalent to the unlink() function.

On success, the remove() function returns 0. On error, it returns -1 and errno is set to indicate the error.

The functionality described here is also in the Extension to the ISO C standard.

Figure 5-5 is a very simple program making use of the remove() function.

Figure 5-5 Remove a file or directory (remove.c)

```
/*
 * Remove a file, symlink, hard link or directory using the remove() function.
```

```
 * Copyright (c) 2013, 2014, 2019 Mr. Jin-Jwei Chen. All rights reserved.
 */

#include <stdio.h>
#include <errno.h>

int main(int argc, char *argv[])
{
  int      ret;

  /* Get the name of the file, link, symlink or directory */
  if (argc <= 1)
  {
    fprintf(stdout, "Usage: %s pathname\n", argv[0]);
    return(-1);
  }

  /* Remove the file, link, symlink or directory */
  ret = remove(argv[1]);
  if (ret == -1)
  {
    fprintf(stderr, "remove() failed, errno=%d\n", errno);
    return(-2);
  }

  return(0);
}
```

5-5-3 The rename() and renameat() Functions

The rename() function changes the name of a file, symlink, hard link or directory.

```
#include <stdio.h>

int rename(const char *oldpath, const char *newpath);
int renameat(int olddirfd, const char *oldpath,
             int newdirfd, const char *newpath);
```

The function takes two arguments. The first argument specifies the name of the existing file or directory and the second argument specifies its new name.

If the newpath argument specifies a link or symlink, that link or symlink will be deleted when the renaming happens.

If oldpath specifies a file and newpath specifies an existing directory, the rename() call will fail with error EISDIR. If oldpath specifies a directory and newpath specifies an existing file, rename() will fail with error ENOTDIR.

If both oldpath and newpath specify a directory, and the directory specified by the newpath is empty, then it will be deleted and the renaming will succeed. However, if the directory specified by newpath is not empty, then rename() function will fail with error ENOTEMPTY.

182

On success, the rename() function returns 0. On error, it returns -1 and errno is set to indicate the error.

Figure 5-6 shows an example program using rename() function.

Figure 5-6 Rename a file or directory (rename.c)

```
/*
 * Rename a file, symlink, hard link or directory using the rename() function.
 * Copyright (c) 2013, 2014, 2019  Mr. Jin-Jwei Chen. All rights reserved.
 */

#include <stdio.h>
#include <errno.h>

int main(int argc, char *argv[])
{
  int       ret;
  char      *oldpath, *newpath;

  /* Get the old and new names */
  if (argc <= 2)
  {
    fprintf(stdout, "Usage: %s old_pathname new_pathname\n", argv[0]);
    return(-1);
  }
  oldpath = argv[1];
  newpath = argv[2];

  /* Change the name */
  ret = rename(oldpath, newpath);
  if (ret == -1)
  {
    fprintf(stderr, "rename() failed, errno=%d\n", errno);
    return(-2);
  }

  return(0);
}
```

The renameat() function operates in exactly the same way as rename() except what is described below.

If the pathname given in oldpath is relative, it is interpreted as relative to the directory referred to by the file descriptor olddirfd, rather than relative to the current working directory of the calling process. This is also true for newpath.

If the pathname given in newpath is relative, it is interpreted as relative to the directory referred to by the file descriptor newdirfd, rather than relative to the current working directory.

If renameat() is passed the special value AT_FDCWD in the olddirfd or newdirfd parameter, the current working directory is used to determine the file for the respective path parameter.

If the pathname given in oldpath is absolute, olddirfd is ignored.

The interpretation of newpath is same as oldpath, except that a relative pathname is interpreted as relative to the directory referred to by the file descriptor newdirfd.

5-6 Get Values of Configurable Parameters

5-6-1 The pathconf() and fpathconf() Functions

```
#include <unistd.h>

long pathconf(const char *pathname, int name);
long fpathconf(int fildes, int name);
```

The pathconf() and fpathconf() functions retrieve the current value of a configurable limit or option (variable) that is associated with a file or directory.

For pathconf(), the pathname argument specifies the pathname of a file or directory. Note that the pathname or file descriptor argument could refer to a regular file, a directory, a FIFO, a terminal file, or a link. The name argument specifies the name of the configurable limit or option. All POSIX defined configurable limits for a file or directory are listed in Figure 5-7.

Figure 5-7 Variables and names of configurable limits of a file or directory

```
-----------------------------------------------------------------------
Variable                      Name  (Description)
-------------       ---------------------------------------------------
{FILESIZEBITS}        _PC_FILESIZEBITS
{LINK_MAX}            _PC_LINK_MAX  (max. number of links to the file)
{MAX_CANON}           _PC_MAX_CANON (max. length of a formatted input line)
{MAX_INPUT}           _PC_MAX_INPUT (max. length of an input line)
{NAME_MAX}            _PC_NAME_MAX  (max. length of a file name)
{PATH_MAX}            _PC_PATH_MAX  (max. length of a relative pathname)
{PIPE_BUF}            _PC_PIPE_BUF  ( size of the pipe buffer)
{POSIX2_SYMLINKS}          _PC_2_SYMLINKS
{POSIX_ALLOC_SIZE_MIN}     _PC_ALLOC_SIZE_MIN
{POSIX_REC_INCR_XFER_SIZE} _PC_REC_INCR_XFER_SIZE
{POSIX_REC_MAX_XFER_SIZE}  _PC_REC_MAX_XFER_SIZE
{POSIX_REC_MIN_XFER_SIZE}  _PC_REC_MIN_XFER_SIZE
{POSIX_REC_XFER_ALIGN}     _PC_REC_XFER_ALIGN
{SYMLINK_MAX}              _PC_SYMLINK_MAX
_POSIX_CHOWN_RESTRICTED    _PC_CHOWN_RESTRICTED (non-zero means chown() may
                             not be used on this file or files in this directory)

_POSIX_NO_TRUNC            _PC_NO_TRUNC
_POSIX_VDISABLE            _PC_VDISABLE
_POSIX_ASYNC_IO            _PC_ASYNC_IO
_POSIX_PRIO_IO             _PC_PRIO_IO
_POSIX_SYNC_IO             _PC_SYNC_IO
_POSIX_TIMESTAMP_RESOLUTION _PC_TIMESTAMP_RESOLUTION
-----------------------------------------------------------------------
```

The fpathconf() function is similar to pathconf() except the first argument is a open file descriptor of the entry instead of a pathname.

On success, both pathconf() and fpathconf() return the current value of the configurable parameter being queried. On failure, they return -1 and errno is set to indicate the error.

Figure 5-8 is a program that gets the values of all configurable limits of the current working directory.

Figure 5-8 Get the values of all configurable limits of a directory (pathconf.c)

```c
/*
 * Example Program for pathconf()
 * Get the current values of all configurable limits of a file or directory.
 * Copyright (c) 2013, 2014, 2020 Mr. Jin-Jwei Chen. All rights reserved.
 */

#include <stdio.h>
#include <errno.h>
#include <unistd.h>     /* pathconf() */
#include <limits.h>

#define  MYPATH  "."    /* use current directory */

int main(int argc, char *argv[])
{
  int    ret;
  long   val;

  /* Get the current values of all configurable limits of a file or directory */
  fprintf(stdout, "FILESIZEBITS = %ld\n", pathconf(MYPATH, _PC_FILESIZEBITS));
  fprintf(stdout, "LINK_MAX = %ld\n", pathconf(MYPATH, _PC_LINK_MAX));
  fprintf(stdout, "MAX_CANON = %ld\n", pathconf(MYPATH, _PC_MAX_CANON));
  fprintf(stdout, "MAX_INPUT = %ld\n", pathconf(MYPATH, _PC_MAX_INPUT));
  fprintf(stdout, "NAME_MAX = %ld\n", pathconf(MYPATH, _PC_NAME_MAX));
  fprintf(stdout, "PATH_MAX = %ld\n", pathconf(MYPATH, _PC_PATH_MAX));
  fprintf(stdout, "PIPE_BUF = %ld\n", pathconf(MYPATH, _PC_PIPE_BUF));
  fprintf(stdout, "POSIX2_SYMLINKS = %ld\n", pathconf(MYPATH, _PC_2_SYMLINKS));
  fprintf(stdout, "POSIX_ALLOC_SIZE_MIN = %ld\n", pathconf(MYPATH,
_PC_ALLOC_SIZE_MIN));
  fprintf(stdout, "POSIX_REC_INCR_XFER_SIZE = %ld\n", pathconf(MYPATH,
_PC_REC_INCR_XFER_SIZE));
  fprintf(stdout, "POSIX_REC_MAX_XFER_SIZE = %ld\n", pathconf(MYPATH,
_PC_REC_MAX_XFER_SIZE));
  fprintf(stdout, "POSIX_REC_MIN_XFER_SIZE = %ld\n", pathconf(MYPATH,
_PC_REC_MIN_XFER_SIZE));
  fprintf(stdout, "POSIX_REC_XFER_ALIGN = %ld\n", pathconf(MYPATH,
_PC_REC_XFER_ALIGN));
  fprintf(stdout, "SYMLINK_MAX = %ld\n", pathconf(MYPATH, _PC_SYMLINK_MAX));
  fprintf(stdout, "_POSIX_CHOWN_RESTRICTED = %ld\n", pathconf(MYPATH,
_PC_CHOWN_RESTRICTED));
  fprintf(stdout, "_POSIX_NO_TRUNC = %ld\n", pathconf(MYPATH, _PC_NO_TRUNC));
  fprintf(stdout, "_POSIX_VDISABLE = %ld\n", pathconf(MYPATH, _PC_VDISABLE));
  fprintf(stdout, "_POSIX_ASYNC_IO = %ld\n", pathconf(MYPATH, _PC_ASYNC_IO));
```

185

```
  fprintf(stdout, "_POSIX_PRIO_IO = %ld\n", pathconf(MYPATH, _PC_PRIO_IO));
  fprintf(stdout, "_POSIX_SYNC_IO = %ld\n", pathconf(MYPATH, _PC_SYNC_IO));
/*
  fprintf(stdout, "_POSIX_TIMESTAMP_RESOLUTION = %ld\n", pathconf(MYPATH,
_PC_TIMESTAMP_RESOLUTION));
*/
  return(0);
}
```

A sample output of the pathconf example program is shown below:

```
$ ./pathconf
FILESIZEBITS = 64
LINK_MAX = 32000
MAX_CANON = 255
MAX_INPUT = 255
NAME_MAX = 255
PATH_MAX = 4096
PIPE_BUF = 4096
POSIX2_SYMLINKS = 1
POSIX_ALLOC_SIZE_MIN = 4096
POSIX_REC_INCR_XFER_SIZE = -1
POSIX_REC_MAX_XFER_SIZE = -1
POSIX_REC_MIN_XFER_SIZE = 4096
POSIX_REC_XFER_ALIGN = 4096
SYMLINK_MAX = -1
_POSIX_CHOWN_RESTRICTED = 1
_POSIX_NO_TRUNC = 1
_POSIX_VDISABLE = 0
_POSIX_ASYNC_IO = -1
_POSIX_PRIO_IO = -1
_POSIX_SYNC_IO = -1
```

5-7 Get and Change Current Working Directory

From time to time a program may need to find out what its current working directory is and change directory. These APIs are discussed in this section.

5-7-1 The getcwd() Function

The getcwd() function gets the pathname of the current working directory.

```
#include <unistd.h>

char *getcwd(char *buf, size_t size);
```

The getcwd() function returns an absolute pathname of the current working directory in the first argument buf. The second argument, size, is also an input. It specifies the size, in bytes, of the buffer given in the first argument.

Upon successful completion, getcwd() returns the starting address of the buf argument. Otherwise, getcwd() returns a null pointer and errno is set to indicate the error.

5-7-2 The chdir() and fchdir() Functions

The chdir() function changes the current working directory.

```
#include <unistd.h>

int chdir(const char *path);
int fchdir(int fd);
```

Upon successful execution of the chdir() function, the calling process' current working directory changes to the directory specified in the path argument.

The fchdir() function is equivalent to chdir() except that the directory that is to be the new current working directory is specified by the file descriptor fd.

On success, the chdir() and fchdir() functions return 0.
On error, they return -1 and errno is set accordingly.

Figure 5-9 shows a program that uses getcwd() and chdir() functions.

Figure 5-9 Change and get current working directory (chdir.c)

```
/*
 * chdir(), getcwd() and pathconf().
 * Copyright (c) 2013, 2014, 2019-2020 Mr. Jin-Jwei Chen. All rights reserved.
 */

#include <stdio.h>
#include <errno.h>
#include <unistd.h>      /* chdir() */
#include <stdlib.h>      /* malloc() */
#include <string.h>      /* memset() */

#define  NEW_WORK_DIR  "/tmp"      /* new working directory */

int main(int argc, char *argv[])
{
  int    ret;
  long   len;
  char   *buf=NULL;   /* buffer to hold the new pathname */
  char   *path;       /* pointer to the new pathname */

  /* Get the maximum length of a pathname */
  len = pathconf(".", _PC_PATH_MAX);
  if (len == (long)(-1))
  {
    fprintf(stderr, "pathconf() failed, errno=%d\n", errno);
    return(-1);
  }

  fprintf(stdout, "Maximum length of a pathname returned by pathconf() = %ld\n",
    len);
```

187

```
/* Allocate memory for holding the pathname */
buf = (char *)malloc((size_t)len);
if (buf == NULL)
{
  fprintf(stderr, "malloc() failed, errno=%d\n", errno);
  return(-2);
}
memset((void *)buf, 0, len);

/* Get and print the current working directory */
path = getcwd(buf, len);
if (path == NULL)
{
  fprintf(stderr, "getcwd() failed, errno=%d\n", errno);
  free(buf);
  return(-3);
}
else
  fprintf(stdout, "Current working directory: %s\n", path);

/* Change the current working directory of this process */
fprintf(stdout, "Trying to change current directory to %s\n", NEW_WORK_DIR);
ret = chdir(NEW_WORK_DIR);
if (ret == -1)
{
  fprintf(stderr, "chdir() failed, errno=%d\n", errno);
  return(-4);
}

/* Get and print the current working directory */
path = getcwd(buf, len);
if (path == NULL)
{
  fprintf(stderr, "getcwd() failed, errno=%d\n", errno);
  free(buf);
  return(-5);
}
else
  fprintf(stdout, "Current working directory: %s\n", path);

/* Free the dynamically allocated memory and return success */
free(buf);
return(0);
}
```

The example program prints the current working directory first.
Then it changes working directory to the "/tmp" directory.
In order to know how big a buffer to allocate for the returned pathname,
it calls the pathconf() function to get the value of the _PC_PATH_MAX
configuration parameter.

5-8 Get Status and Information of a Directory Entry

Very often, a program needs to find out status or information about a file or directory. For example, to check if a file or directory exists or not or who owns it. This section introduces these functions.

5-8-1 The stat(), fstat() and lstat() Functions

```
#include <sys/types.h>
#include <sys/stat.h>
#include <unistd.h>

int stat(const char *path, struct stat *buf);
int fstat(int filedes, struct stat *buf);
int lstat(const char *path, struct stat *buf);
```

The stat() and fstat() functions get the information about a file or directory. Both stat() and fstat() require a second argument, which is a pointer to the 'struct stat', to receive the returned information about the file or directory.

The difference between them is stat() uses the file name to identify the file whereas fstat() uses an open file descriptor. In other words, the calling process must open the file first in order to get the information about a file using fstat(). Note that this has a consequence, though. For example, if the calling process has no permission to even read the file, then the fstat() function won't be able to open it (it would get error EACCES when trying to open it) and thus cannot get information about the file. However, the stat() function still can.

Therefore, in cases where the calling process may not have access to the file, you should try to use the stat() function instead of fstat().

The stat structure is defined in the header file <sys/stat.h>. It includes at least the following fields:

```
struct stat
{
  :
  dev_t st_dev        /* device ID of device containing file */
  ino_t st_ino        /* inode number */
  mode_t st_mode      /* protection mode */
  nlink_t st_nlink    /* number of hard links to the file */
  uid_t st_uid        /* user ID of owner owning the file */
  gid_t st_gid        /* group ID of owner */
  dev_t st_rdev       /* device ID (if character or block special file) */
  off_t st_size       /* For regular files, the total file size in bytes.
                         For symbolic links, the length in bytes of the
                         pathname contained in the symbolic link.
                         For a shared memory object, the length in bytes.

                         For a typed memory object, the length in bytes.
                         For other file types, the use of this field is
                         unspecified. */
  blksize_t st_blksize /* A file system-specific preferred I/O block size
                           for this object. In some file system types, this
                           may vary from file to file. */
  blkcnt_t st_blocks   /* Number of blocks allocated for this object. */
```

```
        struct timespec st_atim    /* last data access timestamp */
        struct timespec st_mtim    /* last data modification timestamp */
        struct timespec st_ctim    /* last file status change timestamp */

             :
        };
```

Note that some of the fields in the 'struct stat', (such as
st_ino, st_size, etc.) are implemented as 'unsigned long' in one platform
(e.g. Linux) and as 'unsigned long long' in another (e.g. Apple Darwin).
Therefore, you may find compiling the example program fstat.c below
might get some warning messages in some platform.

On success, fstat() and stat() return 0. On failure, they return -1 and
errno is set to indicate the error.

The lstat() function is equivalent to stat(), except when path refers to
a symbolic link. In that case lstat() returns information about the symbolic
link, while stat() or fstat() returns information about the file the
symbolic link references.

Figure 5-10 shows an example program that gets information about a file in
two different ways. The two methods do the same thing.

First method employs the stat() function which gets information about a file
using the file name. Second method does the same thing using a file
descriptor. Notice that to be able to use a file descriptor, the program has
to open the file first.

The time of last access, data modification and file status change of a file
are stored as a timestamp in the form of 'struct timespec', which is the
number of seconds and nanoseconds since the base time of 00:00:00 GMT,
1 January 1970. The timespec structure is similar to the tm structure.

```
    struct timespec
    {
      time_t tv_sec;
      long tv_nsec;
    };
```

To convert such a timestamp into a date-time string, the localtime() function
is first invoked to convert a timestamp into a localized broken-down time
stored in a tm structure. Then the strftime() function is called to format
the date and time string.

Figure 5-10 Get information about a file or directory (fstat.c)

```
/*
 * Obtain information about a file using stat() and fstat() function.
 * Copyright (c) 2013, 2014, 2020 Mr. Jin-Jwei Chen. All rights reserved.
 */

#include <stdio.h>
#include <errno.h>
```

190

```c
#include <sys/types.h>
#include <sys/stat.h>
#include <unistd.h>          /* stat(), fstat() */
#include <string.h>          /* memset() */
#include <sys/stat.h>
#include <fcntl.h>           /* open() */
#include <time.h>            /* localtime() */
#include <langinfo.h>        /* nl_langinfo() */

#define   MYFILE    "./myfile"     /* default file name */
#define   DATE_BUFSZ    64         /* size of buffer for date string */
/*
 * Get localized date string.
 * This function converts a time from type time_t to a date string.
 * The input time is a value of type time_t representing calendar time.
 * The output is string of date and time in the following format:
 *    Fri Apr  4 13:20:12 2014
 */
int cvt_time_to_date(time_t *time, char *date, unsigned int len)
{
  size_t       nchars;
  struct tm    *tm;

  if (time == NULL || date == NULL || len <= 0)
    return(-4);

  /* Convert the calendar time to a localized broken-down time */
  tm = localtime(time);

  /* Format the broken-down time tm */
  memset(date, 0, len);
  nchars = strftime(date, len, nl_langinfo(D_T_FMT), tm);
  if (nchars == 0)
    return(-5);
  else
    return(0);
}

int main(int argc, char *argv[])
{
  int   ret;
  struct stat  finfo;      /* information about a file */
  char         *fname;     /* file name */
  int          fd;         /* file descriptor of the opened file */
  char         date[DATE_BUFSZ];

  /* Get the file name from the user, if any */
  if (argc > 1)
    fname = argv[1];
  else
    fname = MYFILE;

  /* Obtain information about the file using stat() */
  ret = stat(fname, &finfo);
  if (ret != 0)
  {
```

```
    fprintf(stderr, "stat() failed, errno=%d\n", errno);
    return(-1);
}

fprintf(stdout, "Information about file %s obtained via stat():\n", fname);
fprintf(stdout, "device ID = %u\n", finfo.st_dev);
fprintf(stdout, "inode number = %lu\n", finfo.st_ino);
fprintf(stdout, "access mode = o%o\n", finfo.st_mode);
fprintf(stdout, "number of hard links = %u\n", finfo.st_nlink);
fprintf(stdout, "owner's user ID = %u\n", finfo.st_uid);
fprintf(stdout, "owner's group ID = %u\n", finfo.st_gid);
fprintf(stdout, "device ID (if special file)= %u\n", finfo.st_rdev);
fprintf(stdout, "total size in bytes = %ld\n", finfo.st_size);
fprintf(stdout, "filesystem block size = %u\n", finfo.st_blksize);
fprintf(stdout, "number of blocks allocated = %ld\n", finfo.st_blocks);
fprintf(stdout, "time of last access = %ld\n", finfo.st_atime);
ret = cvt_time_to_date(&finfo.st_atime, date, DATE_BUFSZ);
fprintf(stdout, "time of last access = %s\n", date);
fprintf(stdout, "time of last modification = %ld\n", finfo.st_mtime);
ret = cvt_time_to_date(&finfo.st_mtime, date, DATE_BUFSZ);
fprintf(stdout, "time of last modification = %s\n", date);
fprintf(stdout, "time of last status change = %ld\n", finfo.st_ctime);
ret = cvt_time_to_date(&finfo.st_ctime, date, DATE_BUFSZ);
fprintf(stdout, "time of last status change = %s\n", date);

/* Need to open the file first when using fstat() */
fd = open(fname, O_RDONLY);
if (fd == -1)
{
    fprintf(stderr, "open() failed, errno=%d\n", errno);
    return(-2);
}

/* Obtain information about the file using fstat() */
memset(&finfo, 0, sizeof(finfo));
ret = fstat(fd, &finfo);
if (ret != 0)
{
    fprintf(stderr, "fstat() failed, errno=%d\n", errno);
    return(-3);
}

fprintf(stdout, "\nInformation about file %s obtained via fstat():\n", fname);
fprintf(stdout, "device ID = %u\n", finfo.st_dev);
fprintf(stdout, "inode number = %lu\n", finfo.st_ino);
fprintf(stdout, "access mode = o%o\n", finfo.st_mode);
fprintf(stdout, "number of hard links = %u\n", finfo.st_nlink);
fprintf(stdout, "owner's user ID = %u\n", finfo.st_uid);
fprintf(stdout, "owner's group ID = %u\n", finfo.st_gid);
fprintf(stdout, "device ID (if special file)= %u\n", finfo.st_rdev);
fprintf(stdout, "total size in bytes = %ld\n", finfo.st_size);
fprintf(stdout, "filesystem block size = %u\n", finfo.st_blksize);
fprintf(stdout, "number of blocks allocated = %ld\n", finfo.st_blocks);
fprintf(stdout, "time of last access = %ld\n", finfo.st_atime);
ret = cvt_time_to_date(&finfo.st_atime, date, DATE_BUFSZ);
fprintf(stdout, "time of last access = %s\n", date);
```

```
fprintf(stdout, "time of last modification = %ld\n", finfo.st_mtime);
ret = cvt_time_to_date(&finfo.st_mtime, date, DATE_BUFSZ);
fprintf(stdout, "time of last modification = %s\n", date);
fprintf(stdout, "time of last status change = %ld\n", finfo.st_ctime);
ret = cvt_time_to_date(&finfo.st_ctime, date, DATE_BUFSZ);
fprintf(stdout, "time of last status change = %s\n", date);

   return(0);
}
```

5-9 Open and Read a Directory

This section talks about how to open a directory and read the entries in a directory.

5-9-1 The opendir(), fdopendir() and closedir() Functions

The opendir() and fdopendir() functions open a directory.

```
#include <dirent.h>

DIR *opendir(const char *dirname);
DIR *fdopendir(int fd);
int closedir(DIR *dirp);
```

The opendir() function opens a directory stream corresponding to the directory named by the dirname argument. The directory stream is positioned at the first entry of the directory.

The fdopendir() function is equivalent to the opendir() function except that the directory is specified by a file descriptor rather than by a name.

Upon successful completion, these functions return a pointer to an object of the DIR type which describes a directory. Otherwise, these functions return a null pointer and errno is set to indicate the error.

A program calls the closedir() function to close the directory opened by opendir() or fdopendir().

5-9-2 The readdir() and readdir_r() Functions

```
#include <dirent.h>

struct dirent *readdir(DIR *dirp);
int readdir_r(DIR *restrict dirp, struct dirent *restrict entry,
    struct dirent **restrict result);
```

Once a directory is opened by the opendir() function, the readdir() function can be invoked to read the entries in that directory, one at a time. Note that the caller normally needs to change directory to that target directory before calling readdir(). This can be done via chdir().
To process all or multiple entries in the target directory, programs usually put the readdir() call in a loop.

193

The readdir() takes an argument, which is a pointer to the target directory and of "DIR *" data type. DIR is defined in the <dirent.h> header file.

The data type DIR represents a directory stream, which is an ordered sequence of all the directory entries in a particular directory.
Directory entries represent files, directories, links, symlinks and others.

The readdir() function returns a pointer to a structure representing the directory entry (i.e. struct dirent) at the current position in the directory stream specified by the argument dirp, and positions the directory stream at the next entry. It returns a null pointer upon reaching the end of the directory stream. The name of a directory entry is stored in the data field named 'd_name' of the structure.

The caller can then invoke the stat() function on the directory entry name to get the information about that directory entry.

The directory entries that readdir() returns are the snapshot of the directory at the time of opendir() (or rewinddir()). Whether changes made to the directory after the opendir() call are reflected in the next readdir() call is operating system implementation dependent. Also, actual implementation of readdir() may read and buffer more than one entry at a time.
This means the directory may not actually be read on each call to readdir().

If the caller does a fork(), then either the parent or the child, but not both, can continue to process the directory stream using readdir().

The readdir() function is not guaranteed to be thread-safe.
To be thread-safe, use the readdir_r() function.

Upon success, readdir() returns a pointer to a 'struct dirent' which represents the directory entry being returned. It returns a null pointer if an error is encountered. In this case, errno is set to indicate the error.

The readdir_r() function requires two more arguments: entry and result.
The storage pointed to by entry shall be large enough for a dirent with an array of char d_name members containing at least {NAME_MAX}+1 elements.

Upon successful return, the pointer returned in the result argument will have the same value as the argument entry.

Figure 5-11 shows an application that uses opendir() and readdir_r() together with stat() to do a 'ls -l' type of operation on a directory.
The program defines and uses a function named get_permstr() that translates the permission values of a file/directory entry from numbers to character strings.

Figure 5-11 Perform a 'ls -l' operation on a directory (readdir_r.c)

```
/*
 * This program does a 'ls -l' type of operation on a directory
 * by using the opendir(), readdir_r() and other functions.
 * Copyright (c) 2013, 2014, 2020 Mr. Jin-Jwei Chen. All rights reserved.
 */
```

```c
#include <stdio.h>
#include <errno.h>
#include <sys/types.h>
#include <dirent.h>          /* readdir(3) */
#include <sys/stat.h>        /* stat(), fstat() */
#include <fcntl.h>
#include <time.h>
#include <pwd.h>
#include <grp.h>
#include <locale.h>
#include <stdint.h>
#include <langinfo.h>
#include <string.h>          /* memset() */
#include <unistd.h>          /* chdir() */

#define   DEFFAULT_DIR   "."     /* to get status info of this directory */
#define   PERMBUFSZ      32      /* length of permission string buffer */
#define   DATEBUFSZ      64      /* length of date string buffer */

/*
 * Convert a file/directory entry's permission value from type mode_t to string.
 * INPUT:
 *   mode - permission value in type of mode_t
 *   permstr - buffer to hold the output permission string
 *   len - length, in bytes, of the output string buffer
 * RETURN: 0 for success, EINVAL for failure.
 */
int get_permstr(mode_t mode, char *permstr, unsigned int len)
{
  char filetype = '?';  /* Set type of file entry to unknown */

  /* Return if we get invalid input arguments */
  if (permstr == NULL || len < 15)
    return(EINVAL);

  /* Determine the type of the file entry */
  if (S_ISDIR(mode))   filetype = 'd';     /* directory */
  if (S_ISREG(mode))   filetype = '-';     /* regular file */
  if (S_ISLNK(mode))   filetype = 'l';     /* symbolic link */
  if (S_ISCHR(mode))   filetype = 'c';     /* character device */
  if (S_ISBLK(mode))   filetype = 'b';     /* block device */
  if (S_ISFIFO(mode))  filetype = '|';     /* FIFO */

  /* Convert the read-write-execute permission bits */
  sprintf(permstr, "%c%c%c%c%c%c%c%c%c%c %c%c%c", filetype,
    mode & S_IRUSR ? 'r' : '-',
    mode & S_IWUSR ? 'w' : '-',
    mode & S_IXUSR ? 'x' : '-',
    mode & S_IRGRP ? 'r' : '-',
    mode & S_IWGRP ? 'w' : '-',
    mode & S_IXGRP ? 'x' : '-',
    mode & S_IROTH ? 'r' : '-',
    mode & S_IWOTH ? 'w' : '-',
    mode & S_IXOTH ? 'x' : '-',
    mode & S_ISUID ? 'U' : '-',
    mode & S_ISGID ? 'G' : '-',
```

195

```
     mode & S_ISVTX ? 'S' : '-');

  return(0);
}

int list_dir_long(char *dirname)
{
  DIR     *thisdir;                /* directory stream pointer */
  char    date[DATEBUFSZ];         /* buffer for date string */
  char    permstr[PERMBUFSZ];      /* buffer for permission string */
  struct dirent entry;             /* directory entry */
  struct dirent *dp=&entry;        /* directory entry pointer */
  struct dirent *result;           /* results return by readdir_r() */
  struct stat    statinfo;         /* status information */
  struct passwd *pwd;              /* password file entry */
  struct group  *grp;              /* group file entry */
  struct tm     *tm;               /* pointer to broken-down time structure */
  int           ret;

  if (dirname == NULL)
    return(EINVAL);

  /* Open the directory */
  errno = 0;
  thisdir = opendir(dirname);

  if (thisdir == NULL)
  {
    fprintf(stderr, "opendir() failed, errno=%d\n", errno);
    return(errno);
  }

  /* Change to that directory */
  ret = chdir(dirname);
  if (ret < 0)
  {
    fprintf(stderr, "chdir() failed, errno=%d\n", errno);
    return(errno);
  }

  /* Loop through all the entries that exist in the directory */
  errno = 0;
  for (ret = readdir_r(thisdir, &entry, &result);
       result != NULL && ret == 0; ret = readdir_r(thisdir, &entry, &result))
  {
    /* Get information of the next entry. Stop if we're done. */
    memset(&statinfo, 0, sizeof(statinfo));
    if (stat(dp->d_name, &statinfo) == -1)
    {
      fprintf(stderr, "stat() failed, errno=%d\n", errno);
      break;
    }

    /* Print the type, permissions, and number of links */
    memset(permstr, 0, PERMBUFSZ);
    if ((get_permstr(statinfo.st_mode, permstr, PERMBUFSZ)) == 0)
```

```
      fprintf(stdout, "%10.10s", permstr);
    fprintf(stdout, "%4d", statinfo.st_nlink);

    /* Print the owner name */
    if ((pwd = getpwuid(statinfo.st_uid)) != NULL)
      fprintf(stdout, " %-8.8s", pwd->pw_name);
    else
      fprintf(stdout, " %-8d", statinfo.st_uid);

    /* Print the group name */
    if ((grp = getgrgid(statinfo.st_gid)) != NULL)
      fprintf(stdout, " %-8.8s", grp->gr_name);
    else
      fprintf(stdout, " %-8d", statinfo.st_gid);

    /* Print the size of the file */
    fprintf(stdout, " %10jd", (intmax_t)statinfo.st_size);

    /* Convert the time to date in string */
    tm = localtime(&statinfo.st_mtime);
    strftime(date, sizeof(date), nl_langinfo(D_T_FMT), tm);

    /* Print the date/time string and entry name */
    fprintf(stdout, " %s %s\n", date, dp->d_name);
    errno = 0;
  }   /* while */

  closedir(thisdir);
  return(errno);
}


/*
 * List the directory specified or the current directory in long form.
 */
int main(int argc, char *argv[])
{
  int     ret = 0;
  char    *dirname = DEFFAULT_DIR;  /* directory to operate on */

  if (argc > 1)
    dirname = argv[1];

  ret = list_dir_long(dirname);

  return(ret);
}
```

To use readdir() instead of readdir_r(), replace the for statement in the list_dir_long() function with the while statement shown below:

```
int list_dir_long(char *dirname)
{
  struct dirent *dp;               /* directory entry pointer */

      :
  /* Loop through all the entries that exist in the directory */
```

```
    errno = 0;

    while ((dp = readdir(thisdir)) != NULL)
    {
        :
    }
}
```

5-10 Change Permission

5-10-1 The chmod(), fchmod() and fchmodat() Functions

The chmod(), fchmod() and fchmodat() functions allow a process to change the permissions of a file system entry, whether it's a file, directory, symlink, or the like.

```
#include <sys/types.h>
#include <sys/stat.h>

int chmod(const char *path, mode_t mode);
int fchmod(int fildes, mode_t mode);
int fchmodat(int fd, const char *path, mode_t mode, int flag);
```

The word chmod stands for change mode. The mode means the modes, or permissions of a file system entry.

The chmod() function changes or sets the permissions of a file system entry.

The pathname provided in the first argument of the chmod() function specifies the file system entry whose permissions are to be changed. It can be an absolute or relative pathname. If it's a relative pathname, then it is relative to the current working directory of the calling process.
The second argument, mode, specifies the new permissions for the entry.

For chmod() to work, the effective UID of the calling process must match the owner of the entry, or the process must be privileged (e.g. the root user).

Upon successful completion, chmod() shall return 0. Otherwise, it shall return -1 and set errno to indicate the error.

Remember to be very careful in changing the permissions using chmod. Normally it would be best to always obtain the current permissions and then add or minus whatever permissions you want to add or drop unless you are certain about the exact permissions you want to set.

There are two flavors of the chmod() function. If the program knows the pathname of the file or directory, then chmod() is easy to use. However, if the program has the open file descriptor for the entry instead of the pathname, then fchmod() function is more convenient to use.
The two functions behave the same except the first argument specifying the file system entry is different. chmod() needs a pathname while fchmod() needs an open file descriptor.

The fchmodat() function is equivalent to the chmod() function except in the case where path specifies a relative pathname. In this case the file or directory to be changed is determined relative to the directory associated with the file descriptor fd instead of the current working directory.

Values for the flag argument to fchmodat() are the result of a bitwise-inclusive OR of flags from the following list, as defined in <fcntl.h>:

AT_SYMLINK_NOFOLLOW
   If path argument names a symbolic link, then the mode of the symbolic link is changed.

Figure 5-12 lists a program that adds write permission for the group and others.

Figure 5-12 Change permissions of a file system entry (chmod.c)

```
/*
 * Change the permissions of a file system entry.
 * Copyright (c) 2013, 2014 Mr. Jin-Jwei Chen. All rights reserved.
 */

#include <stdio.h>
#include <errno.h>
#include <sys/types.h>
#include <sys/stat.h>
#include <unistd.h>          /* stat(), fstat() */

#define  MYFILE  "./mychmodfile"    /* default file name */

int main(int argc, char *argv[])
{
  int   ret;
  struct stat  finfo;         /* information about a file/directory */
  char          *pathname;    /* file/directory name */

  /* Get the file/directory name provided by the user, if there is one. */
  if (argc > 1)
    pathname = argv[1];
  else
    pathname = MYFILE;

  /* Obtain and report the existing permissions */
  ret = stat(pathname, &finfo);
  if (ret != 0)
  {
    fprintf(stderr, "stat() failed, errno=%d\n", errno);
    return(-1);
  }
  fprintf(stdout, "access mode = o%o\n", finfo.st_mode);

  /* Alter the permissions using chmod(). Add write permission for group
     and others. */
  ret = chmod(pathname, finfo.st_mode | S_IWGRP | S_IWOTH);
```

199

```
if (ret == -1)
{
    fprintf(stderr, "chmod() failed, errno=%d\n", errno);
    return(-2);
}

/* Obtain and report the existing permissions again */
ret = stat(pathname, &finfo);
if (ret != 0)
{
    fprintf(stderr, "stat() failed, errno=%d\n", errno);
    return(-3);
}
fprintf(stdout, "access mode = o%o\n", finfo.st_mode);

return(0);
}
```

5-11 Change Owner

5-11-1 The chown(), fchown(), fchownat() and lchown() Functions

```
#include <unistd.h>

int chown(const char *pathname, uid_t owner, gid_t group);
int fchown(int fd, uid_t owner, gid_t group);
int fchownat(int fd, const char *path, uid_t owner, gid_t group,
        int flag);
int lchown(const char *path, uid_t owner, gid_t group);
```

The chown() function changes the user and group ownership of a file system entry. The pathname argument selects the file system entry. Its new owning user and group are set to the user ID and group ID given in the second and third arguments of the call, respectively.

Passing in a value of -1 in the owner (second) or group (third) argument of the chown() call indicates that the calling process has no intention to change that ownership.

If the function call completes successfully, the last file status change timestamp of the file system entry is updated.

Note that the owner of a file system entry cannot change the user ownership of the entry. Otherwise, it would be a security hole because a malicious process would be able to create some bogus or virus files and make them owned by someone else. Only a privileged process (e.g. one with effective user ID being root) can change the ownership of a file system entry.

Similarly, the owner of a file system entry cannot change the group ownership of the entry either unless the owner is also a member of the new group.

If a non-privileged process attempts to change the user or group ownership of a file system entry that it is not allowed to, chown() will fail and the errno is set to EPERM (1).

Figure 5-13 is an example program demonstrating the use of the chown() function. This program invokes the system() function to execute a shell command to display the permissions of a file for demonstration purpose.

The example program changes the group id of the target to the second supplementary group, if there is one. If not, then set it to the primary supplementary group.

Figure 5-13 Change user and group ownership (chown.c)

```c
/*
 * Change the group ownership of a file system entry.
 * Copyright (c) 2013, 2014 Mr. Jin-Jwei Chen. All rights reserved.
 */

#include <stdio.h>
#include <errno.h>
#include <sys/types.h>
#include <sys/stat.h>
#include <unistd.h>          /* chown(), stat(), fstat() */
#include <stdlib.h>          /* system() */
#include <string.h>          /* memset() */

#define  MYFILE  "./mychownfile"     /* default file name */

int main(int argc, char *argv[])
{
  int     ret;
  char    *pathname;          /* file/directory name */
  uid_t   newuid = -1;        /* no intention to change the user ID */
  gid_t   newgid;             /* ID of the new group */
  gid_t   *supgids=NULL;      /* array of IDs of supplementary groups */
  size_t  ngrps;              /* number of supplementary groups */
  char    mycmd[256];         /* buffer of a command to be executed */

  /* Get the file/directory name provided by the user, if there is one. */
  if (argc > 1)
    pathname = argv[1];
  else
    pathname = MYFILE;

  /* Get the number of supplementary groups. In some implementation
     this number may also include the effective group ID as well. */
  ngrps = getgroups(0, supgids);
  if (ngrps == -1)
  {
    fprintf(stderr, "getgroups() failed, errno=%d\n", errno);
    return(-1);
  }

  if (ngrps >= 1)
  {
    supgids = (gid_t *)malloc(sizeof(gid_t) * ngrps);
    if (supgids == NULL)
```

```
  {
    fprintf(stderr, "malloc() failed, errno=%d\n", errno);
    return(-2);
  }
  memset((void *)supgids, 0, (sizeof(gid_t) * ngrps));

  /* Get the IDs of the supplementary groups. Note that in some implementation
     the effective group ID may also be returned in the output list. */
  ret = getgroups(ngrps, supgids);
  if (ret == -1)
  {
    fprintf(stderr, "getgroups() failed, errno=%d\n", errno);
    return(-3);
  }

  /* Pick the second supplementary group if there is one */
  if (ngrps >= 2)
    newgid = supgids[1];
  else
    newgid = supgids[0];
}
else
{
  /* Use the effective group ID if there is no supplementary group ID */
  newgid = getegid();
}

/* List the current user and group ownership before chown() */
sprintf(mycmd, "ls -l %s", pathname);
ret = system(mycmd);
if (ret == -1)
{
  fprintf(stderr, "system() failed, errno=%d\n", errno);
  if (supgids != NULL)
    free(supgids);
  return(-4);
}

/* Change the ownership of user and group */
ret = chown(pathname, newuid, newgid);
if (ret == -1)
{
  fprintf(stderr, "chown() failed, errno=%d\n", errno);
  if (supgids != NULL)
    free(supgids);
  return(-5);
}

/* List the current user and group ownership after chown() */
ret = system(mycmd);
if (ret == -1)
{
  fprintf(stderr, "system() failed, errno=%d\n", errno);
  if (supgids != NULL)
    free(supgids);
  return(-6);
```

```
    }

    /* Free the memory that we have allocated */
    if (supgids != NULL)
        free(supgids);

    return(0);
}
```

The fchown() function is equivalent to chown() except that the file whose owner and group are being changed is specified by the file descriptor fd.

The fchownat() function is equivalent to the chown() function except in the case where the parameter path specifies a relative pathname.
In this case the file to be changed is determined relative to the directory associated with the file descriptor fd instead of the current working directory. If the access mode of the open file description associated with the file descriptor fd is not O_SEARCH, the function shall check whether directory searches are permitted using the current permissions of the directory underlying the file descriptor. If the access mode is O_SEARCH, the function shall not perform the check.

The lchown() function is equivalent to chown() except in the case where the named file is a symbolic link. In this case, lchown() will change the ownership of the symbolic link itself, while chown() changes the ownership of the file or directory which the symbolic link refers to.

5-12 Duplicate a File Descriptor

5-12-1 The dup() and dup2() Functions

The dup() and dup2() functions duplicate a file descriptor, causing the second (new) file descriptor to refer to the same open file as the first (old) one and share the same file offset and file status flags.

```
#include <unistd.h>

int dup(int oldfd);
int dup2(int oldfd, int newfd);
```

Both functions require the caller to pass in an existing file descriptor that represents an existing open file.

The dup2() function requires the new file descriptor to be passed in as the second argument. The dup() function will always return the lowest-numbered file descriptor from the user's open file descriptor table that is available.

The dup2() function causes the file descriptor newfd to refer to the same open file as associated with the file descriptor oldfd and to share any locks. It will return newfd. If newfd is already a valid open file descriptor, it will be closed first, unless oldfd is equal to newfd in which case dup2() will return newfd without closing it.

Upon successful completion of the function call, the two file descriptors shall share the same file offset, file locks, and file status flags except that the FD_CLOEXEC flag associated with the new file descriptor will be cleared.

If necessary, the caller needs to first close the new file descriptor to make it available before calling the dup() or dup2() function. The dup2() function will attempt to close the new file descriptor if it is a valid file descriptor (referring to some open file) before the duplicate operation.

On success, the dup() and dup2() functions return the new file descriptor. On error, they return -1 and errno is set to indicate the error.

If oldfd is not a valid file descriptor, dup2() returns -1 and it will not close newfd. If newfd is less than 0 or greater than or equal to {OPEN_MAX}, dup2() returns -1 with errno set to EBADF (9).
If the close operation fails to close newfd when it tries to do so, then dup2() will return -1 without changing that open file descriptor.

It is worth mentioning that POSIX-compliant operating systems use the dup() and dup2() functions a lot for **I/O redirection** as well as **piping** (connecting one command's output to another's input). For example, the following command redirects the output of the ls command from its standard output, which is the terminal, to the file named ls.out:

```
$ ls > ls.out
```

And following is an example of piping:

```
$ ls | grep my
```

The dup() function provides a service equivalent to that provided by fcntl() using the F_DUPFD command. The call

```
dup(fd);
```

is equivalent to:

```
fcntl(fd, F_DUPFD, 0);
```

Figure 5-14 is an example program using dup2(). It opens a file, reads the first 10 bytes from it. Then it calls dup2() to duplicate the open file descriptor to file descriptor 6 and then reads 26 bytes from file descriptor 6. It gets exactly the next 26 bytes.
This example shows that dup2() returns the new file descriptor you specify and that the current file offset is exactly at where the original file descriptor was.

Figure 5-14 Example program using dup2() -- dup2.c

```
/*
 * Open a data file, read the first few bytes from it.
 * Then duplicate the file descriptor using dup2() and read the next few bytes.
 * Copyright (c) 2019 Mr. Jin-Jwei Chen. All rights reserved.
```

```
  */

#include <stdio.h>
#include <errno.h>
#include <stdlib.h>
#include <sys/types.h>
#include <sys/stat.h>
#include <fcntl.h>
#include <unistd.h>         /* dup() and dup2() */

#define BYTECNT1   10
#define BYTECNT2   26
#define BUFLEN     128

int main(int argc, char *argv[])
{
  int    ret;
  int    fd, fd2, newfd;       /* file descriptors */
  char   buf[BUFLEN] = "";
  char   *fname;                /* name of input data file */

  /* Expect to get the file name from user */
  if (argc > 1)
    fname = argv[1];
  else
  {
    fprintf(stderr, "Usage: %s filename\n", argv[0]);
    return(-1);
  }

  /* Open the data file for read only. */
  fd = open(fname, O_RDONLY, 0644);
  if (fd == -1)
  {
    fprintf(stderr, "open() failed, errno=%d\n", errno);
    return(-2);
  }

  /* Read the first few bytes from the file. */
  ret = read(fd, buf, BYTECNT1);
  if (ret > 0 && ret < BUFLEN)
    buf[ret] = '\0';
  else
  {
    fprintf(stderr, "read() failed, ret = %d\n", ret);
    return(-1);
  }
  fprintf(stdout, "The first %u bytes in the dada file are %s.\n", BYTECNT1, buf);

  /* Duplicate the file descriptor using dup2() */
  fd2 = 6;
  newfd = dup2(fd, fd2);
  fprintf(stdout, "dup2() returned newfd=%d\n", newfd);

  /* Read the next few bytes */
  ret = read(fd, buf, BYTECNT2);
```

```
if (ret > 0 && ret < BUFLEN)
  buf[ret] = '\0';
else
{
  fprintf(stderr, "read() failed, ret = %d\n", ret);
  return(-1);
}
fprintf(stdout, "The next %u bytes in the dada file are %s.\n", BYTECNT2, buf);

close(newfd);
return(0);
}
```

5-13 The fcntl() Function

The fcntl() function performs various operations on an open file. As shown below it has three different formats:

```
#include <unistd.h>
#include <fcntl.h>

int fcntl(int fd, int cmd);
int fcntl(int fd, int cmd, long arg);
int fcntl(int fd, int cmd, struct flock *lock);
```

All three formats take a file descriptor (fd) argument and a command (cmd) argument. The second format requires an additional argument arg while the third format requires an additional argument lock instead.

On success, the value returned by the fcntl() function depends on the command (cmd). On failure, the function returns -1 and errno is set to indicate the error.

In summary, the fcntl() function can perform the following operations or commands on an open file specified by the file descriptor argument fd:

1. Duplicate a file descriptor (cmd = F_DUPFD or F_DUPFD_CLOEXEC)

When a program calls the fcntl() function with an open file descriptor fd and the command F_DUPFD, it duplicates a file descriptor. Specifically, it finds the lowest numbered available file descriptor that is equal to or greater than the value specified in the arg argument and makes it be a copy of fd. The function returns the new file descriptor if success.

In other words,

```
newfd = fcntl(fd, F_DUPFD, 0);
```

is equivalent to

```
newfd = dup(fd);
```

Also, the statements

```
close(fd2);
```

```
    newfd = fcntl(fd, F_DUPFD, fd2);
```

is equivalent to

```
    newfd = dup2(fd, fd2);
```

The F_DUPFD_CLOEXEC command is the same as F_DUPFD except that the FD_CLOEXEC flag associated with the new file descriptor shall be set.

2. Get or set file descriptor flags (cmd = F_GETFD or F_SETFD)

   The third argument of the fcntl() function is not needed by the F_GETFD command. The function's return value is value of flags. However, the F_SETFD command does need the third argument for providing the new value of the flags.

   File descriptor flags include the following:

   FD_CLOEXEC - Setting this flag means to close the file descriptor upon execution of an exec-family function. That is, if the FD_CLOEXEC flag in the third argument is 0, the file descriptor will remain open across the exec functions; otherwise, the file descriptor will be closed upon successful execution of one of the exec() functions.

   The fcntl() function returns a value other than -1 if the F_SETFD command succeeds.

3. Get or set file status flags and file access modes (cmd = F_GETFL or F_SETFL)

   The F_GETFL command gets the file status flags and file access modes. On successful execution of the F_GETFL command, the fcntl() function returns the value of file status flags and access modes. The file access modes can be extracted from the return value using the mask O_ACCMODE. The flags returned may include non-standard file status flags which the application did not set.

   File status flags include the following:

   ```
   O_APPEND - set append mode
   O_NONBLOCK - no delay
   ```

   The F_SETFL command sets the file status flags as specified in the third argument of the function. Bits corresponding to the file access mode and the file creation flags that are set in third argument are ignored.

   On successful execution of the F_SETFL command, the fcntl() function returns a value other than -1.

   For instance, below are two sample return values of the fcntl() F_GETFL command:

   ```
   flags=0x8001   (O_WRONLY)
   flags=0x8401   (O_WRONLY | O_APEEND)
   ```

4. Get or set file segment lock (cmd = F_GETLK, F_SETLK, or F_SETLKW)

F_GETLK: Get the first or any lock that would block the caller from
getting the lock described in the third argument of the call.
The information returned will overwrite third argument.
If no lock is found that would prevent the caller from getting
the lock described in the third argument, then the third argument
will remain unchanged except for the lock type which shall be
set to F_UNLCK.

F_SETLK: Set or clear a file segment lock as described by the third
argument.

F_SETLKW: This command is the same as F_SETLK except that the calling
process blocks and waits if the lock is not available (i.e.
is currently held by another process).

The fcntl() function returns a value other than -1 if the F_GETLK,
F_SETLK, or F_SETLKW command succeeds.

5. Get or set socket ownership (cmd = F_GETOWN or F_SETOWN)

F_GETOWN: If the first argument fd refers to a socket, then this command
gets the process or process group id specified to receive SIGURG signals
when out-of-band data is available. Positive values mean a process
ID; negative values, other than -1, mean a process group ID.
If the file descriptor does not refer to a socket, the result is
unspecified.

F_SETOWN: If the first argument fd refers to a socket, then this command
sets the process or process group id specified to receive SIGURG signals
when out-of-band data is available. Positive values mean a process
ID; negative values, other than -1, mean a process group ID.
If the file descriptor does not refer to a socket, the result is
unspecified.

The fcntl() function returns a value other than -1 if the F_SETOWN command
succeeds. It returns the value of the socket owner process id or process
group id if the F_GETOWN command succeeds.

5-13-1 File Locking Using fcntl()

One of the most useful features of the fcntl() function is to perform
file region locking. This function allows a program to lock a region of
a file so that multiple processes can operate (read or write) on the same
file at the same time without compromising its integrity.

When using the fcntl() function to lock a section of a file, a calling
program can specify a starting byte offset and the number of bytes it wants
to lock and protect. The information needed by the locking operation is
specified in a structure named 'struct flock' as shown below:

```
struct flock {
    :
    short l_type;     /* Type of lock: F_RDLCK, F_WRLCK, F_UNLCK */
    off_t l_start;    /* Starting file offset for lock */
```

```
        short l_whence;   /* How to interpret l_start:
                             SEEK_SET, SEEK_CUR, SEEK_END */
        off_t l_len;      /* Number of bytes to lock */
        pid_t l_pid;      /* process id of process blocking holding the
                             lock (F_GETLK only) */
            :
    };
```

The fields of this structure are explained below:

l_type: INPUT, specifies the type of lock the caller wants to obtain.
    Possible values are F_RDLCK (read or shared lock),
    F_WRLCK (write or exclusive lock), F_UNLCK (to unlock)

l_start: INPUT, specifies a starting byte offset for the file region
    being locked or unlocked.

l_whence: INPUT, specifies how the l_start value should be interpreted.
    Possible values are: SEEK_SET (starting offset is relative to
    beginning of the file), SEEK_CUR (starting offset is relative to
    the current position), SEEK_END (starting offset is relative to
    the end of the file).

l_len: INPUT, specifies the size (in bytes) of the file region/segment
    to be locked/unlocked

l_pid: OUTPUT, returns the process ID of the process holding the lock.
    This is used with F_GETLK.

Figure 5-15 shows a program that demonstrates using fcntl() to lock
a region of a file for update and the regions two program instances
try to lock overlap. The program locks two consecutive blocks (1024 bytes),
the third and fourth blocks, of a file. Once getting the lock, the first
program instance updates the third block and the second instance updates
the fourth block.

If you run two instances of this program, with an input argument of 1 and 2,
respectively, then the two processes will try to place a write (exclusive)
lock on the same file region. Once the process acquires the write lock,
the first process will update the third block with 512 bytes of the
character 'A' while the second process will update the fourth block with
512 bytes of the character 'B'.

To make it easier to see the lock contention, the program sleeps for ten
seconds once it gets the file region locked. This makes it easier to see
the other process has to wait.

The test data file is expected to pre-exist and have at least 2048 bytes
of data in it.

Note that this example locks the file on block boundary. It does not have to
be so. In fact, a program can lock on any byte boundary.

Figure 5-15 Lock file segments using fcntl() (fcntl.c)

```
/*
```

```
 * Locking a file segment using the fcntl() function.
 * Case 1: File regions locked by two processes overlap.
 * This program locks 3rd and 4th blocks of the file. The first instance of
 * this program (with an argument of 1 or no argument) updates the 3rd block
 * and the second program instance (with an argument of 2) updates the
 * 4th block. The two program instances coordinate via a write lock on
 * the shared file region.
 * Note that the data file fcntl.data must pre-exist with at least 2048 bytes
 * of data before you run this program.
 * Copyright (c) 2013, 2014 Mr. Jin-Jwei Chen. All rights reserved.
 */

#include <stdio.h>
#include <errno.h>
#include <sys/types.h>
#include <unistd.h>          /* fcntl() */
#include <fcntl.h>           /* open() */
#include <sys/stat.h>
#include <string.h>          /* memset() */
#include <stdlib.h>          /* atoi() */

#define   FILENAME    "./fcntl.data"    /* name of data file to be updated */
#define   OFFSET2LOCK         (1024)    /* file offset to lock */
#define   SIZE2LOCK           (1024)    /* number of bytes to lock */
#define   MY_UPD_OFFSET       (1024)    /* starting offset of my update */
#define   MY_UPD_SIZE         (512)     /* size of my update */

int main(int argc, char *argv[])
{
  int     fd;
  struct flock  flock;
  char    buf[MY_UPD_SIZE];
  off_t   offset_ret, upd_offset;
  ssize_t bytes;
  int     ret;
  int     instance = 1;      /* program instance */

  /* Get the program instance number */
  if (argc > 1)
    instance = atoi(argv[1]);
  if (instance < 1 || instance > 2)
  {
    fprintf(stderr, "Usage: %s [ 1 or 2 ]\n", argv[0]);
    return(-1);
  }

  /* Open the file */
  fd = open(FILENAME, O_WRONLY);
  if (fd == -1)
  {
    fprintf(stderr, "open() failed on %s, errno=%d\n", FILENAME, errno);
    return(-2);
  }

  /* Set up the flock structure */
  flock.l_type = F_WRLCK;              /* to obtain a write lock */
```

```
  flock.l_whence = SEEK_SET;          /* offset relative to start of file */
  flock.l_start = OFFSET2LOCK;        /* relative offset to lock */
  flock.l_len = SIZE2LOCK;            /* number of bytes to lock */

  /* Acquire the lock on the file segment. Wait if lock not available */
  ret = fcntl(fd, F_SETLKW, &flock);
  if (ret == -1)
  {
    fprintf(stderr, "fcntl() failed to lock, errno=%d\n", errno);
    close(fd);
    return(-3);
  }

  /* Update one block of the file */
  fprintf(stdout, "Program instance %d got the file lock.\n", instance);
  if (instance == 1)
    upd_offset = MY_UPD_OFFSET;
  else
    upd_offset = MY_UPD_OFFSET + 512;
  offset_ret = lseek(fd, upd_offset, SEEK_SET);
  if (offset_ret == -1)
  {
    fprintf(stderr, "lseek() failed, errno=%d\n", errno);
    close(fd);
    return(-4);
  }

  memset((void *)buf, 'A'+(instance-1), MY_UPD_SIZE);
  bytes = write(fd, buf, MY_UPD_SIZE);
  if (bytes == -1)
  {
    fprintf(stderr, "write() failed, errno=%d\n", errno);
    close(fd);
    return(-5);
  }

  fprintf(stdout, "Program instance %d updated one block of the file "
    "but still holding lock.\n", instance);
  sleep(10);   /* Just to make the other process wait */

  /* Release the file lock */
  fprintf(stdout, "Program instance %d releases the lock.\n", instance);
  flock.l_type = F_UNLCK;         /* to release the lock I acquired */
  ret = fcntl(fd, F_SETLK, &flock);
  if (ret == -1)
  {
    fprintf(stderr, "fcntl() failed to unlock, errno=%d\n", errno);
    close(fd);
    return(-6);
  }
  fprintf(stdout, "Program instance %d exiting.\n", instance);

  /* Close the file and return */
  close(fd);
  return(0);
}
```

If you use the fcntl F_SETLK command to try to acquire a file segment lock and the lock is not available, then the function will return right away with errno set to EAGAIN. To wait until the lock becomes available, use the F_SETLKW command instead.

Note that for each byte in the file, there can be at most one type of lock set at a given time. A process having an existing lock in a region can replace the lock with a different type.

All locks owned by a process for a given file shall be released when the file is closed by that process or the process owning the file descriptor terminates.

Deadlock can possibly occur if a process owning a lock on a region is put to sleep while attempting to acquire a lock on another region that is currently held by another process. If the system detects a locking operation would cause deadlock, the fcntl() function will fail with an EDEADLK error.

5-13-2 Other Examples

Figure 5-16 is an example of using the fcntl() function's F_SETFL command to turn on the O_APPEND file status flag. It demonstrates that setting the O_APPEND file status flag has the same effect of using the same flag on the open() function. That is, setting the O_APPEND flag via the following fcntl() call:

```
fcntl(fd, F_SETFL, flags | O_APPEND)
```

achieves the same result as using the same flag in the open function:

```
open(filename, flags | O_APPEND)
```

Figure 5-16 Setting file status flags using fcntl()   (fcntl2.c)

```
/*
 * This program opens a file for writing and then uses the fcntl() function
 * to set the append mode and write a message to it.
 * Copyright (c) 2013, 2014, 2020 Mr. Jin-Jwei Chen.  All rights reserved.
 */

#include <stdio.h>
#include <errno.h>
#include <sys/types.h>
#include <sys/stat.h>
#include <fcntl.h>
#include <unistd.h>
#include <string.h>   /* memset() */

#define  BUFSZ          512

int main(int argc, char *argv[])
{
  char *fname;
```

```
 int    fd;
 ssize_t  bytes;
 size_t   count;
 char      buf[BUFSZ];
 int       flags;            /* file status flags */
 int       ret;

 /* Expect to get the file name from user */
 if (argc > 1)
   fname = argv[1];
 else
 {
   fprintf(stderr, "Usage: %s filename\n", argv[0]);
   return(-1);
 }

 /* Open a file for write only. This open() will fail with errno=2
    if the file does not exist. */
 fd = open(fname, O_WRONLY, 0644);
 if (fd == -1)
 {
   fprintf(stderr, "open() failed, errno=%d\n", errno);
   return(-2);
 }

 /* Fill the buffer with message to write */
 sprintf(buf, "%s", "This is a new string.");
 count = strlen(buf);

 /* Use fcntl() to turn on the APPEND mode */
 flags = fcntl(fd, F_GETFL, 0);
 if (flags == -1)
 {
  fprintf(stderr, "fcntl(F_GETFL) failed, errno=%d\n", errno);
  close(fd);
  return(-3);
 }

 flags = flags | O_APPEND;   /* turn on the APPEND mode */

 ret = fcntl(fd, F_SETFL, flags);
 if (ret == -1)
 {
  fprintf(stderr, "fcntl(F_SETFL) failed, errno=%d\n", errno);
  close(fd);
  return(-4);
 }

 /* Write the contents of the buffer to the file.
  * This will get written to the end of the file due to O_APPEND.
  */
 bytes = write(fd, buf, count);
 if (bytes == -1)
 {
   fprintf(stderr, "write() failed, errno=%d\n", errno);
   close(fd);
```

```
    return(-5);
  }
  fprintf(stdout, "%ld bytes were written into the file\n", bytes);

  /* Close the file */
  close(fd);
  return(0);
}
```

Figure 5-17 is another example that shows how to use some of the fcntl() get commands listed below:

F_GETFD - Get the file descriptor flags defined in <fcntl.h>
F_GETFL - Get the file status flags and file access modes
F_GETOWN - If file descriptor fd refers to a socket, get the process ID
           or process group ID specified to receive SIGURG signals when
           out-of-band data is available. Positive values indicate a process ID;
           negative values, other than -1, indicate a process group ID;
           the value zero indicates that no SIGURG signals are to be sent.
           If fd does not refer to a socket, the results are unspecified.
           For instance, the fcntl() call can get back error 25.

Figure 5-17 Using fcntl() get commands (fcntl3.c)
```

```
/*
 * fcntl() get commands
 * Copyright (c) 2013, 2014 Mr. Jin-Jwei Chen. All rights reserved.
 */

#include <stdio.h>
#include <errno.h>

#include <sys/types.h>
#include <unistd.h>          /* fcntl() */
#include <fcntl.h>           /* open() */
#include <sys/stat.h>

int main(int argc, char *argv[])
{
  int    flags, ret;
  int    fd;
  char   *fname=NULL;

  /* Get the name of the file */
  if (argc <= 1)
  {
    fprintf(stderr, "Usage: %s filename\n", argv[0]);
    return(-1);
  }
  fname = argv[1];

  /* Open the file */
  fd = open(fname, O_RDONLY);
  if (fd == -1)
  {
    fprintf(stderr, "open() failed, errno=%d\n", errno);
```

214
```

```
    return(-1);
}

/* Find file descriptor flags */
flags = fcntl(fd, F_GETFD);
if (flags == -1)
{
   fprintf(stderr, "fcntl() failed, errno=%d\n", errno);
   close(fd);
   return(-2);
}
fprintf(stdout, "File descriptor flags: 0x%x\n", flags);

/* Find file's status flags */
flags = fcntl(fd, F_GETFL);
if (flags == -1)
{
   fprintf(stderr, "fcntl() failed, errno=%d\n", errno);
   close(fd);
   return(-3);
}
fprintf(stdout, "File status flags and access modes: 0x%x\n", flags);

/* Print the file access modes. Note that we do it this way because
   O_RDONLY is defined to be 0, O_WRONLY 1, O_RDWR 2 */
if ((flags & O_ACCMODE) & O_RDWR)
   fprintf(stdout, "File access mode: O_RDWR\n");
else if ((flags & O_ACCMODE) & O_WRONLY)
   fprintf(stdout, "File access mode: O_WRONLY\n");
else
   fprintf(stdout, "File access mode: O_RDONLY\n");

/* Find file descriptor owner */
ret = fcntl(fd, F_GETOWN);
if (ret == -1)
{
   fprintf(stderr, "fcntl() failed, errno=%d\n", errno);
   close(fd);
   return(-4);
}
fprintf(stdout, "Socket file descriptor owner: %d\n", ret);

close(fd);
return(0);
}
```

5-14 The ioctl() Function

The ioctl() function is used to control hardware devices in a system.
It performs a variety of control functions on I/O devices.
In POSIX-compliant systems, all hardware devices are represented by some
device special files, which normally reside in the /dev directory.
System and application software can read and write data to and from these
devices using the read() and write() system calls, which we have introduced
earlier. In addition, software can issue control commands via the ioctl()

system call to control devices.

The ioctl() function is somewhat low level and system dependent. But it is very useful in the development of not only application programs but operating system kernel components such as file systems, network subsystems and device drivers. It can be used to change settings of a file descriptor for almost any kind of regular files and device special files. It is very commonly used with file descriptors representing network sockets, terminal I/O devices, and all kinds of device drivers, for instance, device drivers for disk and tape devices. Note that the device driver can be one that controls a pseudo device or even a kernel subsystem controlling no device at all, too.

Many kernel and/or device driver developers write device drivers that run in the operating system kernel space and then write tools and applications that use the ioctl() function to communicate with their device drivers. The ioctl() function is typically implemented as a system call.

```
#include <sys/ioctl.h>
int ioctl(int d, int request, ...);
```

Because of the device control, the ioctl() function is system dependent. At a high level, the iotcl() function takes two or three arguments. The first argument is always a file descriptor, which is associated with the special device file in the /dev directory that corresponds to the device driver or kernel subsystem in the operating system kernel that actually controls the target physical or pseudo device.

The second argument specifies a control command that is known by the device driver or kernel subsystem. What commands are available is device dependent.

The third argument is optional. Whether it is needed depends on the actual control command. Its actual type is also dependent on the control command. It can be an integer or a pointer to some memory buffer containing the data related to the control command.

Figure 5-18 shows the big picture of the ioctl() function.

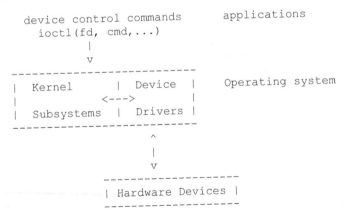

Figure 5-18 Environment of ioctl() function

The POSIX standard includes ioctl() for controlling STREAMS devices.

216

STREAMS is a modular framework for developing networking and character device (e.g. terminal) drivers that originated in Unix System V.

However, the ioctl() function can be used for any devices and even generic kernel subsystems as long as the drivers or kernel subsystems implement the ioctl system call and support the commands. Note that a kernel subsystem may not have a device associated with it, but the device driver framework and ioctl() system call works just fine for it. This works beautifully for kernel developers to dynamically load some new kernel subsystems into the operating system kernel and then develop some user-space applications to communicate with them via ioctl or some system call. ioctl offers a way application programs talk to kernel code. For example, user-space applications can talk to device drivers or kernel subsystems using this call.

Figure 5-19 is a program demonstrating the use of the ioctl() function. This program reads a message from the standard input of the terminal. It prompts the user to enter a message, reads the message and then displays the message. By default, I/O is blocking. Therefore, when the program executes the read() function, it blocks and waits for the user to type in a message. All works just fine.

If you supply an argument when you run the program, then the program will invoke the ioctl() function to turn on nonblocking I/O. Since the nonblocking I/O is on, when the program executes the read() function, it does not block or wait. If data is available for reading, read() will return that. If not, read() returns right away, too. Because of this, you will see the read() function returns before you even get a chance to type in anything.

The effect of this ioctl() call is similar to setting the O_NONBLOCK file status flag with the fcntl() function.

Figure 5-19 Turn on nonblocking I/O using ioctl() (ioctl.c)

```
/*
 * Read from terminal.
 * Enables nonblocking I/O using the ioctl() function.
 * By default, blocking I/O is used when reading from terminal.
 * Pass in an argument to turn on nonblocking I/O.
 * Copyright (c) 2013, 2014 Mr. Jin-Jwei Chen. All rights reserved.
 */

#include <stdio.h>
#include <errno.h>
#include <unistd.h>      /* read() */
#include <sys/ioctl.h>
#include <sys/types.h>
#include <unistd.h>

#define  BUFSZ  256

int main(int argc, char *argv[])
{
  int    ret;
  char   buf[BUFSZ];
  ssize_t  nbytes;
```

```
int    fd=0;        /* standard input (stdin) is the default file descriptor */
int    flags;
int    nbio = 0;    /* by default, nonblocking I/O is off */

/* User can turn on nonblocking I/O by passing in an argument */
if (argc > 1)
{
  nbio = 1;
  fprintf(stdout, "Nonblocking I/O is on\n");
}
else
  fprintf(stdout, "Nonblocking I/O is off\n");

fprintf(stdout, "Enter a message:\n");

/* Enables nonblocking I/O if the user says so */
if (nbio)
{
  flags = 1;
  ret = ioctl(fd, FIONBIO, &flags);
  if (ret == -1)
  {
    fprintf(stderr, "ioctl() failed, errno=%d\n", errno);
    return(-1);
  }
}

/* Read the input message */
nbytes = read(fd, buf, BUFSZ);
fprintf(stdout, "\nJust read this from terminal:\n%s\n", buf);

return(0);
}
```

Figure 5-20 shows another program that employs the ioctl() function to peek into how many bytes are available for read. In order for the user to be able to test this manually, we insert a sleep of six seconds before the ioctl() call. It's only for testing purpose.

Figure 5-20 Peek into number of bytes available for read with ioctl (ioctl2.c)

```
/*
 * Read from terminal.
 * Enables nonblocking I/O using the ioctl() function.
 * Also peek into how many bytes are available for read with ioctl().
 * By default, blocking I/O is used when reading from terminal.
 * Pass in an argument to turn on nonblocking I/O.
 * Copyright (c) 2013, 2014, 2020 Mr. Jin-Jwei Chen. All rights reserved.
 */

#include <stdio.h>
#include <errno.h>
#include <unistd.h>     /* read() */
#include <sys/ioctl.h>
#include <sys/types.h>
#include <unistd.h>
```

```c
#define  BUFSZ  256

int main(int argc, char *argv[])
{
  int    ret;
  char   buf[BUFSZ];
  ssize_t  nbytes=0;
  int    fd=0;      /* standard input (stdin) is the default file descriptor */
  int    flags;
  int    nbio = 0;  /* by default, nonblocking I/O is off */

  /* User can turn on nonblocking I/O by passing in an argument */
  if (argc > 1)
  {
    nbio = 1;
    fprintf(stdout, "Nonblocking I/O is on\n");
  }
  else
    fprintf(stdout, "Nonblocking I/O is off\n");

  fprintf(stdout, "Enter a message:\n");

  /* Enables nonblocking I/O if the user says so */
  if (nbio)
  {
    flags = 1;
    ret = ioctl(fd, FIONBIO, &flags);
    if (ret == -1)
    {
      fprintf(stderr, "ioctl(FIONBIO) failed, errno=%d\n", errno);
      return(-1);
    }
  }

  /* Sleep a few seconds so the user has time to type */
  sleep(3);

  /* Peek into how many bytes are available for read with ioctl() */
  ret = ioctl(fd, FIONREAD, &nbytes);
  if (ret == -1)
    fprintf(stderr, "ioctl(FIONREAD) failed, errno=%d\n", errno);
  fprintf(stdout, "ioctl() found %ld bytes are available for read\n", nbytes);

  /* Read the input message */
  nbytes = read(fd, buf, BUFSZ);
  buf[nbytes] = '\0';
  fprintf(stdout, "\nJust read this from terminal:\n%s\n", buf);

  return(0);
}
```

There are many other ioctl commands available. To get the list of commands available to the ioctl() call, please do a man page on the system you use:

```
$ man ioctl
```

5-15 File and Directory Permission Mask

In a POSIX-compliant operating system, when a process creates a file or directory, the permissions of the file or directory is actually determined by the combination of the **user's file-creation mask** (usually called **umask**) and the mode parameter specified in the API function or command creating the file or directory. The end result is defined to be

```
permissions = mode & ~mask (& 0777)
```

The permission mask can be set in a user's environment by running the umask command or by calling the umask() API from within a program.

5-15-1 Permission Mask Environment Variable

Normally, umask is set as an environment variable. Most users set the umask environment variable in their login shell's startup file.

In UNIX and Linux operating systems, a user's home directory and default shell is set in the system's /etc/passwd file. When the system administrator creates a new user on a system, a new entry in the /etc/passwd file is created for the new user where the user's home directory and login shell are set. Of course, a user's login shell can be changed after the user is created. Editing the /etc/passwd file does that. But one needs to have super user privilege to do so.

Each shell program has a startup file. When a user logins, its login shell's startup file is executed and commands in that shell startup file are run. The login shell startup file resides in the user's home directory. It is where most users set their environment variables. Typically, a user's umask environment variable is set there.

It's worth noting that when a user logins, before the user's login shell startup file is executed, the system usually executes another common login startup file. Environment variables that are common to all users such as HOSTNAME and PATH (most basic pathnames) are often set there. This common login startup file is /etc/profile. Hence, the system-wide login startup file is executed first before the user's local login shell startup file.

If a user does not set the umask environment variable, it gets the default value of 0022. Running the umask command without any argument from the O.S. command prompt will print your current umask setting.

Table 5-3 Name of startup files for different shells

Shell	Name of startup file
bash	.bashrc .bash_profile
csh	.cshrc
sh	.profile

There are different shells in Unix and Linux. Different users prefer different shells. The startup files of the most popular shells are listed in Table 5-3.

5-15-2 The umask() Function

As we said above, in a POSIX-compliant operating system, when a process creates a file or directory, the permissions of the file or directory is actually determined by the combination of a mask (the user's file creation mask) and the mode parameter specified in the function creating the file or directory.

When a program creates a directory or file, it can specify a parameter named mode. The permissions specified by this parameter is adjusted by the process' umask, if there is one defined.

A process can invoke the umask() function to set or change its umask value. The umask() function sets the file creation mask for the current process and returns its previous setting.

```
#include <sys/types.h>
#include <sys/stat.h>

mode_t umask(mode_t mask);
```

By default, the umask value of a process is 0022 (S_IWGRP | S_IWOTH), meaning you want to mask off the write permission for group members and others. If you specify 0644 or 0755 as the permissions when you create the file or directory, respectively, the permissions will be that value because ~mask = 0755, and (0644 & 0755) = 0644 and (0755 & 0755) = 0755.

If you change your process' umask by calling the umask() function, then the file/directory's eventual permissions will change. For instance, if you define umask=026 and still specify the mode as 0644 when you create a file, then the file's permissions will be changed to

```
umask = 026
For files, specifying mode=0644: 0644 & (~026) = 0644 & 0751 = 0640
```

Similarly, if you set your process' umask to be 026 and specify mode=0755 when you create a directory, the permissions of the directory will be:

```
umask = 026
For directories, specifying mode=0755: 0755 & (~026) = 0755 & 0751 = 0751
```

Below are what the file and directory's permissions look like in this case:

```
-rw-r----- 1 jim  devgrp     0 Jul 27 09:57 umask_file
drwxr-x--x 2 jim  devgrp  4096 Jul 27 09:58 umask_dir
```

The umask() call is always successful. It returns the previous umask value.

Figure 5-21 is an example program using the umask() function.

Figure 5-21 Setting/changing a process' umask value (umask.c)

```c
/*
 *  The  parameter mode to umask() specifies the permissions to use.
 *  It is modified by the process' umask in the usual way: the permissions
 *  of the created directory or file are (mode & ~umask & 0777).
 * Copyright (c) 2013, 2014, 2020 Mr. Jin-Jwei Chen. All rights reserved.
 */

#include <stdio.h>
#include <errno.h>
#include <sys/types.h>
#include <sys/stat.h>
#include <fcntl.h>
#include <unistd.h>

#define  UMASK_FILE  "./umask_file"
#define  UMASK_DIR   "./umask_dir"

int main(int argc, char *argv[])
{
  int    ret;
  int    fd;
  mode_t  newmask = 026;
  mode_t  oldmask;
  mode_t  mode1=0644, mode2=0755;

  /* Set new mask */
  oldmask = umask(newmask);
  fprintf(stdout, "old mask=%o new mask=%o\n", oldmask, newmask);

  /* Create a new file */
  fd = open(UMASK_FILE, O_CREAT|O_WRONLY, mode1);
  if (fd == -1)
  {
    fprintf(stderr, "open() failed, errno=%d\n", errno);
    return(-1);
  }
  close(fd);

  /* Create a new directory */
  ret = mkdir(UMASK_DIR, mode2);
  if (ret == -1)
  {
    fprintf(stderr, "mkdir() failed, errno=%d\n", errno);
    return(-2);
  }

  return(0);
}
```

Note that when a process changes its file creation mask, it does not affect its parent's setting at all. In other words, when your program changes its file creation permission mask, its parent (usually this is your shell) is not affected at all because your program is run as a child process of the shell. However, a parent's setting is automatically inherited by its children. Hence, the impact is in one direction (top-down) but not the other (bottom-up).

Normally users do not need to deal with umask. Just take the default or set it in the login shell startup file as below:

    umask 022

That's it. Any time when you notice the permissions of files or directories you or your programs create are wrong, check the umask setting first.

5-16 Set-User-ID, Set-Group-ID and Sticky Bits

Each file has a user owner and a group owner. Normally, when a file is an executable file and a user or program executes the file, the effective user ID of the running process is the ID of the user executing the file, which is usually the real user ID. And the effective group ID of the process is the real group ID of the user.

However, POSIX systems have a feature that if a file has its set-user-ID (SUID for short) bit set, then when a user executes the file, the process' effective ID will **become the owner of the file**, rather than the real user ID.

This is very important because if an executable file is owned by the root user and it also has its SUID bit set, then any user executing this file will assume effective user ID of the root user. That is, the process will have super user privilege. This offers a way to get around the privilege issue in many occasions where a non-root user can temporarily get elevated to have super user privilege and do something requiring root user privilege without actually switching to the root user when it runs certain programs or executable files. It lets ordinary users do something that normally only the root user can do without actually becoming the root user.

A word of warning is that the SUID bit is a double-edged sword. Using it right, it is very handy and solves your problem in a snap. On the other hand, you want to always make sure it does not become a security hole. Therefore, make sure it does not do anything that could damage or endanger the system. And make sure only the super user has the permission to change the file's contents.

The SUID bit is displayed as the 's' character instead of 'x' in the output of the "ls -l" command. For example, the executable file below has its SUID bit set:

    -rwsr-xr-x 1 root   sys   7453 Sep 8 17:22 access

The set-group-ID (SGID, for short) bit does the same for the group owner. If an executable file has its SGID bit set, then when that file is executed the process' effective group ID will be the group owner of the file, not the real group ID of the user.

The SUID and SGID bits of a file are stored in the st_mode word of the file. After calling stat() to get the file's information, a program can test these two bits against the constants S_ISUID and S_ISGID.

Sticky bit

The sticky bit was created for improving performance in the old days.
This bit is not in the POSIX Standard.

As you know by now, the text portion of an executable program must be loaded
from disk into computer physical memory in order for the program to be
executed. After the program terminates, that memory image is discarded.
If the same program is executed again, the same load process will repeat.
The program text loading takes a bit of time.

If the sticky bit of an executable program file is set, then after the first
time it is loaded into memory, its text is saved in the swap area so that
it can be loaded faster the next time the program is executed.
Many common applications such as the compilers and the text editor programs
are executed very often. Setting the sticky bit on these program files
will help improve the performance.

Note that only the superuser can set the sticky bit of a regular file.

5-17 The access() and faccessat() Functions

The access() function allows a process to check if a file system entry exists
and/or if it is accessible by the real UID or GID, rather than effective UID
or GID, of the current process.

```
#include <unistd.h>

int access(const char *pathname, int mode);
int faccessat(int fd, const char *pathname, int amode, int flag);
```

As shown above, the access() function takes two arguments. The first
argument, pathname, specifies the file system entry being checked
or tested. The second argument mode is a combination of R_OK, W_OK, X_OK
and F_OK where each means whether the file system entry is readable,
writable, executable by the current user, or if the entry exists,
respectively.

In other words, access() lets you test if a file exists or if the current
real user has permission to read, write or execute a given file or directory.

The access() function returns 0 if all requested permissions are granted.
It returns -1 if any permission is denied or an error has occurred.
In case of failure, errno is set to indicate the error.

Note that if the file system entry does not exist then the access() function
returns -1 and error is set to ENOENT (2). If the entry exists but the
permission being checked is not granted, the function returns -1 and errno
is set to EACCESS (13) meaning 'Permission denied'.

The faccessat() function is equivalent to the access() function, except in
the case where pathname specifies a relative path. In this case the location
of the file is relative to the directory associated with the file descriptor
fd instead of the current working directory.

If the special value AT_FDCWD is passed in the fd parameter, the current working directory will be used and the behavior is identical to a call to the access() function.

Values for flag parameter are constructed by a bitwise-inclusive OR of the following flags:

AT_EACCESS
The checks for accessibility are performed using the effective user and group IDs instead of the real user and group ID as required in the access() function.

The access() function exists from the very first edition of POSIX standard. The faccessat() function was added later to a newer edition to enable the checking of the accessibility of files in directories other than the current working directory.

One of the applications of the access() function is used in set-user-ID or set-group-ID programs. Sometimes, even when a program is set-user-ID to root user, it still wants to find out who the real UID or GID is and if it is permitted to operate on the file system entry.

Figure 5-22a shows a program illustrating the use of the access() function. It tests if the file or directory, whose name is given as an input argument to the program, exists and if it is readable and writable by the current real user. If it does not exist or is not readable and writable by the current real user, it returns an error. If the file system entry does not exist, the error returned is ENOENT (does not exist). If the real user of the process has no read and write permissions on the entry, the returned error is EACCES (permission denied).

Figure 5-22a Checking if a file exists and is readable and writable using the access() function (access.c)

```
/*
 * Test if a file system entry (a directory or file) exists and whether
 * the current user has Read and Write permission to it.
 * Copyright (c) 2013, 2014, 2019 Mr. Jin-Jwei Chen. All rights reserved.
 */

#include <stdio.h>
#include <errno.h>
#include <unistd.h>

#define   PATHNAME   "./sav1"

int main(int argc, char *argv[])
{
  int   ret;
  char  *pathname = NULL;

  /* Get the name of the file system entry supplied by the user */
  if (argc <= 1)
  {
    fprintf(stderr, "Usage: %s file_or_directory_name\n", argv[0]);
```

```
    return(-1);
}
pathname = argv[1];

/* Test if the file system entry exists and is Readable and Writeable */
ret = access(pathname, F_OK|R_OK|W_OK);
if (ret == -1)
{
    fprintf(stderr, "access() failed, errno=%d\n", errno);
    return(-2);
}

fprintf(stdout, "The entry %s exists and R/W permissions granted for this"
    " user.\n", pathname);

return(0);
}
```

Figure 5-22b shows that it is the real UID, not effective UID, that is used by the access() function. The program named access is owned by the root user and it has SUID bit set so it effectively runs as the root user. But since the real user is jchen, so the access program succeeds on the file testfile1 but fails on the file testfile2, because the first test file is owned by user jchen but the second test file is not.

Figure 5-22b Sample output of running the access example program

```
$ id
uid=1000(jchen) gid=500(oinstall) groups=500(oinstall),501(dba),507(asmdba)
$ ls -ls access testfile?
8 -rwsr-xr-x 1 root    sys 7453 Sep  8 17:22 access
0 -rw-r--r-- 1 jchen  sys    0 Sep  8 19:01 testfile1
0 -rw-r--r-- 1 jchen1 sys    0 Sep  8 19:03 testfile2
$ ./access testfile1
The entry testfile1 exists and R/W permissions granted for this user.
$ ./access testfile2
access() failed, errno=13
```

5-18 Change Access and Modification Times

5-18-1 The utime() function

The utime() function changes the access and modification times of a file.

```
#include <utime.h>

int utime(const char *path, const struct utimbuf *times);
```

The utime() function sets the access and modification times of the file named by the path argument. If the second argument times is not NULL, the access and modification times of the file are set to the time contained in the structure pointed at by that pointer.
If the argument times is NULL, the access and modification times of the file are set to the current time.

Upon successful completion, utime() returns 0. Otherwise, it returns -1 and errno is set to indicate the error, and the file's times should not be affected.

The <utime.h> header declares the utimbuf structure, which includes the following members:

```
time_t     actime    -- Access time.
time_t     modtime   -- Modification time.
```

The times are measured in seconds since the Epoch.

Figure 5-23 shows a program that changes the access and modification times of a file by setting them backward by one minute. It calls the stat() function to get the times of the file first. Then it subtracts 60 seconds from the access and modification times and invokes the utime() function to set the file's access and modification times to the new time values. As you can see, the times go back by one minute.

Figure 5-23 Change access and modification times of a file (utime.c)

```
/*
 * Change access and modification times of a file (setting it backward).
 * Copyright (c) 2019, 2020 Mr. Jin-Jwei Chen. All rights reserved.
 */

#include <stdio.h>
#include <errno.h>
#include <sys/types.h>
#include <sys/stat.h>
#include <unistd.h>        /* stat(), fstat() */
#include <string.h>        /* memset() */
#include <sys/stat.h>
#include <fcntl.h>         /* open() */
#include <time.h>          /* localtime() */
#include <langinfo.h>      /* nl_langinfo(), D_T_FMT */
#include <utime.h>         /* utime() */

#define   DATE_BUFSZ    64        /* size of buffer for date string */

/*
 * Get localized date string.
 * This function converts a time from type time_t to a date string.
 * The input time is a value of type time_t representing calendar time.
 * The output is string of date and time in the following format:
 *    Fri Apr  4 13:20:12 2014
 */
int cvt_time_to_date(time_t *time, char *date, unsigned int len)
{
  size_t        nchars;
  struct tm     *tm;

  if (time == NULL || date == NULL || len <= 0)
    return(-4);
```

```c
    /* Convert the calendar time to a localized broken-down time */
    tm = localtime(time);

    /* Format the broken-down time tm */
    memset(date, 0, len);
    nchars = strftime(date, len, nl_langinfo(D_T_FMT), tm);
    if (nchars == 0)
        return(-5);
    else
        return(0);
}

int main(int argc, char *argv[])
{
    int     ret;
    char    *fname;         /* file name */
    struct  stat   finfo;   /* file information */
    char    date[DATE_BUFSZ];
    struct utimbuf newtime;         /* new access & modification times */

    /* Get the file name from the user */

    if (argc > 1)
        fname = argv[1];
    else
    {
        fprintf(stderr, "Usage: %s filename\n", argv[0]);
        return(-1);
    }

    /* Obtain information about the file using stat() */
    ret = stat(fname, &finfo);
    if (ret != 0)
    {
        fprintf(stderr, "stat() failed, errno=%d\n", errno);
        return(-2);
    }
    fprintf(stdout, "time of last access = %ld\n", finfo.st_atime);
    ret = cvt_time_to_date(&finfo.st_atime, date, DATE_BUFSZ);
    fprintf(stdout, "time of last access = %s\n", date);
    fprintf(stdout, "time of last modification = %ld\n", finfo.st_mtime);
    ret = cvt_time_to_date(&finfo.st_mtime, date, DATE_BUFSZ);
    fprintf(stdout, "time of last modification = %s\n", date);

    /* Set the file's access & modification times backward by one minute */
    newtime.actime = finfo.st_atime -60;
    newtime.modtime = finfo.st_mtime - 60;
    ret = utime(fname, &newtime);
    if (ret < 0)
    {
        fprintf(stderr, "utime() failed, errno=%d\n", errno);
        return(-3);
    }
    fprintf(stdout, "Setting new access and modification times was successful.\n");

    /* Obtain and print the new times of the file */
```

```
ret = stat(fname, &finfo);
if (ret != 0)
{
    fprintf(stderr, "stat() failed, errno=%d\n", errno);
    return(-4);
}
fprintf(stdout, "time of last access = %ld\n", finfo.st_atime);
ret = cvt_time_to_date(&finfo.st_atime, date, DATE_BUFSZ);
fprintf(stdout, "time of last access = %s\n", date);
fprintf(stdout, "time of last modification = %ld\n", finfo.st_mtime);
ret = cvt_time_to_date(&finfo.st_mtime, date, DATE_BUFSZ);
fprintf(stdout, "time of last modification = %s\n", date);

return(0);
}
```

Further Readings

For further details of POSIX system interfaces, please refer to the
document at http://pubs.opengroup.org/onlinepubs/9699919799/

Questions

1. What is a link? What is a symbolic link? What are their differences?

2. List the ways a C program can check if a file exists or not.
   Do you list at least three?

3. How many ways can you remove a directory from within a C program?

Exercises

1. Write a program trying to delete a file system entry using the unlinkat()
   function. Run it to try to remove a file, symlink, hard link and
   directory.

2. Write a program to create a symbolic link using the symlinkat()
   function.

3. Write a program that tests if a file or directory exists using open().
   Return 1 if it does and 0 if it doesn't. Return -1 if error occurs.

4. Write a program to print out the information of a symbolic link
   using the lstat() function.

5. Change the example program chmod.c into using fchmod() function.

6. Modify the program chown.c so that it can change the group ownership
   of a file system entry using the fchown() function.

7. Modify the program fcntl.c so that the two program instances lock and
   update two different blocks of the file such that there is no overlap
   in the file regions they lock. Does the first process block the second

process anymore?

8. Modify the example program ioctl.c to use the fcntl() function to turn on the nonblocking I/O instead.

9. Look up the man page of ioctl() on your system. Pick an ioctl command and write a program using that command to do some I/O control operation.

References

- The Open Group Base Specifications Issue 7, 2018 edition
  IEEE Std 1003.1™-2017 (Revision of IEEE Std 1003.1-2008)
  Copyright © 2001-2018 IEEE and The Open Group
  http://pubs.opengroup.org/onlinepubs/9699919799/

- AT&T UNIX System V Release 4 Programmer's Guide: System Services
  Prentice-Hall, Inc.

- Advanced Programming in the UNIX Environment by W. Richard Stevens,
  Addison Wesley publishing Company

- The Design of The UNIX Operating System, by Maurice J. Bach, Prentice-Hall

6 Signals

POSIX-compliant operating systems, including Unix and Linux, define a set of signals as a way to communicate certain synchronous hardware and software conditions as well as asynchronous events that can occur during the execution of a program.

Signals have existed for a long time. In Unix operating system, signals have existed in AT&T Unix since 1984. However, since the early implementation is not very reliable, the POSIX.1 standard adopted a signal mechanism that is very close to that of 4.2BSD and 4.3BSD.

This chapter introduces POSIX signals to the readers.

6-1 Introduction to Signals

6-1-1 Different Types of Signals

Signals represent events. There are essentially three types of signals based on where and how they originate.

Some signals are generated internally and **synchronous** to the execution of a process. That is, these signals are raised internally from within a process as a result of executing some program instructions that result in erroneous conditions detected and raised by the hardware or operating system. Namely, these signals are a result of programming errors and program bugs. This type of signals is sometimes referred to as synchronous signals.

Internally generated, program bug signals include, but are not limited to, the following:

- Illegal instructions where the processor executes an instruction with , for example, an illegal opcode or operand in it.

- Erroneous arithmetic operations performed by a program such as arithmetic overflow or divide by zero.

- Segmentation faults where a program uses a bad pointer and attempts to access an invalid memory address.

The second type of signals originate from outside a process and are **asynchronous** to the execution of the current process. These signals are essentially generated and sent by some other processes in an attempt to notify the current process of some external events. External processes invoke some special software function to generate (i.e. manufacture) and send a signal.

Here are some examples of asynchronous event signals:

- A user running a program interactively decides to hit the Crtl-C key to quit the execution of the program.

- A user running a job in the background decides to stop the process.

- A system administrator found a runaway process on the system and tries to terminate that process by sending it a KILL signal.

Lastly, a process can invoke a signal generating function and send itself a signal as well. The signal is deliberately manufactured by the process and it is sent to the process itself.

In summary, some of the signals are erroneous conditions detected by the hardware as a result of executing certain buggy instructions in the program while other signals are generated as a result of invoking certain signal-generating software functions by other processes or by the process itself. Signals generated and sent by other processes are asynchronous to the execution of the recipient process.

Most signals a process gets and handles are asynchronous signals.

6-1-2 What Are the Signals

The POSIX.1 standard requires a number of signals to be always supported. All of the required signals must be supported in order for the operating system to be POSIX-compliant. In addition to the required signals, an operating system is allowed to define additional signals.

The signals that are supported in a system are defined in the header file signal.h. All programs dealing with signals must include this header file like the following:

```
#include <signal.h>
```

Each signal is identified by a unique number. However, a symbolic name is defined for each signal to be used inside a program to improve readability. In other words, each signal has a unique name and a unique number. The name is meant to be used from within a program and the number is to be used from a command. Note, though, while the POSIX standard requires the POSIX signals to have unique numbers, it also allows implementation-defined signals to have non-unique overlapping signal numbers.

Table 6-1 lists the signals required by the POSIX standard. We will briefly explain what each of them is all about.

Table 6-1 Signals required by the POSIX standard

Signal   Description

```
SIGABRT      Abnormal termination signal (generated by abort())
SIGALRM      Timeout signal (generated by alarm())
SIGFPE       Error in arithmetic operations (e.g. overflow, divide by zero)
             FPE stands for Floating Point Exceptions. But this signal
             represents error conditions from integer operations as well.
SIGHUP       Hangup signal
SIGILL       Illegal instruction
SIGINT       Interrupt signal from interaction
SIGKILL      Termination signal. This signal cannot be caught or ignored.
SIGPIPE      Writing to a pipe with no readers
SIGQUIT      Quit signal from a controlling terminal
SIGSEGV      Access violation. Attempt to access an invalid memory address.
SIGTERM      Termination signal (the default signal sent by the kill command)
SIGUSR1      Reserved as an application-defined signal
SIGUSR2      Reserved as an application-defined signal
-------------------------------------------------------------------------
```

Each of the POSIX required signals is described below.

SIGABRT

   This is the 'abort the process' signal.
   The SIGABRT signal is a signal to cause an abnormal termination of a
   process. Within a C program, you can abnormally terminate a process
   programmatically by calling the abort() function. The abort() function
   call sends a SIGABRT signal to the process itself. In addition, a SIGABRT
   signal can come from another process, too.

   Note that if the process has set up to ignore or block the SIGABRT signal,
   the abort() function still overrides it. Even if the process sets it up to
   catch the SIGABRT signal, the process will still be terminated after the
   signal handler function returns.

SIGALRM

   This is the alarm signal generated as the result of an invocation of the
   alarm() function. By invoking the alarm() function, a process schedules
   a SIGALRM signal to be delivered to the process after the number of seconds
   specified in the alarm() function call elapses. Therefore, it is indeed
   a timeout signal.

SIGFPE

   FPE stands for Floating Point Exception. In fact, the SIGFPE signal is
   used to represent an error condition resulted from both integer
   and floating-point arithmetic operations. Conditions such as overflow,
   divide by zero, and others.

SIGHUP

   The SIGHUP signal is sent to a process when its controlling terminal goes
   away. HUP stands for HANGUP. In the old days, communication devices such
   as a modem communicate with a computer via a serial line. When a serial
   line drops, a SIGHUP signal is generated.

SIGILL

ILL stands for illegal. When the hardware executes an illegal instruction, say, an instruction with an illegal opcode or operand, it generates the SIGILL signal.

SIGINT

INT stands for interrupt. A SIGINT signal represents the user interrupts the execution of a process. When a user runs a program interactively from a terminal, if he or she hits the Ctrl-c key combination, it will send a SIGINT signal to the process.

```
$ ./myjob
^C
$
```

SIGKILL

SIGKILL is the kill signal. It is meant to kill the recipient process. Note that **the SIGKILL signal cannot be ignored, caught or blocked.** As long as the sender has the permission to do so, sending a SIGKILL signal to a process always kills (i.e. terminates) the receiving process.

SIGPIPE

The SIGPIPE signal is sent to a process when it tries to write to a pipe but there is no process connected to the other end to receive the data.

SIGQUIT

When a user requests termination of an interactive program by pressing the Ctrl-\ key combination from the controlling terminal, a SIGQUIT signal is generated and sent to the process. For example,

```
$ ./myjob
^\
Quit
$
```

SIGQUIT is similar to SIGINT. The difference is that SIGQUIT is generated by a different keystroke, the QUIT character which is usually Ctrl-\. Besides, the SIGQUIT signal may also produce a core dump of the process.

SIGSEGV

SEGV stands for segmentation violation. It means the process attempts to access an invalid memory address. This signal is usually a result of a program bug where the program is using an uninitialized or bad pointer that has a null or garbage address value in it. That is, the pointer has an invalid memory address.

SIGTERM

TERM stands for termination. The SIGTERM signal is sent to a process to tell it to terminate. When you use the kill command to send a signal to a process, by default it sends the SIGTERM signal.

The SIGTERM signal is not as fatal as the SIGKILL signal.
A process can set it up to catch and handle the SIGTERM signal but not
the SIGKILL signal. Hence, a SIGTERM signal can lead to a more graceful
termination of the receiving process.

SIGUSR1 and SIGUSR2

USR stands for user. The SIGUSR1 and SIGUSR2 are signals reserved for
users. That is, their meanings are left up to the application using them
to define.

6-1-3 Job Control

6-1-3-1 Basics of Job Control

Before we go ahead and talk about the job control signals, there is some
background information about job control that we need to mention first.

Job control is a feature of many shells (i.e. operating system command
interpreters). It allows users to manipulate running processes by suspending
them, resuming them, putting them in the background, calling them back to
the foreground, and multiplexing their access to the terminal.

For a given terminal, only one job (a process group) has access to it
and is allowed to read from and write to it at any given time.
Only the foreground process group for the terminal has access to the
terminal. Job control depends on the process groups, sessions, and signals.
It is limited to processes within the same session and to the terminal
associated with the session.

When a user uses a computer running a POSIX-compliant operating system
such as Unix or Linux, he or she typically uses a terminal to login to the
system. When a user logins, a login shell is spawned. A shell is a
operating system command interpreter. It allows users to enter operating
system commands or the names of some programs and execute them.

When a user enters a command or program name, the shell spawns a child
process (via invoking the fork() system call) and then invokes one of the
exec() functions to execute the command or program specified.

A user usually runs a command or program interactively, which ties up the
terminal and the login shell. The user won't get the command prompt back
until the command or program terminates. This means the user can run only
one command or program at a time on one terminal. If the command or program
takes a long time to finish or the user likes to run a number of tasks
in parallel, he/she would add a & character at end of the command such that
the command or program is run in background. A command or program running
in background is called a **'job'**. Running a command in background gives the
command prompt back to the user immediately so that he/she can do other
things at the same time when a job is running in the background.

Once you have jobs running in background, you can use the shell built-in
command fg to call it back to the foreground.

A task running in the foreground can be suspended by the keystroke Ctrl-z.
The example below runs a program named mytask in the foreground first.
The user then types the Ctrl-z. That suspends the process and returns the
command prompt back to the user.

```
$ ./mytask
^z
Suspended
$ ps -ef|grep mytask
jinjche    362 17730  0 14:14 pts/9     00:00:00 ./mytask
```

Note that some operating system prints the word 'Stopped' instead of
'Suspended'.

The Ctrl-z keystroke sends a SIGTSTP signal to the process (or the process
group) and returns control to the shell.

After you stop a job, you can either resume it in the foreground by
typing in the shell built-in command fg or resume it in the background by
entering the shell built-in command bg. In either case, the shell sends
a SIGCONT signal to the process.

```
$ ./mytask
^z
Suspended
$ bg
[1]     ./mytask &
$ ps -ef|grep mytask
jinjche    593 17730  0 14:20 pts/9     00:00:00 ./mytask
```

```
$ ./mytask
^z
Suspended
$ fg
./mytask
```

(The job is running in the foreground now.)

When a job is stopped or suspended, it will remain in that state until
it receives a SIGCONT (continue) signal.

6-1-3-2 Job Control Signals

The POSIX standard defines six signals for job control: SIGTSTP, SIGSTOP,
SIGTTIN, SIGTTOU, SIGCONT and SIGCHLD. Table 6-2 lists the job control
signals.

Table 6-2 Job control signals defined in the POSIX standard

Signal	Description
SIGTSTP	Interactive Stop signal. User enters Ctrl-z from the terminal.

SIGSTOP	Non-interactive Stop signal. Sent via kill() function or kill command.
SIGTTIN	A background process attempts to read from terminal.
SIGTTOU	A background process attempts to write to terminal.
SIGCONT	Continue execution.
SIGCHLD	A child process has terminated or stopped.

The meanings of these job control signals are described below.

SIGTSTP

TSTP stands for terminal (or tty) stop.

While you are running a program from a terminal interactively, if you type the Ctrl-z key combination, it will send a SIGTSTP signal to that process to try to stop it. The command prompt will return and a line of message similar to the following will be printed on the terminal screen:

```
$ ./myjob
^Z
[1]+  Stopped                 ./myjob
```

Some operating system prints the word 'Suspended' instead of 'Stopped'.

The SIGTSTP signal is an interactive stop signal. A SIGTSTP signal can be ignored or caught.

SIGSTOP

Unlike SIGTSTP, a SIGSTOP signal cannot be generated interactively via a key stroke. The SIGSTOP signal can be sent only via the kill() function or the kill command.

A SIGSTOP signal cannot be ignored, caught, or blocked.
Therefore, a SIGSTOP signal always stops the recipient process.

When a process is stopped, the value of its STAT column in the output of the process listing command ('ps' in Unix and Linux) is 'T'.

SIGTTIN

The SIGTTIN signal means terminal (tty) input signal.
A process running as a background job cannot read from the terminal.
If it attempts to do so, it will be sent a SIGTTIN signal.

The default action for getting the SIGTTIN signal is to stop the process.

SIGTTOU

The SIGTTOU signal means terminal (tty) output signal.
When a process running as a background job attempts to write to the

terminal, it will get SIGTTOU signal. To be able to write to a controlling terminal, a process must be in the foreground process group for the terminal.

When a background process attempts an ioctl() call that would change the state of the terminal, it is sent a SIGTTOU signal as well.

The default action for getting the SIGTTOU signal is to stop the process.

As described above, there are four stop signals defined in the POSIX standard for job control: SIGSTOP, SIGTSTP, SIGTTIN and SIGTTOU. They are all terminal-related except SIGSTOP. A SIGSTOP signal can only be sent via the kill() function or kill command.

The default action for the stop signals is to stop a process. If a process is already stopped and a stop signal is delivered, it will have no effect. If a process that is already stopped blocks the stop signal, then the stop signal will never get delivered because it needs to receive a SIGCONT signal in order to continue and the SIGCONT discards all pending stopped signals.

SIGCONT

There are four different signals to stop a process as described above. However, there is only one signal to continue a stopped process. It is the SIGCONT.

When a process receives a SIGCONT signal, if it is currently stopped, then it will continue, even if the SIGCONT signal is blocked or ignored. Otherwise (if the process is not stopped), the signal will be ignored. But if the process has set up to catch the SIGCONT signal, then the signal handler function won't be called until the signal is unblocked.

When any stop signal is generated for a process, any pending SIGCONT signal for that process will be discarded. Similarly, when a SIGCONT signal is generated for a process all pending stop signals for that process will be discarded.

SIGCHLD

Whenever a child process terminates or stops, a SIGCHLD (17) signal is sent to its parent process.

The default action for the SIGCHLD signal is to ignore the signal.

The signal SIGCHLD is provided for a job control shell (the parent) to detect a child process running a job has terminated or stopped. The behavior of the POSIX SIGCHLD signal is close to that of the same signal in 4.2BSD. Traditional AT&T System V Unix has a similar signal named SIGCLD. But its behavior is less conformant to the POSIX semantics. Therefore, you should use the SIGCHLD signal instead.

The POSIX standard requires that **the default action for the SIGCHLD signal be to ignore the signal.** Thus, to avoid a SIGCHLD signal, an application should set the action associated with the signal to SIG_DFL.

A process should not try to change the action of the SIGCHLD signal when it has outstanding children.

The SIGCLD signal is similar to the SIGCHLD signal but it has different semantics. Since it has semantics outside the POSIX standard and is less portable, you should avoid using it.

Figure 6-1 is a program that prints all of the signals required by the POSIX standard and the numbers of these signals. In addition, it also displays the numbers for a handful of signals not required by the POSIX standard.

Figure 6-1 Signals required by the POSIX standard (sig_numbers.c)

```c
/*
 * Signal numbers of required signals.
 * Copyright (c) 2014, 2020 Mr. Jin-Jwei Chen.  All rights reserved.
 */

#include <stdio.h>
#include <signal.h>

/*
 * The main program.
 */
int main(int argc, char *argv[])
{
  printf("Signals required by the POSIX.1 and ISO/IEC 9945 Standards:\n");
  printf("SIGABRT =       %u\n", SIGABRT);
  printf("SIGALRM =       %u\n", SIGALRM);
  printf("SIGFPE  =       %u\n", SIGFPE);
  printf("SIGHUP  =       %u\n", SIGHUP);
  printf("SIGILL  =       %u\n", SIGILL);
  printf("SIGINT  =       %u\n", SIGINT);
  printf("SIGKILL =       %u\n", SIGKILL);
  printf("SIGPIPE =       %u\n", SIGPIPE);
  printf("SIGQUIT =       %u\n", SIGQUIT);
  printf("SIGSEGV =       %u\n", SIGSEGV);
  printf("SIGTERM =       %u\n", SIGTERM);
  printf("SIGUSR1 =       %u\n", SIGUSR1);
  printf("SIGUSR2 =       %u\n", SIGUSR2);

  printf("\nJob control signals defined by the POSIX.1 and ISO/IEC 9945 Standards:\n");
  printf("SIGCHLD =       %u\n", SIGCHLD);
  printf("SIGCONT =       %u\n", SIGCONT);
  printf("SIGSTOP =       %u\n", SIGSTOP);
  printf("SIGTSTP =       %u\n", SIGTSTP);
  printf("SIGTTIN =       %u\n", SIGTTIN);
  printf("SIGTTOU =       %u\n", SIGTTOU);

  printf("\nSome optional signals:\n");
  printf("SIGBUS  =       %u\n", SIGBUS);
  printf("SIGIOT  =       %u\n", SIGIOT);
#ifndef __APPLE__
  printf("SIGPOLL =       %u\n", SIGPOLL);
```

```
#endif
   printf("SIGTRAP =      %u\n", SIGTRAP);
   printf("SIGSYS =       %u\n", SIGSYS);
   return(0);
}
```

Job Control Signals and Orphaned Processes

A process whose parent has terminated is an orphaned process.
Orphaned processes are no longer under the control of their job-control
parent shell. Therefore, if an orphaned process stops, it would normally
not be able to continue. To prevent such a process from lingering around
forever, an orphaned process getting terminal-related stop signals must not
be allowed to stop. This means the system must discard the stop signal.

A SIGHUP signal and a SIGCONT signal are sent to an orphaned process group
if any of its members are stopped when it becomes orphaned by termination
of its parent process, to indicate they've been disconnected from their
session. If such a process catches or ignores the SIGHUP signal, it can
continue to run after becoming orphaned, or it'll be killed by the signal.

6-1-4 How to Send Signals

How does a program or user send a signal to a process?

A program sends a signal to itself or another process by calling the kill()
function. A user sends a signal to a process by using the kill command.
Note that the name of the function and command is a bit of misleading
because the intention is not always to kill (i.e. terminate) the target
process.

For instance, the signal used to reliably kill a runaway process
is signal 9 and its symbolic name is SIGKILL.
In POSIX-compliant operating systems, the command to kill a process is
like the following:

    $ kill -9 4325

This operating system command sends signal 9 (the SIGKILL signal) to
the process whose process id is 4325. Of course, for security reason,
to be able to send a signal to a process, the user or sending process must
either be the super user or have the same effective or real user id as the
target process. (To find out the process id of a process, issue the 'ps -ef'
command.)

Be aware that sending signal 9 to a process always kills the target process
as long as the sender has the permission to do so. This signal cannot be
ignored or caught.

By default, the kill command sends a SIGTERM signal if you don't specify
one. This signal is not absolutely fatal.

We will cover how to use the kill() function to send a signal from within
a program in a later section.

6-2 Signal Actions

A signal represents a condition or an event. When a condition or event occurs, the corresponding signal is generated. A signal generated for a process may not get delivered to the process right away.
The lifetime of a signal begins with the generation of the signal and ends with its delivery to a process. During the time in-between a signal is generated and it is delivered, the signal is said to be **pending**.

When a signal is delivered to a process, the process can take one of the three possible actions on it. The action can be:

- To take the default action of the signal
- To ignore the signal
- To catch and handle the signal

Independently, a process can also block a signal from being delivered.

Note that each signal has a default action associated with it. If a process has not done anything to set its action on a signal, then the default action will be taken once a signal is delivered to the process, which is usually to abruptly terminate the process, which obviously is very undesirable.

Instead of taking the default action, a process can choose to ignore a signal. Ignoring a signal means the signal won't have an effect on the process.

Alternatively, a process can also define a signal handler function and install it to 'catch' (or handle) a signal. Each time a such signal is delivered, the corresponding signal handler function will be called, giving the process a chance to do something with it. Catching a signal gives a process an opportunity to execute some code each time the signal is delivered and to respond to it. It also prevents the default action of the signal from being taken which usually is to terminate the current process.

Note that the SIGKILL and SIGSTOP signals can never be caught.
This means sending the SIGKILL signal (signal number 9) to a process is always guaranteed to kill that process as long as the sender has permission to do so. This provides a way for system administrators to be able to kill runaway processes.

In Linux, if you try to set it up to catch the SIGKILL or SIGSTOP signal, the function call will fail with error EINVAL (22).

Be aware that the action for a signal is determined and carried out at the time of the signal delivery, not the time of the signal generation.
This means the action can still be changed even after the signal is generated.

If a signal is generated and it is not blocked, then it will be delivered as soon as possible. However, there is no specific requirement on how soon it should or could be delivered. There could be delays due to scheduling of other higher priority processes. Applications cannot measure the time interval between the generation and delivery of a signal either.

According to the POSIX standard, if a signal is pending and another occurrence of the same signal is generated, whether the signal is

delivered once or twice is up to the implementation to decide.
The POSIX standard explicitly states that the order in which multiple,
simultaneously pending signals are delivered is undefined.

Effect of Signals

When a signal is delivered to a process, the function being executed at that
time will be interrupted. If the action of the signal is to terminate the
process, then the process will be terminated and the interrupted function
will not resume execution or return. If the action of the signal is to
stop the process, the process will stop until it is continued or terminated.
A SIGCONT signal will cause the process to be continued at the point where
it was stopped.

If the action of the signal is to catch the signal, then the signal-catching
function (i.e. the signal handler function) will be invoked when the signal
is delivered. After the signal handler function returns, the interrupted
function will resume execution at where it was interrupted.

If the action of the signal is to ignore, then the signal will not affect
anything. A blocked signal will not have any effect until it is unblocked
and delivered.

6-2-1 Default Action

Tables 6-3 and 6-4 list the default actions of the required and job control
signals defined by the POSIX and ISO/IEC 9945 Standards.

As you can see, the default action for all of the required signals is all
the same -- to abnormally terminate the process.
This means by default a process will get terminated and die when it receives
one of these required signals unless the process has set to take an action
other than the default action!

This is very important. Because of this, being a programmer, when you
develop an application, it's your responsibility to properly set it up
such that your application can survive various signals, stand on its
feet and continue to operate.

Table 6-3 Default action for POSIX required signals

Signal	Default Action
SIGABRT	To terminate the process abnormally.
SIGALRM	To terminate the process abnormally.
SIGFPE	To terminate the process abnormally.
SIGHUP	To terminate the process abnormally.
SIGILL	To terminate the process abnormally.
SIGINT	To terminate the process abnormally.
SIGKILL	To terminate the process abnormally.
SIGPIPE	To terminate the process abnormally.
SIGQUIT	To terminate the process abnormally.
SIGSEGV	To terminate the process abnormally.
SIGTERM	To terminate the process abnormally.
SIGUSR1	To terminate the process abnormally.

```
SIGUSR2    To terminate the process abnormally.
```

```
   Table 6-4 Default action for POSIX job control signals
```

```
   Signal          Default Action
```

```
   SIGSTOP    To stop the process.
   SIGTSTP    To stop the process.
   SIGTTIN    To stop the process.
   SIGTTOU    To stop the process.
   SIGCONT    To continue the process if it is currently stopped.
              To ignore the signal otherwise.
   SIGCHLD    To ignore the signal.
```

For the job control signals, if the default action of getting a signal is
to stop the process, then the execution of that process is suspended.
When a process is stopped, any additional signals except SIGKILL sent to
the process should not be delivered until the process is continued.

Unless the parent process has set the SA_NOCLDSTOP flag in the sa_flags
field of the sigaction structure when the sigaction() function is called,
when a process stops, a SIGCHLD signal should be generated for its parent
process. This allows a process which has no interest in knowing its
children are stopped to set this flag and avoid the overhead of setting
up a signal handler function to catch the SIGCHLD signal.

6-2-2 Ignore Action

By setting the action for a signal to SIG_IGN (ignore), the delivery of the
signal should have no effect to the process/thread.

Since the signals SIGKILL and SIGSTOP can never be ignored, setting the
action for these signals to SIG_IGN should have no effect or should not
even be allowed.

In addition, some of the signals are generated by erroneous hardware
conditions. These include SIGILL, SIGSEGV and SIGFPE. The POSIX standard says
the behavior of setting the action for these signals to SIG_IGN is undefined.
However, in most implementations the system wouldn't let a program ignore
them. For instance, even if you set the action for the SIGFPE signal to be
SIG_IGN, doing a divide-by-zero arithmetic operation still causes the
program to be terminated.

Also, whether the signal is blocked or not, setting the action to SIG_IGN
for a pending signal should cause the signal to be discarded.
For the sake of consistency, the POSIX standard also requires the same
behavior if the default action of a signal is to ignore and the action
is set to SIG_DFL.

Note that ignoring a signal is not the same as catching the signal (to be
discussed in the next section) and then does nothing.

6-2-3 Catching a Signal

The most proactive way for a process to deal with a signal is perhaps to 'catch' the signal and do something about it.

Catching a signal means the process specifically defines a function that is to be called when the signal is delivered and also explicitly sets it up such that the function becomes the signal handler or signal-catching function of that particular signal. A signal handler function implements the process' intended response to a specific signal.

Setting up a signal handler has two purposes. One is to prevent the process from taking the default action of receiving a signal which is typically terminating the entire process. The other is to do something about it.

The format of a **signal handler** function as defined by POSIX is as follows:

```
void func_name(int sig);
```

You pick the function name. The function has an input argument which is the signal being delivered to the current process by the operating system. It has no return value.

If a process sets up a signal handler for a signal, then when the signal is delivered to the process, the corresponding signal handler function will be executed. After finishing the processing and response to a signal, a signal handler function has two choices at end.

A signal handler function can simply return such that the process can resume execution at where it was interrupted or it can invoke the exit() or _exit() function to terminate the process. It can pass a special value as the argument to the exit()/_exit() function to let the parent process know why and where the process has terminated. Or it can return a value of 0 if it wants the parent to think it is a success.

As we mentioned before, the SIGKILL and SIGSTOP signals cannot be caught.

6-2-4 Calling Functions from a Signal Handler Function

A process responds to a signal by doing whatever processing necessary in the corresponding signal handler function. Typically, a signal handler function does minimum processing, just as much as what is necessary. This is because there are very few functions that can be safely called from a signal handler function.

Be aware that **not every function is callable from within a signal handler function** due to the asynchronous nature. Therefore, to ensure correct behavior all the time, you need to make sure your signal handler function calls only functions that are safe with respect to signals. The functions invoked from within a signal handler function must be reentrant with respect to signals. This is because a process could be in the middle of executing one of these functions when a signal is delivered and the signal handler function is executed. In this case, the first execution of the function is interrupted and the signal handler function may initiate another call into the same function, making it a requirement for the function to be reentrant.

Note that a function is reentrant with respect to signals only means this function can be invoked from within a signal handler function. However, it does not mean invoking this function is recommended. Even though a function is reentrant as far as signal is concerned, there are other issues software developers must worry about. Examples include accessing shared data structures, open files, locks, and accessing global variables. For instance, some of the safe functions may change the global variable errno. Therefore, the signal handler function may need to save and restore it.

Calling the longjmp() and siglongjmp() functions from within a signal handler function (note that these two functions are not in the list of safe functions) is potentially dangerous too because the code executed after these functions can also invoke unsafe functions as well.

If your program uses some non-reentrant functions, to ensure correct results, you need to prevent them from being interrupted by blocking the appropriate signals.

Please remember that **you always need to be extremely careful in calling any function from within a signal handler function.**

Table 6-5 lists some functions that are reentrant with respect to signals.

Table 6-5 Reentrant functions safe from inside a signal handler
```
-------------------------------------------------------------------
_exit() access() alarm(), cfgetispeed(), cfgetospeed(), cfgsetispeed(),
cfgsetospeed(), chdir(), chmod(), chown(), close(), create(), dup2(),
dup(), execle(), execve(), fcntl(), fork(), fstat(), getegid(), geteuid(),
getgid(), getgroups(), getpgrp(), getpid(), getppid(), getuid(),
kill(), link(), lseek(), mkdir(), mkfifo(), open(), pathconf(), pause(),
pipe(), read(), rename(), rmdir(), setgid(), setpgid(), setsid(),
setuid(), sigaction(), sigaddset(), sigdelset(), sigemptyset(),
sigfillset(), sigismember(), sigpending(), sigprocmask(), sigsuspend(),
sleep(), stat(), sysconf(), tcdrain(), tcflow(), tcflush(), tcgetattr(),
tcgetpgrp(), tcsendbreak(), tcsetaatr(), tcsetpgrp(), time(), times(),
umask(), uname(), unlink(), utime(), wait(), waitpid(), write()
-------------------------------------------------------------------
```

In some operating systems (including AIX), the following functions are reentrant and safe to asynchronous signals as well:

```
accept()   readv()   recv()   recvfrom()   recvmsg()
select()   send()   sendmsg()   sendto()
```

For a complete list of functions that are safe for signals, please refer to the documentation of the operating system you are using.

6-2-5 Set a Signal Action Using sigaction()

So far you have learned that taking the default action of a signal is not really a good idea because it typically terminates the process.

In this section we will talk about how to set up an action for a signal.

There are two ways for a program to establish or change its disposition of a signal.

The traditional way of setting an action for a signal is to invoke the signal() function:

```
sighandler_t signal(int signum, sighandler_t handler);
```

However, historical implementations of the signal() function defined by the C Standard has an unreliable feature that the signal action is reset to SIG_DFL before the user-defined signal handler function is entered. Ideally, signals should be blocked during the execution of a signal handler function rather than simply resetting their action to SIG_DFL. For this reason, the POSIX standard recommends using the **sigaction**() function instead:

```
int  sigaction(int  signum,  const struct sigaction *act, struct
        sigaction *oldact);
```

The sigaction() function specifies/changes and/or retrieves the action associated with a signal.

The sigaction() function takes three arguments. The first identifies the signal. The second, if not NULL, specifies the new action for the signal via the sigaction structure. The third, if not NULL, returns the signal's previous action. If the second argument is NULL and the third argument is not NULL, the function retrieves the current action associated with the signal.

If the second argument act is a null pointer, signal handling is unchanged. Hence, the call can be used to inquire about the current handling of a given signal. The SIGKILL and SIGSTOP signals should not be added to the signal mask using this mechanism; this restriction should be enforced by the system without causing an error to be returned.

Note that the POSIX standard requires calling the sigaction() function succeeds if the second argument act is NULL, even if the signal involved cannot be ignored or caught.

The sigaction structure is defined as follows:

```
struct sigaction {
    void (*sa_handler)(int);
    sigset_t sa_mask;
    int      sa_flags;
    void (*sa_sigaction)(int, siginfo_t *, void *);
}
```

The sa_handler field specifies an action for the signal. Its value can be set to SIG_IGN (to ignore the signal), SIG_DFL (to take the default action of the signal), or the address (i.e. name) of a signal handler function (to catch the signal).

When the signal is delivered, the handler function will be automatically invoked and the number of the signal will be passed into the handler function so that it knows which signal is being delivered.
This signal handler function can then execute whatever code deemed appropriate to respond to the signal. Once the signal handler function returns, the process will resume execution from where it was interrupted.

The sa_mask field specifies an additional set of signals that should be added to the process' signal mask before the signal handler function is invoked. The signal(s) it specifies will be blocked during the execution of the signal handler function.

The sa_flags field specifies a set of flags that change the behavior of the signal handling. For instances, specifying the SA_RESTART flag would make certain system calls interrupted by a signal to be automatically restarted to provide a BSD signal semantics, specifying the SA_ONSTACK flag would make the signal handler being invoked on an alternate signal stack specified by the sigaltstack() function, and specifying the SA_NOCLDSTOP flag would say do not receive notification when child processes stop if the signal is SIGCHLD.

If SA_SIGINFO is specified in the sa_flags field, then the sa_sigaction field should specify the signal handler function, rather than the sa_handler field. This parameter exists in Linux but may not exist in other signal implementations.

If the sigaction() call is successful, a value of zero is returned. Otherwise, a value of -1 is returned and errno is set to indicate the real error.

Once an action is set for a signal via the sigaction() function, that action remains in effect until it is changed again by another call to the sigaction() function or until the process invokes one of the exec() functions.

Figures 6-2, 6-3 and 6-4 are three example programs demonstrating the use of the sigaction() function. The programs set the action for the signal SIGQUIT (signal number 3) to be SIG_DFL, SIG_IGN, and catching the signal, respectively. To test the programs, start the program in one window. Then from another window run the 'ps -ef' command to find out the process id of the program and run the 'kill -3 pid' or 'kill -SIGQUIT pid ' command to send the SIGQUIT signal to the program.

As you can see, when taking the default action, getting the SIGQUIT signal kills the process right away. The signal has no effect on the process if the action is set to SIG_IGN. In catching the signal, each time a SIGQUIT signal is delivered, the corresponding signal handler function signal_handler() is automatically invoked and executed.

Figure 6-2 Set to take the default action for a signal (sig_default.c)

```
/*
 * Signal -- taking the default action for SIGQUIT signal.
 * Copyright (c) 2014, 2019-2020 Mr. Jin-Jwei Chen.  All rights reserved.
 */
```

```
#include <stdio.h>
#include <errno.h>
#include <signal.h>

/*
 * The main program.
 */
int main(int argc, char *argv[])
{
  int        ret;
  struct sigaction  oldact, newact;

  /* Set sa_mask such that all signals are to be blocked during execution
     of the signal handler. */
  sigfillset(&newact.sa_mask);
  newact.sa_flags = 0;
  /* Specify to the default action for the signal */
  newact.sa_handler = SIG_DFL;
  ret = sigaction(SIGQUIT, &newact, &oldact);
  if (ret != 0)
  {
    fprintf(stderr, "sigaction failed, errno=%d\n", errno);
    return(-1);
  }

  fprintf(stderr, "Please send me a SIGQUIT signal (kill -3 pid) ...\n");

  while (1 == 1)
  {
    /* Hang around to receive signals */
  }

}
```

```
    $ ./sig_default.lin32
    Please send me a SIGQUIT signal (kill -3 pid) ...
    Quit

    $ kill -SIGQUIT 14182
```

    Figure 6-3 Set to ignore a signal (sig_ignore.c)

```
/*
 * Signal -- ignoring the SIGQUIT signal.
 * Copyright (c) 2014, 2019-2020 Mr. Jin-Jwei Chen.  All rights reserved.
 */

#include <stdio.h>
#include <errno.h>
#include <signal.h>

/*
 * The main program.
 */
int main(int argc, char *argv[])
```

```
{
    int            ret;
    struct sigaction  oldact, newact;

    /* Set sa_mask such that all signals are to be blocked during execution
       of the signal handler. */
    sigfillset(&newact.sa_mask);
    newact.sa_flags = 0;
    /* Specify to ignore the signal as the action */
    newact.sa_handler = SIG_IGN;
    ret = sigaction(SIGQUIT, &newact, &oldact);
    if (ret != 0)
    {
        fprintf(stderr, "sigaction failed, errno=%d\n", errno);
        return(-1);
    }

    fprintf(stderr, "Please send me a SIGQUIT signal (kill -3 pid) ...\n");

    while (1 == 1)
    {
        /* Hang around to receive signals */
    }

}
```

```
$ ./sig_ignore.lin32
Please send me a SIGQUIT signal (kill -3 pid) ...

    (The process stays alive!)

$ kill -SIGQUIT 14199
$ kill -SIGQUIT 14199
$ kill -3 14199
$ kill -3 14199
$
```

As you can see, after sending the SIGQUIT (3) signals to the process
four times in a row, the process continues to stay alive and run because
it has set it up to ignore the signal.

Figure 6-4 Set to catch a signal (sig_handler.c)

```
/*
 * Signal -- to catch a signal by specifying a signal handler.
 * Copyright (c) 2013-4, 2019-2020  Mr. Jin-Jwei Chen. All rights reserved.
 */

#include <stdio.h>
#include <errno.h>
#include <signal.h>

/*
 * Signal handler.
 */
void signal_handler(int sig)
```

```
{
  fprintf(stdout, "This process received a signal %d.\n", sig);
  /* We cannot invoke pthread_exit() here. */
  return;
}


/*
 * The main program.
 */
int main(int argc, char *argv[])
{
  int        ret;
  struct sigaction  oldact, newact;

  /* Set sa_mask such that all signals are to be blocked during execution
     of the signal handler. */
  sigfillset(&newact.sa_mask);
  newact.sa_flags = 0;
  /* Specify my signal handler function */
  newact.sa_handler = signal_handler;
  ret = sigaction(SIGQUIT, &newact, &oldact);
  if (ret != 0)
  {
    fprintf(stderr, "sigaction() failed, errno=%d\n", errno);
    return(-1);
  }

  fprintf(stderr, "Please send me a SIGQUIT signal (kill -3 pid) ...\n");

  while (1 == 1)
  {
    /* Hang around to receive signals */
  }
}
```

Below is a sample output from testing the example program of catching a signal.

First window

```
$ ./sig_handler.lin64
Please send me a SIGQUIT signal (kill -3 pid) ...
Received a signal 3
Received a signal 3
Killed
```

Second window

```
$ kill -SIGQUIT 7402
$ kill -SIGQUIT 7402
$ kill -SIGKILL 7402
$
```

Note that this program catches only one signal. If it gets other signals, the program could be terminated.

Notice that once the signal handler function is installed, it remains good
and continues to work regardless of how many times it has been called.
In some of the old implementations, one needs to re-install the signal
handler function from within the handler itself each time it is called.
There is no need to do that with the POSIX signal implementation.

So, avoid using the less portable signal() function defined in the C Standard.
Instead, use the sigaction() function defined by the POSIX standard
to set the action for a signal. Also don't use both functions for the
same signal in the same program.

Note that the signal disposition is process-wide. In a multithreaded
application, all threads within a process share the same signal disposition.
That is, although each thread has its own signal mask, **the signal
disposition is shared by all threads in the process**. This means that
individual threads can block signals, but when a thread changes the
action associated with a given signal, it affects all threads.

6-2-6 Determine If an Optional Signal Is Supported

Note that the POSIX standard requires a portable way of determining
at run-time whether an optional signal is supported or not.
The method is to call the sigaction() function with NULL second (act)
and third (oldact) arguments. If the function call returns success,
then the signal is supported.

We leave it as an exercise for readers to write a program that determines
whether a particular signal (number) is supported on your system or not.

6-2-7 Summary on Signal Actions

In summary, when a signal condition occurs, the signal is added to the set
of signals pending for the process. If the signal is currently blocked from
delivery, it will be held. If that signal is not currently blocked
for the process, it will be delivered. If the process has not set up
to catch the signal or change its default action, the default action for
the signal will be taken, which usually is to terminate the current process.

If the process has set the signal's action to ignore, then the signal will
have no effect and the signal will be discarded. If the process has set up to
catch the signal, then as part of the signal delivery, the signal and those
blocked for the signal handler function will be added to the list of signals
blocked for the process. Then the current context of the process will be
saved and the signal handler function of the signal will be invoked.

If the signal handler function returns, then the original list of blocked
signals for the process will be restored and the process will resume
execution from where it was interrupted. This is in general what will happen
when a signal is raised for a process.

6-3 Sending a Signal Using kill()

How does a program send a signal to others or even itself?

It is simple. Just invoke the kill() function.

The kill() function sends a signal to a process or a group of processes.

```
int kill(pid_t pid, int sig);
```

As shown, the function takes two arguments. The first argument specifies the process id of the process that is to receive the signal. The second argument specifies the signal being sent. In POSIX, for a program to send a signal to itself, all it needs to do is to call the getpid() function to get its own process id. Therefore, the call would be like the following:

```
kill(getpid(), sig);
```

For a process to be able to send a signal to another process, the real or effective id of the sending process must match the real or effective id of the receiving process(es) or the sending process must have the super-user privilege.

If the signal being sent by the kill() function is 0, then no signal is actually sent. However, error checking is done. Therefore, **sending a process the signal 0 is often used by programmers as a way to check if a process is still alive**.

Depending on the value of the pid argument, the target process(es) receiving the signal varies.

If the value of the pid is greater than 0, then the signal is sent to the process whose pid equals that value.

If the value of the pid argument is 0, the signal is sent to all processes whose process group id equals to the process group id of the sender. This means all processes in the same process group as the sender are targeted.

If pid is -1, the behavior is undefined. (Note: Some operating systems' implementation is such that if the user is a super user then the signal is sent to all processes, and if the user is not a super user then the signal is sent to all processes whose user id matches. However, neither of these is adopted by the POSIX standard.)

If the value of the pid is negative but not -1, then the signal is sent to all processes whose process group id equals to the absolute value of the pid.

However, the POSIX standard says an implementation can place restrictions on sending the signal 0 as well as the processes that the pid can actually get to. Therefore, some of what we said above may not be honored by all implementations.

If at least one signal was sent, then the kill() function will return 0 indicating success. If the kill() function fails, it will return -1. In that case, errno will be set and no signal shall be sent.

Figure 6-5 shows a program that tests if a process is alive by sending it a signal 0 -- the so-called null signal.

Figure 6-5 Test if a process is still alive (sig_isalive.c)

```
/*
 * Signal -- test if a process is still alive using kill()
 * Copyright (c) 2014, 2020 Mr. Jin-Jwei Chen.  All rights reserved.
 */

#include <stdio.h>
#include <errno.h>
#include <sys/types.h>
#include <unistd.h>
#include <signal.h>
#include <sys/wait.h>

int main(int argc, char *argv[])
{
  pid_t  pid;
  int    stat;    /* child's exit value */
  int    ret;

  /* Create a child process */
  pid = fork();

  if (pid == -1)
  {
    fprintf(stderr, "fork() failed, errno=%d\n", errno);
    return(-1);
  }
  else if (pid == 0)
  {
    /* This is the child process. */
    fprintf(stdout, "Child: I'm a new born child.\n");
    /* Perform the child process' task here */
    sleep(2);
    return(0);
  }
  else
  {
    /* This is the parent process. */
    fprintf(stdout, "Parent: I've just spawned a child.\n");

    /* Test to see if the child is still alive. It must be. */
    ret = kill(pid, 0);
    if (ret == 0)
      fprintf(stdout, "Parent: My child is still alive.\n");
    else
      fprintf(stdout, "Parent: My child is dead.\n");

    /* Wait for the child to exit */
    pid = wait(&stat);
    if (pid > 0)
    {
      fprintf(stdout, "My child has exited.\n");

      /* Test to see if the child is still alive again. It should be dead. */
      ret = kill(pid, 0);
      if (ret == 0)
```

```
        fprintf(stdout, "Parent: My child is still alive.\n");
    else
        fprintf(stdout, "Parent: My child is dead.\n");
    }

    return(0);
}
}
```

We must point out that although the POSIX standard considers a process' lifetime includes the process being **defunct** (a process that has terminated but has not been waited for by its parent yet), the actual implementations of using the kill() function to send a signal 0 vary if the target process is in the defunct state. Some return success while others return an error such as ESRCH (meaning no such process).

Therefore, to make your application more portable, if the two processes have a parent-child relationship, the most reliable way for a parent to check if a child process is still alive is to use the waitpid() function. However, this also has a disadvantage of blocking the parent process until the child process terminates. (Be aware that a suspended waitpid() function call can be interrupted by the delivery of a signal.) Of course, if the parent-child relationship does not exist, then this won't help.

Note that signals SIGUSR1, SIGUSR2, SIGKILL, and SIGTERM normally can be generated only by explicitly invoking the kill() function or the kill command.

As we have mentioned before, to send a signal, you use the kill() function from within a program or the kill command from the operating system command prompt. The kill command sends a SIGTERM signal by default.

6-3-1 Killing Self

Ideally, when a process sends a signal to itself via the kill() function, and if that signal is not blocked, then that signal should be delivered before the kill() function returns because that way the kill() function would never return. Old implementations providing only the signal() but not the sigaction() interface could not guarantee this behavior because every time a process' execution enters the operating system kernel mode they deliver only one signal.

To support the sigaction() interface, operating systems normally need to re-enter the O.S. kernel again right after returning from a signal handler function to restore the process' signal mask. This allows the sigaction() interface to support that ideal behavior.

6-3-2 Signal Impacts on Other Functions

When a process receives a signal, that is, when a signal is delivered to a process, very often the process could be in the middle of executing some function call. If the signal is caught then the signal handler function is executed. After the signal handler function returns, the process resumes execution from where it was interrupted. At this point, many functions will return the EINTR (interrupted) error. Some function calls may be automatically restarted by some operating systems. Others don't.

Note that a very small number of functions defined in POSIX never return an error. The getuid() and getpid() functions are among them.

In addition, many POSIX functions are not signal interruptible. While a process executes one of these functions, a signal generated for the process will be delayed in its delivery. For functions that are quick to complete, this may not be an issue. However, for functions that will take quite some time to execute, they should be made interruptible by signals. Examples include I/O functions such as read() and write(), as well as those functions that can suspend the process for a long time, such as sleep(), pause(), wait() and suspend().

6-4 Signal Masks -- Blocked Signals

A signal can be purposely masked or blocked from being delivered. After a signal is generated, if that signal is masked/blocked, that signal won't be delivered until it is unmasked/unblocked. The signal is said to be in the 'pending' state after it is generated and before it is delivered.

Note that the SIGKILL and SIGSTOP signals cannot be blocked. This means they cannot be added to the process' signal mask. This holds true whether the program uses sigaction or sigprocmask (which we will introduce shortly) to alter its signal mask. Attempts to block the SIGKILL or SIGSTOP signal are usually silently ignored.

For example, in Linux, using the sigprocmask() function to add the SIGKILL and SIGSTOP signals to the process's signal mask will execute successfully but the signals are not added to the signal mask afterwards.

Each process or each thread within a process has its own independent signal mask. A signal mask contains the set of signals that are currently masked or blocked from delivery for the process or thread. Therefore, a signal mask is of the type sigset_t -- a signal set, which is actually defined to be an array of unsigned long integers.

6-4-1 Signal Set Functions

There are five operations a process/thread can perform on a signal mask.

First, a signal set can be initialized with a call to sigemptyset() or sigfillset(). The sigemptyset() initializes the signal set to be empty, with no signals included in the set. The sigfillset() function initializes a signal set to be full, with all signals currently supported included in the set. Note that the POSIX standard requires the resulting signal set from the sigemptyset() or sigfillset() operation includes all POSIX defined signals. It is recommended that the resulting signal set includes implementation-defined signals as well.

Once a signal set is initialized, specific signals can be added to or deleted from the set by using the sigaddset() or sigdelset() function, respectively.

You can test to see if a signal is included in a signal set by invoking the sigismember() function. This function returns 1 if the specified signal is in the given signal set. It returns 0 if not.

The five signal set functions are listed below:

    int sigemptyset(sigset_t *set);

    int sigfillset(sigset_t *set);

    int sigaddset(sigset_t *set, int signum);

    int sigdelset(sigset_t *set, int signum);

    int sigismember(const sigset_t *set, int signum);

The sigemptyset() function initializes the signal set pointed to by the set argument such that all signals defined in POSIX.1 standard are excluded.

The sigfillset() function initializes the signal set specified by the set argument such that all signals defined in the POSIX.1 standard are included.

The sigaddset() function adds the individual signal specified by the signum argument to the signal set specified by the set argument.

The sigdelset() function deletes the individual signal specified by signum from the signal set identified by the set argument.

Upon successful completion, these functions return 0; otherwise, they return -1 and set errno to indicate the error.

Figure 6-6 shows a program that demonstrates how to use these functions.

Figure 6-6 Signal Mask (sig_sigset.c)

```
/*
 * Signal set.
 * Copyright (c) 2014, 2019-2020 Mr. Jin-Jwei Chen.  All rights reserved.
 */

#include <stdio.h>
#include <errno.h>
#include <signal.h>

/*
 * Display sample contents of a signal set.
 */
void display_signal_set(sigset_t *sigset)
{
    int     ret;

    if (sigset == (sigset_t *)NULL)
        return;

    fprintf(stdout, "\nSampling current contents of the signal set:\n");
```

```
  ret = sigismember(sigset, SIGINT);
  if (ret == 1)
    fprintf(stdout, "  SIGINT is a member of the current signal set.\n");
  else
    fprintf(stdout, "  SIGINT is not a member of the current signal set.\n");

  ret = sigismember(sigset, SIGQUIT);
  if (ret == 1)
    fprintf(stdout, "  SIGQUIT is a member of the current signal set.\n");
  else
    fprintf(stdout, "  SIGQUIT is not a member of the current signal set.\n");

  ret = sigismember(sigset, SIGPIPE);
  if (ret == 1)
    fprintf(stdout, "  SIGPIPE is a member of the current signal set.\n");
  else
    fprintf(stdout, "  SIGPIPE is not a member of the current signal set.\n");

  ret = sigismember(sigset, SIGKILL);
  if (ret == 1)
    fprintf(stdout, "  SIGKILL is a member of the current signal set.\n");
  else
    fprintf(stdout, "  SIGKILL is not a member of the current signal set.\n");

  ret = sigismember(sigset, SIGTERM);
  if (ret == 1)
    fprintf(stdout, "  SIGTERM is a member of the current signal set.\n");
  else
    fprintf(stdout, "  SIGTERM is not a member of the current signal set.\n");
  fprintf(stdout,"\n");
}


/*
 * The main program.
 */
int main(int argc, char *argv[])
{
  sigset_t     sigset;
  int          ret;

  /* Fill a signal set */
  ret = sigfillset(&sigset);
  if (ret != 0)
  {
    fprintf(stderr, "Failed to fill the signal set, errno=%d\n", errno);
    return(-1);
  }
  fprintf(stdout, "The signal set is just being filled now.\n");
  display_signal_set(&sigset);

  /* Delete a couple of signals from the signal set */
  ret = sigdelset(&sigset, SIGINT);
  if (ret != 0)
  {
    fprintf(stderr, "Failed to delete SIGINT from the signal set, errno=%d\n",
      errno);
```

```
    return(-2);
}
fprintf(stdout, "SIGINT has been successfully deleted from the signal set.\n");

ret = sigdelset(&sigset, SIGQUIT);
if (ret != 0)
{
    fprintf(stderr, "Failed to delete SIGQUIT from the signal set, errno=%d\n",
        errno);
    return(-3);
}
fprintf(stdout, "SIGQUIT has been successfully deleted from the signal set.\n");
display_signal_set(&sigset);

/* Empty a signal set */
ret = sigemptyset(&sigset);
if (ret != 0)
{
    fprintf(stderr, "Failed to empty the signal set, errno=%d\n", errno);
    return(-4);
}
fprintf(stdout, "The signal set is empty now.\n");
display_signal_set(&sigset);

/* Add a couple of signals to the signal set */
ret = sigaddset(&sigset, SIGPIPE);
if (ret != 0)
{
    fprintf(stderr, "Failed to add SIGPIPE to the signal set, errno=%d\n", errno);
    return(-5);
}
fprintf(stdout, "SIGPIPE has been successfully added to the signal set.\n");

ret = sigaddset(&sigset, SIGTERM);
if (ret != 0)
{
    fprintf(stderr, "Failed to add SIGTERM to the signal set, errno=%d\n", errno);
    return(-6);
}
fprintf(stdout, "SIGTERM has been successfully added to the signal set.\n");
display_signal_set(&sigset);

return(0);
}
```

6-4-2 Alter Signal Mask Using the sigprocmask() Function

Remember we said that each process/thread has a signal mask which contains
the set of signals that are currently blocked for delivery.
To add or remove signals to or from an existing signal mask, use the
sigprocmask() function. In a multi-threaded process, use the pthread_sigmask()
function instead. pthread_sigmask() will be discussed in section 8-10-1.

Note that if a signal is set on the signal mask, then it is blocked.
The sigprocmask() or pthread_sigmask() function can be used to block

multiple signals or all signals except SIGKILL and SIGSTOP.

The sigprocmask() function changes and/or retrieves the signal mask of the calling process.

```
    int sigprocmask(int how, const sigset_t *set, sigset_t *oldset);
```

As shown, the function takes three arguments.

The second argument specifies a new set of signals to be acted upon. If this argument is NULL then the current signal mask will not be changed. Note that if the second argument is NULL and the third argument is not NULL, then the sigprocmask() function just returns the current signal mask without changing it.

The first argument, named how, decides how the set of signals specified in the second argument will affect the current signal mask. The effect of the sigprocmask() function totally depends on the value of the first argument -- how.

- If the value of the how argument is SIG_BLOCK, then the signals specified in the second argument are added to the set of currently blocked signals.

  Note that this is a set union operation. The resulting signal mask will be the set union of the existing signal mask and the set of signals specified in the second argument.

- If the value of the how argument is SIG_UNBLOCK, then the signals specified in the second argument are dropped from the set of currently blocked signals.

- If the value of the how argument is SIG_SETMASK, then the set of blocked signals are set to the signals specified in the second argument. That is, the value of the second argument becomes the new signal mask.

If the third argument is not NULL, then the previous value of the signal mask is returned in it. This allows a program to change its signal mask while also get back its previous setting in one function call.

The sigprocmask() returns 0 on success and -1 on error.

Figure 6-7 is a program that tries to add SIGINT and SIGQUIT to the process's signal mask first and then removes SIGINT signal from the signal mask. If you run the program, you will find that when a signal is on the signal mask, sending that signal to the process has no effect on the process. Indeed, the example program survives from both SIGINT and SIGQUIT signals. Also notice the signal set is empty at end of the program after removal.

Figure 6-7 Manipulate signal mask (sig_procmask.c)

```
/*
 * Signal -- the sigprocmask() function.
 * Copyright (c) 2014, 2019, 2020 Mr. Jin-Jwei Chen.  All rights reserved.
 */

#include <stdio.h>
```

```c
#include <errno.h>
#include <signal.h>
#include <unistd.h>

/*
 * Check to see if SIGINT and SIGQUIT are in a signal set/mask.
 */
void check_two(sigset_t sigset)
{
  int         ret;

  ret = sigismember(&sigset, SIGINT);
  if (ret == 1)
    fprintf(stdout, "  SIGINT is a member of the current signal mask.\n");
  else
    fprintf(stdout, "  SIGINT is not a member of the current signal mask.\n");

  ret = sigismember(&sigset, SIGQUIT);
  if (ret == 1)
    fprintf(stdout, "  SIGQUIT is a member of the current signal mask.\n");
  else
    fprintf(stdout, "  SIGQUIT is not a member of the current signal mask.\n");
}


/*
 * The main program.
 */
int main(int argc, char *argv[])
{
  int         ret;
  sigset_t    newset, oldset;

  /* Get the current signal mask */
  ret = sigprocmask(SIG_SETMASK, NULL, &oldset);
  if (ret != 0)
  {
    fprintf(stderr, "Failed to get the current signal mask, errno=%d\n", errno);
    return(-1);
  }
  fprintf(stdout, "This is what we started with:\n");
  check_two(oldset);

  /* Construct a signal set containing SIGINT and SIGQUIT */
  ret = sigemptyset(&newset);
  if (ret != 0)
  {
    fprintf(stderr, "Failed to empty the signal set, errno=%d\n", errno);
    return(-2);
  }
  ret = sigaddset(&newset, SIGINT);
  if (ret != 0)
  {
    fprintf(stderr, "  Failed to add SIGINT to the signal set, errno=%d\n", errno);
    return(-3);
  }
  ret = sigaddset(&newset, SIGQUIT);
```

```
  if (ret != 0)
  {
    fprintf(stderr, "  Failed to add SIGQUIT to the signal set, errno=%d\n", errno);
    return(-4);
  }

  /* Set the signal mask to the new set */
  fprintf(stdout, "Adding SIGINT and SIGQUIT to the current signal mask\n");
  ret = sigprocmask(SIG_BLOCK, &newset, &oldset);
  if (ret != 0)
  {
    fprintf(stderr, "Failed to change the current signal mask, errno=%d\n", errno);
    return(-5);
  }

  /* Retrieve the current signal mask */
  ret = sigprocmask(SIG_SETMASK, NULL, &oldset);
  if (ret != 0)
  {
    fprintf(stderr, "Failed to get the current signal mask, errno=%d\n", errno);
    return(-6);
  }
  check_two(oldset);

  /* Test getting a signal in the signal mask. Notice this does not kill. */
  fprintf(stdout, "Sending myself a SIGINT signal and see if we stay alive\n");
  kill(getpid(), SIGINT);
  fprintf(stdout, "Sending myself a SIGQUIT signal and see if we stay alive\n");
  kill(getpid(), SIGQUIT);
  fprintf(stdout, "Yes, we survived!\n");

  /* Make sure the SIGINT signal is the only thing in the newset */
  ret = sigdelset(&newset, SIGQUIT);
  if (ret != 0)
  {
    fprintf(stderr, "  Failed to drop SIGQUIT from the signal set, errno=%d\n",
errno);
    return(-7);
  }

  /* Remove the SIGINT signal from the current signal mask */
  fprintf(stdout, "Removing SIGINT from the current signal mask\n");
  ret = sigprocmask(SIG_UNBLOCK, &newset, &oldset);
  if (ret != 0)
  {
    fprintf(stderr, "Failed to change the current signal mask, errno=%d\n", errno);
    return(-8);
  }

  /* Retrieve the current signal mask */
  ret = sigprocmask(SIG_SETMASK, NULL, &oldset);
  if (ret != 0)
  {
    fprintf(stderr, "Failed to get the current signal mask, errno=%d\n", errno);
    return(-9);
  }
```

```
check_two(oldset);

return(0);
}
```

The sigprocmask() function is often used before a critical section code segment to block one or more signals and prevent them from interrupting the execution of the critical section by adding these signals to the current process' existing signal mask.

Note that if a process' signal mask is changed in a signal handler function installed by the sigaction() function, that change will be wiped out once the control returns from the signal handler function. This is because **a process's signal mask is restored each time the control returns from a signal handler function**.

The POSIX standard states that signals that cannot be ignored should not be added to a signal mask.

If a signal is blocked and its action is to ignore (either set to SIG_IGN or being so by default), then the behavior is implementation dependent. The POSIX standard does not specify a behavior. Some operating systems discard the generated signal right away while others let it remain pending.

Note that blocking a signal is not the same as ignoring it. When you block a signal, it gets added to a pending signal queue and will be delivered to the process as soon as the signal is unblocked.

Unblocking signals can be done using the following code:

```
#include <signal.h>

sigset_t  mask;
sigemptyset(&mask);
sigprocmask(SIG_SETMASK, &mask, NULL);
```

6-4-3 Ignoring Signals

As we just said above, ignoring a signal is not the same as blocking a signal, although their net effects might be the same under certain circumstances.

How does a program ignore a signal?

There are at least two ways to ignore a signal. First, you can invoke the sigaction() function on a signal and specify SIG_IGN action in the sa_handler field of the sigaction structure to tell the system to ignore a signal.

Second, you can install a signal handler to catch a signal and then choose to do nothing in that signal handler.

Can all signals be ignored? No.

Note that **SIGKILL and SIGSTOP signals cannot be ignored**.

SIGKILL always kills a process without giving it a chance of reacting. SIGSTOP always suspends a process without giving it a chance of reacting, either.

6-4-4 Behavior of Blocking SIGILL, SIGSEGV and SIGFPE Signals

The POSIX standard says that if the SIGILL, SIGSEGV, or SIGFPE signals are generated while they are blocked, the result is undefined, unless the signal was generated by a call to the kill() or raise() function. (Note: The raise() function is like the kill() function but it is defined in the ISO C Standard.)

There are two different ways that these signals get generated.

Normally, a SIGILL, SIGSEGV, SIGFPE or SIGBUS signal is generated as a result of programming errors. Thus, they are "synchronous" to the process execution and they represent serious problems in the program. Therefore, it's impossible to block these signals when they represent real problems. In general, there is no way of ignoring, catching, or blocking these signals.

However, a program can also invoke the kill() or raise() function to deliberately send these signals, too. In this case, it is reasonable for systems to allow them to be blocked.

In Linux, a SIGILL, SIGSEGV, SIGFPE or SIGBUS signal generated as a result of code bugs in a program cannot be blocked. They cause the process to terminate right away even if these signals are blocked. However, if these signals are generated by a call to the kill() or raise() function, they can be blocked.

In addition to SIGILL, SIGSEGV and SIGFPE, there are other signals that are generated as a result of programming errors. They include SIGBUS, SIGSYS, SIGTRAP, SIGIOT, and SIGEMT. However, these are not part of the POSIX standard and their behavior is implementation dependent.

6-5 Receive Pending Blocked Signals

One of the reasons a program wants to block signals is that it may have to execute some critical section which cannot be interrupted by signals. Assuming a program blocks some signals during certain section of its code, what does the program do about those blocked signals if there is any pending once the critical section is finished? To receive them and respond! Otherwise, why blocking them? It would be simpler to just ignore them instead.

This section discusses how to receive pending blocked signals.

6-5-1 The sigpending() Function

Before a process goes ahead to receive a signal, it's best if it can first determine if there is any pending. This is because the functions used to receive a signal are all blocking. They suspend the execution of the caller indefinitely until there is a signal delivery. Such a blocking behavior is not most desirable. A more useful scenario is that if there is a pending signal, I like to receive it. If not, I like to continue execution without being blocked. The sigpending() function allows you to do exactly that.

```
int sigpending(sigset_t *set);
```

The sigpending() function returns the set of signals that are currently pending and blocked from delivery for the current process.
For example, if a process has blocked the SIGQUIT signal and some process has sent a SIGQUIT signal to that process, then the call to the sigpending() function will return a signal set containing that signal.

The sigpending() function returns 0 on success and -1 on error.

Figure 6-8 is an example demonstrating the use of the sigpending() function.

Figure 6-8 Getting the pending blocked signals (sig_sigpending.c)

```c
/*
 * Signal -- the sigpending() function.
 * Copyright (c) 2014, 2020 Mr. Jin-Jwei Chen.  All rights reserved.
 */

#include <stdio.h>
#include <errno.h>
#include <signal.h>
#include <unistd.h>

/*
 * Check to see if a signal is pending.
 */
void check_pending(int sig)
{
  sigset_t sigset;
  int          ret;

  ret = sigpending(&sigset);
  if (ret != 0)
  {
    fprintf(stderr, "Calling sigpending() failed, errno=%d\n", errno);
    return;
  }

  ret = sigismember(&sigset, sig);
  if (ret == 1)
    fprintf(stdout, "A signal %d is pending.\n", sig);
  else
    fprintf(stdout, "No signal %d is pending.\n", sig);
}

/*
 * The main program.
 */
int main(int argc, char *argv[])
{
  int          ret;
  sigset_t     newset, oldset;
```

```
/* Set up to block the SIGQUIT signal */

/* Construct a signal set containing SIGQUIT */
ret = sigemptyset(&newset);
if (ret != 0)
{
  fprintf(stderr, "Failed to empty the signal set, errno=%d\n", errno);
  return(-1);
}
ret = sigaddset(&newset, SIGQUIT);
if (ret != 0)
{
  fprintf(stderr, "  Failed to add SIGQUIT to the signal set, errno=%d\n", errno);
  return(-2);
}

/* Add the SIGQUIT signal to the current signal mask */
fprintf(stdout, "Adding SIGQUIT to the current signal mask\n");
ret = sigprocmask(SIG_BLOCK, &newset, &oldset);
if (ret != 0)
{
  fprintf(stderr, "Failed to change the current signal mask, errno=%d\n", errno);
  return(-3);
}

/* See if blocking the signal works by calling sigpending() */
check_pending(SIGQUIT);
fprintf(stdout, "Sending myself a SIGQUIT signal\n");
kill(getpid(), SIGQUIT);
check_pending(SIGQUIT);

return(0);
}
```

There are two ways for a program to receive a pending blocked signal. We will introduce them in the following sections.

6-5-2 The sigsuspend() Function

The first method for a process to receive a pending, blocked signal is to invoke the sigsuspend() function.

The sigsuspend() function suspends the execution of the caller indefinitely until a signal is delivered whose action is either to terminate the caller or to catch the signal. If the action is to terminate the caller then the sigsuspend() function will never return. If the action is to catch the signal, then when the signal is delivered, the signal handler function will be executed. After the signal handler function returns, the sigsuspend() function will return -1 with errno set to EINTR (4), meaning the call is interrupted. The signal mask of the process is restored to the state before the sigsuspend() call when it returns.

```
int sigsuspend(const sigset_t *mask);
```

Note that the sigsuspend() function requires a signal mask argument. The argument will temporarily replace the signal mask of the process until the sigsuspend() function returns.

Figure 6-9 is an example that demonstrates how a program can set it up to block the delivery of a signal until it is a convenient time to receive it.

Typically, if a program has a critical section that cannot be interrupted by signals, then it would set it up to block signals before the start of the critical section and then when the critical section finishes, it would check to see if any signal is pending. If a signal is pending, it would receive it at that time. The only reason we check if a signal is pending first is that the sigsuspend() function would suspend the caller indefinitely if there is no signal pending and we don't want to be suspended.

Figure 6-9 Receive a signal at convenient time (sig_sigsuspend.c)

```c
/*
 * Signal -- to block a signal and receive it at convenient time
 * using the sigsuspend() function.
 * Copyright (c) 2014, 2020 Mr. Jin-Jwei Chen.  All rights reserved.
 */

#include <stdio.h>
#include <errno.h>
#include <signal.h>
#include <unistd.h>

/*
 * Signal handler.
 */
void signal_handler(int sig)
{
  fprintf(stdout, "Received a signal %d\n", sig);
  /* We cannot invoke pthread_exit() here. */
  return;
}

/*
 * Check to see if a signal is pending.
 */
int check_pending(int sig)
{
  sigset_t sigset;
  int      ret;

  ret = sigpending(&sigset);
  if (ret != 0)
  {
    fprintf(stderr, "Calling sigpending() failed, errno=%d\n", errno);
    return(ret);
  }

  ret = sigismember(&sigset, sig);
```

266

```
  if (ret == 1)
    fprintf(stdout, "A signal %d is pending.\n", sig);
  else
    fprintf(stdout, "No signal %d is pending.\n", sig);

  return(ret);
}

/*
 * The main program.
 */
int main(int argc, char *argv[])
{
  int         ret, ret2, ret3;
  sigset_t    newset, oldset, blkset;
  int         done=0;
  int         sig;
  struct sigaction sigact;

  /* Set up to block the SIGQUIT signal */

  /* Construct a signal set containing SIGQUIT */
  ret = sigemptyset(&newset);
  if (ret != 0)
  {
    fprintf(stderr, "Failed to empty the signal set, errno=%d\n", errno);
    return(-1);
  }
  ret = sigaddset(&newset, SIGQUIT);
  if (ret != 0)
  {
    fprintf(stderr, "  Failed to add SIGQUIT to the signal set, errno=%d\n",
      errno);
    return(-2);
  }

  /* Add the SIGQUIT signal to the current signal mask */
  fprintf(stdout, "Adding SIGQUIT to the current signal mask\n");
  ret = sigprocmask(SIG_BLOCK, &newset, &oldset);
  if (ret != 0)
  {
    fprintf(stderr, "Failed to change the current signal mask, errno=%d\n",
      errno);
    return(-3);
  }

  /* After the signal is blocked, the critical section code can start here */

  /* Send myself the SIGQUIT signal twice. Typically, this is done by some
     other process. */
  fprintf(stdout, "Sending myself a SIGQUIT signal\n");
  kill(getpid(), SIGQUIT);
  fprintf(stdout, "Sending myself a SIGQUIT signal\n");
  kill(getpid(), SIGQUIT);

  /* The critical section ends here */
```

```
/* Set up to catch the signal that we are about to receive.
 * We need to do so because otherwise the default action is to terminate.
 */
sigfillset(&blkset);
sigdelset(&blkset, SIGQUIT);
sigemptyset(&sigact.sa_mask);
sigact.sa_flags = 0;
sigact.sa_handler = signal_handler;
ret = sigaction(SIGQUIT, &sigact, NULL);
if (ret != 0)
{
  fprintf(stderr, "sigaction() failed, errno=%d\n", errno);
  return(-4);
}

/* Check if we have a pending SIGQUIT signal. Receive it if yes. */
while (!done)
{
  ret2 = check_pending(SIGQUIT);
  if (ret2)
  {
    /* Receive the pending signal */
    errno = 0;
    ret3 = sigsuspend(&blkset);
    fprintf(stdout, "sigsuspend() returned %d, errno=%d\n", ret3, errno);
  }
  else
    done = 1;   /* Done if no pending SIGQUIT signal */
}

  return(0);
}
```

As you can see from the example program in Figure 6-9, the process receives the SIGQUIT signal twice but there is only one delivery.
The POSIX standard says that whether multiple occurrences of a pending signal is delivered more than once is defined by implementation (and thus it may vary from one implementation to next). If there are multiple pending signals, the order they are delivered is undefined. Besides, whether they are all delivered at once (one right after another) or one at a time is also undefined in the POSIX standard.

6-5-3 The sigwait() Function

Note that, yes, with the sigsuspend() function, a program can receive a signal at the time it likes. However, it still requires a signal handler.

In fact, a program can choose to receive a signal at the time it likes and to receive it synchronously without using a signal handler function. The sigwait() function enables that.

```
int sigwait( const sigset_t *set, int *sig );
```

The sigwait() function selects a pending signal from the set of signals specified in its first argument, clears it from the set of pending signals for the process/thread, and then returns that signal number in the second argument. If there is no signal in the specified set is pending at the time of the call, the caller is suspended for execution. The caller will resume execution when one or more signals in the set become pending.

Note that the signals specified in the first argument must be blocked.

The sigwait() function returns 0 on success. Otherwise, it returns -1 and the errno is set to indicate the reason for failure.

The sigwait() function is thread safe.

Note that Oracle/Sun Solaris supports two versions of sigwait(). The first version of sigwait() function in Solaris does not use the second argument. Instead the function itself returns the signal number, as it would be returned by the second argument. The second version is the standard version which is the same as what is shown above. To get the second version, you must define the -D_POSIX_PTHREAD_SEMANTICS on the C compiler command.

Figure 6-10 shows an example program using the sigwait() function to synchronously receive a signal without using a signal handler function.

Figure 6-10 Synchronously receive a signal (sig_sigwait.c)

```
/*
 * Signal -- to synchronously receive a signal with the sigwait() function.
 * On Solaris, compile like this:
 *    cc -D_POSIX_PTHREAD_SEMANTICS  -o sig_sigwait sig_sigwait.c
 * Copyright (c) 2014, 2019, 2020 Mr. Jin-Jwei Chen.  All rights reserved.
 */

#include <stdio.h>
#include <errno.h>
#include <signal.h>
#include <unistd.h>

/*
 * Check to see if a signal is pending.
 */
int check_pending(int sig)
{
  sigset_t sigset;
  int         ret;

  ret = sigpending(&sigset);
  if (ret != 0)
  {
    fprintf(stderr, "Calling sigpending() failed, errno=%d\n", errno);
    return(ret);
  }

  ret = sigismember(&sigset, sig);
  if (ret == 1)
    fprintf(stdout, "A signal %d is pending.\n", sig);
  else
```

```
      fprintf(stdout, "No signal %d is pending.\n", sig);

  return(ret);
}

/*
 * The main program.
 */
int main(int argc, char *argv[])
{
  int         ret, ret2, ret3;
  sigset_t    newset, oldset;
  int         done=0;
  int         sig;

  /* Set up to block the SIGQUIT signal */

  /* Construct a signal set containing SIGQUIT */
  ret = sigemptyset(&newset);
  if (ret != 0)
  {
    fprintf(stderr, "Failed to empty the signal set, errno=%d\n", errno);
    return(-1);
  }
  ret = sigaddset(&newset, SIGQUIT);
  if (ret != 0)
  {
    fprintf(stderr, "  Failed to add SIGQUIT to the signal set, errno=%d\n", errno);
    return(-2);
  }

  /* Add the SIGQUIT signal to the current signal mask */
  fprintf(stdout, "Adding SIGQUIT to the current signal mask\n");
  ret = sigprocmask(SIG_BLOCK, &newset, &oldset);
  if (ret != 0)
  {
    fprintf(stderr, "Failed to change the current signal mask, errno=%d\n", errno);
    return(-3);
  }

  /* Send myself the SIGQUIT signal twice */
  fprintf(stdout, "Sending myself a SIGQUIT signal\n");
  kill(getpid(), SIGQUIT);
  fprintf(stdout, "Sending myself a SIGQUIT signal\n");
  kill(getpid(), SIGQUIT);

  /* Wait and process the pending signals */
  while (!done)
  {
    ret2 = check_pending(SIGQUIT);
    if (ret2)
    {
      /* Wait for a signal and process it */
      ret3 = sigwait(&newset, &sig);
      if (ret3 == 0)
      {
```

```
            fprintf(stdout, "sigwait() returned signal %d\n", sig);
            fprintf(stdout, "Handling signal %d here ...\n", sig);
        }
    }
    else
        done = 1;
}

return(0);
}
```

6-5-4 The sigtimedwait() and sigwaitinfo() Functions

Here we introduce two more functions that are related to sigwait().

Three functions can be used to wait for an asynchronous signal.
In addition to sigwait() which we just introduced, the other two are below:

```
   int sigtimedwait(const sigset_t *restrict set,
       siginfo_t *restrict info,
       const struct timespec *restrict timeout);
   int sigwaitinfo(const sigset_t *restrict set,
       siginfo_t *restrict info);
```

The sigwaitinfo() function selects a pending signal from the signal set
specified by the set argument. If there is more than one signal pending,
the lowest numbered one is selected first. The selection order between
realtime and non-realtime signals is not specified by the POSIX standard.
If no signal in set is pending at the time of the call, the calling thread
will be suspended until one or more signals in set become pending or until
it is interrupted by an unblocked, caught signal.

The sigwaitinfo() function is equivalent to the sigwait() function,
except that the return value and the error reporting method are different,
and that it also returns information about the signal if the info argument
is not NULL. If the info argument is not NULL, the signal number will be
returned in the the si_signo member of the siginfo_t structure and
the cause of the signal will be returned in the si_code member of the same
structure.

The sigtimedwait() function is equivalent to sigwaitinfo() except that
if none of the signals specified by set are pending, sigtimedwait() will
wait for the time interval specified in the timeout argument and then return.
Should the timeout value be zero and if none of the signals specified by
set argument are pending, sigtimedwait() will return immediately with an
error. If timeout argument is NULL, the behavior is unspecified.

Upon successful completion these two functions return the number of the
selected signal. Otherwise, they return -1 and errno is set.

Just a quick note here. Most of the signal functions are defined in
POSIX.1 standard. Only three of them sigtimedwait(), sigwaitinfo() and
sigqueue() are defined in POSIX.1b.

6-6 Signals Reserved for Applications

In the POSIX standard, there are two signals reserved for applications to define and use. They are SIGUSR1 and SIGUSR2. These two signals can only be generated through explicit invocations of the kill() function or the kill command. The POSIX standard recommends that the signal implementation should not generate or use these two signals, nor the library functions, completely leaving them for applications to use. Most programmers find these application-defined signals very useful.

For example, one way to use these signals is to use each of them as a specific command. For instance, an application could employ a manager process supervising a group of worker processes. Each time the manager process would send a worker process a SIGUSR1 signal if it wants it to perform task A, and a SIGUSR2 signal if task B.

Another use of one of the application-defined signals is as a process SHUTDOWN command. Often it is the case that an application deploys multiple collaborating processes and at times a process finds it needs to tell another process to shut down. Instead of sending that process a SIGKILL or some other signal which leads to a non-graceful ending of the process, using SIGUSR1 or SIGUSR2 is a very good alternative because the target process can be set up to catch or receive the signal and then does all necessary steps to close all open files, release all locks, free all memories and resources, and does a clean and graceful exit.

Figure 6-11 Using signal SIGUSR1 as a command for clean shutdown (sig_sigusr.c)

```
/*
 * Signal -- using the SIGUSR1 signal as a command to do a clean shutdown.
 * Use two (parent and child) processes.
 * Copyright (c) 1997, 2014, 2019-2020 Mr. Jin-Jwei Chen.  All rights reserved.
 */

#include <stdio.h>
#include <errno.h>
#include <sys/types.h>
#include <unistd.h>
#include <stdlib.h>       /* exit() */
#include <signal.h>

/*
 * Signal handler.
 */
int signal_handler(int sig)
{
  /* Do a cleanup and release all resources held by this process */
  fprintf(stdout, "In signal_handler(), this process received a signal %d.\n",
    sig);
  fprintf(stdout, "In signal_handler(), this process is doing a cleanup and"
    " releasing all resources ...\n");
  /* Release all resources this process holds here */
  fprintf(stdout, "In signal_handler(), cleaning up is done. This process is shutting
down. Bye!\n");
  /* Shut down this process */
```

```
  exit(0);
}

int main(int argc, char *argv[])
{
  pid_t   pid;
  int     stat;     /* child's exit value */
  int     ret;

  /* Create a child process */
  pid = fork();

  if (pid == -1)
  {
    fprintf(stderr, "fork() failed, errno=%d\n", errno);
    return(-1);
  }
  else if (pid == 0)
  {
    /* This is the child process. */
    struct sigaction  newact, oldact;

    fprintf(stdout, "Child: I'm a new born child.\n");
    /* Specify an action for a signal */
    sigfillset(&newact.sa_mask);
    newact.sa_flags = 0;
    /* Specify (i.e. install) my own signal handler function */
    newact.sa_handler =  (void (*)(int))signal_handler;
    ret = sigaction(SIGUSR1, &newact, &oldact);
    if (ret != 0)
    {
      fprintf(stderr, "Child: sigaction() failed on SIGUSR1, errno=%d\n", errno);
      return(-2);
    }
    fprintf(stdout, "Child: A signal handler was successfully installed for "
      "signal SIGUSR1.\n");

    /* Perform the child process' task here and wait for shutdown signal */
    while (1)
      sleep(1);
    return(0);
  }
  else
  {
    /* This is the parent process. */
    fprintf(stdout, "Parent: I've just spawned a child.\n");

    /* Let child get on its feet first before sending it a signal */
    sleep(2);

    /* Test to see if the child is still alive. It must be. */
    ret = kill(pid, SIGUSR1);
    if (ret == 0)
      fprintf(stdout, "Parent: A SIGUSR1 signal was successfully sent to child.\n");
    else
      fprintf(stderr, "Parent: Sending a SIGUSR1 signal to child failed, "
```

```
            "errno = %d\n", errno);

  /* Wait for the child to exit */
  pid = wait(&stat);
  if (pid > 0)
  {
    fprintf(stdout, "Parent: My child has exited.\n");

    /* Test to see if the child is still alive again. It should be dead. */
    ret = kill(pid, 0);
    if (ret == 0)
      fprintf(stdout, "Parent: My child is still alive.\n");
    else
      fprintf(stdout, "Parent: My child is dead.\n");
  }


  return(0);
}
}
```

Figure 6-11 displays a program which demonstrates how to use the SIGUSR1
signal as a command to do a clean shutdown. We show the two-process example
case here by using parent-child processes. We leave it as a programming
assignment for doing it in the single-process case.

Remember that receiving the SIGUSR1 or SIGUSR2 signal terminates the process
by default. Therefore, a program must install a signal handler for these
signals reserved for applications as well.

Note that the signal the parent process sends could get delivered to the
child process before the child finishes installing its signal handler.
In that case the child process will die before it gets to execute its code.
That's why we do a sleep of two seconds in the parent process before it
actually sends the signal to the child. This is so that the child process
has sufficient time to get started and set up its signal handler before the
signal is sent. Another way to avoid this is to block all signals before the
child is spawned.

In order to terminate the entire process, the signal handler function invokes
exit(0) instead of return() at its end. Notice because of that we make the
signal handler returning an int. This requires us to cast the type of the
signal handler.

Since this is a very simple example and the program does not really do much,
there is no actual resource to release. Thus, we simply print a message
saying the process is releasing all of its resources. In real applications,
it should close the open files, release all locks the process has, free
all dynamic memories, and so on.

Some of you might have thought of that it would be nice if you could define
and use many more application-defined signals. It would.
However, although the signal number is an integer, usually only a very small
number of signal numbers are allowed in each implementation.
One of the reasons is that the type sigset_t is normally implemented as
an array of some integer type and it has a limited size.
This means you won't be allowed to use a very large signal number as you

wish. In Linux, the maximum signal number allowed is usually 64.
For instance, if you try to use a signal number greater than this maximum
signal number in a sigaction() call, it would fail with errno set to
EINVAL (22) -- invalid argument value.

6-7 Optional Signals Defined by Implementations

As we mentioned it before, the POSIX standard allows operating systems or
implementations of signals to define optional signals in addition to those
required by the Standard. This on one hand provides flexibility and on the
other might hurt application portability.

Some may argue that applications are more robust if they handle all possible
signals, including those optional ones. Others may say that it does not
make any real difference because SIGKILL is not catchable and an application
can get killed regardless.

The thing is there is no simple and easy way for an application to catch
or ignore optional signals. An application needs to figure out how many
there are and what they are because those could be different from one
implementation to the next.

6-8 Impacts of Signals on the sleep() Function

The sleep() function causes the calling process to sleep for the
number of real-time seconds specified in the argument. The calling
process will be suspended until either the specified time has elapsed,
in this case the function will return 0, or a signal is delivered and its
action is to terminate the process or to execute a signal handler
function.

Figure 6-12 Effect of signals on sleep() function (sig_sleep.c)

```
/*
 * Signal -- catching a signal during the sleep() call.
 * Copyright (c) 2014, 2020 Mr. Jin-Jwei Chen.  All rights reserved.
 */

#include <stdio.h>
#include <errno.h>
#include <sys/types.h>
#include <unistd.h>
#include <signal.h>
#include <sys/wait.h>

/*
 * Signal handler.
 */
void signal_handler(int sig)
{
  fprintf(stdout, "Received a signal %d\n", sig);
  /* We cannot invoke pthread_exit() here. */
  return;
}
```

```c
int main(int argc, char *argv[])
{
  pid_t   pid;
  int     stat;   /* child's exit value */
  int     ret;
  unsigned int  ret2;
  struct sigaction  oldact, newact;

  /* Set it up to catch the SIGQUIT signal */
  /* Set sa_mask such that all signals are to be blocked during execution
     of the signal handler */
  sigfillset(&newact.sa_mask);
  newact.sa_flags = 0;
  /* Specify my signal handler function */
  newact.sa_handler = signal_handler;
  ret = sigaction(SIGQUIT, &newact, &oldact);
  if (ret != 0)
  {
    fprintf(stderr, "sigaction failed, errno=%d\n", errno);
    return(-1);
  }

  /* Create a child process */
  pid = fork();

  if (pid == -1)
  {
    fprintf(stderr, "fork() failed, errno=%d\n", errno);
    return(-2);
  }
  else if (pid == 0)
  {
    /* This is the child process. */
    fprintf(stdout, "Child: I'm a new born child.\n");

    /* Perform the child process' task here */
    fprintf(stdout, "Child: Go to sleep for a few seconds.\n");
    ret2 = sleep(5);
    fprintf(stdout, "Child: sleep() return %u\n", ret2);
    return(ret2);
  }
  else
  {
    /* This is the parent process. */
    fprintf(stdout, "Parent: I've just spawned a child.\n");

    /* Test to see if the child is still alive. It must be. */
    ret = kill(pid, 0);
    if (ret == 0)
      fprintf(stdout, "Parent: My child is still alive.\n");
    else
      fprintf(stdout, "Parent: My child is dead.\n");

    /* Send the child a signal */
    sleep(1);  /* comment this out to see what effect it has */
```

```
    fprintf(stdout, "Parent: Send my child a signal.\n");
    kill(pid, SIGQUIT);

    /* Wait for the child to exit */
    pid = wait(&stat);
    if (pid > 0)
    {
      fprintf(stdout, "My child has exited.\n");

      /* Test to see if the child is still alive again. It should be dead. */
      ret = kill(pid, 0);
      if (ret == 0)
        fprintf(stdout, "Parent: My child is still alive.\n");
      else
        fprintf(stdout, "Parent: My child is dead.\n");
    }

    return(0);
  }
}
```

Figure 6-12 shows an example program where the parent process creates a child process and then sends the child process a signal (SIGQUIT).
In order to let the child process start execution and get into the sleep() function, the parent process sleeps for a second before sending the signal to the child. As you can see when you run the program, when the parent sleeps for a second, the child gets started. It then goes into sleep. Then the parent wakes up from the sleep and sends the child a SIGQUIT signal. The signal gets delivered to the child process. The child's sleep call is interrupted. The signal handler function gets invoked. And then the child process returned prematurely from its sleep() call with a return value of EINTR (4), which means the system call was interrupted.

For an experiment, if you take out the sleep(1) call from the parent right before it sends the signal, you will notice that the signal could be sent and delivered to the child even before the child gets a chance to execute. In that case, the signal handler function will get executed first before the child process' code actually gets executed. And since the signal was already caught and handled, when the child starts its execution, it will execute its full course without an interruption.

Note that during a sleep, if the process gets a signal that is not caught and the action associated with the signal is not SIG_IGN, then the sleep() call can end prematurely too.

Effect of SIGALRM Signal on sleep()

During the execution of the sleep() function, if a SIGALRM signal is generated for the calling process, and

- if the signal is ignored or blocked, then when the signal is scheduled, whether the function returns or not is unspecified.

- if the signal is not ignored or blocked, then it will cause the sleep() function to return. Other than that, whether the signal has an effect or not is unspecified.

6-9 Caveats of Signals

Signals are very easy to use and convenient. They have a role to play, even though they have some caveats.

The first caveat is by default receiving a signal causes a process to terminate, which is fatal and disruptive.

The second caveat of signals is when a signal causes process termination, there is really no mechanism available for programmers to try to clean up the process before it terminates.

The third caveat of signals is because it came before threads, it was designed to work with processes. As a result, in some cases it just does not work perfectly with threads. If a signal causes a thread to terminate, the entire process terminates.

That said, signals are still useful in many cases and applications. One just needs to make sure they are used correctly and safely.

6-10 Summary on Signals

There are essentially two types of signals. Synchronous signals are events that happen as a result of executing the code of current process or thread. Examples include the code trying to do a divide by zero operation, trying to access memory at an invalid address (e.g. dereferencing a NULL pointer), or trying to execute an illegal instruction. When one of these events occurs, the operating system will generate a corresponding signal and deliver it to the process, which will normally lead to termination of the process. These synchronous events are not catch-able or block-able. Nor can they be ignored.

Another type of signals are asynchronous events coming from outside the current running process or thread. These signals are sent by another process or thread asynchronously while the thread or process is running. This chapter mainly discusses dealing with this type of signals.

There are many different signals a process or thread can send to another or self. If a process does not do anything to protect itself, by default, receiving a signal will result in termination of the process.

To protect itself a process can choose to block all or some signals by using the sigprocmask() function so that signals except SIGKILL and SIGSTOP will never get delivered, or it can invoke the sigaction() function to specify an action it wants to take upon receiving a particular signal. To block signals, a thread calls the pthread_sigmask() function instead of sigprocmask().

Three action choices are available. First, it can specify to take the default (SIG_DFL) action, which will normally result in termination of the process. Second, it can specify to take the ignore (SIG_IGN) action, which means the signal will be ignored, effectively having no impact on the process at all. Third, it can specify a signal handler function to "catch" and handle the signal. Whenever that signal is delivered to the process, the signal handler function will be called instead of an automatic termination. Then it's up to the signal handler to decide the fate of the process.

Instead of specifying an action on each individual signal, alternatively, a process can take collective actions as well using the notion of a signal set. A process can specify an action on a particular set of signals using the sigprocmask() API. For instance, with a single function call, it can collectively block or unblock a set of signals or all signals.

A process could make arrangements to receive pending blocked signals at more convenient time by using sigsuspend() and sigwait().

Later in the pthreads chapter, we will introduce an additional solution. There we will talk about how to block all signals and then set up and use a signal handling thread to catch/receive all signals. It offers a simplified and more organized way to deal with signals in a multithreaded process.

In short, to protect itself from being abruptly terminated by asynchronous signals, a process needs to either block or ignore the signals or set up and install a signal handler function for each signal.

In the process model, each process has its own set of signal handlers, signal actions and signal mask. Each process can send signals to other processes using the kill() function. It can also receive signals from other processes. When a process receives a signal, if the action is to terminate, then the entire process terminates.

In the multithreaded model, each thread can have its own signal mask. But the signal disposition is shared among all threads in the same process.

6-11 Other Signal Functions

There are some other signal functions. We are unable to cover them all here. Please refer to the latest POSIX standard. The version of POSIX standard this book is based on is available at the following URL:

https://pubs.opengroup.org/onlinepubs/9699919799/

After you get to this web page, select the "System Interfaces" volume and then click on "3. System Interfaces". You will then get the lists of all system-level APIs defined in the POSIX standard. All the signal functions are named sigXXX().

Review Questions

1. What are signals? How many types of signals are there based on how they are generated? Give some examples in each type.

2. How do you send a signal to a process, from within a program and from a command prompt?

3. What is a pending signal?

4. What are the possible actions that a process can take in response to the delivery of a signal? How do they affect the behavior of the process?

5. What is the default action of each of the POSIX signals and job control signals?

6. What is catching a signal? How does a process catch a signal? What happens to the execution of the process when a signal is caught?

7. What signals can never be caught?

8. Can all signals be ignored? What signals cannot be ignored?

9. How does a process ignore signals?

10. As a programmer what do you need to be concerned about when you invoke other functions from within a signal handler function?

11. How does a process set or alter the action associated with a signal? How does a process get the action associated with a signal?

12. Once an action is set for a signal, it remains until when?

13. What is the signal mask of a process?

14. Why would a process block certain signals?

15. What signals cannot be blocked?

16. How does a process change its signal mask? How does a process get its current signal mask?

17. What happens when you block the SIGFPE signal from within a program and then send that process a such signal? Does it behave the same way as when the program does a divide-by-zero operation (say, x = x/0;) after the signal is blocked?

18. From within a program, how do you find out if a process is still alive or not?

19. How many different ways can a process receive a pending, blocked signal? What are the differences between them?

20. The signal receiving functions are blocking. What do you do if you don't want your code to be blocked when there are no signals to receive?

21. Explain what you can use the application-defined signals (SIGUSR1 and SIGUSR2) for?

22. Is any user or process allowed to send a signal to another process?

23. What signals can never be ignored, caught or blocked no matter what?

Exercises

1. Add a sleep(60) at end of the sig_procmask.c. Recompile and run the program in one window. Then from another window, find out the process id (pid) of the sig_procmask process and send three SIGQUIT signals and one SIGINT signal to it. What happens? Why?

   ```
   $ kill -3 pid
   $ kill -3 pid
   $ kill -3 pid
   $ kill -2 pid
   ```

2. Write a very simple program that blocks all signals.

3. Write a single process program that does a cleanup and then shuts down the process after it receives a SIGUSR1 signal. Use the kill command to send a SIGUSR1 signal to the process to test it.

4. Modify example program sig_sigusr.c and remove the sleep() call in the parent process. Then block signals before spawning the child process so that the child process always has a chance to install its signal handler function before a signal is delivered.

5. Write a program that takes a signal number as input and reports whether the signal is supported or not on your system.

6. Write a program to display all signals that are supported on your system.

7. Write a program to determine whether an optional signal is supported by your operating system.

8. What is the effect of the SIGALRM signal on the sleep() function in the operating system you use when the signal is ignored or blocked? Write a program to demonstrate it. Also, what is the behavior when the signal is not ignored or blocked?

9. Write a program that creates a child process but the parent does not wait for the child. Let the child terminates first. Let the parent sleeps or continues to run for some time so that you can observe the behavior. Set up in the parent to catch the SIGCHLD signal. Use the process list command to observe when the child process becomes a defunct process and when that defunct process disappears.

   Try without calling the wait() function to wait for the child from within the signal handler function first. And then try with calling the wait() from within the signal handler function.
   Explain the difference in the behaviors observed.

10. Modify the program above that creates a zombie/defunct child process such that the parent explicitly sets the action of the SIGCHLD signal to SIG_IGN. Make sure the parent does not call any wait() function. Do you notice any difference in behavior?
    Is the child process still a defunct process?

11. Modify the program above that creates a zombie/defunct child process

such that the parent sets up a signal handler function to catch the SIGCHLD signal and also sets the SA_NOCLDWAIT flag in the sa_flags field of the sigaction structure. Make sure the parent does not call any wait() function to wait for the child.
What is the behavior? Did the terminated child process become a zombie?

References

1. The Open Group Base Specifications Issue 7, 2018 edition
   IEEE Std 1003.1™-2017 (Revision of IEEE Std 1003.1-2008)
   Copyright © 2001-2018 IEEE and The Open Group
   http://pubs.opengroup.org/onlinepubs/9699919799/

2. AT&T UNIX System V Release 4 Programmer's Guide: System Services
   Prentice-Hall, Inc. 1990

7 Processes

In a working big server system, a computer usually has hundreds, if not thousands, of processes running at the same time. How does it get to so many processes?

In some operating systems such as Unix and Linux, when a system starts the operating system kernel, bootstrap code runs first. After the initialization and startup phase, when the system is ready to be up, the kernel then creates the first process, named init, which typically has a user id of root (the super-user), a process id of 1 and parent process id 0.
The init process then creates other operating system processes such as the scheduler, virtual memory management processes, file system daemons, I/O daemons, network daemons, and login server daemons, etc.
At this point, a system usually has dozens of system processes running.

After the system is fully up and running, users start to login and jobs are started. More processes are created. These processes typically further create other processes as well. A hierarchical structure of processes come to exist. Evidently, one central capability of any computer system is to create new processes when needed.

In this chapter we aim to introduce to you how to programmatically create new processes and run new programs. Besides, we also talk about a few other concepts related to process creation, management and communications.

7-1 Some Concepts and Functions Related to Process

Before we jump into the heart of creating new processes and running new programs, let us first go over some process related concepts and then introduce a number of process related functions that get and set user and group information.

In this section, we introduce the concepts of process, process group, session, real user id, effective user id, real group id, effective group id, saved set-user-id, and saved set-group-id.

7-1-1 What Is a Process?

A **process** is an instance of a program in execution. A single program can have multiple instances in execution at the same time, and thus having multiple processes in that case.

When you type a command or a program's name at the OS command prompt, you

start a process (well, at least one. It could sometimes be multiple.)
In this section, we explain what a process looks like.

Each process has a virtual address space which is generated by the compiler
when the program is built. Typically, the virtual address space of a process
consists of code or text segment, data segment, stack, and heap.
It also contains shared library code, shared library data, and the loader's
code and data as well.

Each of these segments starts at a particular virtual address, which is
operating system dependent. There is a limit on the size of each segment
and the entire virtual address space. Some operating system makes it
possible to configure the starting addresses and sizes. The stack and heap
can grow and they typically grow toward different directions.

The code/text segment contains the actual compiled code of the program.
When a program runs, its contents are read into the computer main memory
from the program's executable file on disk. The code/text segment is
typically set to be read only, except in some rare debugging cases
where a program is run under a debugger.

The data segment contains both program initialized data (which will be read
from disk) and the uninitialized data (BSS). The BSS section is for
statically-allocated program variables that are not explicitly initialized
to any value. These include variables and constants declared at file scope
outside any function and uninitialized static local variables.

Normally only the length of the BSS section is stored in the program's
executable file, no data. The program loader allocates the memory for BSS
when it loads the program from disk into memory.

Some operating system initializes the BSS memory to zero while others don't.

The stack segment is the program's stack memory. It is for storage of all
local variables declared within functions (i.e. variables with function
scope) and also function arguments passed between function calls.

The **heap** is the dynamically allocated memory, sometimes called **dynamic memory**.
Any memory that is allocated when a C program invokes malloc(), realloc() or
calloc() function resides in heap. Note that once allocated, the dynamically
allocated memory exists in the heap area forever until either it is explicitly
freed by the free() function or the program terminates. If a program keeps
allocating dynamic memories without freeing them, the memory used by the
process will grow and it could lead to memory leak.

A memory leak is a piece of dynamic memory that is not in use anymore but
it has not been explicitly freed. It is very important that the program you
develop does not have any memory leak. That is, every piece of memory
malloc-ed must be explicitly freed under normal and error conditions.

Just a note that author has seen many engineers tried to make a career out of
memory allocation. They create so many macros and functions around malloc-ed
memory. It's silly. It's only making the code and product unnecessarily
complicated and wasting their own and others' time.

Ultimately, there is only one pair of functions, malloc() and free(), in C

programming. They are so simple, reliable and easy to use. Just use them
directly. Don't make all this fuss out of it. I felt so frustrated that I had
to spend hours and hours trying to understand all the macros, functions, and
unnecessary complexities other engineers have defined and used in managing
dynamic memory. It's a total waste of time. So please don't do the same.
Just use malloc/realloc and free. If your program needs some dynamic memory,
use malloc() to allocate it and call free() to free it after use.
Don't make it much more complicated than that. I found I never had to.
I worked on a component of a product where the designer defined 65 macros
around malloc() for just one component. It makes no sense at all.
It only makes the product more difficult to understand and support.

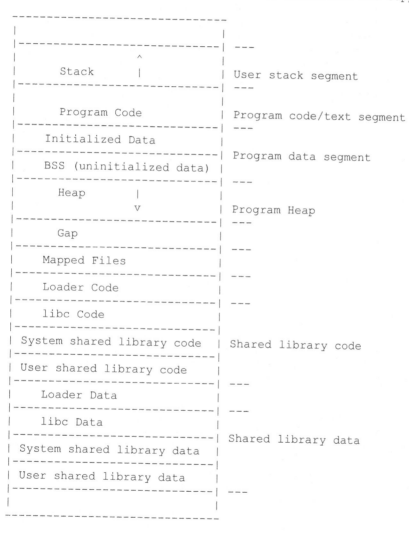

Figure 7-1 Memory map of process virtual address space

Figure 7-1 shows an example of the memory layout of a process's address space.
Please note that the exact layout is operating system dependent. Although the
placements may vary from one system to another, the contents are very similar

between different operating systems.

In addition to the process's virtual address space as shown in Figure 7-1, when a process is created, the operating system kernel also creates some kernel data structures used to track and manage each process, such as process states, process scheduling and accounting information. The operating system kernel has a process table tracking all active processes on the system. One entry in that table will be added for each newly created process. Unix system creates the so-called "u area" which contains information used to control the operation of a process.

Also notice that all addresses in the process's virtual address space are virtual and relative. A program could get loaded into different physical memory location. That's why all virtual addresses are relative addresses. Computer's memory management hardware unit translates virtual addresses generated by the compiler into physical addresses during execution.

7-1-2 The getpid() and getppid() Functions

There is a list of attributes associated with an active process in a system. The first one is a process identifier (id).

Each active process in a system has a unique process id identifying it. A process id is of pid_t type, which is actually defined to be an int. Each process also has a parent process and the parent's process id is also recorded.

The getpid() function returns the process id of the current process. The getppid() function returns the process id of the parent of the calling process. These functions are very straightforward. They take no argument and return a value of type pid_t. To use these functions, a program must include header files sys/types.h and unistd.h.

```
#include <sys/types.h>
#include <unistd.h>

pid_t getpid(void);
pid_t getppid(void);
```

These functions never fail.

7-1-3 The getuid() and geteuid() Functions

Each active process also has a user associated with it for the purpose of access control and accounting. The user attribute of a process determines what privileges the process has in terms of accessing various resources. In a POSIX-compliant operating system, access control is done based on individual users and groups of users.

Each user on a system has a unique login name which is a string and a unique user identifier (uid) which is an integer. In general, user name is for human to use and user number (uid) is for programs to use.

In fact, a process has two user ids associated with it: a **real user id** and an **effective user id.**

Sometimes it comes very handy if a program has some additional privileges when it runs. For instance, some program may need the super-user privilege to do just one thing. Because of this, POSIX operating systems allow the creation of the so-called set-user-identifier (setuid) programs.
A **setuid program** is a program that runs with a different user id -- the user who owns the program (file) instead of the user who runs the program. Similarly, there are set-group-identifier (setgid) programs that run with an additional group privilege.

When a setuid program runs, the privileges of the process are extended to include those of the user id associated with the program.
In this situation, the user id of the program is referred to as the **'effective user id'** of the process, whereas the original user id of the process is called the **'real user id'** (the real user who runs the program).

A program calls the getuid() function to obtain the real user id of the current process, and the geteuid() function to get the effective user id. The specifications of these functions are shown below:

```
#include <unistd.h>
#include <sys/types.h>

uid_t getuid(void);
uid_t geteuid(void);
```

These functions never fail.

7-1-4 The getgid() and getegid() Functions

Parallel to the user id, the getgid() and getegid() functions return the real group id and effective group id of the current process, respectively.

```
#include <unistd.h>
#include <sys/types.h>

gid_t getgid(void);
gid_t getegid(void);
```

These functions never fail.

7-1-5 The setuid() and setgid() Functions

When we said that a process has two user ids in a preceding section, we did not tell the whole story. In fact, in POSIX a process can have a third user id value. It's the saved set-user-id. Similarly, there is a saved set-group-id as well.

If the compile-time symbolic constant _POSIX_SAVED_IDS is defined, each process has a saved set-user-id and a saved set-group-id.

The setuid() function sets the real and effective user ids, and possibly the saved set-user-id of the current process.

```
#include <sys/types.h>
#include <unistd.h>

int setuid(uid_t uid);
int setgid(gid_t gid);
```

If the calling process has appropriate privileges (for instance, the effective user id of the calling process is the root user), the setuid() function sets the real and effective user ids of the current process to the value of the uid argument. If the compile-time symbolic constant _POSIX_SAVED_IDS is defined, the saved set-user-id is also set to the value of the uid argument.

If the calling process does not have appropriate privileges (say, it's not the root user), but the specified uid argument is the same as the real user id of the process, then the setuid() function sets the effective id to the value of the uid argument. The real user id remains unchanged. If _POSIX_SAVED_IDS is defined and the specified uid argument is equal to the saved set-user-id, then the effective id is set to the value of the uid argument; the real user id and the saved set-user-id remain unchanged.

The working of the setgid() function is similar to the setuid(), except it deals with the group instead of user. That is, it resets the real group id, effective group id, and saved set-group-id.

7-1-6 Process Groups and Sessions

Process groups

In a POSIX-compliant operating system, processes are organized into process groups. A **process group** is a set of related processes which have been assigned the same **process group identifier** (gid). Process groups are used in controlling access to terminals and in sending signals.

Normally process groups are created based on inheritance. A process inherits its process group from its parent process. When a parent process creates child processes, it forms a new process group whose process group id is the process id of the parent's process id. The group of processes in a process group is often called a **job**.

Typically, a user starts a process or job from the login shell (an operating system command interpreter) on a terminal. Therefore, a job is controlled from the shell and has an associated terminal, referred to as the **controlling terminal**. A terminal also has a process group id assigned to it at any time. Processes with the same process group id as the terminal are **foreground processes** of the terminal and may read from it.

A job control shell may create multiple process groups associated with the same terminal. In performing I/O, a process may read from its controlling terminal only if the terminal's process group id matches that of the process. If a process attempts to read from a terminal whose process group id does not match, the process will be blocked. By changing the process group id of the terminal, a shell can arbitrate a terminal among multiple jobs.

For instance, below is an example of a process group. In the process family tree, the login shell is the great grandparent and has the process id 7441. Under this shell, a program named mkprocgrp was run, whose process id is 8551 and process group id (the one in parentheses) is also 8551. The program creates a child whose process id is 8552 and process group id is 8551. This child process further creates two children. The first child has a process id of 8553 and process group id of 8551, and the second child has a process id of 8554 and process group id of 8551. As you can see, the mkprocgrp process forms a process group of four processes, all of them have the process group id 8551.

```
     7441 (shell)
       |
     8551 (8551)  (mkprocgrp program)
       |
     8552 (8551)
       |
   --------------
   |            |
 8553 (8551)  8554(8551)
```

Sessions

A session consists of one or more process groups.
A session may be associated with a terminal device.
Sessions have two main uses. One is to group together a user's login shell and all of the jobs it creates. The other is to form an isolated environment for a daemon process and all of its children.

A session can be created by calling the setsid() function.
A process that is not already a leader of a process group may create a session and become the session leader. Thereafter, processes created by this session leader and the children and grandchildren of these processes will become members of this new session.

If a session needs to communicate with the user, it may have a controlling terminal associated with it. The controlling terminal of a session is created by the session leader. After doing so, the session leader becomes the controlling process of the session. Note that a terminal device can be the controlling terminal of only one session at a time. This means only one process group can be the foreground process group for a controlling terminal and is allowed to read from and write to it at a time. All other process groups in the session are in the background, with no access to the terminal.

7-1-7 The getpgid(), setpgid(), getpgrp() and setpgrp() Functions

The following four functions get and set the process group id of a process. To use these functions, a program must include the header file unistd.h.

```
#include <unistd.h>

pid_t getpgrp(void);
int   setpgrp(void);
```

```
pid_t getpgid(pid_t pid);
int    setpgid(pid_t pid, pid_t pgid);
```

The getpgrp() function returns the process group id of the current process.
The getpgid() function returns the process group id of the process specified
by pid argument. The call getpgrp() is equivalent to getpgid(0).

The setpgrp() function sets the process group id of the current process.
The setpgid() function sets the process group id of the process identified
by the pid argument to be the value of the pgid argument.
setpgrp() is equivalent to setpgid(0,0).

If success, setpgid() and setpgrp() return 0. On error, they return -1
and errno is set appropriately.

A process can change its own process group or that of a child process
by creating a new process group via the setpgid() function.
The same function can also be used to move a process into an existing
process group.

Figure 7-2 is a program that displays a process' process id, parent process
id, and process group id.

  Figure 7-2 getpid(), getppid(), getpgrp(), and getpgid() (getpid.c)

```
/*
 * Example on getpid(), getppid(), getpgrp(), and getpgid().
 * Copyright (c) 2013, 2014 Mr. Jin-Jwei Chen. All rights reserved.
 */

#include <stdio.h>
#include <errno.h>
#include <unistd.h>

int main(int argc, char *argv[])
{
  pid_t  pid;

  fprintf(stdout, "My process id, pid=%u\n", getpid());
  fprintf(stdout, "My parent's process id, ppid=%u\n", getppid());
  fprintf(stdout, "My process group id, pgrp=%u\n", getpgrp());
  fprintf(stdout, "My process group id, pgid=%u\n", getpgid(0));
}
```

7-1-8 The setsid() Function

```
#include <unistd.h>

pid_t setsid(void);
```

The setsid() function creates a new session if the calling process is not
a process group leader. The calling process becomes the session leader of
the new session and the process group leader of a new process group.
The process has no controlling terminal. The process group id and session
id of the calling process is set to the process id of the calling process.

The calling process becomes the only process in the new process group and in the new session.

The setsid() function returns the value of the process group id of the calling process on success. It returns -1 on failure and errno is set to indicate the error. The error EPERM is returned if the process group id of some other process equals the process id of the calling process, or if the calling process is already a process group leader.

7-2 Create a New Process with fork()

In POSIX standard, a process creates another new process by invoking the fork() function. The calling process is called the parent process and the new process created by the fork() function is called the child process. The two processes thus have a parent-child relationship.

The fork() interface is as follows:

```
#include <sys/types.h>
#include <unistd.h>

pid_t fork(void);
```

The function takes no argument. It returns a value of pid_t type. To use this function, your program must include the two header files as shown above.

When just created by the fork() function, a child process is an exact copy of its parent except it has its own unique process id and a different parent process id. It also has its own copy of the parent's file descriptors, which point to the same set of files as its parent's file descriptors. However, file locks owned by the parent are not inherited. The parent's pending signals are not inherited by the child, either.

After the fork() function, the parent and the child execute independently. Although they share the same code segment, each has its own stack.

If the fork() function is successful in spawning the new child process, it will return the process id of the child process in the parent and return zero in the child process. A process can tell whether it is the parent or the child by checking if the return value is zero or not.

If the fork() function fails to create a new child process, it will return -1 and the errno global variable will be set to indicate the error.

A fork() call can fail. For example, when the system is very low in memory and the function fails to allocate the memory needed for creating the necessary kernel data structures for the new process, such as the proc and task structures and the virtual memory page tables. A fork() call may also fail if the total number of processes in the system exceeds the limit set inside the operating system kernel.

Figure 7-3 lists a program demonstrating the fork() function.

Figure 7-3 Create a new process (fork.c)

```c
/*
 * Create a child process.
 * Copyright (c) 2013, 2014 Mr. Jin-Jwei Chen. All rights reserved.
 */

#include <stdio.h>
#include <errno.h>
#include <sys/types.h>
#include <unistd.h>

int main(int argc, char *argv[])
{
  pid_t  pid;

  /* Create a child process */
  pid = fork();

  if (pid == -1)
  {
    fprintf(stderr, "fork() failed, errno=%d\n", errno);
    return(1);
  }
  else if (pid == 0)
  {
    /* This is the child process. */
    fprintf(stdout, "Child: I'm a new born child, my pid=%u\n", getpid());
    fprintf(stdout, "Child: my parent is pid=%u\n", getppid());
    /* Perform the child process' task here */
    return(0);
  }
  else
  {
    /* This is the parent process. */
    sleep(2);
    fprintf(stdout, "Parent: I've just spawned a child, its pid=%u\n", pid);
    /* Perform the parent process' task here */
    return(0);
  }
}
```

Why fork()?

You may ask why do fork? Well, it's like child birth.
When the operating system starts, it creates and runs a number of processes
where each performs a specific task such as managing the system's physical
memory, managing file systems, doing process scheduling, user accounting, etc.
When a user logins to the system, the system creates a shell for the user
using fork(). After the user logins, each time he or she issues a command,
a new process is created (again using fork()) to run that command.

Thus, forking a new process happens all the time in an operating system.
Processes come and go, just like birth and death happen all the time in real
life. In computer, calling fork() is how a new process is created.

7-2-1 After the fork() Function

Below is what happens after the fork() function succeeds.

After a successful fork call, the new child process is an exact copy of the parent process except the following:

- The new child process has its own unique process id.
  This process id does not match any active process group id.

- The child process has a different parent process id. It is the process id of the parent process.

- The child process has its own copy of the open file descriptors.
  This is a copy of the parent process' open file descriptors.
  Therefore, both the parent and the child still share the same set of open files.

- The child process has its own copy of the parent's open directory streams.

- All pending signals are cleared for the child process.

- All pending alarms are cleared for the child process.

- File locks owned by the parent process are not inherited by the child process.

- The values of tms_utime, tms_stime, tms_cutime, and tms_cstime are set to zero in the child process.

7-3 Parent Waits for Child

There are three possible scenarios when a parent process creates a child process. The parent could exit itself after creating the child and let the child run its course and does its job. The parent and the child could both continue to run in parallel and each does its own job. Or the parent could simply sit there and wait for the child to complete.

To wait for a child process to complete and collect the child's exit status, a parent process can call either the wait() or waitpid() function.

```
#include <sys/types.h>
#include <sys/wait.h>

pid_t wait(int *status);
pid_t waitpid(pid_t pid, int *status, int options);
```

To use the wait() or waitpid() function, a program must include the header files sys/types.h and sys/wait.h.

Both wait() and waitpid() return the process id of the child process that has terminated.

In general, the two wait() functions are similar. The main difference between the two is that the wait() function waits for any child process. It will return as soon as any child process has terminated. In contrast, as its name implies, the waitpid() function waits for a particular child process whose process id matches the pid specified in the function call. However, if the pid argument has a value of -1 and the options argument has a value of zero, then the waitpid() function shall have the same behavior as the wait() function.

Note that in either function, if the status argument is not NULL, then when the function returns, the terminated child's exit status (that is, the value the child process has returned) will be deposited in the status argument. The child can use this exit status value to convey some information back to the parent and let the parent know how the child has terminated. Notice that although this exit status value is declared as an int type, only the lowest byte (8 bits) is returned back to the parent. In other words, the values that can be returned from a child process to its parent are from 0 to 255. For instance, if the child has returned a value of 260, then the actual exit status value its parent gets through the wait() functions will be (260 % 256) = 4.

There are some macros defined for programmers to use in checking the exit status of a child process. They are described below.

WIFEXITED(status)

This macro evaluates to a nonzero value if the child process has terminated normally (i.e. via executing the return statement from the main() function or invoking one of the exit() functions from anywhere).

WEXITSTATUS(status)

If the value of WIFEXITED(status) is nonzero, then this macro evaluates to the lowest-order byte of the exit status of the terminated child process. The exit status of the child process is the integer value it passed to the return statement or exit()/_exit() function when it terminated.

WIFSIGNALED(status)

If the child process that returns the status value has terminated due to receipt of a signal (that was not caught), this macro evaluates to a nonzero value.

WTERMSIG(status)

If the value of WIFSIGNALED(status) is nonzero, then the value of this macro is the number of the signal that has caused the child process to terminate.

WIFSTOPPED(status)

If the child process that returned the status is currently stopped, this macro evaluates to a nonzero value.

WSTOPSIG(status)

If the value of WIFSTOPPED(status) is nonzero, the value of this macro is the number of the signal that caused the child process to stop.

Figure 7-4 shows a program that creates two child processes, waits for them, and uses the exit status macros to determine how a child has terminated. This example illustrates both normal termination and abnormal termination where the first child process terminates normally via executing the return statement in its main() function and the second child process dies of getting a SIGKILL signal. As you can see from this example, either WIFEXITED(status) or WIFSIGNALED(status) evaluates to a nonzero value, not both.

Figure 7-4 Wait for children to terminate with wait() (wait.c)

```c
/*
 * Create child processes and wait for them to exit using wait.
 * The parent sends a SIGKILL signal to the second child.
 * Copyright (c) 2013, 2014 Mr. Jin-Jwei Chen. All rights reserved.
 */

#include <stdio.h>
#include <errno.h>
#include <sys/types.h>
#include <signal.h>        /* kill() */
#include <unistd.h>
#include <sys/wait.h>

#define NPROCS  2      /* number of child processes to create */

int main(int argc, char *argv[])
{
  pid_t  pid;
  int    i;
  int    stat;    /* child's exit value */

  /* Create the child processes */
  fprintf(stdout, "Parent: to create %u child processes\n", NPROCS);
  for (i = 0; i < NPROCS; i++)
  {
    pid = fork();

    if (pid == -1)
    {
      fprintf(stderr, "fork() failed, errno=%d\n", errno);
      return(1);
    }
    else if (pid == 0)
    {
      /* This is the child process. */
      fprintf(stdout, "Child: I'm a new born child, my pid=%u\n", getpid());
      fprintf(stdout, "Child: my parent is pid=%u\n", getppid());
      sleep(2);
      return(0);
    }
  }

  /* This is the parent */
```

```
/* Send a signal to the last child */
kill(pid, SIGKILL);

/* Wait for all child processes to exit */
for (i = 0; i < NPROCS; i++)
{
    pid = wait(&stat);
    fprintf(stdout, "Child %u has terminated\n", pid);

    /* See if the child terminated normally.
     * WIFEXITED(stat) evaluates to non-zero if a child has terminated normally,
     * whether it returned zero or non-zero.
     */
    if (WIFEXITED(stat))
    {
        fprintf(stdout, "Child %u has terminated normally\n", pid);
        if (WEXITSTATUS(stat))
            fprintf(stdout, "The lowest byte of exit value for child %u is %d\n",
                pid, WEXITSTATUS(stat) );
        else
            fprintf(stdout, "Child %d has returned a value of 0\n", pid);
    }

    /* See if the child terminated due to a signal */
    if (WIFSIGNALED(stat) != 0)
    {
        /* Child terminated due to a signal */
        fprintf(stdout, "Child %d terminated due to a signal\n", pid);
        fprintf(stdout, "Child %d terminated due to getting signal %d\n",
            pid, WTERMSIG(stat));
    }
}
return(0);
}
```

7-3-1 The waitpid() Function

Using the pid argument, the waitpid() function can specify to wait for
either a single child process or a group of child processes.

- If the value of the pid argument is greater than zero, it means to wait
  for a single child process; the one whose process id matches the pid value.

- If the value of the pid argument is -1, it means to wait for any child
  process. In this case, waitpid() is just like wait().

- If the value of the pid argument is 0, it means to wait for any child
  process whose process group ID is equal to that of the calling process.

- If the value of the pid argument is less than -1, it means to wait for any
  child process whose process group ID is equal to the absolute value of
  the pid argument.

The options argument to the waitpid() function is a bitwise inclusive OR of zero or more of the following flags:

- WNOHANG

    Specifying the WNOHANG flag in the options argument makes the waitpid()
    function becomes non-blocking. That is, the calling (i.e. parent) process
    will not be suspended if no status of the child process(es) is immediately
    available. When no child process' status is available, the waitpid()
    function with the WNOHANG options flag returns a value of 0, rather than
    a process id value. Note that in this case a child process continues to
    run even after the parent's waitpid() call returns.

- WUNTRACED

    Specifying this flag makes the waitpid() function returns if the child
    process has stopped.

Figure 7-5 is a program that illustrates the use of waitpid() function with
the WUNTRACED flag as well as the WIFSTOPPED(status) and WSTOPSIG(status)
macros. As you can see, specifying the WUNTRACED options flag makes the
waitpid() function returns when a child process is stopped.

Figure 7-5 Wait for children to terminate with waitpid() (waitpid.c)

```c
/*
 * Create two child processes and wait for them using waitpid() with
 * WUNTRACED flag.
 * The parent sends the second child a SIGSTOP signal.
 * The parent sleeps for one second to let the children get a chance to start.
 * Copyright (c) 2013, 2014, 2020 Mr. Jin-Jwei Chen. All rights reserved.
 */

#include <stdio.h>
#include <errno.h>
#include <sys/types.h>
#include <signal.h>        /* kill() */
#include <unistd.h>
#include <sys/wait.h>

#define NPROCS      2       /* number of child processes to create */
#define SLEEPTIME   20      /* number of seconds a child sleeps */

int main(int argc, char *argv[])
{
  pid_t  pid;
  int    i;
  int    stat;    /* child's exit value */
  int    options = (WUNTRACED); /* options for waitpid() */

  /* Create the child processes */
  fprintf(stdout, "Parent: to create %u child processes\n", NPROCS);
  for (i = 0; i < NPROCS; i++)
  {
    pid = fork();

    if (pid == -1)
```

```
    {
      fprintf(stderr, "fork() failed, errno=%d\n", errno);
      return(1);
    }
    else if (pid == 0)
    {
      /* This is the child process. */
      fprintf(stdout, "Child: I'm a new born child, my pid=%u\n", getpid());
      fprintf(stdout, "Child: my parent is pid=%u\n", getppid());
      sleep(SLEEPTIME);
      return(0);
    }
  }

  /* This is the parent */

  /* Send a signal to the last child */
  sleep(1);
  kill(pid, SIGSTOP);

  /* Wait for all child processes to exit */
  for (i = 0; i < NPROCS; i++)
  {
    pid = waitpid(-1, &stat, options);
    fprintf(stdout, "waitpid() has returned with pid = %d\n", pid);

    /* See if the child terminated normally.
     * WIFEXITED(stat) evaluates to non-zero if a child has terminated normally,
     * whether it returned zero or non-zero.
     */
    if (WIFEXITED(stat))
    {
      fprintf(stdout, "Child %u has terminated normally\n", pid);
      if (WEXITSTATUS(stat))
        fprintf(stdout, "The lowest byte of exit value for child %u is %d\n",
          pid, WEXITSTATUS(stat) );
      else
        fprintf(stdout, "Child %d has returned a value of 0\n", pid);
    }

    /* See if the child terminated due to a signal */
    if (WIFSIGNALED(stat) != 0)
    {
      /* Child terminated due to a signal */
      fprintf(stdout, "Child %d terminated due to a signal\n", pid);
      fprintf(stdout, "Child %d terminated due to getting signal %d\n",
        pid, WTERMSIG(stat));
    }

    /* See if the child was stopped. */
    if (WIFSTOPPED(stat) != 0)
    {
      /* Child was stopped */
      fprintf(stdout, "Child was stopped.\n");
      fprintf(stdout, "Child was stopped by signal %d.\n", WSTOPSIG(stat));
    }
```

```
    }
    return(0);
}
```

7-4 Create a New Process to Run a Different Program

Like we have said, right after the fork() function, a child process is an
exact copy of its parent. This means they have the same code image
although they may execute different sections of the code.
Occasionally, it may be all right to stay with the same code image.
However, most of the time a process creates a child process to perform
some different task. This means the child will need to have a different
personality. For this reason, creating a child process is usually
a two-step process.

First, the parent spawns a new process by invoking the fork() function.

Second, an exec() function is called by the child process to replace
its current process image with a new program image.
This second step overlays the code of a new program on top of the current
process such that it becomes running a completely different program
thereafter. This step gives the new-born child a different personality
than its parent. This means if the exec() function call is successful,
it will never return.

We will go over how to exec a new program in this section.

7-4-1 The exec() Functions

As listed below, there are a family of six exec() functions available
for executing a new program. To use any of these functions, your program
must include the header file unistd.h. We explain how to use them below.

```
#include <unistd.h>

extern char **environ;

int execl(const char *path, const char *arg, ...);
int execlp(const char *file, const char *arg, ...);
int execle(const char *path, const char *arg,
        ..., char * const envp[]);
int execv(const char *path, char *const argv[]);
int execvp(const char *file, char *const argv[]);
int execve(const char *filename, char *const argv[],
        char *const envp[]);
```

Two types of exec functions: execl() and execv(). execl() lists arguments
to the new program one by one. execv() gives them in a string array.

When a process tries to execute a new program, there are essentially four
types of information needed.

1. What is the name of the program?
2. Where is the program?

3. What are the arguments to the new program?
4. What are the environment variables for the new program?

In terms of where to find the program to be executed (bullet 2 above), there are basically two approaches.

1. The exec() function specifies where the program is by providing the pathname of the file containing the program.

2. The operating system searches a list of directories defined by the PATH environment variable for the program file.

   Note: In many operating systems such as Unix and Linux, the PATH environment variable specifies a list of directories where the operating system should search for a program to be executed. As a developer, it's your responsibility to make sure the directories where your programs reside are in that list. If not, then the value of the PATH environment variable should be updated to include them.

This is why essentially there are two flavors of the exec() functions. There are execl() and execlp() functions, as well as execv() and execvp(). The functions with the letter p in their names use the PATH environment variable to search for the program to execute. Because of this, their first argument is supposed to be just a simple file name such as "myprog". The functions without the letter p at the end of their names are specifying the pathname of the program (for example, /home/john/bin/myprog) in their first argument. That's why their first argument is named path instead of file (bullet 1 of 4 above).

In general, the approach of using the PATH environment variable to locate a program file is more flexible because it allows you to place your program in whatever directory convenient for you. All you need to do is to make sure that directory is in the list of the directories contained in the PATH environment variable. If not, you can just add the new directory to the list. With this approach, whenever the exec() function cannot find the program to execute, the first thing you do is to check the value of the PATH environment variable. For example, in Unix or Linux, this is what you do:

```
$ echo $PATH
/sbin:/bin:/usr/sbin:/usr/bin:/usr/local/bin
```

If your program is not located in one of the directories shown, then you must update PATH and add that directory to the list.

Note that given what we said above, with the execlp() and execvp() functions, if you specify the absolute pathname of the program file in the first argument (the one named 'file') of these functions, it works too. In that case, the system will just use the pathname given without searching through the directories listed in the PATH environment variable. In addition, for both the file and the path arguments in all of the exec() functions, you can also specify a relative pathname. But this relative pathname works only in relative to the current working directory. This works even the current working directory (.) is not in the PATH environment variable's value.

The third type of information needed is the list of arguments to the new program to be executed. This list is passed around as a list of character strings or pointers to characters. The first one on the list must always be a string that contains the name of the new program. This is because in C language, every program starts execution at the main() function and the first argument (argv[0]) to the main() function is always the name of the program itself. To conform to the C standard, passing in the name of the program as the very first argument to a program is required. This means the list of arguments to the new program must be at least one at any time.

In addition, the list of arguments to the new program must ALWAYS end with a NULL pointer. This is how the new program is going to know where the list of input arguments ends because the number of arguments is not fixed. If you forget to terminate the argument list with a NULL pointer, the exec() function will fail with a return value of -1 and with errno=14 (EFAULT). (This is bullet 3 of 4 above.)

Redefining the environment variables for the new program constitutes the third flavor of the exec() functions. These are the functions whose names end with the letter e -- execle() and execve().

For the exec() functions whose names do not end with e, there is no way to redefine the environment variables for the new program. Instead, the new program inherits all of the environment variables from its parent.

The execle() and execve() functions allow you to use a different set of environment variables for the new program via their last argument, envp. The argument envp is an array of pointers to character strings where each string is a definition of an environment variable in the following format:

    name=value

For example:

    TERM=xterm

The array must be terminated with a NULL pointer.

From within the new program, the environment variables passed to it can be obtained from the external variable 'environ', which is an array of pointers to character strings. The pointer array is NULL terminated.

In the sections below, we will give a few program examples on how to use these exec() functions.

7-4-2 The execl() Function

Here we first introduce the execl() function to you.

    int execl(const char *path, const char *arg, ...);

As we have explained in the preceding section, the path argument needs to specify the pathname of the new program to be executed. The second argument must always be a string whose value is the name of the new program.

301

Then any arguments you want to pass to the new program follow.
Each argument must be in a character string format. And the last argument
must be (char *)NULL to indicate to the new program that is the end of the
argument list.

If the execl() function succeeds, it never returns. The control is then
transferred to execute the new program. If the execl() function fails,
it will return -1 with the global variable errno set to indicate the error.

Figure 7-6 shows a program using the execl() function to execute a new
program named myprog.

Figure 7-6 Fork and exec a program using execl() (execl.c)

```c
/*
 * Create a child process to run a new program with the execl() function.
 * Copyright (c) 2013, 2014 Mr. Jin-Jwei Chen. All rights reserved.
 */

#include <stdio.h>
#include <errno.h>
#include <sys/types.h>
#include <unistd.h>

#define  PROG_NAME   "myprog"   /* name of my program */
#define  PROG_PATH   "./myprog"  /* path of my program */

int main(int argc, char *argv[])
{
  pid_t  pid;                    /* process id */
  int    ret;

  /* Create a child process */
  pid = fork();

  if (pid == -1)
  {
    fprintf(stderr, "fork() failed, errno=%d\n", errno);
    return(1);
  }
  else if (pid == 0)
  {
    char  arg1[8] = "2";  /* first real argument to the child process */

    /* This is the child process. */
    fprintf(stdout, "Child: I'm a new born child.\n");

    /* Run a new program in the child process */
    ret = execl(PROG_PATH, PROG_NAME, (char *)arg1, (char *)NULL);
    fprintf(stdout, "Child: execl() returned %d, errno=%d\n", ret, errno);
    return(0);
  }
  else
  {
    /* This is the parent process. */
    fprintf(stdout, "Parent: I've just spawned a child.\n");
```

```
      /* Perform the parent process' task here */
      fprintf(stdout, "Parent: exited\n");
      return(0);
   }
}
```

7-4-3 The execlp() Function

The execlp() function is similar to execl() except its first argument only needs to specify a file name - the name of the program file to be executed. There is no path required at all (although it works too if you specify an absolute pathname). As mentioned above, the execlp() function relies on the setting of the PATH environment variable to find a program to execute.

```
      int execlp(const char *file, const char *arg, ...);
```

When you use the execlp() function, make sure the directory where your program resides appears in the list of directories specified by the PATH environment variable.

Figure 7-7 Fork and exec a program using execlp() (execlp.c)

```
/*
 * Create a child process to run a new program with the execlp() function.
 * Copyright (c) 2013, 2014 Mr. Jin-Jwei Chen. All rights reserved.
 */

#include <stdio.h>
#include <errno.h>
#include <sys/types.h>
#include <unistd.h>

#define  PROG_NAME  "myprog"  /* name of my program */

int main(int argc, char *argv[])
{
   pid_t  pid;             /* process id */
   int    ret;

   /* Create a child process */
   pid = fork();

   if (pid == -1)
   {
      fprintf(stderr, "fork() failed, errno=%d\n", errno);
      return(1);
   }
   else if (pid == 0)
   {
      char  arg1[8] = "2";  /* first real argument to the child process */

      /* This is the child process. */
      fprintf(stdout, "Child: I'm a new born child.\n");
```

```
  /* Run a new program in the child process */
  ret = execlp(PROG_NAME, PROG_NAME, (char *)arg1, (char *)NULL);
  fprintf(stdout, "Child: execlp() returned %d, errno=%d\n", ret, errno);
  return(0);
}
else
{
  /* This is the parent process. */
  fprintf(stdout, "Parent: I've just spawned a child.\n");

  /* Perform the parent process' task here */
  fprintf(stdout, "Parent: exited\n");
  return(0);
}
}
```

Figure 7-7 shows a program using the execlp() function. Notice the first
argument to the execlp() function is instead "myprog" now.

Below is the output of a terminal session that demonstrates the execlp()
function uses the PATH environment variable to find a program to execute.
As it shows, initially both programs execlp and myprog reside in the
same directory -- the current working directory. Since the current working
directory (.) is in the value of the PATH variable, the execlp() function
in the execlp program finds the myprog and runs it.
Then after we move the myprog to a subdirectory named tmp, the execlp()
function can no longer finds it. Therefore, the execlp() function fails
and the errno is 2 (No such file).

After we add the full path of the tmp subdirectory to the PATH environment
variable, the same program runs fine again. This demonstrates that the
execlp() function relies on the PATH environment variable to find a program
to execute.

```
$ pwd
/home/oracle/mybk1/proc/lin
$ echo $PATH
/usr/kerberos/bin:/usr/local/bin:/bin:/usr/bin:.::/home/oracle/bin
$ ls -l execlp myprog
-rwxr-xr-x 1 oracle oinstall 7811 Mar 13 18:18 execlp
-rwxr-xr-x 1 oracle oinstall 7480 Mar 13 15:15 myprog
$ ./execlp
Parent: I've just spawned a child.
Parent: exited
Child: I'm a new born child.
Entered my program
My program is going to sleep for 2 seconds.
Exited my program

$ mv myprog tmp/
$  ./execlp
Parent: I've just spawned a child.
Parent: exited
Child: I'm a new born child.
Child: execlp() returned -1, errno=2
```

```
$ ls -l myprog
ls: myprog: No such file or directory
$ ls -l tmp/myprog
-rwxr-xr-x 1 oracle oinstall 7480 Mar 13 15:15 tmp/myprog

$ PATH=$PATH:/home/oracle/mybk1/proc/lin/tmp; export PATH
$ ./execlp
Parent: I've just spawned a child.
Parent: exited
Child: I'm a new born child.
Entered my program
My program is going to sleep for 2 seconds.
Exited my program
```

7-4-4 The execv() and execvp() Functions

The execv() and execvp() functions do the same thing as execl() and execlp() except that instead of providing the list of arguments to the new program one by one in the function call, a single argument is used for that which provides an array of pointers to null-terminated strings that represent the argument list to the new program. Note that the first pointer in this array must point to a string that is the filename of the program file to be executed. Also, the pointer array must end with a NULL pointer.

Again, the main difference between the execv() and execvp() functions is that the execvp() function uses the PATH environment variable to locate the file to be executed. That's why the first argument to execvp() needs to specify only a filename, rather than a pathname as in execv(). Though as we have pointed out, specifying an absolute pathname of the new program in the file argument of the execvp() function works too.

Figure 7-8 is a program that demonstrates how to use the execv() function.

Figure 7-8 Run a new program with execv() (execv.c)

```c
/*
 * Create a child process to run a new program with the execv() function.
 * Copyright (c) 2013, 2014 Mr. Jin-Jwei Chen. All rights reserved.
 */

#include <stdio.h>
#include <errno.h>
#include <sys/types.h>
#include <unistd.h>

#define PROG_PATH  "./myprog" /* path of my program */
#define PROG_NAME  "myprog"   /* name of my program */

int main(int argc, char *argv[])
{
  pid_t  pid;                 /* process id */
  int    ret;

  /* Create a child process */
  pid = fork();
```

```
  if (pid == -1)
  {
    fprintf(stderr, "fork() failed, errno=%d\n", errno);
    return(1);
  }
  else if (pid == 0)
  {
    char *arglst[]= {PROG_NAME, "2", NULL};   /* argument list */

    /* This is the child process. */
    fprintf(stdout, "Child: I'm a new born child.\n");

    /* Run a new program in the child process */
    ret = execv(PROG_PATH, arglst);
    fprintf(stdout, "Child: execv() returned %d, errno=%d\n", ret, errno);
    return(0);
  }
  else
  {
    /* This is the parent process. */
    fprintf(stdout, "Parent: I've just spawned a child.\n");

    /* Perform the parent process' task here */
    fprintf(stdout, "Parent: exited\n");
    return(0);
  }
}
```

7-4-5 The execle() and execve() Functions

Figure 7-9 is a program that demonstrates how to use the execve() function. As you can see, the new program can retrieve the environment variables passed in by the execve() call from the external variable environ.

Figure 7-9 Run a new program with execve() (execve.c)

```
/*
 * Create a child process to run a new program with the execve() function.
 * Copyright (c) 2013, 2014 Mr. Jin-Jwei Chen. All rights reserved.
 */

#include <stdio.h>
#include <errno.h>
#include <sys/types.h>
#include <unistd.h>

#define PROG_PATH   "./myprog2" /* path of my program */
#define PROG_NAME   "myprog2"   /* name of my program */

int main(int argc, char *argv[])
{
  pid_t  pid;                   /* process id */
  int    ret;
```

```
/* Create a child process */
pid = fork();

if (pid == -1)
{
  fprintf(stderr, "fork() failed, errno=%d\n", errno);
  return(1);
}
else if (pid == 0)
{
  char *arglst[]= {PROG_NAME, "2", NULL};   /* argument list */
  char *envp[]= {"TERM=chen", NULL};

  /* This is the child process. */
  fprintf(stdout, "Child: I'm a new born child.\n");

  /* Run a new program in the child process */
  ret = execve(PROG_PATH, arglst, envp);
  fprintf(stdout, "Child: execve() returned %d, errno=%d\n", ret, errno);
  return(0);
}
else
{
  /* This is the parent process. */
  fprintf(stdout, "Parent: I've just spawned a child.\n");

  /* Perform the parent process' task here */
  fprintf(stdout, "Parent: exited\n");
  return(0);
}
}
```

7-4-6 After the exec() Functions

Below is what happens after one of the exec() functions succeeds.

- Files open in the parent process remain open in the child process
  except those with close-on-exec flag FD_CLOEXEC set.
  Attributes of the open files remain unchanged.

- Directory streams open in the parent process are closed in the child
  process.

- **Signals set to be caught by the parent process are set to the default
  action in the child process.** Signals set to be the default action
  (SIG_DFL) or set to be ignored (SIG_IGN) remain unchanged in the child
  process.

- The child process inherits the process signal mask from the parent process.

- The child process inherits the current working directory, root directory,
  and file mode creation mask from the parent process.

- If the set-user-ID mode (SUID) bit of the new program file is set,
  then after the exec() function the effective user ID of the child process

will be the owner ID of the new program file. Similarly, the same is true
for the set-group-ID mode bit on the effective group ID.
Otherwise, if neither of these bits is set, the effective user ID and
effective group ID of the child process remain the same as those of
the parent process.

The real user ID, real group ID, and supplementary group IDs of the child
process remain the same as those of the parent process.

If {POSIX_SAVED_IDS} is defined, the effective user and group IDs of the
child process will be saved for use by the setuid() function.

- The child process inherits from its parent the time left on an alarm clock.

- The new program image file is considered to be having been opened
  and its st_atime (time of last access) is updated.

7-5 Communications Between Parent and Child Processes

There are many different ways a parent process can communicate with a child
process. Most of these communication schemes are available to processes
even without a parent-child relationship. We have discussed some of them
so far. We will introduce more of these inter-process communication
mechanisms in this and later chapters.

Here in this section, we introduce a communication scheme that is
only available to processes with a parent-child relationship -- pipes.

Some may ask if a child process can communicate with its parent via a
global variable and the answer is no because each has a separate copy of
the global variable. Global variables do not exist outside/across the
boundary of a process.

7-5-1 What Is a Pipe?

A pipe is a uni-directional information flow channel. A pipe has two ends:
a write end where information can be written to and a read end where
information can be read from. Information written into a pipe is read on
a First-In-First-Out (FIFO) basis. Hence, a pipe is sometimes referred to
as a FIFO.

In many operating systems, pipes are implemented as files of FIFO type.
Each pipe has a unique inode number identifying it in the file system.

Figure 7-10 A pipe

```
the write end                                          the read end
              ------------------------------
fd[1]    -->             a pipe              --> fd[0]
              ------------------------------
```

A pipe is an anonymous communication channel typically used in between
a parent and a child processes or two processes connected through the use
of the dup() function.

Remember we said a child process shares open file descriptors with its parent process. Therefore, if a parent process creates a pipe before it does a fork, then the child will inherit that pipe as well.
Then if the parent opens the write end and closes the read end of the pipe and the child process does exactly the opposite (closes the write end and opens the read ends), then the two processes will have a one-way communication channel from the parent to the child.

If the parent process creates a pair of pipes, instead of just one, before it invokes the fork() function, and then after the fork, both do exactly opposite of what we describe above on the second pipe, then the parent and the child will have "bidirectional" communications, with the parent sends information to the child using the first pipe and the child sends information to the parent using the second pipe.

In other words, a parent process and a child process can have a private, not available to anyone else, bidirectional communication via a pair of pipes.

Figure 7-11 Bidirectional communications between a parent and a child

```
The parent process                          The child process

the write end                               the read end
            ---------------------------------
fd1[1]   -->            first pipe              --> fd1[0]
            ---------------------------------

the read end                                the write end
            ---------------------------------
fd2[0]   <--            second pipe             <-- fd2[1]
            ---------------------------------
```

7-5-2 Creating and Using a Pipe

A program creates a pipe using the pipe() function, as shown below:

```
#include <unistd.h>

int pipe(int fd[2]);
```

The pipe() function creates a pipe and returns two file descriptors, one in each of the arguments. The file descriptor for the read end of the pipe is placed in fd[0] and the file descriptor for the write end of the pipe is placed in fd[1].

Figure 7-12a is a program that illustrates communications between a parent process and a child process using a pipe and file descriptor duplication. The program first creates a pipe and then spawns a child process so that both the parent and child processes share the pipe.

Figure 7-12a Parent-child process communication using a pipe (pipe.c)

```
/*
```

```
 * Parent and child processes communication using a pipe.
 * The parent process sends a message to the child process using a pipe.
 * Copyright (c) 2013, 2014, 2019-2020 Mr. Jin-Jwei Chen. All rights reserved.
 */

#include <stdio.h>
#include <errno.h>
#include <unistd.h>        /* pipe(), read(), write() */
#include <string.h>        /* strlen() */
#include <sys/types.h>
#include <sys/wait.h>

#define  BUFSIZE  128
#define  MYMSG  "This is a message from the parent."

int main(int argc, char *argv[])
{
  pid_t   pid;             /* process id */
  int     pfd[2];          /* pipe file descriptors */
  int     ret = 0;
  ssize_t  bytes;          /* number of bytes read or written */
  char    buf[BUFSIZE];    /* message buffer */
  int     status;          /* child's exit status */

  /* Create a pipe */
  ret = pipe(pfd);
  if (ret != 0)
  {
    fprintf(stderr, "pipe() failed, errno=%d\n", errno);
    return(1);
  }

  /* Create a child process */
  pid = fork();
  if (pid == (pid_t)-1)
  {
    fprintf(stderr, "fork() failed, errno=%d\n", errno);
    close(pfd[0]);
    close(pfd[1]);
    return(2);
  }
  else if (pid == 0)
  {    /* The child process */
    close(pfd[1]);           /* Close the write end of the pipe */
    bytes = read(pfd[0], buf, BUFSIZE);  /* Read from the pipe */
    if (bytes < 0)
    {
      fprintf(stderr, "Child: read() failed, errno=%d\n", errno);
      return(1);
    }
    if (bytes < BUFSIZE)
      buf[bytes] = '\0';
    else
      buf[BUFSIZE-1] = '\0';
    fprintf(stdout, "Child received below messages from parent:\n%s\n", buf);
```

```
    close(pfd[0]);
    return(ret);
  }
  else
  {     /* The parent process */
    close(pfd[0]);          /* Close the read end of the pipe */
    sprintf(buf, "%s", MYMSG);
    bytes = write(pfd[1], buf, strlen(buf));   /* Write message to the pipe */
    if (bytes < 0)
    {
      fprintf(stderr, "Parent: write() failed, errno=%d\n", errno);
      ret = 3;
    }
    close(pfd[1]);          /* The reader will see EOF after this. */
    pid = wait(&status);    /* Wait for the child */
    return(ret);
  }
}
```

Note that the parent process must create the pipe before it does a fork.
This is so that the child process can inherit the pipe and use that to
communicate with its parent.

After the fork, the parent process closes the read end of the pipe so that
it writes to it but not reads from it. The child does the opposite by
closing the write end of the pipe so that it reads from it but not writes
to it. The parent process sends messages to the child by writing into the
write end of the pipe pfd[1] and the child process gets the messages from
the parent by reading from the read end of the pipe pfd[0].

Although the example sends a character string, the data sent can be
of any type. After the message is sent, the parent closes the write end of
the pipe and exits. After reading and printing the message, the child process
closes the read end of the pipe and exits.

If the parent process creates a second pipe, the two processes can use that
for the child to send messages to the parent as well, establishing a
two-way communications.

When there are multiple writers writing to the same pipe at the same time,
the maximum amount of information that can be atomically written to the
pipe is defined by the configurable parameter PIPE_BUF, which can be
obtained by calling the pathconf() function as we discussed in section 5-6-1.

Note that there is another way of doing the same thing as in pipe.c,
which is to also use **dup()** as shown in pipedup.c in Figure 7-12b. This is
how the command piping is done with dup() in POSIX-compliant systems.

Instead of writing to the pipe file descriptor, the pipe writer closes its
stdout (file descriptor 1) and makes that file descriptor available.
Then it calls the dup() function to duplicate the file descriptor of the
pipe's write end. **Once this is done, writing to stdout (or file descriptor
1) is writing to the pipe.**

Similarly, the pipe reader closes its stdin (file descriptor 0) and then
invokes dup() to duplicate the file descriptor of the read end of the pipe.

This makes the reader reads from the pipe when it reads from stdin (or file descriptor 0).

Figure 7-12b shows an example program that does this.

Figure 7-12b Using pipe() with dup() together (pipedup.c)

```c
/*
 * Parent and child processes communication using a pipe with dup().
 * The parent process sends a message to the child process using a pipe.
 * Copyright (c) 2013, 2014, 2019-2020 Mr. Jin-Jwei Chen. All rights reserved.
 */

#include <stdio.h>
#include <errno.h>
#include <unistd.h>        /* pipe(), read(), write() */
#include <string.h>        /* strlen() */
#include <sys/types.h>
#include <sys/wait.h>

#define   BUFSIZE  128
#define   MYMSG   "This is a message from the parent."

int main(int argc, char *argv[])
{
  pid_t   pid;              /* process id */
  int     pfd[2];           /* pipe file descriptors */
  int     ret = 0;
  ssize_t bytes;            /* number of bytes read or written */
  char    buf[BUFSIZE];     /* message buffer */
  int     status;           /* child's exit status */

  /* Create a pipe */
  ret = pipe(pfd);
  if (ret != 0)
  {
    fprintf(stderr, "pipe() failed, errno=%d\n", errno);
    return(1);
  }

  /* Create a child process */
  pid = fork();
  if (pid == (pid_t)-1)
  {
    fprintf(stderr, "fork() failed, errno=%d\n", errno);
    close(pfd[0]);
    close(pfd[1]);
    return(2);
  }
  else if (pid == 0)
  {     /* The child process */
    close(pfd[1]);           /* Close the write end of the pipe */

    /* Close stdin, duplicate pipe read end fd and read from stdin */
    close(0);
    if (dup(pfd[0]) == -1)
```

```
        {
            fprintf(stderr, "Child: dup() failed, errno=%d\n", errno);
            return(errno);
        }

        bytes = read(0, buf, BUFSIZE);   /* Read from the pipe */
        if (bytes < 0)
        {
            fprintf(stderr, "Child: read() failed, errno=%d\n", errno);
            return(1);
        }
        if (bytes < BUFSIZE)
            buf[bytes] = '\0';
        else
            buf[BUFSIZE-1] = '\0';
        fprintf(stdout, "Child received below messages from parent:\n%s\n", buf);

        close(pfd[0]);
        return(ret);
    }
    else
    {    /* The parent process */
        close(pfd[0]);            /* Close the read end of the pipe */

        /* Close stdout, duplicate pipe write end fd and write to stdout */
        close(1);
        if (dup(pfd[1]) == -1)
        {
            fprintf(stderr, "Parent: dup() failed, errno=%d\n", errno);
            return(errno);
        }

        sprintf(buf, "%s", MYMSG);
        bytes = write(1, buf, strlen(buf));   /* Write message to the pipe */
        if (bytes < 0)
        {
            fprintf(stderr, "Parent: write() failed, errno=%d\n", errno);
            ret = 3;
        }

        close(pfd[1]);            /* The reader will see EOF after this */
        pid = wait(&status);      /* Wait for the child */
        return(ret);
    }
}
```

It is worth pointing out that **piping** -- connecting two processes together
by feeding the output of one process into the input of another -- is very
popular in Unix and Linux operating systems. For instance, the commands
below

```
$ ls | tee ls.out
```

is an example of piping. In this example, the ls and tee commands are
connected via a pipe -- the '|' character. As a result, the output of the
'ls' command is sent to the standard input of the tee command. This allows

the tee command to not only capture the output of the first command in
a file (ls.out) but also display it on the terminal.

At end of this chapter, there is an exercise which is to let the readers
modify the example pipedup.c and get a sense of how piping can be done between
two programs.

7-6 Orphaned and Zombie Processes

We introduce a couple of terminologies related to processes in this section.

Orphaned Processes

An **orphaned process** is a process that is still alive but its parent has
died. In many operating systems including Unix and Linux, Orphaned processes
are adopted by the init process (whose process id is 1). Since the init
process waits for its children, the orphaned process will disappear from the
system after it terminates.

Zombie (Defunct) Processes

A **zombie process** is a process that has completed but has not yet been waited
for or "reaped" by its parent. It is also referred to as a defunct or
inactive process.

In a Unix or Linux system, a zombie process can be identified by the
presence of the letter 'Z' in the STAT column in the output of the
ps command (e.g. ps -efs).

A zombie process continues to exist in the system's process table internally
maintained by the operating system kernel until its parent invokes the wait()
function to read its exit status. After that a zombie process is removed
from the system and its process table slot (and thus its process id)
can be reused by the operating system.

Therefore, a zombie process occupies one entry of the process table in the
operating system kernel, which normally has a limited, fixed size.
As you can probably think of, if too many of the slots in the process
table are occupied by these zombie processes, the process table can become
full and the operating system can no longer create any more new processes
to run any new jobs, which will be a real problem. In case your system
runs out of processes, one thing you might want to check first is whether
it has got any defunct processes hanging around before you actually go
ahead and tune the O.S. kernel to increase the limit on the total number of
processes allowed.

Unlike normal processes, you cannot use the kill command to get rid of
a zombie process. Even 'kill -9' won't work. Once the parent process
has terminated, a zombie child process becomes an orphaned process
which will be adopted by the init process in most systems. Since the init
process periodically waits on its children, the zombie child process will
soon be removed from the system after its new parent calls wait().

So, to avoid letting a terminated child process becomes a zombie process,
a parent process must call one of the wait() functions to collect the child

process' exit status. The parent process could do it either in its normal code path or set it up to catch the SIGCHLD signal and call the wait() function in the signal-catching function. The difference between the two is the former blocks the parent (the wait() function is a blocking call) and the latter does not.

Note that a zombie process hanging around for some time means a bug in the parent process. The parent should have arranged to call the wait() function on each of its children and reap them.

It's worth noting that in many Unix and Linux systems that are compliant with the Single UNIX Specification version 3, if a parent process explicitly (as opposed to by default) specifies the SIG_IGN (to ignore) action for the SIGCHLD signal (which is what the parent gets when a child terminates), then the exit status of a terminated child will be discarded and the child won't become a zombie. Alternatively, the parent can still set up a signal catching function to catch the SIGCHLD signal but specify the SA_NOCLDWAIT flag in doing so. That will have the same effect in preventing the terminated child process from becoming a zombie.

7-7 Process Termination

There are two kinds of process termination.

1. Normal termination. A process terminates normally if it executes the return() statement from the main() function or if it invokes the exit() or _exit() function from anywhere.

2. Abnormal termination. A process terminates abnormally if it invokes the abort() function or if it gets terminated as a result of getting a signal.

In addition to calling the return() function from the main() function, a process can terminate itself by invoking one of the exit(), _exit(), _Exit(), and abort() function from anywhere.
We introduce these process terminating functions in this section.

7-7-1 The exit() Function

The exit() function causes normal termination of the calling process.

As shown below, to use the exit() function, your program must include the header file stdlib.h. The exit() function does not return any value. In fact, this function ends the program so it never returns.

```
#include <stdlib.h>

void exit(int status);
```

When your program calls the exit() function, it can pass in an integer value as the argument. This value will become the return value of the program. If the parent process of this current process waits for its child, this exit status will be passed back to the parent. It is a way for a program to inform its parent how it has ended its life. By convention, an exit

status of 0 means success and a non-zero value means failure.
Different values can be used to indicate the different reasons for
failure. Note that although the exit status is declared as an int,
when the value is passed back to the parent via the wait() or waitpid()
function, only the lowest byte is passed back. So, don't use a value
greater than 255.

Following are what happen during the execution of the exit() function:

- All buffered I/Os are flushed.

- All open files and streams are closed.

- Any functions registered previously for the process by the atexit()
  function are called in the reverse order of their registrations.
  We will discuss the atexit() function in section 7-7-3.

- The exit() function calls the _exit() function to complete the process
  termination. The _exit() function does not return.

7-7-2 The _exit() and _Exit() Functions

The _exit() and _Exit() functions terminate the calling process.
To use the function _exit(), your program must include the unistd.h.
To use the function _Exit(), your program must include the stdlib.h.

```
#include <unistd.h>
void _exit(int status);
```

```
#include <stdlib.h>
void _Exit(int status);
```

The _Exit() function is functionally equivalent to the _exit() function.

The _exit() function is like exit(), but it does not call any functions
registered with atexit().

The effect of calling the _exit() function by a process is as follows:

- All open files and directory streams belonging to the calling process
  are closed.

  Whether the standard I/O buffers are flushed is system dependent.

- If SIGCHLD signal is supported by the signal implementation, a SIGCHLD
  signal is sent to the parent process.

- If the parent process of the process calling _exit() is waiting on the
  child (i.e. executing a wait() or waitpid()), and it has not set its
  SA_NOCLDWAIT flag nor set SIGCHLD to SIG_IGN, it is notified of the calling
  process' termination and the lowest-order byte of the status is made
  available to it. The exiting process dies and is removed from the system
  immediately.

  If the parent process has set SA_NOCLDWAIT flag in the sa_flags field of the sigaction structure, or it has set the SIGCHLD handler to SIG_IGN, the exit status is discarded. The exiting process dies and is removed from the system immediately.

If the parent process of the process calling _exit() is not waiting and has not indicated that it is not interested in the exit status (i.e. has neither set its SA_NOCLDWAIT flag nor set SIGCHLD's action to SIG_IGN), then the exiting process is turned into a zombie process. The exiting process' status will be made available to its parent when it calls wait() or waitpid() later.

- If the process calling exit() or _exit() is a session leader and its controlling terminal is the controlling terminal of the session, then a SIGHUP signal is sent to every process in the foreground process group of this controlling terminal. Furthermore, the controlling terminal is disassociated from the session so that it can be acquired by a new controlling process.

Note that termination of a process does not directly terminate its child processes. But sending the SIGHUP signal can cause some child processes to terminate indirectly.

- The orphaned processes of the process calling the _exit() function are inherited by some other process (the init process with process id 1 in Unix and Linux) and are assigned a new parent process id.

- If the exit of the process causes a process group to become orphaned, and if any member of the newly orphaned process group is stopped, then a SIGHUP signal followed by a SIGCONT signal is sent to each process in the newly orphaned process group.

- Memory mappings that were created in the process are unmapped.

Note that **in most systems, the _exit() or _Exit() function does not call the functions registered via atexit() or on_exit(). For this reason, your program should not call these functions directly.**

7-7-3 The atexit() Function

To meet special needs of some programs in doing cleanup before termination, a program can employ the atexit() function to register some cleanup functions that are automatically called and executed at the time of its termination.

The atexit() function allows you to register a function to be called at normal process termination. This interface is as follows.

```
#include <stdlib.h>

int atexit(void (*function)(void));
```

As shown, your program must include the stdlib.h to use atexit().

To register a function, you simply invoke the atexit() and pass in the pointer to that function (which is the name of the function) as the only argument to atexit(). The function being registered must have been defined.

Note that each function registered by the atexit() must return.
This ensures that all registered functions are called.

**Functions registered by atexit() are called when the process terminates
either via return from main() or via invoking the exit() function.**
If multiple functions are so registered, they are called in the reverse
order of their registrations. Be aware that no arguments can be passed to
these functions.

Note that if a process terminates via calling the _exit() or _Exit()
function, the functions registered by the atexit() are not called.
For this reason, in general it is a better practice to terminate a
program via return from main() or via calling the exit() function
than via invoking the _exit() or _Exit() function.

Figure 7-13 shows a program demonstrating four different ways to exit
a program and which one invokes the function(s) registered by the
atexit() function.

Figure 7-13 Different ways to terminate a program (atexit.c)

```
/*
 * Test which exit function calls the registered cleanup at program termination.
 * Copyright (c) 2013, 2014 Mr. Jin-Jwei Chen. All rights reserved.
 */

#include <stdio.h>
#include <unistd.h>      /* _exit() */
#include <stdlib.h>      /* _Exit(), atexit(), atoi() */

#define  USE_RETURN  1

/* My cleanup function */
void my_cleanup()
{
  fprintf(stdout, "My cleanup function at termination was executed.\n");
}

int main(int argc, char *argv[])
{
  int   ret;
  int   how2exit = USE_RETURN;  /* by default use return() to exit the program */

  fprintf(stdout, "Entered main()\n");

  /* Get the input argument */
  if (argc > 1)
  {
    how2exit = atoi(argv[1]);
    if (how2exit <= 0)
      how2exit = USE_RETURN;
  }

  /* Register the cleanup function */
  ret = atexit(my_cleanup);
```

```
if (ret != 0)
  fprintf(stderr, "atexit() failed, returned value = %d\n", ret);
else
  fprintf(stdout, "My cleanup function was successfully registered.\n");

/* Terminate the program in the way the user wants it */
switch (how2exit)
{
  case 2:
    fprintf(stdout, "To leave main() via exit()\n");
    exit(ret);
    break;
  case 3:
    fprintf(stdout, "To leave main() via _exit()\n");
    _exit(ret);
    fflush(stdout);
    break;
  case 4:
    fprintf(stdout, "To leave main() via _Exit()\n");
    _Exit(ret);
    fflush(stdout);
    break;
  case 5:
    fprintf(stdout, "To leave main() via abort()\n");
    abort();
    break;
  default:
    fprintf(stdout, "To leave main() via return()\n");
    return(ret);
}
}
```

7-7-4 The abort() Function

The abort() function abnormally terminates a process. It has the following specification.

```
#include <stdlib.h>

void abort(void);
```

Note that the abort() function never returns.
It guarantees to abnormally terminate the calling process unless the SIGABRT signal is caught by the process and the signal handler does not return.

The abort() function essentially sends the SIGABRT signal to the calling process. If the action of the SIGABRT signal is SIG_DFL or SIG_IGN, the process is terminated with no hassle. If SIGABRT signal is caught by the process, then when the signal handler function returns, the process is terminated. The signal handler function is executed only once. The exit status made available to the wait() or waitpid() function will be that of a process terminated by a SIGABRT signal.

7-7-5 The assert() Function

```
#include <assert.h>

void assert(scalar expression);
```

The assert() function is used in debugging. It's indeed a macro.
The assert() macro lets developers insert debugging diagnostics into programs.
When using assert(), you always specify a condition. At program execution,
if the condition evaluates to a false (that is, the entire expression
evaluates to zero), then assert() will write to stderr information about the
particular condition that failed and call abort() to abnormally terminate the
current program.

If you know at a particular point of program execution, a certain variable
should never be NULL, and you are suspecting it actually gets that value
sometimes, then you could insert an assert() call to try to catch it.
The call would be

```
assert(pointer != NULL);
```

Adding this assert() statement in your code means you are claiming that
at this execution point, the value of the pointer variable should never
equal to NULL. And if it is, then the program should die right here!

Should the pointer's value become NULL, the expression "(pointer != NULL)"
will evaluate to FALSE, and the assert() will fire, terminating the program
right away.

Figure 7-14 is a program demonstrating exactly this.

Figure 7-14 Using assert() to debug -- assert.c

```
/*
 * A very simple program demonstrating assert().
 * Copyright (c) 2019  Mr. Jin-Jwei Chen. All rights reserved.
 */

#include <stdio.h>
#include <assert.h>

int main(int argc, char *argv[])
{
  char  *ptr = NULL;

  assert(ptr != NULL);

  printf("Program terminates normally.\n");
}
```

Below is an example of the output you will get when assert() fires.

```
$ ./assert
assert: assert.c:9: main: Assertion `ptr != ((void *)0)' failed.
Aborted
```

```
$
```

Please note that whenever the assert condition evaluates to false, the calling program terminates right away. It's like committing suicide.

Make sure you don't mis-use assert(). assert() is mainly for debugging code, not production code.

In one software product I worked on, I saw it calls assert() a lot in order to prevent the application program from continuing and further corrupting data. It's a very bad programming to mis-use or over-use assert(). Good software engineers write programs that work correctly all the time, rather than often throwing up their hands and saying "I give up", which is what assert() does. So in one sense, using assert() in production code indicates the engineer is incapable of resolving the current situation. You should try to always do better than this. I personally have never used assert() anywhere throughout my entire career, whether it's in Unix operating system kernel, database systems, networking code or other applications.

Calling assert() is NOT like encountering an error condition, printing an error, doing something to handle the error and then continuing execution. It is abnormally terminating the entire program immediately right there. Therefore, it is very disruptive. Note that **it terminates the entire program right on spot!** It should not happen in any good software. In other words, good-quality software should not behave like that at all!

Typically, during the software development and debugging phase, people may use assert() to catch bugs. But when the software is shipped and in production mode, all assert() calls are removed because they kill the application program once any of the assert condition is false. Software engineers' job is to make sure the program never encounters any of the conditions that would trigger an assert.

7-8 The getenv() and sysconf() Functions

7-8-1 The getenv() Function

Sometimes a program may need to know the value of a certain environment variable. The getenv() function does just that.

```
#include <stdlib.h>

char *getenv(const char *name);
```

To use the getenv() function, a program must include the stdlib.h header file. To get the value of an environment variable, a program invokes the getenv() function and passes in the name of the environment variable in string form as the argument. The function returns the value of the environment variable. getenv() returns a NULL pointer if the environment variable is not defined or cannot be found.

Figure 7-15 is an example program that demonstrates how to use the getenv() function.

Figure 7-15 Get values of environment variables (getenv.c)

```c
/*
 * Get environment variables via getenv().
 * Copyright (c) 2013, 2014 Mr. Jin-Jwei Chen. All rights reserved.
 */

#include <stdio.h>
#include <stdlib.h>      /* getenv() */

int main(int argc, char *argv[])
{
  int  ret;

  fprintf(stdout, "Environment variable HOSTNAME = %s\n", getenv("HOSTNAME"));
  fprintf(stdout, "Environment variable SHELL = %s\n", getenv("SHELL"));
  fprintf(stdout, "Environment variable TERM = %s\n", getenv("TERM"));
  fprintf(stdout, "Environment variable USER = %s\n", getenv("USER"));

  return(0);
}
```

7-8-2 The sysconf() Function

Each operating system has a number of configurable parameters.
Programs or programmers often need to know the limits of some of these
parameters. The POSIX standard defines a way for applications to query
the system's configurable parameters. It is via the sysconf() function.

```c
#include <unistd.h>

long sysconf(int name);
```

The way it works is each system configurable parameter has a name and a
value. In the sysconf() interface, each name has a macro defined for it
and corresponds to an integer. In POSIX, these names are all in the format
of _SC_PARAMETERNAME. If your program invokes the sysconf() function with
the integer (i.e. macro) corresponding to the parameter as the argument,
the function returns the limit of that parameter as a long integer.

If you specify an invalid value for the parameter, sysconf() returns -1
and the errno global variable is set to EINVAL. If the specified parameter
is not supported, sysconf() returns -1 but the errno is not set.

Figure 7-16 is a program that queries all configurable parameters.

Figure 7-16 Query system configurable parameters (sysconf.c)

```c
/*
 * Print system configurable parameters using sysconf()
 * Copyright (c) 2013, 2014 Mr. Jin-Jwei Chen. All rights reserved.
 */
#include <stdio.h>
#include <unistd.h>
```

322

```c
int main(int argc, char *argv[])
{
  long  val;

  fprintf(stdout, "AIO_LISTIO_MAX = %ld\n", sysconf(_SC_AIO_LISTIO_MAX));
  fprintf(stdout, "AIO_MAX = %ld\n", sysconf(_SC_AIO_MAX));
  fprintf(stdout, "ASYNCHRONOUS_IO = %ld\n", sysconf(_SC_ASYNCHRONOUS_IO));
  fprintf(stdout, "ARG_MAX = %ld\n", sysconf(_SC_ARG_MAX));
  fprintf(stdout, "BC_BASE_MAX = %ld\n", sysconf(_SC_BC_BASE_MAX));
  fprintf(stdout, "BC_DIM_MAX = %ld\n", sysconf(_SC_BC_DIM_MAX));
  fprintf(stdout, "BC_SCALE_MAX = %ld\n", sysconf(_SC_BC_SCALE_MAX));
  fprintf(stdout, "BC_STRING_MAX = %ld\n", sysconf(_SC_BC_STRING_MAX));
  fprintf(stdout, "CHILD_MAX = %ld\n", sysconf(_SC_CHILD_MAX));
  fprintf(stdout, "CLK_TCK = %ld\n", sysconf(_SC_CLK_TCK));
  fprintf(stdout, "COLL_WEIGHTS_MAX = %ld\n", sysconf(_SC_COLL_WEIGHTS_MAX));
  fprintf(stdout, "DELAYTIMER_MAX = %ld\n", sysconf(_SC_DELAYTIMER_MAX));
  fprintf(stdout, "EXPR_NEST_MAX = %ld\n", sysconf(_SC_EXPR_NEST_MAX));
  fprintf(stdout, "JOB_CONTROL = %ld\n", sysconf(_SC_JOB_CONTROL));
  fprintf(stdout, "IOV_MAX = %ld\n", sysconf(_SC_IOV_MAX));
#ifdef AIX
  fprintf(stdout, "LARGE_PAGESIZE = %ld\n", sysconf(_SC_LARGE_PAGESIZE));
#endif
  fprintf(stdout, "LINE_MAX = %ld\n", sysconf(_SC_LINE_MAX));
  fprintf(stdout, "LOGIN_NAME_MAX = %ld\n", sysconf(_SC_LOGIN_NAME_MAX));
  fprintf(stdout, "MQ_OPEN_MAX = %ld\n", sysconf(_SC_MQ_OPEN_MAX));
  fprintf(stdout, "MQ_PRIO_MAX = %ld\n", sysconf(_SC_MQ_PRIO_MAX));
  fprintf(stdout, "MEMLOCK = %ld\n", sysconf(_SC_MEMLOCK));
  fprintf(stdout, "MEMLOCK_RANGE = %ld\n", sysconf(_SC_MEMLOCK_RANGE));
  fprintf(stdout, "MEMORY_PROTECTION = %ld\n", sysconf(_SC_MEMORY_PROTECTION));
  fprintf(stdout, "MESSAGE_PASSING = %ld\n", sysconf(_SC_MESSAGE_PASSING));
  fprintf(stdout, "NGROUPS_MAX = %ld\n", sysconf(_SC_NGROUPS_MAX));
  fprintf(stdout, "OPEN_MAX = %ld\n", sysconf(_SC_OPEN_MAX));
  fprintf(stdout, "PASS_MAX = %ld\n", sysconf(_SC_PASS_MAX));
  fprintf(stdout, "PAGESIZE = %ld\n", sysconf(_SC_PAGESIZE));
  fprintf(stdout, "PAGE_SIZE = %ld\n", sysconf(_SC_PAGE_SIZE));
  fprintf(stdout, "PRIORITIZED_IO = %ld\n", sysconf(_SC_PRIORITIZED_IO));
  fprintf(stdout, "PRIORITY_SCHEDULING = %ld\n", sysconf(_SC_PRIORITY_SCHEDULING));
  fprintf(stdout, "RE_DUP_MAX = %ld\n", sysconf(_SC_RE_DUP_MAX));
  fprintf(stdout, "RTSIG_MAX = %ld\n", sysconf(_SC_RTSIG_MAX));
  fprintf(stdout, "REALTIME_SIGNALS = %ld\n", sysconf(_SC_REALTIME_SIGNALS));
  fprintf(stdout, "SAVED_IDS = %ld\n", sysconf(_SC_SAVED_IDS));
  fprintf(stdout, "SEM_NSEMS_MAX = %ld\n", sysconf(_SC_SEM_NSEMS_MAX));
  fprintf(stdout, "SEM_VALUE_MAX = %ld\n", sysconf(_SC_SEM_VALUE_MAX));
  fprintf(stdout, "SEMAPHORES = %ld\n", sysconf(_SC_SEMAPHORES));
  fprintf(stdout, "SHARED_MEMORY_OBJECTS = %ld\n",
sysconf(_SC_SHARED_MEMORY_OBJECTS));
  fprintf(stdout, "SIGQUEUE_MAX = %ld\n", sysconf(_SC_SIGQUEUE_MAX));
  fprintf(stdout, "STREAM_MAX = %ld\n", sysconf(_SC_STREAM_MAX));
  fprintf(stdout, "SYNCHRONIZED_IO = %ld\n", sysconf(_SC_SYNCHRONIZED_IO));
  fprintf(stdout, "TIMER_MAX = %ld\n", sysconf(_SC_TIMER_MAX));
  fprintf(stdout, "TIMERS = %ld\n", sysconf(_SC_TIMERS));
  fprintf(stdout, "TZNAME_MAX = %ld\n", sysconf(_SC_TZNAME_MAX));
  fprintf(stdout, "VERSION = %ld\n", sysconf(_SC_VERSION));
  fprintf(stdout, "XBS5_ILP32_OFF32 = %ld\n", sysconf(_SC_XBS5_ILP32_OFF32));
  fprintf(stdout, "XBS5_ILP32_OFFBIG = %ld\n", sysconf(_SC_XBS5_ILP32_OFFBIG));
  fprintf(stdout, "XBS5_LP64_OFF64 = %ld\n", sysconf(_SC_XBS5_LP64_OFF64));
```

```
  fprintf(stdout, "XBS5_LPBIG_OFFBIG = %ld\n", sysconf(_SC_XBS5_LPBIG_OFFBIG));
  fprintf(stdout, "XOPEN_CRYPT = %ld\n", sysconf(_SC_XOPEN_CRYPT));
  fprintf(stdout, "XOPEN_LEGACY = %ld\n", sysconf(_SC_XOPEN_LEGACY));
  fprintf(stdout, "XOPEN_REALTIME = %ld\n", sysconf(_SC_XOPEN_REALTIME));
  fprintf(stdout, "XOPEN_REALTIME_THREADS = %ld\n",
sysconf(_SC_XOPEN_REALTIME_THREADS));
  fprintf(stdout, "XOPEN_ENH_I18N = %ld\n", sysconf(_SC_XOPEN_ENH_I18N));
  fprintf(stdout, "XOPEN_SHM = %ld\n", sysconf(_SC_XOPEN_SHM));
  fprintf(stdout, "XOPEN_VERSION = %ld\n", sysconf(_SC_XOPEN_VERSION));
#ifndef HPUX
  fprintf(stdout, "XOPEN_XCU_VERSION = %ld\n", sysconf(_SC_XOPEN_XCU_VERSION));
#endif
  fprintf(stdout, "ATEXIT_MAX = %ld\n", sysconf(_SC_ATEXIT_MAX));
  fprintf(stdout, "PAGE_SIZE = %ld\n", sysconf(_SC_PAGE_SIZE));
#ifdef AIX
  fprintf(stdout, "AES_OS_VERSION = %ld\n", sysconf(_SC_AES_OS_VERSION));
#endif
  fprintf(stdout, "2_VERSION = %ld\n", sysconf(_SC_2_VERSION));
  fprintf(stdout, "2_C_BIND = %ld\n", sysconf(_SC_2_C_BIND));
  fprintf(stdout, "2_C_DEV = %ld\n", sysconf(_SC_2_C_DEV));
#ifndef __APPLE__
  fprintf(stdout, "2_C_VERSION = %ld\n", sysconf(_SC_2_C_VERSION));
#endif
  fprintf(stdout, "2_FORT_DEV = %ld\n", sysconf(_SC_2_FORT_DEV));
  fprintf(stdout, "2_FORT_RUN = %ld\n", sysconf(_SC_2_FORT_RUN));
  fprintf(stdout, "2_LOCALEDEF = %ld\n", sysconf(_SC_2_LOCALEDEF));
  fprintf(stdout, "2_SW_DEV = %ld\n", sysconf(_SC_2_SW_DEV));
  fprintf(stdout, "2_UPE = %ld\n", sysconf(_SC_2_UPE));
#ifndef HPUX
  fprintf(stdout, "NPROCESSORS_CONF = %ld\n", sysconf(_SC_NPROCESSORS_CONF));
  fprintf(stdout, "NPROCESSORS_ONLN = %ld\n", sysconf(_SC_NPROCESSORS_ONLN));
#endif
#ifdef AIX
  fprintf(stdout, "THREAD_DATAKEYS_MAX = %ld\n", sysconf(_SC_THREAD_DATAKEYS_MAX));
#endif
  fprintf(stdout, "THREAD_DESTRUCTOR_ITERATIONS = %ld\n",
sysconf(_SC_THREAD_DESTRUCTOR_ITERATIONS));
  fprintf(stdout, "THREAD_KEYS_MAX = %ld\n", sysconf(_SC_THREAD_KEYS_MAX));
  fprintf(stdout, "THREAD_STACK_MIN = %ld\n", sysconf(_SC_THREAD_STACK_MIN));
  fprintf(stdout, "THREAD_THREADS_MAX = %ld\n", sysconf(_SC_THREAD_THREADS_MAX));
#ifdef AIX
  fprintf(stdout, "REENTRANT_FUNCTIONS = %ld\n", sysconf(_SC_REENTRANT_FUNCTIONS));
#endif
  fprintf(stdout, "THREADS = %ld\n", sysconf(_SC_THREADS));
  fprintf(stdout, "THREAD_ATTR_STACKADDR = %ld\n",
sysconf(_SC_THREAD_ATTR_STACKADDR));
  fprintf(stdout, "THREAD_ATTR_STACKSIZE = %ld\n",
sysconf(_SC_THREAD_ATTR_STACKSIZE));
  fprintf(stdout, "THREAD_PRIORITY_SCHEDULING = %ld\n",
sysconf(_SC_THREAD_PRIORITY_SCHEDULING));
  fprintf(stdout, "THREAD_PRIO_INHERIT = %ld\n", sysconf(_SC_THREAD_PRIO_INHERIT));
  fprintf(stdout, "THREAD_PRIO_PROTECT = %ld\n", sysconf(_SC_THREAD_PRIO_PROTECT));
  fprintf(stdout, "THREAD_PROCESS_SHARED = %ld\n",
sysconf(_SC_THREAD_PROCESS_SHARED));
  fprintf(stdout, "TTY_NAME_MAX = %ld\n", sysconf(_SC_TTY_NAME_MAX));
  fprintf(stdout, "SYNCHRONIZED_IO = %ld\n", sysconf(_SC_SYNCHRONIZED_IO));
```

```
  fprintf(stdout, "FSYNC = %ld\n", sysconf(_SC_FSYNC));
  fprintf(stdout, "MAPPED_FILES = %ld\n", sysconf(_SC_MAPPED_FILES));
#ifdef AIX
  fprintf(stdout, "LPAR_ENABLED = %ld\n", sysconf(_SC_LPAR_ENABLED));
  fprintf(stdout, "AIX_KERNEL_BITMODE = %ld\n", sysconf(_SC_AIX_KERNEL_BITMODE));
  fprintf(stdout, "AIX_REALMEM = %ld\n", sysconf(_SC_AIX_REALMEM));
  fprintf(stdout, "AIX_HARDWARE_BITMODE = %ld\n", sysconf(_SC_AIX_HARDWARE_BITMODE));
  fprintf(stdout, "AIX_UKEYS = %ld\n", sysconf(_SC_AIX_UKEYS));
  /* root user only */
  fprintf(stdout, "AIX_MP_CAPABLE = %ld\n", sysconf(_SC_AIX_MP_CAPABLE));
#endif
}
```

7-9 The system() Function

One of the main topics in this chapter is creating a new process to run a new program. For completeness, we need to mention that there is an alternative way of running a new program. It is simpler but at the same time with less control.

The system() function allows you to run a Bourne shell (/bin/sh or /usr/bin/sh) command from within a program. Note that this function runs the specified command using a Bourne shell. The interface is shown below:

```
#include <stdlib.h>

int system(const char *command);
```

As shown above, the system() function invokes the sh shell to execute the command specified in the only argument to the function. The command can be a binary executable or even a shell script.

The system() function first calls the fork() function to create a child process. It then uses one of the exec() functions to run the /bin/sh or /usr/bin/sh shell, which in turn runs the command specified in the argument.

The calling process waits until the shell has completed and then returns the exit status of the shell. If the specified command was run, the exit status of the shell is indeed the exit status of the command.
The exit status of the shell is returned in the same format as a call to the wait() or waitpid() function. Hence, to extract the actual return status value, the calling process must use the WEXITSTATUS(status) macro.

The output from the command run by the sh shell is displayed on the current terminal.

The system() function returns -1 on error. For instance, if it fails to fork or shell's status can't be obtained. If fork() succeeds but the command can not be executed by the shell, then it returns 127. If the specified command is executed, the function returns the exit status of the command executed.

Figure 7-17 shows a program using the system() function.
Notice that to extract the command's exit status value, the program calling the system() function must use the WEXITSTATUS(status) macro.

Figure 7-17 Run a program using the system() function (system.c)

```c
/*
 * Run a new program using the system() function.
 * Copyright (c) 2013, 2014, 2019  Mr. Jin-Jwei Chen. All rights reserved.
 */

#include <stdio.h>
#include <errno.h>
#include <stdlib.h>
#include <sys/types.h>
#include <sys/wait.h>

#define  MYCMD  "/bin/echo 'Hello, there!'"   /* the command to run by default */

int main(int argc, char *argv[])
{
  int     ret = 0;
  char    *cmd = MYCMD;   /* the command to run */

  /* Get the command from the user if there is one */
  if (argc > 1)
    cmd = argv[1];

  /* Run the command */
  ret = system(cmd);
  if (ret == -1)
  {
    /* The first fork() failed */
    fprintf(stderr, "Calling system() failed, errno=%d\n", errno);
    return(1);
  }
  else
    /* The shell was up */
    fprintf(stdout, "Running the command %s returned %d\n", cmd, WEXITSTATUS(ret));

  return(0);
}
```

7-10 Process Resource Limits

Each process has a limit in using many system resources. Examples of these resources include the maximum number of files a process can open, the maximum amount of CPU time it can use, maximum size of its stack, and so on.

The POSIX standard defines getrlimit() function for querying a process's resource limits and setrlimit() function for changing them.

```c
    #include <sys/resource.h>

    int getrlimit(int resource, struct rlimit *rlp);
    int setrlimit(int resource, const struct rlimit *rlp); [Option End]
```

Each resource has a soft limit and a hard limit. The soft limit is the

current limit value set for the resource. The **hard limit** is the absolute
maximum (i.e. ceiling) value that the soft limit can be up-tuned to.

A resource limit is represented by a rlimit structure.
The structure member rlim_cur specifies the current or soft limit and
the member rlim_max specifies the maximum or hard limit.

```
struct rlimit {
    rlim_t rlim_cur;  /* Soft limit */
    rlim_t rlim_max;  /* Hard limit (ceiling for rlim_cur) */
};
```

The value RLIM_INFINITY denotes no limit on a resource. This value can be
returned by the getrlimit(). It can also be used as an input in setrlimit().
It means the operating system implementation shall not enforce limits on
that resource.

7-10-1 Getting Limits of Process Resources

The following resources are defined in the POSIX standard.

RLIMIT_CORE
  The maximum size of a core file in bytes.
  Setting this limit to 0 prevents creation of a core file.
  If this limit is exceeded, creating a core file should stop at this limit.

RLIMIT_CPU
  The maximum amount of CPU time in seconds that a process can use.
  If this limit is exceeded, signal SIGXCPU is generated for the process.
  If the process is catching or ignoring SIGXCPU, or all threads belonging
  to that process are blocking SIGXCPU, the behavior is undefined.

RLIMIT_DATA
  The maximum size of a data segment of the process, in bytes.
  This is the sum of uninitialized data, initialized data and heap.
  If this limit is exceeded, the malloc() function shall fail with errno
  set to ENOMEM.

RLIMIT_FSIZE
  The maximum size of a file, in bytes, that may be created by a process.
  If a write or truncate operation would cause this limit to be exceeded,
  SIGXFSZ will be generated for the thread. If the thread is blocking, or
  the process is catching or ignoring SIGXFSZ, continued attempts to increase
  the size of a file from end-of-file to beyond the limit will fail with
  the errno set to EFBIG.

RLIMIT_NOFILE
  Maximum number of open files a process can have. The maximum value of an
  open file descriptor is one less than this number. This limit constrains
  the number of files a process may have open.
  If this limit is exceeded, functions that allocate a file descriptor will
  fail with errno set to EMFILE.

  If a process attempts to set the hard limit or soft limit for RLIMIT_NOFILE
  to less than the value of {_POSIX_OPEN_MAX} from <limits.h>,

unexpected behavior may occur.

If a process attempts to set the hard limit or soft limit for RLIMIT_NOFILE
to less than the highest currently open file descriptor +1, unexpected
behavior may occur.

RLIMIT_STACK
    The maximum size of stack of the initial thread in bytes.
    The stack of a thread cannot grow beyond this limit.
    If this limit is exceeded, SIGSEGV signal is generated for the thread.
    If the thread is blocking SIGSEGV, or the process is ignoring or catching
    SIGSEGV and has not made arrangements to use an alternate stack, the
    disposition of SIGSEGV will be set to SIG_DFL before it is generated.

    Note that RLIMIT_STACK applies "at least" to the stack of the initial
    thread in the process, and not to the sum of all the stacks in the process.

RLIMIT_AS
    The maximum size of total available memory of the process, in bytes.
    If this limit is exceeded, the malloc() and mmap() functions will fail
    with errno set to ENOMEM. In addition, the automatic stack growth fails
    with the effects stated above.

Note that many operating systems support querying and/or changing limits of
more resources than the POSIX list above. Below is just a very small sample.
For a complete list of resource limits supported in your operating system,
please reference its documentation or run the 'man getrlimit' command.

RLIMIT_NPROC
    The maximum number of threads/processes that can be created for the real
    user ID of the calling process. Upon encountering this limit, fork()
    fails with the error EAGAIN.

RLIMIT_NICE
    This specifies a ceiling to which the process's nice (scheduling priority)
    value can be raised using setpriority() or nice() function.

RLIMIT_RSS
    This is the limit (in pages) of the process's resident set -- the number
    of memory pages currently resident in physical memory.

The getrlimit() function returns zero on success. On error, it returns -1
and errno is set to indicate the error.

When using the getrlimit() function, if a resource limit can be represented
correctly in an object of type rlim_t, then its representation is returned;
otherwise, if the value of the resource limit is equal to that of the
corresponding saved hard limit, the value returned is RLIM_SAVED_MAX;
otherwise, the value returned is RLIM_SAVED_CUR.

The exec() family of functions causes resource limits to be saved.

Figure 7-18 is a simple program querying some of a process's resource limits.

Figure 7-18 Getting a process's resource limits (getrlimit.c)

```c
/*
 * Get resource limits of a process.
 * Copyright (c) 2019, 2020  Mr. Jin-Jwei Chen. All rights reserved.
 */

#include <stdio.h>
#include <errno.h>
#include <stdlib.h>
#include <sys/types.h>
#include <sys/resource.h>

#define RSCNAME_LEN   24
#define NUM_RSCNAMES 16

struct rscname
{
  unsigned int  idx;
  char          rscname[RSCNAME_LEN+1];
};

struct rscname  names[NUM_RSCNAMES] =
{
  0,   "RLIMIT_CPU",
  1,   "RLIMIT_FSIZE",
  2,   "RLIMIT_DATA",
  3,   "RLIMIT_STACK",
  4,   "RLIMIT_CORE",
  5,   "__RLIMIT_RSS",
  6,   "__RLIMIT_NPROC",
  7,   "RLIMIT_NOFILE",
  8,   "__RLIMIT_MEMLOCK",
  9,   "RLIMIT_AS",
  10,  "__RLIMIT_LOCKS",
  11,  "__RLIMIT_SIGPENDING",
  12,  "__RLIMIT_MSGQUEUE",
  13,  "__RLIMIT_NICE",
  14,  "__RLIMIT_RTPRIO",
  15,  "__RLIMIT_NLIMITS"
};

void print_resrc_limit(unsigned int idx, struct rlimit *limit)
{
  if (limit == NULL)
    return;
  fprintf(stdout, "The limit of %s is \n", names[idx].rscname);
  fprintf(stdout, "  Soft limit: ");
  if (limit->rlim_cur == RLIM_INFINITY)
    fprintf(stdout, "unlimited.\n");
  else
    fprintf(stdout, "%lu.\n", limit->rlim_cur);
  fprintf(stdout, "  Hard limit: ");
  if (limit->rlim_max == RLIM_INFINITY)
    fprintf(stdout, "unlimited.\n");
  else
    fprintf(stdout, "%lu.\n", limit->rlim_max);
}
```

```c
int main(int argc, char *argv[])
{
  int     ret = 0;
  struct rlimit  limit;  /* limit of resource */

  /* Get current limit of the RLIMIT_NOFILE resource */
  ret = getrlimit(RLIMIT_NOFILE, &limit);
  if (ret < 0)
  {
    fprintf(stderr, "getrlimit(RLIMIT_NOFILE) failed , errno=%d\n", errno);
    return(1);
  }
  print_resrc_limit(RLIMIT_NOFILE, &limit);

  /* Get current limit of the RLIMIT_STACK resource */
  ret = getrlimit(RLIMIT_STACK, &limit);
  if (ret < 0)
  {
    fprintf(stderr, "getrlimit(RLIMIT_STACK) failed , errno=%d\n", errno);
    return(1);
  }
  print_resrc_limit(RLIMIT_STACK, &limit);

  /* Get current limit of the RLIMIT_CPU resource */
  ret = getrlimit(RLIMIT_CPU, &limit);
  if (ret < 0)
  {
    fprintf(stderr, "getrlimit(RLIMIT_CPU) failed , errno=%d\n", errno);
    return(1);
  }
  print_resrc_limit(RLIMIT_CPU, &limit);

  /* Get current limit of the RLIMIT_FSIZE resource */
  ret = getrlimit(RLIMIT_FSIZE, &limit);
  if (ret < 0)
  {
    fprintf(stderr, "getrlimit(RLIMIT_FSIZE) failed , errno=%d\n", errno);
    return(1);
  }
  print_resrc_limit(RLIMIT_FSIZE, &limit);

  /* Get current limit of the RLIMIT_DATA resource */
  ret = getrlimit(RLIMIT_DATA, &limit);
  if (ret < 0)
  {
    fprintf(stderr, "getrlimit(RLIMIT_DATA) failed , errno=%d\n", errno);
    return(1);
  }
  print_resrc_limit(RLIMIT_DATA, &limit);

  /* Get current limit of the RLIMIT_AS resource */
  ret = getrlimit(RLIMIT_AS, &limit);
  if (ret < 0)
  {
    fprintf(stderr, "getrlimit(RLIMIT_AS) failed , errno=%d\n", errno);
```

```
      return(1);
   }
   print_resrc_limit(RLIMIT_AS, &limit);

   /* Get current limit of the RLIMIT_CORE resource */
   ret = getrlimit(RLIMIT_CORE, &limit);
   if (ret < 0)
   {
      fprintf(stderr, "getrlimit(RLIMIT_CORE) failed , errno=%d\n", errno);
      return(1);
   }
   print_resrc_limit(RLIMIT_CORE, &limit);

   return(0);
}
```

7-10-2 Setting Limits of Process Resources

An unprivileged process is allowed to set the soft limit of a process resource to a value in the range from 0 up to the hard limit.

However, normally changing the hard limit of a resource requires the process to have a super user privilege except one case.
A process may irreversibly lower its hard limit to any value that is equal to or greater than the current soft limit without super user privilege. But raising a hard limit is not permitted at any time without super user or appropriate privilege. Only a process with appropriate privileges can raise a hard limit.

Both hard and soft limits can be changed in a single call to setrlimit().

Figure 7-19 is another program changing both soft and hard limits of a resource.

   Figure 7-19 Setting a process's resource limits (setrlimit.c)

```
/*
 * Set resource limits of a process.
 * Changing the hard limit of a resource requires super user privilege.
 * Copyright (c) 2019, 2020  Mr. Jin-Jwei Chen. All rights reserved.
 */

#include <stdio.h>
#include <errno.h>
#include <stdlib.h>
#include <sys/types.h>
#include <sys/resource.h>

#define RSCNAME_LEN   24
#define NUM_RSCNAMES 16

struct rscname
{
   unsigned int  idx;
   char          rscname[RSCNAME_LEN+1];
};
```

```
struct rscname  names[NUM_RSCNAMES] =
{
  0,  "RLIMIT_CPU",
  1,  "RLIMIT_FSIZE",
  2,  "RLIMIT_DATA",
  3,  "RLIMIT_STACK",
  4,  "RLIMIT_CORE",
  5,  "__RLIMIT_RSS",
  6,  "__RLIMIT_NPROC",
  7,  "RLIMIT_NOFILE",
  8,  "__RLIMIT_MEMLOCK",
  9,  "RLIMIT_AS",
  10, "__RLIMIT_LOCKS",
  11, "__RLIMIT_SIGPENDING",
  12, "__RLIMIT_MSGQUEUE",
  13, "__RLIMIT_NICE",
  14, "__RLIMIT_RTPRIO",
  15, "__RLIMIT_NLIMITS"
};

void print_resrc_limit(unsigned int idx, struct rlimit *limit)
{
  if (limit == NULL)
    return;
  fprintf(stdout, "The limits of %s are: \n", names[idx].rscname);
  fprintf(stdout, "  Soft limit: ");
  if (limit->rlim_cur == RLIM_INFINITY)
    fprintf(stdout, "unlimited.\n");
  else
    fprintf(stdout, "%lu\n", limit->rlim_cur);
  fprintf(stdout, "  Hard limit: ");
  if (limit->rlim_max == RLIM_INFINITY)
    fprintf(stdout, "unlimited.\n");
  else
    fprintf(stdout, "%lu\n", limit->rlim_max);
}

int main(int argc, char *argv[])
{
  int     ret = 0;
  struct rlimit  limit;  /* limit of resource */

  /* Get current limit of the RLIMIT_NOFILE resource */
  ret = getrlimit(RLIMIT_NOFILE, &limit);
  if (ret < 0)
    {
    fprintf(stderr, "getrlimit(RLIMIT_NOFILE) failed , errno=%d\n", errno);
    return(1);
    }
  print_resrc_limit(RLIMIT_NOFILE, &limit);

  /* Raise the soft limit of the RLIMIT_NOFILE resource */
  fprintf(stdout, "\nTo raise the soft limit of RLIMIT_NOFILE resource...\n");
  limit.rlim_cur = limit.rlim_cur + 256;
  ret = setrlimit(RLIMIT_NOFILE, &limit);
```

```
 if (ret < 0)
 {
   fprintf(stderr, "setrlimit(RLIMIT_NOFILE) failed , errno=%d\n", errno);
   return(2);
 }
 fprintf(stdout, "setrlimit(RLIMIT_NOFILE) succeeded.\n");

 /* Get current limit of the RLIMIT_NOFILE resource */
 ret = getrlimit(RLIMIT_NOFILE, &limit);
 if (ret < 0)
 {
   fprintf(stderr, "getrlimit(RLIMIT_NOFILE) failed , errno=%d\n", errno);
   return(3);
 }
 print_resrc_limit(RLIMIT_NOFILE, &limit);

 /* Raise the hard limit of the RLIMIT_NOFILE resource, and soft limit too */
 fprintf(stdout, "\nTo raise the hard limit of RLIMIT_NOFILE resource...\n");
 limit.rlim_max = limit.rlim_max + (512);
 limit.rlim_cur = limit.rlim_cur + (1024);
 ret = setrlimit(RLIMIT_NOFILE, &limit);
 if (ret < 0)
 {
   fprintf(stderr, "setrlimit(RLIMIT_NOFILE) failed to raise the hard limit,"
     " errno=%d\n", errno);
   return(4);
 }
 fprintf(stdout, "setrlimit(RLIMIT_NOFILE) succeeded in raising the hard limit.\n");

 /* Get current limit of the RLIMIT_NOFILE resource */
 ret = getrlimit(RLIMIT_NOFILE, &limit);
 if (ret < 0)
 {
   fprintf(stderr, "getrlimit(RLIMIT_NOFILE) failed , errno=%d\n", errno);
   return(5);
 }
 print_resrc_limit(RLIMIT_NOFILE, &limit);

 return(0);
}
```

When using the setrlimit() function, if the requested new limit is
RLIM_INFINITY, the new limit will be "no limit"; otherwise, if the requested
new limit is RLIM_SAVED_MAX, the new limit will be the corresponding saved
hard limit; otherwise, if the requested new limit is RLIM_SAVED_CUR, the new
limit will be the corresponding saved soft limit; otherwise, the new limit
is the requested value. In addition, if the corresponding saved limit can be
represented correctly in an object of type rlim_t then it will be overwritten
with the new limit.

The result of setting a limit to RLIM_SAVED_MAX or RLIM_SAVED_CUR is undefined
unless a previous call to getrlimit() returned that value as the soft or hard
limit for that resource.

Determining if a limit can be correctly represented in an object of type
rlim_t is operating system implementation-dependent. For instance, some

implementations permit a limit whose value is greater than RLIM_INFINITY and others do not.

It's worth mentioning that at command line prompt, each Shell has a built-in command for you to get the user's resource limits. The built-in shell command is 'ulimit' for Bourne shell and Korn shell and is 'limit' for C shell.

```
$ sh
sh-3.2$ ulimit -all
core file size          (blocks, -c) 0
data seg size           (kbytes, -d) unlimited
scheduling priority           (-e) 0
file size               (blocks, -f) unlimited
pending signals               (-i) 15985
max locked memory       (kbytes, -l) 64
max memory size         (kbytes, -m) unlimited
open files                    (-n) 1024
pipe size           (512 bytes, -p) 8
POSIX message queues     (bytes, -q) 819200
real-time priority            (-r) 0
stack size              (kbytes, -s) 10240
cpu time               (seconds, -t) unlimited
max user processes            (-u) 2047
virtual memory          (kbytes, -v) unlimited
file locks                    (-x) unlimited

$ csh
$ limit
cputime        unlimited
filesize       unlimited
datasize       unlimited
stacksize      10240 kbytes
coredumpsize   0 kbytes
memoryuse      unlimited
vmemoryuse     unlimited
descriptors    1024
memorylocked   64 kbytes
maxproc        2047
```

In addition, each operating system typically has a system-wide common login environment and startup program. System-wide resource limits that apply to all users are normally set there. For instance, in Linux, it's /etc/profile, /etc/csh.login and /etc/csh.cshrc.

7-11 Other User and Group Related Functions

There are a number of other functions in POSIX that fall in the area of user and group that we need to cover here. These are mostly related to user login names and passwords.

7-11-1 The getlogin() Function

The getlogin() function allows you to find out the name of the user who logins to a controlling terminal.

```
#include <unistd.h>

char *getlogin(void);
int   getlogin_r(char *buf, size_t bufsize);
```

The getlogin() function returns a pointer to a string containing the name of the user logged in on the controlling terminal of the current process. Note that this function returns the original user that logins on the controlling terminal. For example, if the user that logged in was the root user and then it switched to the user smith, then the getlogin() function returns root instead of smith.

If the getlogin() function cannot get the information for some reason, it will return a NULL pointer.

Note that the memory space holding the string value returned by the getlogin() function is statically allocated. Therefore, its value can be overwritten by a subsequent call. For this reason, you should use the getlogin_r() function instead.

The getlogin_r() function is functionally the same as getlogin() except the calling process has to allocate the buffer to hold the returned string value. The starting address of this buffer and its length must be passed in as arguments to the getlogin_r() function. The length of the buffer must include one extra byte for the null character that is used to terminate each string value.

On success, the getlogin_r() function returns 0. On failure, it returns a non-zero value. For instance, if the allocated buffer is not big enough to hold the entire login name string, the getlogin_r() function returns ERANGE (34).

The maximum possible length of a login name is defined by the configurable parameter LOGIN_NAME_MAX, which is usually 256.
To get the macro for this limit so that you can use it in your program, your program must include the header file limits.h:

```
#include <limits.h>
```

Figure 7-20 is a program that demonstrates the use of both getlogin() and getlogin_r().

Figure 7-20 Get login name of current process (getlogin.c)

```
/*
 * The getlogin() and getlogin_r() functions.
 * Copyright (c) 2013, 2014 Mr. Jin-Jwei Chen. All rights reserved.
 */

#include <stdio.h>
#include <errno.h>
#include <unistd.h>     /* getlogin() */
#include <limits.h>     /* LOGIN_NAME_MAX */

int main(int argc, char *argv[])
```

```
{
  int   ret = 0;
  char  *loginname;
#ifdef SPARC_SOLARIS
  char  name[_POSIX_LOGIN_NAME_MAX+1];
#elif defined(__APPLE__)
  char  name[_POSIX_LOGIN_NAME_MAX+1];
#else
  char  name[LOGIN_NAME_MAX+1];
#endif

  /* Get the login name using getlogin() */
  loginname = getlogin();
  if (loginname != NULL)
    fprintf(stdout, "My login name returned from getlogin() is %s\n", loginname);
  else
  {
    fprintf(stderr, "getlogin() failed, ret=%d, errno=%d\n", ret, errno);
    ret = 1;
  }

  /* Get the login name using getlogin_r() */
#ifdef SPARC_SOLARIS
  loginname = getlogin_r(name, _POSIX_LOGIN_NAME_MAX);
#elif defined(__APPLE__)
  loginname = getlogin_r(name, _POSIX_LOGIN_NAME_MAX);
#else
  ret = getlogin_r(name, LOGIN_NAME_MAX);
#endif
  if (ret == 0)
    fprintf(stdout, "My login name returned from getlogin_r() is %s\n", name);
  else
  {
    fprintf(stderr, "getlogin_r() failed, ret=%d, errno=%d\n", ret, errno);
    ret = 2;
  }

  return(ret);
}
```

Note that both getlogin() and getlogin_r() functions are in POSIX standard. But I found there is a slight difference between operating systems on the length of a login name. As shown below, some operating systems (e.g. Linux and AIX) use LOGIN_NAME_MAX while Oracle/Sun Solaris and Apple Darwin use _POSIX_LOGIN_NAME_MAX.

Linux and AIX:

```
  int  ret;
  char  name[LOGIN_NAME_MAX+1];
  ret = getlogin_r(name, LOGIN_NAME_MAX);
```

Solaris and Apple Darwin:
```
  char  *loginname;
  char  name[_POSIX_LOGIN_NAME_MAX+1];
  loginname = getlogin_r(name, _POSIX_LOGIN_NAME_MAX);
```

7-11-2 The getpwnam(), getpwuid() and getpwent() Functions

```
#include <sys/types.h>
#include <pwd.h>

struct passwd *getpwuid(uid_t uid);
struct passwd *getpwnam(const char *name);

int getpwuid_r(uid_t uid, struct passwd *pwbuf,
        char *buf, size_t buflen, struct passwd **pwbufp);
int getpwnam_r(const char *name, struct passwd *pwbuf,
        char *buf, size_t buflen, struct passwd **pwbufp);
```

In a POSIX compliant operating system, there is usually a file (e.g.
/etc/passwd) that stores the name, user id, group id, home directory,
and login shell of each of the users who has an account on the system.
Each time a new user account is created on the system, a new corresponding
entry is added to this file. The format of the entries in this file is
as follows:

```
jsmith:x:1100:500::/home/jsmith:/bin/bash
```

The fields in this entry are: user's login name, password (which is
hidden. That's why it is shown as 'x'.), uid (user id), gid (group id),
home directory, and login shell.

There is a data structure defined to hold this information for processing.
It is the type 'struct passwd', which is typically defined in <pwd.h>.

```
/* The passwd structure.  */
struct passwd
{
  char *pw_name;              /* Username.  */
  char *pw_passwd;            /* Password.  */
  __uid_t pw_uid;            /* User ID.  */
  __gid_t pw_gid;            /* Group ID.  */
  char *pw_gecos;             /* Real name.  */
  char *pw_dir;               /* Home directory.  */
  char *pw_shell;             /* Shell program.  */
};
```

The getpwuid() and getpwnam() functions allow programs to look up this
password file entry by a given user id (uid) or login name, respectively.

Again, there are two versions of these functions. The first version,
getpwuid() and getpwnam(), takes the uid or login name as the input argument
and returns a pointer to struct passwd holding the structure data. However,
the information returned is stored in a static memory area and its value can
be overwritten by subsequent calls to the same function. Therefore, for
safety, it's recommended that you use the second version, getpwuid_r() and
getpwnam_r(). Note that not every operating system supports the second
version yet as of this writing. But most of them do, e.g. Linux and Unix.
In case the operating system you use does not support the getpwuid_r() or

getpwnam_r(), you will have to use the version without the _r and copy the results aside to somewhere else.

The second version is a bit different because it uses a pointer to a structure with many structure elements that are pointers to string values themselves. First, the first four arguments of the functions are input and the last (fifth) is the output. The last argument is like the return value of the getpwuid()/getpwnam(). It returns a pointer to the result in case of success or NULL in case of errors or entry not found. After the function call, in case of success, this returned pointer value should equal to the value of the second input argument (pwbuf).

The rest of arguments are input. First, your program needs to allocate a structure of 'struct passwd' and pass its starting address in the second argument, pwbuf. When the function call returns, if successful, the values of the members in the structure will be filled in. Since many members in the structure are in turn pointers to string values which have variable sizes, your program must allocate another buffer that is big enough to hold all of these string values. And you need to pass the starting address of this buffer in the third argument and its size in the fourth argument.

You are probably already asking "How do I know how much space is needed for this buffer?" Good question. The maximum size of this buffer can be obtained by querying the _SC_GETPW_R_SIZE_MAX configurable parameter using sysconf().

The getpwnam_r() and getpwuid_r() functions return zero on success. They return the error number in case of an error. For instance, if you pass in a NULL buffer, it will return ERANGE (34).

Note that all of the getpwuid(), getpwnam(), getpwuid_r() and getpwnam_r() functions are in the POSIX standard. However, there seems to be a slight difference in Solaris as shown below. The Solaris' _r version of the functions do not use the fifth argument. Instead, a pointer to the 'struct passwd' is returned by the functions. IBM AIX and Apple Darwin are the same as Linux in these two function calls.

Linux, AIX and Apple Darwin:

```
    int getpwuid_r(uid_t uid, struct passwd *pwbuf,
            char *buf, size_t buflen, struct passwd **pwbufp);
    int getpwnam_r(const char *name, struct passwd *pwbuf,
            char *buf, size_t buflen, struct passwd **pwbufp);
```

Solaris:

```
    struct passwd *getpwuid_r(uid_t uid, struct passwd *pwbuf,
            char *buf, size_t buflen);
    struct passwd *getpwnam_r(const char *name, struct passwd *pwbuf,
            char *buf, size_t buflen);
```

Figure 7-21 is a program demonstrating how to use the getpwuid_r() function. Notice that this program uses the sysconf() function to get the maximum size of buffer needed by the getpwuid_r() function. It also invokes the malloc() function to dynamically allocate the buffer space in the process's heap. Then it calls the geteuid() function to get the current process' effective

338

user id and uses the output as the first argument to the getpwuid_r()
function. The program always frees the dynamic memory regardless of whether
it runs successfully or incurs an error so that there is no memory leak.

Exactly the same thing can be done by using the getpwnam_r() function
instead of the getpwuid_r(), as well as using the output of getlogin()
to provide the first argument. We will leave this as a homework.

Figure 7-21 Get password file entry using getpwuid_r() (getpwuid_r.c)

```c
/*
 * The getpwuid_r() function.
 * Copyright (c) 2013, 2014, 2020 Mr. Jin-Jwei Chen. All rights reserved.
 */

#include <stdio.h>
#include <errno.h>
#include <sys/types.h>
#include <pwd.h>            /* getpwuid_r(), getpwnam_r() */
#include <unistd.h>       /* sysconf() */
#include <stdlib.h>       /* malloc(), free() */
#include <string.h>        /* memset() */

int main(int argc, char *argv[])
{
  int    ret;
  long   buflen;      /* maximum buffer size */
  struct passwd   pwbuf;
  struct passwd   *pwbufp = NULL;
  char            *buf = NULL;      /* pointer to the buffer for string values */

  /* Get the value of the _SC_GETPW_R_SIZE_MAX parameter */
  buflen = sysconf(_SC_GETPW_R_SIZE_MAX);
  if (buflen == -1)
  {
    fprintf(stderr, "sysconf() failed, errno=%d\n", errno);
    return(1);
  }
  fprintf(stdout, "buflen=%ld\n", buflen);

  /* Allocate memory for the buffer */
  buf = (char *)malloc(buflen);
  if (buf == NULL)
  {
    fprintf(stderr, "malloc() failed\n");
    return(2);
  }
  memset((void *)buf, 0, buflen);

  /* Get the password file entry using getpwuid_r() */
#ifdef SPARC_SOLARIS
  pwbufp = getpwuid_r(geteuid(), &pwbuf, buf, buflen);
#else
  ret = getpwuid_r(geteuid(), &pwbuf, buf, buflen, &pwbufp);
#endif
  if (ret != 0)
```

```
{
    fprintf(stderr, "getpwuid_r() failed, ret=%d\n", ret);
    free(buf);
    return(3);
}

/* Print the values of 'struct passwd' */
fprintf(stdout, "User name = %s\n", pwbuf.pw_name);
fprintf(stdout, "User id   = %u\n", pwbuf.pw_uid);
fprintf(stdout, "Group id  = %u\n", pwbuf.pw_gid);
fprintf(stdout, "Home directory = %s\n", pwbuf.pw_dir);
fprintf(stdout, "Login shell    = %s\n", pwbuf.pw_shell);

fprintf(stdout, "&pwbuf=%p pwbufp=%p\n", &pwbuf, pwbufp);

/* Free the dynamically allocated memory and return */
free(buf);
return(0);
}
```

The getpwent() Function

By the way, in case your program needs to walk through the entries in the password file (or the so-called user "database" file), use the getpwent() function in that case. It takes no argument and returns a pointer to 'struct passwd' or NULL.

```
#include <sys/types.h>
#include <pwd.h>

struct passwd *getpwent(void);
void setpwent(void);
void endpwent(void);
```

On the first call, the getpwent() function opens the password file/database, reads its first entry and returns a pointer to a passwd structure containing the first entry in the file. Thereafter, on successive calls, the function will return the next entries in the user password file. Therefore, by putting the call in a loop, a program can search the entire password file/database, getting one entry back from the password fie at a time.

The getpwent() function returns a null pointer when an end-of-file or an error is encountered.

The setpwent() function rewinds the user database so that the next getpwent() call returns the first entry, allowing repeated searches.

The endpwent() function closes the password file.

The setpwent() and endpwent() functions do not change the setting of errno if successful.

The errno variable will be set to indicate the error if an error occurs.

7-11-3 The getgrnam() and getgrgid() Functions

Just as there is a /etc/passwd file for the user information, there is also a /etc/group file that stores information about all user groups that exist on the system. The format of the entries in the group file is like the following:

    dba:x:501:oracle,ldap,oracle1

The first field is the name of the group. The second field is the group password. The third field is the id of the group. The fourth field is a list of user names who belong to this group. In this example, the name of the group is 'dba'. The group id of the group is 501. And there are currently three users belonging to this group: oracle, ldap and oracle1.

Similar to the APIs listed in the preceding section for user information, a program can look up the information about a group either via the group id or group name by invoking the getgrgid() or getgrnam() function, respectively. And the information returned here is a 'struct group' structure which is defined in the header file grp.h as follows:

```
/* The group structure.  */
struct group
  {
    char *gr_name;          /* Group name.  */
    char *gr_passwd;        /* Password.    */
    __gid_t gr_gid;         /* Group ID.    */
    char **gr_mem;          /* Member list. */
  };
```

Below are the interfaces of the APIs for obtaining group information.

```
    #include <sys/types.h>
    #include <grp.h>

    struct group *getgrgid(gid_t gid);
    struct group *getgrnam(const char *name);

    int getgrgid_r(gid_t gid, struct group *gbuf,
            char *buf, size_t buflen, struct group **gbufp);
    int getgrnam_r(const char *name, struct group *gbuf,
            char *buf, size_t buflen, struct group **gbufp);
```

Again, there are also two versions of the APIs: one with the returned information stored in a static area allocated by the system and can get overwritten by subsequent calls to the same function, and the other with the information returned in buffers allocated by the calling process.

Note that the getgrgid() and getgrnam() are in the POSIX standard and so are getgrgid_r() and getgrnam_r().

The getgrnam() and getgrgid() functions return a pointer to a group structure on success, or NULL on error or no matching entry can be found. If an error occurs, errno is set to indicate the error.

The getgrnam_r() and getgrgid_r() functions return zero on success.
They return the error number in case of error.

These functions are very similar to the functions in the preceding section.
Readers are encouraged to write programs using them.

Figure 7-22 is a program that looks up information about a group whose name
is provided by the user on the command line.

Figure 7-22 Look up information about a group (getgrnam_r.c)

```c
/*
 * The getgrnam_r() function.
 * Look up information about a group.
 * Copyright (c) 2013, 2014, 2019, 2020 Mr. Jin-Jwei Chen. All rights reserved.
 */

#include <stdio.h>
#include <errno.h>
#include <sys/types.h>
#include <grp.h>
#include <unistd.h>        /* sysconf() */
#include <stdlib.h>        /* malloc(), free() */
#include <string.h>        /* memset() */

#define DEFAULTGRP   "bin"

int main(int argc, char *argv[])
{
  int    ret, i;
  int    buflen;     /* maximum buffer size */
  struct group grpinfo;
  struct group *grpinfop = NULL;
  char         *buf = NULL;     /* pointer to the buffer for string values */
  char         *grpname = NULL;

  /* Get the name of the group from user */
  if (argc > 1)
    grpname = argv[1];
  else
    grpname = DEFAULTGRP;

  /* Get the value of the _SC_GETGR_R_SIZE_MAX parameter */
  buflen = sysconf(_SC_GETGR_R_SIZE_MAX);
  if (buflen == -1)
  {
    fprintf(stderr, "sysconf(_SC_GETGR_R_SIZE_MAX) failed.\n");
    return(1);
  }
  fprintf(stdout, "buflen=%u\n", buflen);

  /* Allocate memory for the buffer */
  buf = (char *)malloc(buflen);
  if (buf == NULL)
  {
    fprintf(stderr, "malloc() failed\n");
```

```
    return(2);
  }
  memset((void *)buf, 0, buflen);
  memset((void *)&grpinfo, 0, sizeof(grpinfo));

  /* Get the /etc/group file entry using getgrnam_r() */
#ifdef SPARC_SOLARIS
  ret = getgrnam_r(getlogin(), &grpinfo, buf, buflen);
#else
  ret = getgrnam_r(grpname, &grpinfo, buf, buflen, &grpinfop);
#endif
  if (ret != 0)
  {
    fprintf(stderr, "getgrnam_r() failed, ret=%d\n", ret);
    free(buf);
    return(3);
  }

  /* Print the values of 'struct passwd' */
  if (grpinfo.gr_name != NULL)
    fprintf(stdout, "Group name = %s\n", grpinfo.gr_name);
  fprintf(stdout, "Group id   = %u\n", grpinfo.gr_gid);
  for (i = 0; (grpinfo.gr_mem != NULL) && (grpinfo.gr_mem[i] != NULL); i++)
    fprintf(stdout, " %s ", grpinfo.gr_mem[i]);
  fprintf(stdout, "\n");

  /* Free the dynamically allocated memory and return */
  free(buf);
  return(0);
}
```

7-11-4 The getgroups() Function

```
#include <unistd.h>

int getgroups(int gidsetsize, gid_t grouplist[]);
```

The getgroups() function gets the current supplementary group IDs of the calling process. Depending on the implementation, getgroups() may also return the effective group ID. These group IDs are returned in the grouplist argument, which is an array of gid_t. The caller must allocate enough space so that grouplist can hold all of the group IDs. If not, getgroups() could fail and errno would be set to EINVAL(22). The gidsetsize argument specifies the number of elements in the array grouplist.

The actual number of group IDs can be obtained by calling the getgroups() function with a 0 in the gidsetsize argument.

Upon successful completion, the number of supplementary group IDs is returned as the return value of the getgroups() function. Upon failure, -1 is returned and errno shall be set to indicate the error. If the effective group ID of the process is returned with the supplementary group IDs, the value returned shall always be greater than or equal to one and less than or equal to the value of {NGROUPS_MAX}+1.

7-11-5 The getgid() and getegid() Functions

```
#include <unistd.h>
#include <sys/types.h>

gid_t getgid(void);
gid_t getegid(void);
```

The getgid() function returns the real group ID of the current process.
The getegid() function returns the effective group ID of the current process.
These two functions are always successful.

Questions

1. What is the real user id of a process?
   What is the effective user id of a process?

2. What is a process group?
   How can you change the process group of a process?

3. What is a session? What is it used for?

4. What is a session leader? How to create a session leader?

5. What is a controlling terminal?
   What privileges does the foreground process group for a controlling
   terminal have?

6. How does a process create a new child process?
   What does that function return?

7. What are the two steps in creating a new process to run a new
   program?

8. What happens after the fork() function succeeds?

9. What are the ways that the exec() functions locate a program to execute?

10. What happens after one of the exec() functions succeeds?

11. How does a parent process wait for a child?

12. What is a pipe? How can a parent process communicate with a child
    process using pipes?

13. What happens during the exit() function?

14. What are the differences between exit() and _exit() functions?

15. What is the advantage of terminating a program via return from main()
    or calling the exit() function instead of calling the _exit() or
    _Exit() function?

16. What does the atexit() function do?

17. What signal is sent to the parent process when a process terminates?

18. If a terminating process is a controlling process, what signal is sent to its children processes in the foreground when it terminates?

19. Does terminating a process automatically kill its children processes? When it does and when it does not?

20. What is a zombie process?
    What effect zombie processes have on the system?

21. What is an orphaned process?
    What happens when a process becomes orphaned?

22. How does a program get the limit of a configurable parameter?

Exercises

1. Write a program that creates a new process and runs a different program using the execvp() function.

2. Write a program that creates a child process but the parent does not wait for the child. Let the child exits before the parent. Use a command that lists processes, such as the 'ps' command in POSIX-compliant systems, to verify that the child process becomes a defunct process.
   You may need to let the parent sleep or continue to run for some time in order for you to observe this.

3. Write a program that creates a pair of pipes and a child process such that the parent process communicates with the child process using the pipes. The child process should accept commands from its parent, execute them and then send the results back to its parent.

4. Write a program that creates an orphaned process. Let the child process continues to run for 10 more seconds after the parent terminates. Use the process listing tool (e.g. the 'ps' command in POSIX systems) to observe the change in the parent process id of the orphaned child process.

5. Modify the example program waitpid.c so that each time it waits a specific process using the child process' process id, rather than to wait for any process.

6. Write a program that creates two child processes and uses the waitpid() function to wait for the child processes to terminate.
   Experiment it with using no options flags, using only the WNOHANG flag, and using only the WUNTRACED flag.

7. After studying the chapter on signals, write a program that creates a child process and sets to ignore the child process' termination by either setting the SA_NOCLDWAIT flag in the sigaction structure or setting the action of the SIGCHLD signal to SIG_IGN.

Don't wait on the child. Observe what happens when the child process terminates. Is the child removed from the system right away?

If you change the above program and make the parent wait on the child, does the behavior change?

8. Write a program that creates a child process which in turn creates two grandchildren. Print out the process group id of each of them. Do you see the three generations share the same process group id?

9. Write a program using the system() function to execute a C-shell shell script and observe what happens.

10. Write a program to get and print the values of fields in the user's password file entry (i.e. 'struct passwd') using the getpwnam_r() and getlogin() functions. (Hint: Use the output of the getlogin() function to provide the first argument to the getpwnam_r().)

11. Write a program to get and print the values of fields in the 'struct group' structure for the group that the user of the current process is in. If your system supports getgrgid_r(), use that. Otherwise, use getgrgid().

12. Write a simple program that writes a message to its stdout (file descriptor 1). Say, call it pipeprog1.c.

Write another small program which does nothing but reads a message from its stdin (file descriptor 0) and prints the message to its stdout. Name it pipeprog2.c.

Change the example program pipedup.c in Figure 7-12b and replace the write() call in the parent with an execlp() that execs pipeprog1. Also replace the read() call in the child with another execlp() that execs pipeprog2.

Do you get the same result from this new program?

13. Write a program that tries to lower the hard limit of a resource first and then tries to raise that same limit again. Run it as an unprivileged user first. Then run it as a privileged user. What is the difference you observe?

14. Write a program to search the password file and return the login home directory and login shell of a user.

References

1. The Open Group Base Specifications Issue 7, 2018 edition
   IEEE Std 1003.1™-2017 (Revision of IEEE Std 1003.1-2008)
   Copyright © 2001-2018 IEEE and The Open Group
   http://pubs.opengroup.org/onlinepubs/9699919799/

2. AT&T UNIX System V Release 4 Programmer's Guide: System Services
   Prentice-Hall, Inc. 1990

8 Pthreads Programming

This chapter introduces multithreaded programming using POSIX threads (pthreads, or pthread, as many people call it). The pthreads introduced here is an API originally defined by the standard POSIX.1c, Threads extensions (IEEE Std 1003.1c-1995). It is now part of "The Open Group Base Specifications Issue 7, 2018".

8-1 Why Multithreaded Programming?

8-1-1 Paradigm of Modern Server Programs

Modern programs, both clients and servers, and especially servers, often need to multitask -- to be able to perform multiple tasks at the same time. For instance, the most common server-side program that everyone is familiar with is probably the Web Server. A web server is a server side program which runs on some server machine that hosts a company's or person's web site. And there are millions of web sites around the world.
A web server's job is to listen to requests from clients (e.g. web browsers) coming in from potentially all over the world and service their requests. Clearly, if a web server is single-tasking and can handle only one request and hence one user at a time, its performance would be extremely slow and unacceptable. And Internet users around the world would not have the good experience they have today.

To service multiple clients at the same time and achieve acceptable performance, modern server programs including web servers are all multi-tasking, accepting and handling multiple requests at the same time. Essentially, the server just sits in a loop listening for connection requests. As soon as a request comes in, the server simply spawns a child process or thread, hands the request to the child, and lets it handles and

Figure 8-1 Main skeleton of a modern server program

```
TypicalServerProgram()
{
  forever
  {
    listen for a client's connect request
    spawn a child process or thread
    service client requests using the child process or thread created
  }
}
```

services that request so that the server itself can quickly go back and listen for the next request. Therefore, the main-line logic of a typical server program is like what is shown in Figure 8-1.

To optimize performance, some server may even pre-create a pool of working threads or processes and re-use them instead of creating them on the fly and destroying them after use each time. That approach will save the time of having to re-create the working children over and over again, at the cost of having to keep track of them.

8-1-2 Processes Versus Threads

As you can imagine, **multitasking can be accomplished by using either multiple processes or multiple threads, or a combination of both.**
Each time there is a new request comes in, the server program can spawn a new either process or thread to handle it. In the old days, many implementations tend to use processes. These days, threads are getting very common, popular, or even standard. We have shown readers how to fork and exec a child process in a previous chapter. We will show you how to create a new thread in this chapter.

There have been debates over using processes versus threads. Each has its own strength and weakness. Both solutions are in use in different products today. We will present a very brief summary of the pros and cons of the two in this section.

Historically, processes were available first in most operating systems. Threads came later and often as an add-on software package or library. When threads were first available, there was no industry standard and many operating systems have their own proprietary thread implementations. For instance, SunOS' offering of Solaris thread is just one example. In early 1990s, the computer industry recognized the need to have a thread standard. As a result, in 1995, the pthreads (POSIX threads) standard was born and published in POSIX 1003.1c standard (IEEE Std 1003.1c-1995). Below is the full name of this standard:

IEEE Std 1003.1c-1995 IEEE Standard for Information Technology--
Portable Operating System Interface (POSIX) - System Application Program
Interface (API) Amendment 2: Threads Extension (C Language)

This chapter introduces multithreaded programming using pthreads because pthreads is the only thread standard today and the pthreads library and implementation is available on almost all operating systems, including all Unix, Linux and Windows.

Below we will discuss the differences between the process model and the thread model from the address space perspective. Besides, we will talk about the pros and cons of the two.

In the process model, each process has its own code, data, heap and stack which are not shared. In the thread model, the code, global data and heap segments of a process are shared by all threads. However, each thread has its own stack. It is extremely important to have this concept and picture in mind in order for you to write correct multithreaded programs. Figure 8-2 shows the address map of a multithreaded process.

Please notice that the left most column would be what a single-thread process looks like. That is, for each additional thread created by the process, there is an additional corresponding stack being added to the process' address space.

Figure 8-2 Address map of a multithreaded process

```
Process address space        Process address space not
shared by all threads        shared between threads (stack)
--------------
|    Code      |
|------------|
| Global Data |
|------------|
|    Heap      |
--------------

    main thread          child thread 1    child thread 2    ...
--------------          -------------    -------------
|    Stack     |          |   Stack    |    |   Stack    |    ...
--------------          -------------    -------------
```

Below is a summary of the advantages and disadvantages of using processes versus threads:

Processes

Advantages

- Better isolation and protection provided by the operating system.
  The operating system guarantees that each process has its own address
  space which is insulated from address spaces of other processes.
  A process cannot intrude or do any harm to any other process's address
  space.

Disadvantages

- Slightly heavier weight
- Must rely on IPC mechanisms for inter-process communications

Threads

Advantages

- Light-weight (less overhead)
- No absolute need to rely on inter-process communication schemes
  provided by the operating system for inter-thread communications.

Disadvantages

- Less isolation and protection between threads than between processes.
  All threads within a process share the same address space.
  One mis-behaving thread can cause the process to die and hence taking
  out all threads.

- Care needs to be taken to ensure the threads do not step on one

351

another's toes. Specifically, synchronization needs to be in place in accessing all data, variables and resources shared between threads.

- Handling of signals may be slightly more challenging with threads.

- Threads may not be available on some systems.

8-1-3 What Is Thread?

A **thread** is a single flow of control within a process.
It is a separate unit of scheduling and execution.
Figure 8-3 shows a process with a single thread and one with multiple.

Figure 8-3 Single-threaded and multithreaded process

```
 --------------             ---------------------------------
|    main()    |           | main() thrd1() thrd2() thrd3()|
|      :       |           |   :       :       :       :    |
|      :       |           |   :       :       :       :    |
|              |           |                                |
 --------------             ---------------------------------
 (a) A traditional          (b) A multi-threaded process with
 process - single-threaded      three child threads
```

A traditional process is single threaded in that it starts its execution from the main() function and progresses through each statement in the program one at a time without creating any additional flow of control. At any given time, there is only one statement in the program that is in execution.
So there exists a single flow of control throughout the entire program.

In a multithreaded process, the process starts the main function with a single thread -- the main thread. However, at some point, the main thread creates additional child threads that can be separately scheduled to run from a specified starter function. For example, if the main thread creates two additional child threads, then the process will have a total of three threads running at the same time -- the main thread plus two child threads.
Each of these threads could perform a different task or the same.
Each thread is a separate scheduling entity and all of the threads in a process can all run at the same time.

Figure 8-4 A multithreaded server in action

```
Clients                    Server Process
                           ---------------------------------
client 1  ---->   | ~~ thread 1 serving client 1 |
                  |                               |
client 2  ---->   | ~~ thread 2 serving client 2 |
                  |                               |
client 3  ---->   | ~~ thread 3 serving client 3 |
                  |                               |
    :             |       :                       |
                   ---------------------------------
```

As shown in Fig. 8-4, a multithreaded program can handle multiple tasks at a time, one by each thread. On a multi-CPU system, the multiple threads can be executed by the CPUs in parallel simultaneously and thus improve performance. A multithreaded program is also more **scalable**. A best program design is to programmatically find out how many CPUs are available on the system at the beginning of the program and then **spawn a number of threads or processes that is equal or proportional to the number of processors. This way the program can automatically scale with the hardware.**

8-2 Pthreads Basics

8-2-1 How to Create and Join a Thread

Using pthreads, you invoke the pthread_create() function to create a child thread. This function has the following specification:

```
int pthread_create(pthread_t *restrict thread,
        const pthread_attr_t *restrict attr,
        void *(*start_routine)(void*), void *restrict arg);
```

The pthread_create() function takes four arguments. The first argument is an output. It will return the thread id of the new thread which you can later use to, for example, join the thread. The second argument is an input. It specifies a pthreads attributes object of type pthread_attr_t. This object contains many attributes that you can define to be associated with the thread being created. If this argument is NULL, then all thread attributes take the default values. We will further discuss this object in a later section.

The third argument is the name of the start routine that you want the thread to begin execution at. The fourth argument is the beginning address of the arguments that you would like to pass to the thread's start routine. Specify NULL if there is no argument to pass to the child thread's start routine.

Figure 8-5 Creating a child thread (pt_create.c)

```
/*
 * Creating a child thread.
 * Copyright (c) 2014, 2019 Mr. Jin-Jwei Chen.  All rights reserved.
 */

#include <stdio.h>
#include <pthread.h>

/*
 * The child thread.
 */
void child_thread(void *args)
{
  fprintf(stdout, "Enter the child thread\n");
  fprintf(stdout, "My thread id is %ul\n", pthread_self());
  fprintf(stdout, "Child thread exiting ...\n");
  pthread_exit((void *)NULL);
}

/*
```

```
 * The main program.
 */
int main(int argc, char *argv[])
{
  pthread_t       thrd;
  int             ret=0;

  /* Create a child thread to run the child_thread() function. */
  ret = pthread_create(&thrd, (pthread_attr_t *)NULL,
        (void *(*)(void *))child_thread, (void *)NULL);
  if (ret != 0)
  {
    fprintf(stderr, "Error: failed to create the child thread, ret=%d\n", ret);
    return(ret);
  }

  /* Wait for the child thread to finish. */
  ret = pthread_join(thrd, (void **)NULL);
  if (ret != 0)
    fprintf(stderr, "Error: failed to join the child thread, ret=%d\n", ret);

  fprintf(stdout, "Main thread exiting ...\n");
  return(ret);
}
```

Figure 8-5 shows an example program that creates a child thread in pthreads. As you run this program you will notice that the child thread is not invoked by anyone. But it runs from start to finish. This is because it is automatically scheduled to run by the system once it is created. All the main program has to do is to create the thread and specify a start routine for it. After that, the thread will run automatically.

Also notice that the main thread invokes the pthread_join() function to wait for the child thread to finish. This is very important. Without this, the main thread may exit and terminate the entire program before the child thread even gets a chance to start itself and run.

As shown below, the pthread_join() function takes two arguments. First argument is the id of the thread it intends to wait for. This value is returned by the pthread_create() function earlier. The second argument is an output. It is used to receive the value returned from the child thread. Note that the data type of this returned value parameter is pointer-to-pointer.

```
        int pthread_join(pthread_t thread, void **value_ptr);
```

When the pthread_join() function is called, the calling thread will be suspended until the target thread specified in the function's first argument terminates. If the target thread has already terminated, the pthread_join() call will return immediately. Upon return, the target thread's exit status will be stored into the location specified by the second argument of the pthread_join() function. Joining a thread is the only way to get its return value. Once a thread is joined, its memory and resources are reclaimed.

Note that a thread can be joined by its parent thread or any thread in the same process that knows its thread id. Also, **the pthread_join() function**

can join only the specific thread specified. It does not have the flexibility to join simply the next terminating thread.

Note on pthread_join()

Notice that there is an implementation/behavior difference in the way the pthread_join() API collecting a child thread's returned value between 64-bit Oracle/Sun SPARC Solaris and other platforms. Specifically, calling pthread_exit() from a child thread to return a numeric constant as below:

```
pthread_exit((void *)0);
```

works on all of the Linux, IBM AIX, HPUX and Apple Darwin in both 32-bit and 64-bit modes. It also works in 32-bit Solaris. However, it causes the pthread_join() API to dump core in 64-bit Solaris 11. Hence, as shown in Fig. 8-6, our code tries to accommodate both by using the SUN64 macro. You need to define the SUN64 macro if you are compiling the program on Oracle/SUN SPARC Solaris 64-bit mode. Notice the difference seems to be the implementation of the pthread_join() function. Unless I do it the way it is in this program, pthread_join() dumps core on Oracle/SUN SPARC Solaris 64-bit platform. You probably notice already, simply returning a constant works just fine in the main() function. There is no need to put the return value in a variable and return the address of that variable.

How To Exit The Main Thread

One thing to remember is that you should not call the exit() or return() function to terminate the main thread. If you do, that call will terminate the entire process immediately including all of the child threads even if the child threads may not even get a chance to run yet.
The correct way to exit the main thread of your program is to use the pthread_exit() function. For example,

```
pthread_exit((void *)0);
```

When you invoke the pthread_exit() function to exit the main thread, it will terminate only the main thread itself, rather than the entire process. That way, all the child threads will continue to run even after the main thread has terminated. Figure 8-5 uses return() since no child thread running.

8-2-2 How to Pass Arguments to a Thread

A creator thread is allowed to pass no data, a scalar value or an aggregate to a child thread as long as it places the data at a single starting address. A child thread's start function can take a single argument which is a pointer. As long as you fill in the data before creating the thread and pass the starting address of the data to the child thread's start routine, the child thread can retrieve the input arguments one by one as they were laid out.

Figure 8-6 shows an example of passing two integers to a thread's startup routine. In the example, we pass two pieces of information to each child thread: an id for the thread and the number of tasks the thread has to perform.

Figure 8-6 Passing two integers to a child thread (pt_args_ret.c)

```
/*
 * Passing an array of integers to a child thread and returning one integer.
 * Copyright (c) 2014, Mr. Jin-Jwei Chen.  All rights reserved.
 */

#include <stdio.h>
#include <pthread.h>

#define   NTHREADS     2
#define   NTASKS       3

/*
 * The worker thread.
 */
int worker_thread(void *args)
{
  unsigned int   *argp;
  unsigned int   myid;
  unsigned int   ntasks;
#ifdef SUN64
  int            ret = 0;
#endif

  /* Extract input arguments (two unsigned integers) */
  argp = (unsigned int *)args;
  if (argp != NULL)
  {
    myid = argp[0];
    ntasks = argp[1];
  }
  else
#ifdef SUN64
  {
    ret = (-1);
    pthread_exit((void *)&ret);
  }
#else
    pthread_exit((void *)(-1));
#endif

  fprintf(stdout, "Worker thread: myid=%u ntasks=%u\n", myid, ntasks);
#ifdef SUN64
  pthread_exit((void *)&ret);
#else
  pthread_exit((void *)0);
#endif
}

/*
 * The main program.
 */
int main(int argc, char *argv[])
{
  pthread_t       thrds[NTHREADS];
  unsigned int    args[NTHREADS][2];
```

356

```
  int           ret, i;
  int           retval = 0;   /* each child thread returns an int */
#ifdef SUN64
  int           *retvalp = &retval;          /* pointer to returned value */
#endif

  /* Load up the input arguments for each child thread */
  for (i = 0; i < NTHREADS; i++)
  {
    args[i][0] = i;
    args[i][1] = NTASKS;
  }

  /* Create new threads to run the worker_thread() function and pass in args */
  for (i = 0; i < NTHREADS; i++)
  {
    ret = pthread_create(&thrds[i], (pthread_attr_t *)NULL,
          (void *(*)(void *))worker_thread, (void *)args[i]);
    if (ret != 0)
    {
      fprintf(stderr, "Failed to create the worker thread, ret=%d\n", ret);
      pthread_exit((void *)-1);
    }
  }

  /*
   * Wait for each of the child threads to finish and retrieve its returned
   * value.
   */
  for (i = 0; i < NTHREADS; i++)
  {
#ifdef SUN64
    ret = pthread_join(thrds[i], (void **)&retvalp);
#else
    ret = pthread_join(thrds[i], (void **)&retval);
#endif
    fprintf(stdout, "Thread %u exited with return value %d\n", i, retval);
  }

  pthread_exit((void *)0);
}
```

Note that there may exist some potential danger here in the argument passing to a child thread and it is related to a couple of things.

First, due to the operating system scheduling, the order in which all threads are executed typically is unpredictable. This means after the pthread_create() call, a new child thread is created. But when the pthread_create() function returns, where the child thread's execution stands is typically unknown. The child thread may have finished execution and terminated, or it could be still running, or it may not even be started yet.

Second, it is also related to the life span of the storage (i.e. memory) holding the arguments being passed.

Very often a program would use some local variables in the creator function to store the values of arguments to be passed on to the child thread(s), just like what we did in pt_args_ret.c, because that's the easiest thing to do. As you might have known, storage of a function's local variables is allocated on stack which comes and goes as the function is entered and exits. This means as soon as a function exits, the storage of its local variables is deallocated and gone. Any thread or process trying to access that memory afterwards will get a Segmentation Fault error which will kill the calling thread and process!

Therefore, using local variables to store the arguments passed to a child thread may not be the best idea but it's easy to do and it will work as long as the following two conditions hold:

1. The creator function holding the arguments passed to a child thread does not exit until the child thread has finished accessing the arguments or has terminated. This ensures that the memory holding the arguments still exists when the child thread accesses it.

2. The values of the arguments do not change until after the child thread has accessed the arguments or terminates. This ensures that the values of the arguments do not get altered from underneath until after the child thread uses them.

If the above conditions cannot be met, then a program should use other means to store the arguments. For example, try to store the arguments in the process' heap by dynamically allocating the memory using the malloc() function because the heap memory lasts as long as the process or until it is freed. The only thing is that this malloc-ed memory must be freed or memory leak will occur.

8-2-3 How to Return Values from a Thread

A child thread uses the pthread_exit() function to return a value back to its parent:

```
void pthread_exit(void *value_ptr);
```

And the parent uses the pthread_join() function to retrieve a child thread's return value.

Note that to be flexible and be able to return more than just a very simple data item such as an integer, the pthread_exit() function takes an argument of (void *). This allows a thread to return a simple data like a number or a pointer to a buffer containing more complex data.

A child thread can easily return a scalar value such as an integer to its parent. Our example program in Figure 8-6 demonstrates that.
To return an integer, you declare the thread start routine as returning an int. And within the thread start routine, you invoke the pthread_exit() function to terminate the thread and return a value. You pass the value to be returned as the only argument to the pthread_exit() function and type cast it to (void *).

To return an aggregate value such as a structure, it needs to be carefully thought out and designed.

First, one may think of using a global variable.
Well, since a global variable is shared by all threads within a process,
all threads including the main thread have access to it. Therefore, there is
no need to pass in as an argument or return it as a return value.
The danger though is how do you ensure the child threads won't step on one
another's toes and overwrite one another in using the same global variable
to return a value to the parent? So this is not a good idea.

Second, some may think of having the parent thread allocates the
buffer space and passes its address to each child thread.
Again, this will have the same access control issue as we just mentioned
in the preceding paragraph unless the parent uses a separate buffer for
each child thread. If the parent thread allocates a separate copy of the
buffer for each child thread, this should work.

A third approach for each thread to return a structure back to its parent
is to have the child thread dynamically allocate the needed memory, fill
in the structure's values, pass its starting address back to the parent,
and have the parent free that memory afterwards. Since a dynamically
allocated memory resides in the heap area, which remains after a child
thread exits and it is shared by all threads within the same process,
the parent will have no problem accessing it at all.

Note that some of you might have thought of this, but a child thread can
never return anything stored in its local memory back to its parent.
This is because once a child thread exits, its local memory will no longer
exist. So, it would be impossible for the parent to access that memory.
The local variables of a thread start routine or any function are usually
stored on stack. A function's stack is deallocated once the function exits.
Therefore, it could be a bug if a thread attempts to return anything from
its local memory or stack back to its parent except you know for sure that
the parent always waits for the child thread, in which case a child thread's
memory won't get deallocated until it is waited for.

Program 8-7 shows an example that returns a structure from a child thread
using dynamic memory. The child thread dynamically allocates the memory
for the values of the structure being returned.
If the memory allocation succeeds, the thread fills in the returned values
and then passes the starting address of the buffer to the pthread_exit()
function. The starting address is then returned to the parent.
If the memory allocation fails, a NULL pointer is returned.

To receive the structure being returned, the parent declares a variable
named retval as a pointer to the structure. It passes the address of this
variable to the second argument of the pthread_join() function.
When the pthread_join() function returns, the retval variable will have the
starting address of the returned structure in it. The parent then consumes
the values in the returned structure and frees the buffer space afterwards
such that there is no memory leak.

Figure 8-7 Example of thread returning a structure to its parent (pt_args_ret2.c)

```
/*
 * Passing an array of integers to a child thread and returning a structure
 * from each child thread.
```

```
#include <stdio.h>
#include <string.h>
#include <stdlib.h>          /* malloc() */
#include <string.h>          /* memset() */
#include <pthread.h>

#define  NTHREADS      2
#define  NTASKS        3

struct mydata
{
  char msg[32];
  int  num;
};
typedef struct mydata mydata;

/*
 * The worker thread.
 */
mydata *worker_thread(void *args)
{
  unsigned int   *argp;
  unsigned int    myid=0;
  unsigned int    ntasks=0;
  mydata         *outdata;

  /* Extract input arguments (two unsigned integers) */
  argp = (unsigned int *)args;
  if (argp != NULL)
  {
    myid = argp[0];
    ntasks = argp[1];
  }
  fprintf(stdout, "Worker thread: myid=%u ntasks=%u\n", myid, ntasks);

  /* Do some real work here */

  /* Return a structure of data to caller */
  outdata = (mydata *)malloc(sizeof(mydata));
  if (outdata != NULL)
  {
    memset((void *)outdata, 0, sizeof(mydata));
    outdata->num = (myid *100);
    sprintf(outdata->msg, "%s %u", "From child thread ", myid);
  }

  pthread_exit((void *)outdata);
}

/*
 * The main program.
 */
int main(int argc, char *argv[])
```

360

```
{
  pthread_t       thrds[NTHREADS];
  unsigned int    args[NTHREADS][2];
  int             ret, i;
  mydata          *retval;  /* each child thread returns an int */

  /* Load up the input arguments for each child thread */
  for (i = 1; i <= NTHREADS; i++)
  {
    args[i-1][0] = i;
    args[i-1][1] = NTASKS;
  }

  /* Create new threads to run the worker_thread() function and pass in args */
  for (i = 0; i < NTHREADS; i++)
  {
    ret = pthread_create(&thrds[i], (pthread_attr_t *)NULL,
          (void *(*)(void *))worker_thread, (void *)args[i]);
    if (ret != 0)
    {
      fprintf(stderr, "Failed to create the worker thread, ret=%d\n", ret);
      pthread_exit((void *)-1);
    }
  }

  /*
   * Wait for each of the child threads to finish and retrieve its returned
   * value.
   */
  for (i = 1; i <= NTHREADS; i++)
  {
    ret = pthread_join(thrds[i-1], (void **)&retval);
    if (retval == NULL)
      fprintf(stdout, "Child thread %u exited with return value NULL\n", i);
    else
    {
      fprintf(stdout, "Child thread %u exited with following return value:\n", i);
      fprintf(stdout, "  msg = %s\n", retval->msg);
      fprintf(stdout, "  num = %d\n", retval->num);
      free(retval);
    }
  }

  pthread_exit((void *)0);
}
```

8-3 Pthreads Attributes

There are a number of attributes in the pthreads attributes object.
They are:

  - thread contention scope
  - thread detached state
  - thread stack size
  - thread stack address

- thread scheduling information, which includes thread scheduling policy, thread scheduling priority and the inheritsched attribute

1. Thread Contention Scope

The thread (contention) scope attribute is used in thread scheduling. In pthreads, a thread can be created in one of the two contention scopes:

- PTHREAD_SCOPE_SYSTEM
- PTHREAD_SCOPE_PROCESS

A thread with PTHREAD_SCOPE_SYSTEM scope means the thread has system scheduling contention scope. It means this thread will compete for the processor with other system and kernel threads. That is, this thread itself will get its fair share of the processor time among all threads at the system level. It competes for the processor at the system level.

A thread with PTHREAD_SCOPE_PROCESS scope has process scheduling contention scope. It means the thread will compete for the processor with other threads within the current process. In other words, it will share the time of the processor that is allocated to the containing process with other threads within the same process.

As of this writing, by default, a thread is created with the PTHREAD_SCOPE_SYSTEM scope on Linux, AIX, HPUX and Apple Darwin. On Oracle/Sun SPARC Solaris, the default is PTHREAD_SCOPE_PROCESS scope.

To get or set a thread's scope, use the pthread_attr_getscope() or pthread_attr_setscope() function, respectively.

```
    int pthread_attr_getscope(const pthread_attr_t *restrict attr,
            int *restrict contentionscope);
    int pthread_attr_setscope(pthread_attr_t *attr, int contentionscope);
```

This thread contention scope attribute enables programmers to decide on at what level a thread should be allowed to compete for CPU time.

Note that in some implementation, system scope threads are bounded with kernel threads within the operating system to provide true real-time behavior. In contrast, process scope threads are unbound threads. This is system dependent.

2. Thread Detach State

In pthreads, a thread can be in PTHREAD_CREATE_JOINABLE or PTHREAD_CREATE_DETACHED state.

A thread created in the PTHREAD_CREATE_JOINABLE state can be joined by another thread (usually by its parent) and can return a value. A thread created in the PTHREAD_CREATE_DETACHED state cannot be joined by another thread and cannot return a value. If it returns a value, it will be ignored.

By default, a thread is created in the PTHREAD_CREATE_JOINABLE state.
To get or set the detached state of a thread, invoke the pthread_attr_getdetachstate() or pthread_attr_setdetachstate() function.

```
int pthread_attr_getdetachstate(const pthread_attr_t *attr,
        int *detachstate);
int pthread_attr_setdetachstate(pthread_attr_t *attr, int detachstate);
```

In general, it is a good idea for the parent thread to join its child
threads and retrieve their return values. But if the child threads do not
return values or they run forever and never return, then creating them
as detached threads may make more sense.

3. Thread Stack Size

The stack size attribute defines the size of the stack for the thread.
The unit is in bytes.

The default value for the stack size attribute is NULL, meaning it is
size of the system default.

To get or set a thread's stack size, use the pthread_attr_getstacksize()
or pthread_attr_setstacksize() function, respectively.
The value specified in the pthread_attr_setstacksize() function must be
equal to or greater than PTHREAD_STACK_MIN.

```
int pthread_attr_getstacksize(const pthread_attr_t *restrict attr,
        size_t *restrict stacksize);
int pthread_attr_setstacksize(pthread_attr_t *attr, size_t stacksize);
```

Often the default stack size is too small for some applications and
running the application results in the "stack overflow" error.
This thread attribute allows your application to set a bigger stack size
that satisfies the specific requirement of your application.

4. Stack Address

The thread stack address attribute defines the starting address of the
thread's stack. A program seldom does this.

By default, the value of the stack address attribute is NULL.
This means the stack starting address is assigned by the system.

To get or set the stack address for a thread, invoke the
pthread_attr_getstackaddr() or pthread_attr_setstackaddr() function:

```
int pthread_attr_getstackaddr(const pthread_attr_t *restrict attr,
        void **restrict stackaddr);
int pthread_attr_setstackaddr(pthread_attr_t *attr, void *stackaddr);
```

5. Scheduling Policy

Each process or thread is controlled by an associated scheduling policy and
priority. Associated with each policy is a priority range. Each policy
definition specifies the priority range for that policy.
The priority range for each policy may overlap the priority range of
other policies. Operating systems are also allowed to define other policies.

The scheduling policies supported by an operating system are defined in the header file sched.h.

Pthreads defines three different scheduling policies:

    SCHED_FIFO   (First-In-First-Out)
    SCHED_RR   (Round Robin)
    SCHED_OTHER

A thread's scheduling policy is specified by the pthreads **schedpolicy**
attribute. SCHED_OTHER is the default.

Note that some operating systems map SCHED_OTHER to other policy.
For example, Oracle/Sun SPARC Solaris maps SCHED_OTHER to traditional
time-sharing scheduling policy. HPUX maps SCHED_OTHER to SCHED_HPUX which
is the same as SCHED_TIMESHARE which is a traditional timesharing
non-realtime scheduling policy.

You call the pthread_attr_getschedpolicy() and pthread_attr_setschedpolicy()
functions, respectively, to get and set the thread's scheduling policy.

    int pthread_attr_getschedpolicy(const pthread_attr_t *restrict attr,
            int *restrict policy);
    int pthread_attr_setschedpolicy(pthread_attr_t *attr, int policy);

If successful, the pthread_attr_getschedpolicy() and
pthread_attr_setschedpolicy() functions return zero; otherwise, an error
number is returned to indicate the error.

As of this writing, no operating system supports the SCHED_SPORADIC
scheduling policy yet as mentioned in POSIX Issue 7.

6. Scheduling Priority

A thread's scheduling priority is defined by a scheduling parameter
attribute which is the sched_param structure (struct sched_param).
The sched_param structure normally contains only the sched_priority
field, which is an integer.

To get or set a thread's scheduling parameter, you invoke the
pthread_attr_getschedparam() or pthread_attr_setschedparam() function
as below, respectively:

    int pthread_attr_getschedparam(const pthread_attr_t *restrict attr,
            struct sched_param *restrict param);
    int pthread_attr_setschedparam(pthread_attr_t *restrict attr,
            const struct sched_param *restrict param);

The pthread_attr_setschedparam() function sets the scheduling parameters
in the thread attributes object. The value of the sched_priority in the
param parameter must be in between PRIORITY_MIN and PRIORITY_MAX.

If successful, the pthread_attr_getschedparam() and
pthread_attr_setschedparam() functions return zero; otherwise, an error
number is returned to indicate the error.

Note that if you already set the priority of the process or thread outside

of the pthreads API, you probably don't want to use
pthread_attr_setschedparam() to interfere with it.

The minimum and maximum priorities associated with each scheduling policy
can be queried by calling the following APIs:

```
int     sched_get_priority_min(int);
int     sched_get_priority_max(int);
```

The priority ranges of the POSIX scheduling policies on various operating
systems are listed in Figure 8-8.

Figure 8-8 Thread scheduling priority ranges

Operating system	Scheduling policy	Minimum priority	Maximum priority
Linux	SCHED_FIFO	1	99
	SCHED_RR	1	99
	SCHED_OTHER	0	0
AIX	SCHED_FIFO	1	127
	SCHED_RR	1	127
	SCHED_OTHER	1	127
Solaris	SCHED_FIFO	0	59
	SCHED_RR	0	59
HPUX	SCHED_FIFO	0	31
	SCHED_RR	0	31
Apple Darwin	SCHED_FIFO	15	47
	SCHED_RR	15	47
	SCHED_OTHER	15	47

7. The inheritsched Attribute

The inheritsched attribute determines how the other scheduling attributes
of the created thread will be set.

Valid values for the pthreads inheritsched attribute are below:

PTHREAD_INHERIT_SCHED
  When you use a pthreads attributes object with the pthread_create() call,
  this value means that the thread scheduling attributes are inherited from
  the creating thread, and the scheduling attributes in the attr argument
  will be ignored. This is the default.

PTHREAD_EXPLICIT_SCHED
  The value PTHREAD_EXPLICIT_SCHED means that the thread scheduling
  attributes will be set to the corresponding values from this attributes
  object.

Use the pthread_attr_getinheritsched() and pthread_attr_setinheritsched()
functions, respectively, to get and set the value of inheritsched attribute.

```
 int pthread_attr_getinheritsched(const pthread_attr_t *restrict attr,
      int *restrict inheritsched);
 int pthread_attr_setinheritsched(pthread_attr_t *attr,
```

```
            int inheritsched);
```

Upon success, the pthread_attr_getinheritsched() and
pthread_attr_setinheritsched() functions return zero; otherwise, an error
number is returned to indicate the error.

Figure 8-9 is an example program which prints the default values of
all pthreads attributes.

Figure 8-9 Print default values of pthreads attributes (pt_prt_thrd_attr.c)

```
/*
 * Print pthread attributes.
 * Copyright (c) 2014, 2019, 2020 Mr. Jin-Jwei Chen.  All rights reserved.
 */
#include <stdio.h>
#include <stdlib.h>
#include <unistd.h>
#include <string.h>
#include <errno.h>
#include <pthread.h>

/* Print pthread attributes */
void print_pthread_attr(pthread_attr_t *attr)
{
  int   ret;
  int   val = 0;
  struct sched_param    pri;   /* scheduling priority */
  void   *stkaddr = NULL;      /* stack address */
  size_t stksz = 0;            /* stack size */
  size_t guardsz = 0;          /* guard size */

  if (attr == NULL)
    return;

  /* Get and print detached state */
  ret = pthread_attr_getdetachstate(attr, &val);
  if (ret == 0)
    fprintf(stdout, "  Detach state = %s\n",
      (val == PTHREAD_CREATE_DETACHED) ? "PTHREAD_CREATE_DETACHED" :
      (val == PTHREAD_CREATE_JOINABLE) ? "PTHREAD_CREATE_JOINABLE" :
      "Unknown");
  else
    fprintf(stderr, "print_pthread_attr(): pthread_attr_getdetachstate() "
      "failed, ret=%d\n", ret);

  /* Get and print contention scope */
  val = 0;
  ret = pthread_attr_getscope(attr, &val);
  if (ret == 0)
    fprintf(stdout, "  Contention scope = %s\n",
      (val == PTHREAD_SCOPE_SYSTEM) ? "PTHREAD_SCOPE_SYSTEM" :
      (val == PTHREAD_SCOPE_PROCESS) ? "PTHREAD_SCOPE_PROCESS" :
      "Unknown");
  else
    fprintf(stderr, "print_pthread_attr(): pthread_attr_getscope() "
```

```
          "failed, ret=%d\n", ret);

  /* Get and print inherit scheduler */
  val = 0;
  ret = pthread_attr_getinheritsched(attr, &val);
  if (ret == 0)
    fprintf(stdout, "  Inherit scheduler = %s\n",
      (val == PTHREAD_INHERIT_SCHED) ? "PTHREAD_INHERIT_SCHED" :
      (val == PTHREAD_EXPLICIT_SCHED) ? "PTHREAD_EXPLICIT_SCHED" :
      "Unknown");
  else
    fprintf(stderr, "print_pthread_attr(): pthread_attr_getinheritsched() "
      "failed, ret=%d\n", ret);

  /* Get and print scheduling policy */
  val = 0;
  ret = pthread_attr_getschedpolicy(attr, &val);
  if (ret == 0)
    fprintf(stdout, "  Scheduling policy = %s\n",
      (val == SCHED_RR) ? "SCHED_RR" :
      (val == SCHED_FIFO) ? "SCHED_FIFO" :
      (val == SCHED_OTHER) ? "SCHED_OTHER" :
      "Unknown");
  else
    fprintf(stderr, "print_pthread_attr(): pthread_attr_getschedpolicy() "
      "failed, ret=%d\n", ret);

  /* Get and print scheduling priority */
  memset(&pri, 0, sizeof(pri));
  ret = pthread_attr_getschedparam(attr, &pri);
  if (ret == 0)
    fprintf(stdout, "  Scheduling priority = %d\n", pri.sched_priority);
  else
    fprintf(stderr, "print_pthread_attr(): pthread_attr_getschedparam() "
      "failed, ret=%d\n", ret);

  /* Get and print stack address and stack size */
  ret = pthread_attr_getstack(attr, &stkaddr, &stksz);
  if (ret == 0)
  {
    fprintf(stdout, "  Stack address = %p\n", stkaddr);
    fprintf(stdout, "  Stack size = %lu bytes\n", stksz);
  }
  else
    fprintf(stderr, "print_pthread_attr(): pthread_attr_getstack() "
      "failed, ret=%d\n", ret);

  /* Get and print guard size */
  ret = pthread_attr_getguardsize(attr, &guardsz);
  if (ret == 0)
    fprintf(stdout, "  Guard size = %lu bytes\n", guardsz);
  else
    fprintf(stderr, "print_pthread_attr(): pthread_attr_getguardsize() "
      "failed, ret=%d\n", ret);
}
```

```c
int main(int argc, char *argv[])
{
  pthread_attr_t   attr1;
  int              ret;

  /* Initialize thread attributes */
  ret = pthread_attr_init(&attr1);
  if (ret != 0)
  {
    fprintf(stderr, "Failed to initialize thread attributes, ret=%d\n", ret);
    return(-1);
  }

  print_pthread_attr(&attr1);

  /* Destroy thread attributes */
  ret = pthread_attr_destroy(&attr1);
  if (ret != 0)
  {
    fprintf(stderr, "Failed to destroy thread attributes, ret=%d\n", ret);
    return(-2);
  }
  return(0);
}
```

8-3-1 Detached Thread

There are two types of threads based on whether it can be joined or not by another thread:

1. joinable (or nondetached) thread
2. detached thread

Joinable threads can be joined by their parent or others. They can also return values. Detached threads cannot be joined and thus they cannot return values. Trying to join a detached thread by calling pthread_join() will get an error.

By default, a thread is created in the PTHREAD_CREATE_JOINABLE state unless it is explicitly set to the PTHREAD_CREATE_DETACHED state. This means if you wish to create a thread in detached state, you must create a variable of type pthread_attr_t, call the pthread_attr_init() function to initialize its value, then call the pthread_attr_setdetachstate() function to set the state to PTHREAD_CREATE_DETACHED, and pass in this pthreads attributes object when you invoke the pthread_create() function to create the thread.

Figure 8-10 shows an example program that uses thread attributes to create a detached thread.

Figure 8-10 Creating a detached thread (pt_detached.c)

```
/*
 * Creating a detached child thread.
 * Copyright (c) 2014, Mr. Jin-Jwei Chen.  All rights reserved.
```

```c
 */

#include <stdio.h>
#include <pthread.h>

/*
 * The child thread.
 */
void child_thread(void *args)
{
  fprintf(stdout, "Enter the child thread\n");
  fprintf(stdout, "Child thread exiting ...\n");
  pthread_exit((void *)NULL);
}


/*
 * The main program.
 */
int main(int argc, char *argv[])
{
  pthread_t        thrd;
  int              ret;
  pthread_attr_t   attr;   /* thread attributes */

  /* Initialize the pthread attributes */
  ret = pthread_attr_init(&attr);
  if (ret != 0)
  {
    fprintf(stderr, "Failed to init thread attributes, ret=%d\n", ret);
    pthread_exit((void *)-1);
  }

  /* Set up to create a detached thread */
  ret = pthread_attr_setdetachstate(&attr, PTHREAD_CREATE_DETACHED);
  if (ret != 0)
  {
    fprintf(stderr, "Failed to set detach state, ret=%d\n", ret);
    pthread_exit((void *)-2);
  }

  /* Create a detached child thread to run the child_thread() function. */
  ret = pthread_create(&thrd, (pthread_attr_t *)&attr,
       (void *(*)(void *))child_thread, (void *)NULL);
  if (ret != 0)
  {
    fprintf(stderr, "Failed to create the child thread\n");
    pthread_exit((void *)-3);
  }

  /* Destroy the pthread attributes */
  ret = pthread_attr_destroy(&attr);
  if (ret != 0)
  {
    fprintf(stderr, "Failed to destroy thread attributes, ret=%d\n", ret);
    pthread_exit((void *)-4);
  }
```

```
    fprintf(stdout, "Main thread exiting ...\n");

    /*
     * Make sure you don't call return() or exit() here to terminate the main
     * thread. If you do, it will terminate the entire process including the
     * child thread even if the child thread may not even get a chance to run yet.
     */
    pthread_exit((void *)0);
}
```

Keep in mind that one difference between a detached thread and a joinable thread is that a detached thread will clean up and release its memory upon exit. In contrast, a joinable thread will not clean up and release its memory until after it is joined because its return value must still be passed back to the joining thread at the time of join. Therefore, if your program creates a lot of joinable/nondetached threads without actually joining them, the program's memory usage will grow quickly.

Therefore, if a thread's returned value is needed and/or synchronizing with the thread upon termination is needed, then use joinable threads. Use detached threads if a thread's returned value is not needed and/or there is no need to synchronize with its termination.

8-4 Types of Problems in Concurrency Control

There are different types of synchronizations between concurrent, competing or collaborating processes/threads in computer programming. Here we quickly introduce two because pthreads includes APIs for solving three kinds of concurrency problems including these two.

8-4-1 Update Loss Problem

We will dive deep into the update loss problem later in this book in the concurrency control chapter. Here we just briefly touch upon this subject.

One of the very common problems almost all software products face is that two or more processes/threads try to update the same piece of shared data. To guarantee the integrity of the shared data and correctness of the computation result, mutual exclusion is required. That is, only one process/thread can exclusively perform the update at a time.

In pthreads, the synchronization primitive that guarantees data integrity under concurrent updates is a mutual exclusion lock. Whoever finds the lock available and is able to grab it first gets access to the shared data. All other processes/threads have to wait.

A mutual exclusion lock is usually implemented as an integer variable with only two values. Indeed, it can be as small as a single bit. The implementation typically requires a single or a pair of assembly language instructions from the processor that can perform a test-and-set or compare-and-swap operation on the integer variable atomically.

The key thing is there is a single lock shared by all processes/threads and only one process/thread can have it at a time. Other processes/threads are blocked by the unavailability of the lock.

Depending on what kind of systems are available to you, you may have a number of options to choose from for implementing your mutual exclusion solution.

Fundamentally, you can always implement the locking/unlocking functions in the machine's assembly language yourself without relying on the facilities that the underlying operating system or certain software package such as pthreads provides.

Almost all operating systems provide some mutual exclusion APIs to application developers. You may want to choose to use the operating system APIs for a number of reasons. For example, you don't want to implement your own locking/unlocking functions in assembly languages. Or the performance of your product is not that important.

In cases where you have to support multiple different operating systems and you want to code it the same way across all platforms, or where you have no choice but to use an existing software package, then you may want to choose to use APIs from a software package. For example, the POSIX standard has a standard on how to do multithreaded programming. It defines a pthreads library, which is very widely implemented on the popular operating systems. Therefore, using the thread package and the mutex comes with it would be a very sensible choice.

The update loss problem is simply a mutual exclusion issue. Using a mutual exclusion lock will solve the problem. In pthreads, mutex is exactly for this application. We will discuss mutex and demonstrate how to use mutex to solve update loss problems in the next section.

8-4-2 Producer-consumer Problem

A second type of concurrency problems involves multiple collaborating processes/threads sharing a pool of resources where some processes/threads producing resources while others consuming them. This is the famous producer-consumer problem.

There are two pieces of data shared in this type of problems.

First is the counter indicating how many resources or buffers are available. The second piece of shared data is the resource pool itself. To guarantee integrity of the shared data, mutual exclusion using a mutex is required. Any process/thread needing to access and modify the shared data must lock the mutex first and release it after.

There are typically two ways to solve this problem.

First, an application can code it like this in Figure 8-11 below.

Figure 8-11 Skeleton of solution to a producer-consumer problem

The MAXCAPACITY represents the capacity of the system. For instance,

the maximum number of buffers available to hold the produced resources.
The integer variable count represents the current number of resources
that are already produced but not consumed yet.

Producer:

```
loop
{
  lock the mutex;
  if (count < MAXCAPACITY)
  {
    produce();
    count = count + 1;
  }
  unlock the mutex;
}
```

Consumer:

```
loop
{
  lock the mutex;
  if (count > 0)
  {
    consume();
    count = count - 1;
  }
  unlock the mutex;
}
```

Solving the producer-consumer problem this way requires only support of
a mutex from the underlying system and nothing else. However, it is not
the optimal solution. This is especially true when the system is full
or empty. When the system is full, the producer threads may waste a lot
of CPU time in getting the mutex, finding the resource pool is already
full, releasing the mutex and accomplishing nothing.
Similarly, when the resource pool is empty, the consumer threads
may waste a lot of time in acquiring the mutex, finding the resource pool
is empty, releasing the mutex and accomplishing nothing.

For this reason, many operating systems and programming languages,
including Pthreads, provide a more sophisticated facility and APIs that
allow application developers to solve the producer-consumer problem more
efficiently.

In the POSIX threads standard and in the Java programming language, the
answer to this is the condition variable. We will talk about condition
variables in the section after next. And then we will have our example
of solving the producer-consumer problem using pthreads at that time.
In Unix/Linux, the counting semaphore in System V IPC may help solve this
problem, too. We'll introduce System V IPC in the next chapter.

The condition variable solution aims at freeing the applications from
having to keep looping and checking under the conditions where the resource
pool is full or empty! Hence, the loops shown above won't exist anymore.
An application thread simply calls the APIs. And if the resource pool is

full (if the thread is a producer thread) or empty (if the thread is
a consumer thread), the system will automatically block the calling thread
and put the thread to sleep. Later the system will automatically wake up
the thread when the blocking condition no longer holds.

8-5 Mutex

8-5-1 What Is Mutex?

The POSIX thread standard uses mutex for concurrency control.

Mutex stands for **mutual exclusion**. A mutex is an object that allows multiple
threads to synchronize their accesses to a shared resource.

Mutex is a synchronization primitive that provides mutual exclusion among
the competing threads that try to lock the same mutex.
A mutex is like a mutual exclusive lock but is a bit more complex than a lock.
Mutexes and locks have different names but perform similar functions.

When programming using pthreads, it's very natural to use mutex as the
concurrency control facility because it comes with the pthreads package.
However, you don't have to use mutex. Other synchronization primitives
can also be used. For instance, you could use locking routines that you build
by yourself. We will show you how to do exactly this in the next chapter.

In pthreads, a mutex is of pthread_mutex_t type. For instance, the statement
below declares a mutex named mutex1:

```
pthread_mutex_t  mutex1;
```

8-5-2 Initialize a Mutex

Every mutex must be initialized before it can be used.
Every mutex should be initialized exactly once.

Unlike a regular lock which has a variable name and a simple integer value
associated with it, each mutex has a number of attributes associated with it.
So to initialize a mutex, you must invoke the pthread_mutex_init() function
and provide a mutex attributes object. The mutex attributes object contains
the initial values for various attributes of the mutex. Below is the
synopsis of this function:

```
int pthread_mutex_init(pthread_mutex_t *restrict mutex,
      const pthread_mutexattr_t *restrict attr);
```

This means in order to initialize a mutex, one may need to define and
initialize a mutex attributes object first. A mutex attributes object
contains all the attributes of a mutex. And this is done by calling the
pthread_mutexattr_init() function:

```
int pthread_mutexattr_init(pthread_mutexattr_t *attr);
```

Using this pthread_mutexattr_init() function to initialize a mutex attributes object allows you to set mutex attributes to the values you want to specialize. When the pthread_mutexattr_init() call returns successfully, the mutex attributes object that is just initialized contains the system's default values for the mutex attributes. At this point, you can change and set some of the attribute values before you use it to initialize your mutex. This is the most flexible and powerful way of initializing a mutex. At the same time, it is also the one that needs most lines of code.

To initialize a mutex using nondefault mutex attributes, you call the pthread_mutexattr_init() function to initialize a mutex attributes object first, then you change/set some of the attribute values by calling one or more of the pthread_mutexattr_setXXX() functions, and then you call pthread_mutex_init() to initialize the mutex with the attribute values you set.

A mutex attributes object may be used to initialize more than one mutex. After a mutex attributes object has been used to initialize one or more mutexes, any change affecting the attributes object (including destruction) shall not affect any previously initialized mutexes.

Normally if you just like to take all the default values for all of the mutex attributes, you can skip the pthread_mutexattr_init() call and simply passing in a NULL mutex attributes object to the pthread_mutex_init() call.

In fact, if you like to take all the default values for all of the mutex attributes, there is yet another way of initializing a mutex, which is to statically initialize a mutex as the following:

```
pthread_mutex_t mymutex = PTHREAD_MUTEX_INITIALIZER;
```

That is, when you declare your mutex variable, initialize it with the static initializer PTHREAD_MUTEX_INITIALIZER. This is the simplest way of initializing a mutex. It saves you from using the pthread_mutex_init() and pthread_mutexattr_init() calls.

In summary, there are **three different ways to initialize a mutex**.

1. Using dynamic mutex initialization and setting your own mutex attribute values

```
pthread_mutex_t   mutex;                /* the mutex */

pthread_mutexattr_t  mutexattr;     /* mutex attributes */

/* Initialize mutex attributes object with system's default values */
ret = pthread_mutexattr_init(&mutexattr);

/* Perhaps setting/changing some mutex attribute values in-between here */

/* Initialize the mutex with the attribute values we just set */
ret = pthread_mutex_init(&mutex, &mutexattr);
```

2. Using dynamic mutex initialization and getting default mutex attribute values

```
pthread_mutex_t   mutex;                /* the mutex */
```

```
/* Passing in a NULL mutex attributes object to get all system default's */
ret = pthread_mutex_init(&mutex, (pthread_mutexattr_t *)NULL);
```

3. Use static mutex initializer (getting default mutex attribute values)

```
pthread_mutex_t mymutex = PTHREAD_MUTEX_INITIALIZER;
```

8-5-3 Mutex Attributes

The POSIX Standard defines the following mutex attributes:

1. The type attribute

A mutex has a type attribute, indicating what type of mutex it is. Valid mutex types include the following:

```
PTHREAD_MUTEX_NORMAL
PTHREAD_MUTEX_ERRORCHECK
PTHREAD_MUTEX_RECURSIVE
PTHREAD_MUTEX_DEFAULT
```

Mutexes of **PTHREAD_MUTEX_NORMAL** type are normal mutual exclusive locks. **They can be locked only once. Attempting to relock a mutex already locked will result in deadlock.**

Mutexes of PTHREAD_MUTEX_ERRORCHECK do a bit more for you. It will check and return an error if the calling thread tries to relock a mutex that is already locked.

Mutexes of PTHREAD_MUTEX_RECURSIVE type allow a thread to recursively lock on the same mutex. So, it won't cause deadlock, nor is it an error.

An implementation may map PTHREAD_MUTEX_DEFAULT to one of the other mutex types.

The mutex type affects the behavior of calls which lock and unlock the mutex.

Use the pthread_mutexattr_gettype() and pthread_mutexattr_settype() APIs to get and set the mutex type attribute, respectively.

```
int pthread_mutexattr_gettype(const pthread_mutexattr_t *restrict attr,
        int *restrict type);
int pthread_mutexattr_settype(pthread_mutexattr_t *attr, int type);
```

The pthread_mutexattr_gettype() and pthread_mutexattr_settype() functions return zero on success; otherwise, an error number is returned to indicate the error.

2. The process-shared attribute

The process-shared attribute specifies whether a mutex is to be used only by threads within the same process or shared by threads in multiple processes. In the first version of the POSIX.1c standard, this was the only mutex attribute defined.

The value PTHREAD_PROCESS_PRIVATE means the mutex will be used only by
threads in the calling process. The value PTHREAD_PROCESS_SHARED means
the mutex is to be shared by threads in multiple processes.
The POSIX.1c standard says the default value of the attribute should
be PTHREAD_PROCESS_PRIVATE. If the value of this attribute is
PTHREAD_PROCESS_SHARED, then it's the application program's responsibility
to allocate the mutex in memory shared by these multiple processes.

Use the pthread_mutexattr_getpshared() and pthread_mutexattr_setpshared()
functions to get and set the process-shared attribute, respectively.

```
int pthread_mutexattr_getpshared(const pthread_mutexattr_t
        *restrict attr, int *restrict pshared);
int pthread_mutexattr_setpshared(pthread_mutexattr_t *attr,
        int pshared);
```

Upon successful completion, pthread_mutexattr_setpshared() returns zero;
otherwise, an error number is returned to indicate the error.
Same for pthread_mutexattr_getpshared().

3. The prioceiling attribute

The prioceiling attribute contains the priority ceiling of initialized
mutexes. The values of prioceiling are within the maximum range of
priorities defined by SCHED_FIFO.

The prioceiling attribute specifies the priority ceiling of initialized
mutexes, which is the minimum priority level at which the critical section
guarded by the mutex is executed. To avoid priority inversion,
the priority ceiling of the mutex should be set to a priority higher than
or equal to the highest priority of all the threads that may lock that
mutex.

Use the pthread_mutexattr_getprioceiling() and
pthread_mutexattr_setprioceiling() functions to get and set the value of
the prioceiling attribute of the mutex attributes object, respectively.

```
int pthread_mutexattr_getprioceiling(const pthread_mutexattr_t
        *restrict attr, int *restrict prioceiling);
int pthread_mutexattr_setprioceiling(pthread_mutexattr_t *attr,
        int prioceiling);
```

Upon successful completion, the pthread_mutexattr_getprioceiling() and
pthread_mutexattr_setprioceiling() functions return zero; otherwise,
an error number is returned to indicate the error.

4. The protocol attribute

The protocol attribute defines the protocol to be followed in utilizing
mutexes. It concerns with the priority and scheduling of a thread
owning a mutex. This attribute was added in The Open Group Base
Specifications Issue 6 of 2004.

The value of protocol attribute can be one of the following:

```
PTHREAD_PRIO_NONE
PTHREAD_PRIO_INHERIT
PTHREAD_PRIO_PROTECT
```

The default value of the protocol attribute is PTHREAD_PRIO_NONE. When a thread with the PTHREAD_PRIO_NONE protocol attribute owns a mutex, its priority and scheduling will not be affected by its mutex ownership.

When a thread is blocking other higher priority threads because of owning one or more robust mutexes with the PTHREAD_PRIO_INHERIT protocol attribute, it will execute at the higher of its priority or the priority of the highest priority thread waiting on any of the robust mutexes owned by this thread and initialized with this protocol.

When a thread owns one or more robust mutexes initialized with the PTHREAD_PRIO_PROTECT protocol, it will execute at the higher of its priority or the highest of the priority ceilings of all the robust mutexes owned by this thread and initialized with this attribute, regardless of whether other threads are blocked on any of these robust mutexes or not.

When a thread calls pthread_mutex_lock(), assuming the mutex was initialized with the PTHREAD_PRIO_INHERIT protocol, when the calling thread is blocked because the mutex is owned by another thread, that owner thread shall inherit the priority level of the calling thread as long as it continues to own the mutex. The implementation will update its execution priority to the maximum of its assigned priority and all its inherited priorities. Furthermore, if this owner thread itself becomes blocked on another mutex with the protocol attribute having the value PTHREAD_PRIO_INHERIT, the same priority inheritance effect should be propagated to this other owner thread, in a recursive manner.

Use pthread_mutexattr_getprotocol() and pthread_mutexattr_setprotocol() functions to get and set the value of the protocol attribute of the mutex attributes object, respectively.

```
int pthread_mutexattr_getprotocol(const pthread_mutexattr_t
     *restrict attr, int *restrict protocol);
int pthread_mutexattr_setprotocol(pthread_mutexattr_t *attr,
     int protocol);
```

If success, the pthread_mutexattr_getprotocol() and pthread_mutexattr_setprotocol() functions return zero; otherwise, an error number is returned to indicate the error.

5. The robust attribute

The robust attribute was added in Issue 7 of the POSIX.1 Standard in 2018. Because of it's recent, some operating systems have not supported this attribute yet. Though it is expected that they will soon catch up because this is a very important feature.

The robust attribute was added in an effort to make cleaning up inconsistent mutex state easier. From time to time, a process or thread holding the lock on a mutex may die, making no one else is able to use the same mutex again and resulting in deadlock or hang. With the **robust attribute**, you can make your mutex a robust mutex. And if this situation occurs, the next thread calling pthread_mutex_lock() will get the EOWNERDEAD error. And it will be able to invoke the pthread_mutex_consistent() function to clean up, make the mutex state consistent, and make the mutex usable again.

Valid values for the robust attribute and their meanings are listed below:

PTHREAD_MUTEX_STALLED
   No special actions are taken if the owner of the mutex is terminated while holding the mutex lock. If no other thread can unlock the mutex, this can lead to deadlocks. This is the default value.

PTHREAD_MUTEX_ROBUST
   If the owning thread of a robust mutex terminates while holding the mutex lock, the next thread that tries to acquire the mutex will be notified about it and the locking function will return **EOWNERDEAD**.

   The notified thread can then attempt to make the state of the mutex consistent again, and if successful can mark the mutex state as consistent by calling **pthread_mutex_consistent**(). After a subsequent successful call to pthread_mutex_unlock(), the mutex lock shall be released and can be used normally by other threads.

   If the mutex is unlocked without a call to pthread_mutex_consistent(), it will be in a permanently unusable state and all attempts to lock the mutex will fail with the error ENOTRECOVERABLE.
   The only operation allowed on such a mutex is pthread_mutex_destroy().

Use the pthread_mutexattr_getrobust() and pthread_mutexattr_setrobust() functions, respectively, to get and set the mutex robust attribute.

```
int pthread_mutexattr_getrobust(const pthread_mutexattr_t *restrict
      attr, int *restrict robust);
int pthread_mutexattr_setrobust(pthread_mutexattr_t *attr,
      int robust);
```

On success, pthread_mutexattr_getrobust() and pthread_mutexattr_setrobust() functions return zero; otherwise, an error number is returned on failure.

Note that as of this writing, not every operating system supports the robust attribute yet. Linux and Solaris do but AIX, HPUX and Apple Darwin don't. Apple Darwin does not support the pthread_mutex_consistent() function yet. But they'll probably catch up soon on this because it's a very nice feature.

The pthread_mutexattr_init() function will initialize a mutex attributes object with the default values for all of the attributes defined by the implementation.

Figure 8-12 shows an example of initialize a mutex in most general and flexible way.

Figure 8-12 Initialize a mutex in a general and flexible way (pt_mutex_init.c)

```
/*
 * Initialize a mutex with specialized mutex attributes.
 * As of this writing, AIX and HPUX do not support mutex robust attribute.
```

```
 * Copyright (c) 2019-2020 Mr. Jin-Jwei Chen.  All rights reserved.
 */

#include <stdio.h>
#include <pthread.h>

void prt_mutex_attrs(pthread_mutexattr_t *attr)
{
  int     type = 0;       /* mutex type attribute */
  int     pshared = 0;    /* mutex pshared attribute */
  int     prot = 0;       /* mutex protocol attribute */
  int     pric = 0;       /* mutex prioceiling attribute */
  int     robust = 0;     /* mutex robust attribute */
  int     ret;

  if (attr == NULL) return;

  ret = pthread_mutexattr_gettype(attr, &type);
  fprintf(stdout, " mutex type attribute = %s\n",
      (type == PTHREAD_MUTEX_NORMAL) ? "PTHREAD_MUTEX_NORMAL" :
      (type == PTHREAD_MUTEX_RECURSIVE) ? "PTHREAD_MUTEX_RECURSIVE" :
      (type == PTHREAD_MUTEX_ERRORCHECK) ? "PTHREAD_MUTEX_ERRORCHECK" :
      (type == PTHREAD_MUTEX_DEFAULT) ? "PTHREAD_MUTEX_DEFAULT" :
      "Unknown");
  ret = pthread_mutexattr_getpshared(attr, &pshared);
  fprintf(stdout, " mutex pshared attribute = %s\n",
      (pshared == PTHREAD_PROCESS_PRIVATE) ? "PTHREAD_PROCESS_PRIVATE" :
      (pshared == PTHREAD_PROCESS_SHARED ) ? "PTHREAD_PROCESS_SHARED " :
      "Unknown");
  ret = pthread_mutexattr_getprotocol(attr, &prot);
  fprintf(stdout, " mutex protocol attribute = %s\n",
      (prot == PTHREAD_PRIO_NONE) ? "PTHREAD_PRIO_NONE" :
      (prot == PTHREAD_PRIO_INHERIT) ? "PTHREAD_PRIO_INHERIT" :
      (prot == PTHREAD_PRIO_PROTECT ) ? "PTHREAD_PRIO_PROTECT " :
      "Unknown");

  ret = pthread_mutexattr_getprioceiling(attr, &pric);
  fprintf(stdout, " mutex prioceiling attribute = %d\n", pric);

#ifndef NOROBUST
  ret = pthread_mutexattr_getrobust(attr, &robust);
  fprintf(stdout, " mutex robust attribute = %s\n",
      (robust == PTHREAD_MUTEX_STALLED) ? "PTHREAD_MUTEX_STALLED" :
      (robust == PTHREAD_MUTEX_ROBUST) ? "PTHREAD_MUTEX_ROBUST" :
      "Unknown");
#endif
}

pthread_mutex_t      mutex1;       /* global mutex shared by all threads */

/*
 * The main program.
 */
int main(int argc, char *argv[])
{
  int           ret;
```

379

```
pthread_mutexattr_t  mutexattr1;   /* mutex attributes */
int         pshared;               /* mutex pshared attribute */
int         prot;                  /* mutex protocol attribute */

/* Initialize mutex attributes */
ret = pthread_mutexattr_init(&mutexattr1);
if (ret != 0)
{
  fprintf(stderr, "Failed to initialize mutex attributes, ret=%d\n", ret);
  pthread_exit((void *)-1);
}

/* Set mutex pshared attribute to be PTHREAD_PROCESS_SHARED */
pshared = PTHREAD_PROCESS_SHARED;
ret = pthread_mutexattr_setpshared(&mutexattr1, pshared);
if (ret != 0)
  fprintf(stderr, "failed to set mutex pshared attribute, ret=%d\n", ret);

/* Set mutex protocol attribute to be PTHREAD_PRIO_INHERIT */
prot = PTHREAD_PRIO_INHERIT;
ret = pthread_mutexattr_setprotocol(&mutexattr1, prot);
if (ret != 0)
  fprintf(stderr, "failed to set mutex protocol attribute, ret=%d\n", ret);

/* Initialize the mutex */
ret = pthread_mutex_init(&mutex1, &mutexattr1);
if (ret != 0)
{
  fprintf(stderr, "Failed to initialize mutex, ret=%d\n", ret);
  pthread_exit((void *)-2);
}
fprintf(stdout, "The mutex initialization was successful!\n");

/* Print mutex attributes */
prt_mutex_attrs(&mutexattr1);

/* Create the child threads to do the work here */

/* Join the child threads */

/* Destroy mutex attributes */
ret = pthread_mutexattr_destroy(&mutexattr1);
if (ret != 0)
{
  fprintf(stderr, "Failed to destroy mutex attributes, ret=%d\n", ret);
  pthread_exit((void *)-3);
}

/* Destroy the mutex */
ret = pthread_mutex_destroy(&mutex1);
if (ret != 0)
{
  fprintf(stderr, "Failed to destroy mutex, ret=%d\n", ret);
  pthread_exit((void *)-4);
}
```

```
pthread_exit((void *)0);
}
```

8-5-4 Destroy a Mutex

Object initialization (creation) and destruction always come in pair.
After a program is done with using a mutex, it must destroy the mutex and
the mutex attributes object associated with it. They are carried out by the
pthread_mutex_destroy() and pthread_mutexattr_destroy() functions,
respectively. For instance, one might destroy the attribute first
and then the mutex after.

```
int pthread_mutexattr_destroy(pthread_mutexattr_t *attr);

int pthread_mutex_destroy(pthread_mutex_t *mutex);
```

Note that, **a mutex should be destroyed when it is unlocked.**
Trying to destroy a mutex when it is locked, or a mutex that another thread
is attempting to lock, or a mutex that is being used in a
pthread_cond_timedwait() or pthread_cond_wait() call by another thread,
will result in undefined behavior.

Hence, ensure that no other thread may be referencing the mutex before
destroying it.

Note that calling pthread_mutexattr_destroy() to try to destroy a mutex
attributes works just fine in all platforms except it seems to get error
number 22 in the 64-bit mode of HPUX IA64 platform. Even if the order
of the two functions is reversed, it makes no difference.
Because of that, we put the function call under the '#ifndef HPUX64' macro.

8-5-5 Lock and Unlock a Mutex

When using a mutex to synchronize accesses to a shared resource, a thread
must successfully lock the mutex first before it can access or update the
shared resource. And when the thread is done using the shared resource,
it must unlock the mutex such that other threads can use the shared resource.
All threads involved in using the same shared resource must do so in order to
protect and preserve the integrity of the shared resource.

In other words, the standard way of accessing a shared resource from within
a program is like this:

```
lock the mutex
access the shared resource (the so-called critical section)
unlock the mutex
```

A mutex has two states: locked and unlocked.

There are three possible ways to lock a mutex:

```
#include <pthread.h>
#include <time.h>
```

```
int pthread_mutex_lock(pthread_mutex_t *mutex);
int pthread_mutex_trylock(pthread_mutex_t *mutex);
int pthread_mutex_timedlock(pthread_mutex_t *restrict mutex,
    const struct timespec *restrict abstime);
```

The pthread_mutex_lock() function is synchronous and it does busy-waiting. That is, should the mutex be unavailable (i.e. it has been locked by some other thread or the current thread), calling this function will block the thread forever or until the mutex becomes available. When this call completes and returns successfully, the mutex is in the locked state and is owned by the calling thread.

To avoid wasting time, a thread my invoke the pthread_mutex_trylock() function instead. This function is the same as the pthread_mutex_lock() function except one thing. That is, the pthread_mutex_trylock() function will return right away and let the caller decide what it wants to do if the mutex is currently not available, as opposed to blocking as in the case of pthread_mutex_lock(). This gives the caller an option of not having to wait when the mutex is not available.

Alternatively, a calling thread or process can specify a time limit for how long it is willing to wait if the mutex is already locked (again, either by another thread or by the current thread itself). This is done by the pthread_mutex_timedlock() API. The caller specifies the time it's willing to wait in the second argument of the function call. If after that time expires and the mutex is still not available, the call will return with the error ETIMEDOUT. To use the pthread_mutex_timedlock() function, applications need to include the header file <time.h> as well.

Both of pthread_mutex_trylock() and pthread_mutex_timedlock() are asynchronous, meaning they don't block until the mutex is successfully locked by the caller as in the case of pthread_mutex_lock(). Rather, when they return, it could mean the mutex is successfully locked by the caller or the mutex is not available. Therefore, the calling program must check to see which case it is.

When successful, all of pthread_mutex_lock(), pthread_mutex_trylock(), and pthread_mutex_timedlock() return zero. In this case, the mutex is successfully locked by the calling thread. Otherwise, an error is returned to indicate the error.

Always make sure a mutex lock is released (i.e. unlocked) when it is no longer needed.

To release an acquired mutex lock, a thread or process invokes the pthread_mutex_unlock() function:

```
int pthread_mutex_unlock(pthread_mutex_t *mutex);
```

When a mutex is unlocked, if there are other threads waiting, the scheduling policy will determine which thread gets the mutex next.

When successful, the pthread_mutex_unlock() function returns zero. Otherwise, an error is returned to indicate the error.

Figure 8-13 is a program demonstrating the use of pthreads mutex.
The example program creates a number of threads (the default value is 4)
to update a shared variable global_count for a certain number of times.
Each time a thread increases the value of the shared variable by one.
The update operation is guarded by a pair of mutex lock and unlock calls.
As you can see, the program produces correct result at end and there is
no update loss.

Figure 8-13 Program example using mutex (pt_mutex.c)

```c
/*
 * Update shared data with synchronization using pthread mutex.
 * Copyright (c) 2014, 2019 Mr. Jin-Jwei Chen.  All rights reserved.
 */

#include <stdio.h>
#include <pthread.h>

#define  NTHREADS    4
#define  NTASKS      500000
#define  DELAY_COUNT 1000

unsigned int  global_count=0;     /* global data shared by all threads */

pthread_mutex_t        mutex1;     /* global mutex shared by all threads */

/*
 * The worker thread.
 */

int worker_thread(void *args)
{
  unsigned int  *argp;
  unsigned int  myid;
  unsigned int  ntasks;
  int           i, j, ret=0;

  /* Extract input arguments (two unsigned integers) */
  argp = (unsigned int *)args;
  if (argp != NULL)
  {
    myid = argp[0];
    ntasks = argp[1];
  }
  else
#ifdef SUN64
  {
    ret = (-1);
    pthread_exit((void *)&ret);
  }
#else
    pthread_exit((void *)(-1));
#endif

  fprintf(stdout, "Worker thread: myid=%u ntasks=%u\n", myid, ntasks);
```

```
  /* Do my job */
  for (i = 0; i < ntasks; i++)
  {
    ret = pthread_mutex_lock(&mutex1);
    if (ret != 0)
    {
      fprintf(stderr, "Thread %u failed to lock the mutex, ret=%d\n", myid, ret);
      continue;
    }

    /* Update the shared data */
    global_count = global_count + 1;
    /* insert a bit of delay */
    for (j = 0; j < DELAY_COUNT; j++);

    ret = pthread_mutex_unlock(&mutex1);
    if (ret != 0)
      fprintf(stderr, "Thread %u failed to unlock the mutex, ret=%d\n", myid, ret);
  }

#ifdef SUN64
  pthread_exit((void *)&ret);
#else
  pthread_exit((void *)0);
#endif
}

/*
 * The main program.
 */
int main(int argc, char *argv[])
{
  pthread_t        thrds[NTHREADS];
  unsigned int     args[NTHREADS][2];
  int              ret, i;
  int              retval = 0;      /* each child thread returns an int */
  pthread_mutexattr_t  mutexattr1;  /* mutex attributes */
#ifdef SUN64
  int              *retvalp = &retval; /* pointer to returned value */
#endif

  /* Load up the input arguments for each child thread */
  for (i = 0; i < NTHREADS; i++)
  {
    args[i][0] = i;
    args[i][1] = NTASKS;
  }

  /* Initialize mutex attributes */
  ret = pthread_mutexattr_init(&mutexattr1);
  if (ret != 0)
  {
    fprintf(stderr, "Failed to initialize mutex attributes, ret=%d\n", ret);
    pthread_exit((void *)-1);
  }
```

```c
  /* Initialize the mutex */
  ret = pthread_mutex_init(&mutex1, &mutexattr1);
  if (ret != 0)
  {
    fprintf(stderr, "Failed to initialize mutex, ret=%d\n", ret);
    pthread_exit((void *)-2);
  }

  /* Create new threads to run the worker_thread() function and pass in args */
  for (i = 0; i < NTHREADS; i++)
  {
    ret = pthread_create(&thrds[i], (pthread_attr_t *)NULL,
          (void *(*)(void *))worker_thread, (void *)args[i]);
    if (ret != 0)
    {
      fprintf(stderr, "Failed to create the worker thread, ret=%d\n", ret);
      pthread_exit((void *)-3);
    }
  }

  /*
   * Wait for each of the child threads to finish and retrieve its returned
   * value.
   */
  for (i = 0; i < NTHREADS; i++)
  {
#ifdef SUN64
    ret = pthread_join(thrds[i], (void **)&retvalp);
#else
    ret = pthread_join(thrds[i], (void **)&retval);
#endif
    fprintf(stdout, "Thread %u exited with return value %d\n", i, retval);
  }

  /* Destroy mutex attributes */
#ifndef HPUX64
  ret = pthread_mutexattr_destroy(&mutexattr1);
  if (ret != 0)
  {
    fprintf(stderr, "Failed to destroy mutex attributes, ret=%d\n", ret);
    pthread_exit((void *)-4);
  }
#endif

  /* Destroy the mutex */
  ret = pthread_mutex_destroy(&mutex1);
  if (ret != 0)
  {
    fprintf(stderr, "Failed to destroy mutex, ret=%d\n", ret);
    pthread_exit((void *)-5);
  }

  fprintf(stdout, "global_count = %u\n", global_count);
  pthread_exit((void *)0);
}
```

Some Notes

If a signal is delivered to a thread waiting for a mutex, upon return from the signal handler the thread will resume waiting for the mutex as if it was not interrupted.

As we said above, the pthread_mutex_lock() function is synchronous, meaning the call will block until the mutex becomes available. When the call returns, the mutex should be in locked state with the caller being the owner of it. This is the behavior of this call with respect to a normal mutex.

With the advent of robust mutexes in Issue 7 of the POSIX Standard 2018, if the mutex is a robust mutex, this call may return EOWNERDEAD error should the mutex be in the dangling state (i.e. locked by a dead thread) which we will discuss very soon next. In fact, all of pthread_mutex_lock(), pthread_mutex_trylock(), and pthread_mutex_timedlock() functions will return error EOWNERDEAD if the mutex is locked by a dead thread.

We will discuss robust mutex in the next section.

8-5-5-1 Lock Recursively or Wrongly Unlock

By definition, a mutex is a mutual exclusive lock. It can be locked only once. However, this is the normal mutex's behavior. POSIX defines different types of mutexes and some types do not behave this way.

Figure 8-14 shows the behavior of different types of mutexes.

If a thread attempts to relock a mutex that it has already locked, pthread_mutex_lock() should behave as described in the 'Relock' column of the table. If a thread attempts to unlock a mutex that it has not locked or a mutex which is unlocked, pthread_mutex_unlock() shall behave as described in the 'Unlock When Not Owner' column of the table.

Figure 8-14 Behavior of different types of mutex

Mutex type	Robustness	Relock	Unlock when not owner
NORMAL	non-robust	deadlock	undefined behavior
NORMAL	robust	deadlock	error returned
ERRORCHECK	either	error returned	error returned
RECURSIVE	either	recursive	error returned
DEFAULT	non-robust	undefined behavior*	undefined behavior*
DEFAULT	robust	undefined behavior*	error returned

(Courtesy of The Open Group)

* If the mutex type is PTHREAD_MUTEX_DEFAULT, the behavior of pthread_mutex_lock() may correspond to one of the three other standard mutex types. And if not, the behavior is undefined.

Where the table indicates recursive behavior, the mutex will maintain the concept of a lock count. When a thread successfully acquires a mutex for the first time, the lock count is set to one. Every time a thread relocks this mutex, the lock count is incremented by one. Each time

the thread unlocks the mutex, the lock count is decremented by one.
When the lock count reaches zero, the mutex will become available for
other threads to acquire.

Figure 8-15 is a program example demonstrating how to make a mutex a RECURSIVE
mutex such that if the same thread relocks the same mutex it has held a lock
on, it's OK; it will work rather than deadlock. A recursive mutex maintains
an internal lock count and this will just cause the internal lock count
to be incremented by one. **Note that by default, a mutex is a NORMAL mutex
which is not a RECURSIVE mutex.** To create a recursive mutex, you have to
invoke the pthread_mutexattr_settype() API and set the type of the mutex
to be PTHREAD_MUTEX_RECURSIVE.

Figure 8-15 Creating and using a recursive type of mutex (pt_recursive_mutex.c)

```c
/*
 * PTHREAD_MUTEX_RECURSIVE mutex.
 * An attempt to recursively lock a PTHREAD_MUTEX_RECURSIVE type of mutex
 * works just fine rather than deadlocks.
 * Copyright (c) 2019 Mr. Jin-Jwei Chen.  All rights reserved.
 */

#include <stdio.h>
#include <stdlib.h>
#include <pthread.h>
#include <time.h>

#define   MAXNTHREADS   10       /* maximum number of threads */
#define   DEFNTHREADS   2        /* default number of threads */
#define   MAXTASKS      3000     /* maximum number of tasks */
#define   DEFNTASKS     5        /* default number of tasks */

pthread_mutex_t      mutex1;     /* global mutex shared by all threads */

int recursive(unsigned int myid, unsigned int cnt)
{
  struct timespec   slptm;
  int     ret;

  slptm.tv_sec = 0;
  slptm.tv_nsec = 500000000;   /* 5/10 second */

  if (cnt <= 0)
    return(0);

  /* Acquire the mutex lock */
  ret = pthread_mutex_lock(&mutex1);
  if (ret != 0)
  {
    fprintf(stderr, "recursive(): thread %u failed to lock the mutex,"
      " ret=%d\n", myid, ret);
    return(-8);
  }

  /* Do some work. Here we do nothing but sleep and then call ourself. */
  fprintf(stdout, "Thread %u in recursive(), cnt=%u\n", myid, cnt);
```

```
    nanosleep(&slptm, (struct timespec *)NULL);
    ret = recursive(myid, --cnt);

    /* Release the lock */
    ret = pthread_mutex_unlock(&mutex1);
    if (ret != 0)
    {
      fprintf(stderr, "recursive(): thread %u failed to unlock the mutex,"
        " ret=%d\n", myid, ret);
      return(-9);
    }

  return(0);
}

/* The worker thread */
int worker_thread(void *args)
{
  unsigned int  *argp;
  unsigned int  myid;          /* my id */
  unsigned int  ntasks;        /* number of tasks to perform */
  int           i, ret=0;

  /* Extract input arguments (two unsigned integers) */
  argp = (unsigned int *)args;
  if (argp != NULL)
  {
    myid = argp[0];
    ntasks = argp[1];
  }
  else
#ifdef SUN64
  {
    ret = (-1);
    pthread_exit((void *)&ret);
  }
#else
    pthread_exit((void *)(-1));
#endif

  fprintf(stdout, "worker_thread(): myid=%u ntasks=%u\n", myid, ntasks);

  /* Do the work */
  ret = recursive(myid, ntasks);

#ifdef SUN64
  pthread_exit((void *)&ret);
#else
  pthread_exit((void *)ret);
#endif
}

/*
 * The main program.
 */
int main(int argc, char *argv[])
```

```
{
  pthread_t      thrds[MAXNTHREADS];
  unsigned int   args[MAXNTHREADS][2];
  int            ret, i;
  int            retval = 0;   /* each child thread returns an int */
#ifdef SUN64
  int            *retvalp = &retval;          /* pointer to returned value */
#endif
  int            nthreads = DEFNTHREADS;     /* default # of threads */
  int            ntasks = DEFNTASKS;         /* default # of tasks */
  int            mtype = PTHREAD_MUTEX_RECURSIVE;  /* recursive mutex */
  pthread_mutexattr_t  mutexattr1;  /* mutex attributes */

  /* Get number of threads and tasks from user */
  if (argc > 1)
  {
    nthreads = atoi(argv[1]);
    if (nthreads < 0 || nthreads > MAXNTHREADS)
      nthreads = DEFNTHREADS;
  }
  if (argc > 2)
  {
    ntasks = atoi(argv[2]);
    if (ntasks < 0 || ntasks > MAXTASKS)
      ntasks = DEFNTASKS;
  }

  /* Initialize mutex attributes */
  ret = pthread_mutexattr_init(&mutexattr1);
  if (ret != 0)
  {
    fprintf(stderr, "Failed to initialize mutex attributes, ret=%d\n", ret);
    pthread_exit((void *)-1);
  }

  /* Create a recursive type of mutex */
  ret = pthread_mutexattr_settype(&mutexattr1, mtype);
  if (ret != 0)
  {
    fprintf(stderr, "Failed to set mutex type to be recursive, ret=%d\n", ret);
    pthread_exit((void *)-2);
  }

  /* Initialize the mutex */
  ret = pthread_mutex_init(&mutex1, &mutexattr1);
  if (ret != 0)
  {
    fprintf(stderr, "Failed to initialize mutex, ret=%d\n", ret);
    pthread_exit((void *)-3);
  }

  /* Load up the input arguments for each child thread */
  for (i = 0; i < nthreads; i++)
  {
    args[i][0] = (i + 1);
    args[i][1] = ntasks;
```

```
   }

   /* Create new threads to run the worker_thread() function and pass in args */
   for (i = 0; i < nthreads; i++)
   {
      ret = pthread_create(&thrds[i], (pthread_attr_t *)NULL,
            (void *(*)(void *))worker_thread, (void *)args[i]);
      if (ret != 0)
      {
         fprintf(stderr, "Failed to create the worker thread, ret=%d\n", ret);
         pthread_exit((void *)-4);
      }
   }

   /*
    * Wait for each of the child threads to finish and retrieve its returned
    * value.
    */
   for (i = 0; i < nthreads; i++)
   {
#ifdef SUN64
      ret = pthread_join(thrds[i], (void **)&retvalp);
#else
      ret = pthread_join(thrds[i], (void **)&retval);
#endif
      fprintf(stdout, "Thread %u exited with return value %d\n", (i+1), retval);
   }

   /* Destroy mutex attributes */
#ifndef HPUX64
   ret = pthread_mutexattr_destroy(&mutexattr1);
   if (ret != 0)
   {
      fprintf(stderr, "Failed to destroy mutex attributes, ret=%d\n", ret);
      pthread_exit((void *)-5);
   }
#endif

   /* Destroy the mutex */
   ret = pthread_mutex_destroy(&mutex1);
   if (ret != 0)
   {
      fprintf(stderr, "Failed to destroy mutex, ret=%d\n", ret);
      pthread_exit((void *)-6);
   }

   pthread_exit((void *)0);
}
```

8-5-5-2 Fix a Dangling Mutex – Robust Mutex

Normally, with a regular mutex, if a thread holding the lock on a mutex
dies, the mutex becomes being locked forever and if any other threads try
to obtain the same lock again, it will deadlock and hang forever,
assuming a synchronous call is made. Killing the entire application usually

is the only solution in this case. However, with the introduction of the so-called "robust" mutex, not anymore.

If a mutex is a **robust mutex** and the thread owning the lock on the mutex terminates while holding the mutex lock, a call to pthread_mutex_lock() on the mutex will return the error value EOWNERDEAD, as opposed to block and deadlock forever. This allows the thread needing the same mutex lock to go in and clean it up so that the mutex becomes usable and available again. This is a very nice feature added in The Open Group Base Specifications Issue 7, 2018 edition.

In this case, the mutex is locked by a dead thread but the state it protects is marked as inconsistent. The application should ensure that the state is made consistent so that the mutex becomes usable again.

The way to do this is as follows:

1. After you initialize the mutex attributes object and before you initialize the mutex, call the **pthread_mutexattr_setrobust**() function to make the mutex a "robust" mutex by passing in **PTHREAD_MUTEX_ROBUST** as the value of the second argument.

2. In all threads, check the return value from pthread_mutex_lock(). If pthread_mutex_lock() returns the error EOWNERDEAD (which is defined in errno.h), then invoke both pthread_mutex_consistent() and pthread_mutex_unlock() functions on the mutex. This should make the mutex available again after its lock was held by a dead thread.

```
ret = pthread_mutex_consistent(&mutex1);
ret = pthread_mutex_unlock(&mutex1);
```

As we said it earlier, if you make a mutex a robust mutex, then after a thread holding a lock on the mutex dies, another thread calling the pthread_mutex_lock() function on this mutex will get the error EOWNERDEAD returned. And that's when it can go in and make these two calls to clean it up and make the mutex available again.

The first call pthread_mutex_consistent() makes the mutex's state consistent and the second call releases the lock held by the dead thread. These two calls together clean up the mutex's state and make the mutex unlocked and available again.

The key here is that if an owner of a robust mutex terminates while holding the mutex lock, the mutex becomes inconsistent and the next thread that tries to acquire the mutex lock will be notified of the situation by the return **error code EOWNERDEAD**.

Figure 8-16 shows an example program that does exactly this.
Two threads are created in this program. Thread 1 is the worker thread and thread 2 is the manager thread. The worker thread holds the mutex lock while doing its work. The manager thread cancels the worker thread.
So, the worker thread terminates while holding the lock on the mutex.

After canceling the worker thread, the manager thread tries to acquire the mutex lock itself. It gets the error EOWNERDEAD returned. Therefore, it calls pthread_mutex_consistent() and pthread_mutex_unlock() on the mutex to fix its state and release the lock. Then the manager thread tries to obtain the same mutex lock and it gets it successfully.

As of this writing, this example program works on Linux 3.10 and Solaris 11.5, but not AIX 7.1, HPUX 11.31 or Apple Darwin 19.3 because they do not support robust mutex yet. That is, functions pthread_mutexattr_setrobust() and pthread_mutex_consistent() are not yet supported. But they may soon catch up.

Figure 8-16 Clean up a mutex whose lock was held by a dead thread (pt_mutex_cleanup.c)

```c
/*
 * Clean up the state of a dangling mutex whose lock is held by a dead thread
 * using pthread_mutex_consistent() and pthread_mutex_unlock().
 * Copyright (c) 2019, 2020 Mr. Jin-Jwei Chen.  All rights reserved.
 * pthread_mutex_consistent() is not supported in Apple Darwin.
 */

#include <stdio.h>
#include <stdlib.h>
#include <pthread.h>
#include <errno.h>
#include <time.h>
#include <unistd.h>

#define   MAXNTHREADS   10        /* maximum number of threads */
#define   DEFNTHREADS   2         /* default number of threads */
#define   MAXTASKS      9000      /* maximum number of tasks */
#define   DEFNTASKS     500       /* default number of tasks */
#define   LOOPCNT       10000

pthread_mutex_t       mutex1;       /* global mutex shared by all threads */

/* Thread cancellation cleanup handler function */
void cancel_cleanup(char *bufptr)
{
  fprintf(stdout, "Enter thread cancellation cleanup routine.\n");
  if (bufptr)
  {
    free(bufptr);
    fprintf(stdout, "cancel_cleanup(): memory at address %p was freed.\n",
      bufptr);
  }
}

/* The worker thread */
int worker_thread(void *args)
{
  unsigned int   *argp;
  unsigned int   myid;        /* my id */
  unsigned int   ntasks;      /* number of tasks to perform */
  int            i, j, ret=0;
  unsigned int   count = 0;   /* counter */
  int            curstate;    /* thread's current cancelstate */
  int            oldstate;    /* thread's previous cancelstate */
  int            curtype;     /* thread's current canceltype */
```

```
   int           oldtype;       /* thread's previous canceltype */
   char          *bufptr=NULL;  /* address of malloc-ed memory */
   struct timespec  slptm;      /* time to sleep */

   /* Extract input arguments (two unsigned integers) */
   argp = (unsigned int *)args;
   if (argp != NULL)
   {
     myid = argp[0];
     ntasks = argp[1];
   }
   else
#ifdef SUN64
   {
     ret = (-1);
     pthread_exit((void *)&ret);
   }
#else
     pthread_exit((void *)(-1));
#endif

   fprintf(stdout, "worker_thread(): myid=%u ntasks=%u\n", myid, ntasks);

   /* Set thread's cancelstate -- disable cancellation */
   curstate = PTHREAD_CANCEL_DISABLE;
   ret = pthread_setcancelstate(curstate, &oldstate);
   fprintf(stdout, "worker_thread(): thread cancellation is disabled.\n");

   /* Set thread's canceltype */
   curtype = PTHREAD_CANCEL_DEFERRED;
   ret = pthread_setcanceltype(curtype, &oldtype);

   /* To demo cancellation cleanup, we allocate some memory here. */
   bufptr = malloc(512);
   if (bufptr != NULL)
     fprintf(stdout, "worker_thread(): memory at address %p was allocated.\n",
       bufptr);
   else
     fprintf(stderr, "worker_thread(): failed to allocate memory.\n");

   /* Install the thread cancellation cleanup handler */
   pthread_cleanup_push((void (*)())cancel_cleanup, (void *)bufptr);

   /* Acquire the mutex lock */
   ret = pthread_mutex_lock(&mutex1);
   if (ret != 0)
   {
     fprintf(stderr, "Thread %u failed to lock the mutex, ret=%d\n", myid, ret);
   }

   /* Do the work */
   slptm.tv_sec = 0;
   slptm.tv_nsec = 100000000;  /* 1/10 second */
   for (i = 0; i < ntasks; i++)
   {
     for (j = 0; j < LOOPCNT; j++)
```

```
      count++;
   nanosleep(&slptm, (struct timespec *)NULL);
   fprintf(stdout, "worker_thread(): count=%u\n", count);

   if (count == (5*LOOPCNT))
     sleep(1);

   if (count == (10*LOOPCNT))
   {
      /* Set thread's cancelstate -- enable cancellation */
      curstate = PTHREAD_CANCEL_ENABLE;
      ret = pthread_setcancelstate(curstate, &oldstate);
      fprintf(stdout, "worker_thread(): thread cancellation is enabled.\n");
   }
 }

 /* Release the mutex lock */
 ret = pthread_mutex_unlock(&mutex1);
 if (ret != 0)
   fprintf(stderr, "Thread %u failed to unlock the mutex, ret=%d\n", myid, ret);

 /* Remove the thread cancellation cleanup handler */
 pthread_cleanup_pop(0);
 if (bufptr != NULL)
   free(bufptr);

#ifdef SUN64
  pthread_exit((void *)&ret);
#else
  pthread_exit((void *)ret);
#endif
}

/* The manager thread */
int manager_thread(void *args)
{
   pthread_t   *argp;
   int          ret=0;
   pthread_t   targetThread;   /* thread id of the target thread */

   /* Extract input argument */
   argp = (pthread_t *)args;
   if (argp != NULL)
     targetThread = *(pthread_t *)argp;
   else
#ifdef SUN64
   {
     ret = (-1);
     pthread_exit((void *)&ret);
   }
#else
     pthread_exit((void *)(-1));
#endif

   sleep(1);   /* Let the worker thread run first */
```

```
  /* Cancel the worker thread */
  fprintf(stdout, "manager_thread(), canceling worker thread ...\n");
  fflush(stdout);
  ret = pthread_cancel(targetThread);
  if (ret != 0)
    fprintf(stderr, "manager_thread(), pthread_cancel() failed, ret=%d.\n", ret);


  /* Dead worker thread should still hold the lock.  Try to acquire that lock */
  fprintf(stdout, "Manager thread tries to acquire the same mutext lock ...\n");
  fflush(stdout);
  ret = pthread_mutex_lock(&mutex1);
  if (ret == EOWNERDEAD)
  {
    fprintf(stderr, "Manager thread got error EOWNERDEAD from "
      "pthread_mutex_lock(). Try to clean up ...\n");
#ifndef NOROBUST
    /* Make mutex state consistent */
    ret = pthread_mutex_consistent(&mutex1);
    if (ret != 0)
      fprintf(stderr, "Manager thread failed in pthread_mutex_consistent(),"
        " ret=%d.\n", ret);
    else
      fprintf(stdout, "Manager thread fixed mutex state so it's consistent.\n");
#endif

    /* Release the lock held by the dead thread */
    ret = pthread_mutex_unlock(&mutex1);
    if (ret != 0)
      fprintf(stderr, "Manager thread failed to release the mutex lock, "
        "ret=%d.\n", ret);
    else
      fprintf(stdout, "Manager thread successfully released the mutex lock.\n");

    fprintf(stdout, "Manager thread tries to lock the mutex again.\n");
    ret = pthread_mutex_lock(&mutex1);
    if (ret != 0)
      fprintf(stderr, "Manager thread failed to lock the mutex again, "
        "ret=%d.\n", ret);
    else
      fprintf(stdout, "Manager thread successfully acquired the mutext lock!\n");
  }
  else if (ret != 0)
  {
    fprintf(stderr, "Manager thread failed to lock the mutex, ret=%d.\n", ret);
  }
  else
    fprintf(stdout, "Manager thread successfully acquire the mutext lock.\n");

  ret = pthread_mutex_unlock(&mutex1);
  if (ret != 0)
    fprintf(stderr, "Manager thread failed to unlock the mutex, ret=%d.\n", ret);
  else
    fprintf(stdout, "Manager thread successfully released the mutex lock.\n");

#ifdef SUN64
  ret = (0);
```

```
  pthread_exit((void *)&ret);
#else
  pthread_exit((void *)(0));
#endif
}


/*
 * The main program.
 */
int main(int argc, char *argv[])
{
  pthread_t        thrds[MAXNTHREADS];
  unsigned int     args1[2];
  pthread_t        args2;
  int              ret, i;
  int              retval = 0;  /* each child thread returns an int */
#ifdef SUN64
  int              *retvalp = &retval;            /* pointer to returned value */
#endif
  int              nthreads = DEFNTHREADS;    /* default # of threads */
  int              ntasks = DEFNTASKS;        /* default # of tasks */
  pthread_mutexattr_t  mutexattr1;            /* mutex attributes */

  /* Get number of threads and tasks from user */
  if (argc > 1)
  {
    nthreads = atoi(argv[1]);
    if (nthreads < 0 || nthreads > MAXNTHREADS)
      nthreads = DEFNTHREADS;
  }
  if (argc > 2)
  {
    ntasks = atoi(argv[2]);
    if (ntasks < 0 || ntasks > MAXTASKS)
      ntasks = DEFNTASKS;
  }

  /* Initialize mutex attributes */
  ret = pthread_mutexattr_init(&mutexattr1);
  if (ret != 0)
  {
    fprintf(stderr, "Failed to initialize mutex attributes, ret=%d.\n", ret);
    pthread_exit((void *)-1);
  }

#ifndef NOROBUST
  /* Set robust mutex */
  ret = pthread_mutexattr_setrobust(&mutexattr1, PTHREAD_MUTEX_ROBUST);
  if (ret != 0)
  {
    fprintf(stderr, "pthread_mutexattr_setrobust() failed, ret=%d.\n", ret);
    pthread_exit((void *)-2);
  }
#endif

  /* Initialize the mutex */
```

```
  ret = pthread_mutex_init(&mutex1, &mutexattr1);
  if (ret != 0)
  {
    fprintf(stderr, "Failed to initialize mutex, ret=%d.\n", ret);
    pthread_exit((void *)-3);
  }

  /* Load up the input arguments for the worker thread */
  args1[0] = (1);
  args1[1] = ntasks;

  /* Create a worker thread */
  ret = pthread_create(&thrds[0], (pthread_attr_t *)NULL,
         (void *(*)(void *))worker_thread, (void *)args1);
  if (ret != 0)
  {
    fprintf(stderr, "Failed to create the worker thread, ret=%d.\n", ret);
    pthread_exit((void *)-4);
  }

  /* Create the manager thread */
  args2 = thrds[0];
  ret = pthread_create(&thrds[1], (pthread_attr_t *)NULL,
         (void *(*)(void *))manager_thread, (void *)&args2);
  if (ret != 0)
  {
    fprintf(stderr, "Failed to create the manager thread, ret=%d.\n", ret);
    pthread_exit((void *)-5);
  }

  /*
   * Wait for each of the child threads to finish and retrieve its returned
   * value.
   */
  for (i = 0; i < nthreads; i++)
  {
#ifdef SUN64
    ret = pthread_join(thrds[i], (void **)&retvalp);
#else
    ret = pthread_join(thrds[i], (void **)&retval);
#endif
    fprintf(stdout, "Thread %u exited with return value %d\n", (i+1), retval);
  }

  /* Destroy mutex attributes */
  ret = pthread_mutexattr_destroy(&mutexattr1);
  if (ret != 0)
  {
    fprintf(stderr, "Failed to destroy mutex attributes, ret=%d.\n", ret);
    pthread_exit((void *)-6);
  }

  /* Destroy the mutex */
  ret = pthread_mutex_destroy(&mutex1);
  if (ret != 0)
  {
```

```
        fprintf(stderr, "Failed to destroy mutex, ret=%d.\n", ret);
        pthread_exit((void *)-7);
    }


    pthread_exit((void *)0);
}
```

In summary, **if you create and use a robust mutex, then should a thread holding a lock on the mutex terminate while holding the lock, the state of that mutex becomes inconsistent. The next thread attempting to acquire a lock on this mutex will get the error EOWNERDEAD returned, rather than being blocked forever. This thread can then invoke the pthread_mutex_consistent() API to make the mutex's state consistent. And then it can invoke the pthread_mutex_unlock() function to release the lock on behalf of the dead thread. After these two steps the dangling mutex will become normal and available again.**
Note that only the robust type of mutexes have this feature. The regular, normal type of mutexes, which is the default, do not.

8-5-6 Avoiding Deadlock

As we will discuss in the concurrency control chapter, using locks or mutexes can result in deadlock if it is not done right.

One very common deadlock arises in applications where a thread has to acquire and own multiple locks at the same time. In this situation, applications need to order the locks so that all participants request the locks strictly in that order to prevent deadlock.

In addition, the unlocking operations must be in exactly the reverse order so that it is completely symmetric. For instance, if a thread has to acquire three locks or mutexes in order to do its job, then the locking and unlocking operations must look like the following to not cause deadlock:

```
    :
  pthread_mutex_lock(&mutex1);
  pthread_mutex_lock(&mutex2);
  pthread_mutex_lock(&mutex3);
    :
  pthread_mutex_unlock(&mutex3);
  pthread_mutex_unlock(&mutex2);
  pthread_mutex_unlock(&mutex1);
```

8-5-7 Performance Considerations in Mutex Implementation

Note that the decision on whether or not to busy wait and spin on a mutex when it is not available partly depends on the hardware architecture of the system. For instance, in a single-core single processor system, since there is only one hardware execution unit in the CPU on the entire system, there is only one thread can run at a time. Given that the mutex is already held by another thread, busy-waiting and spinning on the unavailable mutex could be fruitless. It is possible to get nowhere and to just waste the CPU time because the other thread holding the mutex cannot run (because it cannot get the CPU) and cannot unlock the mutex. Therefore, in that case, to yield the processor without spinning may be a more productive implementation. It may avoid wasting some CPU time.

In contrast, in a multi-core or multi-processor system, since there are multiple hardware CPU execution units available on the same system, while one thread is spinning on an unavailable mutex, another thread holding the lock on that same mutex can get executed on another CPU or CPU core and release it afterwards. So, there is a hope of actually getting it before too long if the current thread busy waits and spins on it. In this case, all three implementations could make sense. You might then ask which one result in the best throughput? The answer depends on how long the mutex is held on average and how long each CPU's time quantum is. For example, if a CPU's time quantum won't expire until after 1 millisecond and the mutex usually is held for 500 microseconds, then even spinning forever might make sense. In other words, if a thread spinning on a mutex has a good chance of locking the mutex before it gets context switched out of the CPU due to CPU scheduling time quantum expiration, then it is probably worth of spinning and busy waiting for it.

8-6 Condition Variables

8-6-1 What Is a Condition Variable?

A condition variable is a synchronization primitive that allows a thread to wait for a particular event. The POSIX pthreads package has this. The condition variable and its associated APIs enable applications to solve problems that involve threads waiting for events to occur.

Condition variables provide a way to stop threads from proceeding if certain condition is not met or certain event has not occurred yet. In other words, they provide conditional processing. They offer a way for multiple threads depending on one another to nicely coordinate with one another and to synchronize.

A condition variable is typically used in an application where there are interactions between multiple collaborating threads. Some threads have to wait for other threads to do something and satisfy certain condition before they can proceed.

A condition variable supports two operations: wait and signal.
Some thread waits on a condition variable to wait for an event to occur. Another thread makes an event happen and then signals the threads waiting for it. This is generally how multiple threads use a condition variable to coordinate and synchronize with one another.

A condition variable cannot be used alone. It requires a mutex to work.

Condition variables provide a way to solve some very special type of problems such as the producer-consumer problem. It combines a number of elements together and offers a simple and elegant solution to the problems. In addition, it also improves the efficiency and performance.

While mutexes are designed to solve mutually exclusive concurrency problems, condition variables are used to tackle event-waiting type of problems.

We briefly explain what a condition variable is here.
After reading through the following sections and seeing how we use it to solve producer-consumer problem, you will have a better understanding of what it is, what it does and how to use it.

Before we delve into how to use it to solve the producer-consumer problem, let's look at how to define and initialize a condition variable first.

8-6-2 Condition Variable Attributes

Just as there is a mutex attributes object associated with each mutex, there is a condition variable attributes object associated with each condition variable. Each condition variable attributes object contains the attributes associated with a condition variable. Condition variable attributes object is optional. If you don't specify any specialized attributes, a default condition variable will be automatically created.

A program invokes the pthread_condattr_init() and pthread_condattr_destroy() functions to initialize and destroy a condition variable attributes object, respectively.

```
int pthread_condattr_init(pthread_condattr_t *attr);
int pthread_condattr_destroy(pthread_condattr_t *attr);
```

Initializing a condition variable attributes object gives it all the system default values. Once a condition variable attributes object is initialized, individual attributes can be changed to have nondefault values.

After a condition variable attributes object has been used to initialize one or more condition variables, any function affecting the attributes object (including destruction) will not affect any previously initialized condition variables.

POSIX.1-2017 requires two condition variable attributes to be defined: the process-shared attribute and the clock attribute.

1. The process-shared (pshared) attribute

The process-shared (pshared) attribute can have one of the two values: PTHREAD_PROCESS_SHARED and PTHREAD_PROCESS_PRIVATE.
The default value of the attribute is PTHREAD_PROCESS_PRIVATE.

The value PTHREAD_PROCESS_PRIVATE specifies the condition variable is to be shared within the current process only. In contrast, the value PTHREAD_PROCESS_SHARED specifies that the condition variable is to be shared among multiple processes. In this case, the memory of the condition variable must be allocated in shared memory that is accessible by the multiple processes sharing the condition variable.

The value of the process-shared attribute can be obtained or changed using the pthread_condattr_getpshared() or pthread_condattr_setpshared() function, respectively.

```
int pthread_condattr_getpshared(const pthread_condattr_t *restrict attr,
    int *restrict pshared);
```

```
int pthread_condattr_setpshared(pthread_condattr_t *attr, int pshared);
```

These two functions return zero on success. Otherwise, an error number is returned to indicate the error.

2. The clock attribute

The clock attribute is the clock ID of the clock that is used to measure the timeout service of pthread_cond_timedwait(). The default value of the clock attribute will refer to the system clock.

The value of the clock attribute can be queried or set by invoking the pthread_condattr_getclock() and pthread_condattr_setclock() functions, respectively.

```
int pthread_condattr_getclock(const pthread_condattr_t *restrict attr,
    clockid_t *restrict clock_id);
int pthread_condattr_setclock(pthread_condattr_t *attr,
    clockid_t clock_id);
```

Upon success, these two functions return zero. Otherwise, an error is returned to indicate the error.

To destroy a condition variable attributes object, invoke the pthread_condattr_destroy() API.

On success, both of the pthread_condattr_init() and pthread_condattr_destroy() functions return zero; otherwise, an error is returned to indicate the error.

8-6-3 Initializing and Destroying a Condition Variable

A condition variable must be initialized before it can be used. A program invokes the pthread_cond_init() and pthread_cond_destroy() functions to initialize and destroy a condition variable, respectively.

```
int pthread_cond_init(pthread_cond_t *restrict cond,
    const pthread_condattr_t *restrict attr);
int pthread_cond_destroy(pthread_cond_t *cond);
```

Once a condition variable has been initialized, its attributes cannot be changed anymore.

Similar to a mutex initialization, there are **three different ways to initialize a condition variable**.

1. Most general way

The most general way of initializing a condition variable is to declare a variable for a condition variable attributes object, initialize that object first, and then use that object to initialize the condition variable. This is most flexible because it allows you to set specialized condition variable attribute values.

```
pthread_condattr_t    convarattr;    /* condition variable attributes */
pthread_cond_t        convar;        /* condition variable */
```

401

```
/* Initialize the condition variable attributes object */
ret = pthread_condattr_init(&convarattr);

/* Perhaps set some condition variable attribute in-between here */

/* Initialize the condition variable */
ret = pthread_cond_init(&convar, &convarattr);
```

2. Use a NULL condition variable attributes object

```
pthread_cond_t   convar;              /* the condition variable */

ret = pthread_cond_init(&convar, (pthread_condattr_t  *)NULL);
```

3. Use the static condition variable initializer

```
pthread_cond_t cond = PTHREAD_COND_INITIALIZER;
```

To destroy a condition variable, invoke the pthread_cond_destroy() function.

```
int pthread_cond_destroy(pthread_cond_t *cond);
```

8-6-4 How Condition Variables Work?

Here we go deeper and explain how a condition variable really works.

As we said it earlier, condition variables are typically used to solve the type of problems such as the producer-consumer problem.

A factory production pipeline is one example. The worker at stage n+1 of a production assembly pipeline has to wait until the worker at stage n to finish his/her work before he or she can do his or hers. So, there are interrelated dependencies between the workers. This is a unique type of problem to solve.

A more typical and generic problem is that there are multiple workers at each stage. And a typical situation is there could be multiple semi-products output at a time by workers at stage n and there are multiple workers waiting to grab them at stage n+1. In other words, it's a shared pool. Not only that. Typically, the shared pool has a limited capacity. It's not unlimited. This is a typical producer-consumer problem. Condition variables are used to solve exactly this type of problems.

Since the workers are working on a shared pool, to ensure the integrity of the shared pool, there needs to be a mutex to protect its access. Hence, before each worker can access the shared pool, adding a semi-product to it or taking one out, he or she must acquire the mutex lock. **Thus, the solution requires an associated mutex. This is the first component.**

The thing is that after a worker has acquired the mutex lock and gained access to the shared pool, the pool itself could be empty or full. If the shared pool is full, no worker (i.e. producer) can further add any additional semi-product to it. If the shared pool is empty, no worker (i.e. consumer) can take any semi-product out of it. In both of these situations, the worker will have to wait. This is the second component of it.

There exists a condition that must be true (satisfied) before a worker can really do his or her job. If the condition is not true, the worker will have to wait.

But he or she is holding the mutex lock, which prevents all other workers from accessing the shared pool. Because of this, this worker, holding the mutex lock but can't do anything, has to release the mutex lock while he or she waits. This will allow some other worker to come in and hopefully change the situation. Therefore, the worker waiting for his/her condition to become true must also release the mutex lock. **This is the 'release mutex lock and wait' part of the protocol.**

Figure 8-17 Typical solution using a condition variable

(a)   pseudo code of each thread:

```
Repeat following until done
   acquire the mutex lock
   while (my condition is not true)
   {
      release the mutex lock
      go to sleep and wait

      after being awakened
      try to grab the lock again
   }
   /* Falling through, I have mutex lock and my condition is true */
   do the work
   release the mutex lock
```

(b) flow chart of each thread:

```
         |<-------------------------------------------------------------
         V                                                             |
   -----------------------------                                       |
   |try to acquire the mutex lock|                                     |
   -----------------------------                                       |
         | got the lock                                                |
------->|                                                              |
|        v                                                             |
|   --------------------- Y ---------  -----------------------         |
|   |Is my condition true?|-->|do work|->|release the mutex lock|----
|   ---------------------   ---------  -----------------------
|        | N
|        v
|   -----------------------------
|   |release mutex lock and wait|
|   -----------------------------
|        | being awakened
|        v
|   -----------------------------
|   |acquire the mutex lock again|
|   -----------------------------
|        |
---------
```

And when some worker does come in and change the situation, for instance, adding a semi-product to an empty pool or taking one out of a pool that is full, he or she should signal it so that those workers waiting for the condition to change can all be awakened. **This is the signaling part of the protocol**.

Note that there could be multiple workers waiting for the same condition to become true, but only one should be allowed to work on the shared pool at a time. Hence, whoever is awakened must try to grab the mutex lock again before it can go back, peek at the pool again and see if the condition he or she has been waiting for is met now.

The pseudo-code and flow chart of the solution look like what are in Figure 8-17 (a) and (b), respectively.

In summary, a solution using a condition variable typically requires a few components:

1. a condition variable (so that threads can do wait and signal operations)
2. an associated mutex (to protect the integrity of the shared data)
3. a condition or predicate (to make sure there is really something to do)
   For consumers, the predicate is the buffer is not empty.
   For producers, the condition to be met is the buffer is not full.
4. releasing the mutex lock and wait if my condition is not met
5. re-acquire the mutex lock again after being awakened

Fortunately, the fourth and fifth parts all happen behind the scene and are taken care of by implementation of condition variables. A programmer only needs to take care of the first three parts.

We will give a program example solving the famous producer-consumer problem using a pthreads condition variable in the next section. Before then, let's quickly look at some of the major condition variable APIs.

8-6-5 Major Functions on Condition Variable

In a program using condition variables, normally you define one mutex and one condition variable. These are typically defined as global variables so that all threads share them.

As shown in the pseudo code above in Figure 8-17, in each thread, the first thing it does is typically acquiring a lock on the mutex using the pthread_mutex_lock() API, which we discussed earlier.

8-6-5-1 Condition Wait

The second thing each thread does is to check if its predicate is true. And wait if it is not. This condition wait is done by invoking the pthread_cond_wait() or pthread_cond_timedwait() function. For instance,

```
while (my condition is not met)
  pthread_cond_wait(&convar, &mutex);
```

The synopses of these two functions are as below:

```
int pthread_cond_wait(pthread_cond_t *restrict cond,
    pthread_mutex_t *restrict mutex);

int pthread_cond_timedwait(pthread_cond_t *restrict cond,
    pthread_mutex_t *restrict mutex,
    const struct timespec *restrict abstime);
```

The pthread_cond_timedwait() function is equivalent to pthread_cond_wait() except that it does not try to wait forever. Instead, an error ETIMEDOUT is returned if the absolute time specified by abstime argument passes (that is, system time equals or exceeds abstime) before the condition variable is signaled or broadcasted, or if the absolute time specified by abstime has already been passed at the time of the call.

These functions specify both the condition variable and the associated mutex. Make sure the caller has already held a lock on the mutex before one of these two functions is called.

While the condition is not met, these functions will automatically release the mutex lock and cause the calling thread to block on the condition variable.

A condition wait (whether timed or not) is a cancellation point. A thread that has been unblocked because it has been canceled while blocked in a call to pthread_cond_timedwait() or pthread_cond_wait() will not consume any condition signal. However, when a thread is canceled while blocked in one of these two condition wait functions, a lock on the condition variable's associated mutex is re-acquired before the cancellation cleanup handler is invoked. Therefore, make sure the cancellation cleanup handler always releases the lock on the condition variable's associated mutex.

These condition wait functions return zero on success. They return an error code otherwise.

It's very important that the condition predicate is always re-evaluated after returning from the pthread_cond_wait() or pthread_cond_timedwait() function because condition waits are subject to spurious wakeups. For instance, a signal is delivered to a thread blocked in pthread_cond_wait() or pthread_cond_timedwait().

8-6-5-2 Condition Signal

When the caller's condition is met, the control will fall through the while statement. In that case, the caller also owns the mutex lock. So, it's ready to do its work. After the thread finishes its work, it will have to invoke one of the following two functions to send a condition signal.

```
int pthread_cond_signal(pthread_cond_t *cond);
int pthread_cond_broadcast(pthread_cond_t *cond);
```

Sending a condition signal will unblock threads blocked on the condition variable.

The pthread_cond_signal() function unblocks at least one of the threads that are blocked on the specified condition variable.

The pthread_cond_broadcast() function will unblock all threads currently
blocked on the specified condition variable. Use this function
if the caller needs all blocked threads to wake up and continue executing.
If there are no threads currently blocked on the condition variable,
these two functions should have no effect.

If more than one thread is blocked on a condition variable, the scheduling
policy determines the order in which threads are unblocked. When a thread
unblocked as a result of a pthread_cond_signal() or pthread_cond_broadcast()
returns from its call to pthread_cond_wait() or pthread_cond_timedwait(),
the thread will own the mutex with which it called pthread_cond_wait() or
pthread_cond_timedwait(). The threads that are unblocked will contend for
the mutex according to the scheduling policy.

Note that calling the pthread_cond_signal() or pthread_cond_broadcast()
function does not require owning a mutex lock. These condition signal
functions can be called regardless the caller owns the lock on the mutex
associated with the condition variable or not.

If successful, the pthread_cond_signal() and pthread_cond_broadcast()
functions return zero; otherwise, an error number is returned to indicate
the error.

8-6-6 Solving Producer-Consumer Problem

We provide an example program which uses condition variables to solve
the producer-consumer problem in this section.

Figure 8-18 lists a program that does exactly this, employing a condition
variable to solve the producer-consumer problem.

Figure 8-18 Solving producer-consumer problem (pt_produce_consume.c)

```
/*
 * Solving the Producer-Consumer problem using one pthread condition variable
 * (and mutex).
 * Copyright (c) 2014, 2019, 2020 Mr. Jin-Jwei Chen.  All rights reserved.
 */

#include <stdio.h>
#include <stdlib.h>
#include <pthread.h>

#define   DEFBUFSZ      2     /* Maximum # of buffers to hold resources */
#define   DEFNTHREADS   3     /* default number threads of each type to run */
#define   MAXNTHREADS   12    /* max. number threads of each type allowed */
#define   DEFNTASKS     5     /* number of tasks to perform for each thread */
#define   MILLISECS25   25000 /*  25 milliseconds */

/*
 * Global data structures shared by all threads.
 */
pthread_cond_t    convar = PTHREAD_COND_INITIALIZER;     /* the condition variable */
pthread_mutex_t   mutex;                /* the associated mutex */
unsigned int      product_count=0;   /* the number of resources available */
```

406

```c
void random_sleep(unsigned int maxusec);

/*
 * The producer thread.
 */
int producer_thread(void *args)
{
  unsigned int  *argp;
  unsigned int  myid;
  unsigned int  ntasks;
  unsigned int  maxbufs;
  int      ret = 0;

  /* Extract arguments (two unsigned integers) */
  argp = (unsigned int *)args;
  if (argp != NULL)
  {
    myid = argp[0];
    ntasks = argp[1];
    maxbufs = argp[2];
  }
  else
#ifdef SUN64
  {
    ret = (-1);
    pthread_exit((void *)&ret);
  }
#else
    pthread_exit((void *)(-1));
#endif

  fprintf(stdout, "Producer: myid=%u ntasks=%u maxbufs=%u\n",
    myid, ntasks, maxbufs);

  /* Do my job */
  while (ntasks > 0)
  {
    /* Lock the mutex */
    ret = pthread_mutex_lock(&mutex);
    if (ret != 0)
    {
      fprintf(stderr, "Producer %3u failed to lock the mutex, ret=%u\n",
        myid, ret);
#ifdef SUN64
      ret = (-2);
      pthread_exit((void *)&ret);
#else
      pthread_exit((void *)-2);
#endif
    }
    fprintf(stdout, "Producer %3u locked the mutex\n", myid);

    /* Wait for buffers to become available */
    while (product_count >= maxbufs)
      pthread_cond_wait(&convar, &mutex);
```

```
    /* Do whatever it takes to produce the resource */

    /* Produce and add one resource to the pool */
    random_sleep(MILLISECS25);   /* It takes time to produce. */
    product_count = product_count + 1;
    fprintf(stdout, "Producer %3u added one resource, product_count=%u\n",
      myid, product_count);

    /* Without this, the awaiting consumer threads waiting on the same
     * condition variable won't get waken up even though the mutex
     * is properly released and re-acquired by the system automatically.
     */
    pthread_cond_signal(&convar);

    /* Unlock the mutex */
    ret = pthread_mutex_unlock(&mutex);
    if (ret != 0)
    {
      fprintf(stderr, "Producer %3u failed to unlock the mutex, ret=%u\n",
        myid, ret);
#ifdef SUN64
      ret = (-3);
      pthread_exit((void *)&ret);
#else
      pthread_exit((void *)-3);
#endif
    }
    fprintf(stdout, "Producer %3u unlocked the mutex\n", myid);

    /* Reduce my task count by one */
    ntasks = ntasks - 1;

  }  /* while */

#ifdef SUN64
  ret = 0;
  pthread_exit((void *)&ret);
#else
  pthread_exit((void *)0);
#endif
}

/*
 * The consumer thread.
 */
int consumer_thread(void *args)
{
  unsigned int  *argp;
  unsigned int   myid;
  unsigned int   ntasks;
  unsigned int   maxbufs;
  int      ret = 0;

  /* Extract arguments (two unsigned integers) */
  argp = (unsigned int *)args;
```

```
   if (argp != NULL)
   {
     myid = argp[0];
     ntasks = argp[1];
     maxbufs = argp[2];
   }
   else
#ifdef SUN64
   {
     ret = (-1);
     pthread_exit((void *)&ret);
   }
#else
     pthread_exit((void *)-1);
#endif

   fprintf(stdout, "Consumer: myid=%u ntasks=%u maxbufs=%u\n",
     myid, ntasks, maxbufs);

   /* Do my job */
   while (ntasks > 0)
   {
     /* Lock the mutex */
     ret = pthread_mutex_lock(&mutex);
     if (ret != 0)
     {
       fprintf(stderr, "Consumer %3u failed to lock the mutex, ret=%u\n",
         myid, ret);
#ifdef SUN64
       ret = (-2);
       pthread_exit((void *)&ret);
#else
       pthread_exit((void *)-2);
#endif
     }
     fprintf(stdout, "Consumer %3u locked the mutex\n", myid);

     /* Wait for resources to become available */
     while (product_count <= 0)
       pthread_cond_wait(&convar, &mutex);

     /* Consume and remove one resource from the pool */
     random_sleep(MILLISECS25);  /* It takes time to consume. */
     product_count = product_count - 1;
     fprintf(stdout, "Consumer %3u removed one resource, product_count=%u\n",
       myid, product_count);

     /* Without this, the awaiting producer threads waiting on the same
      * condition variable won't get waken up even though the mutex
      * is properly released and re-acquired by the system automatically.
      */
     pthread_cond_signal(&convar);

     /* Unlock the mutex */
     ret = pthread_mutex_unlock(&mutex);
     if (ret != 0)
```

```
      {
         fprintf(stderr, "Consumer %3u failed to unlock the mutex, ret=%u\n",
           myid, ret);
#ifdef SUN64
         ret = (-3);
         pthread_exit((void *)&ret);
#else
         pthread_exit((void *)-3);
#endif
      }
      fprintf(stdout, "Consumer %3u unlocked the mutex\n", myid);

      /* Decrement my task count by one */
      ntasks = ntasks - 1;

      /* Could actually consume the resource here if it takes long */

   }   /* while */

#ifdef SUN64
   ret = 0;
   pthread_exit((void *)&ret);
#else
   pthread_exit((void *)0);
#endif
}

int main(int argc, char *argv[])
{
   pthread_t        prthrds[MAXNTHREADS];
   unsigned int     prargs[MAXNTHREADS][3];
   pthread_t        csthrds[MAXNTHREADS];
   unsigned int     csargs[MAXNTHREADS][3];
   int              ret, i;
   int              retval = 0;              /* Each child thread returns an int */
   int              nbufs = DEFBUFSZ;        /* number of total buffers */
   int              nthrds = DEFNTHREADS;    /* number of threads */
   int              ntasks = DEFNTASKS;      /* number of tasks per thread */
   pthread_mutexattr_t  mutexattr;          /* mutex attributes */
#ifdef SUN64
   int              *retvalp = &retval;      /* pointer to returned value */
#endif

   /* Get the number of buffers to use from user */
   if (argc > 1)
   {
      nbufs = atoi(argv[1]);
      if (nbufs <= 0)
         nbufs = DEFBUFSZ;
   }

   /* Get the number of threads to run from user */
   if (argc > 2)
   {
      nthrds = atoi(argv[2]);
      if ((nthrds <= 0) || (nthrds > MAXNTHREADS))
```

```
      nthrds = DEFNTHREADS;
  }

  /* Get the number of tasks per thread to perform from user */
  if (argc > 3)
  {
    ntasks = atoi(argv[3]);
    if (ntasks <= 0)
      ntasks = DEFNTASKS;
  }

  fprintf(stdout, "Run %d threads, %u tasks per thread using %u buffers\n",
      nthrds, ntasks, nbufs);

  /* Initialize mutex attributes */
  ret = pthread_mutexattr_init(&mutexattr);
  if (ret != 0)
  {
    fprintf(stderr, "Failed to initialize mutex attributes, ret=%d\n", ret);
    pthread_exit((void *)-1);
  }

  /* Initialize the mutex */
  ret = pthread_mutex_init(&mutex, &mutexattr);
  if (ret != 0)
  {
    fprintf(stderr, "Failed to initialize mutex, ret=%d\n", ret);
    pthread_exit((void *)-2);
  }

  /* Load up the input arguments to each child thread */
  for (i = 0; i < nthrds; i++)
  {
    prargs[i][0] = (i + 1);
    csargs[i][0] = (i + 1);
    prargs[i][1] = ntasks;
    csargs[i][1] = ntasks;
    prargs[i][2] = nbufs;
    csargs[i][2] = nbufs;
  }

  /* Create the consumer threads */
  for (i = 0; i < nthrds; i++)
  {
    ret = pthread_create(&csthrds[i], (pthread_attr_t *)NULL,
        (void *(*)(void *))consumer_thread, (void *)csargs[i]);
    if (ret != 0)
    {
      fprintf(stderr, "Failed to create the consumer thread %d, ret=%d\n",
        i, ret);
      pthread_exit((void *)-3);
    }
  }

  /* Create the producer threads */
  for (i = 0; i < nthrds; i++)
```

```c
  {
    ret = pthread_create(&prthrds[i], (pthread_attr_t *)NULL,
            (void *(*)(void *))producer_thread, (void *)prargs[i]);
    if (ret != 0)
    {
      fprintf(stderr, "Failed to create the producer thread, ret=%d\n", ret);
      pthread_exit((void *)-4);
    }
  }

  /* Wait for the child threads to finish. */
  for (i = 0; i < nthrds; i++)
  {
#ifdef SUN64
    ret = pthread_join(prthrds[i], (void **)&retvalp);
#else
    ret = pthread_join(prthrds[i], (void **)&retval);
#endif
    fprintf(stdout, "Producer thread %u exited with return value %d\n",
      i, retval);
  }
  for (i = 0; i < nthrds; i++)
  {
#ifdef SUN64
    ret = pthread_join(csthrds[i], (void **)&retvalp);
#else
    ret = pthread_join(csthrds[i], (void **)&retval);
#endif
    fprintf(stdout, "Consumer thread %u exited with return value %d\n",
      i, retval);
  }

  fprintf(stdout, "main(), product_count = %d\n", product_count);

  /* Destroy mutex attributes */
#ifndef HPUX64
  ret = pthread_mutexattr_destroy(&mutexattr);
  if (ret != 0)
  {
    fprintf(stderr, "Failed to destroy mutex attributes, ret=%d\n", ret);
    pthread_exit((void *)-5);
  }
#endif

  /* Destroy the mutex */
  ret = pthread_mutex_destroy(&mutex);
  if (ret != 0)
  {
    fprintf(stderr, "Failed to destroy mutex, ret=%d\n", ret);
    pthread_exit((void *)-6);
  }

  pthread_exit((void *)0);
}
```

By default, the program runs 3 threads, 5 tasks per thread using 2 buffers.

This means there are 3 producers and each of them will produce 5 goods. There are also 3 consumers and each of them will consume 5 goods. There are only two buffers available. If the buffer is full then the producers will have to wait until some consumer comes along and consumes some goods. If the buffer is empty, the consumers will have to wait until some producer comes along and produces some more goods.

Under these two situations, the producer or consumer calls pthread_cond_wait() to wait. This call will automatically release the mutex lock held by the caller such that some other thread (producer or consumer) can come in and work to consume or produce more goods and remove the buffer full or empty condition. Once that happens, this second thread (a consumer in buffer full situation or a producer in buffer empty situation) will do a pthread_cond_signal() so that the first thread blocked on the pthread_cond_wait() has a chance to wake up.

In other words, after producing a new goods, that producer invokes pthread_cond_signal() to wake up the consumers blocked and waiting in pthread_cond_wait() because the buffer was empty.
Similarly, after consuming a goods, that consumer calls pthread_cond_signal() to wake up the producers blocked on pthread_cond_wait() and waiting for a buffer space to become available. **Adding the condition variable and the pthread_cond_wait() and pthread_cond_signal() APIs on top of mutex eliminates the fruitless busy waiting that would otherwise occur under the buffer full or buffer empty situation, which is all due to a limited buffer**. If the buffer is unlimited, this extra condition variable synchronization wouldn't be needed! Yet, nothing in this world is unlimited!

One thing to note here is that since there is no need to hold the mutex lock while doing condition signaling using pthread_cond_signal() or pthread_cond_broadcast(), in the producer-consumer program, we could have moved pthread_mutex_unlock() one line up to right before the pthread_cond_signal() call in both of the producer_thread() and consumer_thread(). That is, trying to release the mutex lock right before calling the condition signal function. That may improve performance a little bit in case the thread gets a context switch right after pthread_cond_signal() and right before pthread_mutex_unlock().
But the way the example program does it is guaranteed to be free of race conditions under any circumstances.

From the program output, one can see each producer has produced the number of goods it is supposed to. And each consumer has consumed exactly the number of goods it should. Therefore, the program works correctly.

Figure 8-19 shows a sample output of running the pt_produce_consume program.

Figure 8-19 Sample output from pt_produce_consume program

```
$ ./pt_produce_consume.lin32
Run 3 threads, 5 tasks per thread using 2 buffers
Producer: myid=2 ntasks=5 maxbufs=2
Consumer: myid=1 ntasks=5 maxbufs=2
Producer: myid=1 ntasks=5 maxbufs=2
Producer: myid=3 ntasks=5 maxbufs=2
Consumer: myid=2 ntasks=5 maxbufs=2
Producer    2 locked the mutex
```

```
Consumer: myid=3 ntasks=5 maxbufs=2
Producer    2 added one resource, product_count=1
Producer    2 unlocked the mutex
Producer    2 locked the mutex
Producer    2 added one resource, product_count=2
Producer    2 unlocked the mutex
Producer    2 locked the mutex
Consumer    1 locked the mutex
Consumer    1 removed one resource, product_count=1
Consumer    1 unlocked the mutex
Consumer    1 locked the mutex
Consumer    1 removed one resource, product_count=0
Consumer    1 unlocked the mutex
Consumer    1 locked the mutex
Consumer    3 locked the mutex
Producer    1 locked the mutex
Producer    1 added one resource, product_count=1
Producer    1 unlocked the mutex
Producer    1 locked the mutex
Producer    1 added one resource, product_count=2
Producer    1 unlocked the mutex
Producer    1 locked the mutex
Consumer    2 locked the mutex
Consumer    2 removed one resource, product_count=1
Consumer    2 unlocked the mutex
Consumer    2 locked the mutex
Consumer    2 removed one resource, product_count=0
Producer    3 locked the mutex
Consumer    2 unlocked the mutex
Producer    3 added one resource, product_count=1
Producer    3 unlocked the mutex
Consumer    3 removed one resource, product_count=0
Consumer    3 unlocked the mutex
Consumer    3 locked the mutex
Producer    2 added one resource, product_count=1
Producer    2 unlocked the mutex
Consumer    3 removed one resource, product_count=0
Consumer    3 unlocked the mutex
Consumer    3 locked the mutex
Consumer    2 locked the mutex
Producer    3 locked the mutex
Producer    3 added one resource, product_count=1
Producer    3 unlocked the mutex
Consumer    3 removed one resource, product_count=0
Consumer    3 unlocked the mutex
Producer    1 added one resource, product_count=1
Producer    1 unlocked the mutex
Producer    1 locked the mutex
Producer    1 added one resource, product_count=2
Producer    1 unlocked the mutex
Producer    1 locked the mutex
Consumer    3 locked the mutex
Consumer    3 removed one resource, product_count=1
Consumer    3 unlocked the mutex
Consumer    3 locked the mutex
Consumer    3 removed one resource, product_count=0
```

```
Consumer    3 unlocked the mutex
Producer    2 locked the mutex
Producer    2 added one resource, product_count=1
Producer    2 unlocked the mutex
Producer    3 locked the mutex
Producer    3 added one resource, product_count=2
Producer    3 unlocked the mutex
Producer    3 locked the mutex
Producer    2 locked the mutex
Consumer    2 removed one resource, product_count=1
Consumer    2 unlocked the mutex
Producer    1 added one resource, product_count=2
Producer    1 unlocked the mutex
Consumer    2 locked the mutex
Producer thread 0 exited with return value 0
Consumer    2 removed one resource, product_count=1
Consumer    2 unlocked the mutex
Consumer    1 removed one resource, product_count=0
Consumer    1 unlocked the mutex
Consumer    1 locked the mutex
Producer    3 added one resource, product_count=1
Producer    3 unlocked the mutex
Consumer    1 removed one resource, product_count=0
Consumer    1 unlocked the mutex
Consumer    1 locked the mutex
Producer    2 added one resource, product_count=1
Producer    2 unlocked the mutex
Producer thread 1 exited with return value 0
Consumer    1 removed one resource, product_count=0
Consumer    1 unlocked the mutex
Consumer    2 locked the mutex
Producer    3 locked the mutex
Producer    3 added one resource, product_count=1
Producer    3 unlocked the mutex
Producer thread 2 exited with return value 0
Consumer thread 0 exited with return value 0
Consumer    2 removed one resource, product_count=0
Consumer    2 unlocked the mutex
Consumer thread 1 exited with return value 0
Consumer thread 2 exited with return value 0
main(), product_count = 0
```

8-7 Read-Write Locks

So far, we have discussed two very different types of concurrency problems that are very commonly seen in computer programming -- the update loss problem and the producer-consumer problem -- and how to solve them. In this section we will introduce a third type.

Sometimes the concurrent access problem is not all updates.
One type of applications that is also commonly seen is readers and writers mixing together. That is, some threads want to update the shared data while others want to just read. For data integrity, updating shared data requires exclusive access. Therefore, as long as there is a writer updating the data, no other writers or readers are allowed. But since the readers do not change

the shared data, multiple readers are allowed to read the shared data at the same time. To improve performance and allow multiple readers to access the data at the same time instead of one reader at a time, we need to distinguish whether a thread or process is doing read-only or write operation.
This is achieved through implementing both read locks and write locks, as opposed to exclusive locks only. Write locks are exclusive.

Pthreads offers read-write locks. A caller can try to acquire a read or write lock on a lock by calling different functions with the lock.
Taking a write lock means the caller wants to have exclusive access to the shared resource. In contrast, taking a read lock means the caller won't modify the shared resource and it can share it with other readers at the same time during the period while it holds the lock.

In pthreads, a read-write lock is of the data type pthread_rwlock_t.
For instance, the following statement declares a read-write lock named rwlock1:

```
pthread_rwlock_t    rwlock1;
```

A thread or process invokes the pthread_rwlock_rdlock() or pthread_rwlock_wrlock() function to acquire a read or write lock on the resource being protected, respectively:

```
#include <pthread.h>

int pthread_rwlock_rdlock(pthread_rwlock_t *rwlock);
int pthread_rwlock_wrlock(pthread_rwlock_t *rwlock);
```

Both of these functions also have a non-blocking version as shown below:

```
int pthread_rwlock_tryrdlock(pthread_rwlock_t *rwlock);
int pthread_rwlock_trywrlock(pthread_rwlock_t *rwlock);
```

To release a read-write lock, a thread or process calls the following function:

```
int pthread_rwlock_unlock(pthread_rwlock_t *rwlock);
```

All these functions return zero on success and an error number on failure.
The non-blocking version, pthread_rwlock_trywrlock() or pthread_rwlock_tryrdlock() returns error EBUSY if it fails to acquire the lock because the lock has already been taken by some other thread or process.

Figure 8-20 shows a program running one writer and two reader threads.

Figure 8-20 Reader/Writer locks (pt_rwlock.c)

```
/*
 * Read-write locks in pthread.
 * Copyright (c) 2014-2020, Mr. Jin-Jwei Chen.  All rights reserved.
 */

#include <stdio.h>
#include <pthread.h>
```

```
#define   NREADERS    2        /* number of readers */
#define   NWRITERS    1        /* number of writers */
#define   NTASKS      4
#define   DELAY_COUNT_RD 200000000
#define   DELAY_COUNT_WR 100000000


unsigned int   global_count=0;      /* global data shared by all threads */

/* Global read-write lock shared by all threads */
pthread_rwlock_t    rwlock1 = PTHREAD_RWLOCK_INITIALIZER;


/*
 * The reader thread.
 */
int reader_thread(void *args)
{
  unsigned int   *argp;
  unsigned int   myid;
  unsigned int   ntasks;
  int            i, ret;
  unsigned long long j;

  /* Extract input arguments (two unsigned integers) */
  argp = (unsigned int *)args;
  if (argp != NULL)
  {
    myid = argp[0];
    ntasks = argp[1];
  }
  else
    pthread_exit((void *)(-1));

  fprintf(stdout, "Reader thread %u started: ntasks=%u\n", myid, ntasks);

  /* Do my job */
  for (i = 0; i < ntasks; i++)
  {
    fprintf(stdout, "Reader thread %u tries to get the read lock\n", myid);
    ret = pthread_rwlock_rdlock(&rwlock1);
    if (ret != 0)
    {
      fprintf(stderr, "Reader thread %u failed to get a read lock, ret=%d\n",
        myid, ret);
      continue;
    }
    fprintf(stdout, "Reader thread %u successfully get the read lock\n", myid);
    fflush(stdout);

    /* Read the shared data */
    fprintf(stdout, "   Reader thread %u read global_count, count = %u\n",
      myid, global_count);
    fflush(stdout);
    /* insert a bit of delay */
    for (j = 0; j < DELAY_COUNT_RD; j++);

    fprintf(stdout, "Reader thread %u successfully released the read lock\n",
```

417

```
        myid);
    fflush(stdout);

    ret = pthread_rwlock_unlock(&rwlock1);
  }

  pthread_exit((void *)0);
}

/*
 * The writer thread.
 */
int writer_thread(void *args)
{
  unsigned int    *argp;
  unsigned int    myid;
  unsigned int    ntasks;
  int             i, ret;
  unsigned long long j;

  /* Extract input arguments (two unsigned integers) */
  argp = (unsigned int *)args;
  if (argp != NULL)
  {
    myid = argp[0];
    ntasks = argp[1];
  }
  else
    pthread_exit((void *)(-1));

  fprintf(stdout, "Writer thread %u started: ntasks=%u\n", myid, ntasks);

  /* Do my job */
  for (i = 0; i < ntasks; i++)
  {
    fprintf(stdout, "Writer thread %u tries to get the write lock\n", myid);
    ret = pthread_rwlock_wrlock(&rwlock1);
    if (ret != 0)
    {
      fprintf(stderr, "Writer thread %u failed to get a write lock, ret=%d\n",
        myid, ret);
      continue;
    }
    fprintf(stdout, "Writer thread %u successfully get the write lock\n", myid);
    fflush(stdout);

    /* Update the shared data */
    global_count = global_count + 1;
    fprintf(stdout, "  Writer thread %u updated global_count, count = %u\n",
      myid, global_count);
    /* insert a bit of delay */
    for (j = 0; j < DELAY_COUNT_WR; j++);

    fprintf(stdout, "Writer thread %u successfully released the write lock\n",
      myid);
    fflush(stdout);
```

```
      ret = pthread_rwlock_unlock(&rwlock1);
   }

   pthread_exit((void *)0);
}

/*
 * The main program.
 */
int main(int argc, char *argv[])
{
   pthread_t      thrds[NREADERS+NWRITERS];
   unsigned int   args[NREADERS+NWRITERS][2];
   int            ret, i;
   int            retval;   /* each child thread returns an int */

   /* Load up the input arguments */
   for (i = 0; i < NREADERS; i++)
   {
      args[i][0] = (i+1);
      args[i][1] = NTASKS;
   }
   for (i = NREADERS; i < (NREADERS+NWRITERS); i++)
   {
      args[i][0] = (i+1);
      args[i][1] = NTASKS;
   }

   /* Create the reader threads */
   for (i = 0; i < NREADERS; i++)
   {
      ret = pthread_create(&thrds[i], (pthread_attr_t *)NULL,
           (void *(*)(void *))reader_thread, (void *)args[i]);
      if (ret != 0)
      {
         fprintf(stderr, "Failed to create the reader thread, ret=%d\n", ret);
         pthread_exit((void *)-1);
      }
   }

   /* Create the writer threads */
   for (i = NREADERS; i < (NREADERS+NWRITERS); i++)
   {
      ret = pthread_create(&thrds[i], (pthread_attr_t *)NULL,
           (void *(*)(void *))writer_thread, (void *)args[i]);
      if (ret != 0)
      {
         fprintf(stderr, "Failed to create the writer thread, ret=%d\n", ret);
         pthread_exit((void *)-2);
      }
   }

   /*
    * Wait for each of the child threads to finish and retrieve its returned
    * value.
```

```
    */
  for (i = 0; i < (NREADERS+NWRITERS); i++)
  {
    ret = pthread_join(thrds[i], (void **)&retval);
    fprintf(stdout, "Thread %u exited with return value %d\n", (i+1), retval);
  }

  fprintf(stdout, "global_count = %u\n", global_count);
  pthread_exit((void *)0);
}
```

From the output of running the pt_rwlock program, one can see that
more than one reader is allowed in at the same time.
One can also see that any reader blocks the writer or vice versa.

There are two different ways to initialize a read-write lock and its
attribute. In Figure 8-20, pt_rwlock.c shows the simple way that uses the
PTHREAD_RWLOCK_INITIALIZER to initialize the read-write lock, which
saves you from doing pthread_rwlockattr_init() and pthread_rwlock_init().
In cases where default read-write lock attributes are appropriate,
the macro PTHREAD_RWLOCK_INITIALIZER can be used to initialize a read-write
lock that is statically allocated. Its effect is equivalent to a dynamic
initialization by actually calling pthread_rwlock_init() with the parameter
attr being NULL, except that no error checks are performed.

Figure 8-21 shows a second way of initializing a read-write lock,
which explicitly invokes both pthread_rwlockattr_init() and
pthread_rwlock_init(). Comparing to using the static initializer
PTHREAD_RWLOCK_INITIALIZER, this is a bit more work but more general.

Figure 8-21 General way of initializing a Reader/Writer locks (pt_rwlock_attr.c)

```
/*
 * Read-write locks in pthread with lock attribute init.
 * Copyright (c) 2014-2020, Mr. Jin-Jwei Chen.  All rights reserved.
 */

#include <stdio.h>
#include <pthread.h>

#define   NREADERS    2          /* number of readers */
#define   NWRITERS    1          /* number of writers */
#define   NTASKS      4
#define   DELAY_COUNT_RD 200000000
#define   DELAY_COUNT_WR 100000000

unsigned int  global_count=0;      /* global data shared by all threads */

/* Global read-write lock shared by all threads */
pthread_rwlock_t    rwlock1;

/*
 * The reader thread.
 */
int reader_thread(void *args)
{
```

```
  unsigned int   *argp;
  unsigned int   myid;
  unsigned int   ntasks;
  int            i, ret;
  unsigned long long j;

  /* Extract input arguments (two unsigned integers) */
  argp = (unsigned int *)args;
  if (argp != NULL)
  {
    myid = argp[0];
    ntasks = argp[1];
  }
  else
    pthread_exit((void *)(-1));

  fprintf(stdout, "Reader thread %u started: ntasks=%u\n", myid, ntasks);

  /* Do my job */
  for (i = 0; i < ntasks; i++)
  {
    fprintf(stdout, "Reader thread %u tries to get the read lock\n", myid);
    ret = pthread_rwlock_rdlock(&rwlock1);
    if (ret != 0)
    {
      fprintf(stderr, "Reader thread %u failed to get a read lock, ret=%d\n",
        myid, ret);
      continue;
    }
    fprintf(stdout, "Reader thread %u successfully get the read lock\n", myid);
    fflush(stdout);

    /* Read the shared data */
    fprintf(stdout, "  Reader thread %u read global_count, count = %u\n",
      myid, global_count);
    fflush(stdout);
    /* insert a bit of delay */
    for (j = 0; j < DELAY_COUNT_RD; j++);

    fprintf(stdout, "Reader thread %u successfully released the read lock\n",
        myid);
    fflush(stdout);

    ret = pthread_rwlock_unlock(&rwlock1);
  }

  pthread_exit((void *)0);
}

/*
 * The writer thread.
 */
int writer_thread(void *args)
{
  unsigned int   *argp;
  unsigned int   myid;
```

```
  unsigned int   ntasks;
  int            i, ret;
  unsigned long long j;

  /* Extract input arguments (two unsigned integers) */
  argp = (unsigned int *)args;
  if (argp != NULL)
  {
    myid = argp[0];
    ntasks = argp[1];
  }
  else
    pthread_exit((void *)(-1));

  fprintf(stdout, "Writer thread %u started: ntasks=%u\n", myid, ntasks);

  /* Do my job */
  for (i = 0; i < ntasks; i++)
  {
    fprintf(stdout, "Writer thread %u tries to get the write lock\n", myid);
    ret = pthread_rwlock_wrlock(&rwlock1);
    if (ret != 0)
    {
      fprintf(stderr, "Writer thread %u failed to get a write lock, ret=%d\n",
        myid, ret);
      continue;
    }
    fprintf(stdout, "Writer thread %u successfully get the write lock\n", myid);
    fflush(stdout);

    /* Update the shared data */
    global_count = global_count + 1;
    fprintf(stdout, "   Writer thread %u updated global_count, count = %u\n",
      myid, global_count);
    /* insert a bit of delay */
    for (j = 0; j < DELAY_COUNT_WR; j++);

    fprintf(stdout, "Writer thread %u successfully released the write lock\n",
      myid);
    fflush(stdout);

    ret = pthread_rwlock_unlock(&rwlock1);
  }

  pthread_exit((void *)0);
}

/*
 * The main program.
 */
int main(int argc, char *argv[])
{
  pthread_t      thrds[NREADERS+NWRITERS];
  unsigned int   args[NREADERS+NWRITERS][2];
  int            ret=0, i;
  int            retval;  /* each child thread returns an int */
```

422

```
   pthread_rwlockattr_t      rwlattr;      /* read-write lock attribute */

   /* Initialize a read-write lock attribute */
   ret = pthread_rwlockattr_init(&rwlattr);
   if (ret != 0)
   {
     fprintf(stderr, "pthread_rwlockattr_init() failed, error=%d\n", ret);
     pthread_exit((void *)-1);
   }

   /* Initialize a read-write lock */
   ret = pthread_rwlock_init(&rwlock1, &rwlattr);
   if (ret != 0)
   {
     fprintf(stderr, "pthread_rwlock_init() failed, error=%d\n", ret);
     pthread_exit((void *)-2);
   }

   /* Load up the input arguments */
   for (i = 0; i < NREADERS; i++)
   {
     args[i][0] = (i+1);
     args[i][1] = NTASKS;
   }
   for (i = NREADERS; i < (NREADERS+NWRITERS); i++)
   {
     args[i][0] = (i+1);
     args[i][1] = NTASKS;
   }

   /* Create the reader threads */
   for (i = 0; i < NREADERS; i++)
   {
     ret = pthread_create(&thrds[i], (pthread_attr_t *)NULL,
           (void *(*)(void *))reader_thread, (void *)args[i]);
     if (ret != 0)
     {
       fprintf(stderr, "Failed to create the reader thread\n");
       pthread_exit((void *)-3);
     }
   }

   /* Create the writer threads */
   for (i = NREADERS; i < (NREADERS+NWRITERS); i++)
   {
     ret = pthread_create(&thrds[i], (pthread_attr_t *)NULL,
           (void *(*)(void *))writer_thread, (void *)args[i]);
     if (ret != 0)
     {
       fprintf(stderr, "Failed to create the writer thread\n");
       pthread_exit((void *)-4);
     }
   }

   /*
    * Wait for each of the child threads to finish and retrieve its returned
```

423

```
 * value.
 */
for (i = 0; i < (NREADERS+NWRITERS); i++)
{
  ret = pthread_join(thrds[i], (void **)&retval);
  fprintf(stdout, "Thread %u exited with return value %d\n", (i+1), retval);
}

fprintf(stdout, "global_count = %u\n", global_count);

/* Destroy the read-write lock attribute */
#ifndef HPUX64
  ret = pthread_rwlockattr_destroy(&rwlattr);
  if (ret != 0)
  {
    fprintf(stderr, "Destroying read-write lock attribute failed, ret=%d\n",
      ret);
    pthread_exit((void *)-5);
  }
#endif

/* Destroy the read-write lock */
ret = pthread_rwlock_destroy(&rwlock1);
if (ret != 0)
{
  fprintf(stderr, "Destroying read-write lock failed, ret=%d\n", ret);
  pthread_exit((void *)-6);
}

pthread_exit((void *)0);
}
```

Read-Write Lock Attributes

Note that destroying a read-write lock attributes object does not affect the read-write locks that have been initialized with the attributes object. Because of that, as soon as all read-write locks have been initialized, a read-write lock attributes object can be destroyed. A program should not use a read-write lock attributes object after it is destroyed.

In the read-write lock attributes object, there is one attribute worth mentioning, which is 'process-shared'. The process-shared attribute can take one of the following two values:

1. PTHREAD_PROCESS_PRIVATE

   This is the default value. This means the read-write lock will be used by threads within the calling process only.

2. PTHREAD_PROCESS_SHARED

   Setting the process-shared attribute to this value means the read-write lock is meant to be used by multiple processes. In this case, it is the application's responsibility to allocate the read-write lock variable in memory that is accessible to all these processes (for example, in System V shared memory which we will discuss in a later chapter).

A program invokes the following pthreads functions to retrieve or set the value of the process-shared attribute, respectively:

```
int pthread_rwlockattr_getpshared(const pthread_rwlockattr_t
    *restrict attr, int *restrict pshared);
int pthread_rwlockattr_setpshared(pthread_rwlockattr_t *attr,
    int pshared);
```

8-8 Thread-Specific Data

Initially, in the old days before threads came along, there was only one way of using a global variable. That is to declare the variable outside the scope of any function so that it becomes a global and thus is accessible globally from anywhere in the program. This way, since the data of the global variable is shared across the entire process, to ensure its integrity, concurrent accesses (especially updates) to the data must be synchronized using a lock. When such a program becomes multithreaded, the global data is accessible to all threads and all threads see the same value. One slight variation of this is to add the 'static' keyword in front of the declaration of the variable to reduce its scope from the entire program to a single source file.

When threads came alone, it brings a new feature where all threads can share a same variable but each thread has its own private, separate value. It's called thread specific data and it's very useful in some situations. We introduce this feature in this section.

Note that the similarities between the two are (a) they are all typically declared as a global variable and (b) they are accessible from any threads and anywhere using the same variable name. But the differences are (1) each thread sees a private copy of the value in thread specific data whereas all threads see the same value in a traditional global variable, (2) no use of synchronization primitives is needed to access thread-specific data while synchronization is required in the other case, and (3) special APIs are used to read or write a thread-specific data.

8-8-1 What Is Thread-Specific Data

Thread specific data, or **thread local storage** as it is sometimes called, is a pthreads feature that allows programmers to use global data variables in a multithreaded program like private ones and access them without using any synchronization primitives.

It is a feature that allows all threads in the same process to use exactly the same global variable name and not worry about stepping on one another's toes because behind the scene, the implementation ensures that **each thread has its own private copy of the variable's value**. As a result, no synchronization measure is needed at all when all threads all use and access the same global variable for a thread-specific data.

The only catch, though, is you cannot read or write the thread-specific data variable like before. To assign a value to it, you have to call the

pthread_setspecific() function to do it. And to use its value, you have to call the **pthread_getspecific() function** to retrieve its value first.

Thread specific data offers a path to quickly convert a traditional single threaded application using global variables into a multithreaded application and continue to work correctly. The conversion essentially involves making each existing global variable become a thread specific data key.

Thread specific data uses the model of a key with a set of values. You need to define a key for each thread specific data item. A key is essentially a variable name, a global one so that all threads can access it. Each key has a value, one for each thread. **The thread-specific data implementation ensures each individual thread has a separate private copy of the key value, although all threads use the same key (i.e. the same variable name).** This key needs to be created only once before the thread specific data is used. It is usually created in the main thread.

In other words, each thread has a different value of the key. The key's value for a given thread is independent of any other thread. For example, if we have a thread-specific data key named key1 and the process has four threads, then at any given time, there will be four different copies of the value, one for each thread. And the values can all be different as shown below:

thread	value of key1
thread 1	10
thread 2	5
thread 3	0
thread 4	190

In other words, a thread-specific data is like a private global when you declare it global. It is private because each thread has a separate copy of the data which other threads don't see. It is a global in terms of its scope because a thread can access it from anywhere. And it's like a global or static in terms of its lifetime because its existence is beyond one function.

8-8-2 Examples of Using Thread-Specific Data

Figure 8-22 shows an example program of how to create and use thread-specific data in pthreads. It declares a global thread-specific data key named gvar1 (stands for global variable 1). Since it is global, every thread has access to it and they can all use the same variable (i.e. key) name gvar1 to access it. Besides, since it is a thread-specific data (declared as the pthread_key_t), each thread has a private copy of the data value that is independent of that of any other threads. Therefore, each thread can change the value of the same variable without affecting any other threads and no synchronization (e.g. mutex) is needed at all to coordinate the updates between different threads!

Figure 8-22 Using thread-specific data (pt_tsd.c)

```
/*
 * Thread-specific data in pthread.
```

```c
 * Note that all threads share the same key or global variable gvar1, but each
 * thread has a private copy of the data. Changes to the data in one thread is
 * never seen by any other thread.
 * Copyright (c) 2014, 2019, 2020 Mr. Jin-Jwei Chen.  All rights reserved.
 */

#include <stdio.h>
#include <unistd.h>
#include <pthread.h>

#define  NTHREADS    4
#define  NTASKS      3

pthread_key_t       gvar1;              /* thread-specific data (the key) */

/*
 * The worker thread.
 */
int worker_thread(void *args)
{
  unsigned int  *argp;
  unsigned int  myid;        /* my id */
  unsigned int  ntasks;      /* number of tasks to perform */
  int           i, ret=0;
  unsigned int  *valptr;     /* pointer returned by pthread_getspecific() */
  unsigned int  mynewval;    /* value of thread-specific key */

  /* Extract input arguments (two unsigned integers) */
  argp = (unsigned int *)args;
  if (argp != NULL)
  {
    myid = argp[0];
    ntasks = argp[1];
  }
  else
#ifdef SUN64
  {
    ret = (-1);
    pthread_exit((void *)&ret);
  }
#else
    pthread_exit((void *)(-1));
#endif

  fprintf(stdout, "Worker thread: myid=%u ntasks=%u\n", myid, ntasks);

  ret = pthread_setspecific(gvar1, (void *)&myid);
  if (ret != 0)
    fprintf(stderr, "worker_thread: pthread_setspecific() failed, ret=%d\n",
      ret);

  /* Do my job */
  for (i = 0; i < ntasks; i++)
  {
    /* Get and print the current value of the thread-specific data */
    valptr =  pthread_getspecific(gvar1);
```

427

```
      if (valptr == NULL)
      {
          fprintf(stderr, "worker_thread: pthread_getspecific() returned NULL\n");
#ifdef SUN64
          ret = (-2);
          pthread_exit((void *)&ret);
#else
          pthread_exit((void *)(-2));
#endif
      }
      mynewval = (*(unsigned int *)valptr);
      fprintf(stdout, "In thread %u gvar1 = %u \n", myid, mynewval);

      /* Double the value of the thread-specific data */
      mynewval = (2 * mynewval);
      ret = pthread_setspecific(gvar1, (void *)&mynewval);
      if (ret != 0)
      {
          fprintf(stderr, "worker_thread: pthread_setspecific() failed, ret=%d\n",
          ret);
#ifdef SUN64
          ret = (-3);
          pthread_exit((void *)&ret);
#else
          pthread_exit((void *)(-3));
#endif
      }
      sleep(1);
  }

#ifdef SUN64
  pthread_exit((void *)&ret);
#else
  pthread_exit((void *)0);
#endif
}


/*
 * The main program.
 */
int main(int argc, char *argv[])
{
  pthread_t       thrds[NTHREADS];
  unsigned int    args[NTHREADS][2];
  int             ret, i;
  int             retval = 0;   /* each child thread returns an int */
#ifdef SUN64
  int             *retvalp = &retval;          /* pointer to returned value */
#endif

  /* Load up the input arguments for each child thread */
  for (i = 0; i < NTHREADS; i++)
  {
    args[i][0] = (i + 1);
    args[i][1] = NTASKS;
  }
```

```
/* Create thread-specific data key: gvar1 */
ret = pthread_key_create(&gvar1, (void *)NULL);
if (ret != 0)
{
  fprintf(stderr, "Failed to create thread-specific data key, ret=%d\n", ret);
  pthread_exit((void *)-1);
}

/* Create new threads to run the worker_thread() function and pass in args */
for (i = 0; i < NTHREADS; i++)
{
  ret = pthread_create(&thrds[i], (pthread_attr_t *)NULL,
        (void *(*)(void *))worker_thread, (void *)args[i]);
  if (ret != 0)
  {
    fprintf(stderr, "Failed to create the worker thread, ret=%d\n", ret);
    pthread_exit((void *)-2);
  }
}

/*
 * Wait for each of the child threads to finish and retrieve its returned
 * value.
 */
for (i = 0; i < NTHREADS; i++)
{
#ifdef SUN64
  ret = pthread_join(thrds[i], (void **)&retvalp);
#else
  ret = pthread_join(thrds[i], (void **)&retval);
#endif
  fprintf(stdout, "Thread %u exited with return value %d\n", (i+1), retval);
}

/* Delete thread-specific data key: gvar1 */
ret = pthread_key_delete(gvar1);
if (ret != 0)
{
  fprintf(stderr, "Failed to delete thread-specific data key, ret=%d\n", ret);
  pthread_exit((void *)-3);
}

pthread_exit((void *)0);
}
```

The example program creates the thread-specific data key in the main function
before it actually spawns any thread. It then creates all the child threads.
In the middle of the thread start routine, which is shared by all threads,
it sets/initializes the value of the thread-specific data item to each
thread's thread number -- myid, which is different for each thread.
Every thread then goes into a loop which iterates NTASKS times.
In each iteration, the thread gets and prints its own value of the key
and then doubles that value.

As you can see from the program output, since each thread has the key's

value stored in its own thread local storage, the value of the thread-specific data of each thread is different!
When each thread doubles the value of the global variable gvar1, it doubles the thread's own copy of the value, not any other thread's.
Also changes to the same variable in a thread is not seen by any other thread! Thread local storage is usually implemented as dynamic memory behind the scene.

A Single Scalar or Pointer Value

A thread-specific data key can store either a scalar data such an integer or a pointer. If you have a integer variable whose value is different for each thread, you could store that under a thread-specific data key.

```
pthread_key_t  someVar;   /* Thread specific data key */

unsigned int  myval=0;   /* value for a thread-specific data key */

pthread_setspecific(someVar, (void *)&myval); /* save this thread's value */
```

If you have allocated memory space for a structure of data which every thread has its own private copy, you can store the pointer (i.e. address) of that structured data in a thread-specific data key too.

```
static pthread_key_t  somePtr;      /* Thread specific data key */

struct xyz  *myptr=0;   /* value for a thread-specific data key */

myptr = malloc(sizeof(struct xyz));
pthread_setspecific(somePtr, (void *)myptr); /* save thread's ptr value */
```

Figure 8-23 is an example of storing a buffer pointer returned by malloc() in a thread-specific data. In this program, each thread calls malloc() to allocate space for the value of a structure. It then stores the pointer value returned by the malloc() function in the thread specific data named bufptr.
Each thread then fills in a different value for the structure.
Every thread calls print_buf() to print its own copy of the structure value. To show the value is not affected by other threads, print_buf() sleeps about half second between each print.

Figure 8-23 Using thread-specific data to store a buffer pointer (pt_tsd_ptr.c)

```
/*
 * Thread-specific data in pthread.
 * Using thread-specific data to store a pointer to a thread specific buffer.
 * Copyright (c) 2014, 2019 Mr. Jin-Jwei Chen.  All rights reserved.
 */

#include <stdio.h>
#include <stdlib.h>
#include <pthread.h>
#include <time.h>

#define  MAXNTHREADS  10      /* maximum number of threads */
#define  DEFNTHREADS  3       /* default number of threads */
#define  MAXTASKS     3000    /* maximum number of tasks */
```

```c
#define  DEFNTASKS    2           /* default number of tasks */

pthread_key_t        bufptr;      /* thread-specific data (the key) */
struct mybuf {
  unsigned int      myid;
  char              text[32];
};

/* Print contents of 'struct mybuf' */
int print_buf(unsigned int myid, unsigned int cnt)
{
  struct timespec  slptm;
  int    i;
  char  *valptr;        /* pointer returned by pthread_getspecific() */
  struct mybuf  *mybufptr;   /* value of thread-specific key */

  slptm.tv_sec = 0;
  slptm.tv_nsec = 500000000;  /* 5/10 second */

  if (cnt <= 0)
    return(-1);

  for (i = 0; i < cnt; i++)
  {
    /* Retrieve thread-specific buffer pointer */
    valptr = pthread_getspecific(bufptr);
    if (valptr == NULL)
    {
      fprintf(stderr, "print_buf(): pthread_getspecific() returned NULL\n");
      return(-2);
    }
    mybufptr = (struct mybuf *)valptr;

    /* Do something */
    fprintf(stdout, "Contents of the thread-specific buffer are:\n");
    fprintf(stdout, "  myid = %u\n", mybufptr->myid);
    fprintf(stdout, "  text = %s\n", mybufptr->text);

    nanosleep(&slptm, (struct timespec *)NULL);
  }

  return(0);
}

/* The worker thread */
int worker_thread(void *args)
{
  unsigned int  *argp;
  unsigned int  myid;      /* my id */
  unsigned int  ntasks;    /* number of tasks to perform */
  int           i, ret=0;
  char          *ptr1;
  struct mybuf  *ptr2;

  /* Extract input arguments (two unsigned integers) */
  argp = (unsigned int *)args;
```

431

```
  if (argp != NULL)
  {
    myid = argp[0];
    ntasks = argp[1];
  }
  else
#ifdef SUN64
  {
    ret = (-1);
    pthread_exit((void *)&ret);
  }
#else
    pthread_exit((void *)(-1));
#endif

  fprintf(stdout, "Worker thread: myid=%u ntasks=%u\n", myid, ntasks);

  /* Initialize thread specific data. First, allocate buffer memory. */
  ptr1 = (char *)malloc(sizeof(struct mybuf));
  if (ptr1 == NULL)
  {
#ifdef SUN64
    ret = (-2);
    pthread_exit((void *)&ret);
#else
    pthread_exit((void *)(-2));
#endif
  }

  /* Save the pointer in thread-specific data. No & because ptr1 is a pointer */
  ret = pthread_setspecific(bufptr, (void *)ptr1);
  if (ret != 0)
  {
    fprintf(stderr, "worker_thread: pthread_setspecific() failed, ret=%d\n",
        ret);
#ifdef SUN64
    ret = (-3);
    pthread_exit((void *)&ret);
#else
    pthread_exit((void *)(-3));
#endif
  }

  /* Set thread-specific data */
  ptr2 = (struct mybuf *)ptr1;
  ptr2->myid = myid;
  sprintf(ptr2->text, "This is thread %2d.\n", myid);

  /* Do the work -- just print the data. */
  print_buf(myid, ntasks);
  free(ptr1);

  ret = 0;
#ifdef SUN64
  pthread_exit((void *)&ret);
#else
```

```
  pthread_exit((void *)0);
#endif
}


/*
 * The main program.
 */
int main(int argc, char *argv[])
{
  pthread_t        thrds[MAXNTHREADS];
  unsigned int     args[MAXNTHREADS][2];
  int              ret, i;
  int              retval = 0;   /* each child thread returns an int */
#ifdef SUN64
  int              *retvalp = &retval;          /* pointer to returned value */
#endif
  int              nthreads = DEFNTHREADS;      /* default # of threads */
  int              ntasks = DEFNTASKS;          /* default # of tasks */

  /* Get number of threads and tasks from user */
  if (argc > 1)
  {
    nthreads = atoi(argv[1]);
    if (nthreads < 0 || nthreads > MAXNTHREADS)
      nthreads = DEFNTHREADS;
  }
  if (argc > 2)
  {
    ntasks = atoi(argv[2]);
    if (ntasks < 0 || ntasks > MAXTASKS)
      ntasks = DEFNTASKS;
  }

  /* Load up the input arguments for each child thread */
  for (i = 0; i < nthreads; i++)
  {
    args[i][0] = (i + 1);
    args[i][1] = ntasks;
  }

  /* Create thread-specific data key: bufptr */
  ret = pthread_key_create(&bufptr, (void *)NULL);
  if (ret != 0)
  {
    fprintf(stderr, "Failed to create thread-specific data key, ret=%d\n", ret);
    pthread_exit((void *)-3);
  }

  /* Create new threads to run the worker_thread() function and pass in args */
  for (i = 0; i < nthreads; i++)
  {
    ret = pthread_create(&thrds[i], (pthread_attr_t *)NULL,
          (void *(*)(void *))worker_thread, (void *)args[i]);
    if (ret != 0)
    {
      fprintf(stderr, "Failed to create the worker thread, ret=%d\n", ret);
```

```
        pthread_exit((void *)-4);
    }
}

/*
 * Wait for each of the child threads to finish and retrieve its returned
 * value.
 */
for (i = 0; i < nthreads; i++)
{
#ifdef SUN64
    ret = pthread_join(thrds[i], (void **)&retvalp);
#else
    ret = pthread_join(thrds[i], (void **)&retval);
#endif
    fprintf(stdout, "Thread %u exited with return value %d\n", (i+1), retval);
}

/* Delete thread-specific data key: bufptr */
ret = pthread_key_delete(bufptr);
if (ret != 0)
{
    fprintf(stderr, "Failed to delete thread-specific data key, ret=%d\n", ret);
    pthread_exit((void *)-5);
}

pthread_exit((void *)0);
}
```

A Real-life Example

Here we give an example from real-life. This was exactly what the author did when working at a very big company. Author found a deadlock bug in someone else's code and used thread specific data to fix it.

Thread-specific data comes very handy in some cases. Sometimes a function calls itself. That is, it's recursive. Many times, the function itself also takes a lock. A thread calling a recursive function obtaining a mutual exclusive lock will deadlock itself when it tries to obtain the same lock after it has already done so the very first time around.

This kind of self-deadlock can be avoided by using a thread-specific data key. The function could use a thread-specific data to remember whether it has acquired the lock yet or not. If yes, then it can simply skip the operation to acquire the lock because it has already had the lock. Trying to acquire the same lock again while holding it already will deadlock itself. This way, self-deadlocking is avoided and the code becomes reentrantable.
And it is thread-safe because each thread has its own copy of the data independent of any other threads, thanks to thread-specific data.
And the code still works correctly because it still ensures mutual exclusion between different threads. All it does is eliminating the self-deadlock within a thread itself, due to recursion or nested calls.

Figure 8-24 is an example demonstrating exactly this.

To see the self-deadlock problem first, compile the program by defining the

SHOWDEADLOCK macro:

```
cc -DSHOWDEADLOCK pt_tsd_reentrant.c -o pt_tsd_reentrant -lpthread
```

When you run the program, you will see the entire program deadlocks forever. When the first thread runs, it calls recursive(). During the very first call into recursive(), the thread will call pthread_mutex_lock() to acquire the lock. It will then have the lock. Then on its second call to recursive(), it will call pthread_mutex_lock() again. This time it will block forever because the lock is no longer available -- it has already been taken by the thread itself. Hence, this first executing thread blocks and deadlocks itself.

Then the second thread will run, this thread will call pthread_mutex_lock() on its first entry into recursive() and that call will block forever because the lock is already held by the first thread. So, the first thread blocks itself and can never makes any progress. And since the first thread has taken the lock but it cannot make any progress, that blocks all other threads on their pthread_mutex_lock() call. That's why the entire program becomes permanently blocked, not any thread can make any progress.

Then recompile the same program without defining the SHOWDEADLOCK macro (taking out the -DSHOWDEADLOCK from the above command line).
You will see the program runs to completion. Each thread remembers whether it has acquired the lock or not in a thread specific data key named **haslock** and uses that value to decide when to call, or not to call, pthread_mutex_lock() and pthread_mutex_unlock().

Figure 8-24 Using thread-specific data to avoid self-deadlock (pt_tsd_reentrant.c)

```c
/*
 * Thread-specific data in pthread.
 * Using thread-specific data to prevent a thread from deadlock itself.
 * Remember if a thread has obtained a lock or not in a thread-specific data
 * and check that so that a thread won't deadlock itself in trying to get same
 * lock and the function becomes reentrantable.
 * To see self-deadlock, recompile with SHOWDEADLOCK defined using
 *   $ cc -DSHOWDEADLOCK pt_tsd_reentrant.c -o pt_tsd_reentrant -lpthread
 * Copyright (c) 2014, 2019-2020 Mr. Jin-Jwei Chen.  All rights reserved.
 */

#include <stdio.h>
#include <stdlib.h>
#include <pthread.h>
#include <time.h>

#define   MAXNTHREADS   10        /* maximum number of threads */
#define   DEFNTHREADS   2         /* default number of threads */
#define   MAXTASKS      3000      /* maximum number of tasks */
#define   DEFNTASKS     5         /* default number of tasks */

pthread_key_t       haslock;    /* thread-specific data (the key) */
pthread_mutex_t     mutex1;     /* global mutex shared by all threads */

int recursive(unsigned int myid, unsigned int cnt)
{
```

```
  struct timespec  slptm;
  int     ret;
  unsigned int  *valptr;       /* pointer returned by pthread_getspecific() */
  unsigned int  ihaslock;      /* value of thread-specific key */
  unsigned int  myval;

  slptm.tv_sec = 0;
  slptm.tv_nsec = 500000000;  /* 5/10 second */

  if (cnt <= 0)
    return(0);

  /* To avoid deadlocking self, take the lock only if myself has not done so */
  valptr = pthread_getspecific(haslock);
  if (valptr == NULL)
  {
    fprintf(stderr, "recursive(): pthread_getspecific() returned NULL\n");
    return(-3);
  }
  ihaslock = (*(unsigned int *)valptr);
#ifndef SHOWDEADLOCK
  if (ihaslock == 0)
  {
#endif
    ret = pthread_mutex_lock(&mutex1);
    if (ret != 0)
    {
      fprintf(stderr, "recursive(): thread %u failed to lock the mutex,"
        " ret=%d\n", myid, ret);
      return(-4);
    }

    /* Remember in thread-specific data that I have the lock already */
    myval = 1;
    ret = pthread_setspecific(haslock, (void *)&myval);
    if (ret != 0)
    {
      fprintf(stderr, "recursive(): thread %u pthread_setspecific() failed,"
        " ret=%d\n", myid, ret);
      return(-5);
    }
#ifndef SHOWDEADLOCK
  }
#endif

  /* Do some work. Here we do nothing but sleep and then call ourselves. */
  fprintf(stdout, "Thread %u in recursive(), cnt=%u\n", myid, cnt);
  nanosleep(&slptm, (struct timespec *)NULL);
  ret = recursive(myid, --cnt);

  /* Release the lock and clear our memory */
#ifndef SHOWDEADLOCK
  if (ihaslock == 0)
  {
#endif
    ret = pthread_mutex_unlock(&mutex1);
```

```c
    if (ret != 0)
    {
      fprintf(stderr, "recursive(): thread %u failed to unlock the mutex,"
        " ret=%d\n", myid, ret);
      return(-6);
    }
    /* Reset the value in thread specific data */
    myval = 0;
    ret = pthread_setspecific(haslock, (void *)&myval);
    if (ret != 0)
    {
      fprintf(stderr, "recursive(): thread %u pthread_setspecific() failed,"
        " ret=%d\n", myid, ret);
      return(-7);
    }
#ifndef SHOWDEADLOCK
  }
#endif
  return(0);
}


/* The worker thread */
int worker_thread(void *args)
{
  unsigned int  *argp;
  unsigned int  myid;          /* my id */
  unsigned int  ntasks;        /* number of tasks to perform */
  int           i, ret=0;
  unsigned int  myval = 0;     /* initial value for thread-specific data */

  /* Extract input arguments (two unsigned integers) */
  argp = (unsigned int *)args;
  if (argp != NULL)
  {
    myid = argp[0];
    ntasks = argp[1];
  }
  else
#ifdef SUN64
  {
    ret = (-1);
    pthread_exit((void *)&ret);
  }
#else
    pthread_exit((void *)(-1));
#endif

  fprintf(stdout, "worker_thread(): myid=%u ntasks=%u\n", myid, ntasks);

  /* Initialize thread specific data */
  ret = pthread_setspecific(haslock, (void *)&myval);
  if (ret != 0)
  {
    fprintf(stderr, "worker_thread(): pthread_setspecific() failed, ret=%d\n",
      ret);
#ifdef SUN64
```

437

```
      ret = (-2);
      pthread_exit((void *)&ret);
#else
      pthread_exit((void *)(-2));
#endif
  }

  /* Do the work */
  ret = recursive(myid, ntasks);

#ifdef SUN64
  pthread_exit((void *)&ret);
#else
  pthread_exit((void *)ret);
#endif
}

/*
 * The main program.
 */
int main(int argc, char *argv[])
{
  pthread_t       thrds[MAXNTHREADS];
  unsigned int    args[MAXNTHREADS][2];
  int             ret, i;
  int             retval = 0;   /* each child thread returns an int */
#ifdef SUN64
  int             *retvalp = &retval;          /* pointer to returned value */
#endif
  int             nthreads = DEFNTHREADS;      /* default # of threads */
  int             ntasks = DEFNTASKS;          /* default # of tasks */
  pthread_mutexattr_t  mutexattr1;  /* mutex attributes */

  /* Get number of threads and tasks from user */
  if (argc > 1)
  {
    nthreads = atoi(argv[1]);
    if (nthreads < 0 || nthreads > MAXNTHREADS)
      nthreads = DEFNTHREADS;
  }
  if (argc > 2)
  {
    ntasks = atoi(argv[2]);
    if (ntasks < 0 || ntasks > MAXTASKS)
      ntasks = DEFNTASKS;
  }

  /* Initialize mutex attributes */
  ret = pthread_mutexattr_init(&mutexattr1);
  if (ret != 0)
  {
    fprintf(stderr, "Failed to initialize mutex attributes, ret=%d\n", ret);
    pthread_exit((void *)-1);
  }

  /* Initialize the mutex */
```

```c
  ret = pthread_mutex_init(&mutex1, &mutexattr1);
  if (ret != 0)
  {
    fprintf(stderr, "Failed to initialize mutex, ret=%d\n", ret);
    pthread_exit((void *)-2);
  }

  /* Load up the input arguments for each child thread */
  for (i = 0; i < nthreads; i++)
  {
    args[i][0] = (i + 1);
    args[i][1] = ntasks;
  }

  /* Create thread-specific data key: haslock */
  ret = pthread_key_create(&haslock, (void *)NULL);
  if (ret != 0)
  {
    fprintf(stderr, "Failed to create thread-specific data key, ret=%d\n", ret);
    pthread_exit((void *)-3);
  }

  /* Create new threads to run the worker_thread() function and pass in args */
  for (i = 0; i < nthreads; i++)
  {
    ret = pthread_create(&thrds[i], (pthread_attr_t *)NULL,
        (void *(*)(void *))worker_thread, (void *)args[i]);
    if (ret != 0)
    {
      fprintf(stderr, "Failed to create the worker thread, ret=%d\n", ret);
      pthread_exit((void *)-4);
    }
  }

  /*
   * Wait for each of the child threads to finish and retrieve its returned
   * value.
   */
  for (i = 0; i < nthreads; i++)
  {
#ifdef SUN64
    ret = pthread_join(thrds[i], (void **)&retvalp);
#else
    ret = pthread_join(thrds[i], (void **)&retval);
#endif
    fprintf(stdout, "Thread %u exited with return value %d\n", (i+1), retval);
  }

  /* Delete thread-specific data key: haslock */
  ret = pthread_key_delete(haslock);
  if (ret != 0)
  {
    fprintf(stderr, "Failed to delete thread-specific data key, ret=%d\n", ret);
    pthread_exit((void *)-5);
  }
```

```
  /* Destroy mutex attributes */
#ifndef HPUX64
  ret = pthread_mutexattr_destroy(&mutexattr1);
  if (ret != 0)
  {
    fprintf(stderr, "Failed to destroy mutex attributes, ret=%d\n", ret);
    pthread_exit((void *)-6);
  }
#endif

  /* Destroy the mutex */
  ret = pthread_mutex_destroy(&mutex1);
  if (ret != 0)
  {
    fprintf(stderr, "Failed to destroy mutex, ret=%d\n", ret);
    pthread_exit((void *)-7);
  }

  pthread_exit((void *)0);
}
```

Alternatively, this can be solved **using a recursive lock**. See assignment #6.

Thread Specific Data Versus Global Variable

Notice that there are a couple of main coding differences between using
a thread-specific data key and using a traditional, regular global variable.
First, before spawning any of the child threads, the main thread has to
invoke the pthread_key_create() function to create the thread-specific data
key or data item. Second, accessing the thread-specific data must be done via
calling a pthreads function rather than direct accessing the variable name.
Specifically, setting or changing the value of a thread-specific data key
(i.e. variable) is done via calling the pthread_setspecific() function and
getting the value of a thread-specific data key is done through invoking
the pthread_getspecific() function, respectively.

It is worth pointing out that in a multithreaded process, **the global
variable errno (defined in errno.h) is an example of thread-specific data**.
When a thread retrieves the value of the global variable errno, each thread
gets its own copy of the variable's value that is specific to that particular
thread. Notice that the POSIX thread standard has made errno an exception
in that a thread can directly access the variable without going through
the standard thread-specific data APIs so that the old legacy code
continues to work without changes.

8-8-3 Destructor Function of Thread-Specific Data Key

Note that the design of thread-specific data allows a destructor function to
be specified at the time of the data key creation. If specified, this
function will be automatically called whenever a thread terminates.
It is typically used to release all resources associated with a thread.
For instance, if a thread allocates dynamic memory using malloc, then
the destructor function should always try to free the memory to ensure
there is no memory leak even when a thread terminates unexpectedly.

Figure 8-25 is an example program that demonstrates how to allocate memory for complex structure data for thread local storage and how to define and use a destructor function so that pthreads will automatically free that memory for you.

Figure 8-25 Using destructor function of a thread-specific data key (pt_tsd_destroy.c)

```c
/*
 * Providing destructor function for thread-specific data.
 * Note that all threads share the same global variable gvar1, but each thread
 * has a private copy of the data. Changes to the data in one thread is
 * never seen by any other thread.
 * Copyright (c) 2014, 2019 Mr. Jin-Jwei Chen.  All rights reserved.
 */

#include <stdio.h>
#include <stdlib.h>     /* malloc */
#include <string.h>     /* memset() */
#include <unistd.h>     /* sleep() */
#include <pthread.h>

#define  NTHREADS    2
#define  NTASKS      2
#define  MSGSIZE     64

pthread_key_t       gvar1;           /* thread-specific data */

struct mystruct
{
  unsigned int mynum;
  char         mymsg[MSGSIZE];
};
typedef struct mystruct mystruct;

/*
 * Destructor function for thread-specific data key, gvar1.
 */
void destroy_gvar1(void *ptr)
{
  if (ptr != NULL)
  {
    fprintf(stdout, "In destroy_gvar1(), free the memory at address %p\n", ptr);
    free(ptr);
  }
}

/*
 * The worker thread.
 */
int worker_thread(void *args)
{
  unsigned int  *argp;
  unsigned int  myid;
  unsigned int  ntasks;
  int           i;
```

```
  mystruct        *mydata;
#ifdef SUN64
  int             ret = 0;
#endif

  /* Extract input arguments (two unsigned integers) */
  argp = (unsigned int *)args;
  if (argp != NULL)
  {
    myid = argp[0];
    ntasks = argp[1];
  }
  else
#ifdef SUN64
  {
    ret = (-1);
    pthread_exit((void *)&ret);
  }
#else
    pthread_exit((void *)(-1));
#endif

  fprintf(stdout, "Worker thread: myid=%u ntasks=%u\n", myid, ntasks);

  /* Dynamically allocate memory for the thread-specific data key, gvar1 */
  mydata = (mystruct *)malloc(sizeof(mystruct));
  if (mydata == NULL)
  {
    fprintf(stderr, "Thread %u failed to allocate memory\n", myid);
#ifdef SUN64
    ret = (-2);
    pthread_exit((void *)&ret);
#else
    pthread_exit((void *)-2);
#endif
  }
  memset((void *)mydata, 0, sizeof(mystruct));
  fprintf(stdout, "Thread %u, address of thread-specific data %p\n", myid, mydata);

  /* Set the value of the thread-specific data key */
  mydata->mynum = myid;
  sprintf(mydata->mymsg, "This is a message from thread %u.", myid);
  pthread_setspecific(gvar1, (void *)mydata);

  /* Do my job */
  for (i = 0; i < ntasks; i++)
  {
    mydata = pthread_getspecific(gvar1);
    fprintf(stdout, "In thread %u :\n", myid);
    fprintf(stdout, "  mynum = %u\n", mydata->mynum);
    fprintf(stdout, "  mymsg = %s\n", mydata->mymsg);
    sleep(1);
  }

  /* Note that: We would need to free the memory here if we had not
   * called pthread_key_create() with destroy_gvar1 in its second argument.
```

```
   *    free(mydata);
   * Since we did that, pthread will invoke destroy_gvar1() automatically
   * for us when each thread exits.
   */
#ifdef SUN64
  pthread_exit((void *)&ret);
#else
  pthread_exit((void *)0);
#endif
}


/*
 * The main program.
 */
int main(int argc, char *argv[])
{
  pthread_t       thrds[NTHREADS];
  unsigned int    args[NTHREADS][2];
  int             ret, i;
  int             retval = 0;  /* each child thread returns an int */
#ifdef SUN64
  int             *retvalp = &retval;           /* pointer to returned value */
#endif

  /* Load up the input arguments for each child thread */
  for (i = 0; i < NTHREADS; i++)
  {
    args[i][0] = (i + 1);
    args[i][1] = NTASKS;
  }

  /* Create thread-specific data key: gvar1 and specify destructor function */
  ret = pthread_key_create(&gvar1, (void *)destroy_gvar1);
  if (ret != 0)
  {
    fprintf(stderr, "Failed to create thread-specific data key, ret=%d\n", ret);
    pthread_exit((void *)-1);
  }

  /* Create new threads to run the worker_thread() function and pass in args */
  for (i = 0; i < NTHREADS; i++)
  {
    ret = pthread_create(&thrds[i], (pthread_attr_t *)NULL,
         (void *(*)(void *))worker_thread, (void *)args[i]);
    if (ret != 0)
    {
      fprintf(stderr, "Failed to create the worker thread, ret=%d\n", ret);
      pthread_exit((void *)-2);
    }
  }

  /*
   * Wait for each of the child threads to finish and retrieve its returned
   * value.
   */
  for (i = 0; i < NTHREADS; i++)
```

443

```
    {
#ifdef SUN64
    ret = pthread_join(thrds[i], (void **)&retvalp);
#else
    ret = pthread_join(thrds[i], (void **)&retval);
#endif
    fprintf(stdout, "Thread %u exited with return value %d\n", (i+1), retval);
    }

    /* Delete thread-specific data key: gvar1 */
    ret = pthread_key_delete(gvar1);
    if (ret != 0)
    {
        fprintf(stderr, "Failed to delete thread-specific data key, ret=%d\n", ret);
        pthread_exit((void *)-3);
    }

    pthread_exit((void *)0);
}
```

As demonstrated by this example program, thread local storage can store the value of a structure, rather than just a simple integer. The thread start routine, worker_thread(), has code to dynamically allocate the memory for the structure data and use it. And when it comes to free the dynamic memory of the structure data, there are two choices.

The first choice is the thread could choose to free the memory itself, simply by invoking the free() function at whatever spot appropriate or desired.

The second choice is to take advantage of a feature provided by pthreads. When a program creates a thread-specific data key, it has the option to specify a destructor function for the thread-specific data. If you do that, then when the thread terminates that destructor function will be automatically invoked by pthreads. So, if you free the memory in the destructor function, this pthreads feature will end up freeing the memory for you automatically and you don't need to free it at other places.

As you can see from the example program, we do four things. (1) We define the function destroy_gvar1(). (2) When the main() function calls the pthread_key_create() to create the thread-specific data key, it passes destroy_gvar1 in the second argument as its destructor function. (3) After a thread successfully allocating the memory, it invokes pthread_setspecific() and saves the starting address of that dynamic memory in the thread-specific data key. This pointer value (value of the data key) will get passed to the destructor function later by Pthreads. (4) In the destructor function we free the memory at the address specified by the input argument.

So, if you specify a destructor when calling pthread_key_create() then Pthreads will always call that destructor for you when the thread terminates and it will pass the value of the data key as the input argument into that function. The order of destructor calls is unspecified if more than one destructor exists.

8-9 Pthreads Cancellation

Pthreads has a cancellation API, the pthread_cancel() function.

```
#include <pthread.h>

int pthread_cancel(pthread_t thread);
```

It allows one thread in a process to terminate another thread in the same process. To ensure threads are cancelled in a very controlled and clean manner, pthreads cancellation feature allows programmers to install cancellation cleanup handlers which will be automatically executed when the canceled thread terminates.

When a thread is canceled, that thread's (called the target thread) cancelability state and type determine when the cancellation takes effect. When the cancellation is acted on, the cancellation cleanup handlers for the thread are called. After all of the cancellation cleanup handlers are executed and the last cancellation cleanup handler returns, the thread-specific data destructor functions are called for thread. When the last destructor function returns, thread will be terminated.

The cancellation processing in the target thread runs asynchronously with respect to the returning of pthread_cancel() call in the thread calling the function.

If successful, the pthread_cancel() function returns zero; otherwise, it returns an error number to indicate the error. The error number shall not be EINTR.

8-9-1 Pthreads Cancellation Attributes

In pthreads, a thread is able to control if and when it is canceled. Two cancellation attributes are associated with each POSIX thread: **cancelstate** and **canceltype**.

1. Cancelstate

   Thread cancellation can be enabled or disabled. These are represented in a thread's cancelability state by the values PTHREAD_CANCEL_ENABLE and PTHREAD_CANCEL_DISABLE, respectively. If the value of a thread's Cancelstate attribute is PTHREAD_CANCEL_ENABLE, cancellation of the thread is enabled. If the value is PTHREAD_CANCEL_DISABLE cancellation is disabled.

   If a thread is about to carry out some very important operation and cannot or should not be terminated, it can set the value of its Cancelstate attribute to PTHREAD_CANCEL_DISABLE to disable cancellation. When cancellation is disabled, any cancellation requests for the thread are held pending until cancellation is enabled again.

   Enabling/disabling thread cancellation is done via the pthread_setcancelstate() API.

   ```
   #include <pthread.h>
   int pthread_setcancelstate(int state, int *oldstate);
   ```

2. Canceltype

When thread cancellation is enabled, a thread can also control when it is canceled via the canceltype attribute.
There are two options: **asynchronous** or **deferred**, represented by the value PTHREAD_CANCEL_ASYNCHRONOUS and PTHREAD_CANCEL_DEFERRED, respectively.

With asynchronous cancelability, a thread's cancellation requests are acted upon at any time. That means the thread can be canceled at any given time. In contrast, with deferred cancelability, a thread's cancellation requests are processed only at certain predefined cancellation points.

Canceltype is set by invoking the pthread_setcanceltype() API:

```
#include <pthread.h>
int pthread_setcanceltype(int type, int *oldtype);
```

Here we give an example of how to cancel a running thread.
Figure 8-26 is an example program that starts two threads: a worker thread and a manager thread. The manager thread cancels the worker thread.

You can see worker_thread() sets its canceltype to PTHREAD_CANCEL_DEFERRED. It also has its cancellation disabled in the beginning. As a result, the cancel request from the manager_thread() has been pending and not acted on. Later the worker thread enables its cancellation. As soon as that happens, the cancellation request that has been pending is acted upon.
At that point, the worker thread is canceled. In processing the cancellation, the cancellation handler routine is called and executed. The dynamic memory that the worker thread allocates is freed by the cancellation handler routine and the worker thread terminates.

Notice that the program defines a thread cancellation cleanup handler function named cancel_cleanup(). And the worker thread invokes the pthread_cleanup_push() and pthread_cleanup_pop() functions to install and remove the cleanup function, respectively.

When a thread is canceled, its return value varies from one system to another. They include 0, -1, -3 and -19.

Figure 8-26 Cancel a thread (pt_cancel.c)

```
/*
 * Thread cancellation.
 * Copyright (c) 2014, 2019, 2020 Mr. Jin-Jwei Chen.  All rights reserved.
 */

#include <stdio.h>
#include <stdlib.h>
#include <pthread.h>
#include <time.h>
#include <unistd.h>

#define   MAXNTHREADS   10        /* maximum number of threads */
#define   DEFNTHREADS   2         /* default number of threads */
#define   MAXTASKS      9000      /* maximum number of tasks */
#define   DEFNTASKS     500       /* default number of tasks */
#define   LOOPCNT       10000
```

```c
/* Thread cancellation cleanup handler function */
void cancel_cleanup(char *bufptr)
{
  fprintf(stdout, "Enter thread cancellation cleanup routine.\n");
  if (bufptr)
  {
    free(bufptr);
    fprintf(stdout, "cancel_cleanup(): memory at address %p was freed.\n",
      bufptr);
  }
}


/* The worker thread */
int worker_thread(void *args)
{
  unsigned int  *argp;
  unsigned int  myid;         /* my id */
  unsigned int  ntasks;       /* number of tasks to perform */
  int           i, j, ret=0;
  unsigned int  count = 0;    /* counter */
  int           curstate;     /* thread's current cancelstate */
  int           oldstate;     /* thread's previous cancelstate */
  int           curtype;      /* thread's current canceltype */
  int           oldtype;      /* thread's previous canceltype */
  char          *bufptr=NULL; /* address of malloc-ed memory */
  struct timespec  slptm;     /* time to sleep */

  /* Extract input arguments (two unsigned integers) */
  argp = (unsigned int *)args;
  if (argp != NULL)
  {
    myid = argp[0];
    ntasks = argp[1];
  }
  else
#ifdef SUN64
  {
    ret = (-1);
    pthread_exit((void *)&ret);
  }
#else
    pthread_exit((void *)(-1));
#endif

  fprintf(stdout, "worker_thread(): myid=%u ntasks=%u\n", myid, ntasks);

  /* Set thread's cancelstate -- disable cancellation */
  curstate = PTHREAD_CANCEL_DISABLE;
  ret = pthread_setcancelstate(curstate, &oldstate);
  fprintf(stdout, "worker_thread(): thread cancellation is disabled.\n");

  /* Set thread's canceltype */
  curtype = PTHREAD_CANCEL_DEFERRED;
  ret = pthread_setcanceltype(curtype, &oldtype);

  /* To demo cancellation cleanup, we allocate some memory here. */
```

447

```
bufptr = malloc(512);
if (bufptr != NULL)
  fprintf(stdout, "worker_thread(): memory at address %p was allocated.\n",
    bufptr);
else
  fprintf(stderr, "worker_thread(): failed to allocate memory.\n");

/* Install the thread cancellation cleanup handler */
pthread_cleanup_push((void (*)())cancel_cleanup, (void *)bufptr);

/* Do the work */
slptm.tv_sec = 0;
slptm.tv_nsec = 100000000;   /* 1/10 second */
for (i = 0; i < ntasks; i++)
{
  for (j = 0; j < LOOPCNT; j++)
    count++;
  nanosleep(&slptm, (struct timespec *)NULL);
  fprintf(stdout, "worker_thread(): count=%u\n", count);

  if (count == (5*LOOPCNT))
    sleep(1);

  if (count == (10*LOOPCNT))
  {
    /* Set thread's cancelstate -- enable cancellation */
    curstate = PTHREAD_CANCEL_ENABLE;
    ret = pthread_setcancelstate(curstate, &oldstate);
    fprintf(stdout, "worker_thread(): thread cancellation is enabled.\n");
  }
}

/* Remove the thread cancellation cleanup handler */
pthread_cleanup_pop(0);
if (bufptr != NULL)
  free(bufptr);

#ifdef SUN64
  pthread_exit((void *)&ret);
#else
  pthread_exit((void *)ret);
#endif
}

/* The manager thread */
int manager_thread(void *args)
{
  pthread_t   *argp;
  int         ret=0;
  pthread_t   targetThread;   /* thread id of the target thread */

  /* Extract input argument */
  argp = (pthread_t *)args;
  if (argp != NULL)
    targetThread = *(pthread_t *)argp;
  else
```

```
#ifdef SUN64
    {
      ret = (-1);
      pthread_exit((void *)&ret);
    }
#else
      pthread_exit((void *)(-1));
#endif

    sleep(1);   /* Let the worker thread run first */

    /* Cancel the worker thread */
    fprintf(stdout, "manager_thread(), canceling worker thread ...\n");
    fflush(stdout);
    ret = pthread_cancel(targetThread);
    if (ret != 0)
      fprintf(stderr, "manager_thread(), pthread_cancel() failed, ret=%d\n", ret);

#ifdef SUN64
  ret = (0);
  pthread_exit((void *)&ret);
#else
  pthread_exit((void *)(0));
#endif
}


/*
 * The main program.
 */
int main(int argc, char *argv[])
{
  pthread_t       thrds[MAXNTHREADS];
  unsigned int    args1[2];
  pthread_t       args2;
  int             ret, i;
  int             retval = 0;   /* each child thread returns an int */
#ifdef SUN64
  int             *retvalp = &retval;            /* pointer to returned value */
#endif
  int             nthreads = DEFNTHREADS;      /* default # of threads */
  int             ntasks = DEFNTASKS;          /* default # of tasks */

  /* Get number of threads and tasks from user */
  if (argc > 1)
  {
    nthreads = atoi(argv[1]);
    if (nthreads < 0 || nthreads > MAXNTHREADS)
      nthreads = DEFNTHREADS;
  }
  if (argc > 2)
  {
    ntasks = atoi(argv[2]);
    if (ntasks < 0 || ntasks > MAXTASKS)
      ntasks = DEFNTASKS;
  }
```

```
/* Load up the input arguments for the worker thread */
args1[0] = (1);
args1[1] = ntasks;

/* Create a worker thread */
ret = pthread_create(&thrds[0], (pthread_attr_t *)NULL,
      (void *(*)(void *))worker_thread, (void *)args1);
if (ret != 0)
{
  fprintf(stderr, "Failed to create the worker thread, ret=%d\n", ret);
  pthread_exit((void *)-3);
}

/* Create the manager thread */
args2 = thrds[0];
ret = pthread_create(&thrds[1], (pthread_attr_t *)NULL,
      (void *(*)(void *))manager_thread, (void *)&args2);
if (ret != 0)
{
  fprintf(stderr, "Failed to create the manager thread, ret=%d\n", ret);
  pthread_exit((void *)-4);
}

/*
 * Wait for each of the child threads to finish and retrieve its returned
 * value.
 */
for (i = 0; i < nthreads; i++)
{
#ifdef SUN64
    ret = pthread_join(thrds[i], (void **)&retvalp);
#else
    ret = pthread_join(thrds[i], (void **)&retval);
#endif
    fprintf(stdout, "Thread %u exited with return value %d\n", (i+1), retval);
}

  pthread_exit((void *)0);
}
```

Note that this example program (pt_cancel.c) works fine in all platforms
we tested except it failed at end in the 64-bit mode of HPUX IA64 platform.
The pthread_join() got a 'bus error' in joining the thread that was canceled.
It might be a bug in the implementation on HPUX 64-bit platform.

8-9-2 Thread Cancellation Points

As we said, if a thread has its cancellation enabled and its canceltype set
as deferred, its cancellation occurs only at certain predefined cancellation
points.

What is a cancellation point? A **cancellation point** is a place, an execution
point, where a thread must act upon a pending cancellation request if its
cancellation is enabled. In other words, cancellation points are the only
places where a thread may be canceled if its canceltype is

450

PTHREAD_CANCEL_DEFERRED.

There are a small number of pthreads functions and a large number of functions outside pthreads that are cancellation points. They are listed at end of this chapter.

The pthreads functions containing a cancellation point include pthread_join(), pthread_testcancel(), pthread_cond_wait() and pthread_cond_timedwait(). Note that pthread_mutex_lock() is not on the list. It would put a huge burden on programmers on the cleanup if it is. This means a thread blocked on mutexes cannot be canceled.

A lot of functions outside pthreads are thread cancellation points too. They include almost all of the I/O functions. The list includes but is not limited to open(), creat(), close(), read(), write(), fcntl(), fsync(), recv(), recvfrom(), send(), sendmsg(), sendto(), msgsnd(), msgrcv(), sleep(), nanosleep(), system(), wait(), waitpid(), sigwait() and many others.

Note that lots of the C standard I/O functions such as fopen(), fclose(), fgetc(), fgets(), fputc(), fputs(), fread(), fwrite(), fscanf(), fstat(), fprintf(), printf(), ioctl() and so on are thread cancellation points as well.

For a complete list of the functions with thread cancellation points, please refer to the subsection named "Cancellation Points" under "Section 2 General Information" of the following POSIX Standard documentation:

The Open Group Base Specifications Issue 7, 2018 edition
IEEE Std 1003.1-2017 (Revision of IEEE Std 1003.1-2008)

at URL: https://pubs.opengroup.org/onlinepubs/9699919799/

In general, if a function can block for some time or if it could return error EINTR, it's likely to be a cancellation point. When a thread is blocked in one of these functions, it could get terminated by a cancellation request.

Note that any function that calls one of these functions containing a cancellation point is itself a cancellation point too. Hence, if you deliver a software with some of your own library functions, make sure you document those functions containing a cancellation point.

Creating a Cancellation Point

Sometimes a thread may want to check if there is any pending cancellation request and to process it if yes. That is done via the following API:

    void pthread_testcancel(void);

Each time the pthread_testcancel() function is called, if the thread has its cancelability disabled, then nothing will happen. But if the thread has its cancellation enabled, a pending thread cancellation request against the thread will be acted upon if there is one and the calling thread will be terminated.

So effectively, the pthread_testcancel() function creates a cancellation point.

8-9-3 Cancel-safe

If your program invokes pthread_cancel() function, then you must make it cancel-safe.

A function is cancel-safe if a thread executing the function is canceled and no state is left behind from the canceled thread.

To make a function cancel-safe, you need to install and use the cancellation cleanup handler. You need to examine all of the functions the thread calls and see what resources it could leave behind once a thread executing the functions is cancelled. Typical resources include but are not limited to locks/mutexes, allocated dynamic memory and opened files.
The cancellation cleanup handler must release these resources.
In pthreads, an application can install more than one cancellation cleanup handler.

If a thread executing a function taking a lock, when the thread is canceled, if the lock it holds is not released, deadlock could occur.
If a function allocates dynamic memory and it is not freed, it could cause memory leak. If an opened file is not closed, it is taking up open file resources.

You can install a cancellation cleanup handler routine for the calling thread by calling the pthread_cleanup_push() function and remove one from the top of the cancellation stack by calling the pthread_cleanup_pop() function. Pthreads manages a thread's cancellation cleanup handlers using the stack data structure. The one you just push in goes to top of the stack and the one you just pop up comes from top of the stack too.

```
#include <pthread.h>

void pthread_cleanup_pop(int execute);
void pthread_cleanup_push(void (*routine)(void*), void *arg);
```

8-10 Signal Handling with Threads

As we all know from the chapter on signals, in a single-treaded process, unless a process has blocked or ignored all signals, or has set up and installed a signal handler, when it receives a signal, normally the default action is to terminate the process.

This is essentially true too in a multithreaded process.
In a multithreaded process, the way signals work remains mostly the same. Unless a signal is blocked or ignored, or there is a signal handler installed for it, a signal still terminates the entire multithreaded process.

The main differences between the process model and the thread model are:
(1) Pthreads has a function to kill a specific thread, as opposed to killing the entire process. (2) Pthreads allows setting up a signal thread to handle all signals.

Specifically, the signal behavior in a multithreaded process is as below.

If a multithreaded process does not do anything about signals, it will be getting the default behavior which is the entire process will terminate when it receives a signal.

If a multithreaded process invokes the sigaction() function to specify the action for some signal but using the SIG_DFL (default) action, the result is the same as doing nothing. The entire process will terminate when it receives a signal.

If a multithreaded process invokes the sigaction() function to install a specific signal handler for some signals, then whenever the process receives one of these signals, execution of the process will get interrupted and the signal handler will be called. After returning from the signal handler, the process continues to run. If the process gets other signals which it does not block, ignore or install a signal handler for, the process will terminate.

Signal handlers are maintained at the process level even in multithreaded applications.

If a multithreaded process creates a signal handling thread and blocks all signals in all other threads, then all signals sent to the process will be received and handled by the signal handling thread.
The signal handling thread essentially sits in a loop and waits for signals to come. This is a neat way to handle signals in a multithreaded process.

If a multithreaded process blocks all signals and does not create a signal handling thread, then all signals except the SIGKILL (9) signal will be blocked (or effectively ignored). In this case, the only way to forcefully terminate the process is to send a SIGKILL signal to it (kill -9 pid).

We will talk about how to use a signal handling thread in just a moment. For now, let's look at how one sends a signal and changes a signal set in the pthreads environment.

8-10-1 pthread_sigmask() and pthread_kill() Functions

In a single-threaded process, you block or unblock signals by invoking the sigprocmask() function. The sigprocmask() function examines and/or changes the signal mask of the calling process.

In a multithreaded application, you invoke the pthread_sigmask() function to do the same. This function is equivalent to the sigprocmask() function except it examines or changes (or both) the signal mask of the calling thread.

```
int pthread_sigmask(int how, const sigset_t *restrict set,
    sigset_t *restrict oset);
int sigprocmask(int how, const sigset_t *restrict set,
    sigset_t *restrict oset);
```

The first argument to the pthread_sigmask() function specifies how you want the signal set be changed. It must be one of the following three values:

SIG_SETMASK
    The resulting set will be the signal set pointed to by the second argument.

SIG_BLOCK
The resulting set will be the union of the current set and the signal set pointed to by the set argument.

SIG_UNBLOCK
The resulting set will be the intersection of the current set and the complement of the signal set pointed to by second argument (set).

Upon successful completion pthread_sigmask() returns 0; otherwise, an error is returned to indicate the error.

As for sending a signal, one uses the kill() function in a single-threaded process but the pthread_kill() function in a multithreaded process.

```
int pthread_kill(pthread_t thread, int sig);
```

The pthread_kill() function requests that a signal be sent to the specified thread within the same process. Note that since a pthread id is unique only within the current process, one cannot use the pthread_kill() function to send a signal to another thread in a different process.

Remember that when using the pthread_kill() function to send a signal to a particular thread, if the signal sent results in the thread being continued, stopped or terminated, the entire process is continued, stopped or terminated. So be careful. It affects the entire process, not just one thread. Therefore, make sure the target thread has a signal handler function set up for it such that the entire process won't terminate as a result of receiving the signal.

As in kill(), if the specified signal number is zero, error checking should be done by the operating system implementation and no signal should actually be sent.

If the pthread_kill() function fails, no signal is sent.

Upon success, the pthread_kill() function returns zero; otherwise, an error number is returned to indicate the error.

8-10-2 Using a Signal Handling Thread

Figure 8-27 is an example program of creating and using a signal handling thread. In the chapter on signals, we learned that a process or thread can invoke the sigwait() function to synchronously receive a signal. This program example creates a signal handling thread, blocks all signals, and then sits in a loop calling sigwait() to receive signals one by one.

Figure 8-27 Using signal handling thread (pt_signal_thread.c)

```
/*
 * Create and use a signal handling thread.
 * Update shared data with synchronization using pthread mutex.
 * Copyright (c) 2014, 2019-2020 Mr. Jin-Jwei Chen.  All rights reserved.
 */
```

```c
#include <stdio.h>
#include <pthread.h>
#include <errno.h>
#include <signal.h>


#define   NTHREADS    4
#define   NTASKS      5000000
#define   DELAY_COUNT 1000


unsigned int  global_count=0;      /* global data shared by all threads */
pthread_mutex_t       mutex1;      /* global mutex shared by all threads */

/* Signal handling thread */
void signal_handling_thread()
{
  int       signal;    /* signal number */
  sigset_t  sigset;    /* signal set */
  int       ret = 0;   /* return code */

  /* Block all signals */
  sigfillset(&sigset);
  pthread_sigmask(SIG_SETMASK, &sigset, (sigset_t *)NULL);
#ifdef AIX
  sigdelset(&sigset, SIGKILL);
  sigdelset(&sigset, SIGSTOP);
  sigdelset(&sigset, SIGWAITING);
#endif
  /* Wait for a signal to arrive and then handle it */
  while (1)
  {
    ret = sigwait((sigset_t *)&sigset, (int *)&signal);
    if (ret != 0)
      fprintf(stderr, "signal_handling_thread(): sigwait() failed, ret=%d\n",
        ret);
    else
      fprintf(stdout, "signal_handling_thread() received signal %d.\n",
        signal);
  }
#ifdef SUN64
  pthread_exit((void *)&ret);
#else
  pthread_exit((void *)0);
#endif
}


/*
 * The worker thread.
 */

int worker_thread(void *args)
{
  unsigned int  *argp;
  unsigned int  myid;
  unsigned int  ntasks;
  int           i, j, ret=0;
```

```
  /* Extract input arguments (two unsigned integers) */
  argp = (unsigned int *)args;
  if (argp != NULL)
  {
    myid = argp[0];
    ntasks = argp[1];
  }
  else
#ifdef SUN64
  {
    ret = (-1);
    pthread_exit((void *)&ret);
  }
#else
    pthread_exit((void *)(-1));
#endif

  fprintf(stdout, "Worker thread: myid=%u ntasks=%u\n", myid, ntasks);

  /* Do my job */
  for (i = 0; i < ntasks; i++)
  {
    ret = pthread_mutex_lock(&mutex1);
    if (ret != 0)
    {
      fprintf(stderr, "Thread %u failed to lock the mutex, ret=%d\n", myid, ret);
      continue;
    }

    /* Update the shared data */
    global_count = global_count + 1;
    /* insert a bit of delay */
    for (j = 0; j < DELAY_COUNT; j++);

    ret = pthread_mutex_unlock(&mutex1);
    if (ret != 0)
      fprintf(stderr, "Thread %u failed to unlock the mutex, ret=%d\n", myid, ret);
  }

#ifdef SUN64
  pthread_exit((void *)&ret);
#else
  pthread_exit((void *)0);
#endif
}

/*
 * The main program.
 */
int main(int argc, char *argv[])
{
  pthread_t       thrds[NTHREADS];
  unsigned int    args[NTHREADS][2];
  int             ret, i;
  int             retval = 0;          /* each child thread returns an int */
  pthread_mutexattr_t  mutexattr1;     /* mutex attributes */
```

456

```
#ifdef SUN64
  int           *retvalp = &retval; /* pointer to returned value */
#endif
  sigset_t      sigset;
  pthread_t     sigthrd;

  /* Block all signals */
  sigfillset(&sigset);
  pthread_sigmask(SIG_SETMASK, &sigset, (sigset_t *)NULL);

  /* Load up the input arguments for each child thread */
  for (i = 0; i < NTHREADS; i++)
  {
    args[i][0] = i;
    args[i][1] = NTASKS;
  }

  /* Initialize mutex attributes */
  ret = pthread_mutexattr_init(&mutexattr1);
  if (ret != 0)
  {
    fprintf(stderr, "Failed to initialize mutex attributes, ret=%d\n", ret);
    pthread_exit((void *)-2);
  }

  /* Initialize the mutex */
  ret = pthread_mutex_init(&mutex1, &mutexattr1);
  if (ret != 0)
  {
    fprintf(stderr, "Failed to initialize mutex, ret=%d\n", ret);
    pthread_exit((void *)-3);
  }

  /* Create new threads to run the worker_thread() function and pass in args */
  for (i = 0; i < NTHREADS; i++)
  {
    ret = pthread_create(&thrds[i], (pthread_attr_t *)NULL,
        (void *(*)(void *))worker_thread, (void *)args[i]);
    if (ret != 0)
    {
      fprintf(stderr, "Failed to create the worker thread, ret=%d\n", ret);
      pthread_exit((void *)-4);
    }
  }

  /* Create the signal handling thread */
  ret = pthread_create(&sigthrd, (pthread_attr_t *)NULL,
      (void *(*)(void *))signal_handling_thread, NULL);
  if (ret != 0)
    fprintf(stderr, "Failed to create the signal handling thread, ret=%d\n",
      ret);

  /* Send a signal to the worker thread */
  ret = pthread_kill(thrds[0], SIGINT);
  if (ret != 0)
  {
```

```
      fprintf(stderr, "Failed to send a signal to first worker thread, ret=%d\n",
        ret);
    }

    /*
     * Wait for each of the child threads to finish and retrieve its returned
     * value.
     */
    for (i = 0; i < NTHREADS; i++)
    {
#ifdef SUN64
        ret = pthread_join(thrds[i], (void **)&retvalp);
#else
        ret = pthread_join(thrds[i], (void **)&retval);
#endif
        fprintf(stdout, "Thread %u exited with return value %d\n", i, retval);
    }

    /* Destroy mutex attributes */
#ifndef HPUX64
    ret = pthread_mutexattr_destroy(&mutexattr1);
    if (ret != 0)
    {
        fprintf(stderr, "Failed to destroy mutex attributes, ret=%d\n", ret);
        pthread_exit((void *)-5);
    }
#endif

    /* Destroy the mutex */
    ret = pthread_mutex_destroy(&mutex1);
    if (ret != 0)
    {
        fprintf(stderr, "Failed to destroy mutex, ret=%d\n", ret);
        pthread_exit((void *)-6);
    }

    fprintf(stdout, "global_count = %u\n", global_count);

    /* Cancel the signal handling thread */
    ret = pthread_cancel(sigthrd);
    if (ret != 0)
    {
        fprintf(stderr, "Failed to cancel signal handling thread, ret=%d\n",
          ret);
    }

    pthread_exit((void *)0);
}
```

As you can see the main thread blocks all the signals of interest before it
creates the child threads such that all these signals are also blocked
in the child threads through inheritance. The child threads inherit the
signal mask of their parent thread. We block all signals at the start of
the signal handling thread too.

The sigwait() function, and sigtimedwait() and sigwaitinfo() too, blocks

458

the calling thread until one of the signals specified in the signal set argument is delivered to the calling thread or the process.
If more than one thread is waiting for the same signal, only one of them will return.

Note that although a signal handling thread can perform operations like locking a mutex which normally cannot be done in a signal handler function, be careful about its impact to the signal receiving.

8-11 Further Readings

This chapter intends to introduce the basic concepts of multithreading and how to write basic multi-threaded programs using pthreads. It aims to prepare the readers with the basic knowledge and skills and get them off the ground. Pthreads itself is a rich set of APIs. It is beyond the scope of this book to cover every detail of it. For further details and other APIs please refer to your system's documentation on pthreads or other books on pthreads.

As an example, there are many attributes in a pthreads attributes object of the pthread_attr_t type. There are many pthreads APIs for it. They are all named as pthread_attr_getXXX() and pthread_attr_setXXX(), where XXXX is usually the name of the pthreads attribute.
Similarly, there are also many mutex attributes which we just cannot discuss all of them in details. The mutex attribute APIs are named pthread_mutexattr_getXXX() and pthread_mutexattr_setXXX(). And of course, there are others.

We leave it to the readers to further seek and consult corresponding documentations (e.g. man pages) and look into further details when you actually get to use this stuff.

The subject of POSIX threads warrants a book by itself. Obviously, a book like this just cannot cover all of the details in a chapter.

For a complete list of the pthreads APIs, please visit the following web site:

https://pubs.opengroup.org/onlinepubs/9699919799/

All of the pthreads APIs are named as pthread_XXX().

8-12 List of Pthreads APIs

We list all of the pthreads APIs here in this section for a quick reference for the readers. On a Unix or Linux system, please do a man command to get the documentation on these APIs. For example,

```
$ man pthread_create
```

POSIX Threads APIs

```
int pthread_atfork(void (*prepare)(void), void (*parent)(void),
    void (*child)(void));
int pthread_attr_destroy(pthread_attr_t *attr);
```

```
int pthread_attr_init(pthread_attr_t *attr);
int pthread_attr_getdetachstate(const pthread_attr_t *attr,
        int *detachstate);
int pthread_attr_setdetachstate(pthread_attr_t *attr, int detachstate);
int pthread_attr_getguardsize(const pthread_attr_t *restrict attr,
        size_t *restrict guardsize);
int pthread_attr_setguardsize(pthread_attr_t *attr,
        size_t guardsize);
int pthread_attr_getinheritsched(const pthread_attr_t *restrict attr,
        int *restrict inheritsched);
int pthread_attr_setinheritsched(pthread_attr_t *attr,
        int inheritsched); [Option End]
int pthread_attr_getschedparam(const pthread_attr_t *restrict attr,
        struct sched_param *restrict param);
int pthread_attr_setschedparam(pthread_attr_t *restrict attr,
        const struct sched_param *restrict param);
int pthread_attr_getschedpolicy(const pthread_attr_t *restrict attr,
        int *restrict policy);
int pthread_attr_setschedpolicy(pthread_attr_t *attr, int policy);
int pthread_attr_getscope(const pthread_attr_t *restrict attr,
        int *restrict contentionscope);
int pthread_attr_setscope(pthread_attr_t *attr, int contentionscope);
int pthread_attr_getstack(const pthread_attr_t *restrict attr,
        void **restrict stackaddr, size_t *restrict stacksize);
int pthread_attr_setstack(pthread_attr_t *attr, void *stackaddr,
        size_t stacksize);
int pthread_attr_getstacksize(const pthread_attr_t *restrict attr,
        size_t *restrict stacksize);
int pthread_attr_setstacksize(pthread_attr_t *attr, size_t stacksize);
int pthread_attr_destroy(pthread_attr_t *attr);
int pthread_attr_init(pthread_attr_t *attr);
int pthread_barrierattr_destroy(pthread_barrierattr_t *attr);
int pthread_barrierattr_init(pthread_barrierattr_t *attr);
int pthread_barrierattr_getpshared(const pthread_barrierattr_t
        *restrict attr, int *restrict pshared);
int pthread_barrierattr_setpshared(pthread_barrierattr_t *attr,
        int pshared);
int pthread_barrierattr_destroy(pthread_barrierattr_t *attr);
int pthread_barrierattr_init(pthread_barrierattr_t *attr);
int pthread_barrier_destroy(pthread_barrier_t *barrier);
int pthread_barrier_init(pthread_barrier_t *restrict barrier,
        const pthread_barrierattr_t *restrict attr, unsigned count);
int pthread_barrier_wait(pthread_barrier_t *barrier);
int pthread_cancel(pthread_t thread);
void pthread_cleanup_pop(int execute);
void pthread_cleanup_push(void (*routine)(void*), void *arg);
int pthread_condattr_destroy(pthread_condattr_t *attr);
int pthread_condattr_init(pthread_condattr_t *attr);
int pthread_condattr_getclock(const pthread_condattr_t *restrict attr,
        clockid_t *restrict clock_id);
int pthread_condattr_setclock(pthread_condattr_t *attr,
        clockid_t clock_id);
int pthread_condattr_getpshared(const pthread_condattr_t *restrict attr,
        int *restrict pshared);
int pthread_condattr_setpshared(pthread_condattr_t *attr,
        int pshared)
```

```
int pthread_cond_broadcast(pthread_cond_t *cond);
int pthread_cond_signal(pthread_cond_t *cond);
int pthread_cond_destroy(pthread_cond_t *cond);
int pthread_cond_init(pthread_cond_t *restrict cond,
       const pthread_condattr_t *restrict attr);
pthread_cond_t cond = PTHREAD_COND_INITIALIZER;
int pthread_cond_timedwait(pthread_cond_t *restrict cond,
       pthread_mutex_t *restrict mutex,
       const struct timespec *restrict abstime);
int pthread_cond_wait(pthread_cond_t *restrict cond,
       pthread_mutex_t *restrict mutex);
int pthread_create(pthread_t *restrict thread,
       const pthread_attr_t *restrict attr,
       void *(*start_routine)(void*), void *restrict arg);
int pthread_detach(pthread_t thread);
int pthread_equal(pthread_t t1, pthread_t t2);
void pthread_exit(void *value_ptr);
int pthread_getconcurrency(void);
int pthread_setconcurrency(int new_level);
int pthread_getcpuclockid(pthread_t thread_id, clockid_t *clock_id);
int pthread_getschedparam(pthread_t thread, int *restrict policy,
       struct sched_param *restrict param);
int pthread_setschedparam(pthread_t thread, int policy,
       const struct sched_param *param);
void *pthread_getspecific(pthread_key_t key);
int pthread_setspecific(pthread_key_t key, const void *value);
int pthread_join(pthread_t thread, void **value_ptr);
int pthread_key_create(pthread_key_t *key, void (*destructor)(void*));
int pthread_key_delete(pthread_key_t key);
int pthread_kill(pthread_t thread, int sig);
int pthread_mutexattr_destroy(pthread_mutexattr_t *attr);
int pthread_mutexattr_init(pthread_mutexattr_t *attr);
int pthread_mutexattr_getprioceiling(const pthread_mutexattr_t
       *restrict attr, int *restrict prioceiling);
int pthread_mutexattr_setprioceiling(pthread_mutexattr_t *attr,
       int prioceiling);
int pthread_mutexattr_getprotocol(const pthread_mutexattr_t
       *restrict attr, int *restrict protocol);
int pthread_mutexattr_setprotocol(pthread_mutexattr_t *attr,
       int protocol);
int pthread_mutexattr_getpshared(const pthread_mutexattr_t
       *restrict attr, int *restrict pshared);
int pthread_mutexattr_setpshared(pthread_mutexattr_t *attr,
       int pshared);
int pthread_mutexattr_getrobust(const pthread_mutexattr_t *restrict
       attr, int *restrict robust);
int pthread_mutexattr_setrobust(pthread_mutexattr_t *attr,
       int robust);
int pthread_mutexattr_gettype(const pthread_mutexattr_t *restrict attr,
       int *restrict type);
int pthread_mutexattr_settype(pthread_mutexattr_t *attr, int type);
int pthread_mutex_consistent(pthread_mutex_t *mutex);
int pthread_mutex_destroy(pthread_mutex_t *mutex);
int pthread_mutex_init(pthread_mutex_t *restrict mutex,
       const pthread_mutexattr_t *restrict attr);
pthread_mutex_t mutex = PTHREAD_MUTEX_INITIALIZER;
```

```
int pthread_mutex_getprioceiling(const pthread_mutex_t *restrict mutex,
        int *restrict prioceiling);
int pthread_mutex_setprioceiling(pthread_mutex_t *restrict mutex,
        int prioceiling, int *restrict old_ceiling);
int pthread_mutex_lock(pthread_mutex_t *mutex);
int pthread_mutex_trylock(pthread_mutex_t *mutex);
int pthread_mutex_unlock(pthread_mutex_t *mutex);
int pthread_mutex_timedlock(pthread_mutex_t *restrict mutex,
        const struct timespec *restrict abstime);
int pthread_once(pthread_once_t *once_control,
        void (*init_routine)(void));
pthread_once_t once_control = PTHREAD_ONCE_INIT;
int pthread_rwlockattr_destroy(pthread_rwlockattr_t *attr);
int pthread_rwlockattr_init(pthread_rwlockattr_t *attr);
int pthread_rwlockattr_getpshared(const pthread_rwlockattr_t
        *restrict attr, int *restrict pshared);
int pthread_rwlockattr_setpshared(pthread_rwlockattr_t *attr,
        int pshared);
int pthread_rwlock_destroy(pthread_rwlock_t *rwlock);
int pthread_rwlock_init(pthread_rwlock_t *restrict rwlock,
        const pthread_rwlockattr_t *restrict attr);
pthread_rwlock_t rwlock = PTHREAD_RWLOCK_INITIALIZER;
int pthread_rwlock_rdlock(pthread_rwlock_t *rwlock);
int pthread_rwlock_tryrdlock(pthread_rwlock_t *rwlock);
int pthread_rwlock_timedrdlock(pthread_rwlock_t *restrict rwlock,
        const struct timespec *restrict abstime);
int pthread_rwlock_timedwrlock(pthread_rwlock_t *restrict rwlock,
        const struct timespec *restrict abstime);
int pthread_rwlock_trywrlock(pthread_rwlock_t *rwlock);
int pthread_rwlock_wrlock(pthread_rwlock_t *rwlock);
int pthread_rwlock_unlock(pthread_rwlock_t *rwlock);
pthread_t pthread_self(void);
int pthread_setcancelstate(int state, int *oldstate);
int pthread_setcanceltype(int type, int *oldtype);
void pthread_testcancel(void);
int pthread_sigmask(int how, const sigset_t *restrict set,
        sigset_t *restrict oset);
int sigprocmask(int how, const sigset_t *restrict set,
        sigset_t *restrict oset);
int pthread_spin_destroy(pthread_spinlock_t *lock);
int pthread_spin_init(pthread_spinlock_t *lock, int pshared);
int pthread_spin_lock(pthread_spinlock_t *lock);
int pthread_spin_trylock(pthread_spinlock_t *lock);
int pthread_spin_unlock(pthread_spinlock_t *lock);
```

8-13 Functions with Cancellation Points

Cancellation points shall occur when a thread is executing the following
 functions:

```
accept()
aio_suspend()
clock_nanosleep()
close()
connect()
```

462

```
creat()
fcntl()
fdatasync()
fsync()
getmsg()
getpmsg()
lockf()
mq_receive()
mq_send()
mq_timedreceive()
mq_timedsend()
msgrcv()
msgsnd()
msync()

nanosleep()
open()
openat()
pause()
poll()
pread()
pselect()
pthread_cond_timedwait()
pthread_cond_wait()
pthread_join()
pthread_testcancel()
putmsg()
putpmsg()
pwrite()
read()
readv()
recv()
recvfrom()
recvmsg()

select()
sem_timedwait()
sem_wait()
send()
sendmsg()
sendto()
sigsuspend()
sigtimedwait()
sigwait()
sigwaitinfo()
sleep()
tcdrain()
wait()
waitid()
waitpid()
write()
writev()
```

A cancellation point may also occur when a thread is executing the following functions:

```
access()
asctime_r()
catclose()
catopen()
chmod()
chown()
closedir()
closelog()
ctermid()
ctime_r()
dlclose()
dlopen()
dprintf()
endhostent()
endnetent()
endprotoent()
endservent()
faccessat()
fchmod()
fchmodat()
fchown()
fchownat()
fclose()
fcntl()
fflush()
fgetc()
fgetpos()
fgets()
fgetwc()
fgetws()
fmtmsg()
fopen()
fpathconf()
fprintf()
fputc()
fputs()
fputwc()
fputws()
fread()
freopen()
fscanf()
fseek()
fseeko()
fsetpos()
fstat()

fstatat()
ftell()
ftello()
futimens()
fwprintf()
fwrite()
fwscanf()
getaddrinfo()
getc()
getc_unlocked()
```

```
getchar()
getchar_unlocked()
getcwd()
getdelim()
getgrgid_r()
getgrnam_r()
gethostid()
gethostname()
getline()
getlogin_r()
getnameinfo()
getpwnam_r()
getpwuid_r()
gets()
getwc()
getwchar()
glob()
iconv_close()
iconv_open()
ioctl()
link()
linkat()
lio_listio()
localtime_r()
lockf()
lseek()
lstat()
mkdir()
mkdirat()
mkdtemp()
mkfifo()
mkfifoat()
mknod()
mknodat()

mkstemp()
mktime()
opendir()
openlog()
pathconf()
perror()
popen()
posix_fadvise()
posix_fallocate()
posix_madvise()
posix_openpt()
posix_spawn()
posix_spawnp()
posix_trace_clear()
posix_trace_close()
posix_trace_create()
posix_trace_create_withlog()
posix_trace_eventtypelist_getnext_id()
posix_trace_eventtypelist_rewind()
posix_trace_flush()
posix_trace_get_attr()
```

```
posix_trace_get_filter()
posix_trace_get_status()
posix_trace_getnext_event()
posix_trace_open()
posix_trace_rewind()
posix_trace_set_filter()
posix_trace_shutdown()
posix_trace_timedgetnext_event()
posix_typed_mem_open()
printf()
psiginfo()
psignal()
pthread_rwlock_rdlock()
pthread_rwlock_timedrdlock()
pthread_rwlock_timedwrlock()
pthread_rwlock_wrlock()
putc()
putc_unlocked()
putchar()
putchar_unlocked()
puts()
putwc()
putwchar()
readdir_r()

readlink()
readlinkat()
remove()
rename()
renameat()
rewind()
rewinddir()
scandir()
scanf()
seekdir()
semop()
sethostent()
setnetent()
setprotoent()
setservent()

sigpause()
stat()
strerror_l()
strerror_r()
strftime()
strftime_l()
symlink()
symlinkat()
sync()
syslog()
tmpfile()
tmpnam()
ttyname_r()
tzset()
ungetc()
```

```
ungetwc()
unlink()
unlinkat()
utime()
utimensat()
utimes()
vdprintf()
vfprintf()
vfwprintf()
vprintf()
vwprintf()
wcsftime()
wordexp()
wprintf()
wscanf()
```

Review Questions

1. What is a thread?

2. What are the differences in address space between a process and a thread?

3. What are the advantages and disadvantages of processes and threads?

4. Does your system support threads? Is it standard pthreads or proprietary?

5. What is the skeleton of a typical server program like a web server?

6. What threads can help in a server program doing I/O?

7. What is thread-specific data? What can it be used for?
   How does a thread access a thread-specific data?

8. What pthreads provides for concurrency control?

9. What pthreads attributes are there?

10. What is a detached thread?

11. How does a main thread wait for all of its child threads?

12. What is a condition variable? What type of problems are condition variables best suited for?

13. What issues are present when using signals with threads?

14. What are thread cancellation points?
    What functions are cancellation points?

15. Does the system you use support all of the mutex attributes including robust?

Programming Assignments

1. Modify the example program pt_mutex.c and use pthread_mutex_trylock()
   instead of pthread_mutex_lock().

2. Modify the example program pt_mutex.c and use pthread_mutex_timedlock()
   instead of pthread_mutex_lock().

3. Modify the example program pt_mutex.c to use detached threads.
   What do you have to do to make the program work? And why?
   Do you run into a situation where the mutex is destroyed before all
   child threads finish? Explain why.

4. Write a program using a PTHREAD_MUTEX_ERRORCHECK type of mutex and
   show that an attempt to recursively lock the same mutex will get
   an error returned instead of deadlock.

5. Write a program using a PTHREAD_MUTEX_RECURSIVE mutex and try to
   recursively lock the mutex. What happens?

6. Reimplement the example program pt_tsd_reentrant.c. Use a
   PTHREAD_MUTEX_RECURSIVE mutex instead to avoid the self-deadlock.

7. Write a program with two writer threads. Design it to show that only
   one writer is allowed in at any given time.

8. Write a program with one writer thread and one reader thread. Design it
   to show that the reader thread blocks the writer thread as well.

9. Write a program with multiple reader threads and show that multiple reader
   threads can obtain and hold the same reader lock at the same time.

10. Write a program to get and set the value of a process-shared attribute
    in a read-write lock attributes object.

11. Write a program that demonstrates use of the pthread_testcancel() function.

12. Write a program which changes the mutex prioceiling attribute.

13. Research into sched.h and the following APIs. Write a program to print out
    the minimum and maximum scheduling priorities of the scheduling policies
    defined in POSIX.1c Standard.

    ```
    int    sched_get_priority_max(int);
    int    sched_get_priority_min(int);
    ```

14. Write a program that uses a robust mutex. Create a condition where the
    mutex is in an inconsistent state and then use the pthread_mutex_consistent()
    function to clean up the mutex's state and fix the deadlock situation.

15. Write a program that changes value of the process-shared (pshared) attribute
    of a condition variable to either PTHREAD_PROCESS_SHARED or
    PTHREAD_PROCESS_PRIVATE. Does it work in both cases?

16. Modify the example program pt_produce_consume.c to use a non-NULL condition variable attributes object. Make sure your program invokes both the pthread_condattr_init() and pthread_cond_init() APIs. And don't forget the destruction side of it.

References

1. THREADTIME, by Scott J. Norton and Mark D. Dipasquale, Hewlett-Packard Professional Books, Hewlett-Packard Company 1997

2. Threads Primer, byBil Lewis and Daniel J. Berg, Prentice Hall

3. The Open Group Base Specifications Issue 7, 2018 edition IEEE Std 1003.1â™-2017 (Revision of IEEE Std 1003.1-2008) Copyright â© 2001-2018 IEEE and The Open Group http://pubs.opengroup.org/onlinepubs/9699919799/ https://pubs.opengroup.org/onlinepubs/9699919799/

9 Concurrency Control and Locking

9-1 Introduction to Concurrency Control

Computers are very fast. They execute millions of instructions per second. Modern computers are also multitasking, meaning they execute multiple programs simultaneously or at least concurrently. On a single processor computer with a single arithmetic/logical unit, the processor interleaves between multiple programs by going around them and executing each of them a small slice of time (the so-called time quantum) to create the illusion of running multiple programs at the same time. In this case, the computer is executing multiple programs **concurrently**.

In a multiple-processor or a single-processor with multi-core computer, two or more programs can be executed in parallel by the processors or processing units at exactly the same time. There is a true parallelism in this case and we say the programs are executed **simultaneously**.

Since computer is so fast, when two or more programs are executed either concurrently or simultaneously, any possible interleaving scenario can and does really occur. If the programs that are executed concurrently or simultaneously do not share any data or resources, then there is nothing to worry about. However, most of the time, programs do collaborate and share data and/or resources. In this case, extreme care must be taken to ensure that the programs always produce correct results under all circumstances no matter what the interleaving is. This is the task of **concurrency control**.

In short, concurrency happens inside a computer all the time. Care needs to be taken and control must be exercised over concurrent activities to guarantee correct results at all times. It is the responsibility of software developers to code it correctly such that the integrity of data and computation correctness are always guaranteed.

This is exactly what we'll discuss in this chapter. This chapter talks about **what update loss is, how to prevent it, and how to do it the fastest way**.

Notice that concurrency control is one of the most basic fundamentals in computers. Therefore, it's paramount that it is done right.

There are multiple types of concurrency problems in computers. In chapter 8, we introduced to readers how to solve update loss, producer-consumer and reader-writer problems using pthreads. In this chapter, we will discuss update loss in further details and also introduce three other technologies that are often used to solve update loss problems without using pthreads.

9-1-1 The Update Loss Problem

The most famous problem in the concurrent update space in computer science is **the Update Loss problem.** The essence of the issue is that **when there are two or more entities trying to update the same data, some update can end up being lost and the end result being incorrect unless proper concurrency control is done.**

One example is that John and Mary are a couple. They have a joint bank account. One day, both of them try to deposit some money into their joint account from two different ATM machines at exactly the same time.
Let us say the balance of their joint account starts at $4,000. John tries to deposit $1,000 and Mary tries to deposit $500. It is entirely possible that the two update events can be interleaved in a way such that what Figure 9-1 shows is exactly what happens:

Figure 9-1 The update loss problem

Starting balance: $4,000

John deposits $1,000 from ATM1	Mary deposits $500 from ATM2
ATM1 reads current balance ($4,000)	
	ATM2 reads current balance ($4,000)
ATM1 adds $1,000 to balance ($5,000)	
	ATM2 adds $500 to balance ($4,500)

Balance ends up being 4500!

As you can see, in the end the total balance becomes $4,500 instead of $5,500. In other words, John's deposit is lost because it gets overwritten by Mary's. If the order is reversed, that is, Mary's update goes right before John's, then the ending balance would be $5,000 and Mary's update would be lost due to being overwritten by John's.

Note that as shown in Figure 9-2 this kind of interleaving and update loss can happen at the assembly language instruction level, too. For example, assuming the bank account balance is stored in the memory location labelled as balance and register A and B are used in the computation.

Figure 9-2 The update loss problem at assembly instruction level

(a) John deposits $1,000 and Mary deposits $500 to the same bank account
    at the same time (initial balance $4000)

John deposits $1,000 from ATM1	Mary deposits $500 from ATM2
load A, balance (A <- 4000)	
	load B, balance (B <- 4000)
addi A, 1000 (A=5000)	
	addi B, 500 (B=4500)
store A, balance (balance=5000)	
	store B, balance (balance=4500)

```
-->  Balance ends up being 4500 rather than 5500!
```

(b) Two threads or processes try to increment the value of a shared
    variable X by one (initial value 5)

```
      X = X + 1;                    X = X + 1;

      Thread/Process #1        Thread/Process #2
      -----------------        -----------------
                        X=5
      Read X (X=5)             Read X (X=5)
      Increment X (6)          Increment X (6)
      Write X (6)              Write X (6)
```

```
-->  The result is X=6 instead of 7!
```

These execution scenarios above are entirely possible to happen in a real
computer. If the computer has two or more CPUs, it is possible that the
two threads or processes are running on two separate CPUs in parallel
at the same time. Or even on a single-core single-CPU system, the
interleaving could very well end up being the first thread/process reads
the original value (5) of X, then its time quantum expires. Then the
second thread/process gets to run. It finishes its update sequence.
X becomes 6. Later the first thread/process resumes its execution.
It gets to finish the second and third instructions in its update sequence.
The value of X becomes 6 again. One of the updates is overwritten and lost!

This is the concurrent update loss problem which concerns the fundamental
data integrity of any and all computer systems.

Concurrent updates to the same data or shared data by multiple threads
or processes happen in computer processing all the time and everywhere,
not just in O.S. or database applications! As you see here, the computations
can often end up with wrong results and be useless unless the concurrent/
simultaneous updates are correctly coordinated and synchronized.

Keep in mind that concurrent updates of shared data or resources happen
almost in every software product. Therefore, what you learn from this
chapter should be very useful and can be applied to many things you do as
a software developer. The issue is to ensure data integrity and correct
results under concurrent or simultaneous updates.

9-1-2 Solve Concurrency Problems via Locking

From analyzing the concurrent activities as depicted above, we know that
**the only way to guarantee there is no update loss is to always perform
only one update at a time. That is, the updates must be mutually exclusive.**
In other words, we must **serialize** the update activities.

To achieve serialization, locking must be used during each update.
Imagine we can put a lock on each shared data such that the first process
or thread that finds it is unlocked can turn on the lock and lock everyone
else out and thus gets exclusive access to the data. Since only one process
or thread can update the data at a time, the update loss problem won't occur.

In other words, whoever being the first to find the lock being free, grab the lock itself, and lock everyone else out gets the exclusive right to do the update. When it is done, it unlocks to set the lock free so that the next process or thread can perform its update.

To implement the serialization of concurrent updates, locking is typically used. We create an entity that serves as the lock and associate each shared data with a distinct lock. Any process or thread that wants to update the shared data must try to acquire the lock associated with that piece of data first. And it does the update only after having successfully acquired the lock. When a process or thread has the lock, all other processes or threads will have to wait because they do not have the lock. Once the process or thread owning the lock finishes the update, it must release the lock so that one of the other processes or threads still waiting can proceed.

The application of locking is such that only one process or thread can obtain the lock at a time. In other words, via locking, the concurrent updates are serialized and the possibility of their overlapping and thus causing update loss is eliminated.

Note that for locking to work, all processes and/or threads that try to update the same piece of data must all follow the same protocol. That is, all of them must use locking and do the following three steps:

LOCK
   update operation
UNLOCK

If any of them does not follow the same rule, then update loss will occur and the data will end up being incorrect.

9-1-3 Terms

The terms used in the concurrency control land can often be confusing. We will try to clarify them here in this section.

Note that there is the entity that is used as a lock to achieve serialization to guarantee data integrity under concurrent updates. In its simplest form, this entity is essentially an integer variable inside the program regardless of languages or operating systems used. However, it has many different names for it. **Some of the terms used to mean a lock include lock, mutex, and semaphore.** 'Lock' is a generic term. Mutex is used in the POSIX Thread environment. Semaphore is used in POSIX-compliant operating systems as part of System V interprocess communication facility. All of these can be used to achieve mutual exclusion.

Besides the entity, there are also two operations that can be performed on each lock entity.

1. To acquire the lock (i.e. to perform the lock operation)
2. To release the lock (i.e. to perform the unlock operation)

Instead of saying 'to acquire the lock', many people and articles use the expression "to lock the lock" or simply "to lock". Similarly, rather than saying "to release the lock", they say "to unlock the lock" or simply "to unlock". Some implementations even name the functions that allow a process/thread to obtain and release a lock as lock() and unlock(), respectively.

Therefore, depending on the context, the word 'lock' could mean one of the three things:

1. It's a noun and it means the entity used for guarding access to a piece of shared data or resource.
2. It's a verb and it means to obtain the right to access the shared data or resource.
3. It is the name of the routine that a process/thread can invoke to obtain the right to access the shared data or resource.

9-1-4 Three Required Elements

It is extremely important to note that for concurrency control using locking to work, there are three requirements:

1. Locking must be used to serialize the updates of the shared data. Otherwise, two or more concurrent updates of the shared data may result in update loss.

2. Any and all processes/threads involved in updating the same piece of shared data must all follow the same locking protocol and rule. If all other processes/threads do the required locking/unlocking but one or more does not, then update loss can still occur and the data integrity can be in jeopardy. All participants must all follow the same protocol/rule, or it won't work.

3. The operation of acquiring or releasing a lock must be atomic (i.e. inseparable). If not, then one cannot guarantee only one contending process/thread will get the lock at a time.

   Unless the implementation of the lock used to protect the shared data guarantees the operation in obtaining or releasing the lock is always atomic, exclusive access to the shared data by only one process/thread at a time cannot be guaranteed and thus update loss can still occur.

9-1-5 Many Concurrency Control Facilities Are Available

Then how do I do locking in my program? You may ask.
Well, you may use the locking facility provided by the operating system or by the programming language you use. Or you may even implement your own locking facilities. We will cover both of these in this chapter.

If you do multithreaded programming and use pthreads, then pthreads has the so-called mutex as a locking facility. You can use mutex to implement concurrency control between the process threads within your program. We have just discussed pthreads and mutex in the preceding chapter.

If you program in C, then the most common practice is to use the locking facilities provided by the operating system. For instance, POSIX systems all support traditional AT&T Unix System V semaphore. Besides, POSIX

introduces its own semaphore facility as well. We will introduce both types
of semaphores below because they are all included in the POSIX standard.

If you program in Java, the Java language provides many locking primitives
you can use. They are in the java.util.concurrent package.
For instance, the java.util.concurrent.locks, java.util.concurrent.atomic
and java.util.concurrent.locks.ReentrantReadWriteLock classes.

Here in this chapter, we will talk about how to use two types of semaphores
to achieve concurrency control within a C/C++ program. In addition,
we will also show you how to design and implement your own concurrency
control functions in assembly language to achieve the best performance.

9-2 Introduction to System V IPC Resources

One of the very typical features of an operating system is isolation and
protection. This means within an operating system every process is isolated
and protected from against any other processes. It is isolated in that
each process has its own address space and executes within its own address
space. Whatever a process does to its own address space (and thus memory)
is not visible to other processes and shall not impact others. This
isolation and protection provides fundamental security to programs running
on the same system using the same physical main memory at the same time.
It's hard to imagine how much additional work programmers would have to do
without this protection.

While the isolation and protection is good and necessary, there are times
when processes need to collaborate and thus communicate with one another.
This is exactly what System V IPC (Inter-Process Communication) facilities
and resources are for.

The System V IPC was originally available in the traditional AT&T Unix
System V back in 1980s. It was later included in the POSIX standard
and available in all Unix, Linux and other operating systems.
It has made writing complex system software easier and has been widely used
in many system and application software products for decades.

System V IPC facilities or resources are designed for different processes
and programs on the same system, potentially developed by different vendors,
to communicate with one another. Therefore, once created, they exist outside
the boundary of the creator process and are globally available within
the boundary of the operating system.

Three System V IPC facilities/resources are available. They are:

    message queue
    shared memory
    semaphore

Message queues allow different processes to communicate with one another
by sending messages. Shared memory allows different processes to communicate
or collaborate by sharing a piece of memory in their address space and
working on shared data in the shared memory. Semaphores are typically used
for concurrency control and for synchronizing concurrent accesses and
updates to shared memory or shared data.

This book will introduce all of these System V IPC facilities to you
in the chapters to come, with semaphore being discussed in this chapter.
We will talk about some basic knowledge common to all System V IPC
facilities in this current section and then show you how to create and use
semaphore in the next.

9-2-1 Identifier of a System V IPC Resource

Within a process, each System V IPC resource is uniquely identified by a
key value of the type key_t, which is essentially an integer.

The idea around the System V IPC is that on a given system, there may be
multiple applications developed by different vendors using the System V IPC
at the same time. In order for them not to step on one another, each
vendor's application is supposed to pick a **unique pathname** on the system
and tie the System V IPC resources it uses to that unique pathname.
Collisions between System V IPC resources used by different applications
are meant to be avoided this way with the use of a unique pathname on the
system. Each software vendor should pick and create a unique pathname on
the system for its application(s) that creates and uses System V IPC
resources.

To allow more flexibility, under a given pathname, a **project id** can be
further specified to distinguish between the different applications from
the same vendor, between different components of the same application,
or between the different resources. The project id itself is an integer, too.

In other words, each System V IPC resource is uniquely identified by a
(pathname, project_id) pair. For simplicity, within a program, each program
feeds the (pathname, project_id) pair into the ftok() function and converts
the pair into a unique **key value**. The program then uses that key value to
identify the System V IPC resource it wants to access.

Figure 9-3 How System V IPC key value and identifier are derived

a unique pathname for the application + a unique project id
                          |
                    ftok()
                          |
                    IPC **key** (an integer)
                          |
                    Resource creation API (XXXget())
                          |
                    IPC resource's **identifier** (an integer too)

So below is how it works:

1. Pick a unique pathname for your application.
2. Pick a unique project id, which is an integer, for your project,
   component or resource.
3. Invoke the ftok() function to convert the pathname and the project id
   into a unique key value.
4. Use the key value to create the resource and/or get its identifier.
5. Use the IPC resource's **identifier** to access and perform all operations.

Apparently, the ftok() function hashes the pathname and the project id into a unique integer. Obviously, it is easier to use an integer as the identifier than to use a pathname and an integer together throughout a program.

Note that three things must be done right in order for this to always work:

1. The pathname you pick to associate with your application must be **unique**. You want to make sure it does not collide with those used by any other applications, either from other vendors or your own company. Therefore, you might want to use the names of your company and your application in the pathname.

2. The pathname must **pre-exist and be online** before you can create the associated System V IPC resource. At customer sites, the creation of the corresponding pathname can be done as part of the installation of the application. For your own testing, you can manually create it on your system (for instance, under your own home directory, or in the /tmp directory, or somewhere else that you have a permission to do so.)

3. To ensure that your application can always run and is available all the time, you must pick a pathname that is **always available.** For instance, you certainly don't want to pick a directory or file name that exists in a file system that may be unmounted. For this reason, it's always a good idea to use a pathname that exists in the system's root (/) file system because the root file system has to be mounted all the time in order for the system to operate.

9-2-2 Access to System V IPC Resources

Remember that System V IPC resources are available system-wide. This presents two issues. First, how do we ensure the IPC resources one application creates do not collide with those created by other applications? Second, how do we ensure security and privacy? That is, System V IPC resources created by one application cannot be accessed from other applications.

The first issue is resolved by the pathname. Hopefully, different vendors won't collide with one another in picking the unique pathnames for their applications. With care this should work reasonably well.

The second issue is addressed by the permission of the resource itself. When a program creates a System V IPC resource, it can specify the permission for that resource (by using the lowest 9 bits of the flags argument). The creator of the resource can use the permission setting to control who are allowed to access the resource and who are not, at the granularity of owner, group and others. An application can create its own user and group.

For instance, using a permission of octal 0600 would block all other users (except the root (super) user) from accessing the resource. As an example, if user John creates the resource and sets the resource's permission to 0600, then any process running as any other user except the root user won't be able to access it. Say, if a process running as the user Mary attempts to access the resource, it will get the 'Permission denied' error

(EACCESS, errno 13). Only processes running as John or the super user have access to this System V IPC resource.

It's worth pointing out that the permission of the pathname associated with the IPC resource does not play a role in controlling the accesses to the IPC resource. In fact, the permission on the pathname itself does not really matter. **It is the permission that is specified within the function call that actually creates the IPC resource that counts**! It's that permission that actually controls the accesses of the IPC resource.

In summary, for a process to be able to access a System V IPC resource created on a system, all of the following must be true:

1. The process must know the pathname and project id associated with the IPC resource. This is so that it can derive the key value of the IPC resource and use it to create the resource and/or get its identifier.

2. The effective user of the running process must be allowed to access the resource by the permission set on the resource by its creator when it is created or after creation.

9-2-3 Useful Commands Related to System V IPC

A couple of operating system commands related to System V IPC resources on a POSIX-compliant system are very useful.

First, to find out what System V IPC resources currently exist on a system, you can run the ipcs command from the operating system prompt:

```
$ ipcs
```

This ipcs command will list all of the System V IPC resources currently exist on the system.

As a real-world example, the Oracle relational database management system (the so-called Oracle RDBMS or Oracle database system) uses three System V shared memories and one System V semaphore set with 120+ semaphores in it. So, when the Oracle database system is running, the output of the ipcs command would look like the following (look for those resources owned by the user jinchen who is the user owning the Oracle installation):

```
$ ipcs

------ Shared Memory Segments --------
key         shmid       owner     perms       bytes        nattch      status
0x00000000  327681      root      644         80           2
0x00000000  360450      root      644         16384        2
0x00000000  393219      root      644         280          2
0xe6198994  372375556   jinchen   660         16785408     132
0x00000000  372408325   jinchen   660         1073741824   66
0x00000000  372441094   jinchen   660         167772160    66

------ Semaphore Arrays --------
key         semid       owner     perms       nsems
0x7142075c  4325377     jinchen   660         124
```

```
------ Message Queues --------
key          msqid        owner        perms        used-bytes   messages
```

Second, many times a program may fail and the System V IPC resources it has
created will continue to exist and hang around on the system even after
the death of their creator or no one is using them. A manual cleanup may
be necessary in this case. If you have the permission to do so (for example,
you are the creator of the resources) you can invoke the ipcrm command to
manually delete the System V IPC resources.

For example, the following ipcrm command deletes the semaphore whose
semid is 32768:

```
$ ipcs

------ Semaphore Arrays --------
key          semid        owner        perms        nsems
0x4101f745   32768        john         600          2

$ ipcrm -s 32768
```

9-3 System V Semaphore

Speaking of semaphore, POSIX Standard includes two semaphore implementations.
First, there is System V semaphore originated in AT&T Unix and it has been in
The Open Group Base Specifications since Issue 2. Then there is the so-called
POSIX semaphore that was introduced later in Issue 5, included for alignment
with the POSIX Realtime Extension. Conceptually, they are very similar,
although they use separate sets of APIs. We will introduce System V semaphore
in this section and talk about POSIX semaphore later in this chapter.

9-3-1 What Is a Semaphore?

Semaphore is one of the UNIX System V interprocess communication mechanisms
that have been available in Unix since 1983, and now in Linux too.
It is the concurrency control mechanism of the System V IPC.

A **semaphore** is an integer variable whose value can be increased or decreased.
It usually takes a non-negative value and the system guarantees incrementing
or decrementing its value is an atomic operation. Because of this,
a semaphore is usually used as a lock.

In its simplest form, a System V IPC semaphore functions as a lock. It's
meant to be used for synchronizing concurrent updates of a shared data or
resource. For instance, it is often used to control accesses to System V IPC
shared memory by multiple processes. We'll discuss shared memory in next
chapter.

Perhaps due to the fact that most programs usually need more than just
one semaphore, System V IPC semaphore exists in sets. A program creates
a set, or array, of semaphores at a time. Hence, if all the program needs is
one semaphore, then it would create a semaphore set with only one semaphore
in it.

Just like every other System V IPC resources, each semaphore set is identified by a key value, which is of type key_t, which is defined as an int in C. As we mentioned before, this key value is derived from a combination of a pathname and a project id by using the ftok() function. Each semaphore set is uniquely identified by a key value. This key value is later converted into a **semaphore set identifier** by the system when the semaphore set is created. This identifier is usually referred to as 'semid'.

Within each semaphore set, each individual semaphore is further identified by a number. The semaphores in a semaphore set are numbered starting at 0. For example, if a semaphore set has 5 semaphores in it, then these semaphores are numbered as 0, 1, 2, 3, 4. In other words, the first semaphore in a semaphore set has a semaphore number 0.
This semaphore number that identifies an individual semaphore within a set is often referred to as the 'semnum'.

Each semaphore in a semaphore set is essentially an integer of the 'unsigned short' type and has a value. (well, it indeed has a set of other values associated with it, too. But we will talk about that later. For now, we are mainly interested in only one -- the most important one.) A program uses a semaphore by performing operations that alter the semaphore's value. There are a number of operations a program can perform on a semaphore's value. It does so by invoking the semop() function or system call. The value of an individual semaphore is generally referred to as the 'semval'.

Figure 9-4 shows the three basic numbers associated with a System V semaphore.

```
    Figure 9-4 Three most important values associated with a semaphore
    ----------------------------------------------------------------------
    semid - identifies the semaphore set containing the individual semaphores.
            This value is returned by semget() function.
    semnum - identifies an individual semaphore within a semaphore set.
            This number starts with 0. It's indeed an index value.
    semval - the current value of an individual semaphore (an integer)
    ----------------------------------------------------------------------
```

9-3-2 Binary Semaphore and Counting Semaphore

Since a System V IPC semaphore is an integer by itself and can take a range of values, it has multiple usages. Based on the range of its values, there are two types of semaphores:

1. Binary semaphore

2. Counting semaphore

A **binary semaphore** is restricted to take only two values, for example, 0 and 1, and is intended to be used as a lock, controlling exclusive access to some shared data or resource.

A **counting semaphore** can take a range of values and is intended to be used as a counter of the number of resources available for use or consumption. It is intended to be used in solving a slightly different type of problems such as the Producer-Consumer problem.

Perhaps due to a semaphore is also meant to be used as a counting semaphore, the operating system does not allow its value to go below zero.

Binary semaphores are used a lot more often than counting ones.

In this section, we will focus on using a semaphore as a binary semaphore. That is, use it as an exclusive lock.

9-3-3 Create a Semaphore Set

Before a semaphore can be used, it must be created. As we mentioned before, a semaphore can only be created as part of a semaphore set.
A program invokes the semget() system call to create a semaphore set.

The **semget**() function creates a semaphore set if it does not already exist and returns its semid. If the specified semaphore set already exists, the semget() function simply returns its semid without creating it.

As shown below, the semget() function has three arguments. The first argument specifies the key value of the semaphore set. This key value should be a value returned by the ftok() function and is computed from the pathname and project id associated with the semaphore set.

```
int semget(key_t key, int nsems, int semflg);
```

The second argument specifies the number of semaphores in the semaphore set. It can be 1 or many.

The third argument specifies a combination of flags and permission.
Flags that can be specified in the third argument to the semget() function are similar to those for the open() function of files.
They include the following:

  IPC_CREAT : This flag means you want to create the semaphore set
    if it does not already exist. Only the creator of the semaphore set
    needs to specify this flag.

  IPC_EXCL : This flag means you want to create the semaphore set
    only if it does not already exist. The semget() function will fail with
    errno=EEXIST (17) (File exists) if the semaphore set already exists.
    In this case, the old, existing semaphore set must be removed before
    the semget() function can succeed.

On creation, the least significant nine bits of the argument 'semflg' define the permissions (for owner, group and others) of the semaphore set. This value is very important because it concerns security.
It determines what processes are allowed to read/write the IPC resource in the granularity of owner, group and others. For instance, a permission of 0640 in octal means the owner can read and write the resource, the members in the group can read and no access for others.

In one sense, the semget() function to a semaphore set is similar to the open function to a file. Before any process/thread can access a shared file, some process/thread must call the open() function to create it if it does not already exist. Similarly, before any process/thread can access a semaphore set, some process/thread must call the semget() function to create it if it does not already exist. When a file already exists, a process/thread must call the open() function to get the file descriptor of the file before it can access it. Similarly, when a semaphore set already exists, a process/thread must call the semget() function to get the semaphore id (semid) before it can access it.

Note that although some implementation may initialize the semaphore values to 0 upon creation, the POSIX.1-2001 standard says their values are indeterminate. Therefore, to ensure application portability, it is wise to always initialize the semaphores' values right after creation.

The program in Figure 9-5 demonstrates how to create a semaphore set.

   Figure 9-5 Creating a semaphore set (semcreate.c)

```
/*
 * Create a semaphore set.
 * Copyright (c) 2013, 2020 Mr. Jin-Jwei Chen.  All rights reserved.
 */

#include <stdio.h>
#include <errno.h>
#include <stdlib.h>
#include <sys/types.h>
#include <sys/ipc.h>
#include <sys/sem.h>

#define  IPCKEYPATH  "/var/xyzinc/app1"  /* this file or directory must exist */
#define  IPCSUBID    'A'                 /* project id identifying the semaphore set */
#define  NSEMS       3                   /* number of semaphores in our semaphore set */

int main(int argc, char *argv[])
{
  key_t  ipckey;
  int    projid;
  int    semid;
  int    ret;

  if (argc > 1)
  {
    projid = atoi(argv[1]);
  }
  else
    projid = IPCSUBID;

  /* Compute the IPC key value from the pathname and project id */
  /* ftok() got error 2 if the pathname does not exist. */
  if ((ipckey = ftok(IPCKEYPATH, projid)) == (key_t)-1) {
    fprintf(stderr, "ftok() failed, errno=%d\n", errno);
    return(-1);
  }

  /* Create the semaphore set */
```

```
semid = semget(ipckey, NSEMS, IPC_CREAT|0600);
if (semid == -1)
{
   fprintf(stderr, "semget() failed, errno=%d\n", errno);
   return(-2);
}
fprintf(stdout, "The semaphore set was successfully created.\n");

return(0);
}
```

To verify the creation of the semaphore set is successful on a POSIX-compliant system, you can run the ipcs command from another window after starting the semcreate program.

```
$ ipcs

------ Semaphore Arrays --------
key         semid     owner     perms     nsems
0x4101f745 32768      john       600        2
```

The command should show the semaphore set created.
To manually remove the semaphore set, run the ipcrm command and specify the semid. For example,

```
$ ipcrm -s 32768
```

9-3-4 Remove a Semaphore Set

Note that all of the System V IPC resources are designed to be created by one process and used by many others. Therefore, they don't just disappear when the creator process exits. Each System V IPC has to be explicitly removed. It will continue to exist and thus consume system resources until either it is removed or the system goes down.

To remove a semaphore set, a process or thread calls the **semctl**() system call with the IPC_RMID in the third argument.

```
int semctl(int semid, int semnum, int cmd, ...);
```

The semctl() function has three or four arguments. When there are four, the fourth has the type union semun. The first argument is the semaphore id which identifies the semaphore set. It should be the semid value returned by the semget() call. The second argument selects a semaphore within the semaphore set. The third argument specifies a command to be performed. It can be IPC_STAT (getting info from associated internal kernel data structure), IPC_SET (setting semaphore's value), IPC_RMID (removing semaphore set), IPC_INFO (getting system-wide semaphore parameters and their limits), and many others. Please refer to man page for all the commands supported.

Note that with IPC_RMID command, the second argument is ignored. It does not matter whether you provide a value of 0 or 1.

When a semaphore set is removed, all processes blocked in the semop() call of this semaphore set will be awakened.

Note that in order to be able to remove a semaphore set, the effective user ID of the process must match the creator or owner of the semaphore set, or it must be a privileged user. Even if the permission of the semaphore set is set to, for instance, 0660, as group writeable, a different user in the same group still cannot remove the semaphore set.

Figure 9-6 shows a program that creates a semaphore set and then removes it.

Figure 9-6 Create and remove a semaphore set (semcrerm.c and mysemutil.h)

(a) semcrerm.c

```c
/*
 * Create and remove a semaphore set.
 * Copyright (c) 2013, Mr. Jin-Jwei Chen.  All rights reserved.
 */

#include "mysemutil.h"

int main(int argc, char *argv[])
{
  key_t  ipckey;
  int    projid;
  int    semid;
  int    ret;

  if (argc > 1)
  {
    projid = atoi(argv[1]);
  }
  else
    projid = IPCSUBID;

  /* Compute the IPC key value from the pathname and project id */
  /* ftok() got error 2 if the pathname does not exist. */
  if ((ipckey = ftok(IPCKEYPATH, projid)) == (key_t)-1) {
    fprintf(stderr, "ftok() failed, errno=%d\n", errno);
    return(-1);
  }

  /* Create the semaphore set */
  semid = semget(ipckey, NSEMS, IPC_CREAT|0600);
  if (semid == -1)
  {
    fprintf(stderr, "semget() failed, errno=%d\n", errno);
    return(-2);
  }
  fprintf(stdout, "The semaphore set was successfully created.\n");

  /* Wait a few seconds so you can check the semaphore set created. */
  sleep(5);

  /* Remove the semaphore set */
  /* The second argument, semnum, is ignored for removal. */
  ret = semctl(semid, 0, IPC_RMID);
```

```
  if (ret == -1)
  {
    fprintf(stderr, "semctl() failed to remove, errno=%d\n", errno);
    return(-3);
  }
  fprintf(stdout, "The semaphore set was successfully removed.\n");

  return(0);
}
```

        (b) mysemutil.h

```
/*
 * Include files, defines and utility functions for semaphore example programs.
 * Copyright (c) 2013, 2020 Mr. Jin-Jwei Chen.  All rights reserved.
 */

#include <stdio.h>
#include <errno.h>
#include <sys/types.h>
#include <sys/stat.h>
#include <fcntl.h>
#include <unistd.h>
#include <stdlib.h>
#include <string.h>   /* memset and strcmp */

#include <sys/ipc.h>
#include <sys/sem.h>

#include <sys/wait.h>
#include <pthread.h>

/*
 * Defines
 */

#define  IPCKEYPATH  "/var/xyzinc/app1"  /* this file or directory must exist */
#define  IPCSUBID    'A'             /* project id identifying the semaphore set */
#define  NSEMS       3               /* number of semaphores in our semaphore set */
#define  ONESEM      1               /* only one semaphore in the semaphore set */
#define  MAXSEMS     128             /* maximum number of semaphores in our set */

#define  BLKSZ       512             /* block size */
#define  BUFSZ       (2*BLKSZ)       /* buffer size */
#define  INIT_VALUE  '0'             /* initial byte value */

/* Apple Darwin does not define struct seminfo. */
#ifdef __APPLE__
struct seminfo {
    int     semmap,                  /* # of entries in semaphore map */
            semmni,                  /* # of semaphore identifiers */
            semmns,                  /* # of semaphores in system */
            semmnu,                  /* # of undo structures in system */
            semmsl,                  /* max # of semaphores per id */
            semopm,                  /* max # of operations per semop call */
            semume,                  /* max # of undo entries per process */
```

```
            semusz,                 /* size in bytes of undo structure */
            semvmx,                 /* semaphore maximum value */
            semaem;                 /* adjust on exit max value */
};
#endif


/* Trying to undefine "union semun" does not seem to work. */
#ifdef __APPLE__
#define _POSIX_C_SOURCE
#undef _DARWIN_C_SOURCE
#endif


/* Apple Darwin wrongly defines this in user space, against POSIX standard */
/* Besides, its definition is missing member "struct seminfo *__buf" */
#ifndef __APPLE__
/*
 * The data type for the fourth argument to semctl() function.
 * The type 'union semun'.
 */
union semun {
    int               val;     /* Value for SETVAL */
    struct semid_ds *buf;      /* Buffer for IPC_STAT, IPC_SET */
    unsigned short  *array;    /* Array for GETALL, SETALL */
    struct seminfo  *__buf;    /* Buffer for IPC_INFO
                                  (Linux specific) */
};
typedef union semun semun;
#else
typedef union semun semun;
#endif


/*
 * -----------------------------------------------------------------------
 * Declaration of utility functions.
 * -----------------------------------------------------------------------
 */


/*
 * This function gets and returns the identifier of the semaphore set specified.
 * It also creates the semaphore set if it does not already exist.
 */
int get_semaphore_set(char *pathname, int projid, int nsems, size_t perm);

/* This function sets the value of each semaphore in a semaphore set. */
int init_semaphore_set(int semid, int nsems, int semval);

/*
 * This function creates a file of the specified name, size (in bytes) and
 * permission and fills it with the value specified.
 */
int create_file(char *fname, size_t fsize, unsigned char val, int perm);

/*
 * This function randomly picks a block from a file and updates the very
 * first byte of it that is not the initial value as specified by the
 * parameter oldval. It replaces the initial byte value with the new byte
```

```
 * value specified by the newval parameter.
 */
int random_file_update(int fd, size_t fsize, unsigned char oldval, unsigned char
newval);

/*
 * This function randomly picks a block from a file and updates the very
 * first byte of it that is not the initial value as specified by the
 * parameter oldval. It replaces the initial byte value with the new byte
 * value specified by the newval parameter.
 * The update repeats for the number of times specified by the updcnt
 * parameter.
 */
int random_file_update_all(char *fname, size_t fsize, unsigned char oldval, unsigned
char newval, size_t updcnt);

/*
 * Count the number of occurrences of each character in '1' ... '9',
 * 'a' ... 'z' in a file.
 */
int count_char_occurrences(char *fanme);

/*
 * Semaphore functions.
 */
int lock_semaphore(int semid, int semnum);
int unlock_semaphore(int semid, int semnum);
int print_semaphore_set(int semid, int nsems);
```

After running this program, to verify that the program works correctly, you want to issue the ipcs command to make sure the semaphore set created by the program is actually deleted and no longer exists on the system.

9-3-5 How to Use a Semaphore

One can use a System V semaphore in at least a couple of different ways. The most common way is to use it as a binary semaphore and for controlling exclusive access to a shared data/resource. In this usage, a semaphore is an exclusive lock.

A semaphore is typically shared and used by multiple processes or threads. Before it can be used, it must be created. Typically, the manager process/thread or the process/thread that runs first creates it. After being created, a semaphore can be used by many processes/threads that know its key and have permission to do so. Therefore, a semaphore has one creator and typically many user processes.

Remember, a binary semaphore is meant to synchronize concurrent updates/accesses to a shared data/resource. As a programmer, you need to know which semaphore protects what shared data/resource.

To use a semaphore as a lock, we adopt the convention where the semval is 1 means the semaphore is available (it is unlocked) and the semval being 0 means the semaphore is unavailable (i.e. it is locked).

This means, after the semaphore is created, its value must be initialized to 1. And acquiring the lock is to find its current value of being 1 and decrement it to 0. Releasing the lock is to change the semaphore's value from 0 to 1.

Altering the semval is done via the semop() system call. This function has the following specification:

```
int semop(int semid, struct sembuf *sops, unsigned nsops);
```

The first argument semid specifies the semaphore set containing the semaphores. The second argument is a pointer to a structure or an array of structures that specifies which semaphore(s) is to receive the operation and what the operation is. This structure is of type 'struct sembuf', containing the following members:

```
unsigned short sem_num;   /* semaphore number */
short          sem_op;    /* semaphore operation */
short          sem_flg;   /* operation flags */
```

The first member of the structure is the what we call semnum (although named as sem_num), specifying the individual semaphore within the set to receive the operation. The second member is the sem_op, which specifies the operation to be performed on the selected semaphore. In fact, it specifies a value that will be 'added' to the current value of the semaphore. Specifying a positive value means to increase the semaphore's value by that amount and a negative value means to decrement the current value by that amount. A value of 0 means to wait for the semval to become 0. In that case, if the semval is currently 0, then the operation will proceed. Otherwise, if IPC_NOWAIT is specified in sem_flg, semop() fails with errno set to EAGAIN.

Note that the system will not let a semaphore's value fall below 0. For example, if the current semval is 1 and you pass in -2 in the sem_op, then the operation will be blocked, potentially forever if the IPC_NOWAIT flag is not specified, or until some other process has increased the semaphore's value to 2 or above.

If IPC_NOWAIT is specified in sem_flg, semop() will fail and return with errno set to EAGAIN (11) and none of the operations in sops is performed. If IPC_NOWAIT is not specified in sem_flg, then the counter of processes waiting for this semaphore's value to increase is incremented by one and the process is put to sleep and wait until the semval becomes greater than or equal to the absolute value of the sem_op, or until the process catches a signal, or the semaphore set is removed.

With the convention we set above regarding the semaphore's values (i.e. 1 means lock is available and 0 means the lock is unavailable), we will pass in a value of -1 in sem_op in our locking operation because to acquire the lock we want to change the semaphore's value from 1 to 0. If the current value of the semaphore is 0 and a process/thread attempts to decrement it by 1, it will block unless the IPC_NOWAIT flag is specified. In our unlock operation, we will pass in a value of 1 in sem_op because to release a lock we want to change the semaphore's value from 0 to 1.

Remember we said that for locking to work, the operation to acquire or release a lock must be atomic. Because of this, the implementation of the semop() function is such that the set of operations contained in the second argument to the semop() call is performed atomically. The operations are performed as all or nothing. That is, they are done at the same time, and only if they can all be done simultaneously. In case the operations cannot all be done simultaneously, the behavior then depends on whether the IPC_NOWAIT flag is present in the sem_flg field.

There are two flags one can set in the sem_flg field of the 'struct sembuf':

IPC_NOWAIT: indicates the caller does not want to be blocked. If this flag is specified and the requested operation cannot be performed, instead of putting the calling process/thread to sleep and wait, the semop() function returns right away with errno set to EAGAIN.

SEM_UNDO: This flag is used for cleanup when a process terminates. Specifying this flag means the caller wants the requested operation to be undone by the operating system in case this process terminates unexpectedly.

In general, it's always a good practice to specify the SEM_UNDO flag so that the operating system can undo the effect of the semaphore operation your program has performed in the case of unexpected termination. For example, you don't want this situation to happen where a process holding the semaphore (i.e. lock) dies before it can unlock the semaphore and thus causing all other processes needing the same semaphore to hang. By specifying the SEM_UNDO flag, the operating system would be able to go in and clean it up on behalf of the dead process and allow the other processes to continue to function. This is how a good quality software should behave!

So always remember that you set the SEM_UNDO flag in the second argument whenever your program calls the semop() function.

Of course, there is a potential issue of what if the undo operation needs to be blocked, too. Would that hold up the termination process? This behavior is implementation dependent. In Linux, it tries to decrease the semaphore's value as far as it can during the undo operation and let the termination proceed.

In summary, the steps that a program using a semaphore for locking takes are listed below:

• create the semaphore set (using semget()) and initialize its value (using semctl()) or simply get the semid (using semget())
• lock the semaphore (using semop())
• perform the processing on the shared data/resource
• unlock the semaphore (using semop())
• remove the semaphore set if appropriate (using semctl())(normally not done)

Figure 9-7 lists a program that performs the lock and unlock operations on a semaphore.

Figure 9-7 Lock and unlock a semaphore (semlock.c)

/*

```c
 * Lock and unlock a semaphore.
 * Copyright (c) 2013, Mr. Jin-Jwei Chen.  All rights reserved.
 */

#include "mysemutil.h"

int main(int argc, char *argv[])
{
  key_t  ipckey;
  int    projid;
  int    semid;
  int    ret;
  int    exit_code=0;
  semun  semarg;
  struct sembuf   semoparg;
  int    i;

  if (argc > 1)
  {
    projid = atoi(argv[1]);
  }
  else
    projid = IPCSUBID;

  /* Compute the IPC key value from the pathname and project id */
  if ((ipckey = ftok(IPCKEYPATH, projid)) == (key_t)-1) {
    fprintf(stderr, "ftok() failed, errno=%d\n", errno);
    return(-1);
  }

  /* Create the semaphore */
  semid = semget(ipckey, 1, IPC_CREAT|0600);
  if (semid == -1)
  {
    fprintf(stderr, "semget() failed, errno=%d\n", errno);
    return(-2);
  }
  fprintf(stdout, "The semaphore was successfully created.\n");

  /* Initialize the value of the semaphore */
  semarg.val = 1;
  ret = semctl(semid, 0, SETVAL, semarg);
  if (ret == -1)
  {
    fprintf(stderr, "semctl() failed to set value, errno=%d\n", errno);
    exit_code = (-3);
    goto exit;
  }
  fprintf(stdout, "Initializing the semaphore value was successful.\n");

  /* Lock the semaphore */
  semoparg.sem_num = 0;    /* select the semaphore */
  semoparg.sem_op  = -1;   /* change its value from 1 to 0 to lock */
  semoparg.sem_flg = (SEM_UNDO);
  if ((ret = semop(semid, &semoparg, 1)) == -1) {
    fprintf(stderr, " semop() failed to lock the semaphore, errno=%d\n",
```

```
    errno);
  exit_code = (-errno);
  goto exit;
}
fprintf(stdout, "We have successfully acquired the lock!\n");

fprintf(stdout, "  Updating the shared data ...\n");

/* Unlock the semaphore */
semoparg.sem_num = 0;    /* select the semaphore */
semoparg.sem_op  = 1;    /* increment its value by 1 to unlock */
semoparg.sem_flg = (SEM_UNDO);
if ((ret = semop(semid, &semoparg, 1)) == -1) {
  fprintf(stderr, " semop() failed to unlock the semaphore, errno=%d\n",
    errno);
  exit_code = (-errno);
}
fprintf(stdout, "We have successfully released the lock!\n");

exit:

/* Remove the semaphore */
ret = semctl(semid, 0, IPC_RMID);
if (ret == -1)
{
  fprintf(stderr, "semctl() failed to remove, errno=%d\n", errno);
  return(-6);
}
fprintf(stdout, "The semaphore set was successfully removed.\n");

return(exit_code);
}
```

To allow users to be able to find out what is going on with a semaphore at any given time, each semaphore in a semaphore set has the following management attribute values associated with it:

```
unsigned short  semval;    /* current value of the semaphore */
pid_t           sempid;    /* pid of the process performed the last op */
unsigned short  semzcnt;   /* # of processes waiting for it to become zero */
unsigned short  semncnt;   /* # of processes waiting for it to increase */
```

In other words, the operating system maintains the value of each semaphore (semval), the process id (pid) of the process that performs the last operation on the semaphore (sempid), the number of processes that are waiting for the semaphore's value to become zero (semzcnt), and the number of processes blocked and waiting for the semaphore's value to increase.

For instance, if the semop() call is successful, then the sempid value associated with the semaphore will be set to the pid value of the current process.

9-3-6 Perform Various Operations on Semaphores

There are a number of control operations one can perform on a semaphore.

They are all performed by invoking the semctl() function.
We will talk about some of these operations in this section.

The **semctl**() function allows a program to perform various control operations
on a semaphore set or on an individual semaphore. The semctl() function has
the following specification:

```
int semctl(int semid, int semnum, int cmd, semun semarg);
```

This function typically has four arguments except in one case (when the
cmd is IPC_RMID).

The first argument identifies the semaphore set to be operated on.

The second argument identifies an individual semaphore to be operated on
if the operation is to be performed on only one semaphore rather than the
entire semaphore set. If the operation is for the entire semaphore set,
this second argument is ignored. Whether the operation is for one or multiple
semaphores is really determined by the third argument, cmd, which we will
discuss in just a moment.

The fourth argument provides the input values needed by the operation or
the buffer that holds the return values of the operation.
It must be of type 'union semun'. According to POSIX.1-2001 standard, the
program that invokes the semctl() function must declare this type as below:

```
/* data type for the fourth argument of semctl() function */
union semun {
    int                 val;    /* input only, value for SETVAL */
    struct semid_ds *buf;       /* input/output buffer for IPC_STAT, IPC_SET */
    unsigned short  *array;     /* input buffer for SETALL, output buffer for
                                   GETALL */
    struct seminfo  *__buf;     /* Buffer for IPC_INFO -- Linux specific */
} semarg;
```

As you can see, the fourth argument to the semctl() function is a
multi-purpose argument and is thus declared as a union of multiple data
types. It is used as one of the many types in the union depending on the
different command specified by the third argument cmd.

Also notice that the first member (val) of the union is a single scalar
value. So, it has only one use, which is to provide the input semaphore
value for the SETVAL command. It cannot be used as an output at all
because the value, instead of the address, of the union is passed in as
the fourth argument to the semctl() function.

Besides, be very careful! Since this is a union and it takes only a single
value, either an integer or an address. If after you use the val field for
the SETVAL operation you want to perform other operations, make sure you
set the semarg.buf, semarg.array or semarg.__buf again or your program may
die because it will try to interpret that scalar integer value as an address,
which is totally wrong!

If the command is GETVAL, the semaphore value returned is the value
returned by the function itself.

The type 'struct semid_ds' is defined in <sys/sem.h>. The last union member is Linux specific. The type 'struct seminfo' is defined in /usr/include/linux/sem.h and /usr/include/bits/sem.h on Linux. That structure has a field for each of the Linux operating system tunable parameters related to semaphore.

The third argument specifies the operation or command to be performed. Its value can be one of the following. As you can tell, some of these operations are for one individual semaphore only and others are for the entire semaphore set.

IPC_RMID: This operation removes the semaphore set. It will wake up all processes that are still blocked in the semop() call on the semaphore set. Those processes will return with errno set to EIDRM. In order to be able to remove a semaphore set, the effective user ID of the caller must match the creator or owner of the semaphore set. The second argument semnum of the semctl() call is ignored and the fourth argument is not needed.

We have shown an example on how to use this operation in a previous section.

GETVAL: This command queries and returns the current value of the semaphore. The individual semaphore is identified by the combination of the first and second arguments, that is, semid and semnum. The caller must have a read permission on the semaphore set. The function's return value is the semaphore's current value.

SETVAL: This command sets the current value of the semaphore. The individual semaphore is identified by the combination of the first and second arguments, that is, semid and semnum.

You provide the new value of the semaphore in the val field of the semun union. The caller must have a write permission on the semaphore set. If this value change would allow some processes blocked on the semop() call on this semaphore to proceed, they will be woken up.

GETALL: This command queries the current values of all semaphores in the set.

To perform this operation, the fourth argument will have to provide the buffer for holding the values of the semaphores in the set that are being returned. The caller will have to allocate memory for an array of unsigned short and put the starting address of the array in the field named 'array' in the 'union semun'. The size of the array must equal to the number of semaphores in the set. The second argument semnum is ignored.

The caller must have a read permission on the semaphore set.

SETALL: This command sets the current values of all semaphores in the set. To perform this operation, the fourth argument will have to provide an array of values for the semaphores in the set using the member array in the 'union semun'. The caller will have to allocate memory for an array of unsigned short, fill the new value for each semaphore in the set into the corresponding array element, and put the starting address of

the array in the field named 'array' in the 'union semun'.
The size of the array must equal to the number of semaphores in the set.
The second argument semnum is ignored.

The caller must have a write permission on the semaphore set.
This command updates the last change time (sem_ctime) of the semaphore
set.

If this operation would allow some processes blocked on the semop()
call on the semaphores in the set to proceed, they will be woken up.

GETPID: This operation returns the PID (process id) of the process that
executed the last semop() call on the semaphore.
The caller must have read permission on the semaphore set.

GETNCNT: This operation returns the number of processes that are currently
waiting for the value of the semaphore to increase.
The caller must have read permission on the semaphore set.

GETZCNT: This operation returns the number of processes that are currently
waiting for the value of the semaphore to become zero.
The caller must have read permission on the semaphore set.

IPC_STAT: query and return the information about the semaphore set as
defined in 'struct semid_ds' structure.

This information includes the number of semaphores in the set, owner
and permission, the timestamp of last semop() call, and the timestamp
of last change. The values are returned in the buf field of the fourth
argument. The second argument semnum of the semctl() call is ignored

IPC_SET: change and set the information about the semaphore set as
defined in 'struct semid_ds' structure. This operation updates the
last change time (sem_ctime) of the semaphore set.
The input values are provided in the buf field of the fourth argument.
The second argument semnum of the semctl() call is ignored.

The operations below are Linux specific. To perform the following Linux
specific operations, you must add the following line at the beginning of
your program before including the <sys/ipc.h> :

```
#define  _GNU_SOURCE    /* to get Linux specific semctl commands */
```

IPC_INFO: This command is Linux specific. It queries and returns
information about the current values and limits of semaphore-related
operating system parameters as defined in the 'struct seminfo'
structure. These values include semmni (maximum number of semaphore
sets allowed), semmsl (maximum number of semaphores allowed in a set),
semmns (maximum number of semaphores allowed in all sets on the system),
semvmx (maximum value of a semaphore), and others.

SEM_INFO: similar to IPC_INFO except that the semusz field returns the
number of semaphore sets that currently exist on the system and the
semaem field returns the total number of semaphores currently exist
on the entire system. This command is Linux specific, too.

SEM_STAT: similar to IPC_STAT, except that the semid is not a semaphore
set identifier. Instead, it is an index into the Linux kernel's
internal array that maintains information about all semaphore sets
on the system. This operation is Linux specific as well.

Note that the semctl() function can be used to operate on one individual
semaphore or all semaphores in the entire semaphore set. If it's one
semaphore, then the second argument, semnum, selects it. Otherwise,
the second argument is ignored for an operation targeting the entire set.

In this section, we give examples of how to use some of these commands.
For further details on these and other operations, please refer to the
man page or documentation of the semctl() function.

Figure 9-8 is a program that demonstrates the use of the SETVAL and GETVAL
operations with the semctl() function.

Figure 9-9 is a program demonstrates the SETALL and GETALL commands
with the semctl() function.

Figure 9-8 Set and get a semaphore's value (semsetone.c)

```
/*
 * Demonstrate the GETVAL and SETVAL operations of the semctl function.
 * Copyright (c) 2013, Mr. Jin-Jwei Chen.  All rights reserved.
 */

#include "mysemutil.h"

int main(int argc, char *argv[])
{
  key_t  ipckey;
  int    projid;
  int    semid;
  int    ret;
  int    exit_code=0;
  semun  semarg;
  struct sembuf    semoparg;
  int    i;

  if (argc > 1)
  {
    projid = atoi(argv[1]);
  }
  else
    projid = IPCSUBID;

  /* Compute the IPC key value from the pathname and project id */
  /* ftok() got error 2 if the pathname does not exist. */
  if ((ipckey = ftok(IPCKEYPATH, projid)) == (key_t)-1) {
    fprintf(stderr, "ftok() failed, errno=%d\n", errno);
    return(-1);
  }

  /* Create the semaphore */
```

```
semid = semget(ipckey, 1, IPC_CREAT|0600);
if (semid == -1)
{
   fprintf(stderr, "semget() failed, errno=%d\n", errno);
   return(-2);
}
fprintf(stdout, "The semaphore was successfully created.\n");

/* Get and print the initial values of the semaphore. */
ret = semctl(semid, 0, GETVAL, semarg);
if (ret == -1)
{
   fprintf(stderr, "semctl() failed to GETVAL, errno=%d\n", errno);
   exit_code = (-3);
   goto exit;
}
fprintf(stdout, "  The initial semaphore value is:\n");
fprintf(stdout, "     semval=%d\n",  ret);

/* Set the value of the semaphore */
semarg.val = 1;
ret = semctl(semid, 0, SETVAL, semarg);
if (ret == -1)
{
   fprintf(stderr, "semctl() failed to SETVAL, errno=%d\n", errno);
   exit_code = (-4);
   goto exit;
}
fprintf(stdout, "Setting the semaphore value was successful.\n");

/* Get and print the current values of the semaphore. */
ret = semctl(semid, 0, GETVAL, semarg);
if (ret == -1)
{
   fprintf(stderr, "semctl() failed to GETVAL, errno=%d\n", errno);
   exit_code = (-5);
   goto exit;
}
fprintf(stdout, "  The new semaphore value is:\n");
fprintf(stdout, "     semval=%d\n",  ret);

exit:

/* Remove the semaphore */
/* The second argument, semnum, is ignored for removal. */
ret = semctl(semid, 0, IPC_RMID);
if (ret == -1)
{
   fprintf(stderr, "semctl() failed to remove, errno=%d\n", errno);
   return(-6);
}
fprintf(stdout, "The semaphore set was successfully removed.\n");

return(exit_code);
}
```

Figure 9-9 Set and get all semaphores' values (semsetall.c)

```c
/*
 * Set and get all semaphore values in a semaphore set.
 * Copyright (c) 2013, Mr. Jin-Jwei Chen.  All rights reserved.
 */

#include "mysemutil.h"

int main(int argc, char *argv[])
{
  key_t  ipckey;
  int    projid;
  int    semid;
  int    ret;
  int    exit_code=0;
  semun  semarg;
  unsigned short semval[NSEMS];
  int    i;

  if (argc > 1)
  {
    projid = atoi(argv[1]);
  }
  else
    projid = IPCSUBID;

  /* Compute the IPC key value from the pathname and project id */
  /* ftok() got error 2 if the pathname does not exist. */
  if ((ipckey = ftok(IPCKEYPATH, projid)) == (key_t)-1) {
    fprintf(stderr, "ftok() failed, errno=%d\n", errno);
    return(-1);
  }

  /* Create the semaphore set */
  semid = semget(ipckey, NSEMS, IPC_CREAT|0600);
  if (semid == -1)
  {
    fprintf(stderr, "semget() failed, errno=%d\n", errno);
    return(-2);
  }
  fprintf(stdout, "The semaphore set was successfully created.\n");

  /* Get and print the initial values of all semaphores in the semaphore set */
  semarg.array = (unsigned short *)semval;
  ret = semctl(semid, 0, GETALL, semarg);
  if (ret == -1)
  {
    fprintf(stderr, "semctl() failed, errno=%d\n", errno);
    exit_code = (-3);
    goto exit;
  }
  fprintf(stdout, "The initial semaphore values are:\n");
  for (i=0; i < NSEMS; i++)
    fprintf(stdout, "  semval[%5u]=%d\n", i, semarg.array[i]);
```

```
/* Set the semaphores' values */
for (i=0; i < NSEMS; i++)
  semarg.array[i] = (i + 1);
ret = semctl(semid, 0, SETALL, semarg);
if (ret == -1)
{
  fprintf(stderr, "semctl() failed to set all, errno=%d\n", errno);
  exit_code = (-4);
  goto exit;
}
fprintf(stdout, "Setting semaphore values was successful.\n");

/* Get and print the current values of the semaphores. */
for (i=0; i < NSEMS; i++)
  semarg.array[i] = 0;
ret = semctl(semid, 0, GETALL, semarg);
if (ret == -1)
{
  fprintf(stderr, "semctl() failed to get all, errno=%d\n", errno);
  exit_code = (-5);
  goto exit;
}
fprintf(stdout, "The current semaphore values are:\n");
for (i=0; i < NSEMS; i++)
  fprintf(stdout, "  semval[%5u]=%d\n", i, semarg.array[i]);

exit:

/* Remove the semaphore set */
/* The second argument, semnum, is ignored for removal. */
ret = semctl(semid, 0, IPC_RMID);
if (ret == -1)
{
  fprintf(stderr, "semctl() failed to remove, errno=%d\n", errno);
  return(-6);
}
fprintf(stdout, "The semaphore set was successfully removed.\n");

  return(exit_code);
}
```

Return Values of the semctl() Function

The return value of the semctl() function is worth noting here.

On a POSIX-compliant system, the semctl() function returns -1 on failure and errno is set to indicate the error, which is typical of a Unix/Linux function.

On success, the semctl() function returns a nonnegative value depending on the operation performed:

```
GETVAL - semctl() returns the value of the semaphore (semval)
GETPID - semctl() returns the pid of the process that executed the last
          semop() operation on the semaphore (sempid)
GETNCNT - semctl() returns the number of processes waiting for the
```

499

value of the semaphore to increase (semncnt)

GETZCNT - semctl() returns the number of processes waiting for the semaphore value to become zero (semzcnt)

Please refer to the documentation (e.g. man page) of the semctl() function on your system for its return value in other operations as well as its possible error codes.

9-3-7 A Concurrent Update Example

Here we give an example of using System V semaphores in synchronizing concurrent updates. This program demonstrates multiple processes concurrently update a shared file. At end it verifies no updates are lost.

The program first creates the shared file by calling the create_file() function. For easy identification purpose, the file is filled with the ASCII character '0' to begin with.

It then creates the semaphore that will be used to synchronize the concurrent updates of the shared file by calling the get_semaphore_set() function. The semaphore's value is initialized to 1 by the init_semaphore_set() function.

The program then creates a number of child processes (four of them, by default) that will try to update the same file at the same time. The parent process will then wait for all of its children to finish and then remove the semaphore.

Before the program exits, it calls the count_char_occurrences() function to count the numbers of updates on the shared file by each of the child processes.

After being created (via the fork() system call), each child process will start running the update_shared_file() function to update the shared file.

Again, for easy identification purpose, when a child process updates the shared file, it writes its own id into the selected block of the file. Each file update essentially picks a random block of the file and writes the id of the process into the next un-updated byte of the block as an ASCII character. That's why at end of the updates, the count_char_occurrences() function can simply count the ids to tally the number of updates made by each process. The id of each process and the number of updates it is supposed to perform are passed in as arguments to the update_shared_file() function.

Note that because when a child process is created via the fork system call in a POSIX-compliant system it inherits all the resources its parent has, all the child processes share the same file and same semaphore. That's why the program can demonstrate concurrent updates of a shared resource (the file) using the shared concurrency control entity (the semaphore) by creating the shared file and semaphore in the parent process before it spawns the children.

The utility functions employed by the semupdf program are grouped in the source file semlib.c as shown in Figure 9-10(b).

Please notice that we intentionally insert a delay after each update in the update_shared_file() function. This is mainly because the shared file we use is very small by default, only 2 MB. With today's systems, such a small file can easily be cached in memory and therefore updating a file runs almost as fast as updating the memory. Users can adjust the delay based on the file size to make it most appropriate.

Figure 9-10 Concurrent updates of a shared file by multiple processes (semupdf.c and semlib.c)

(a) semupdf.c

```c
/*
 * Concurrent updates of a shared file by multiple processes using semaphore.
 * Copyright (c) 2013, 2020 Mr. Jin-Jwei Chen.  All rights reserved.
 */

#include "mysemutil.h"

/* Default values related to the shared file */
#define   NMB          2                /* number of megabytes */
#define   ONEMB        (1024*1024)      /* one megabytes */
#define   DEFFILESZ    (NMB*ONEMB)      /* default file size in bytes */
#define   NPROC        4                /* number of concurrent processes */
#define   DEF_FNAME    "semsharedf1"    /* name of the shared file */
#define   DEFUPDCNT    40               /* default update count */
#define   MAXDELAYCNT  100000000        /* delay count */

int update_shared_file(char *fname, size_t fsize, int newval, size_t updcnt, int semid);

int main(int argc, char *argv[])
{
  key_t   ipckey;
  int     nproc;
  int     semid;
  int     ret;
  int     exit_code=0;
  semun   semarg;
  unsigned short semval[ONESEM];
  int     i;
  int     projid = IPCSUBID;
  char    def_fname[64] = DEF_FNAME;
  char    *fname;
  size_t  filesz;
  size_t  updcnt = DEFUPDCNT;
  pid_t   pid;
  int     stat;    /* child's exit value */

  if ((argc > 1) &&
      ((strcmp(argv[1], "-h") == 0) || (strcmp(argv[1], "-help") == 0)))
  {
    fprintf(stdout, "Usage: %s [nproc] [MBs] [updcnt] [fname]\n", argv[0]);
    return(-1);
  }
```

501

```
/*
 * Get the number of concurrent processes, update count, file size and
 * file name from the user, if any.
 */
nproc = NPROC;
if (argc > 1)
  nproc = atoi(argv[1]);
if (nproc <= 0)
  nproc = NPROC;

filesz = DEFFILESZ;
if (argc > 2)
{
  filesz = atoi(argv[2]);
  if (filesz > 0)
    filesz = (filesz * ONEMB);
}
if (filesz <= 0)
  filesz = DEFFILESZ;

updcnt = DEFUPDCNT;
if (argc > 3)
  updcnt = atoi(argv[3]);
if (updcnt <= 0)
  updcnt = DEFUPDCNT;

fname = def_fname;
if (argc > 4)
  fname = argv[4];

fprintf(stdout, "Updating file %s of %lu bytes using %u concurrent processes,"
  " %lu updates each.\n" , fname, filesz, nproc, updcnt);

/* Create the shared file */
ret = create_file(fname, filesz, INIT_VALUE, 0644);
if (ret < 0)
{
  fprintf(stderr, "Failed to create the shared file\n");
  return(-2);
}

/* Create the semaphore */
semid = get_semaphore_set(IPCKEYPATH, IPCSUBID, ONESEM, 0600);
if (semid < 0)
{
  fprintf(stderr, "Failed to create the semaphore set, errno=%d\n", semid);
  return(-3);
}

/* Initialize the value of the semaphore (to be 1) */
ret = init_semaphore_set(semid, ONESEM, 1);
ret = print_semaphore_set(semid, ONESEM);

/* Create the worker processes and let them go to work */
```

```
  for (i = 1; i <= nproc; i++)
  {
    pid = fork();

    if (pid == -1)
    {
      fprintf(stderr, "fork() failed, i=%u, errno=%d\n", i, errno);
    }
    else if (pid == 0)
    {
      /* This is the child process. */
      /* Perform the child process' task here */
      ret = update_shared_file(fname, filesz, '0'+i, updcnt, semid);
      return(ret);
    }
    else
    {
      /* This is the parent process. */
      /* Simply continue */
    }
  }

  /* Wait for all worker processes to finish */
  for (i = 0; i < nproc; i++)
  {
    pid = wait(&stat);
  }

  /* Remove the semaphore */
  ret = semctl(semid, 0, IPC_RMID);
  if (ret == -1)
  {
    fprintf(stderr, "semctl() failed to remove the semaphore set, errno=%d\n",
      errno);
    return(-9);
  }
  fprintf(stdout, "The semaphore set was successfully removed.\n");

  /* Report the update counts from all processes */
  ret = count_char_occurrences(fname);
}

/*
 * Code for the worker process to execute.
 * This function updates a shared file, one block at a time.
 */
int update_shared_file(char *fname, size_t fsize, int newval, size_t updcnt, int
semid)
{
  int    fd;
  int    i;
  int    ret=0;
  unsigned long long  j, k=0;
  struct timeval  tm1, tm2, tm3;

  /* Open the file for read and write */
```

```
    fd = open(fname, O_RDWR, 0644);
    if (fd == -1)
    {
      fprintf(stderr, "open() failed, errno=%d\n", errno);
      return(-errno);
    }

    /* Do the file update until done */
    for (i = updcnt; i > 0; i--)
    {
      /* Acquire the lock */
      ret = lock_semaphore(semid, 0);
      if (ret != 0)
        break;

      /* Update the file */
      ret = random_file_update(fd, fsize, INIT_VALUE, newval);

      /* Introduce some delay here to be a bit more real */
      for (j = 0; j < MAXDELAYCNT; j++)
        k = k + 2;

      /* Release the lock */
      ret = unlock_semaphore(semid, 0);

      if (ret != 0)
        break;
    }

    /* close the file */
    close(fd);
    return(ret);
}
```

        (b) semlib.c

```
/*
 * Utility functions for semaphore example programs.
 * Copyright (c) 2013, 2020 Mr. Jin-Jwei Chen.  All rights reserved.
 */

#include "mysemutil.h"
#include <string.h>        /* memset() */

/*
 * This function gets and returns the identifier of the semaphore set specified.
 * It also creates the semaphore set if it does not already exist.
 * It returns a negative value on failure.
 * Parameters:
 *    pathname (IN) : a pathname identifying the semaphore set
 *    projid   (IN) : combined with pathname to uniquely identifying the
 *                    semaphore set
 *    nsems    (IN) : number of semaphores in the semaphore set
 *    perm     (IN) : permission of the semaphore set
 * Return value:
 *    on success: semaphore id (a non-negative integer)
```

```
 *    on failure: negative value of the errno
 */

int get_semaphore_set(char *pathname, int projid, int nsems, size_t perm)
{
  key_t   ipckey;
  int     semid;

  if (pathname == NULL)
    return(-EINVAL);

  /* Compute the IPC key value from the pathname and project id */
  /* ftok() got error 2 if the pathname does not exist. */
  if ((ipckey = ftok(pathname, projid)) == (key_t)-1) {
    fprintf(stderr, "ftok() failed, errno=%d\n", errno);
    return(-errno);
  }

  /* Create the semaphore if it doesn't exist and get the identifier */
  semid = semget(ipckey, nsems, IPC_CREAT|perm);
  if (semid == -1)
  {
    fprintf(stderr, "semget() failed, errno=%d\n", errno);
    return(-errno);
  }

  return(semid);
}

/*
 * This function sets the value of each semaphore in a semaphore set.
 * Parameters:
 *    semid  (IN) : identifier of the semaphore set
 *    nsems  (IN) : number of semaphores in the semaphore set
 *    semval (IN) : new value of each semaphore
 * Return value:
 *    on success: 0
 *    on failure: the negative value of errno
 */
int init_semaphore_set(int semid, int nsems, int semval)
{
  semun   semarg;
  int     ret;
  int     i;

  if ((semid < 0) || (nsems <= 0))
    return(-EINVAL);

  semarg.array = (unsigned short *)malloc((size_t) (nsems * sizeof(short)));
  if (semarg.array == NULL)
    return(-ENOMEM);
  memset((void *)semarg.array, 0, (size_t) (nsems * sizeof(short)));

  /* Set the semaphores' values */
  for (i=0; i < nsems; i++)
    semarg.array[i] = semval;
```

```c
  ret = semctl(semid, 0, SETALL, semarg);
  if (ret == -1)
  {
    fprintf(stderr, "semctl() failed to set all, errno=%d\n", errno);
    free(semarg.array);
    return(-errno);
  }

  free(semarg.array);
  return(0);
}

/*
 * This function prints the value of each semaphore in a semaphore set.
 * Parameters:
 *    semid   (IN) : identifier of the semaphore set
 *    nsems   (IN) : number of semaphores in the semaphore set
 * Return value:
 *    on success: 0
 *    on failure: the negative value of errno
 */
int print_semaphore_set(int semid, int nsems)
{
  semun   semarg;
  int     ret;
  int     i;

  if ((semid < 0) || (nsems <= 0))
    return(-EINVAL);

  semarg.array = (unsigned short *)malloc((size_t) (nsems * sizeof(short)));
  if (semarg.array == NULL)
    return(-ENOMEM);

  /* Get the semaphores' values */
  for (i=0; i < nsems; i++)
    semarg.array[i] = 0;

  ret = semctl(semid, 0, GETALL, semarg);
  if (ret == -1)
  {
    fprintf(stderr, "semctl() failed to get all, errno=%d\n", errno);
    free(semarg.array);
    return(-errno);
  }

  for (i=0; i < nsems; i++)
    fprintf(stdout, "  semval[%5u]=%d\n", i, semarg.array[i]);

  free(semarg.array);
  return(0);
}

/*
 * This function acquires the lock on a binary semaphore.
```

```
 * A semaphore value of 1 means the lock is available.
 * A semaphore value of 0 means the lock is unavailable.
 * This expects the semaphore's value to be initialized to 1 to begin with.
 * This function attempts to decrement the semaphore's value by 1 to obtain
 * the lock.
 */
int lock_semaphore(int semid, int semnum)
{
  struct sembuf    semoparg;
  int              ret;

  /* See if we can decrement the semaphore's value from 1 to 0 */
  semoparg.sem_num = semnum;    /* starting from 0 */
  semoparg.sem_op  = -1;   /* assume semval is 1 when the lock is not taken */
  semoparg.sem_flg = (SEM_UNDO);
  if ((ret = semop(semid, &semoparg, 1)) == -1) {
    fprintf(stderr, "semop() failed to lock, errno=%d\n", errno);
    return(-errno);
  }

  return(0);
}


/*
 * This function releases the lock on a binary semaphore.
 * A semaphore value of 1 means the lock is available.
 * A semaphore value of 0 means the lock is unavailable.
 * This expects the semaphore's value to be initialized to 1 to begin with.
 * This function attempts to increment the semaphore's value by 1 to make
 * it available.
 */
int unlock_semaphore(int semid, int semnum)
{
  struct sembuf    semoparg;
  int              ret;

  /* Increment the semaphore's value by 1 */
  semoparg.sem_num = semnum;    /* starting from 0 */
  semoparg.sem_op  = 1;   /* assume semval is 1 when the lock is not taken */
  semoparg.sem_flg = (SEM_UNDO);
  if ((ret = semop(semid, &semoparg, 1)) == -1) {
    fprintf(stderr, "semop() failed to unlock, errno=%d\n", errno);
    return(-errno);
  }

  return(0);
}


/*
 * This function creates a file of the specified name, size (in bytes) and
 * permission and fills it with the value specified.
 * Parameters:
 *    fname (IN) - pathname of the file to be created
 *    fsize (IN) - size of the file in bytes
 *    val   (IN) - initial byte value for the entire file
 *    perm  (IN) - permission of the file
```

507

```c
 * Return value:
 *    0 if success, or a negative value if failure
 */

int create_file(char *fname, size_t fsize, unsigned char val, int perm)
{
  char    buf[BUFSZ];
  size_t  count, chunk;
  ssize_t bytes;
  int     fd;
  int     ret=0;
  char    *bufadr;      /* starting address of the buffer to write */

  if (fname == NULL || (fsize <= 0))
    return(-1);

  /* Open the file for write only. Create it if it does not already exist.
   * Truncate it if it exists already.
   */
  fd = open(fname, O_WRONLY|O_CREAT|O_TRUNC, perm);
  if (fd == -1)
  {
    fprintf(stderr, "open() failed, errno=%d\n", errno);
    return(-2);
  }

  /* Fill the buffer with the value to write */
  memset(buf, val, BUFSZ);
  count = fsize;

  /* For easy identification, we start each block with a 'A'.
   * Remove this inserted additional step if you want a uniform file.
   */
  buf[0] = buf[BLKSZ] = 'A';

  /* Fill the file with the initial value specified */
  while (count > 0)
  {
    if (count > BUFSZ)
      chunk = BUFSZ;
    else
      chunk = count;
    count = count - chunk;

    bufadr = buf;
    while (chunk > 0)
    {
      bytes = write(fd, bufadr, chunk);
      if (bytes == -1)
      {
        fprintf(stderr, "failed to write to output file, errno=%d\n", errno);
        close(fd);
        return(-3);
      }
      chunk = chunk - bytes;
      bufadr = bufadr + bytes;
```

```
    }   /* inner while */
  }   /* outer while */

  /* Close the file */
  close(fd);
  return(ret);
}


/*
 * This function randomly picks a block from a file and updates the very
 * first byte of it that is not the initial value as specified by the
 * parameter oldval. It replaces the initial byte value with the new byte
 * value specified by the newval parameter.
 * The update repeats for the number of times specified by the updcnt
 * parameter.
 * Parameters:
 *    fd      (IN) - file descriptor of the file to be updated
 *    fsize   (IN) - size of the file in bytes
 *    oldval  (IN) - initial byte value to be updated
 *    newval  (IN) - new byte value to replace the old value
 * Return value:
 *     0 on success or a negative value if failure
 */

int random_file_update(int fd, size_t fsize, unsigned char oldval, unsigned char
newval)
{
  char   buf[BLKSZ];
  size_t    count;         /* number of bytes to read/write */
  ssize_t   bytes_done;    /* number of bytes that were read/written */
  size_t    i, j;
  off_t     offset;
  size_t    nblks;
  size_t    blkno;
  char      *bufadr;

  if ((fd <= 0) || (fsize <= 0))
     return(-1);

  /* Compute the total number of full blocks in the file */
  nblks = (fsize / BLKSZ);
  if (nblks < 1)
     return(-1);

  /* Randomly select a block */
  blkno = (size_t) (rand() % nblks);

  /* Seek to the block selected */
  offset = lseek(fd, (blkno * BLKSZ), SEEK_SET);
  if (offset == (off_t)-1)
  {
    fprintf(stderr, "lseek() failed, errno=%d\n", errno);
    close(fd);
    return(-3);
  }
```

```c
/* Read the file block */
count = BLKSZ;
bufadr = buf;
while (count > 0)
{
  bytes_done = read(fd, bufadr, count);
  if (bytes_done == -1)
  {
    fprintf(stderr, "failed to read from file, errno=%d\n", errno);
    close(fd);
    return(-4);
  }
  count = count - bytes_done;
  bufadr = bufadr + bytes_done;
}  /* while */

/* Update the block by replacing first original byte with the new byte */
for (j = 0; j < BLKSZ; j++)
  if (buf[j] == oldval)
    break;
if (j < BLKSZ)
  buf[j] = newval;

/* Seek to the block selected */
offset = lseek(fd, (blkno * BLKSZ), SEEK_SET);
if (offset == (off_t)-1)
{
  fprintf(stderr, "lseek() failed before write, errno=%d\n", errno);
  close(fd);
  return(-5);
}

/* Write back the block */
count = BLKSZ;
bufadr = buf;
while (count > 0)
{
  bytes_done = write(fd, bufadr, count);
  if (bytes_done == -1)
  {
    fprintf(stderr, "failed to write to output file, errno=%d\n", errno);
    close(fd);
    return(-6);
  }
  count = count - bytes_done;
  bufadr = bufadr + bytes_done;
}  /* while */

sync();

return(0);
}

/*
 * This function randomly picks a block from a file and updates the very
 * first byte of it that is not the initial value as specified by the
```

```
 * parameter oldval. It replaces the initial byte value with the new byte
 * value specified by the newval parameter.
 * The update repeats for the number of times specified by the updcnt
 * parameter.
 * Parameters:
 *    fname   (IN) - pathname of the file to be updated
 *    fsize   (IN) - size of the file in bytes
 *    oldval  (IN) - initial byte value to be updated
 *    newval  (IN) - new byte value to replace the old value
 *    updcnt  (IN) - number of updates to be performed
 * Return value:
 *     0 on success or a negative value if failure
 */

int random_file_update_all(char *fname, size_t fsize, unsigned char oldval, unsigned
char newval, size_t updcnt)
{
  char      buf[BLKSZ];
  size_t    count;          /* number of bytes to read/write */
  ssize_t   bytes_done;     /* number of bytes that were read/written */
  int       fd;
  size_t    i, j;
  off_t     offset;
  size_t    nblks;
  size_t    blkno;
  char      *bufadr;

  if ((fname == NULL) || (fsize <= 0))
    return(-1);

  /* Compute the total number of full blocks in the file */
  nblks = (fsize / BLKSZ);
  if (nblks < 1)
    return(-1);

  /* Open the file for read and write */
  fd = open(fname, O_RDWR, 0644);
  if (fd == -1)
  {
    fprintf(stderr, "open() failed, errno=%d\n", errno);
    return(-2);
  }

  /* Do the file update until done */
  for (i = updcnt; i > 0; i--)
  {
    /* Randomly select a block */
    blkno = (size_t) (rand() % nblks);

    /* Seek to the block selected */
    offset = lseek(fd, (blkno * BLKSZ), SEEK_SET);
    if (offset == (off_t)-1)
    {
      fprintf(stderr, "lseek() failed, errno=%d\n", errno);
      close(fd);
      return(-3);
```

```
    }

    /* Read the file block */
    count = BLKSZ;
    bufadr = buf;
    while (count > 0)
    {
      bytes_done = read(fd, bufadr, count);
      if (bytes_done == -1)
        {
          fprintf(stderr, "failed to read from file, errno=%d\n", errno);
          close(fd);
          return(-4);
        }
      count = count - bytes_done;
      bufadr = bufadr + bytes_done;
    }  /* while */

    /* Update the block by replacing first original byte with the new byte */
    for (j = 0; j < BLKSZ; j++)
      if (buf[j] == oldval)
        break;
    if (j < BLKSZ)
      buf[j] = newval;

    /* Seek to the block selected */
    offset = lseek(fd, (blkno * BLKSZ), SEEK_SET);
    if (offset == (off_t)-1)
    {
      fprintf(stderr, "lseek() failed before write, errno=%d\n", errno);
      close(fd);
      return(-5);
    }


    /* Write back the block */
    count = BLKSZ;
    bufadr = buf;
    while (count > 0)
    {
      bytes_done = write(fd, bufadr, count);
      if (bytes_done == -1)
        {
          fprintf(stderr, "failed to write to output file, errno=%d\n", errno);
          close(fd);
          return(-6);
        }
      count = count - bytes_done;
      bufadr = bufadr + bytes_done;
    }  /* while */
  }  /* for */

  close(fd);
  return(0);
}

/*
```

```
 * This function counts the number of occurrences of each character among
 * '1' ... '9', 'a' ... 'z'.
 */
#define  NCHARS  46
int count_char_occurrences(char *fname)
{
  char    buf[BLKSZ];
  unsigned int occurrences[NCHARS];
  size_t   count;          /* number of bytes to read/write */
  ssize_t  bytes;          /* number of bytes that were read */
  ssize_t  bytes_tot;      /* accumulated number of bytes that were read */
  int      fd;
  size_t   i;
  int      done=0, j;
  char     *bufadr;

  if (fname == NULL)
    return(-1);

  /* Open the file for read */
  fd = open(fname, O_RDONLY, 0644);
  if (fd == -1)
  {
    fprintf(stderr, "open() failed, errno=%d\n", errno);
    return(-2);
  }

  /* Reset the counters */
  for (i = 0; i < NCHARS; i++)
    occurrences[i] = 0;

  /* Read the file block by block and count the character occurrences */
  while (!done)
  {
    /* Read the next block */
    count = BLKSZ;
    bufadr = buf;
    bytes_tot = 0;
    while (count > 0)
    {
      bytes = read(fd, bufadr, count);
      if (bytes == -1)
      {
        fprintf(stderr, "failed to read from file, errno=%d\n", errno);
        close(fd);
        return(-3);
      }
      else if (bytes == 0)
      {
        done = 1;
        break;
      }
      count = count - bytes;
      bufadr = bufadr + bytes;
      bytes_tot = bytes_tot + bytes;
    } /* while */
```

513

```
/* Count the characters in the current blocks */
for (i = 0; i < bytes_tot; i++)
{
  j = -1;
  if ((buf[i] >= '1') && (buf[i] <= '9'))
    j = buf[i] - '0';
  else if ((buf[i] >= 'a') && (buf[i] <= 'z'))
    j = buf[i] - 'a' + 10;
  if (j >= 0)
    occurrences[j] = occurrences[j] + 1;
}
}

/* Print the count -- starting from index 1 */
fprintf(stdout, "Process/Thread  Updates\n");
for (i = 1; i < NCHARS; i++)
  fprintf(stdout, "%8lu %12u\n", i, occurrences[i]);

close(fd);
return(0);
}
```

9-4 Different Types of Locks

Using a lock to synchronize or coordinate the concurrent accesses to a shared data that can be modified to ensure the data integrity and computation correctness is the central concept in concurrency control. Under this concept, there are a number of different types of applications that require a slightly different implementation of the lock involved. As a result, there are different types of locks.

As discussed below, there are at least a couple of ways to classify locks.

9-4-1 Exclusive (Writer) Lock Versus Shared (Reader) Lock

The first classification is based on whether the process/thread with the lock has exclusive access to the shared data/resource or not.
In this classification, a lock can be exclusive or shared.

In some applications, for instance, database, there often exist many client programs where some of them may update the database while others are just interested in reading it. To allow all of them to co-exist and work at the optimal performance at the same time, the locks available on the shared data will have to be both exclusive and shared.

The key thing here is that a writer requires exclusive access to the shared data while a reader requires only shared access. In other words, a writer must block out the rest of the world but a reader can allow many other readers in at the same time. The readers are just querying or reading the data. None of them is going to modify the data. Thus, it is OK for all of them to access (i.e. read) the shared data all at the same time.

Obviously, the compatibility between the two types of locks is as shown in Figure 9-11a.

Figure 9-11a Compatibility between shared(read) and exclusive(write) locks
```
------------------------------------------------
process/thread 1   process/thread 2   compatible
----------------   ----------------   ----------
shared             shared             yes
shared             exclusive          no
exclusive          shared             no
exclusive          exclusive          no
------------------------------------------------
```

Many systems go even a step further by offering more than one type of
shared lock and more than one type of exclusive lock. The goal is to
increase the degree of parallelism or concurrency and thus increasing
throughput by maximizing the sharing through use of more types of locks.
For example, Figure 9-11b below is one possible implementation of the
lock in more than just two modes by introducing the sub-shared and
sub-exclusive modes:

Figure 9-11b Compatibility between sub-shared and sub-exclusive locks

	sub-shared	sub-exclusive	shared	exclusive
sub-shared	Yes	Yes	Yes	No
sub-exclusive	Yes	Yes	No	No
shared	Yes	No	Yes	No
exclusive	No	No	No	No

The exclusive lock is sometimes called the write lock and the shared lock
is called the read lock. A process/thread using a write lock is called
a writer and one using a read lock is referred to as a reader.

Therefore, an update application needs to take a write or exclusive lock
whereas a query application needs to take only a shared, read lock.

For Reader Application:

```
lock(mylock_in_shared_mode);
use (read only) the shared data
unlock(mylock_in_shared_mode);
```

For Writer Application:

```
lock(mylock_in_exclusive_mode);
modify the shared data
unlock(mylock_in_exclusive_mode);
```

9-4-2 Trylock, Spinlock and Timeoutlock

Another classification of locks is based on what the locking routine
does when it tries to acquire a lock but the lock is not available.
There are normally three different ways to implement a lock function.

1. Return right away and don't even try to wait if the lock is unavailable.

   Let the caller decides what to do if the lock happens to be unavailable. This type of locking function is known as a **try lock**. Just try to get the lock, return right away either way, and let the caller decide what it wants to do when the lock is unavailable.

   The advantage of this is the caller is never blocked even if the lock is not available. In case the lock is not available, the caller can decide to try it again, sleep for a very short period of time and try again, or do something else.

   The try lock gives the caller maximum flexibility. However, the caller must have code to handle the case of 'should the lock be unavailable".

   ```
   has_lock = FALSE;
   while (! has_lcok)
   {
       has_lock = try_lock(mylock);
       if (! has_lock)
       {
         sleep(one_millisecond);
         (or do something else)
         /* here you can decide for how long you want to keep trying it */
       }
   }
   do the concurrent update or whatever processing
   unlock(mylock);
   ```

2. Be persistent, keep trying forever and wait until the lock is available.

   This kind of lock is called **'spin lock'**.
   It is based on the philosophy that the lock should be available soon. For applications where the lock is held for only a short period of time, this is a very reasonable implementation.

   The disadvantage of spin locks is that all the time spent by this process/thread on spinning/looping and busy waiting for the lock to become available again is sort of wasted in terms of the CPU resource. That CPU resource could have been used by some other processes/threads for getting some real work done.

   In addition, should there be a program error or bug that the lock is lost or becomes permanently unavailable, any and all processes/threads that try to acquire this lock this way will hang and block indefinitely. This would be a very bad situation to have.

   On the positive side, spin lock is very easy and simple to use. All the application needs to do is this:

   ```
   spin_lock(mylock);
   do the concurrent update or whatever processing.
   unlock(mylock);
   ```

   As you can see, this code is extremely simple and straightforward. As long as there is no bug that results in hang, this is the simplest and it works great.

3. Try to be persistent, spin and wait, though not forever.

   This type of lock is known as **timeout lock**. It's a spin lock with a timeout.

   The idea is that in case the lock is not available, keep trying to get it for some limited amount of time. Once that time period expires, give up and return.

   This is a middle ground solution. The locking routine makes some best effort but does not go extreme to try forever.
   Usually the timeout period is variable and can be specified by the caller. Thus, it is flexible.

   The caller's logic is somewhat similar to that in case 1 above.

   ```
   has_lock = FALSE;
   while (! has_lcok)
   {
      has_lock = timeout_lock(mylock, time_out_period);
      if (! has_lock)
      {
        sleep(one_millisecond);
        (or do something else or return error)
      }
   }
   do the concurrent update or whatever processing
   unlock(mylock);
   ```

In terms of how many times or how long it re-tries when the lock is not available, there are essentially three types of locks as we have just described, as shown in Figure 9-12.

Figure 9-12 Trylock, spinlock, timeoutlock

```
------------------------------------------------------------------

   Lock Type              Characteristics
   ---------------        -------------------------------------------
1. Try lock            try it only once
2. Spin lock           try forever until it acquires the lock
3. Timeout lock        try it for up to some period of time
------------------------------------------------------------------
```

In the following section, we will demonstrate how to implement some of these types of locks by writing our own locking functions in assembly language to get a 30-80+% performance gain over semaphores.

9-5 Design and Implement Your Own Locking Routines

It comes handy when the operating systems (such as Linux and Unix), the languages (such as Java), or the software libraries (such as the pthreads library) you use provide locking facilities for your program to use.

However, there are situations where you may want to or have to develop your own locking routines. For instance, if the operating system or programming language you use does not provide any locking functions. Or they do but its performance is not as desirable, or they do not have exactly what you need.

In this section, we will show you how to design and implement some of the basic locking functions on your own in assembly language. Doing so achieves both guaranteed correctness and best performance. It not only lets you truly understand how computer achieves the most fundamental data integrity, and at its highest speed, but also lets you become a concurrency control provider. What we demonstrate here is exactly many current commercial database management systems do internally to achieve **data integrity** and **best performance**.

This coverage offers at least two benefits. First, it lets the readers really understand how computer concurrency control is actually done at the lowest level -- the assembly language instruction level. Second, as we will show later in section 9-5-2-8 in this chapter, these assembly language routines that we design and implement ourselves provide a big performance advantage over the System V semaphore locking facility offered by the operating systems.

According to our own performance measurements, the performance of these locking functions ranges from 25% to 80+% faster than the System V semaphore, depending on the processors, operating systems and versions.

9-5-1 Designing Your Own Locking Routines

A lock is normally implemented by using an integer variable. Although in its simplest form, only a single bit is needed, a memory location of 8-bit, 16-bit, 32-bit or 64-bit is normally used for availability and efficiency reasons. (Some processors may have bit instructions available for use while others may not.) In general, you want to use a memory location whose size is the same as the processor's word size. For instance, in a 32- or 64-bit processor, you may want to use a 4-byte integer. But it will depend on what word size is actually supported by the instruction(s) we use.

In our example, we will use an integer variable of an int type in C as the lock variable. (Note that a C int type variable occupies a memory location that is normally 4 bytes (32 bits) in a 32-bit or 64-bit computer.) Since only a single bit is needed, we will use the lowest bit (bit 0) (i.e. the least significant bit) of it if such a bit manipulation instruction is available. If not, we will use the whole word for it -- setting the value of the entire integer to 1 or 0.

The convention we will use is that if the lock's value is 0, it means the lock is free and available. If the lock's value is 1, it means the lock is taken and not available.

Based on this convention we set, to acquire a lock, the locking function will have to 'peek into' the current value of the lock variable and see if it is 0, and set it to 1 if it is currently 0. If it can do so, then it can declare it has successfully acquired the lock.
To release a lock, the unlocking function will have to peek into the current value of the lock variable and see if it is 1 and set it to 0 if it is currently 1, or simply always set it to 0 regardless.

Note that the locking or unlocking operation itself must be atomic! That is, the operation must be inseparable. It has to be atomic (all or nothing) for the whole concept to work. Otherwise, two or more simultaneous processes/threads could all find the lock value being 0 and set it to 1. And all of them will think they get the lock. Hence, it could end up with two or more processes/threads getting the same lock at the same time. This completely breaks the basic premise of the locking concept that only one process/thread is allowed to hold the lock at any given time! When two or more processes/threads can hold the same lock at the same time, there is no exclusive access to the same data/resource and the update operations are not serialized anymore. And consequently, the integrity of the shared data/resource is no longer guaranteed.

Although we write our own locking routines in assembly language, our goal is to make it also callable from a C program, which is exactly how we will demonstrate it in this section.

To be consistent with the convention used in Unix/Linux and C, our locking functions will return 0 for success and -1 for failure. For a routine trying to obtain a lock, success means it has found the lock available and changed it to be unavailable. That is, it has successfully acquired the lock. Failure means it fails to get the lock. (Some of you might find returning 1 for success and 0 for failure more desirable because that way the caller can check the return result as a boolean value. But it's a matter of choice and preference. Here we choose to be consistent with the traditional Unix/Linux and C interface convention.)

In this section, we will design and implement the following three locking functions:

1. int spinlock(int *lockvar)
2. int unlock(int *lockvar)
3. int trylock(int *lockvar)

These functions are implemented in the following three assembly language programs:

1. spinlock.s
2. unlock.s
3. trylock.s

The unlock() function releases the lock by setting the value of the lock variable to 0. If it finds the original value was already 0, it returns -1. Otherwise, it returns 0 for success.

The trylock() function attempts to acquire the lock by setting the lock variable's value to 1. If it finds the original value was 0, it returns 0 for success, meaning successfully getting the lock. If it finds the original value of the lock variable was already 1, it returns -1 for failing to obtain the lock. Whether getting the lock or not, the trylock() function makes only one attempt to obtain the lock. It returns right away after that.

The spinlock() function is similar to the trylock() function except if it finds the lock unavailable it will loop and continue to try to get the lock until it has successfully done so or forever.

9-5-1-1 What Is Required?

What is required to implement your own super-efficient locking routines in assembly language is an atomic assembly language instruction or sequence from the processor that allows you to test-and-set or swap the value of some memory location (i.e. an integer variable).

Ultimately, computers execute instructions at machine or assembly language level to get work done. Therefore, update loss problems occur at that level and must be analyzed and solved at that same level, too. **This is why assembly language instructions that can perform the atomic test-and-set or swap operation is what is needed to implement the locking.**

So, to write your own locking routine, the first thing you need to do is to search the assembly language instruction set of the computer processor you are using for such an instruction. Once you get that, then the next task is to understand it and learn how to use it.

If you adopt the convention that the value 0 in the lock variable means the lock is available and the value 1 means the lock is not available, then your locking function is to test if the current value of the lock variable is 0 and set it to 1 if it is. Being able to do so means it has successfully acquired the lock. The unlocking function is to set the lock variable's value to 0.

Both of the locking and unlocking functions should return a value indicating success or failure. Failure of the locking function means it does not obtain the lock. Failure of the unlocking function means it discovers the the lock was not taken, i.e. the original value is already 0.

Figure 9-13 Atomic assembly instructions for lock implementation

Processor	Assembly language instruction(s) for locking
Intel x86	bts, btr
IBM PowerPC	lwarx and stwcx.
Oracle/Sun SPARC	cas
HP PARISC	LDCW and CMPIB
HP/DEC Alpha	ldq_l and stq_c (or ldl_l and stl_c)

The table in Figure 9-13 lists the atomic assembly language instruction(s) that can be used to implement the locking and unlocking functions for some of the most popular processors. As you can see, it is the bit-test-and-set (bts) instruction on Intel x86 microprocessors, the lwarx and stwcx. instruction pair on IBM PowerPC processor, compare and swap (cas) instruction on Oracle Sun SPARC processor, LDCW and CMPIB instruction pair on HP PARISC processor, and the load locked and store conditional instruction pair on HP/DEC Alpha processor.

9-5-1-2 Don't Implement the Locking Routine in High Level Language

Normally, an assembly language instruction is atomic. That is, the operation it carries out occurs all or nothing. For locking to work, the lock and unlock operations must be atomic.

This atomicity is the reason why we have to implement our own locking functions in assembly language. We have to pick and use only some very specific assembly language instructions to get our job done. Usually each processor has only one or two of this kind of instructions. Some processors in the old days did not even have such instructions and it has to be emulated.

Don't ever try to implement your own locking and unlocking functions in a high level programming language, for instance C. One of my first assignments in the industry was to fix a RDBMS hang problem. After my analysis, I found it was caused by the following C statement in the RDBMS source code:

```
if (lockvar == 0)    /* if the lock is available */
    lockvar = 1;     /* lock it */
```

This simple C statement tries to get the lock represented by the variable named lockvar. You may think this looks OK and should work. But it doesn't!

As we mentioned above, for locking to work, the lock and unlock operations must both be atomic.

The problem with the above statement is that no compiler is that smart to know that this entire statement above must be translated into a single assembly language instruction for it to work. As a result, it's typically translated into a read instruction first followed by another write one. So, the problem shown in Figure 9-2 occurs.

Even on a single processor with single execution unit, the interleaving of executing this statement between multiple processes or threads will often result in either two or more of them acquire the same lock at the same time (which will cause update loss or data corruption), or they will step on each other's toes and cause the lock to be forever lost and thus lead to hang.

After replacing the above C statement with the locking function in assembly language like the one we show in this section, the hang problem was forever fixed. Of course, similar thing was done for the unlock operation, too.

The only way that it works in a high-level language implementation is to call assembly language locking/unlocking routines like the ones we show below, or to invoke locking/unlocking functions that lock/unlock a semaphore, a pthreads mutex, or alike!

9-5-2 Implement Your Own Locking Routines

To implement your own locking routines in assembly language, you need to know at least a few things.

1. The names of the general-purpose registers that you can use.

2. Where you can retrieve the arguments to the function.
3. How do you return a value to the caller
4. What instruction(s) you can use to perform an atomic test-and-set
   or swap operation.

Writing assembly language code requires using some of the CPU registers.
Therefore, in order for us to implement our own locking functions in
assembly language, we need to get familiar with what CPU registers are
available for use on the processor we are programming.

Each processor puts the input argument(s) to a function in a different place.
They also use different registers to return a value.

Be aware that the memory location of the lock variable must be accessible
from all threads or processes that will use the lock. In a multithreaded
application, this can be a global variable within the program that all
threads have access to. In a multi-process environment, the lock variable
would have to exist in some shared memory that is shared among the
processes.

9-5-2-1 Intel x86 Architecture (Linux and Unix)

The Intel x86 processors have four general-purpose registers for programmers
to use. They are registers A, B, C and D.
Depending on whether you are on a 8-, 16-, 32-, or 64-bit processor,
their names are listed below:

```
8-bit:  AH AL  BH BL  CH CL  DH DL
16-bit: AX      BX     CX     DX     BP   SI   DI   SP
32-bit: EAX     EBX    ECX    EDX    EBP  ESI  EDI  ESP
64-bit: RAX     RBX    RCX    RDX    RBP  RSI  RDI  RSP
```

On Intel x86 processors, upon entry into an assembly language routine, the
input arguments are deposited on stack. Upon exit, the EAX register is used
to hold the return value.

The atomic instructions you can use to implement locking on the Intel x86
family of processors are the following:

```
BTS (Bit Test and Set)
BTR (Bit Test and Reset)
```

The BTS instruction saves the current value of the selected bit into the
carry flag (the CF flag) and then sets the value of that bit to 1.
It performs the test-and-set operation for the selected bit and saves the
original value of the selected bit in the carry flag of the status register.
The code can then decide what to do based on the value of the carry flag.
Clearly, you use the BTS instruction to obtain a lock.

The BTR instruction is sort of the opposite of the BTS instruction.
It performs the test and clear operation. The BTR instruction saves the
current value of the selected bit into the carry flag (the CF flag) and
then clears that bit (i.e. resetting its value to 0).
Clearly, you use the BTR instruction to release a lock.

Figure 9-14 shows the 32-bit version of spinlock() routine for the Intel
x86 architecture. Its 64-bit version can be easily obtained by slight
modifications to 64-bit spinlock.s or 64-bit trylock.s of the Apple Mac Pro
Darwin as shown in Figure 9-17.

Upon entry, the ESP register points to the top of the stack.
The first thing we do is to save the original contents of the EBP register
by pushing it onto stack. We then make a copy of the contents of the ESP
register into the EBP register so that we can use it.
Then we retrieve the first argument to this function from the stack
(at offset 8 from top of the stack) and save it in the EAX register.

The 'bts $0,(%eax)' instruction tests the value of bit 0 (the lowest bit)
of the memory location selected by the address held in the EAX register.
If that value is 1, the carry flag will be set after the bts instruction.
In that case, we did not get the lock and thus branch back and try it again.
(The jc instruction does a jump to the specified destination if the Carry
Flag is set.) Otherwise, if the original value is 0 (i.e. the Carry Flag
is not set), the jump won't happen and we fall through and continue to
execute the next instruction. Since the bts instruction has set the bit value
to 1, we have just successfully acquired the lock. Hence, we put a 0 in
the EAX register and return that to the caller after we restore the original
contents of the EBP register.

Note that the LOCK prefix in front of the BTS instruction is used to prevent
the instruction from being interrupted for any reason when it modifies
memory.

Figure 9-14 Spinlock() function for Intel x86 architecture (32-bit)

```
spinlock:
        pushl    %ebp             # Save current contents of EBP register
        movl     %esp, %ebp       # Copy contents of stack pointer to EBP register
        movl     8(%ebp), %eax    # Get the input memory address into EAX
spin:
        lock bts $0, (%eax)       # Set the lowest bit of that location to 1
        jc       spin             # Loop if the Carry Flag (old value) is set (1)
        movl     $0, %eax         # Return success (0) if old value was 0
        popl     %ebp             # Restore contents of the temp register we used
        ret                       # Return
```

Figure 9-15 further shows the trylock() and unlock() functions for
the Intel x86 architecture, both 32-bit and 64-bit.

Figure 9-15 Trylock() and unlock() functions for Intel x86 Architecture

(a) unlock.s

(1) 32-bit

```
# This routine performs an unlock operation by clearing the bit value
# (i.e. setting it to 0) representing the lock.
# We are using the lowest bit of an integer variable as the lock.
# The address of this integer variable is the input argument to this function.
# This function returns 0 if the old bit value is 1, meaning successfully freeing
```

```
# the lock. It returns -1 if the old bit value is 0, meaning the lock was
# already freed before us. The returned value is 32-bit (of C type int).
# 32-bit version for Intel x86 processors.
# Authored by Mr. Jin-Jwei Chen.
# Copyright (c) 1989-2016, Mr. Jin-Jwei Chen. All rights reserved.
#
        .file   "unlock.s"
        .text
.globl unlock
        .type   unlock, @function
unlock:
        pushl   %ebp                # Save current contents of EBP register
        movl    %esp, %ebp          # Copy contents of stack pointer to EBP register
        movl    8(%ebp), %eax       # Get the input memory address into EAX
        lock btr $0, (%eax)         # Set the lowest bit of that location to 0
        jnc     missit              # Jump if the Carry Flag (old value) is not 1
        movl    $0, %eax            # Return success (0) if old value was 1
        popl    %ebp                # Restore contents of the temp register we used
        ret                         # Return
missit:
        movl    $-1, %eax           # Return error (-1) if old value was 0 already
        popl    %ebp                # Restore contents of the temp register we used
        ret                         # Return
```

(2) 64-bit

```
# This routine performs an unlock operation by clearing the bit value
# (i.e. setting it to 0) representing the lock.
# We are using the lowest bit of an integer variable as the lock.
# The address of this integer variable is the input argument to this function.
# This function returns 0 if the old bit value is 1, meaning successfully freeing
# the lock. It returns -1 if the old bit value is 0, meaning the lock was
# already freed before us. The returned value is 32-bit (of C type int).
# 64-bit version for Intel x86 processors.
# Authored by Mr. Jin-Jwei Chen.
# Copyright (c) 1989-2016, Mr. Jin-Jwei Chen. All rights reserved.
#
        .file   "unlock.s"
        .text
.globl unlock
        .type   unlock, @function
unlock:
        pushq   %rbp
        movq    %rsp, %rbp
        movq    %rdi, -8(%rbp)
        movq    -8(%rbp), %rax      # Save value of input address (argument) in RAX
        lock btr $0, (%rax)         # Set the lowest bit of that location to 0
        jnc     missit              # Jump if the Carry Flag (old value) is not 1
        movl    $0, %eax            # Return success (0) if old value was 1
        leave                       # This restores contents of RBP from stack.
        ret
missit:
        movl    $-1, %eax           # Return error (-1) if old value was 0 already
        leave                       # This restores contents of RBP from stack.
        ret
```

(b) `trylock.s`

(1) 32-bit

```
# This routine performs a lock operation by setting the bit value
# representing the lock to 1 if its current value is 0.
# We are using the lowest bit of an integer variable as the lock.
# The address of this integer variable is the input argument to this function.
# This function returns 0 if the old bit value is 0, meaning successfully
# acquiring the lock. It returns -1 if the old bit value is 1, meaning the lock
# was already taken before us. The returned value is 32-bit (of C type int).
# 32-bit version for Intel x86 processors.
# Authored by Mr. Jin-Jwei Chen.
# Copyright (c) 1989-2016, Mr. Jin-Jwei Chen. All rights reserved.
#
        .file   "trylock.s"
        .text
.globl trylock
        .type   trylock, @function
trylock:
        pushl   %ebp            # Save current contents of EBP register
        movl    %esp, %ebp      # Copy contents of stack pointer to EBP register
        movl    8(%ebp), %eax   # Get the input memory address into EAX
        lock bts $0, (%eax)     # Set the lowest bit of that location to 1
        jc      missit          # Jump if the Carry Flag (old value) is set (1)
        movl    $0, %eax        # Return success (0) if old value was 0
        popl    %ebp            # Restore contents of the temp register we used
        ret                     # Return
missit:
        movl    $-1, %eax       # Return error (-1) if old value was 1 already
        popl    %ebp            # Restore contents of the temp register we used
        ret                     # Return
```

(2) 64-bit

```
# This routine performs a lock operation by setting the bit value
# representing the lock to 1 if its current value is 0.
# We are using the lowest bit of an integer variable as the lock.
# The address of this integer variable is the input argument to this function.
# This function returns 0 if the old bit value is 0, meaning successfully
# acquiring the lock. It returns -1 if the old bit value is 1, meaning the lock
# was already taken before us. The returned value is 32-bit (of C type int).
# 64-bit version for Intel x86 processors.
# Authored by Mr. Jin-Jwei Chen.
# Copyright (c) 1989-2016, Mr. Jin-Jwei Chen. All rights reserved.
#
        .file   "trylock.s"
        .text
.globl trylock
        .type   trylock, @function
trylock:
        pushq   %rbp
        movq    %rsp, %rbp
        movq    %rdi, -8(%rbp)
        movq    -8(%rbp), %rax  # Save value of input address (argument) in RAX
        lock bts $0, (%rax)     # Set the lowest bit of that location to 1
```

```
        jc      missit              # Jump if the Carry Flag (old value) is set (1)
        movl    $0, %eax            # Return success (0) if old value was 0
        leave
        ret
missit:
        movl    $-1, %eax           # Return error (-1) if old value was 1 already
        leave
        ret
```

Figure 9-16 is a new version of the semupdf.c. This semupdf_mylock.c is
the same as semupdf.c except that it replaces the locking and unlocking
routines using semaphore with our own locking and unlocking routines in
assembly language. As you can see, the program becomes simpler and shorter,
although it works the same way.

Figure 9-16 Concurrent updates of shared file using our own lock routines
(semupdf_mylock.c)

```
/*
 * Concurrent updates of a shared file by multiple threads using
 * our own locking routines in assembly language.
 * cc -o semupdf_mylock semupdf_mylock.c semlib.o spinlock.o unlock.o -lpthread
 * Copyright (c) 2013, 2020 Mr. Jin-Jwei Chen.  All rights reserved.
 */

#include "mysemutil.h"

/* Default values related to the shared file */
#define   NMB         2                 /* number of megabytes */
#define   ONEMB       (1024*1024)        /* one megabytes */
#define   DEFFILESZ   (NMB*ONEMB)        /* default file size in bytes */
#define   NTHREADS    4                 /* number of concurrent threads */
#define   MAXNTHREADS 12                /* max. number of concurrent threads */
#define   DEF_FNAME   "semsharedf1"      /* name of the shared file */
#define   DEFUPDCNT   1000              /* default update count */
#define   MAXDELAYCNT 10000            /* delay count */

/* Shared lock variable */
int       lockvar=0;

/* Shared file name and file size */
char     *fname;
size_t    filesz;

/* These are our own locking functions in assembly language. */
int spinlock(int *lockvar);
int unlock(int *lockvar);

int update_shared_file(char *fname, size_t fsize, int newval, size_t updcnt, int
*lockvar);

/*
 * The worker thread.
 */

int worker_thread(void *args)
```

```
{
  unsigned int   *argp;
  unsigned int   myid;
  unsigned int   updcnt;
  int            ret;
  int            newval;

  /* Extract input arguments (two unsigned integers) */
  argp = (unsigned int *)args;
  if (argp != NULL)
  {
    myid = argp[0];
    updcnt = argp[1];
  }
  else
    pthread_exit((void *)(-1));

  fprintf(stdout, "Worker thread: myid=%u updcnt=%u\n", myid, updcnt);

  /* Do my job */
  if (myid < 10)
    newval = '0' + myid;
  else
    newval = 'a' + (myid - 10);

  ret = update_shared_file(fname, filesz, newval, updcnt, &lockvar);
  if (ret != 0)
  {
    fprintf(stderr, "Worker thread: myid=%u, update_shared_file() failed, "
      "ret=%d\n", myid, ret);
    pthread_exit((void *)(-2));
  }

  pthread_exit((void *)0);
}

int main(int argc, char *argv[])
{
  int      nthrd;                         /* actual number of worker threads */
  int      ret, retval;
  int      i;
  char     def_fname[64] = DEF_FNAME;   /* default file name */
  size_t   updcnt = DEFUPDCNT;          /* each thread's file update count */
  pthread_t      thrds[MAXNTHREADS];       /* threads */
  unsigned int   args[MAXNTHREADS][2];     /* arguments for each thread */

  if ((argc > 1) &&
      ((strcmp(argv[1], "-h") == 0) || (strcmp(argv[1], "-help") == 0)))
  {
    fprintf(stdout, "Usage: %s [nthrd] [MBs] [updcnt] [fname]\n", argv[0]);
    return(-1);
  }

  /*
   * Get the number of concurrent threads, update count, file size and
   * file name from the user, if any.
```

```
  */
  nthrd = NTHREADS;
  if (argc > 1)
  {
    nthrd = atoi(argv[1]);
    if (nthrd <= 0)
      nthrd = NTHREADS;
    if (nthrd > MAXNTHREADS)
      nthrd = MAXNTHREADS;
  }

  filesz = DEFFILESZ;
  if (argc > 2)
  {
    filesz = atoi(argv[2]);
    if (filesz > 0)
      filesz = (filesz * ONEMB);
  }
  if (filesz <= 0)
    filesz = DEFFILESZ;

  updcnt = DEFUPDCNT;
  if (argc > 3)
    updcnt = atoi(argv[3]);
  if (updcnt <= 0)
    updcnt = DEFUPDCNT;

  fname = def_fname;
  if (argc > 4)
    fname = argv[4];

  fprintf(stdout, "Updating file %s of %lu bytes using %u concurrent threads,"
    " %lu updates each.\n" , fname, filesz, nthrd, updcnt);

  /* Create the shared file */
  ret = create_file(fname, filesz, INIT_VALUE, 0644);
  if (ret < 0)
  {
    fprintf(stderr, "Failed to create the shared file\n");
    return(-2);
  }

  /* Load up the input arguments for each worker thread */
  for (i = 0; i < nthrd; i++)
  {
    args[i][0] = i+1;          /* worker id starts with 1 */
    args[i][1] = updcnt;
  }

  /* Create the worker threads to concurrently update the shared file */
  for (i = 0; i < nthrd; i++)
  {
    ret = pthread_create(&thrds[i], (pthread_attr_t *)NULL,
        (void *(*)(void *))worker_thread, (void *)args[i]);
    if (ret != 0)
    {
```

```
        fprintf(stderr, "Failed to create the worker thread\n");
        return(3);
    }
}

/*
 * Wait for each of the child threads to finish and retrieve its returned
 * value.
 */
for (i = 0;  i < nthrd;  i++)
{
    ret = pthread_join(thrds[i], (void **)&retval);
    fprintf(stdout, "Thread %u exited with return value %d\n", i, retval);
}

/* Report the update counts from all threads */
ret = count_char_occurrences(fname);
}

/*
 * Code for the worker process to execute.
 * This function updates a shared file, one block at a time.
 */
int update_shared_file(char *fname, size_t fsize, int newval, size_t updcnt, int
*lockvar)
{
    int     fd;
    int     i;
    int     ret=0;
    unsigned long long  j, k=0;
    struct timeval  tm1, tm2, tm3;

    /* Open the file for read and write */
    fd = open(fname, O_RDWR, 0644);
    if (fd == -1)
    {
        fprintf(stderr, "open() failed, errno=%d\n", errno);
        return(-errno);
    }

    /* Do the file update until done */
    for (i = updcnt; i > 0; i--)
    {
        /* Acquire the lock */
        ret = spinlock(lockvar);
        if (ret != 0)
            break;

        /* Update the file */
        ret = random_file_update(fd, fsize, INIT_VALUE, newval);

        /* Introduce some delay here to create more overlap and contention */
        for (j = 0; j < MAXDELAYCNT; j++)
            k = k + 2;

        /* Release the lock */
```

```
        ret = unlock(lockvar);

    if (ret != 0)
        break;
    }

    /* close the file */
    close(fd);
    return(ret);
}
```

This program example demonstrates how you can replace the semaphore with
your own locking routines in assembly language for doing concurrency control
within a program.

In the following sections, we will discuss how to implement our own locking
routines in assembly language in IBM PowerPC architecture, Oracle Sun SPARC
architecture, HP PARISC and Alpha processors, and Apple Mac Pro on Intel x86
with Darwin.

9-5-2-2 Apple Mac Pro on Intel x86 (Darwin)

As of this writing, Apple Mac is using Intel x86 processors. Therefore,
the assembly language code is the same as listed in the preceding section
for Intel Linux except a couple of very minor differences.

The only thing is Apple Darwin has a couple of syntactic differences.
As shown in Figure 9-17, each routine name must start with the underscore
character. Besides, you define the routine using a directive like this:

```
        .globl _spinlock
```

Figure 9-17 Spinlock() function for Intel x86 architecture in Apple Darwin

(a) spinlock.s (64-bit)

```
        .file    "spinlock.s"
        .text
.globl _spinlock
#       .type    spinlock, @function
_spinlock:
        pushq    %rbp
        movq     %rsp, %rbp
        movq     %rdi, -8(%rbp)
        movq     -8(%rbp), %rax    # Save value of input address (argument) in RAX
spin:
        lock bts $0, (%rax)        # Set the lowest bit of that location to 1
        jc       spin              # Loop if the Carry Flag (old value) is set (1)
        movl     $0, %eax          # Return success (0) if old value was 0
        leave
        ret
```

(b) unlock.s (64-bit)

```
        .file    "unlock.s"
```

```
        .text
.globl _unlock
#       .type   unlock, @function
_unlock:
        pushq   %rbp
        movq    %rsp, %rbp
        movq    %rdi, -8(%rbp)
        movq    -8(%rbp), %rax    # Save value of input address (argument) in RAX
        lock btr  $0, (%rax)      # Set the lowest bit of that location to 0
        jnc     missit            # Jump if the Carry Flag (old value) is not 1
        movl    $0, %eax          # Return success (0) if old value was 1
        leave                     # This restores contents of RBP from stack.
        ret
missit:
        movl    $-1, %eax         # Return error (-1) if old value was 0 already
        leave                     # This restores contents of RBP from stack.
        ret
```

(c) trylock.s (64-bit)

```
        .file   "trylock.s"
        .text
.globl _trylock
#       .type   trylock, @function
_trylock:
        pushq   %rbp
        movq    %rsp, %rbp
        movq    %rdi, -8(%rbp)
        movq    -8(%rbp), %rax    # Save value of input address (argument) in RAX
        lock bts  $0, (%rax)      # Set the lowest bit of that location to 1
        jc      missit            # Jump if the Carry Flag (old value) is set (1)
        movl    $0, %eax          # Return success (0) if old value was 0
        leave
        ret
missit:
        movl    $-1, %eax         # Return error (-1) if old value was 1 already
        leave
        ret
```

9-5-2-3 IBM PowerPC Architecture (AIX)

IBM PowerPC processor has 32 general-purpose registers, from r0 to r31.

On entry, register r3 contains the first input argument to the routine.
On exit, register r3 is used for holding the return value.

On IBM AIX machines with the PowerPC processor, there is no single assembly
language instruction that does the test-and-set operation like the
Intel x86 bts instruction does.

Instead, a sequence of instructions consisting of the lwarx and stwcx. pair
is used. The lwarx instruction loads the current contents of a memory
location into a CPU register and creates a reservation on the memory
location for use by a subsequent stwcx. instruction.
If the locking routine can read a current value of 0 from the lock variable

memory location with the lwarx instruction and then successfully stores a
new value of 1 into the same location with the stwcx. instruction,
then it successfully acquires the lock.

For instance, Figure 9-18 is the spin lock routine for IBM PowerPC
architecture.

Figure 9-18 Spinlock() function for IBM PowerPC architecture

```
spinlock:                       # caller pass in addr of lock variable (in r3)
        addi    r4,r0,1         # put 1 in r4
loop:   lwarx   r5,0,r3         # load lock variable's value into r5
        cmpwi   r5,0            # compare r5 with 0
        bc      4,2,loop        # spin if lock is not available (not 0)
        stwcx.  r4,0,r3         # try to store 1
        bc      4,2,loop        # loop if lost reservation
        isync                   # Got the lock
        li      r3, 0           # return 0 in r3 on success
        blr                     # return to caller
```

Upon entry to this routine, the general-purpose register r3 contains the
input argument to the locking function, which is the memory address of the
lock variable.

The addi instruction puts a 1 in register r4.
The 'lwarx r5,0,r3' instruction loads the contents of the memory location
addressed by the contents of register r3, which is the current value of
the lock variable, into register r5.

The 'cmpwi   r5,0' checks if the current value of the lock variable is 0.
It branches to loop if not. If the current value is 0, then the
'stwcx. r4,0,r3' instruction attempts to store the value in register r4
(which is 1) into the memory location of the lock variable.
If the reservation is still there, then it means it has just successfully
acquired the lock by turning the lock variable's value from 0 to 1.
In this case, it puts a 0 in register r3 and returns that 0 to the caller.
If it has lost the reservation, it starts over by looping again.

Figure 9-19 shows the trylock() and unlock() functions for
IBM PowerPC architecture.

Figure 9-19 Trylock() and unlock() functions for IBM PowerPC Architecture

(a) unlock.s

```
# AIX unlock.s
# Set value of memory location addressed by first input argument to 0.
# Return 0 if its old value was 1. Return -1 otherwise.
# Authored by Mr. Jin-Jwei Chen
# Copyright (c) 2002-2016 Mr. Jin-Jwei Chen. All rights reserved.
#
        .machine    "ppc"
        .globl      .unlock[PR];
        .csect      .unlock[PR]

        .set        r0, 0
```

```
                .set        r6, 6
                .set        r3, 3
                .set        r4, 4
                            # caller pass in addr of lock variable (in r3)
unlock:   dcs               # dcs or sync, supposed to be msync
          addi    r6,r0,0   # Put 0 in r6
          l       r4,0(r3)  # Save lock variable's old value in r4
          stw     r6,0(r3)  # Clear the lock variable (location)
          cmpwi   r4,1      # compare r4 with 1
          bc      4,2,notone    # return error if the old lock value was not 1
          addi    r3,r0,0   # Return 0 for unlocking successfully
          blr               # return
notone:
          addi    r3,r0,-1  # Return -1
          blr               # return
```

(b) trylock.s

```
# AIX trylock.s
# Try to acquire the lock by setting the lock variable's value to 1.
# The only input argument to this function specifies the address of the lock.
# Return right away either way. Return 0 if it successfully acquires the
# lock. Return -1 if the lock is not available.
# Authored by Mr. Jin-Jwei Chen
# Copyright (c) 2002-2016 Mr. Jin-Jwei Chen. All rights reserved.
#
          .machine    "ppc"
          .globl      .trylock[PR];
          .csect      .trylock[PR]

          .set        r0, 0
          .set        r3, 3
          .set        r4, 4
          .set        r5, 5
          .set        r6, 6
          .set        LR, 6

trylock:                      # caller pass in addr of lock variable (in r3)
          addi    r4,r0,1     # put 1 in r4
loop:     lwarx   r5,0,r3     # read the lock variable's value into r5
          cmpwi   r5,0        # compare r5 with 0
          bc      4,2,done    # return if lock has been taken (not 0)
          stwcx.  r4,0,r3     # try to store 1
          bc      4,2,loop    # loop if lost reservation
                              # successfully store it! Got the lock
          isync               # Got the lock. Instruction sync.
          li      r3, 0       # return 0 in r3 on success
          blr                 # return
done:                         # fail if r5=1, got it if r5=0
          li      r3,-1       # return -1 in r3 on failure
          blr
```

9-5-2-4 Oracle Sun SPARC Architecture (Solaris)

Atomic Instructions -- CAS (Compare and Swap)

On Oracle/Sun SPARC processors, the atomic assembly language instruction to use for locking implementation is the cas (compare and swap) instruction. It takes three arguments, two registers and one memory.

The CAS instruction deals with one memory location and two CPU registers. It first compares the value of a register with that of a memory location. If they are equal, it then swaps the contents of the memory location with a second register. In other words, it tests to see if the value in the memory location designated as the lock variable is equal to a particular value as specified in the first register. If yes, then it changes the value of that memory location to another value as specified in the second register. Therefore, the single instruction really does a Compare and Swap If Equal operation, which is a lot!

In summary, the cas instruction in SPARC compares the contents of a memory location with that of a register and if they are equal, it then swaps the contents of another register with that memory location. Obviously, the system must not allow testing of same memory location during execution of this.

The SPARC's cas instruction is similar to the Intel x86 bts instruction. If we put a 0 in the first register and a 1 in the second register, then in one cas instruction, it will be able to test if the memory location corresponding to the lock variable has a current value of 0. And if it does, then set it to 1 by swapping it with the contents of the second register specified in the instruction. That's a test-and-set operation in one instruction. A subtle difference is this does it at word size level, not bit.

Note: Some previous SPARC processors used the ldstub (Load Store Unsigned Byte) instruction which saves the current value of a single-byte memory location into a CPU register and then stores the new value 0xFF into that same location. The program can then check the value in the register to see if it is not 0xFF to determine if it gets the lock.
Some old SPARC processors also used the swap instruction which swaps the contents of a CPU register with a memory location.
Both of these instructions were also for lock implementations.

CPU Registers

Oracle Sun SPARC processor has 32 (0-31) general-purpose registers.

On entry, register o0 contains the first input argument to the routine.
On exit, register o0 is used for holding the return value.

Program Examples

For example, Figure 9-20 is the spinlock() function for the SPARC architecture.

Figure 9-20 Spinlock routine for SPARC architecture

```
spinlock:
                        ! %g0 is always 0. Reg %o0 has input argument
                        ! which is the address of the lock variable.
                        ! Assume the lock variable is initialized to 0.
    spin: mov    0,%r1  ! put 0 in Reg. %r1
          mov    1,%r4  ! put 1 in Reg. %r4
```

```
        cas        [%o0],%r1,%r4    ! Compare memory location addressed by [%o0]
                                    ! w/ Reg. %r1. If equal, then swap the contents
                                    ! %r4 and the memory location.
                                    ! (Test if 0. And if yes, then set it to 1)
        cmp        %r4,0            ! Compare old value with 0
        bne,a,pn %icc,spin          ! If not equal, then lock was already taken.
                                    ! Else we got the lock.
        nop                         ! We need this magic.
        retl                        ! return from leaf subroutine
        mov        0,%o0            ! return 0 for SUCCESS
```

Upon entry to this locking routine, register o0 has the input argument to
the function, which is the address of the memory location corresponding to
the lock variable.

The first two mov instructions set up the two registers for the cas
instruction by putting a 0 in register r1 and a 1 in register r4.
Then the cas instruction compares the contents of the memory location
selected by the address in the o0 register with the value in register r1.
If they are equal, then swap the contents of register r4 and the memory
location. All this does is that if the current value of the lock variable
is 0, then set it to 1 to acquire the lock!

After the execution of the cas instruction, the cmp instruction checks to
see if register r4 has a 0. If yes, then it means we have just successfully
acquired the lock. In that case, we put a 0 in register o0 and return that
value to the caller. Otherwise, we branch to the beginning of the routine
and try it again.

Figure 9-21 shows the trylock() and unlock() functions for the
Oracle Sun SPARC architecture.

Figure 9-21 Trylock() and unlock() functions for Oracle Sun SPARC Architecture

(a) unlock.s

```
! SPARC unlock.s
! This function sets the value of the lock variable to 0 to release a lock.
! The address of this lock variable is the input argument to this function.
! The function returns 0 if the old value of the lock variable was 1.
! It returns -1 otherwise.
! Authored by Mr. Jin-Jwei Chen
! Copyright (c) 2002 Mr. Jin-Jwei Chen
! All rights reserved.

        .section   ".text"
        .proc      0                ! r0 contains return value
        .global    unlock
        .align     8
unlock:
                                    ! %g0 is always 0. Reg %o0 has input argument??
        ld         [%o0],%g1        ! save lock's old value in %g1
        st         %g0,[%o0]        ! store 0 in lock variable location
        cmp        %g1,1            ! is the old value 1?
        bne        errexit          ! branch if not equal
```

```
        nop             ! we need this
        retl            ! return from leaf procedure
        mov    0,%o0    ! return 0 for success
errexit:
        mov    -1,%o0   ! return -1 for failure
        retl            ! return from leaf procedure
        nop
```

(b) trylock.s

```
! SPARC trylock.s
! This function tests if the value of the lock variable is 0.
! If yes, set it to 1 using the V9 CAS instruction and return 0 for success.
! Otherwise, it returns -1.
! If the lock is not available, this function does not retry.
! Authored by Mr. Jin-Jwei Chen
! Copyright (c) 2002-2016, 2019 Mr. Jin-Jwei Chen. All rights reserved.

        .section  ".text"
        .proc     0          ! r0 contains return value
        .global   trylock
        .align    8
trylock:
                             ! %g0 is always 0. Reg %o0 has input argument
                             ! which is the address of the lock variable.
                             ! Assume the lock variable is initialized to 0.
        mov    0,%r1         ! put 0 in Reg. %r1
        mov    1,%r4         ! put 1 in Reg. %r4
        casa   [%o0],%r1,%r4 ! Compare memory location addressed by [%o0]
                             ! w/ Reg. %r1. If equal, then swap the contents
                             ! %r4 and the memory location.
                             ! (Test if 0. And if yes, then set it to 1)
        cmp    %r4,0         ! Compare old value with 0
        bne,a,pn %icc,missit ! If not equal, then lock was already taken.
                             ! Else we got the lock.
        nop                  ! We need this magic.
        retl                 ! return from leaf subroutine
        mov    0,%o0         ! return 0 for SUCCESS
missit:
        retl                 ! return from leaf procedure
        mov    -1,%o0        ! return -1 for FAILURE
```

Note: For 32-bit SPARC, change the casa instruction to cas.

9-5-2-5 HP PARISC Architecture (HP-UX)

In the HP PARISC architecture, the atomic locking operation can be implemented by using the load lock and compare instruction pair: LDCW and CMPIB.

Figure 9-22 shows the assembly language routines for trylock, unlock and spinlock on the HP PARISC platform.

Figure 9-22 Lock routines for HP PARISC architecture

9 Concurrency Control and Locking

(a) spinlock.s

```
                 ; spinlock.s (spin lock) for HPUX PARISC 2
                 ; lockvar is 1 when lock is available, 0 when not avail.
                 ; Return SUCCESS if it gets the lock. Return FAILURE otherwise.
                 ;
success   .EQU   0    ; declare a symbolic constant
failure   .EQU   1
inuse     .EQU   0
free      .EQU   1


          .CODE                  ; start code space
          .EXPORT    lock
          .PROC                  ; begin a procedure
          .CALLINFO ENTRY_GR=4   ; save up to %r4
spinlock  .ENTER                 ; auto save necessary registers
spin    LDW        0(%arg0),%r3  ;
        CMPIB,=    inuse,%r3,spin ; if not available, goto spin
        STBY,e     %r0,0(%arg0)  ; Dirty the cache line first (magic)
        LDCW,co    0(%arg0),%r3  ; load & lock the lockvar location
        CMPIB,=,n  inuse,%r3,spin ; if lock is in use, go to spin
                                 ; got the lock!
        LDI        success,%ret0 ; return SUCCESS
exit    .LEAVE                   ; auto restore registers
        .PROCEND                 ; end of procedure
        .END
```

(b) unlock.s

```
                 ; unlock.s for  HPUX PARISC 2
success   .EQU   0
failure   .EQU   1
inuse     .EQU   0
free      .EQU   1


        .CODE
        .EXPORT    unlock
        .PROC
        .CALLINFO ENTRY_GR=4
unlock  .ENTER
        LDI        free,%r3      ;
        STW        %r3,0(%arg0)  ; set lock free
        SYNC                     ;
        LDI        success,%ret0 ; return SUCCESS
exit    .LEAVE
        .PROCEND
        .END
```

(c) trylock.s

```
                 ; trylock.s for HPUX PARISC 2
                 ;
success   .EQU   0    ; declare a symbolic constant
failure   .EQU   1
inuse     .EQU   0
free      .EQU   1
```

```
        .CODE                       ; start code space
        .EXPORT   trylock
        .PROC                       ; begin a procedure
        .CALLINFO ENTRY_GR=4        ; save up to %r4
trylock .ENTER                      ; auto save necessary registers
        LDI       failure,%ret0     ; set return code to FAILURE
        LDW       0(%arg0),%r3      ;
        CMPIB,=   inuse,%r3,exit    ; is busy, goto exit
        STBY,e    %r0,0(%arg0)      ; Dirty the cache line first (magic)
        LDCW,co   0(%arg0),%r3      ; load & lock the lockvar location
        CMPIB,=,n inuse,%r3,exit    ; if lock in use, goto exit
                                    ; got the lock!
        LDI       success,%ret0     ; return SUCCESS
exit    .LEAVE                      ; auto restore registers
        .PROCEND
        .END
```

9-5-2-6 HP/DEC Alpha Architecture (Tru64 Unix or Digital Unix)

Atomic Instruction Pair -- Load Locked and Store Conditional

On the world's first 64-bit microprocessor Alpha that was originally created by DEC (Digital Equipment Corporation) and later acquired by Compaq and HP, Load Locked and Store Conditional instruction pair should be used to implement a locking function. For 32-bit, use the ldl_l and stl_c instruction pair. For 64-bit operations, use the ldq_l and stq_c pair. Alpha calls a 32-bit integer a Longword and a 64-bit integer a Quadword. That's why the letter l and q in these instructions, respectively.

The Load Locked instruction (ldl_l or ldq_l) locks the memory location specified, loads the contents of that memory location into the CPU register specified in the instruction, loads the value 1 into the lock_flag CPU register, and saves the physical memory address of the locked memory location into the locked_physical address register.

If the lock_flag register has the value of 1, then the Store Conditional instruction stores the value in the specified CPU register into the specified memory location. The value of the lock_flag is copied into the specified register. And the lock_flag register's value is set to 0. Otherwise, if the lock_flag register's value is not equal to 1, the store operation does not happen.

Therefore, by using the load locked and store conditional instruction pair, a program can essentially read the value of a memory location into a CPU register, examine it, change it, and store it back. If no other process/thread has changed (i.e. stored into) that same memory location or range during the period, then the store conditional instruction will get executed and succeed. Otherwise, the store conditional will not happen and hence it won't have any real effect. The instruction pair basically does an atomic read-modify-write operation of the memory location used by the lock variable if no conflict occurs at the same time; that is, no other process/thread stores into the same memory location during the time window when the instruction pair is executed.

Note that on a multiprocessor system, if processor A loads locked a memory location and then processor B successfully does a store into that same memory location, then the processor A's lock_flag will be cleared, meaning its subsequent store conditional instruction won't actually modify that memory location at all. In other words, whenever there is a conflict between two processors, the first one that does the store will win and the other processor loses and does no store. This guarantees only one processor can atomically change the contents of the memory location at a time.

Code Examples

Figure 9-23 shows the assembly language routines for trylock, unlock and spinlock on the HP/DEC Alpha processor.

Note that the instruction sequence LDx_L, modify, STx_C, BEQ xyz executed on an Alpha processor performs an atomic read-modify-write operation on the data in the memory location involved if the branch instruction falls through. If the branch takes place, it means the store conditional instruction did not actually modify the contents of the memory location and it failed to acquire the lock. In that case, the entire sequence can be repeated until it succeeds (i.e. until the lock is obtained).

Also notice that for performance reason, as shown in the example program, a forward branch should be always used to handle the failure case right after the stl_c/stq_c instruction. This is because a backward branch would go against the prediction of the Alpha processor and thus disrupt the instruction pipeline flow and lengthen the execution.

Figure 9-23 Locking functions for HP/DEC Alpha architecture

(a) trylock.s

```
          # On entry, R16 has 1st argument - addr of lockvar
          # Value of the lock variable is initialized to 0
          # On return, r0 has return value, 0 - SUCCESS (got the lock)
          .text
          .align    4
          .globl    trylock
          .ent      trylock
trylock:
          ldgp     $gp, 0($27)
          ldq_l    $1, 0($16)      # load the lock variable into r1
          blbs     $1, taken       # branch if taken (lower bit set)
          ldiq     $2, 1           # set value of $2 to be 1
          stq_c    $2, 0($16)      # try to set the lock bit
          beq      $2, taken       # due to exception, interrupt, or
                                   # write by other CPU
          mb                       # ensure memory coherence
                                   # get the lock, return to caller

          ldil     $0, 0           # set r0 to 0 for SUCCESS.
          ret      $31, ($26), 1
taken:                            # lock is already taken or
                                   # stq_c has failed due to..
          ldil     $0, 1           # set r0 to 1 for FAILURE.
```

```
        ret     $31, ($26), 1
        .end    trylock
```

(b) unlock.s

```
        .text
        .align   4
        .globl   unlock
        .ent     unlock
unlock:
        ldgp    $gp, 0($27)
        #.frame $sp, 0, $26, 0  # $26 contains return address.
        mb
        stq     $31, 0($16)
        ldil    $0, 0           # set r0 to 0 for SUCCESS.
        ret     $31, ($26), 1
        .end    unlock
```

(c) spinlock.s (spin lock)

```
        # On entry, R16 has 1st argument - addr of lockvar
        # Value of the lock variable is initialized to 0
        # On return, r0 has return value, 0 - SUCCESS (got the lock)
        .text
        .align   4
        .globl   lock
        .ent     lock
spinlock:
        ldgp    $gp, 0($27)

spinloop:
        ldq_l   $1, 0($16)      # load the lock variable into r1
        blbs    $1, taken       # branch if taken (lower bit set)
        ldiq    $2, 1           # set value of $2 to be 1
        stq_c   $2, 0($16)      # try to set the lock bit
        beq     $2, taken       # due to exception, interrupt, or
                                # write by other CPU
        mb                      # ensure memory coherence
                                # get the lock, return to caller

        ldil    $0, 0           # set r0 to 0 for SUCCESS.
        ret     $31, ($26), 1
taken:                          # lock is already taken or
                                # stq_c has failed due to..
        br      spinloop
        .end    lock
```

9-5-2-7 Concurrent Updates Using Our Own Lock

Figure 9-24 lists a program which demonstrates using our own lock routines in concurrent updates. It also demonstrates the update loss problem. This C program does concurrent updates of some shared variables using multiple threads. Each thread tries to increment the values of the two shared global variables by a certain number of times.

The program takes three input variables. First argument is about using
locking to protect the updates or not, with 1 means use locking and 0 means
does not use locking. The second command-line argument specifies how many
threads you want to run. The third argument specifies how many updates
you want each thread to perform. By default, the program runs 4 threads to
concurrently update the two shared variables by 10000000 times each with
locking to serialize the concurrent updates.

If the program works correctly, then at end the values of both shared
variables should be at 4 * 10000000 = 40000000.
If it gets any other number, it's wrong. If the result is less then it means
some update loss has occurred.

As you can see from running the program, and as it can be seen from
Figure 9-25, without using locking, the resultant number is always less than
40000000. That means update losses have occurred. That is, some thread(s)
has read the value of a shared variable trying to increment it.
But since there is no locking, other thread(s) has come in at that time
and read the same value and tried to increment it too. As a result,
they step on one another and some's updates are lost.

However, as Figure 9-26 shows, as long as you apply locking for the updates,
the result is always consistent and correct. We show the test results in
the following three different platforms with our own locking and unlocking
assembly language routines:

    Intel x86 Linux
    IBM Power AIX
    Oracle/Sun SPARC Solaris

This example clearly demonstrates the update loss problem and how to prevent
it. This is extremely important! It is the basis that all database
systems are built upon -- applying locking such that concurrent updates
always produce consistent, correct results. Without this, database systems
or many programs won't produce correct results and would be useless.

Note: We have two slightly different versions of semupd_mylock.c.
Figure 9-24(a) shows a version that works for Linux 32-bit and 64-bit,
, AIX 32-bit and 64-bit and Sun SPARC 32-bit. 9-24(b) lists a version
which is for Sun SPARC 64-bit. For some reason, the pthread_join() function
got a bus error on SPARC 64-bit. To fix that, we have to change the way
that the worker_thread() returns its value.

    Figure 9-24 Concurrent updates using our own lock routines

    (a) semupd_mylock.c

```
/*
 * Concurrent updates of two shared variables by multiple threads using
 * our own locking routines in assembly language.
 * Copyright (c) 2013, 2019, 2020 Mr. Jin-Jwei Chen.  All rights reserved.
 */

#include "mysemutil.h"

/* Default values related to the shared file */
```

```c
#define   NTHREADS    4            /* number of concurrent threads */
#define   MAXNTHREADS 12           /* max. number of concurrent threads */
#define   DEFUPDCNT   10000000     /* default update count */
#define   MAXDELAYCNT 1000         /* delay count */

/* Shared lock variable */
int     lockvar=0;

/* Shared data */
unsigned int globalcnt = 0;
unsigned int globalcnt2 = 0;

/* These are our own locking functions in assembly language. */
int spinlock(int *lockvar);
int unlock(int *lockvar);

/*
 * The worker thread.
 */

int worker_thread(void *args)
{
  unsigned int    *argp;
  unsigned int    myid;
  unsigned int    updcnt;
  int             ret = 0;
  int             i, j;
  int             uselock=1;

  /* Extract input arguments (two unsigned integers and one signed) */
  argp = (unsigned int *)args;
  if (argp != NULL)
  {
    myid = argp[0];
    updcnt = argp[1];
    uselock = argp[2];
  }
  else
#ifdef SUN64
  {
    ret = (-1);
    pthread_exit((void *)&ret);
  }
#else
    pthread_exit((void *)(-1));
#endif

  fprintf(stdout, "Worker thread: myid=%u updcnt=%u\n", myid, updcnt);

  /* Do my job */
  for (i = 0; i < updcnt; i++)
  {
    if (uselock)
      spinlock(&lockvar);
    globalcnt = globalcnt + 1;           /* update shared variable 1 */
    for (j=0; j < MAXDELAYCNT; j++);     /* create a bit of delay */
```

542

```
      globalcnt2 = globalcnt2 + 1;        /* update shared variable 2 */
      if (uselock)
        unlock(&lockvar);
    }

#ifdef SUN64
  pthread_exit((void *)&ret);
#else
  pthread_exit((void *)0);
#endif
}

int main(int argc, char *argv[])
{
  int      nthrd;                         /* actual number of worker threads */
  int      ret, retval;
#ifdef SUN64
  int      *retvalp = &retval;            /* pointer to returned value */
#endif
  int      i;
  size_t   updcnt = DEFUPDCNT;            /* each thread's file update count */
  pthread_t      thrds[MAXNTHREADS];      /* threads */
  unsigned int   args[MAXNTHREADS][3];    /* arguments for each thread */
  int            uselock;                 /* use locking for update or not */
  pthread_attr_t attr;                    /* pthread attributes */

  if ((argc > 1) &&
      ((strcmp(argv[1], "-h") == 0) || (strcmp(argv[1], "-help") == 0)))
  {
    fprintf(stdout, "Usage: %s [uselock] [nthrd] [updcnt]\n", argv[0]);
    return(-1);
  }

  /*
   * Get the lock switch, number of concurrent threads and update count
   * from the user, if any.
   */
  uselock = 1;
  if (argc > 1)
  {
    uselock = atoi(argv[1]);
    if (uselock != 0)
      uselock = 1;
  }

  nthrd = NTHREADS;
  if (argc > 2)
    nthrd = atoi(argv[2]);
  if (nthrd <= 0 || nthrd > MAXNTHREADS)
    nthrd = NTHREADS;

  updcnt = DEFUPDCNT;
  if (argc > 3)
    updcnt = atoi(argv[3]);
  if (updcnt <= 0)
    updcnt = DEFUPDCNT;
```

```
  fprintf(stdout, "Increment the values of two shared variables using %u "
    "threads, with each doing it %lu times.\n", nthrd, updcnt);
  if (uselock)
    fprintf(stdout, "Locking is used during the updates.\n");
  else
    fprintf(stdout, "Locking is not used during the updates.\n");
  printf("At start, globalcnt=%d globalcnt2=%d\n", globalcnt, globalcnt2);

  /* Load up the input arguments for each worker thread */
  for (i = 0; i < nthrd; i++)
  {
    args[i][0] = i+1;        /* worker id starts with 1 */
    args[i][1] = updcnt;
    args[i][2] = uselock;
  }

  /* Initialize the pthread attributes */
  ret = pthread_attr_init(&attr);
  if (ret != 0)
  {
    fprintf(stderr, "pthread_attr_init() function failed, ret=%d\n", ret);
    return(-2);
  }

  /* Create the worker threads to concurrently update the shared variables */
  for (i = 0; i < nthrd; i++)
  {
    ret = pthread_create(&thrds[i], (pthread_attr_t *)&attr,
          (void *(*)(void *))worker_thread, (void *)args[i]);
    if (ret != 0)
    {
      fprintf(stderr, "Failed to create the worker thread\n");
      return(-3);
    }
  }


  /*
   * Wait for each of the child threads to finish and retrieve its returned
   * value.
   */
  for (i = 0; i < nthrd; i++)
  {
#ifdef SUN64
    ret = pthread_join(thrds[i], (void **)&retvalp);
#else
    ret = pthread_join(thrds[i], (void **)&retval);
#endif
    fprintf(stdout, "Thread %u exited with return value %d\n", i, retval);
  }

  /* Report the end results */
  printf("At end, globalcnt=%d globalcnt2=%d\n", globalcnt, globalcnt2);

  return(0);
}
```

(b) semupd_mylock_sun64.c

```c
/*
 * Concurrent updates of two shared variables by multiple threads using
 * our own locking routines in assembly language.
 * Copyright (c) 2013, 2019-2020 Mr. Jin-Jwei Chen.  All rights reserved.
 */

#include "mysemutil.h"

/* Default values related to the shared file */
#define   NTHREADS    4              /* number of concurrent threads */
#define   MAXNTHREADS 12             /* number of concurrent threads */
#define   DEFUPDCNT    10000000      /* default update count */
#define   MAXDELAYCNT 1000           /* delay count */

/* Shared lock variable */
int       lockvar=0;

/* Shared data */
unsigned int globalcnt = 0;
unsigned int globalcnt2 = 0;

/* These are our own locking functions in assembly language. */
int spinlock(int *lockvar);
int unlock(int *lockvar);

/*
 * The worker thread.
 */

int worker_thread(void *args)
{
  unsigned int  *argp;
  unsigned int  myid;
  unsigned int  updcnt;
  int           ret = 0;
  int           i, j;
  int           uselock=1;

  /* Extract input arguments (two unsigned integers) */
  argp = (unsigned int *)args;
  if (argp != NULL)
  {
    myid = argp[0];
    updcnt = argp[1];
    uselock = argp[2];
  }
  else
  {
    ret = (-1);
    pthread_exit((void *)&ret);
  }

  fprintf(stdout, "Worker thread: myid=%u updcnt=%u\n", myid, updcnt);
```

```
  /* Do my job */
  for (i = 0; i < updcnt; i++)
  {
    if (uselock)
      spinlock(&lockvar);
    globalcnt = globalcnt + 1;          /* update shared variable 1 */
    for (j=0; j < MAXDELAYCNT; j++);    /* create a bit of delay */
    globalcnt2 = globalcnt2 + 1;        /* update shared variable 2 */
    if (uselock)
      unlock(&lockvar);
  }

  pthread_exit((void *)&ret);
}

int main(int argc, char *argv[])
{
  int       nthrd;                      /* actual number of worker threads */
  int       ret, retval;
  int       *retvalp = &retval;         /* pointer to returned value */
  int       i;
  size_t    updcnt = DEFUPDCNT;         /* each thread's file update count */
  pthread_t       thrds[MAXNTHREADS];   /* threads */
  unsigned int  args[MAXNTHREADS][3];   /* arguments for each thread */
  int           uselock;                /* use locking for update or not */
  pthread_attr_t  attr;                 /* pthread attributes */

  if ((argc > 1) &&
      ((strcmp(argv[1], "-h") == 0) || (strcmp(argv[1], "-help") == 0)))
  {
    fprintf(stdout, "Usage: %s [uselock] [nthrd] [updcnt]\n", argv[0]);
    return(-1);
  }

  /*
   * Get the number of concurrent threads, update count and lock switch
   * from the user, if any.
   */
  uselock = 1;
  if (argc > 1)
  {
    uselock = atoi(argv[1]);
    if (uselock != 0)
      uselock = 1;
  }

  nthrd = NTHREADS;
  if (argc > 2)
    nthrd = atoi(argv[2]);
  if (nthrd <= 0 || nthrd > MAXNTHREADS)
    nthrd = NTHREADS;

  updcnt = DEFUPDCNT;
  if (argc > 3)
    updcnt = atoi(argv[3]);
```

546

```
  if (updcnt <= 0)
    updcnt = DEFUPDCNT;

  fprintf(stdout, "Increment the values of two shared variables using %u "
    "threads, with each doing it %u times.\n", nthrd, updcnt);
  if (uselock)
    fprintf(stdout, "Locking is used during the updates.\n");
  else
    fprintf(stdout, "Locking is not used during the updates.\n");
  printf("At start, globalcnt=%d globalcnt2=%d\n", globalcnt, globalcnt2);

  /* Load up the input arguments for each worker thread */
  for (i = 0; i < nthrd; i++)
  {
    args[i][0] = i+1;          /* worker id starts with 1 */
    args[i][1] = updcnt;
    args[i][2] = uselock;
  }

  /* Initialize the pthread attributes */
  ret = pthread_attr_init(&attr);
  if (ret != 0)
  {
    fprintf(stderr, "pthread_attr_init() function failed, ret=%d\n", ret);
    return(-2);
  }

  /* Create the worker threads to concurrently update the shared file */
  for (i = 0; i < nthrd; i++)
  {
    ret = pthread_create(&thrds[i], (pthread_attr_t *)&attr,
         (void *(*)(void *))worker_thread, (void *)args[i]);
    if (ret != 0)
    {
      fprintf(stderr, "Failed to create the worker thread\n");
      return(-3);
    }
  }

  /*
   * Wait for each of the child threads to finish and retrieve its returned
   * value.
   */
  for (i = 0; i < nthrd; i++)
  {
    ret = pthread_join(thrds[i], (void **)&retvalp);
    fprintf(stdout, "Thread %u exited with return value %d\n", i, retval);
  }

  /* Report the update counts from all threads */
  printf("At end, globalcnt=%d globalcnt2=%d\n", globalcnt, globalcnt2);

  return(0);
}
```

Figure 9-25 Without locking, update losses occur at concurrent updates

```
$ ./semupd_mylock.lin64 0
Increment the values of two shared variables using 4 threads, with each doing it
10000000 times.
Locking is not used during the updates.
At start, globalcnt=0 globalcnt2=0
Worker thread: myid=2 updcnt=10000000
Worker thread: myid=1 updcnt=10000000
Worker thread: myid=3 updcnt=10000000
Worker thread: myid=4 updcnt=10000000
Thread 0 exited with return value 0
Thread 1 exited with return value 0
Thread 2 exited with return value 0
Thread 3 exited with return value 0
At end, globalcnt=37244611 globalcnt2=37223599
```

```
$ ./semupd_mylock.aix64 0
Increment the values of two shared variables using 4 threads, with each doing it
10000000 times.
Locking is not used during the updates.
At start, globalcnt=0 globalcnt2=0
Worker thread: myid=1 updcnt=10000000
Worker thread: myid=4 updcnt=10000000
Worker thread: myid=3 updcnt=10000000
Worker thread: myid=2 updcnt=10000000
Thread 0 exited with return value 0
Thread 0 exited with return value 0
Thread 1 exited with return value 0
Thread 0 exited with return value 0
Thread 1 exited with return value 0
Thread 2 exited with return value 0
Thread 0 exited with return value 0
Thread 1 exited with return value 0
Thread 2 exited with return value 0
Thread 3 exited with return value 0
At end, globalcnt=39973602 globalcnt2=39961776
```

```
$ ./semupd_mylock.sun32 0
Increment the values of two shared variables using 4 threads, with each doing it
10000000 times.
Locking is not used during the updates.
At start, globalcnt=0 globalcnt2=0
Worker thread: myid=1 updcnt=10000000
Worker thread: myid=2 updcnt=10000000
Worker thread: myid=3 updcnt=10000000
Worker thread: myid=4 updcnt=10000000
Thread 0 exited with return value 0
Thread 1 exited with return value 0
Thread 2 exited with return value 0
Thread 3 exited with return value 0
At end, globalcnt=39800851 globalcnt2=39756173
```

```
$ ./semupd_mylock.sun64 0 4 10000000 Increment the values of two shared variables
using 4 threads, with each doing it 10000000 times.
Locking is not used during the updates.
```

```
At start, globalcnt=0 globalcnt2=0
Worker thread: myid=1 updcnt=10000000
Worker thread: myid=2 updcnt=10000000
Worker thread: myid=3 updcnt=10000000
Worker thread: myid=4 updcnt=10000000
Thread 0 exited with return value 0
Thread 1 exited with return value 0
Thread 2 exited with return value 0
Thread 3 exited with return value 0
At end, globalcnt=39732575 globalcnt2=39681540
```

Figure 9-26 With locking, concurrent updates produce correct results

```
$ ./semupd_mylock.lin64 1
Increment the values of two shared variables using 4 threads, with each doing it
10000000 times.
Locking is used during the updates.
At start, globalcnt=0 globalcnt2=0
Worker thread: myid=1 updcnt=10000000
Worker thread: myid=2 updcnt=10000000
Worker thread: myid=3 updcnt=10000000
Worker thread: myid=4 updcnt=10000000
Thread 0 exited with return value 0
Thread 1 exited with return value 0
Thread 2 exited with return value 0
Thread 3 exited with return value 0
At end, globalcnt=40000000 globalcnt2=40000000
```

```
$ ./semupd_mylock.aix64 1
Increment the values of two shared variables using 4 threads, with each doing it
10000000 times.
Locking is used during the updates.
At start, globalcnt=0 globalcnt2=0
Worker thread: myid=1 updcnt=10000000
Worker thread: myid=4 updcnt=10000000
Worker thread: myid=3 updcnt=10000000
Worker thread: myid=2 updcnt=10000000
Thread 0 exited with return value 0
Thread 0 exited with return value 0
Thread 1 exited with return value 0
Thread 0 exited with return value 0
Thread 1 exited with return value 0
Thread 2 exited with return value 0
Thread 0 exited with return value 0
Thread 1 exited with return value 0
Thread 2 exited with return value 0
Thread 3 exited with return value 0
At end, globalcnt=40000000 globalcnt2=40000000
```

```
$ ./semupd_mylock.sun32
Increment the values of two shared variables using 4 threads, with each doing it
10000000 times.
Locking is used during the updates.
At start, globalcnt=0 globalcnt2=0
Worker thread: myid=1 updcnt=10000000
```

549

```
Worker thread: myid=2 updcnt=10000000
Worker thread: myid=3 updcnt=10000000
Worker thread: myid=4 updcnt=10000000
Thread 0 exited with return value 0
Thread 1 exited with return value 0
Thread 2 exited with return value 0
Thread 3 exited with return value 0
At end, globalcnt=40000000 globalcnt2=40000000

$ ./semupd_mylock.sun64
Increment the values of two shared variables using 4 threads, with each doing it
10000000 times.
Locking is used during the updates.
At start, globalcnt=0 globalcnt2=0
Worker thread: myid=1 updcnt=10000000
Worker thread: myid=2 updcnt=10000000
Worker thread: myid=3 updcnt=10000000
Worker thread: myid=4 updcnt=10000000
Thread 0 exited with return value 0
Thread 1 exited with return value 0
Thread 2 exited with return value 0
Thread 3 exited with return value 0
At end, globalcnt=40000000 globalcnt2=40000000
```

The scope of impact of using our own locking routines depends on where you place the lock variable. If you place the lock variable as a global variable within a process, as we have demonstrated in the example above, it will be able to synchronize multiple threads within a process.
But if you place the shared lock variable in a shared memory, then it will be able to synchronize multiple processes having accesses to the shared memory, which we will discuss and provide examples in the next chapter.

9-5-2-8 Performance Comparison of Semaphore and Our Own Lock

Figure 9-28 lists the concurrent update program using System V semaphore, which is the same as semupd_mylock.c in Fig. 9-24 except lock implementation.

By running the two example programs semupd_sema and semupd_mylock on four different platforms: Intel Linux, IBM Power AIX, Oracle/Sun SPARC Solaris, and Apple Darwin 19.3, we found there is a significant performance improvement seen by using our own assembly language locking routines over using the System V semaphore provided by the underlying operating system.

The performance improvements observed are shown in Figure 9-27.

```
Figure 9-27 Performance improvements of our own locking routines
----------------------------------------------------------------
29-33% on IBM Power AIX
85-88% on Oracle/Sun SPARC Solaris
25-80+% on Intel Linux
25-80+% in Apple x86 Darwin 19.3
----------------------------------------------------------------
```

Figure 9-28 Concurrent Update Program using semaphores (semupd_sema.c)

```
/*
 * Concurrent updates of two shared variables by multiple threads using
 * System V semaphore as locking facility.
 * Create the path "/var/xyzinc/app1" before running the program.
 * Copyright (c) 2013, 2019, 2020 Mr. Jin-Jwei Chen.  All rights reserved.
 */

#include "mysemutil.h"

/* Default values related to the shared file */
#define   NTHREADS    4              /* number of concurrent threads */
#define   MAXNTHREADS 12             /* number of concurrent threads */
#define   DEFUPDCNT   10000000       /* default update count */
#define   MAXDELAYCNT 1000           /* delay count */

/* Shared data */
unsigned int globalcnt = 0;
unsigned int globalcnt2 = 0;

/* These are our own locking functions in assembly language. */
int spinlock(int *lockvar);
int unlock(int *lockvar);

/*
 * The worker thread.
 */

int worker_thread(void *args)
{
  unsigned int  *argp;
  unsigned int  myid;
  unsigned int  updcnt;
  int           ret;
  int           i, j;
  int           uselock=1;
  int           semid;

  /* Extract input arguments (two unsigned integers and one signed) */
  argp = (unsigned int *)args;
  if (argp != NULL)
  {
    myid = argp[0];
    updcnt = argp[1];
    uselock = argp[2];
    semid = argp[3];
  }
  else
    pthread_exit((void *)(-1));

  fprintf(stdout, "Worker thread: myid=%u updcnt=%u semid=%u\n",
    myid, updcnt, semid);

  /* Do my job */
  for (i = 0; i < updcnt; i++)
  {
```

```
    if (uselock)
    {
      ret = lock_semaphore(semid, 0);
      if (ret == -1)
      {
          fprintf(stderr, "semop() failed to lock, errno=%d\n", errno);
          pthread_exit((void *)-1);
      }
    }
    globalcnt = globalcnt + 1;          /* update shared variable 1 */
    for (j=0; j < MAXDELAYCNT; j++);    /* create a bit of delay */
    globalcnt2 = globalcnt2 + 1;        /* update shared variable 2 */
    if (uselock)
    {
      ret = unlock_semaphore(semid, 0);
      if (ret == -1)
      {
          fprintf(stderr, "semop() failed to unlock, errno=%d\n", errno);
          pthread_exit((void *)-1);
      }
    }
  }

  pthread_exit((void *)0);
}

int main(int argc, char *argv[])
{
  int       nthrd;                      /* actual number of worker threads */
  int       ret, retval;
  int       i;
  size_t    updcnt = DEFUPDCNT;         /* each thread's file update count */
  pthread_t       thrds[MAXNTHREADS];   /* threads */
  unsigned int  args[MAXNTHREADS][4];   /* arguments for each thread */
  int             uselock;              /* use locking for update or not */
  key_t  ipckey;
  int       semid;
  semun  semarg;

  if ((argc > 1) &&
      ((strcmp(argv[1], "-h") == 0) || (strcmp(argv[1], "-help") == 0)))
  {
    fprintf(stdout, "Usage: %s [uselock] [nthrd] [updcnt]\n", argv[0]);
    return(-1);
  }

  /*
   * Get the lock switch, number of concurrent threads and update count
   * from the user, if any.
   */
  uselock = 1;
  if (argc > 1)
  {
    uselock = atoi(argv[1]);
    if (uselock != 0)
      uselock = 1;
```

```
    }

    nthrd = NTHREADS;
    if (argc > 2)
        nthrd = atoi(argv[2]);
    if (nthrd <= 0 || nthrd > MAXNTHREADS)
        nthrd = NTHREADS;

    updcnt = DEFUPDCNT;
    if (argc > 3)
        updcnt = atoi(argv[3]);
    if (updcnt <= 0)
        updcnt = DEFUPDCNT;

    fprintf(stdout, "Increment the values of two shared variables using %u "
        "threads, with each doing it %lu times.\n", nthrd, updcnt);
    if (uselock)
        fprintf(stdout, "Locking is used during the updates.\n");
    else
        fprintf(stdout, "Locking is not used during the updates.\n");
    printf("At start, globalcnt=%d globalcnt2=%d\n", globalcnt, globalcnt2);

    /* Create the semaphore */
    semid = get_semaphore_set(IPCKEYPATH, IPCSUBID, ONESEM, 0600);
    if (semid == -1)
    {
        fprintf(stderr, "get_semaphore_set() failed\n");
        return(-2);
    }
    fprintf(stdout, "The semaphore was successfully created, semid=%d.\n", semid);

    /* Initialize the value of the semaphore -- value 1 means available */
    ret = init_semaphore_set(semid, ONESEM, 1);
    if (ret == -1)
    {
        fprintf(stderr, "init_semaphore_set() failed\n");
        ret = (-3);
        goto exit;
    }
    fprintf(stdout, "Initializing the semaphore value was successful.\n");

    /* Load up the input arguments for each worker thread */
    for (i = 0; i < nthrd; i++)
    {
        args[i][0] = i+1;          /* worker id starts with 1 */
        args[i][1] = updcnt;
        args[i][2] = uselock;
        args[i][3] = semid;
    }

    /* Create the worker threads to concurrently update the shared variables */
    for (i = 0; i < nthrd; i++)
    {
        ret = pthread_create(&thrds[i], (pthread_attr_t *)NULL,
            (void *(*)(void *))worker_thread, (void *)args[i]);
        if (ret != 0)
```

```
    {
        fprintf(stderr, "Failed to create the worker thread\n");
        ret = (-4);
        goto exit;
    }
}

/*
 * Wait for each of the child threads to finish and retrieve its returned
 * value.
 */
for (i = 0; i < nthrd; i++)
{
    ret = pthread_join(thrds[i], (void **)&retval);
    fprintf(stdout, "Thread %u exited with return value %d\n", i, retval);
}

exit:
    /* Remove the semaphore */
    ret = semctl(semid, 0, IPC_RMID);
    if (ret == -1)
    {
        fprintf(stderr, "semctl() failed to remove, errno=%d\n", errno);
    }
    fprintf(stdout, "The semaphore set was successfully removed.\n");

    /* Report the end results */
    printf("At end, globalcnt=%d globalcnt2=%d\n", globalcnt, globalcnt2);

    return(ret);
}
```

9-6 POSIX Semaphore

In addition to System V semaphore, POSIX Standard added the so-called **POSIX
semaphore** in issue 5 to be used with POSIX threads. POSIX semaphores can
also be used for synchronization between multiple threads within the same
process or between multiple processes running on the same system.
It's slightly easier to use and a little bit faster than System V semaphores.

The names of the POSIX semaphore APIs are all called sem_xxx(). On most
systems, they exist in the rt library librt.so. To link with it, use -lrt
on the linker command line.

Just like a System V semaphore, a POSIX semaphore is an integer variable
whose value is never allowed to fall below zero. Two operations can be
performed on each semaphore: to decrement the semaphore's value by one
(for a binary semaphore, this is to lock the semaphore) and to increment
the semaphore's value by one (for a binary semaphore, this is to release
the lock on the semaphore).

Note that there is a difference between System V semaphores and POSIX
semaphores. With System V semaphores, the semop() API allows a caller to
add or subtract an integer value from the current value of the semaphore.
In contrast, the APIs of POSIX semaphores (specifically, sem_post() and

sem_wait() functions) only allow a caller to add one to or subtract one from current value of a semaphore, respectively. So it's to increment by one or decrement by one in POSIX semaphores, but to increment by one or more or decrement by one or more in System V semaphores. With POSIX semaphores, there is no API available for incrementing or decrementing a semaphore's value by more than one.

POSIX semaphores come in two forms: **unnamed semaphores** and **named semaphores**. Essentially, unnamed semaphores are for synchronization between multiple threads within the same process and named semaphores are for synchronization between multiple processes. This is because POSIX named semaphores are implemented as virtual file system entries which are accessible by multiple processes. To use a POSIX unnamed semaphore for synchronization between multiple processes, the semaphore must be created in a shared memory that is accessible to all sharing processes.

We introduce both of them below.

9-6-1 Unnamed POSIX Semaphores

A POSIX unnamed semaphore does not have a universal name associated with it.

A POSIX unnamed semaphore can be created as shared between multiple threads or processes. A thread-shared semaphore is usually placed in a global variable which is shared between all threads within a process.
A process-shared semaphore must be placed in a shared memory region (e.g., a System V shared memory segment created by semget(), or a POSIX shared memory object created using shm_open()).

Before it can be used, a POSIX unnamed semaphore must be initialized by the sem_init() function. It can then be operated on by the sem_wait() and sem_post() functions. When a POSIX unnamed semaphore is no longer needed, it must be destroyed by invoking the sem_destroy() function.

Using a POSIX unnamed semaphore involves the following four steps.

```
#include <semaphore.h>

int sem_init(sem_t *sem, int pshared, unsigned value);
int sem_wait(sem_t *sem);
int sem_post(sem_t *sem);
int sem_destroy(sem_t *sem);
```

We describe each of these functions below.

1. The sem_init() Function

The sem_init() function initializes the unnamed semaphore specified by the function's first argument, setting its initial value to be the value specified by the function's third argument. The second argument indicates whether the semaphore is to be shared between threads or processes.
A zero value means the semaphore is shared between threads of the process and a non-zero value means the semaphore is shared between processes.

On success, the sem_init() function returns 0. Otherwise, it returns -1 with errno containing the error number.

Note that sem_init() is for POSIX unnamed semaphores only, just as sem_open() is for POSIX named semaphores only.

2. The sem_wait() Function

The sem_wait() attempts to decrement the semaphore's value by one. If the semaphore's value is currently positive, the decrement will occur and the caller has just locked the semaphore. If the semaphore's value is currently zero, then the lock is considered not available and the calling process or thread will be blocked until it either locks the semaphore or is interrupted by a signal.

Upon success, sem_wait() returns zero and the state of the semaphore is locked and it will remain locked until the sem_post() function is executed. If the call is unsuccessful, the function returns -1 with errno set to indicate the error. In that case, the state of the semaphore is unchanged.

3. The sem_trywait() Function

```
#include <semaphore.h>
int sem_trywait(sem_t *sem);
```

The sem_trywait() function is the same as sem_wait() except that it will return without waiting if the function cannot immediately lock the semaphore.

4. The sem_timedwait() Function

```
#include <semaphore.h>
#include <time.h>

int sem_timedwait(sem_t *restrict sem,
    const struct timespec *restrict abstime);
```

The sem_timedwait() function tries to lock the semaphore specified in the first argument. It will wait until either it successfully locks the semaphore or the time period specified in the second argument expires. The timeout is based on the CLOCK_REALTIME clock. The resolution of the timeout is the resolution of the clock on which it is based.

If the semaphore can be locked immediately, the function will return success regardless of the validity of the timeout value.

The sem_timedwait() function returns zero if the call successfully locks the semaphore. Otherwise, it returns -1 with errno having the error number.

5. The sem_post() Function

The sem_post() function increments the semaphore's value by one. It essentially unlocks the semaphore.

If this call results in the semaphore's value consequently becomes greater than zero, then another process or thread blocked in a sem_wait() call will be woken up and proceed to lock the semaphore.

The sem_post() call returns zero on success; otherwise, it returns -1 and errno is set to indicate the error.

6. The sem_destroy() Function

The sem_destroy() function destroys the unnamed semaphore specified in the argument. Only an unnamed POSIX semaphore that was created using sem_init() may be destroyed using sem_destroy(); the effect of calling sem_destroy() with a named semaphore is undefined.

The effect of destroying a semaphore upon which other threads are currently blocked is undefined.

On success, sem_destroy() returns zero. Otherwise, it returns -1 and errno is set to indicate the error.

Example

Figure 9-29 shows a program using a POSIX unnamed semaphore to synchronize multiple threads updating shared data.

Figure 9-29 Concurrent updates using POSIX unnamed semaphore (semupd_posix_sema.c)

```
/*
 * Concurrent updates of shared variables by multiple threads using
 * POSIX unnamed semaphore as synchronization facility.
 * Copyright (c) 2013, 2019, 2021 Mr. Jin-Jwei Chen.  All rights reserved.
 */

#include <stdio.h>
#include <errno.h>
#include <stdlib.h>
#include <pthread.h>
#include <semaphore.h>    /* for POSIX semaphore */

/* Default values related to the shared file */
#define  NTHREADS     4                /* number of concurrent threads */
#define  MAXNTHREADS 12                /* max. number of concurrent threads */
#define  DEFUPDCNT    100000000        /* default update count */
#define  MAXDELAYCNT 1000              /* delay count */

/* Shared data */
unsigned int globalcnt = 0;
unsigned int globalcnt2 = 0;

/*
 * This function acquires the lock on a binary semaphore.
 * A semaphore value of 1 means the lock is available.
 * A semaphore value of 0 means the lock is unavailable.
 * This expects the semaphore's value to be initialized to 1 to begin with.
 * This function attempts to decrement the semaphore's value by 1 to obtain
 * the lock.
 */
int lock_posix_semaphore(sem_t *mysem)
```

```
{
  int    ret;

  if (mysem == NULL)
     return(EINVAL);
  ret = sem_wait(mysem);

  return(ret);
}

/*
 * This function releases the lock on a binary semaphore.
 * A semaphore value of 1 means the lock is available.
 * A semaphore value of 0 means the lock is unavailable.
 * This expects the semaphore's value to be initialized to 1 to begin with.
 * This function attempts to increment the semaphore's value by 1 to make
 * it available.
 */
int unlock_posix_semaphore(sem_t *mysem)
{
  int    ret;

  if (mysem == NULL)
     return(EINVAL);
  ret = sem_post(mysem);

  return(ret);
}

/*
 * The worker thread.
 */

int worker_thread(void *args)
{
  unsigned long   *argp;
  unsigned long    myid;
  unsigned long    updcnt;
  int              ret;
  int              i, j;
  long             uselock=1;
  sem_t            *mysemptr;    /* address of POSIX semaphore */

  /* Extract input arguments (two unsigned long integers and one signed) */
  argp = (unsigned long *)args;
  if (argp != NULL)
  {
     myid = argp[0];
     updcnt = argp[1];
     uselock = argp[2];
     mysemptr = (sem_t *)argp[3];
  }
  else
     pthread_exit((void *)(-1));

  fprintf(stdout, "Worker thread: myid=%u updcnt=%u \n", myid, updcnt);
```

```
  /* Do my job */
  for (i = 0; i < updcnt; i++)
  {
    if (uselock)
    {
      ret = lock_posix_semaphore(mysemptr);
      if (ret == -1)
      {
          fprintf(stderr, "lock_posix_semaphore() failed, ret=%d\n", ret);
          pthread_exit((void *)-1);
      }
    }
    globalcnt = globalcnt + 1;              /* update shared variable 1 */
    globalcnt2 = globalcnt2 + 1;            /* update shared variable 2 */
    if (uselock)
    {
      ret = unlock_posix_semaphore(mysemptr);
      if (ret == -1)
      {
          fprintf(stderr, "unlock_posix_semaphore() failed, ret=%d\n", ret);
          pthread_exit((void *)-1);
      }
    }
  }

  pthread_exit((void *)0);
}

int main(int argc, char *argv[])
{
  int       nthrd;                          /* actual number of worker threads */
  int       ret, retval;
  int       i;
  size_t    updcnt = DEFUPDCNT;             /* each thread's file update count */
  pthread_t       thrds[MAXNTHREADS];       /* threads */
  unsigned long args[MAXNTHREADS][4];       /* arguments for each thread */
  int             uselock;                  /* use locking for update or not */
  sem_t           mysem;                    /* my POSIX semaphore */

  if ((argc > 1) &&
      ((strcmp(argv[1], "-h") == 0) || (strcmp(argv[1], "-help") == 0)))
  {
    fprintf(stdout, "Usage: %s [uselock] [nthrd] [updcnt]\n", argv[0]);
    return(-1);
  }

  /*
   * Get the lock switch, number of concurrent threads and update count
   * from the user, if any.
   */
  uselock = 1;
  if (argc > 1)
  {
    uselock = atoi(argv[1]);
    if (uselock != 0)
```

```
      uselock = 1;
}

nthrd = NTHREADS;
if (argc > 2)
   nthrd = atoi(argv[2]);
if (nthrd <= 0 || nthrd > MAXNTHREADS)
   nthrd = NTHREADS;

updcnt = DEFUPDCNT;
if (argc > 3)
   updcnt = atoi(argv[3]);
if (updcnt <= 0)
   updcnt = DEFUPDCNT;

fprintf(stdout, "Increment the values of two shared variables using %u "
   "threads, with each doing it %u times.\n", nthrd, updcnt);
if (uselock)
   fprintf(stdout, "Locking is used during the updates.\n");
else
   fprintf(stdout, "Locking is not used during the updates.\n");
printf("At start, globalcnt=%d globalcnt2=%d\n", globalcnt, globalcnt2);

/* Initialize the value of the semaphore -- value 1 means available */
/* To be shared between threads and initial value is 1. */
ret = sem_init(&mysem, 0, 1); // initialize POSIX semaphore
if (ret == -1)
{
   fprintf(stderr, "sem_init() failed, errno=%d\n", errno);
   ret = (-3);
   goto exit;
}
fprintf(stdout, "Initializing the semaphore value was successful.\n");

/* Load up the input arguments for each worker thread */
for (i = 0; i < nthrd; i++)
{
   args[i][0] = i+1;          /* worker id starts with 1 */
   args[i][1] = updcnt;
   args[i][2] = uselock;
   args[i][3] = (unsigned long)&mysem;
}

/* Create the worker threads to concurrently update the shared variables */
for (i = 0; i < nthrd; i++)
{
   ret = pthread_create(&thrds[i], (pthread_attr_t *)NULL,
         (void *(*)(void *))worker_thread, (void *)args[i]);
   if (ret != 0)
   {
      fprintf(stderr, "Failed to create the worker thread\n");
      ret = (-4);
      goto exit;
   }
}
```

```
/*
 * Wait for each of the child threads to finish and retrieve its returned
 * value. Using a for loop tends to terminate after the first thread exits.
 */
ret = pthread_join(thrds[0], (void **)&retval);
   fprintf(stdout, "Thread %u exited with return value %d\n", 0, retval);
ret = pthread_join(thrds[1], (void **)&retval);
   fprintf(stdout, "Thread %u exited with return value %d\n", 1, retval);
ret = pthread_join(thrds[2], (void **)&retval);
   fprintf(stdout, "Thread %u exited with return value %d\n", 2, retval);
ret = pthread_join(thrds[3], (void **)&retval);
   fprintf(stdout, "Thread %u exited with return value %d\n", 3, retval);

exit:
/* Remove the semaphore */
ret = sem_destroy(&mysem);
if (ret == -1)
{
   fprintf(stderr, "sem_destroy() failed to remove, errno=%d\n", errno);
}
fprintf(stdout, "The semaphore set was successfully removed.\n");

/* Report the end results */
printf("At end, globalcnt=%d globalcnt2=%d\n", globalcnt, globalcnt2);

return(ret);
}
```

Summary

From the example, we can summarize the steps for using a POSIX unnamed semaphore as follows:

Steps in Using POSIX Unnamed Semaphore as Binary Semaphore

(1) include the header file

```
#include <semaphore.h>
```

(2) declare the semaphore variable

```
sem_t  mysem;     /* my POSIX semaphore */
```

To use the POSIX semaphore between processes, this allocation would have to be made within a shared memory accessible to all processes.

(3) init:

```
/* Initialize the value of the semaphore -- value 1 means available */
/* To be shared between threads and initial value is 1. */
ret = sem_init(&mysem, 0, 1);  /* initialize POSIX semaphore */
```

Do the above steps in the main thread only once.

(4) Lock and unlock the semaphore

To lock:

```
ret = sem_wait(&mysem);
```

To unlock:

```
ret = sem_post(&mysem);
```

(5) Destroy the semaphore

To destroy:

```
ret = sem_destroy(&mysem);
```

Do steps 1-3 and 5 in the main thread and do the lock and unlock steps in the worker threads.

9-6-2 Named POSIX Semaphores

A POSIX named semaphore has a universal name associated with it that a process can open it. It's normally created as a virtual file system object. Two processes running on the same system can operate on the same named semaphore by invoking the sem_open() function and providing the same semaphore name.

The format of a POSIX semaphore's name is /NameofMyPosixNamedSemaphore. This name must start with a / character and with no slash character after that. Its maximum length is NAME_MAX-4 because the system uses 4 characters. For example, some operating system prepends the name given by the application with this prefix "sem.".

For instance, in Linux, the file representing a POSIX named semaphore can be seen in the /dev/shm/ directory.

```
[root@srv4 ~]# ls -l /dev/shm/
-rw-r-----. 1 jim oinstall   32 Feb 23 11:16 sem.emupdf2_posix_named_sem
```

However, this is system implementation-dependent. For example, in Apple Darwin, the name is nowhere to be seen.

Also note that even if a POSIX named semaphore exists, one cannot use regular file system APIs to access it. For instance, if you try to use the access() function to test if it exists or not, it won't work. The file system function just doesn't see it. So, it always says it does not exist. But sem_open() can open it.

A POSIX named semaphore can be created or opened by invoking the sem_open() function. After that, the process uses sem_wait() and sem_post() functions to operate on the semaphore. When a process is done using the semaphore, it must invoke the sem_close() function to close it. And when all processes have finished using the semaphore, it can be removed from the system using the sem_unlink() function.

Using POSIX named semaphores involves the following five steps.

```
#include <semaphore.h>

sem_t *sem_open(const char *name, int oflag, ...);
int sem_wait(sem_t *sem);
int sem_post(sem_t *sem);
int sem_close(sem_t *sem);
int sem_unlink(const char *name);
```

The sem_wait() and sem_post() are the same as discussed above. We introduce the other three functions here.

1. The sem_open() Function

The sem_open() function establishes a connection between a POSIX named semaphore and a process. It creates and opens or just opens the named semaphore.

The second argument oflag may contain the following flags OR-ed together.

O_CREAT
  Specifying this flag means the caller would like to create the semaphore if it does not already exist. If O_CREAT is set and the semaphore already exists, then O_CREAT has no effect, except O_EXCL flag is also set.

  Note that specifying the O_CREAT flag requires the third and the fourth arguments for the function. The third argument is mode, which is of type mode_t. It specifies the permission. The fourth argument is value, which is of type unsigned. It specifies the initial value of this semaphore.

O_EXCL
  If O_CREAT and O_EXCL flags are both set, and if the semaphore name already exists, then the sem_open() call will fail. If the semaphore doesn't exist, then the check for the existence of the semaphore and the creation of the semaphore are atomic with respect to other processes executing sem_open() with O_EXCL and O_CREAT set. If O_EXCL is set and O_CREAT is not set, the effect is undefined.

The POSIX Standard does not specify whether the semaphore's name should appear in the file system or whether it is visible to functions taking pathname as an argument. In fact, the semaphore name appears under /dev/shm in Linux but no file system APIs can get to it. This means a program cannot even call a file function to test and see if it exists or not. The entry is nowhere to be seen in Apple Darwin. It's essentially invisible.

Once created, a named semaphore will exist until some program calls sem_unlink() to explicitly remove it.

Each sem_open() call must be matched by a corresponding sem_close() call.

If a process makes multiple successful calls to sem_open() with the same value for name, the same semaphore address will be returned for each such successful call, provided that there have been no calls to sem_unlink() to remove this semaphore.

For instance, all processes sharing a POSIX named semaphore can all make the following call to create or open a named semaphore:

```
mysemptr = sem_open(pathname, O_CREAT, 0660, 1);
```

It will create and initialize the semaphore if it does not already exist. And it will just open it without initialization if it already exists. If successful, the call returns the address of the semaphore.

2. The sem_close() Function

The sem_close() function indicates that the caller is finished using the named POSIX semaphore. It deallocates system resources allocated by the system for use by the caller for this named semaphore.

Every sem_open() call must be matched by a corresponding sem_close() call.

On success, sem_close() returns zero. Otherwise, it returns -1 and errno is set to indicate the error.

3. The sem_unlink() Function

The sem_unlink() function removes the named POSIX semaphore from the system.

If one or more processes have the semaphore open when sem_unlink() is called, destruction of the semaphore is postponed until all references to the semaphore have been destroyed by calls to sem_close(), _exit(), or exec. Calls to sem_open() to recreate or reconnect to the semaphore refer to a new semaphore after sem_unlink() is called. The sem_unlink() call does not block until all references have been destroyed; it will return immediately.

sem_unlink() returns zero on success. Otherwise, it returns -1 and errno is set to indicate the error.

Figure 9-30 is a program demonstrating the use of POSIX named semaphores. The program spawns 4 processes which update an integer in a file at the same time using a POSIX named semaphore as the synchronization facility.

Figure 9-30 Synchronizing multiple processes using a POSIX named semaphore (semupdf2_posix_named_sem.c)

```
/*
 * Concurrent updates of a shared file by multiple processes using
 * POSIX named semaphore as synchronization facility.
 * Read a number in ASCII form from a file, increment its value by one and
 * then write it back.
 * Copyright (c) 2019, 2021 Mr. Jin-Jwei Chen.  All rights reserved.
 */

#include <stdio.h>
#include <errno.h>
#include <sys/types.h>      /* sem_open() */
#include <sys/stat.h>
#include <fcntl.h>
```

```
#include <unistd.h>        /* read(), write(), getpid() */
#include <stdlib.h>        /* atoi(), atol(), atoll() */
#include <string.h>
#include <semaphore.h>     /* for POSIX semaphore */

#define MYSEMNAME  "/emupdf2_posix_named_sem"  /* name of POSIX semaphore */
#define MYDATAFILE "semupf2_datafile"  /* name of shared file */
#define BUFSZ 128              /* maximum length of shared data in file */
#define NPROC    4             /* number of concurrent processes */
#define UPDCNT 1000000         /* default update count */

/* Lock POSIX semaphore */
int acquire_lock(sem_t *mysemptr)
{
  if (mysemptr == NULL)
    return(EINVAL);
  return(sem_wait(mysemptr));
}

/* Unlock POSIX semaphore */
int release_lock(sem_t *mysemptr)
{
  if (mysemptr == NULL)
    return(EINVAL);
  return(sem_post(mysemptr));
}

/* Update shared data value in a file */
int update_shared_file_data(int fd, long updcnt, sem_t *mysemptr)
{
  ssize_t    bytes;
  char       indata[BUFSZ];
  char       outdata[BUFSZ];
  long       dataval, i;
  int        ret;
  size_t     len;

  if (fd <= 0)
    return(EINVAL);

  for (i = 0; i < updcnt; i++)
  {
    /* Acquire the lock */
    ret = acquire_lock(mysemptr);
    if (ret != 0)
    {
      fprintf(stderr, "In update_shared_file_data(), acquire_lock() failed, "
        "ret=%d\n", ret);
      return(ret);
    }

    /* Read the data from the file */
    ret = lseek(fd, 0, SEEK_SET);
    bytes = read(fd, indata, BUFSZ);
    if (bytes < 0)
    {
```

```
        fprintf(stderr, "In update_shared_file_data(), read() failed, errno=%d\n",
          errno);
        release_lock(mysemptr);
        return(errno);
    }

    /* Update the data */
    indata[bytes] = '\0';
    dataval = atol(indata);
    dataval++;

    /* Write the data back into the file */
    sprintf(outdata, "%ld", dataval);
    len = strlen(outdata);
    outdata[len] = '\0';
    ret = lseek(fd, 0, SEEK_SET);
    bytes = write(fd, outdata, (len+1));
    if (bytes < 0)
    {
        fprintf(stderr, "In update_shared_file_data(), write() failed, errno=%d\n",
          errno);
        release_lock(mysemptr);
        return(errno);
    }

    /* Release the lock */
    release_lock(mysemptr);
}

    return(0);
}

int main(int argc, char *argv[])
{
    int     ret = 0;
    int     fd = 0;
    int     nproc;
    long    updcnt = UPDCNT, i;
    char    *pathname = MYSEMNAME;      /* name od POSIX named semaphore */
    sem_t   *mysemptr=SEM_FAILED;       /* pointer to my POSIX semaphore */
    pid_t   pid;
    int     stat;    /* child's exit value */

    /* Get command-line arguments */
    nproc = NPROC;
    if (argc > 1)
        nproc = atoi(argv[1]);
    if (nproc <= 0)
        nproc = NPROC;

    updcnt = UPDCNT;
    if (argc > 2)
        updcnt = atol(argv[2]);
    if (updcnt <= 0)
        updcnt = UPDCNT;
```

```
    fprintf(stdout, "Update shared data in a file for %d times each with %d "
        " processes using POSIX named semaphore.\n", updcnt, nproc);

    /* Create a named POSIX semaphore for synchronization between processes */
    mysemptr = sem_open(pathname, O_CREAT, 0660, 1);
    if (mysemptr == SEM_FAILED)
    {
        fprintf(stderr, "sem_open() failed, errno=%d\n", errno);
        return(-1);
    }
    fprintf(stdout, "Creating/Opening POSIX named semaphore was successful.\n");

    /* Open the file */
    fd = open(MYDATAFILE, (O_CREAT|O_RDWR), 0600);
    if (fd < 0)
    {
        fprintf(stderr, "open('%s') failed, errno=%d\n", MYDATAFILE, errno);
        ret = -2;
        goto exit;
    }

    /* Create the worker processes and let them go to work */
    for (i = 1; i <= nproc; i++)
    {
        pid = fork();

        if (pid == -1)
        {
            fprintf(stderr, "fork() failed, i=%u, errno=%d\n", i, errno);
        }
        else if (pid == 0)
        {
            /* This is the child process. */
            /* Perform the child process' task here */
            /* Update the file */
            ret = update_shared_file_data(fd, updcnt, mysemptr);
            if (ret != 0)
            {
                fprintf(stderr, "update_shared_file_data() failed, ret=%d\n", ret);
                close(fd);
                return(ret);
            }
            return(0);
        }
        else
        {
            /* This is the parent process. */
            /* Simply return */
            return(0);
        }
    }

    /* Wait for all worker processes to finish */
    for (i = 0; i < nproc; i++)
    {
        pid = wait(&stat);
```

```
    }

exit:

    sem_close(mysemptr);

    /* Close the file */
    if (fd > 0) close(fd);
    return(ret);
}
```

9-6-3 Comparison of System V and POSIX Semaphores

Ease of Use

Some may argue that POSIX semaphore is a bit easier to use than System V semaphore but others say it's a toss-up.

The advantage of using System V semaphore is that a System V semaphore, once created, exists in the system and it works for both intraprocess and interprocess situations in exactly the same way. That is, you do it one way and it works for both situations.

In contrast, POSIX semaphore requires different sets of APIs being used between unnamed and named semaphores.

Availability

Although POSIX unnamed semaphores seem to be straightforward to use and provide good performance, not every platform supports them.
For instance, as of the writing of this book, Apple Darwin 19.3 still does not support POSIX unnamed semaphores yet. When the test program is compiled, it says sem_init() was deprecated. But when the program is run, it gets the following error code:

```
    sem_init() failed, errno=78 (ENOSYS)
```

meaning it's not supported.

In contrast, System V semaphore is available in all platforms we did tests on, including Apple Darwin 19.3.

9-7 Comparison of Mutual Exclusion Technologies

Here we do a comparison of all mutual exclusion technologies we have introduced so far in this book.

- our own locking routines
- pthreads mutex
- System V semaphore
- POSIX semaphore (named and unnamed)

Performance Comparisons

Below are some performance numbers obtained from running four threads
where each thread updates two shared variables 100 million times.
The table lists five different technologies used for synchronization
and the times it took.

Figure 9-31 Time it took to update shared data 100M times with 4 threads

```
----------------------------------------------------------------------
synchronization facility         time to update shared variables 100M times
----------------------------     ------------------------------------------
our own locking routines         37.0 secs  (base)
POSIX unnamed semaphore          47.0 secs  (27% slower)
pthreads mutex                   61.4 secs  (66% slower)
POSIX named semaphore            94.0 secs  (254% slower)
System V semaphore               1209 secs  (3267% slower)*
----------------------------------------------------------------------
```

* It looks System V semaphore implementation may have some issue with
  extremely high loop count on some x86 Linux? It was observed that it is
  up to 8 to 32 times slower than our own lock routines on some x86 Linux.

Summary

Figure 9-32 Summary of different mutual exclusion technologies

technology	support multithreads	support multi-processes	performance
our locking routines	Yes	Yes if w/ shared memory	fastest
POSIX unnamed semaphore	Yes	Yes if w/ shared memory	
pthreads mutex	Yes	Yes if w/ shared memory	
POSIX named semaphore	Yes	Yes	
System V semaphore	Yes	Yes	slowest

9-8 Semaphores and Mutexes in Windows

Microsoft Windows operating system makes its kernel services available to
application programs via the so-called Win32 API.
This section gives a quick introduction to the concurrency control
primitives provided by the Windows operating system.
Since this section is Windows specific, it is OK to skip this section
if you are not interested in Windows.

Microsoft Win32 APIs include programming interfaces for both semaphores
and mutexes. Mutexes are like binary semaphores. They are used for mutual
exclusion between processes/threads. Semaphores are superset of mutexes.
A semaphore can take a value between zero and a maximum value specified
at creation time. It is a counting semaphore. A semaphore with a maximum
value of 1 functions as a binary semaphore and can be used in place of
a mutex.

9-8-1 Mutexes in Windows

Mutexes are often used for mutual exclusion between multiple processes or
threads.

A mutex can have a name or no name. It can have no name if it is used only within a single process. If it is used between multiple processes, then it needs to have a name so other processes can access it using the name.

Win32 API has the following functions that allow a program to create, open, release and wait for a mutex.

(1) HANDLE CreateMutex(LPSECURITY_ATTRIBUTES SecurityAttr, BOOL initialOwner, LPCTSTR mutexName)

The CreateMutex() function creates a mutex if it does not already exist and returns a handle to it. It opens a mutex if it already exists. If the third parameter is 0, then the mutex has no name.

(2) HANDLE OpenMutex(DWORD access, BOOL inherit, LPCTSTR mutexName)

The OpenMutex() function opens a mutex by name if it already exists.

(3) BOOL ReleaseMutex(HANDLE mutex)

The ReleaseMutex() function releases a mutex. This performs the unlock operation.

(4) DWORD WaitForSingleObject(HANDLE obj, DWORD time)

The WaitForSingleObject() function waits for the specified object to be available or the so-called "signaled". The wait will last until either the object becomes available or the time specified in the second argument expires. The timeout value is in the unit of milliseconds. To wait as long as the object becomes available, you pass in the value INFINITE.

A mutex is initially set to be in the available or the so-called signaled state unless when it is created the CreateMutex() function specifies TRUE in the initialOwner parameter. In that case, the creator will own the mutex to begin with.

The WaitForSingleObject() function performs the lock operation.

Note that the WaitForSingleObject() function supports nested operations. That is, it is OK for a process/thread that already owns the mutex to call the WaitForSingleObject() function again on the same mutex. In that case, the process/thread will continue to execute, rather than block. However, the process/thread must remember to release the mutex an equal number of times.

Program Example on Locking and Unlocking Mutex

```
MyMutexFunc()
{
  HANDLW mutex;
  mutex = CreateMutex(0, FALSE, "mymutx");

  /* Critical section */

  /* Acquire the mutex */
```

```
    WaitForSingleObject(mutex, INFINITE);

      /* update the shared data or resource here */

    /* Release the mutex */
    ReleaseMutex(mutex);

    CloseHandle(mutex);
  }
```

9-8-2 Semaphores in Windows

In Windows, a semaphore can have a value from zero to a maximum value set at creation. A semaphore of maximum value 1 functions like a mutex.

When the value of a semaphore is zero, the semaphore is considered not "signaled" or not available. In this state, any process/thread waiting on the semaphore will block until the semaphore's value rises above zero, normally as a result of another thread releasing the semaphore. Releasing a semaphore adds a count to the semaphore's current value.

A semaphore in Windows can be named or unnamed, just like mutex.

Win32 API has the following functions for programs to create and use semaphores.

(1) CreateSemaphore(LPSECURITY_ATTRIBUTES securityAttribute,
    LONG initialValue, LONG maxValue, LPCTSTR semaphoreName)

The CreateSemaphore() function creates a semaphore and returns a handle to it if it does not already exist. It opens the semaphore and returns its handle if it already exists.

(2) OpenSemaphore(DWORD access, BOOL inherit, LPCTSTR semaphoreName)

The OpenSemaphore() function opens a semaphore and returns a handle to it if the semaphore already exists. It returns NULL if the semaphore does not already exist.

(3) ReleaseSemaphore(HANDLE semaphoreHandle, LONG valueToAdd, LPLONG oldValue)

This ReleaseSemaphore() function adds the value specified in the second parameter to the current value of the semaphore and releases the semaphore. The semaphore's original value before the incrementing is returned in the third parameter.

Program Example on Semaphore Operation

```
MySemaphoreFunc()
{
  HANDLE  mySemaphore;
  LONG oldSemVal;  /* for holding returned semaphore's old value */

  mySemaphore = CreateSemaphore(0, 1, 1, 0);
```

```
    /* Critical section */
    WaitForSingleObject(mySemaphore, INFINITE);

        /* update the shared data/resource here */

    ReleaseSemaphore(mySemaphore, 1, &oldSemVal);

    CloseHandle(mySemaphore);
}
```

9-9 Deadlock

It's just invaluable that locking/unlocking solves the update loss problem and ensures integrity of shared data during concurrent updates. It works beautifully when there is only one lock involved. However, in a more complicated situation where two or more locks are involved, a serious problem can occur if it is not done correctly. This situation involves a process or thread holding some lock and trying to acquire another.

Unless being handled correctly, a potential problem, deadlock, could occur in these scenarios of multiple locks. For example, in a very simple case, let us say there are two resources that are shared between multiple processes or threads. Each resource has its own lock. Assuming two processes/threads, each needs both resources to do its job. It's entirely possible that the interleaving could end up with a deadlock.

9-9-1 What Is Deadlock?

Deadlock is a situation where two or more processes/threads are waiting for each other to progress and neither can.

Figure 9-33 Deadlock

```
Process/thread 1                    Process/thread 2
-----------------------------       -----------------------------
acquire lockA
                                    acquire lockB
try to acquire lockB (blocked)
                                    try to acquire lockA (blocked)

(can never proceed)                 (can never proceed)

==> deadlock!
----------------------------------------------------------------
```

Here is a simple example. Assuming to complete the computation, a process/thread needs to obtain two locks. It needs to acquire lockA for shared resource 1 and lockB for shared resource 2. If two processes/threads are running side by side at the same time and the interleaving ends up being what is shown in Figure 9-33, then it is a deadlock.

Deadlock is a situation where two or more processes or threads are waiting for each other but none can actually proceed.

In the example above, process/thread 1 is waiting for the resource held by process/thread 2 being released before it can proceed and yet process/thread 2 is waiting for the resource being held by process/thread 1 to be released. Hence, neither one can proceed. It's a deadlock -- no progress can be made forever.

9-9-2 Necessary Conditions for Deadlocks

The paper titled "System Deadlocks" published in Computing Surveys in June of 1971 by E.G. Coffman, M.J. Elphick and A. Shoshani showed that four necessary conditions must hold for a deadlock to occur:

1. Hold and wait.

   At least one of the processes/threads involved in a deadlock must be holding some lock/resource and at the same time waiting for another. In the example, process/thread 1 is holding lockA and waiting for lockB whereas process/thread 2 is holding lockB and waiting for lockA.

2. Circular wait.

   The wait conditions must form a cycle for a deadlock to occur. In the very simple example above, process/thread 1 is waiting for process/thread 2 and process/thread 2 is also waiting for process/thread1, forming a cycle. In a more complicated example, more processes/threads can be involved. For instance, process/thread 1 is waiting for process/thread 2, 2 waiting for 3, 3 waiting for 4, and then 4 waiting for 1.

3. Mutual exclusion.

   The lock/resource that processes/threads are contending for is not sharable. That is, it can only be held by one process/thread at a time. The deadlock would not have occurred if either lockA or lockB in Figure 9-33 is sharable.

4. No preemption.

   The lock/resource held cannot be preempted. It has to be voluntarily released by the process/thread holding it. The deadlock in Fig 9-33 would be able to be eliminated if one can take away either lockA from process/thread 1 or lockB from process/thread 2.

9-9-3 Three Approaches to Deadlocks

There are three different approaches to dealing with the deadlock problem.

1. Deadlock detection:

   Deadlock detection allows a deadlock to occur but tries to detect it and then recover from it.

2. Deadlock prevention:

Deadlock prevention defines and deploys certain protocol that places restrictions on how locks/resources are requested such that one of the necessary conditions causing deadlocks won't ever hold.

3. Deadlock avoidance:

A deadlock avoidance algorithm dynamically examines the system to ensure there is no circular wait condition. It relies on certain information being available when the system makes decision on whether to grant a lock/resource to a requester. The algorithm essentially maintains a state table and makes sure the system does not get into a deadlock or unsafe state.

9-9-4 Deadlock Detection and Recovery

Deadlock can be detected by constructing the transaction wait-for graph in which a node represents a transaction involved and an edge represents one transaction waiting for another to release the lock/resource. A cycle in the graph means a deadlock.

When implemented, a deadlock detection can be continuous or periodic. A continuous deadlock detection results in a rapid detection but consumes more resources. A periodic one results in a slower detection but consumes less resources.

Deadlock Recovery

Once a deadlock is detected, recovering from it involves picking one or more victim deadlocked processes/threads to terminate or rollback and then terminating them.

A deadlock recovery algorithm must ensure it is free of some of the following potential issues.

First, in selecting a victim to terminate or abort, it makes sense to pick the least expensive process/thread from the cost point of view. However, if cost is the only factor used in the determination, it is possible that the same process, after it is picked as a victim and terminated, can get into a repeated deadlock and being picked as a rollback victim again after it is re-started. In other words, starvation can happen to the least expensive process(es) or thread(s).

Second, in actually implementing the rollback, the recovery algorithm needs to be very careful when terminating a victim process. The termination must ensure the locks or shared resources held by that process/thread do not end up being in an incorrect or inconsistent state. For example, you definitely don't want a lock being held by the process being terminated becomes lost, or the data it was modifying become corrupted, after the termination! The actual implementation must carefully guard against these.

There are various kinds of deadlock detection algorithms: centralized, distributed and hierarchical. Some of them may have potential issues such as overhead and phantom (i.e. false) deadlock to be dealt with.

It's beyond the scope of this book to cover these algorithms. Readers interested in this topic are encouraged to read related books and papers. A good starting point is the book: 'Operating Systems -- Advanced Concepts' by Mamoru Maekawa, Arthur E. Oldehoeft and Rodney R. Oldehoeft, published by The Benjamin/Cummings Publishing Company, Inc.

9-9-5 Deadlock Prevention

Deadlock avoidance is practically very difficult to implement. Therefore, most existing software uses deadlock prevention.

There are a number of techniques that can be used to prevent deadlocks. We will introduce three very common ones in this section.

9-9-5-1 Request All Needed Resources at Once

The first technique for preventing deadlocks is to eliminate the Hold And Wait condition causing deadlocks. In other words, if all processes/threads know in advance what locks/resources they need in completing their tasks and request them all at once, then there won't be a hold and wait situation. Hence, there will not be any deadlock.

The problem with this solution is that most processes/threads do not know all the locks/resources they need in advance. Typically, what they actually need is very dynamic. And it all depends on the values of a number of variables, which change from time to time. Yes, one can program it in such a way that it always takes the most pessimistic approach and always requests all of the locks/resources it can potentially ever need. But this would lead to very low degree of parallelism or concurrency between the contending tasks and result in very poor resource utilization and performance.

9-9-5-2 Ordering All Resources

A better solution in deadlock prevention can be provided by eliminating the circular wait condition. One technique is to define and deploy a strict order in which all locks/resources can be requested and require all processes/threads to follow that same order in requesting them. With this, the circular wait condition will never occur and thus there won't be any deadlock. To implement this requires analyzing the system, sorting out and deriving a global order that works for all applications needing the locks/resources.

Author has worked on a couple of Unix kernels that actually deploy this deadlock prevention technique.

As an example, if the system or application has to use 100 different locks. You would number them from 1 to 100 and determine a strict order in which they can be requested. For instance:

```
Shared resource 1      -- Lock 1
Shared resource 2      -- Lock 2
     :
Shared resource 99     -- Lock 99
Shared resource 100    -- Lock 100
```

:

Say, if a task needs shared resource 3, 5 and 20 to finish a computation. Then it must acquire Lock 3 before it tries to acquire Lock 5 or 20. It must also acquire Lock 5 after it has acquired Lock 3 and before it tries to acquire Lock 20. In short, no matter how many locks a process/thread needs, the order it requests them must comply with the order defined.

Just another example. If process/thread 1 needs lock5 and lock7 and process/thread 2 needs lock5, lock7 and lock 12 to do their jobs, then process/thread 1 must try to acquire the locks it needs in this order:

```
Process/Thread 1
----------------
    :
acquire lock5
    :
acquire lock7
```

and process/thread 2 must try to acquire the locks it needs in this order:

```
Process/Thread 2
----------------
    :
acquire lock5
    :
acquire lock7
    :
acquire lock12
```

As you can see in this example, only one of the two processes/threads will eventually be able to obtain lock5, not both. And the other one will have to wait. Assuming all processes/threads follow the same ordering protocol, the process/thread having lock5 will be the one to get lock7 as well once it is available. And it will be the one being able to get both lock5 and lock7 and be able to proceed. As you can see, the blocking each other scenario illustrated earlier in Fig 9-33 is avoided here because of the enforced ordering.

You may ask "What order is the right one?" Well, it's all application dependent. It takes some analysis and perhaps also some trial and error to figure out what the best order is. In general, the analysis involves examining what order most or all of the applications would use in acquiring the locks. In some cases, you may have to change the application or even reorganize some locks to make the defined order work for all applications.

9-9-5-3 Preemption

One of the necessary conditions for deadlocks to occur is no preemption. That is, resources held by threads/processes are only voluntarily released. So, one of the deadlock prevention techniques works by preventing the "No preemption" condition from occurring.

Preemption involves taking a lock/resource away from one process/thread that currently owns it and giving it to another.

There are at least two ways to implement preemption.

First, if a process/thread already holds some locks/resources
and is requesting for another which is not immediately available,
then all the locks/resources held by the process/thread will be preempted.
That is, they will be released so that other processes/threads can get them
and they are added to the list of locks/resources this process is waiting
for.

Another way to implement the preemption is that if process/thread A is
requesting some lock/resource which is currently held by another process/
thread B and if that process is waiting for some other additional resource,
then the algorithm will rob it from process/thread B and assign it to
process/thread A.

9-9-6 Livelock

Although it almost never happens, one potential risk of deploying locking
with busy waiting is that if there is a program bug that leads to the lock
never becomes available, then a task waiting on getting this lock will spin
forever and never get out of that state of looping and testing. This
situation is referred to as a 'livelock'. The task is still running but it
loops and tests a condition that will never turn true. That is, the process/
thread is not blocking but there is no possibility of making progress either.

However, only a program bug can create this situation. If the lock is
implemented correctly and there is no bug in the program logic, this would
not happen.

9-9-7 Starvation

On a system, it's very typical that multiple tasks are waiting for a
pool of resources at the same time, with different resource requirements.
To optimize on achieving maximum throughput, it may make sense to give the
available resources to smaller tasks first because they can complete faster.
However, this has a possibility of making tasks with large resource
requirements being starved, too. Therefore, the system's resource allocation
policy must be very careful about not always favoring tasks with smaller
resource requirements and thus ending up with leaving tasks with larger
resource requirements starved. This situation can also be called livelock.

So be careful when you try to optimize system performance.
Make sure it does not have a side effect of causing certain jobs to starve,
which is different from deadlock but may look like deadlock.

9-9-8 Preventing Deadlock in Reentrant Situation

In this section, we present an example of deadlock and how to prevent it
by making a function reentrant.

Programs from time to time use recursive functions that call themselves in
the middle of the function. If the involved function taking locks, it could

lead to deadlock because it could be that the calling process or thread has already acquired the lock on the first entry and the subsequent calls try to acquire the same lock again and thus a deadlock occurs.

Nested calls could lead to the same deadlock situation too as described above. For example, resource XYZ must be used exclusively. A program could have function A and function B both depend on resource XYZ. And function A could call function B or vice versa. Let us say function A is called and has acquired the exclusive lock on resource XYZ already. If it then calls function B, when function B tries to acquire the lock on resource XYZ again, it will deadlock unless it's a lock supporting recursive locking.

Figure 9-34 shows an example program illustrating deadlock from nested calls.

Figure 9-34 Deadlock caused by nested calls (semupd_mylock_deadlock.c)

```
/*
 * Demonstration of deadlocks
 * Copyright (c) 2013, 2019-2020 Mr. Jin-Jwei Chen.  All rights reserved.
 */

#include "mysemutil.h"

/* Default values related to the shared file */
#define   NTHREADS    2              /* number of concurrent threads */
#define   MAXNTHREADS 12             /* max. number of concurrent threads */
#define   NTASKS      5              /* number of tasks */
#define   MAXDELAYCNT 1000000        /* delay count */

/* Shared lock variable */
int     lockvar=0;

/* These are our own locking functions in assembly language. */
int spinlock(int *lockvar);
int unlock(int *lockvar);

int funcA(unsigned int  myid, int nestedcall);
int funcB(unsigned int  myid);

void lockXYZ()
{
    spinlock(&lockvar);
}

void unlockXYZ()
{
    unlock(&lockvar);
}

int funcA(unsigned int  myid, int nestedcall)
{
  fprintf(stdout, "Thread %2d execute part 1 in function A\n", myid);
  lockXYZ();
  /* Do some funcA specific processing */
  fprintf(stdout, "Thread %2d execute part 2 in function A\n", myid);
  if (nestedcall)
```

```
    funcB(myid);
  unlockXYZ();
  fprintf(stdout, "Thread %2d return from function A\n", myid);
  return(0);
}

int funcB(unsigned int  myid)
{
  fprintf(stdout, "Thread %2d execute part 1 in function B\n", myid);
  lockXYZ();
  /* Do some funcB specific processing */
  fprintf(stdout, "Thread %2d execute part 2 in function B\n", myid);
  unlockXYZ();
  fprintf(stdout, "Thread %2d return from function B\n", myid);
  return(0);
}

/*
 * The worker thread.
 */

int worker_thread(void *args)
{
  unsigned int  *argp;
  unsigned int  myid;
  unsigned int  ntasks;
  int           ret;
  int           i, j;
  int           nestedcall=1;

  /* Extract input arguments (two unsigned integers) */
  argp = (unsigned int *)args;
  if (argp != NULL)
  {
    myid = argp[0];
    ntasks = argp[1];
    nestedcall = argp[2];
  }
  else
    pthread_exit((void *)(-1));

  fprintf(stdout, "Worker thread: myid=%u ntasks=%u\n", myid, ntasks);

  /* Do my job */
  for (i = 0; i < NTASKS; i++)
  {
    funcA(myid, nestedcall);
    for (j=0; j < MAXDELAYCNT; j++);    /* create a bit of delay */
  }

  pthread_exit((void *)0);
}

int main(int argc, char *argv[])
{
  int     nthrd;                        /* actual number of worker threads */
```

```
int      ret, retval;
int      i;
size_t   ntasks = NTASKS;                /* each thread's task count */
pthread_t       thrds[MAXNTHREADS];      /* threads */
unsigned int  args[MAXNTHREADS][3];  /* arguments for each thread */
int          nestedcall;                 /* use locking for update or not */

if ((argc > 1) &&
    ((strcmp(argv[1], "-h") == 0) || (strcmp(argv[1], "-help") == 0)))
{
  fprintf(stdout, "Usage: %s [nestedcall] [nthrd] [ntasks]\n", argv[0]);
  return(-1);
}

/*
 * Get the number of concurrent threads, number of tasks and nested call
 * switch from the user, if any.
 */
nestedcall = 1;
if (argc > 1)
{
  nestedcall = atoi(argv[1]);
  if (nestedcall != 0)
    nestedcall = 1;
}

nthrd = NTHREADS;
if (argc > 2)
  nthrd = atoi(argv[2]);
if (nthrd <= 0 || nthrd > MAXNTHREADS)
  nthrd = NTHREADS;

ntasks = NTASKS;
if (argc > 3)
  ntasks = atoi(argv[3]);
if (ntasks <= 0)
  ntasks = NTASKS;

fprintf(stdout, "Demonstrating deadlock from nested calls of trying to "
  "acquire the same lock using %u threads, with each doing it %lu times.\n",
  nthrd, ntasks);
if (nestedcall)
  fprintf(stdout, "Nested call is used in the demo.\n");
else
  fprintf(stdout, "Nested call is not used in the demo.\n");

/* Load up the input arguments for each worker thread */
for (i = 0; i < nthrd; i++)
{
  args[i][0] = i+1;          /* worker id starts with 1 */
  args[i][1] = ntasks;
  args[i][2] = nestedcall;
}

/* Create the worker threads to concurrently update the shared file */
for (i = 0; i < nthrd; i++)
```

```
   {
      ret = pthread_create(&thrds[i], (pthread_attr_t *)NULL,
            (void *(*)(void *))worker_thread, (void *)args[i]);
      if (ret != 0)
      {
         fprintf(stderr, "Failed to create the worker thread\n");
         return(-2);
      }
   }

   /*
    * Wait for each of the child threads to finish and retrieve its returned
    * value.
    */
   for (i = 0; i < nthrd; i++)
   {
      ret = pthread_join(thrds[i], (void **)&retval);
      fprintf(stdout, "Thread %u exited with return value %d\n", i, retval);
   }

   return(0);
}
```

The deadlock in these two situations can be prevented or avoided by making the function A and B reentrant with respect to the lock on resource XYZ. For the same process or thread, it does not need to acquire the same lock more than once. That is, as long as a process or thread has acquired a particular lock, if it hits the code trying to acquire the same lock again, it should just skip it because it has already owned that lock.
And when it hits the unlocking code for the same lock, it should skip the unlock function unless it (the current invocation) is the one that actually acquired the lock earlier.

Figure 9-35 shows an example program that demonstrates this.

Figure 9-35 Preventing deadlock due to reentrance (semupd_mylock_reentrant.c)

```
/*
 * Making functions taking and releasing locks reentrantly.
 * Copyright (c) 2013, 2019, 2020 Mr. Jin-Jwei Chen.  All rights reserved.
 */

#include "mysemutil.h"

/* Default values related to the shared file */
#define  NTHREADS     2                    /* number of concurrent threads */
#define  MAXNTHREADS 12                     /* max. number of concurrent threads */
#define  NTASKS       5                    /* number of tasks */
#define  MAXDELAYCNT 10000000               /* delay count */

/* Shared lock variable */
int      lockvar=0;

/* Shared data for making locking functions thread reentrant */
static pthread_key_t   has_lock;           /* Thread specific data */
```

```c
/* These are our own locking functions in assembly language. */
int spinlock(int *lockvar);
int unlock(int *lockvar);

int funcA(unsigned int  myid, int nestedcall);
int funcB(unsigned int  myid);

/* Routine used to lock resource XYZ */
void lockXYZ()
{
    spinlock(&lockvar);
}

/* Routine used to unlock resource XYZ */
void unlockXYZ()
{
    unlock(&lockvar);
}

/* Function A updates resource XYZ and also calls function B which
 * updates resource XYZ. too. */
int funcA(unsigned int  myid, int nestedcall)
{
  unsigned int  islocked=0;
  unsigned int  2unlock=0;  /* remember if this invocation gets the lock */

  fprintf(stdout, "Thread %2d execute part 1 in function A\n", myid);

  /* Get information about if this thread has the lockXYZ or not */
  islocked = pthread_getspecific(has_lock);

  /* Try to acquire the lock only if this thread does not have the lock */
  if (islocked <= 0)
  {
    lockXYZ();
    islocked = 1;
    pthread_setspecific(has_lock, (void *)islocked);
    2unlock++;
  }

  /* Do some funcA specific processing */
  fprintf(stdout, "Thread %2d execute part 2 in function A\n", myid);
  if (nestedcall)
    funcB(myid);

  /* Try to release the lock only if this thread has the lock AND
   * it's this invocation that actually acquired the lock */
  if (islocked > 0 && 2unlock > 0)
  {
    unlockXYZ();
    islocked = 0;
    pthread_setspecific(has_lock, (void *)islocked);
    2unlock--;
  }
  fprintf(stdout, "Thread %2d return from function A\n", myid);
  return(0);
```

```
}

/* Function B updates resource XYZ, too. */
int funcB(unsigned int  myid)
{
  unsigned int  islocked=0;
  unsigned int  2unlock=0;  /* remember if this invocation gets the lock */

  fprintf(stdout, "Thread %2d execute part 1 in function B\n", myid);

  /* Get information about if this thread has the lockXYZ or not */
  islocked = pthread_getspecific(has_lock);

  /* Try to acquire the lock only if this thread does not have the lock */
  if (islocked <= 0)
  {
    lockXYZ();
    islocked = 1;
    pthread_setspecific(has_lock, (void *)islocked);
    2unlock++;
  }

  /* Do some funcB specific processing */
  fprintf(stdout, "Thread %2d execute part 2 in function B\n", myid);

  /* Try to release the lock only if this thread has the lock AND
   * it's this invocation that actually acquired the lock */
  if (islocked > 0 && 2unlock > 0)
  {
    unlockXYZ();
    islocked = 0;
    pthread_setspecific(has_lock, (void *)islocked);
    2unlock--;
  }
  fprintf(stdout, "Thread %2d return from function B\n", myid);
  return(0);
}

/*
 * The worker thread.
 */

int worker_thread(void *args)
{
  unsigned int  *argp;
  unsigned int  myid;
  unsigned int  ntasks;
  int           ret = 0;
  int           i, j;
  int           nestedcall=1;
  unsigned int  islocked=0;        /* initial value of thread-specific data */

  /* Extract input arguments (two unsigned integers) */
  argp = (unsigned int *)args;
  if (argp != NULL)
  {
```

583

```
      myid = argp[0];
      ntasks = argp[1];
      nestedcall = argp[2];
    }
  else
#ifdef SUN64
    {
      ret = (-1);
      pthread_exit((void *)&ret);
    }
#else
      pthread_exit((void *)(-1));
#endif

  fprintf(stdout, "Worker thread: myid=%u ntasks=%u\n", myid, ntasks);

  /* Initialize thread-specific data */
  ret = pthread_setspecific(has_lock, (void *)islocked);
  if (ret != 0)
    {
      fprintf(stderr, "worker_thread(): pthread_setspecific() failed, ret=%d\n",
        ret);
#ifdef SUN64
      ret = (-2);
      pthread_exit((void *)&ret);
#else
      pthread_exit((void *)(-2));
#endif
    }

  /* Do my job */
  for (i = 0; i < NTASKS; i++)
    {
      funcA(myid, nestedcall);
      for (j=0; j < MAXDELAYCNT; j++);    /* create a bit of delay */
    }

#ifdef SUN64
  pthread_exit((void *)&ret);
#else
  pthread_exit((void *)0);
#endif
}

int main(int argc, char *argv[])
{
  int      nthrd;                        /* actual number of worker threads */
  int      ret, retval;
#ifdef SUN64
  int      *retvalp = &retval;           /* pointer to returned value */
#endif
  int      i;
  size_t   ntasks = NTASKS;              /* each thread's task count */
  pthread_t       thrds[MAXNTHREADS];    /* threads */
  unsigned int  args[MAXNTHREADS][3];    /* arguments for each thread */
  int             nestedcall;            /* use locking for update or not */
```

```
if ((argc > 1) &&
    ((strcmp(argv[1], "-h") == 0) || (strcmp(argv[1], "-help") == 0)))
{
  fprintf(stdout, "Usage: %s [nestedcall] [nthrd] [ntasks]\n", argv[0]);
  return(-1);
}

/*
 * Get the number of concurrent threads, number of tasks to perform for
 * each thread and doing nested calls or not from the user, if any.
 */
nestedcall = 1;
if (argc > 1)
{
  nestedcall = atoi(argv[1]);
  if (nestedcall != 0)
    nestedcall = 1;
}

nthrd = NTHREADS;
if (argc > 2)
  nthrd = atoi(argv[2]);
if (nthrd <= 0 || nthrd > MAXNTHREADS)
  nthrd = NTHREADS;

ntasks = NTASKS;
if (argc > 3)
  ntasks = atoi(argv[3]);
if (ntasks <= 0)
  ntasks = NTASKS;

fprintf(stdout, "Demonstration of making functions reentrant to prevent "
  "deadlock using %u threads, with each doing it %lu times.\n",
  nthrd, ntasks);
if (nestedcall)
  fprintf(stdout, "Nested call is used in the demo.\n");
else
  fprintf(stdout, "Nested call is not used in the demo.\n");

/* Create the thread-specific data key and initialize its value to 0 */
ret = pthread_key_create(&has_lock, (void *)NULL);
if (ret != 0)
{
  fprintf(stderr, "pthread_key_create() failed, ret=%d\n", ret);
  return(ret);
}

/* Load up the input arguments for each worker thread */
for (i = 0; i < nthrd; i++)
{
  args[i][0] = i+1;        /* worker id starts with 1 */
  args[i][1] = ntasks;
  args[i][2] = nestedcall;
}
```

```
/* Create the worker threads to concurrently update the shared file */
for (i = 0; i < nthrd; i++)
{
    ret = pthread_create(&thrds[i], (pthread_attr_t *)NULL,
            (void *(*)(void *))worker_thread, (void *)args[i]);
    if (ret != 0)
    {
        fprintf(stderr, "Failed to create the worker thread\n");
        return(-2);
    }
}

/*
 * Wait for each of the child threads to finish and retrieve its returned
 * value.
 */
for (i = 0; i < nthrd; i++)
{
#ifdef SUN64
    ret = pthread_join(thrds[i], (void **)&retvalp);
#else
    ret = pthread_join(thrds[i], (void **)&retval);
#endif
    fprintf(stdout, "Thread %u exited with return value %d\n", i, retval);
}

/* Destroy the thread-specific data key */
ret = pthread_key_delete(has_lock);
if (ret != 0)
{
    fprintf(stderr, "pthread_key_delete() failed, ret=%d\n", ret);
    return(ret);
}

return(0);
}
```

In this example program, we declare and use a global variable lockvar as
the lock variable for resource XYZ. The functions lockXYZ() and unlockXYZ()
acquire and release the lock on resource XYZ, respectively.

To make the functions A and B become reentrantable with respect to the lock,
we declare and use another global variable of pthread_key_t type named
has_lock. This is the key for thread specific data that we will use to
remember whether a particular thread has already obtained the lock on
resource XYZ. A value of 1 means the thread has, 0 means no.
Since each thread is different on whether it has acquired this particular
lock or not, we use a thread-specific data (i.e. thread local storage) to
keep track of it.

The main() function of the program invokes pthread_key_create() to create
the thread-specific data key in the beginning so that it is available to
all child threads. It also invokes pthread_key_delete() to destroy it at
the end of the program.

The value of the thread-specific data is initialized to 0 in each thread at the very beginning in the worker_thread() function.

At top of functions A and B, a thread calls the pthread_getspecific(has_lock) function to retrieve the current value of has_lock. If the value is 0, it will actually attempt to acquire the lock on resource XYZ. Otherwise, it will skip the lockXYZ() call to prevent from deadlocking itself. If the thread actually calls lockXYZ(), then it will invoke pthread_setspecific() to set the value of has_lock to 1, indicating this thread has already acquired the lock.

We introduce a second local variable named 2unlock to solve the problem on the unlock side. Note that with our design and implementation, a thread's execution may result in nested calls of function A and/or B multiple times. But there is only one call (the first one) that will result in actually calling lockXYZ(). Since the call to lockXYZ() and unlockXYZ() must be completely symmetrical (i.e. always in pair), we must ensure the unlockXYZ() is called only once, too. Not more than once. And exactly in the invocation that first acquires the lock, not any other. Therefore, we introduce the 2unlock local variable to track this. This is a local variable and it is initialized to 0. It is set to 1 only if the current invocation actually calls lockXYZ(). So, by examining this value, it knows whether it should call unlockXYZ() or not. This ensures it ends up calling the unlockXYZ() in the right invocation. If the current thread has a value of 1 in has_lock and 2unlock is also 1, then it must call the unlockXYZ() to release the lock!

In short, **this example program demonstrates how to use thread-specific data to make functions reentrant with respect to locks and prevent them from deadlocking themselves**.

How do you make a function with locking and unlocking operations reentrant for threads so that a thread won't deadlock itself? This is how you do it. In short, each thread uses thread specific data (i.e. thread local storage) to remember whether it has acquired a particular lock or not. If yes, then a nested or recursive lock operation will be skipped, because the same thread has already held that lock and there is no need to do it again because that would deadlock itself. Similarly, an attempt to release a lock in a nested or recursive call will be skipped if during that call the corresponding lock operation was skipped. **This solves the self-deadlock problem that occurs in a nested or recursive call scenario.**

9-10 System Tuning Parameters Related to System V Semaphore

In a typical Unix or Linux operating system, there are a number of operating system configurable kernel parameters that are related to System V IPC resources. In general, these parameters place a cap on the maximum number of instances of a particular type of resource a system can have.

For instance, on some Linux operating system, the default value for the maximum number of semaphores in a semaphore set is 128. In that case, if a program tries to create a semaphore set with 200 semaphores in it, the semget() function would get an error with errno set to EINVAL.

Many software products use the System V IPC resources. They all have different requirements of these resources. For these resources, two types of operating system kernel tuning normally need to be done. First, you may need to increase the default values of some of these kernel parameters just to be able to install or start up the application. Second, you may also need to adjust the values of some of these parameters to achieve better performance. We discuss this tuning in this section.

The kernel parameters related to System V semaphores in a Linux system are listed below. Most, if not all, of these parameters exist in Unix, too. These are all integers.

```
semmni - maximum number of semaphore sets the system can have
         This limit may affect the semget() call.
semmsl - maximum number of semaphores a semaphore set can have
         This limit may affect the semget() call.
semmns - maximum number of semaphores all semaphore sets can have in total
         This limit may affect the semget() call.
semvmx - maximum value a semaphore value can be. This limit affects
         the semctl() call.
semopm - maximum number operations semop() can perform
semaem - maximum value that can be recorded for semaphore adjustment
         (SEM_UNDO)
semmnu - maximum number of undo structures system-wide
semume - maximum number of undo entries per process
semusz - size of sem_undo structure
semmap - number of entries in semaphore map
```

9-10-1 Querying Kernel Parameters

Querying the current values of kernel tunable parameters is not a standard. On some systems there is a command for it. On others, you have to do it programmatically. This section shows how to do it in some of the popular operating systems.

Linux

In Linux, to query the current values of all kernel parameters, run this following command:

```
$ /sbin/sysctl -a
```

To query the current values of the semaphore kernel parameters, run:

```
$ cat /proc/sys/kernel/sem
```

To query the current setting of a particular kernel parameter (say, shmmni) run:

```
$ cat /proc/sys/kernel/shmmni
```

Oracle/Sun Solaris

On Solaris, you can display the list of the drivers and modules currently loaded and some kernel parameter values by using the /usr/sbin/sysdef command:

```
# sysdef -i
```

IBM AIX

To query all of the configurable kernel parameters and their current values, run the following lsattr command:

```
# /etc/lsattr -E -l sys0
```

To query the current setting of a particular kernel parameter, run the following lsattr command with the parameter name:

```
# /etc/lsattr -E -l sys0 -a semmni
```

HP HP-UX

In HP-UX, current settings of kernel parameters can be viewed via the menu-based system management utility named SAM.

A Programming Example in Linux

Figure 9-36 is a program that displays the current settings of all of the semaphore related kernel parameters in Linux.

Figure 9-36 Program displaying Linux kernel semaphore parameters (semipcinfo.c)

```c
/*
 * Demonstrate the IPCINFO command of the semctl function.
 * Note: The semctl() IPC_INFO command is not supported in AIX or Solaris.
 * Copyright (c) 2013, Mr. Jin-Jwei Chen.  All rights reserved.
 */

#define  _GNU_SOURCE    /* to get IPC_INFO, which is Linux specific */

#include "mysemutil.h"

void print_seminfo(struct seminfo *p);

int main(int argc, char *argv[])
{
  key_t  ipckey;
  int    projid;
  int    semid;
  int    ret;
  int    exit_code=0;
  semun  semarg;
  struct seminfo  seminfo;
  int    i;

  if (argc > 1)
    projid = atoi(argv[1]);
  else
    projid = IPCSUBID;

  /* Compute the IPC key value from the pathname and project id */
  /* ftok() got error 2 if the pathname does not exist. */
```

```c
if ((ipckey = ftok(IPCKEYPATH, projid)) == (key_t)-1) {
  fprintf(stderr, "ftok() failed, errno=%d\n", errno);
  return(-1);
}

/* Create the semaphore */
semid = semget(ipckey, 1, IPC_CREAT|0600);
if (semid == -1)
{
  fprintf(stderr, "semget() failed, errno=%d\n", errno);
  return(-2);
}
fprintf(stdout, "The semaphore was successfully created.\n");

/* Get the system-wide semaphore limits and parameters */
semarg.__buf = &seminfo;
ret = semctl(semid, 0, IPC_INFO, semarg);
if (ret == -1)
{
  fprintf(stderr, "semctl() failed to do IPC_INFO, errno=%d\n", errno);
  exit_code = (-3);
}
else
  print_seminfo(&seminfo);

/* Remove the semaphore */
/* The second argument, semnum, is ignored for removal. */
ret = semctl(semid, 0, IPC_RMID);
if (ret == -1)
{
  fprintf(stderr, "semctl() failed to remove, errno=%d\n", errno);
  return(-4);
}
fprintf(stdout, "The semaphore set was successfully removed.\n");

  return(exit_code);
}

void print_seminfo(struct seminfo *p)
{
  if (p == NULL)
    return;
  fprintf(stdout, "semmap = %d\n", p->semmap);
  fprintf(stdout, "semmni = %d\n", p->semmni);
  fprintf(stdout, "semmns = %d\n", p->semmns);
  fprintf(stdout, "semmnu = %d\n", p->semmnu);
  fprintf(stdout, "semmsl = %d\n", p->semmsl);
  fprintf(stdout, "semopm = %d\n", p->semopm);
  fprintf(stdout, "semume = %d\n", p->semume);
  fprintf(stdout, "semusz = %d\n", p->semusz);
  fprintf(stdout, "semvmx = %d\n", p->semvmx);
  fprintf(stdout, "semaem = %d\n", p->semaem);
}
```

Below is the output of the program:

```
$ ./semipcinfo

semmap = 32000
semmni = 128
semmns = 32000
semmnu = 32000
semmsl = 250
semopm = 100
semume = 32
semusz = 20
semvmx = 32767
semaem = 32767
```

Note that the semipcinfo program is not supported in all platforms.
For instance, it does not compile in Apple Darwin because of two reasons.
(1) The IPC_INFO operation of semctl() is not defined in Apple Darwin.
(2) The definition of 'union semun' in Apple Darwin does not include the
__buf member.

This program is not supported in AIX or Solaris either. The semctl()
function does not support the IPC_INFO command in AIX or Solaris.

9-10-2 Changing Kernel Parameters

If the default or current setting of some kernel parameter(s) leads to
the application either fails to start or not performs well, then you will
need to tune the kernel and change the value of the parameter(s).

To change kernel tunable parameters, you must login as the root user --
the super user, or as a user with the super user privilege.

Below is how you change the operating system kernel parameters to suit the
need of your application in various systems.

Linux

    In Linux, to change a kernel parameter, use an editor to set or change
    the parameter' value directly in the file /etc/sysctl.conf and then
    run the 'sysctl -p' command to make your changes take effect.

    # vi /etc/sysctl.conf

    e.g.

      kernel.semmni = 256

    # /sbin/sysctl -p /etc/sysctl.conf

    The filename at end of this command is optional.

Oracle/Sun Solaris

    In Oracle/Sun Solaris, kernel parameters are modified by directly editing
    the /etc/system file using a text editor. The parameters are set by

using the following syntax:

```
set  semmni=256
```

In order for the changes you make to take effect, you must reboot the system (e.g. with the '/sbin/shutdown -r now' command).

IBM AIX

There are two ways to change a kernel parameter's value in IBM AIX. One is to use the chdev command and the other is to use the AIX's menu-based system administration tool named SMIT.

For example, the following command set the value of the semmni kernel parameter to 256.

```
# /etc/chdev -l sys0 -a semmni = 256
```

AIX dynamically allocates and reallocates most kernel parameter resources up to a predefined limit. Therefore, no manual reconfiguration is needed. No system reboot is necessary.

HP HP-UX

On HP HP-UX systems, the kernel parameters can be modified via a tool called SAM. SAM is a menu-driven system administration management tool.

9-11 Summary of Concurrency Problems and Solutions

9-11-1 Locking Facilities

9-11-1-1 Update Loss Problem

(a) Using your own locking routines

- This can be done on virtually any modern operating system as long as the underlying processor has atomic instruction(s) to support. And most modern processors do.

- This always works within the same process. It works between processes if the lock variable is placed in shared memory.

(b) Using operating system kernel services

- Unix/Linux: Use binary semaphore from System V or POSIX semaphore -- This works within a single process or between processes.

- Windows: Use mutex or semaphore.

(c) Using software packages

- Unix/Linux: pthreads mutex
- Windows: pthreads mutex

Figure 9-37 Different locking facilities for update loss problem

using	environment	facility	between threads	between processes
your own lock routines	any	atomic instruction(s)	Yes	Yes, if in shared memory
OS services	Unix/Linux	binary semaphore	Yes	Yes **
	Windows	mutex, binary semaphore	Yes	Yes
SW packages	Unix/Linux: Pthreads	mutex	Yes	Yes if in shared memory
	Windows: Pthreads	mutex	Yes	Yes if in shared memory

** Yes for System V semaphores and POSIX named semaphores. Yes for POSIX unnamed semaphores if they are placed in shared memory.

9-11-2 A Quick Recap

In this chapter, we learn what update loss is, update loss occurs at assembly language instruction level, the assembly language instruction(s) that provides the foundation for mutual exclusion in today's most popular computer processors, and how to design and implement your own locking routines in assembly language to achieve mutual exclusion and best performance.

Besides, we also introduce System V and POSIX semaphores and compare various mutual exclusion technologies.

To ensure data integrity and no update loss, mutual exclusion is required for concurrent or simultaneous updates of shared data.

That is, when two or more processes or threads are accessing the same shared data either concurrently or simultaneously and some of them are modifying it, there can be only one access of the data at any instant of time. In other word, mutual exclusion protects data integrity (i.e. correctness) from concurrent or simultaneous updates. Without mutual exclusion, update loss could occur and the data would become incorrect.

Mutual exclusion is accomplished via locking. A lock is associated with a piece of shared data. Whoever needs to modify the shared data must acquire the lock on the shared data first. Everyone else not holding the lock on the shared data must wait until the lock is released.

A lock is usually an integer variable while indeed only a single bit is really needed. The operation of acquiring a lock involves testing or checking if the lock is currently free and setting it to taken if it is free. Intuitively, coding this locking operation like the following

```
    if (lockvar == 0)
      lockvar = 1;
```

in a high-level language should work just fine, but it doesn't.

The reason is that it's entirely possible that interleaving in a single-processor computer or parallel processing in a multiprocessor system could, and often will, result in two or more processes or threads getting the same lock at the same time, which breaks mutual exclusion or may cause the lock to be lost. This results in either data corruption or program hang.

The key to implementing a locking function is that the test-and-set operation must be atomic, i.e. inseparable. Otherwise, the problematic scenario described above will occur. The above high-level language code does not guarantee atomicity at all. The atomicity can only be achieved via some specially designed assembly language instruction, instruction pair or instruction sequence. In other words, it requires hardware support and must be solved at assembly language instruction level.

As shown in this chapter, implementing locking functions in assembly language using each processor's specially-designed instruction(s) guarantees that mutual exclusion always works correctly. This is the fundamental basis of data correctness in so many computer software products including database management systems. Not only that, these assembly language locking functions offer significant performance improvements as well, as we have shown.

Questions

1. Describe the update loss problem. Why there is a such problem? And how do you prevent update loss?

2. What is locking for? What are the requirements for locking to work?

3. Describe the differences between a try lock, a spin lock and a timeout lock. What are their advantages and disadvantages?

4. Describe the differences between read locks and write locks.

5. What is a semaphore? How many types of semaphores are there? What are they used for?

6. What is a deadlock?

7. How many approaches are there to dealing with deadlocks?

8. What are the typical ways to avoid a deadlock?

9. What are the System V IPC resources?

10. How are System V IPC resources uniquely identified on a system?

11. On the system you are using, what are the operating system kernel parameters related to semaphores?

12. What are the three technologies used to solve update loss problems that you just learned from this chapter?

Exercises

1. Write a program that finds how many processes on the system are waiting on a particular semaphore. Print out the process ids of those processes. To test this, you may have to write and run programs that create a contentious situation for the semaphore such that some processes are waiting for it.

2. Write a program that finds and displays the process id of the last process that executed the last semop() operation on a semaphore.

3. Write a program that displays the information about the semaphore set as defined in the 'struct semid_ds' structure.

4. Write a program that displays the current settings and limits of all system parameters that are related to semaphores.

5. Write the spinlock and unlock routines in assembly language for the computer you are using.

6. Design and implement a tmlock() (timeout locking) assembly language routine for the processor of the computer you are using.
It should take an additional argument specifying how many times or how long it should keep trying if the lock is not available.
After that, if it still cannot acquire the lock, it should return -1.

7. Write programs to measure the performance differences in locking between using the locking facilities provided by the operating system you use and using your own locking routines written in assembly language.

8. Adjust the time delay in the update_shared_file() function to explore its effect. Explain what you observe.

9. Run the semupdf program with different number of processes and explain what you observe.

10. Run the semupdf program with different file sizes and explain what you observe.

11. Change semupd_posix_sema.c to use a POSIX named semaphore.

12. After studying the shared memory chapter, change semupd_posix_sema.c to use multiple processes.

13. Derive the 64-bit spinlock.s and trylock.s of Intel x86 from Apple Mac version.

Projects

1. Design and implement reader and writer locks in assembly language for the computer you are using. Writer locks are mutually exclusive. But reader locks should allow multiple concurrent readers to hold the

same lock at the same time.

Apply the reader and writer locks in a concurrent read and write application.

2. Design and implement a counting semaphore in assembly language on the computer you are using.

References

1. The Open Group Base Specifications Issue 7, 2018 edition
   IEEE Std 1003.1™-2017 (Revision of IEEE Std 1003.1-2008)
   Copyright © 2001-2018 IEEE and The Open Group
   http://pubs.opengroup.org/onlinepubs/9699919799/

   "Portable Operating System Interface (POSIX) -- Part 1: System Application Program Interface (API)" by the Institute of Electrical and Electronics Engineers, Inc. (IEEE Std 1003.1)(ISO/IEC 9945-1)

2. AT&T UNIX System V Release 4 Programmer's Guide: System Services
   Prentice-Hall, Inc. 1990

3. C. J. Dates "An Introduction to Database Systems Volume II"
   Addison-Wesley Publishing Company, Inc.

4. Maurice J. Bach "The Design of the UNIX Operating System", Prentice-Hall, Inc.

5. A. Silberschatz, J. Peterson, P. Galvin "Operating System Concepts",
   Third Edition, by Addison-Wesley Publishing Company, Inc. 1992

6. Andrew S. Tanenbaum "Modern Operating Systems", Prentice Hall

7. Andrew S. Tanenbaum "Operating Systems Design and Implementation",
   Prentice-Hall, Inc.

8. Intel 80386 System Software Writer's Guide

9. Intel i486 Microprocessor Programmer's Reference Manual

10. Intel i486 Microprocessor Hardware Reference Manual

11. DEC Alpha Architecture Handbook 1992

12. Oracle/Sun The SPARC Architecture Manual

13. IBM AIX 6.1 Assembly Language Reference Manual

14. https://en.wikipedia.org/wiki/Deadlock, Wikipedia.

10 Shared Memory

10-1 Introduction to Shared Memory

What is shared memory? What is it for? And how does it work? You may wonder.

Process Isolation Is a Main Operating System Feature

As you know already, all processes running on a computer system share all processors and physical memory equipped on the system.

Also, as we all know, isolation is one of the many features every operating system provides. This feature guarantees that on a system whatever a process does to its memory is completely isolated from any other processes running on the same system at the same time.

This is very important because it would be a disaster if one process corrupting its memory ends up with spitting over to another process. Note that this protection is in memory only. Of course, if one process writes some bad data out to disk, it will certainly impact other processes which later use that same data.

The isolation feature is achieved because each process has a virtual memory address space which gets translated into its own separate set of physical memory segments or pages. Although the virtual memory addresses of different processes may overlap, because virtual memory addresses from different processes running on the same system always get translated into different, non-overlapping physical pages and addresses, whatever a process does to its memory won't affect any other processes.

This operating system isolation feature protects processes from accidentally hurting one another by putting up a wall between them. However, on the flip side, it also makes it impossible for them to very efficiently share data by simply accessing memory, as they really need to in some cases. This gives birth to shared memory.

```
|  ----------  |  ----------  |  ----------  |  ----------  |
|  |Process 1|  |  |Process 2|  |  |Process 3|  |  |Process 4|  |  ...
|  ----------  |  ----------  |  ----------  |  ----------  |
```

Figure 10-1 Isolation between processes provided by an operating system

Shared Memory Goes Opposite Direction of Isolation

In other words, although the isolation and protection feature provided by

the virtual memory component of the operating system is extremely important,
it would be also very useful that if some processes running on the same
system could communicate with one another by directly accessing the other's
memory because that would mean a large amount of information can be exchanged
between these processes in the shortest amount of time possible!
That's exactly the idea behind shared memory.

Some applications, for example, database management systems, run as a set
of processes where they collaborate on managing a large amount of data
(for instance, a database). It will be very efficient if they could share
the piece of their memory holding this data because accessing a common,
shared memory is always much faster than having to send the shared data
over some networking communication channel or write it out to shared disks
in order to share.

Figure 10-2 is a diagram illustrates the concept of shared memory.
The idea is that each process still has its own private virtual memory
address space. But part of its data segment in that address space gets
mapped to a piece of physical memory that is actually shared between
a number of processes who have access and have attached to it.
The contents of this shared memory are seen simultaneously by each of these
processes. That is, if any of the processes updates a certain byte in
the shared memory, each sharing process will see it right away.

As the diagram shows, shared memory allows processes to share
parts of their virtual address space.

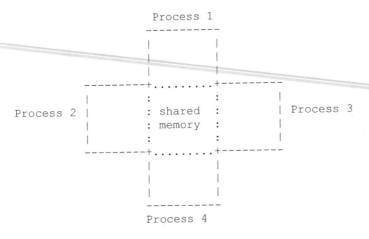

Figure 10-2 Concept of shared memory

In other words, process isolation is achieved by sharing nothing among
the processes. In contrast, shared memory shares part of the memory address
space of each of the multiple processes involved.

How Is Shared Memory Achieved

Shared memory is achieved in the process of address translation during which
a virtual address is translated into a physical memory address.

Specifically, shared memory between processes is done through mapping part of the data segment in each of these processes' virtual address space into the same physical memory area, same set of physical memory pages or segments. As a result, when each process accesses this portion of its virtual address space, they end up with accessing a physical memory area that is actually shared with other processes. (Note: Again, this is very different from how typically virtual memory to physical memory address translation works! Normally virtual addresses from different processes are translated into different, non-overlapping physical addresses so that different processes are isolated from one another in memory usage.) That is, when one of these processes writes data into some location in this shared memory, it is immediately seen by all processes sharing this memory.

Remember that the processes access their virtual memory to use the shared memory. This shared memory may correspond to different virtual addresses in different processes. But there is only a single copy of the shared (physical) memory and its contents are seen simultaneously by all of the processes sharing it.

Logically, shared memory is done in the unit of segments. A segment can be one or more physical memory pages. The actual implementation of the shared memory is hardware dependent because the memory management hardware (which does virtual memory to physical memory mapping/translation) is all processor dependent. Some CPUs support segmentation only, some support paging only, and some support both in their memory management architecture. And the sizes of segments and pages may differ too. The good thing is that as a software developer you don't really need to know its implementation details. You just need to learn how to use it. And that's what you will learn from this chapter.

All Sharing Processes Must Have Exactly the Same View of the Shared Memory

Apparently, for shared memory to work, all the processes sharing the memory must know exactly what data is contained in the shared memory and exactly what its layout is. This is extremely important because if any process were to have a different view of the layout of the data contained in the shared memory and to start to use or manipulate it in a way different from the rest of the processes, it would all mess up the data and break the sharing!

Therefore, extreme caution is required in programming the shared memory, especially in manipulating the shared memory data.

Concurrency Control is Required for Data Integrity of the Shared Memory

In addition, concurrency control is almost always needed in using shared memory. These two usually go hand in hand. This is because typically more than one process or thread is allowed to modify the shared memory. And whenever two or more processes or threads are allowed to update the same shared data, to ensure data integrity, concurrency control (i.e. locking) must be used. In other words, only one process or thread should be allowed to change the same shared data at any instant of time. Never two or more can do updates at the same time. Otherwise, the integrity of the data can be compromised. This is called 'mutual exclusion'. Mutual exclusion protects data integrity. This is very basic fundamental of computer science.

Of course, to increase the level of parallelism and improve performance in processing the data stored in a shared memory, you want to lower the granularity of data that each process or thread is allowed to update at a time. It would be very slow if every time a process or thread needs to do an update, it has to lock the entire shared memory segment or region. Instead, only the smaller individual shared data item should be locked. This allows multiple updates of separate data items within the shared memory to occur at the same time, achieves a higher degree of parallelism, and results in higher performance.

Shared Memory Is for Sharing Large Amount of Data Between Processes

So now you know that shared memory is for a set of collaborating processes running on the same system to very efficiently share a large amount of data they are collectively working on. Conceptually, they go against the isolation concept of an operating system. But it is very useful and in common use especially in large system software such as database management systems including Oracle Relational Database Management System (RDBMS), commonly referred to as Oracle Database.

Shared Memory Works Only Within a Single System

Note that shared memory is used for interprocess communication between processes running on the same system only. Processes running on different systems cannot use this scheme to communicate with one another.
This perhaps is the only disadvantage of shared memory comparing with other IPC mechanisms.

Processes running on different systems typically communicate with one another using network protocols such as TCP/IP and UDP/IP.
We will talk about socket programming in chapter 12 which is exactly for interprocess communications between programs running on different systems or computers.

Performance Is the Key Advantage of Using Shared Memory

One may ask "Why use shared memory?"

The key advantages of using shared memory are performance and simplicity.

Shared memory makes it extremely efficient for a set of processes to share data and collaborate in working on same set of data because reading and writing memory is the fastest communication scheme one can get.
There is no question that accessing memory is much faster than having to share the data by accessing some shared disks or sending it across network. The performance advantage is even greater when there is a large amount of data to be shared.

Shared memory allows a large amount of information to be exchanged between multiple processes in the fastest way. As soon as one process does a memory write to update some data in the shared memory area, all processes sharing the same shared memory area get it and have access to it immediately. Of course, the accesses need to be coordinated and synchronized to ensure data integrity.

Shared memory also makes it simple as well because all the processes need to

do is access memory. There is no network send/receive or disk read and write
involved.

How to Achieve Optimal Performance in Using Shared Memory

Shared memory has the advantage of fast performance because exchanging
data between the processes involves reading and writing memory, which
no other mechanisms can beat in terms of performance.

The only thing standing in the way of optimal performance is the concurrency
control. As mentioned earlier, to protect the integrity of the shared data,
concurrency control (or locking) must be done. In fact, one of the major
tasks in implementing shared memory IPC is to minimize the concurrency
control overhead; that is, to minimize the contention in acquiring the locks
between the competing processes or threads.

For read-only or read-mostly applications, this is not a big issue because
reader and writer locks can be implemented. A reader lock can be shared among
multiple readers so they won't have contentions among themselves because
they won't lock one another out. For heavy update applications, the
efficiency of concurrency control can have a big impact on the overall
performance of the shared memory.

As for the efficiency of concurrency control, there are two aspects.
One is the performance of the locking primitives and the other is the
granularity of data being protected by each lock.

For efficiency of locking primitives, there are usually two options.
The first option is to use the locking primitives provided by the operating
system. On systems that support System V IPC and/or POSIX semaphores,
semaphores are meant for use in concurrency control of the shared memory.
Although this comes handy, the performance of semaphores is not that optimal.
As we introduced in chapter 9, the other option is to implement the locking
primitives yourself and write them in assembly language. This can achieve
much better performance. Indeed, many database management systems author
worked on took this approach.

As for the granularity of data each lock (especially write lock) protects,
this concerns the degree of parallelism. In general, you want the degree
of parallelism among the competing processes or threads to be as high as
possible because greater parallelism leads to greater performance.
To achieve higher degree of parallelism, you want to design the locks
such that each lock protects a smaller granularity of data.
However, there is a balance to strike because there would be too many locks
to implement if every lock protects only one byte of data.

In other words, one extreme is the entire shared memory is protected by
a single lock in which there is only one lock to implement but at the same
time the degree of parallelism is minimal. For most applications, this
level of granularity is absolutely too coarse.

The other extreme is each byte of data is protected by a separate lock.
In this case, the degree of parallelism may be the highest but the number
of locks needed is perhaps way beyond one can handle. Hence, the solution
lies somewhere in-between and the balance to strike is in your hands.
Normally, it all depends on applications in terms of what needs to be

protected together as a single unit of shared data (e.g. a structure).

Typical Applications of Shared Memory

In summary, shared memory allows multiple processes running on the same system to be able to share large amount of data stored in computer memory. It's very fast.

Some processes produce the shared data and store it in shared memory while other processes consume them simply by reading it from shared memory. Or multiple processes can concurrently update the same set of data stored in shared memory. Of course, to guarantee integrity of the shared data, concurrent updates are synchronized via some concurrency control mechanism. The locks needed for the synchronization are stored in shared memory too.

Many RDBMSes implement their own database cache (the most recently referenced database data) in shared memory such that as long as one process reads in the data, it is in memory and is shared by all other processes. Using shared memory avoids reading the same data from disk more than once because that would be slow.

For example, each Oracle RDBMS instance consists of many server programs (the so-called background processes) working together. These processes operate on database data stored in the database cache implemented in System V shared memory, called SGA (System Global Area).

Shared memory is one of the major System V IPC mechanisms originated from the early AT&T System V Unix. Together with semaphores, shared memory has been very critically important and has been at the heart of many very popular and important products, including Oracle RDBMS database and others.

Availability

System V shared memory is part of the System V IPC facilities. It comes standard on almost all UNIX and Linux operating systems, including Apple Darwin, these days. On FreeBSD, your kernel must have option SYSVSHM to use shared memory.

Memory-mapped File Is Not Shared Memory

As explained in section 11-4, memory-mapped file is not shared memory.

We introduce the System V shared memory in the next section.

10-2 System V Shared Memory APIs

As mentioned above, shared memory allows two or more processes running on the same system to share some physical memory space and thus the data contained in it. It offers very high-performance data sharing and exchanges between these processes.

The most commonly used shared memory is the System V IPC shared memory, which is part of the POSIX Standard and is what the following sections will talk about. It is the AT&T Unix System V implementation of the shared memory technology. It was originally implemented in AT&T Unix System V Release 1

(SVR1) in 1983 and has long been supported in all Unix and Linux operating systems and others that support the POSIX standard.

In this section, we will explain how to create and use System V shared memory in a C program as defined in the POSIX Standard.

10-2-1 How to Use System V Shared Memory

The steps involved in using a System V shared memory IPC are below:

1. Create the shared memory
2. Attach to the shared memory
3. Read and/or write the shared memory
4. Detach the shared memory
5. Destroy (i.e. remove) the shared memory (This is rarely done.)

Shared memory normally exists in units of segments. Before a shared memory segment can be used, some process (typically is the very first of the processes sharing the shared memory) must create it first. Once a shared memory segment is created and exists, processes must attach to it before they can use it. Once attaching to it, as long as they have permissions, processes can read from and/or write to the shared memory depending on what permissions they have.

Once a process is done using a shared memory segment, it must detach from it.

Typically, a shared memory hangs around such that other processes can continue to use it. Because of this a shared memory is seldom removed.

Below we will introduce how to do each of these steps in a C program.

10-2-2 Creating Shared Memory -- shmget()

Before a shared memory can be shared, it must be created. Typically, a process which is the first to run would create the shared memory and then the other processes will share it.

A C program invokes the shmget() function to create a shared memory segment and/or get its identifier. The function's specification is as follows:

```
#include <sys/ipc.h>
#include <sys/shm.h>

int shmget(key_t key, size_t size, int shmflg);
```

The argument key specifies a key value of type key_t, which is an int, that uniquely identifies the shared memory segment to be created and shared. We will further discuss how to derive this key value in just a little bit.

The argument size specifies the size of the shared memory segment in bytes.

The argument shmflg specifies a number of things by OR-ing them together.

First, it specifies the permissions of the shared memory segment granted

to the owner, group, and world in its least significant 9 bits.
By default, this value is 0, meaning no one can access it.
The permissions of a System V IPC facility, including shared memory segment,
are typical Unix/Linux permissions where read, write and execute permissions
can be specified for the user, group and others.

In addition, the shmflg argument can also specify a number of flags (read
the man page of shmget() for a complete list) including two very important
ones: IPC_CREAT and IPC_EXCL. Specifying the IPC_CREAT flag means the caller
wants to create the shared memory segment if it does not already exist.
The IPC_EXCL flag means the caller wants an exclusive creation.

When the shmget() function is called, if a shared memory segment
corresponding to the key specified (assuming it is not IPC_PRIVATE) does not
already exist and the shmflg argument has the IPC_CREAT bit set,
and no related kernel system tunable parameters would be exceeded,
then a new shared memory segment is created, a shmid_ds data structure is
created in the operating system kernel, and a new shared memory identifier
(shmid) is generated and returned. However, if a shared memory segment
corresponding to the key given has already existed in the system, the
function simply returns the shared memory identifier (shmid) of the
corresponding shared memory segment.

If the IPC_EXCL flag is set in the shmflg argument and a shared memory
segment for the key provided already exists, the shmget() call will fail
if IPC_CREAT flag is set. In that case, the function will return -1 with
errno being set to EEXIST.

In other words, the flag value (IPC_CREAT | IPC_EXCL) together means to
create but does so only if it does not already exist. Thus, the function call
will fail and return -1 if the shared memory segment already exists.
So please be aware of the implication of using the IPC_EXCL flag.

On success the shmget() function returns the shared memory identifier (shmid)
which is an integer. On failure, it returns -1 and errno is set to indicate
the error.

10-2-2-1 Key and Id of System V IPC Resources

Each shared memory segment has two things that are interesting to the
processes that want to use it:

- a **key** – A shared memory key is an identifier that the operating system
  uses to uniquely identify the resource. A process needing to create
  a shared memory segment or just get its id needs to know this key and
  provide that. A process provides the shared memory key when it invokes
  the shmget() function to first create the shared memory or simply obtain
  its identifier which it can then use to access it.

- a **shmid** – A shared memory id (shmid, for short) is a number that the
  operating system generates to uniquely identify a shared memory segment.
  Once a shared memory is created, the operating system generates a
  unique shared memory id, which is a number, for it.
  Processes use the shared memory id to attach to the shared memory or
  perform other control operations.

Since the type of the shared memory key is key_t which is actually defined to be a 'int' (i.e. an integer), it is very likely that two or more different programs may have a collision and accidentally pick the same integer number as the key of the shared memory segments they intend to create. That would fail the unique identifier requirement and thus fail the creation of the System V IPC resource, be it shared memory, semaphore, or message queue.

To avoid or prevent this potential key collision, the designers of System V IPC provide a ftok() function which maps a pathname to a key. In other words, the way a key is used to uniquely identify a System V IPC resource is supposed to work like this. First, an application picks a pathname which it believes could uniquely identify the application, or the shared memory segment should it create multiple System V IPC resources. The application then invokes the ftok() function to convert that into an integer number, which is then used as the key. The ftok() function guarantees that if the corresponding pathname is unique then the returned integer will be unique. Therefore, how well this uniqueness works comes down to whether the pathname an application picks is really unique or not.

A program needs to know the key and provide the key in order to create a shared memory and/or get its id via shmget(). Once a process has a shared memory's id, it then uses the shared memory id to access it and do everything.

What we describe so far in this section applies to all System V IPC resources including shared memory, semaphores and message queues.

To create a shared memory segment, the operating system first generates a unique shared memory identifier (shmid) based on the key value specified. It also creates a kernel data structure representing the shared memory segment if such a data structure does not already exist. This data structure consists of many fields including shm_nattch which indicates how many processes are currently attached to the shared memory segment. This O.S. kernel data structure takes a small amount of memory. The type of this data structure is defined in the <sys/shm.h> header file as 'struct shmid_ds' and the POSIX standard says it must contain at least the following information:

```
struct shmid_ds {
    struct ipc_perm shm_perm;    /* Ownership and permissions */
    size_t          shm_segsz;   /* Size of segment (bytes) */
    shmatt_t        shm_nattch;  /* No. of current attaches */
    pid_t           shm_cpid;    /* PID of creator */
    pid_t           shm_lpid;    /* PID of last shmat()/shmdt() */
    time_t          shm_atime;   /* Last attach time */
    time_t          shm_dtime;   /* Last detach time */
    time_t          shm_ctime;   /* Last change time */
    ...
};

struct ipc_perm {
    uid_t uid;                   /* Effective UID of owner */
    gid_t gid;                   /* Effective GID of owner */
    uid_t cuid;                  /* Effective UID of creator */
    gid_t cgid;                  /* Effective GID of creator */
```

```
        mode_t mode;              /* Read/write permission */
    };
```

Notice that in this data structure, the operating system kernel records information about the shared memory segment including permission of the IPC facility, its size, how many processes are currently attached to the shared memory facility (shm_nattch), who is the creator of the facility -- what its process id is (shm_cpid), the process id of the process who last did a shmat()/shmdt() call on the segment, the last time a shmat() is called, the last time a shmdt() is called, the last time a change is made.

10-2-2-2 Converting Shared Memory Key to Shared Memory Id

For each shared memory segment, there are at least two identifiers used to uniquely identify the resource at different times and occasions. This could be a little confusing.

The way this was designed to work is as follows.

First, to guarantee uniqueness, an application is expected to pick a unique key for identifying the shared memory segment it wants to create and use. Since a key is just an integer, it's likely that two different applications could potentially have a collision and pick the same integer as their keys. In order to avoid that, **an application should pick a unique pathname in a file system, create and reserve that pathname only for this purpose, and use the ftok() function to convert that unique pathname into a unique integer key value.**

Remember, don't create this pathname in a directory where anyone has the permission to remove it. It would be a security bug if you do. For example, **don't create it under /tmp or /var/tmp directory** because that would allow anyone to be able to remove it.

The application then uses the unique key value in the shmget() call to get back a shared memory identifier, shmid, generated by the operating system kernel, and possibly also create the shared memory if it does not already exist. **From this point on, shmid is meant to be used in other shared memory API functions such as attaching and control functions.**

Hence, it's a three-layer mapping and translation:

   unique pathname -> ftok() -> key -> shmget() -> shmid

- ftok() maps a pathname into a numeric key value

- shmget() returns the shmid of the shared memory segment associated with the specified key. It may also create the shared memory if IPC_CREAT is specified in the shmflg and the segment does not already exist.

- From this point on, shmid is used in all other shared memory functions such as shmat() and shmctl() to uniquely identify the shared memory.

10-2-2-3 Special Shared Memory Key IPC_PRIVATE

If an application doesn't want to generate the key by itself, it can choose to pass in the value IPC_PRIVATE (which is 0) as the key value while calling shmget(). In that case, the operating system will generate a unique shmid that has not been taken for the shared memory segment.

So shmget() returns the shmid of the shared memory segment associated with the key value specified if the key value is not IPC_PRIVATE. If the specified key value is IPC_PRIVATE, the function returns a different, unused shmid each time.

In addition, if the IPC_CREAT flag is specified in the third argument, then the shared memory segment is created if one associated with the provided key does not already exist.

Using IPC_PRIVATE as the key to create shared memory segments is not as useful because the creator of the segment would need to find a way to pass the shmid to other processes who want to share the same segment. They cannot just call shmget() with a key value equal to IPC_PRIVATE to get the same shmid because each invocation of shmget() with IPC_PRIVATE being the key value returns a new, different shmid.

In contrast, if an application generates its own key, then as long as every process does the same and uses that same key in calling shmget(), they will all get back the same shmid and get to the same shared memory segment.

10-2-2-4 Example Program

We give an example of how to create a shared memory segment here in this section.

Figure 10-3a shows a program creating a shared memory segment. Figure 10-3b lists the header file myshm.h which contains the definitions of the constants and function prototypes of library functions used in this chapter. Figure 10-3c displays shmlib.c which has the library functions used in example programs in this chapter.

Figure 10-3a Creating a shared memory segment (shmget.c)

```
/*
 * Create shared memory segment.
 * Authored by Mr. Jin-Jwei Chen
 * Copyright (c) 2015, Mr. Jin-Jwei Chen. All rights reserved.
 */

#include <stdio.h>
#include <sys/types.h>
#include <sys/ipc.h>
#include <sys/shm.h>
#include <errno.h>

#include "myshm.h"
```

```
int main (int argc, char *argv[])
{
  int        shmid = 0;

  /* Create the shared memory segment. Note: The file specified by
     MYSHMKEY must already exist. */
  shmid = do_shmget(MYSHMKEY, MYSHMSIZE, 0);

  if (shmid == -1)
  {
    fprintf(stderr, "shmget() failed. Exiting ...\n");
    return(shmid);
  }

  fprintf(stdout, "Shared memory segment was created, shmid = %d.\n", shmid);

  /* Note that at this point the shared memory segment just created
     remains in the system. */

  return(0);
}
```

Figure 10-3b Declarations of constants and library functions (myshm.h)

```
/*
 * Header file for shared memory example programs
 * Authored by Mr. Jin-Jwei Chen
 * Copyright (c) 2015, 2019, 2020 Mr. Jin-Jwei Chen. All rights reserved.
 */

/*
 * Types
 */
#define  uint unsigned int

/*
 * Constants
 */

/* The pathname used to uniquely identify the shared memory segment */
#define MYSHMKEY "/var/tmp/AppXyzShmAbc"
/* Default size for the shared memory segment (in bytes) */
#define MYSHMSIZE  2048000
/* Default permissions and flags for the shared memory segment */
#define MYDEFFLAGS (00660 | IPC_CREAT)

/*
 * Contents of shared memory
 */
#define  SHMMAGIC      75432018
#define  BANNER_LEN  64
#define  MANNER_STR   "This is shared memory for application XYZ."
#define  TASKNAME_LEN  64
#define  NTASKS          2
#define  SHMDEFUPDCNT  500
```

```c
/* Update counts for different tasks */
#define   LOOPCNT1   1000
#define   LOOPCNT2   1000
#define   LOOPCNT3   1000

#define   DELAYCNT   8000000   /* loop count for introducing some delay */

/* A simple data structure for shared memory updates */
struct task
{
  uint   taskid;   /* id of the task */
  char   taskname[TASKNAME_LEN];   /* name of the task */
  uint   count;   /* a local counter */
  int    lock;    /* a lock meant to protect concurrent updates of this data */
};

/*
 * Utility functions
 */

/* Create or get a shared memory segment */
int do_shmget(char *pathname, size_t size, int shmflag);

/* Get and print the status of a shared memory segment */
int do_shmstat(int shmid);

/* Get, print and return the status of a shared memory segment */
int do_shmstat2(int shmid, struct shmid_ds *buf);

/* Initialize shared memory contents */
int init_shm(char *shmaddr, int force);

/* Initialize shared memory contents without initializing task data */
int init_shm1(char *shmaddr, int force);

/* Read and print the contents of shared memory by taking a lock */
int read_shm(char *shmaddr);

/* Read and print the contents of shared memory without taking a lock */
int read_shm1(char *shmaddr);

/* Update (write to) shared memory */
int update_shm(char *shmaddr, int updcnt, unsigned int delaycnt, int uselock);

/* Our own lock/unlock routines */
int spinlock (int *lockvar);
int trylock (int *lockvar);
int unlock (int *lockvar);
```

Figure 10-3c Library functions for shared memory (shmlib.c)

```c
/*
 * Utility functions for shared memory example programs.
 * Authored by Mr. Jin-Jwei Chen
 * Copyright (c) 2015, 2019, 2020 Mr. Jin-Jwei Chen. All rights reserved.
 */
```

609

```
#include <stdio.h>
#include <sys/types.h>
#include <sys/ipc.h>
#include <sys/shm.h>
#include <errno.h>
#include <string.h>

#include "myshm.h"

/*
 * This function creates a shared memory segment corresponding to the pathname
 * provided if it does not already exist.
 * In either case it returns the id (shmid) of the shared memory segment.
 * INPUT parameters:
 *   pathname: A pathname used to uniquely identify the shared memory segment.
 *             This value is converted into a key of type key_t.
 *             If this input is NULL then IPC_PRIVATE is used as key.
 *   size: The size of the shared memory segment in bytes.
 *   shmflag: Flags used to create the shared memory segment.
 * OUTPUT:
 *   Return shmid on success and -1 on failure.
 */
int do_shmget(char *pathname, size_t size, int shmflag)
{
  key_t  key = 0;
  int    shmid = 0;
  int    projid = 1;   /* This cannot be 0 on AIX. */

  /* Always create the shared memory segment if it does not already exist. */
  if (shmflag == 0)
    shmflag = MYDEFFLAGS;
  shmflag = (shmflag | IPC_CREAT);

  /* Set the size to default size if it is not provided */
  if (size == 0)
    size = MYSHMSIZE;

  /* Convert the unique pathname provided to a System V IPC key */
  if (pathname == (char *)NULL)
    key = IPC_PRIVATE;
  else
  {
    errno = 0;
    key = ftok(pathname, projid);
    if (key == -1)
    {
      fprintf(stderr, "do_shmget(): ftok() failed, errno=%d\n", errno);
      return(key);
    }
  }

  /* Create/get the shared memory segment */
  errno = 0;
  shmid = shmget(key, size, shmflag);
  if (shmid == -1)
```

```
    {
        /* Unable to create/get the shared memory segment */
        fprintf(stderr, "do_shmget(): shmget() failed, errno=%d\n", errno);
        return(shmid);
    }


    return(shmid);
}

/*
 * This function gets and prints some (not all) of the status information
 * of a shared memory segment.
 */
int do_shmstat(int shmid)
{
    int             cmd = IPC_STAT;
    struct shmid_ds buf;
    int             ret = 0;

    ret = shmctl(shmid, cmd, &buf);
    if (ret == -1)
    {
        fprintf(stderr, "do_shmstat(): shmctl() failed, errno=%d\n", errno);
        return(errno);
    }

    fprintf(stdout, "Current status of the shared memory of shmid %d:\n", shmid);
    fprintf(stdout, "  shm_perm.uid = %d\n", buf.shm_perm.uid);
    fprintf(stdout, "  shm_perm.gid = %d\n", buf.shm_perm.gid);
    fprintf(stdout, "  shm_perm.mode = 0%o\n", buf.shm_perm.mode);
    fprintf(stdout, "  shm_segsz = %lu\n", buf.shm_segsz);
    fprintf(stdout, "  shm_nattch = %d\n", buf.shm_nattch);
    fprintf(stdout, "  shm_cpid = %d\n", buf.shm_cpid);
    fprintf(stdout, "  shm_lpid = %d\n", buf.shm_lpid);
    return(0);
}

/*
 * Get, print and return the status of a shared memory segment.
 */
int do_shmstat2(int shmid, struct shmid_ds *buf)
{
    int             cmd = IPC_STAT;
    int             ret = 0;

    if (buf == (struct shmid_ds *)NULL)
    {
        fprintf(stderr, "do_shmstat(): error, input buffer pointer is NULL\n");
        return(EINVAL);
    }

    /* Get the status */
    ret = shmctl(shmid, cmd, buf);
    if (ret == -1)
    {
        fprintf(stderr, "do_shmstat(): shmctl() failed, errno=%d\n", errno);
```

```
    return(errno);
  }

  fprintf(stdout, "Current status of the shared memory of shmid %d:\n", shmid);
  fprintf(stdout, "   shm_perm.uid = %d\n", buf->shm_perm.uid);
  fprintf(stdout, "   shm_perm.gid = %d\n", buf->shm_perm.gid);
  fprintf(stdout, "   shm_perm.mode = 0%o\n", buf->shm_perm.mode);
  fprintf(stdout, "   shm_segsz = %lu\n", buf->shm_segsz);
  fprintf(stdout, "   shm_nattch = %d\n", buf->shm_nattch);
  fprintf(stdout, "   shm_cpid = %d\n", buf->shm_cpid);
  fprintf(stdout, "   shm_lpid = %d\n", buf->shm_lpid);
  return(0);
}


/*
 * Initialize shared memory contents
 * This function does nothing and returns right away if the contents of the
 * shared memory have already been initialized (i.e. its magic number has
 * already been set) unless the force argument has a non-zero value
 * in which case the shared memory will be re-initialized again..
 * Parameters:
 *    shmaddr (input): starting address of the shared memory.
 *    force (input): flag indicating whether to re-initialize it or not
 *                   if it has been initialized before.
 */
int init_shm(char *shmaddr, int force)
{
  char   *shmptr = shmaddr;
  uint   *magic = (uint *)shmaddr;
  uint   *gcount;
  int    *glock;
  struct task *ptask;
  uint   i;

  if (shmaddr == NULL)
    return(EINVAL);

  /* If it has been initialized before, return unless force is true. */
  if ((*magic == (uint)SHMMAGIC) && (!force))
    return(0);

  /* Set the magic number and advance the pointer */
  fprintf(stdout, "Initialize the shared memory contents...\n");
  *magic = (uint)SHMMAGIC;
  shmptr = shmptr + sizeof(uint);

  /* Set the banner string */
  strcpy(shmptr, MANNER_STR);
  shmptr = shmptr + BANNER_LEN;

  /* Initialize the global count and global lock */
  gcount = (uint *)shmptr;
  *gcount = (uint)0;
  shmptr = shmptr + sizeof(uint);
  glock  = (int *)shmptr;
  *glock = (int)0;
```

```
  shmptr = shmptr + sizeof(int);

  /* Initialize the task data structures */
  ptask = (struct task *)shmptr;
  for (i = 0; i < NTASKS; i++)
  {
    ptask->taskid = (i + 1);
    sprintf(ptask->taskname, "%s%2d", "Task #", (i+1));
    ptask->count = 0;
    ptask->lock = 0;
    ptask = ptask + 1;
  }

  return(0);
}

/*
 * Read and print the contents of shared memory.
 */
int read_shm(char *shmaddr)
{
  char   *shmptr = shmaddr;
  uint   *magic = (uint *)shmaddr;
  uint   *gcount;
  int    *glock;
  struct task  *ptask;
  int    i;

  /* Print the header portion */
  if (shmaddr == NULL)
    return(EINVAL);
  glock  = (int *)(shmptr + (2*sizeof(uint)) + BANNER_LEN);
  fprintf(stdout, "Contents of the shared memory are:\n");
  spinlock(glock);  /* lock */
  fprintf(stdout, "  magic = %u\n", *magic);
  shmptr = shmptr + sizeof(uint);
  fprintf(stdout, "  banner = %s\n", shmptr);
  shmptr = shmptr + BANNER_LEN;
  gcount = (uint *)shmptr;
  fprintf(stdout, "  gcount = %u\n", *gcount);
  shmptr = shmptr + sizeof(uint);
  fprintf(stdout, "  glock = %u\n", *glock);
  unlock(glock);  /* unlock */
  shmptr = shmptr + sizeof(int);

  /* Print the task data structures */
  ptask = (struct task *)shmptr;
  for (i = 0; i < NTASKS; i++)
  {
    spinlock(&ptask->lock);  /* lock */
    fprintf(stdout, "  taskid[%2d]   = %u\n", i, ptask->taskid);
    fprintf(stdout, "  taskname[%2d] = %s\n", i, ptask->taskname);
    fprintf(stdout, "  count[%2d] = %u\n", i, ptask->count);
    fprintf(stdout, "  lock[%2d]   = %u\n", i, ptask->lock);
    unlock(&ptask->lock);  /* unlock */
    ptask = ptask + 1;
```

```
   }

   return(0);
}

/*
 * Initialize shared memory contents -- a simple, shorter version.
 * This version does not initialize the task data structures.
 * This function does nothing and returns right away if the contents of the
 * shared memory have already been initialized (i.e. its magic number has
 * already been set) unless the force argument has a non-zero value
 * in which case the shared memory will be re-initialized again..
 * Parameters:
 *    shmaddr (input): starting address of the shared memory.
 *    force (input): flag indicating whether to re-initialize it or not
 *                   if it has been initialized before.
 */
int init_shm1(char *shmaddr, int force)
{
   char   *shmptr = shmaddr;
   uint    *magic = (uint *)shmaddr;
   uint    *gcount;
   int     *glock;

   if (shmaddr == NULL)
      return(EINVAL);

   /* If it has been initialized before, return unless force is true */
   if ((*magic == (uint)SHMMAGIC) && (!force))
      return(0);

   /* Set the magic number and advance the pointer */
   fprintf(stdout, "Initialize the shared memory contents...\n");
   *magic = (uint)SHMMAGIC;
   shmptr = shmptr + sizeof(uint);

   /* Set the banner string */
   strcpy(shmptr, MANNER_STR);
   shmptr = shmptr + BANNER_LEN;

   /* Initialize the global count and global lock */
   gcount = (uint *)shmptr;
   *gcount = (uint)0;
   shmptr = shmptr + sizeof(uint);
   glock  = (int *)shmptr;
   *glock = (int)0;

   return(0);
}

/*
 * Read and print the contents of shared memory -- a simple, shorter version
 * and without concurrency control.
 */
int read_shm1(char *shmaddr)
{
```

```
char    *shmptr = shmaddr;
uint    *magic = (uint *)shmaddr;
uint    *gcount;
int     *glock;

if (shmaddr == NULL)
   return(EINVAL);
fprintf(stdout, "Contents of the shared memory are:\n");
fprintf(stdout, "  magic = %u\n", *magic);
shmptr = shmptr + sizeof(uint);
fprintf(stdout, "  banner = %s\n", shmptr);
shmptr = shmptr + BANNER_LEN;
gcount = (uint *)shmptr;
fprintf(stdout, "  gcount = %u\n", *gcount);
shmptr = shmptr + sizeof(uint);
shmptr = shmptr + sizeof(uint);
glock  = (int *)shmptr;
fprintf(stdout, "  glock = %u\n", *glock);

return(0);
}


/*
 * Update (write to) shared memory
 * Each process updates a few data items within the shared memory.
 * It increments the counter in task1 by one, the counter in task2 by 2,
 * the counter of in task3 by 3, and so on.
 * And then it increments the global counter gcount by 1.
 */
int update_shm(char *shmaddr, int updcnt, unsigned int delaycnt, int uselock)
{
  uint n, i;
  uint loopcnt;   /* number of updates to be performed */
  uint *gcount;
  struct task  *ptask_start, *ptask;
  int     *glock;
  void some_delay(unsigned int);   /* remove this in real code */

  /* Get the offset of the data items to be updated */
  gcount = (uint *)(shmaddr + sizeof(uint) + BANNER_LEN);
  glock = (int *)(shmaddr + (2*sizeof(uint)) + BANNER_LEN);
  ptask_start = (struct task *)((shmaddr + (3*sizeof(uint)) + BANNER_LEN));

  /* Update the local counter of corresponding task structure */
  for (n = 0; n < updcnt; n++)
  {
    /* Update the local counters in task areas */
    /* Note: Make locking optional is only for demo purpose! */
    ptask = ptask_start;
    for (i = 0; i < NTASKS; i++)
    {
      if (uselock)
        spinlock(&ptask->lock);   /* lock */
      some_delay(delaycnt);         /* remove this in real code */
      ptask->count = ptask->count + (i + 1);
      if (uselock)
```

615

```
        unlock(&ptask->lock);      /* unlock */
      ptask = ptask + 1;           /* advance to next task */
    }

    /* Increment the global counter */
    if (uselock)
      spinlock(glock);        /* lock */
    some_delay(delaycnt);   /* remove this in real code */
    *gcount = (*gcount + 1);
    if (uselock)
      unlock(glock);          /* unlock */
  }

  return(0);
}

/*
 * Introduce some delay.
 */
void some_delay(unsigned int count)
{
  uint  i, x, y=2;

  for (i = 0; i < count; i++)
    x = (y-1);
}
```

This program creates a shared memory segment uniquely identified by the pathname "/var/tmp/AppXyzShmAbc". This file name stands for application Xyz and shared memory segment Abc. The program converts this pathname string into a key value using the ftok() function before it calls the shmget() function to actually create the shared memory segment with that key value. The file /var/tmp/AppXyzShmAbc must exist before the program can run successfully. In a POSIX-compliant system, you can run this following shell command to create this file:

```
$ touch /var/tmp/AppXyzShmAbc
```

Please make sure you do so before running any of the example programs in this chapter.

Please be warned that when you develop a real application, don't create this file for your application in /tmp or /var/tmp directory. It would be a security issue if you do because usually any user can remove a file from these directories. You don't really want any user to be able to remove the file(s) your application depends on. Hence, create your own directory somewhere else and set the ownership and permission appropriately for security sake. It's a good idea to create and use a directory or subdirectory that is specific to your company and put all of the System V IPC related files there. Make sure you protect the directory and files so that they won't get removed by unwanted people.

We use /var/tmp here only for simplicity and portability reasons. By creating the file in this directory, anyone can run our example program. This is because everyone should have permissions to create file in the /var/tmp directory. The directory should already exist because it is a directory that exists in all Unix and Linux systems.

Please note that at end of successfully running the program shmget.c,
the shared memory segment created by this program remains on the system.
It will stay until it is removed by a program, a command (e.g. 'ipcrm -m'),
or the system shuts down. To remove a shared memory segment by hand, run the
'ipcs' command to find out the shmid of the segment, and then execute the
'iprm -m xxx' command to delete it where xxx is the shmid of the segment.
For example, the following ipcrm command removes the shared memory segment
whose shmid is 2031616:

```
$ ipcs
$ ipcrm -m 2031616
```

We like to point out three things in the do_shmget() function of our own.

First, if the caller passes in a zero value for shmflg, we set it to a
default value which is (00660|IPC_CREAT), meaning it is to create and set
permissions of the segment to be readable and writeable by owner and group.

Second, if the caller passes in a zero value for the size of the shared
memory segment then it is set to a default value of 2 MB.

Third, if the caller passes in a non-NULL string in the pathname argument,
then the key of the shared memory segment is derived from it. Otherwise,
IPC_PRIVATE is used if the caller passes in a NULL value. In this case,
the shmid will be determined by the system.

10-2-3 Attaching to Shared Memory -- shmat()

Before a process can access a shared memory segment, it must attach to it
first. Attaching to a shared memory segment "maps" the shared memory
segment into the calling process' virtual address space so that the process
knows where it is; that is, knowing its starting address.

The shmat() function attaches a shared memory segment to the calling process'
address space. It returns the shared memory segment's starting address.
Of course, this address is a virtual (as opposed to physical) address.
After the shmat() call succeeds, the calling process can then use the
returned address to access the shared memory.

In short, attaching to a shared memory segment associates a process with
the shared memory so that it can read from and/or write to it.

```
#include <sys/types.h>
#include <sys/shm.h>

void *shmat(int shmid, const void *shmaddr, int shmflg);
```

First argument shmid is an input. It identifies the shared memory segment to
be attached. This is the value returned by the shmget() call that should
occur before the shmat() call.

A process can attach to a shared memory segment at the address it specifies
or one picked by the operating system.

If the second argument, shmaddr, is a null pointer, then the address
within the caller's address space that the shared memory segment is attached
to is selected by the operating system, which is normally the first address
available.

If shmaddr is not null and SHM_RND (round attach address) flag is specified
in the third argument shmflg, then the attach address is equal to shmaddr
rounded down to the nearest multiple of SHMLBA. SHMLBA is the size of
a memory page. In other words, the address is
(shmaddr - ((uintptr_t)shmaddr % SHMLBA)).

If shmaddr is not null and SHM_RND flag is cleared (with a value 0), then
the segment is attached at the address given by shmaddr argument.
In this case, the address value specified must be a page-aligned address.

A process can attach to a shared memory segment with a permission of
read and write or read only. It does so by setting the shmflg argument to
0 or SHM_RDONLY, respectively. If the SHM_RDONLY flag is set in the shmflg
argument, the segment is attached for read only. Otherwise, it's for read
and write.

Return Value

On success, the shmat() function returns the starting address of the shared
memory segment attached. It also increments the value of the shm_nattch
(attachment count) field corresponding to the shared memory id of the
segment by one, indicating that now there is one more process attaching to
the shared memory. Also, the shm_atime field (timestamp) of the same
structure is set to the current time.

If the shmat() function fails to attach to the shared memory segment,
it returns -1. In that case, errno will be set to indicate the error.
Possible errors include the following:

EINVAL - This error could mean the value of shmid passed in is not a valid
    shared memory identifier, or the address specified by the shmaddr argument
    is an illegal memory address.

EACCES - The calling process has no permission to use the shared memory
    segment.

ENOMEM - The available data address space of the calling process is not big
    enough to accommodate the shared memory segment.

EMFILE - The number of shared memory segments attached to the calling process
    would exceed the system-imposed limit for a process.
    On most systems (e.g. UNIX and Linux) this is controlled by SHMSEG
    kernel tunable parameter. On Linux, the SHMSEG parameter inherits its value
    from SHMMNI.

Note that in original Unix man pages, shmat() and shmdt() are co-listed
under the entry shmop.

10-2-4 Detaching from Shared Memory -- shmdt()

When a process is done using a shared memory, it must detach from the shared memory segment by invoking the shmdt() function.

```
#include <sys/types.h>
#include <sys/shm.h>
int shmdt(const void *shmaddr);
```

Detaching from a shared memory segment disassociates a process with the shared memory so that it can no longer read from and/or write to it. This step is important because a shared memory segment exists in the system until it is explicitly removed or the system is shut down.

Note that when a process invokes shmctl() with IPC_RMID command to remove a shared memory segment, the segment is not actually removed until all processes having attached to it are done with using it and either call shmdt() to detach from it or exit. That is, even after some process has called shmctl() to remove the shared memory, as long as other processes are still using it, the shared memory will remain. Also, not all processes have to remove. As long as one of the processes sharing the segment removes and that operation is successful (the calling process must have permission), the shared memory will eventually be removed once all processes using it detach from it or exit.

10-2-5 Controlling Shared Memory -- shmctl()

```
#include <sys/types.h>
#include <sys/shm.h>
int shmctl(int shmid, int cmd, struct shmid_ds *buf);
```

The shmctl() function allows a process to perform some control operations on a shared memory segment. The list of operations that can be performed via the shmctl() call, as defined by the POSIX standard, is given below. Note that only a process with an effective user id of the creator/owner of the facility or the superuser (i.e. the root user) is allowed to perform the IPC_SET or IPC_RMID commands.

IPC_STAT - Query the status information of the shared memory segment. This command gets and returns current value of each member of the shmid_ds data structure from the operating system kernel.

IPC_SET - Set or change the ownership and permissions of the shared memory segment. The ids of the owner and the group of the shared memory segment as well as the read/write/execute permissions of the segment can be set by this command to be the values specified in the buf argument of the call. This command changes the values of the following members of the shmid_ds data structure associated with the shared memory segment:

```
shm_perm.uid
shm_perm.gid
shm_perm.mode     (Low-order nine bits)
```

Use this command to set or change the owner, group, and permissions of the shared memory segment.

IPC_RMID - Remove the shared memory id, delete the shared memory segment
corresponding to the shmid, and destroy the kernel shmid_ds data structure
associated with the segment. After a successful execution of this command,
the shared memory segment is destroyed and will disappear when its attach-
ments get 0. Use this to remove a shared memory segment from the system.

Some operating systems support other commands in this shmctl() call.

Figure 10-4 shows a program that creates a shared memory segment, attaches
to it, gets the status, detaches from the shared memory segment,
and then destroys it. This program uses all of the steps needed to create,
use and cleanly remove a shared memory segment.

Figure 10-4 All steps in using a shared memory segment (shmapi.c)

```
/*
 * Full-range shared memory operations -- this does it all.
 * Authored by Mr. Jin-Jwei Chen
 * Copyright (c) 2015, Mr. Jin-Jwei Chen. All rights reserved.
 */

#include <stdio.h>
#include <sys/types.h>
#include <sys/ipc.h>
#include <sys/shm.h>
#include <errno.h>

#include "myshm.h"

int main (int argc, char *argv[])
{
    int       shmid = 0;
    key_t     key=5;
    size_t    size = 1;
    int       ret;
    void      *shmaddr = (void *)0;

    /* Create/get the shared memory segment */
    shmid = do_shmget(MYSHMKEY, MYSHMSIZE, 0);
    if (shmid == -1)
    {
        fprintf(stderr, "do_shmget() failed. Exiting ...\n");
        return(shmid);
    }
    fprintf(stdout, "Successfully created the shared memory segment, shmid=%d\n",
        shmid);

    /* Attach to the shared memory segment */
    errno = 0;
    shmaddr = shmat(shmid, (void *)NULL, 0);
    if (shmaddr == (void *)-1)
        fprintf(stderr, "shmat() failed, errno=%d\n", errno);
    else
        fprintf(stdout, "Attached to shared memory at address %p\n", shmaddr);
```

620

```
/* Get status of the shared memory segment */
ret = do_shmstat(shmid);
if (ret != 0)
  fprintf(stderr, "do_shmstat() failed, ret=%d\n", ret);

/* Typically you do some shared memory read/write operations here. */

/* Detach from the shared memory segment */
errno = 0;
ret = shmdt(shmaddr);
if (ret == -1)
  fprintf(stderr, "shmdt() failed, errno=%d\n", errno);
else
  fprintf(stdout, "Detached from shared memory at address %p\n", shmaddr);

/* Get status of the shared memory segment */
ret = do_shmstat(shmid);
if (ret != 0)
  fprintf(stderr, "do_shmstat() failed, ret=%d\n", ret);

/* Remove the shared memory segment */
errno = 0;
ret = shmctl(shmid, IPC_RMID, 0);
if (ret == -1)
  fprintf(stderr, "shmctl() failed, errno=%d\n", errno);
else
  fprintf(stdout, "Successfully removed the shared memory segment of "
    "shmid %d\n", shmid);

  return(0);
}
```

From the output of this program you can see that after the shmat() call,
the number of attachment count goes up by one. And after the program
runs successfully, if you run the ipcs command to check, the shared memory
no longer exists on the system. Hence, it is clean.

In the program we insert a couple of calls to the do_shmstat() function
which gets and prints the status information of the shared memory segment,
just to demonstrate the use of the shmctl() function. A typical program
may not always do this IPC_STAT step. However, a typical program would
normally perform some read and/or write operations on the shared memory
in between the shmat() and shmdt() steps which the next examples will show.

10-2-6 Changing the Ownership and Permission of a Shared Memory Segment

The original creator of a shared memory is the owner of it.
It can transfer the ownership to another user and/or group.
It can also change the permissions of the shared memory segment.
All of these can be done via the shmctl() function with a buffer containing
the new settings.

Figure 10-5 is a program that demonstrates how to change the ownership
and permissions of a shared memory segment.

Figure 10-5 Change ownership and permissions of shared memory (shmowner.c)

```c
/*
 * Change ownership and permissions of shared memory segment.
 * Authored by Mr. Jin-Jwei Chen
 * Copyright (c) 2015, 2020 Mr. Jin-Jwei Chen. All rights reserved.
 */

#include <stdio.h>
#include <sys/types.h>
#include <sys/ipc.h>
#include <sys/shm.h>
#include <errno.h>
#include <string.h>
#include "myshm.h"

int main (int argc, char *argv[])
{
  int       shmid = 0;
  key_t     key=5;
  size_t    size = 1;
  int       ret;
  struct shmid_ds  buf;

  /* Create/get the shared memory segment */
  shmid = do_shmget(MYSHMKEY, MYSHMSIZE, 0);
  if (shmid == -1)
  {
    fprintf(stderr, "do_shmget() failed. Exiting ...\n");
    return(shmid);
  }
  fprintf(stdout, "The shared memory segment was successfully created."
    " shmid=%d\n", shmid);

  /* Get status of the shared memory segment */
  memset((void *)&buf, 0, sizeof(struct shmid_ds));
  ret = do_shmstat2(shmid, &buf);
  if (ret != 0)
    fprintf(stderr, "do_shmstat2() failed, ret=%d\n", ret);

  /* Change the ownership and permissions of the shared memory segment */
  buf.shm_perm.uid = 1100;
  buf.shm_perm.mode = 00600;

  errno = 0;
  ret = shmctl(shmid, IPC_SET, &buf);
  if (ret == -1)
    fprintf(stderr, "shmctl() failed, errno=%d\n", errno);
  else
    fprintf(stdout, "Ownership and permissions were successfully changed.\n");

  /* Get status of the shared memory segment */
  ret = do_shmstat2(shmid, &buf);
  if (ret != 0)
    fprintf(stderr, "do_shmstat2() failed, ret=%d\n", ret);
```

```
/* Remove the shared memory segment */
errno = 0;
ret = shmctl(shmid, IPC_RMID, 0);
if (ret == -1)
   fprintf(stderr, "shmctl() failed, errno=%d\n", errno);
else
   fprintf(stdout, "The shared memory segment of shmid %d was successfully"
      " removed.\n", shmid);

   return(0);
}
```

Note that to ensure you change only the values of the fields you want to change, the best practice is to get the existing value of the entire shmid_ds structure (by making a shmctl() call with the IPC_STAT command), change only the fields you want to change in the buffer and then pass the same buffer to the shmctl() call with the IPC_SET command. That way you won't touch the values of the other fields.

Note that for shmctl() to work, the calling process must have the same effective UID of the owner (shm_perm.uid) or creator (shm_perm.cuid) of the segment or it must be the super user.

10-2-7 Operating System Tunable Parameters

There are five operating system tunable parameters in Unix and Linux which are related to shared memory:

   shmmni - maximum number of shared memory segments allowed system-wide
   shmmax - maximum size of a shared memory segment in bytes
   shmall - maximum total amount of shared memory available (in bytes or pages)
   shmseg - maximum number of shared memory segments per process
   shmmin - minimum size of a shared memory segment in bytes

Certain situations in which a shmget() call can fail include the number of shared memory segments exist in the system would exceed the value set by the shmmni tunable, or the size of the shared memory segment specified exceeds the maximum value set by the shmmax tunable.
For instance, if the value of the shmmax kernel parameter is set to be 1024000 and the size argument of the shmget() call is 8192000, the call would fail with errno set to be EINVAL (22 in Linux), meaning "invalid argument value provided".

For example, if you install or run Oracle RDBMS database system software on your system, you may need to increase the values of these shared memory kernel tunable parameters. Oracle RDBMS uses System V shared memory at its core. Therefore, it has required minimum values for these parameters. Indeed, Oracle RDBMS installation checks and verifies these kernel parameters to make sure the current system's settings meet its requirements. The installation will fail if they do not. Below is a sample setting:

   kernel.shmmni = 4096
   kernel.shmmax = 2147483648
   kernel.shmall = 4294967296

```
kernel.shmseg = 1024
```

10-3 Shared Memory Examples

In this section we provide a couple of examples of using shared memory.
First example reads contents of a shared memory and second example
updates contents of shared memory.

10-3-1 Design of Shared Memory Contents

In using shared memory, what data is to be stored and its layout in the
shared memory must be designed and documented so that all users know
exactly what data items are in it and where they are.

In our example of shared memory, the layout of its memory contents is
very simple as shown in Figure 10-6. It contains a magic number, a banner
string, a global counter, a global lock, followed by a couple of task
structures.

Figure 10-6 Layout of example shared memory contents

```
Contents of example shared memory
-------------------------------------
| magic number (unsigned int)       |
| banner string (char[BANNER_LEN])  |
| global counter (unsigned int)     |
| global lock (unsigned int)        |
| struct task[0]                    |
| struct task[1]                    |
|    :                              |
-------------------------------------
```

magic - a magic number specific to the shared memory segment.
          Setting it indicates the shared memory segment has been initialized.
banner - a string identifying the shared memory segment.
          64 bytes of memory are reserved for it.
gcount - a global counter to be updated by concurrent processes
glock - a global lock to protect the integrity of gcount by ensuring
          mutual exclusion of the concurrent updates
struct task - a number of task structures follow.

Each task structure is defined as follows:

```
struct task
{
  uint  taskid;  /* id of the task */
  char  taskname[TASKNAME_LEN];  /* name of the task */
  uint  count;   /* a local counter */
  int   lock;  /* a lock to protect concurrent updates of this structure */
};
```

Each task has an id, a name, a counter and a lock. The count is meant to be
updated by all concurrent processes. And the lock field is the guardian of
the count. It serves as a lock for the count or entire structure so that all

updates to the same count or entire structure can be synchronized. The value of the lock field will be initialized to 0 to indicate the lock is free. Whoever needs to update the count field or entire structure will need to grab this lock by discovering its current value being 0 and then changing its value to 1 in an atomic operation, such as using the test-and-set assembly language instruction in Intel x86 architecture as shown in Figure 9-13.

In shmlib.c (Fig. 10-3c), we have a library function named init_shm() which can be used to initialize the contents of the shared memory when it is first created. There is also a read_shm() function to read the contents of the shared memory. The library function do_shmstat() gets and prints current status information of the shared memory.

10-3-2 Read Shared Memory

Figure 10-7 is an example program that demonstrates how to create a shared memory and read its contents.

Note that the program deliberately does not remove the shared memory. It demonstrates that once created a shared memory exists "forever" until it is explicitly removed or the system shuts down. This is so that even after the creator of a shared memory terminates, other processes can continue to use it.

Figure 10-7 Read shared memory contents -- shmread.c

```c
/*
 * Read shared memory.
 * Authored by Mr. Jin-Jwei Chen
 * Copyright (c) 2015, Mr. Jin-Jwei Chen. All rights reserved.
 */

#include <stdio.h>
#include <sys/types.h>
#include <sys/ipc.h>
#include <sys/shm.h>
#include <errno.h>
#include <string.h>

#include "myshm.h"

int main (int argc, char *argv[])
{
  int       shmid = 0;
  key_t     key=5;
  size_t    size = 1;
  int       ret;
  void      *shmaddr = (void *)0;  /* starting address of shared memory */
  int       force = 0;  /* force initialization or not */

  /* Create/get the shared memory segment */
  shmid = do_shmget(MYSHMKEY, MYSHMSIZE, 0);
  if (shmid == -1)
  {
    fprintf(stderr, "do_shmget() failed. Exiting ...\n");
```

```
   return(shmid);
}
fprintf(stdout, "Successfully created the shared memory segment, shmid=%d\n",
   shmid);

/* Attach to the shared memory segment */
errno = 0;
shmaddr = shmat(shmid, (void *)NULL, 0);
if (shmaddr == (void *)-1)
   fprintf(stderr, "shmat() failed, errno=%d\n", errno);
else
   fprintf(stdout, "Attached to shared memory at address %p\n", shmaddr);

/* Read shared memory contents */
ret = read_shm(shmaddr);

/* Detach from the shared memory segment */
errno = 0;
ret = shmdt(shmaddr);
if (ret == -1)
   fprintf(stderr, "shmdt() failed, errno=%d\n", errno);
else
   fprintf(stdout, "Detached from shared memory at address %p\n", shmaddr);

return(0);
}
```

Notice how we access the shared memory data. This is different from
non-shared-memory programming. **In shared memory accesses, you don't use
pointer variables anymore. Instead you use offsets.** This is because you
don't declare the data items stored in a shared memory directly in your
program anymore. The data has only one copy and is shared across many
different programs now. The only thing a process knows is the starting
address of the shared memory. Shared memory contents have a specific
layout and are initialized by the shared memory initialization code which
is executed exactly once by only one program. All programs having access
to the shared memory must know the layout and understand what data item
is at what offset into the shared memory segment in order to access it.

We know where the shared memory segment starts; it's remembered in shmaddr.
For each data member in the shared memory, you need to know its offset.
**Programs use the shared memory starting address and the data member's
offset to access each data member.** You do pointer arithmetic a lot in
shared memory accesses. Of course, a process needs to know the data type
of each data item it is accessing.

Note that all addresses you have accesses to in a program are all virtual.
They are program specific. They get translated into physical memory
addresses only at run-time. Processes having access to the shared memory
typically have a different virtual address for the same data member
in the shared memory, but at run time they all get translated to the same
physical address pointing to the same data item.

You can try to run the shmread program while the shared memory update
program (shmupd) introduced in the next section is running to monitor
how the update program is progressing.

Figure 10-8 shows another program that reads shared memory status information.

Figure 10-8 Read shared memory status information -- shmstat.c

```
/*
 * Example program of reading shared memory status information.
 * Authored by Mr. Jin-Jwei Chen
 * Copyright (c) 2015, Mr. Jin-Jwei Chen. All rights reserved.
 */

#include <stdio.h>
#include <sys/types.h>
#include <sys/ipc.h>
#include <sys/shm.h>
#include <errno.h>
#include <string.h>

#include "myshm.h"

int main (int argc, char *argv[])
{
  int       shmid = 0;
  key_t     key=5;
  size_t    size = 1;
  int       ret;
  void      *shmaddr = (void *)0;  /* starting address of shared memory */
  int       force = 0;  /* force initialization or not */

  /* Create/get the shared memory segment */
  shmid = do_shmget(MYSHMKEY, MYSHMSIZE, 0);
  if (shmid == -1)
  {
    fprintf(stderr, "do_shmget() failed. Exiting ...\n");
    return(shmid);
  }
  fprintf(stdout, "Successfully created the shared memory segment, shmid=%d\n",
    shmid);

  /* Attach to the shared memory segment */
  errno = 0;
  shmaddr = shmat(shmid, (void *)NULL, 0);
  if (shmaddr == (void *)-1)
    fprintf(stderr, "shmat() failed, errno=%d\n", errno);
  else
    fprintf(stdout, "Attached to shared memory at address %p\n", shmaddr);

  /* Get status of the shared memory segment */
  ret = do_shmstat(shmid);
  if (ret != 0)
    fprintf(stderr, "do_shmstat() failed, ret=%d\n", ret);

  /* Read shared memory contents */
  ret = read_shm1(shmaddr);
  if (ret != 0)
```

```
    fprintf(stderr, "read_shm1() failed, ret=%d\n", ret);

/* Initialize shared memory contents */
ret = init_shm1(shmaddr, force);
if (ret != 0)
    fprintf(stderr, "init_shm1() failed, ret=%d\n", ret);

/* Read shared memory contents */
ret = read_shm1(shmaddr);
if (ret != 0)
    fprintf(stderr, "read_shm1() failed, ret=%d\n", ret);

/* Detach from the shared memory segment */
errno = 0;
ret = shmdt(shmaddr);
if (ret == -1)
    fprintf(stderr, "shmdt() failed, errno=%d\n", errno);
else
    fprintf(stdout, "Detached from shared memory at address %p\n", shmaddr);

return(0);
}
```

10-3-3 Update Shared Memory

As shown in Figure 10-9, in this section we give another example which involves multiple processes updating the same shared memory at the same time.

This example resembles many real applications. In fact, it does what many real-world applications do at their core -- concurrently updating shared variables in shared memory.

The shared data being updated in this example include a global counter and two local counters -- the gcount and the count fields in the two task structures.

The example program tries to update all these shared data items for a given number of times. Each time, it increments the global counter's value by 1, the local counter of the first task structure by one and the local counter of the second task structure by two. The shared memory update function is update_shm() in our library.

For example, if you run four instances of this program to have four processes trying to update the values of these three shared variables at the same time, and each process tries to increment these values by 500 times. Then at end, the values of the global counter and the first task counter should be 4*500=2000 and the value of the second task counter should be 4000. If it gets this result, then the computation is correct. Otherwise, it's incorrect.

We deliberately make the program taking in two arguments. The first argument can be 1 or 0, meaning using lock or not to protect the updates. The second argument represents the number of updates each process will perform on the shared variables. When you run the program yourself, you will see that with locking the program always delivers correct results.

And without locking, the end results are always less than the expected numbers, meaning update losses have occurred without locking!

This again clearly demonstrates why the concurrent updates of the shared variables need to be protected by locks!

Please be aware that we make locking optional in our program example only for demonstration purpose. To ensure data integrity from concurrent updates, make sure you always use locking in your code.

Here we use our own locking routines written in assembly language on Intel Linux, IBM Power AIX, Oracle/Sun SPARC Solaris and Apple Darwin platforms, which we discussed in an early chapter.

Note that if you are on a 64-bit machine building 64-bit executables, then you need to use the 64-bit versions of these locking routines. Also, for absolute consistency the shared memory readers must use locking as well.

For best performance, ideally it is very desirable to implement reader and writer locks such that multiple readers can be allowed in at the same time. For that we will leave it as a project.

Figure 10-10 shows sample outputs from running the shmupd program on different platforms using our own locking routines. Notice that at end of the test, gcount = 2000, count[0] = 2000 and count[1] = 4000.

When the shmupd application is running, you could use another window to run shmread to monitor progress of the test.

Figure 10-9 Concurrent updates of shared variables in shared memory -- shmupd.c

```
/*
 * Update shared memory.
 * Authored by Mr. Jin-Jwei Chen
 * Copyright (c) 2015, 2019, 2020 Mr. Jin-Jwei Chen. All rights reserved.
 */

#include <stdio.h>
#include <sys/types.h>
#include <sys/ipc.h>
#include <sys/shm.h>
#include <errno.h>
#include <string.h>
#include <stdlib.h>

#include "myshm.h"

int main (int argc, char *argv[])
{
  int       shmid = 0;
  key_t     key=5;
  size_t    size = 1;
  int       ret;
  void      *shmaddr = (void *)0;  /* starting address of shared memory */
```

```
int         force = 0;               /* force initialization or not */
int         taskid = 0;
int         uselock = 1;             /* use locking for update or not */
int         delaycnt = DELAYCNT;     /* delay loop count */
size_t      updcnt = SHMDEFUPDCNT;   /* each thread's file update count */

if ((argc > 1) &&
    ((strcmp(argv[1], "-h") == 0) || (strcmp(argv[1], "-help") == 0)))
{
  fprintf(stdout, "Usage: %s [uselock] [updcnt] [delaycnt]\n", argv[0]);
  return(-1);
}

/* Get command line arguments */
if (argc > 1)
{
  uselock = atoi(argv[1]);
  if (uselock != 0)
    uselock = 1;
}

if (argc > 2)
  updcnt = atoi(argv[2]);
if (updcnt <= 0)
  updcnt = SHMDEFUPDCNT;

if (argc > 3)
  delaycnt = atoi(argv[3]);
if (delaycnt <= 0)
  delaycnt = DELAYCNT;

/* Create/get the shared memory segment */
shmid = do_shmget(MYSHMKEY, MYSHMSIZE, 0);
if (shmid == -1)
{
  fprintf(stderr, "do_shmget() failed. Exiting ...\n");
  return(shmid);
}
fprintf(stdout, "\nThe shared memory segment was successfully created/got. "
  "shmid=%d\n", shmid);

/* Attach to the shared memory segment */
errno = 0;
shmaddr = shmat(shmid, (void *)NULL, 0);
if (shmaddr == (void *)-1)
  fprintf(stderr, "shmat() failed, errno=%d\n", errno);
else
  fprintf(stdout, "Attached to shared memory at address %p\n", shmaddr);

/* Get status of the shared memory segment */
ret = do_shmstat(shmid);
if (ret != 0)
  fprintf(stderr, "do_shmstat() failed, ret=%d\n", ret);

/* Initialize shared memory contents if it's not done yet */
ret = init_shm(shmaddr, force);
```

```
if (ret != 0)
  fprintf(stderr, "init_shm() failed, ret=%d\n", ret);

/* Update shared memory contents */
if (uselock)
  fprintf(stdout, "\nTo update shared variables in shared memory %lu times "
    "with locking and delaycnt=%u.\n", updcnt, delaycnt);
else
  fprintf(stdout, "\nTo update shared variables in shared memory %lu times "
    "without locking and delaycnt=%u.\n", updcnt, delaycnt);
ret = update_shm(shmaddr, updcnt, delaycnt, uselock);
if (ret != 0)
  fprintf(stderr, "update_shm() failed, ret=%d\n", ret);

/* Read shared memory contents */
ret = read_shm(shmaddr);
if (ret != 0)
  fprintf(stderr, "read_shm() failed, ret=%d\n", ret);

/* Detach from the shared memory segment */
errno = 0;
ret = shmdt(shmaddr);
if (ret == -1)
  fprintf(stderr, "shmdt() failed, errno=%d\n", errno);
else
  fprintf(stdout, "Detached from shared memory at address %p\n\n", shmaddr);

return(0);
}
```

Figure 10-10 Sample output from running shmupd

1. Intel x86 Linux

```
$ cat testupd
./shmupd &
./shmupd &
./shmupd &
./shmupd &


$ ./testupd

Successfully created/got the shared memory segment, shmid=1867776
Attached to shared memory at address 0xf75de000
Current status of the shared memory of shmid 1867776:
  shm_perm.uid = 1000
  shm_perm.gid = 500
  shm_perm.mode = 0660
  shm_segsz = 2048000
  shm_nattch = 1
  shm_cpid = 5801
  shm_lpid = 5801
Initialize the shared memory contents...
To update shared variables in shared memory 500 times with locking.
  :
  : (omitting outputs from second and third processes)
```

```
      :
Successfully created/got the shared memory segment, shmid=1867776
Attached to shared memory at address 0xf7590000
Current status of the shared memory of shmid 1867776:
   shm_perm.uid = 1000
   shm_perm.gid = 500
   shm_perm.mode = 0660
   shm_segsz = 2048000
   shm_nattch = 2
   shm_cpid = 5801
   shm_lpid = 5803
To update shared variables in shared memory 500 times with locking.

Contents of the shared memory are:
   magic = 75432018
   banner = This is shared memory for application XYZ.
   gcount = 1995
   glock = 1
   taskid[ 0]   = 1
   taskname[ 0] = Task # 1
   count[ 0] = 1998
   lock[ 0]   = 1
   taskid[ 1]   = 2
   taskname[ 1] = Task # 2
   count[ 1] = 3994
   lock[ 1]   = 1
Detached from shared memory at address 0xf7594000
      :
      : (omitting the outputs by processes finished second and third)
      :
Contents of the shared memory are:
   magic = 75432018
   banner = This is shared memory for application XYZ.
   gcount = 2000
   glock = 1
   taskid[ 0]   = 1
   taskname[ 0] = Task # 1
   count[ 0] = 2000
   lock[ 0]   = 1
   taskid[ 1]   = 2
   taskname[ 1] = Task # 2
   count[ 1] = 4000
   lock[ 1]   = 1
Detached from shared memory at address 0xf7590000
```

2. IBM Power AIX

```
bash-4.2$ cat testshmupd.aix64
./shmupd.aix64 &
./shmupd.aix64 &
./shmupd.aix64 &
./shmupd.aix64 &
bash-4.2$ ./testshmupd.aix64

Successfully created/got the shared memory segment, shmid=919601154
Attached to shared memory at address 700000000000000
```

632

```
Current status of the shared memory of shmid 919601154:
  shm_perm.uid = 505921
  shm_perm.gid = 8500
  shm_perm.mode = 0100660
  shm_segsz = 2048000
  shm_nattch = 1
  shm_cpid = 12583054
  shm_lpid = 12583054
Initialize the shared memory contents...
To update shared variables in shared memory 500 times with locking.
  :
  :   (omitting outputs by second and third processes)
  :
Successfully created/got the shared memory segment, shmid=919601154
Attached to shared memory at address 700000000000000
Current status of the shared memory of shmid 919601154:
  shm_perm.uid = 505921
  shm_perm.gid = 8500
  shm_perm.mode = 0100660
  shm_segsz = 2048000
  shm_nattch = 4
  shm_cpid = 12583054
  shm_lpid = 11075608
To update shared variables in shared memory 500 times with locking.
  :
  :  (omitting outputs from processes finished first, second and third)
  :
Contents of the shared memory are:
  magic = 75432018
  banner = This is shared memory for application XYZ.
  gcount = 2000
  glock = 1
  taskid[ 0]   = 1
  taskname[ 0] = Task # 1
  count[ 0] = 2000
  lock[ 0]   = 1
  taskid[ 1]   = 2
  taskname[ 1] = Task # 2
  count[ 1] = 4000
  lock[ 1]   = 1
Detached from shared memory at address 700000000000000
```

3. Oracle/Sun SPARC Solaris

```
bash-4.1$ cat testshmupd.sun64
./shmupd.sun64 &
./shmupd.sun64 &
./shmupd.sun64 &
./shmupd.sun64 &
bash-4.1$ ./testshmupd.sun64

Successfully created/got the shared memory segment, shmid=6
Attached to shared memory at address ffffffff7e800000
Current status of the shared memory of shmid 6:
  shm_perm.uid = 505921
  shm_perm.gid = 8500
```

```
  shm_perm.mode = 0100660
  shm_segsz = 2048000
  shm_nattch = 1
  shm_cpid = 4235
  shm_lpid = 4235
Initialize the shared memory contents...
To update shared variables in shared memory 500 times with locking.
    :
    : (omitting outputs from second and third processes)
    :
Successfully created/got the shared memory segment, shmid=6
Attached to shared memory at address ffffffff7e800000
Current status of the shared memory of shmid 6:
  shm_perm.uid = 505921
  shm_perm.gid = 8500
  shm_perm.mode = 0100660
  shm_segsz = 2048000
  shm_nattch = 4
  shm_cpid = 4235
  shm_lpid = 4237
To update shared variables in shared memory 500 times with locking.
    :
    : (omitting outputs from processes finished first, second and third)
    :
Contents of the shared memory are:
  magic = 75432018
  banner = This is shared memory for application XYZ.
  gcount = 2000
  glock = 1
  taskid[ 0]   = 1
  taskname[ 0] = Task # 1
  count[ 0] = 2000
  lock[ 0]   = 1
  taskid[ 1]   = 2
  taskname[ 1] = Task # 2
  count[ 1] = 4000
  lock[ 1]   = 1
Detached from shared memory at address ffffffff7e800000
```

4. Apple Darwin on MacBook

```
jim@Jims-MacBook-Air mac % cat testupd
#!/bin/sh
./shmupd &
./shmupd &
./shmupd &
./shmupd &
jim@Jims-MacBook-Air mac % ./testupd

The shared memory segment was successfully created/got. shmid=65536
Attached to shared memory at address 0x1024f0000
Current status of the shared memory of shmid 65536:
  shm_perm.uid = 501
  shm_perm.gid = 20
  shm_perm.mode = 04660
  shm_segsz = 2048000
```

```
   shm_nattch = 1
   shm_cpid = 479
   shm_lpid = 479
Initialize the shared memory contents...
```

```
The shared memory segment was successfully created/got. shmid=65536
The shared memory segment was successfully created/got. shmid=65536
Attached to shared memory at address 0x10174c000
Attached to shared memory at address 0x1058c4000
```

```
The shared memory segment was successfully created/got. shmid=65536
Attached to shared memory at address 0x10defa000
```

```
   :
   : (omitting outputs from processes finished first, second and third)
   :
Contents of the shared memory are:
   magic = 75432018
   banner = This is shared memory for application XYZ.
   gcount = 2000
   glock = 1
   taskid[ 0]   = 1
   taskname[ 0] = Task # 1
   count[ 0] = 2000
   lock[ 0]   = 1
   taskid[ 1]   = 2
   taskname[ 1] = Task # 2
   count[ 1] = 4000
   lock[ 1]   = 1
Detached from shared memory at address 0x10defa000
```

10-3-4 Summary

System V shared memory is one of the most important IPC mechanisms.
It uses the following APIs defined in POSIX Standard to create, attach,
detach and control a shared memory:

```
shmget() - get shared memory id (shmid) and create the shared memory if not
           created yet
shmat()  - attach to a shared memory
shmdt()  - detach from a shared memory
shmctl() - control shared memory
```

Shared memory offers the fastest means for sharing and exchanging data
between unrelated processes running on the same system. It is done through
setting up a physical memory address space (a shared memory segment) that
can be shared between multiple processes.

The granularity of memory shared is usually one or more segments.
Accessing data stored in the shared memory is accessing memory.
That is why it's the fastest IPC mechanism.

Once a shared memory is created by one process, it can then be used by
any process that has a permission to read/write it. The shared memory and
its contents remain in physical memory until it is explicitly removed.

Only one copy of each shared memory segment exists on a system.
Any update of its contents by any process is immediately seen by all
processes sharing it. Each shared memory segment is identified by a
unique identifier called shared memory identifier (shmid). For uniqueness,
an application should create a unique pathname, invoke the ftok() function
to convert that pathname into a unique key and use that to create the
shared memory segment and get back a unique shmid. For security, never
place the pathname in /tmp or /var/tmp directory.

The user who originally creates the shared memory is the creator of the
shared memory. It is also the original owner. Via the shmctl() system call,
the owner of a shared memory can pass on the ownership to another user
and/or group. Nonetheless, the creator remains the same.
Permissions of the shared memory can be changed via shmctl() as well.

Concurrency control is essential in reading and/or writing shared memory.
Its efficiency has a direct impact on performance. Updates of same data
items in shared memory must be protected by locks to ensure data integrity.
System V or POSIX semaphores can be used for this purpose. But self-written
assembly language lock routines, as we learned, provide better performance.

The way to access a piece of data in a shared memory from within a program
is different. One no longer uses the name of a variable or pointer directly
as in a traditional C program. Instead, offset into the shared memory is
used.

The data stored at a particular location of a shared memory is typically
defined by a data structure. Usually, there are multiple pieces of data
defined by multiple data structures stored at different locations in a
shared memory. The processes sharing the memory need to know both the
locations and the structures of the data in order to correctly read and/or
write the data. The data location is typically an offset from the start
of the shared memory, rather than a variable name as in traditional programs.
From the offset, a program computes the starting address of the data.
It then casts that address to a pointer to the structure type of the data
and uses that pointer to access the data.

Notice the power of shared memory. Multiple processes can easily access
and update the same piece of memory and cooperate with one another,
providing the most efficient and high-performance way of sharing data
and collaborating between multiple processes running on the same computer.

After some processes finish, contents of the shared memory stay because
the shared memory is not removed. So more processes can attach to the
same shared memory segment and continue to use data from that memory.
It is the most high-performance means of sharing data between multiple
collaborating processes. Many today's most powerful database management
systems (e.g. Oracle RDBMS) employ the shared memory technology at their
cores. Oracle RDBMS maintains its database buffer cache in shared memory
so that all Oracle RDBMS server processes (database writer, log writer,
etc.) all have access to it.

Review Questions

1. What is shared memory?

2. What is shared memory used for?

3. How is shared memory achieved?

4. What characteristics shared memory has?

5. Why concurrency control is usually needed in using shared memory?

6. What is the typical challenge in optimizing performance of shared memory?

7. How do you change the ownership and/or permissions of a shared memory segment?

8. What are the steps in using System V shared memory?
   What are the APIs for these steps?

9. When a program calls shmget(), does it always create the shared memory segment? If not, under what circumstances it does?

10. How do different applications using shared memory ensure they don't step on one another's toes?

Exercises

1. Run multiple instances of the shmupd program with same taskid. Explain what you observe.

2. Run multiple instances of the shmupd program with different taskids. Explain what you observe.

3. Run an arbitrary number of the shmupd program and use the shmread program to see what is going on.

4. Modify the length of the time delay introduced by the some_delay() function. Then run multiple instances of the shmupd program again. Observe if it makes any difference in CPU scheduling of the tasks.

5. Replace the some_delay() function with sleep(1) and then run multiple instances of the shmupd program again. Do you notice any differences in CPU scheduling of the tasks?

6. Replace the some_delay() function with nanosleep() to sleep less than a second and then run multiple instances of the shmupd program again. Vary the sleep time.

Programming Assignments

1. Write two programs that demonstrate a shared memory segment is not actually removed from the system until all processes having attached to it detach from it or terminate.

2. Write a program that allows multiple processes to update a simple

database at the same time. The database contains the employee records of a small company. Each employee record should contain at least the following fields: employee id, social security number, name, address, birthdate, department, salary. This program must use shared memory.

3. Design and implement reader locks and writer locks. Write an application to run multiple readers and multiple writers that read and update shared data stored in shared memory, respectively.

References

1. The Open Group Base Specifications Issue 7, 2018 edition
   IEEE Std 1003.1™-2017 (Revision of IEEE Std 1003.1-2008)
   Copyright © 2001-2018 IEEE and The Open Group
   http://pubs.opengroup.org/onlinepubs/9699919799/

2. AT&T UNIX System V Release 4 Programmer's Guide: System Services
   Prentice-Hall, Inc. 1990

11 More on Interprocess Communication Mechanisms

This chapter discusses **Interprocess Communication (IPC) mechanisms.**
There exist many different interprocess communication mechanisms.
They are used at different occasions for solving different problems or
solving problems in different ways. We have discussed some of them
so far. They include signals, semaphores, shared memory and pipes.

We will give a very brief overview of all of the commonly used
interprocess communication mechanisms first and then talk about
the rest of them except one in this chapter. System V messages queues,
named pipes, and memory-mapped files are discussed here and socket
will be introduced in chapter 12.

Typically, a big, complex software system or product includes many programs
or processes working together, collaborating with one another and serving
clients. Because multiple processes are collaborating, they need to
communicate and/or synchronize with one another. Therefore, interprocess
communication is at the core of almost every software product.

Just like Linux is the "open" operating system today, since early 1980s,
Unix has been the open system. In Unix world, AT&T Unix System V was kind
of the de facto standard. System V Unix defined a set of IPC mechanisms
very early on. They have been widely used. What we discuss here are IPC
mechanisms defined in the POSIX standard. They are generally available
in all POSIX-compliant systems including Unix and Linux.

**IPC is like the plumbing, piping or major communication highway of a
software product. Therefore, it's very important that you do it right.
Make sure you fully understand the characteristics of each IPC mechanism
and choose the right and best ones to use at different places in the
software you design so that it has the best architecture, infrastructure,
quality and performance.**

11-1 Overview of IPC Mechanisms

11-1-1 Signals

Signals are asynchronous notification IPC mechanism.
It works between processes running on the same computer. It does not work
beyond one system. It is not for use between multithreads of the same
process either.

639

A process can send a signal of its choice to another process running on the same system as long as it knows that target process's process id (pid) and has the permission to do so. It is completely independent of what the target process is doing. Hence, it is completely asynchronous (with respect to the processing of the target process). Synchronous signals are not for IPC.

Every signal has a signal number and its own meaning. There are two types of signals. Most signals have a specific meaning predefined by the operating system, or the POSIX standard. They have a predefined behavior which is already implemented in the operating system. You use them for the situations they are defined for. Besides, there are a very small number of user-defined signals. Behavior of these signals are not defined. Users (i.e. you as programmers) can use them for whatever purposes you want. These often come very handy.

Signals allow arbitrary processes running on the same system to communicate. The involved two processes do not have to have a relationship. The message being communicated is just a number, the signal number. It's like event in that each signal represents a different event. Sending a signal to another process is like notifying that process of a particular event, sort of.

Signals are sent via the kill() system call.

Signals are designed to be used with processes before threads even exist. Special care must be taken when using signals with threads.

11-1-2 Semaphores

Semaphores are used for synchronization purposes between processes running on the same system. They do not work beyond one system. Of course, they work between different threads of the same process too.

Based on usage, there are two types of semaphores: binary semaphores and counting semaphores. Each semaphore is essentially an integer variable having an integer value. A binary semaphore has a value of 0 or 1. A counting semaphore has a range of integer values.

Binary semaphores are used for mutual exclusion between competing processes. They work as locks. Binary semaphores are typically used in concurrent updates of shared data to prevent update loss and ensure data integrity

Counting semaphores are used to coordinate accesses to shared resources (e.g. buffers or workers) between collaborating processes where the value of a counting semaphore represents the number of a particular resource available. Counting semaphores are best for solving producer-consumer problems and the like.

POSIX Standard includes two different sets of semaphore APIs: System V semaphores and POSIX semaphores.

System V semaphores come in sets. It was designed with the expectation that most processes would need many semaphores to guard many shared data items. A program creates a semaphore set with a single semaphore in it if all it needs is one semaphore.

Once created, a semaphore (set) exists in the operating system until it is explicitly removed. So, it lives beyond its creator or any single process. Namely, until it is explicitly removed, a System V semaphore lives in memory as long as the system stays up, even after its creator has terminated.

Multiple processes can access the same semaphore as long as they use the same key. A System V IPC key is created by the ftok() function using a unique (pathname, project_id) pair. Please see section 9-2-1 for details.

As we discussed in Section 9-6, POSIX semaphore is slightly easier to use and has better performance than System V semaphore. It includes unnamed and named semaphores and does not exist in sets.

As we've demonstrated, writing your own locking functions in assembly language typically gives you a performance boost of 25% or even higher.

11-1-3 Shared Memory

Shared memory is used to store data shared by multiple processes running on the same system. It does not work beyond one system.

Shared memory exists as segments. One can create one or more shared memory segments, with a size of your choice. Of course, there is an upper limit of how big each shared memory segment can be, which is typically a kernel tunable parameter.

Once created by a creator, a shared memory segment exists in the operating system until it is explicitly removed. So, it lives beyond its creator or any single process. That is, until it is explicitly removed by someone or some program, a shared memory segment lives in memory as long as the system stays up. Furthermore, unless updated by some process, the contents of a shared memory segment remain unchanged in memory. Any update to the shared memory is immediately seen by all processes sharing the shared memory.

Multiple processes can access the same shared memory segment as long as they use the same key. A System V IPC key is created by the ftok() function using a unique (pathname, project_id) pair, as explained in section 9-2-1.

Shared memory indeed is the fastest way of sharing information between multiple processes. It is widely used in most database systems (e.g. Oracle Relational database system). So, the technology is invaluable.

The shared memory technology has existed in Unix operating systems since AT&T UNIX System V Release 1 (SVR1) in 1983, and in POSIX since 1993.

Typical modern software products employ multiple processes collaborating and/or synchronizing with one another where each process may also have multiple threads synchronizing and collaborating with one another. The information sharing and exchanges between multiple processes can be done using shared memory. The synchronization can be achieved through using semaphores, or lock variables stored in shared memory (as in case of multiple processes), or using process globals (in the case of multithreaded process). Shared memory can be used to share large amount of information.

11-1-4 Socket

Socket IPC mechanism works between processes running on different systems connected via a computer network or on the same system.

The socket code is the same regardless of whether the processes communicating with one another using socket run on the same system or on different systems connected by a computer network. This is the IPC mechanism that works across the network or even the globe. Everyone knows that the Internet is so powerful and popular. In fact, the entire Internet is based on the TCP/IP protocol and almost all of the Internet applications are some sort of network applications using socket at bottom. That's the power socket communication has! Hence, the value of socket IPC can never be overstated! This technology is at the core of the entire Internet. We will discuss socket programming in the next chapter.

11-1-5 Pipes

There are two types of pipes defined by POSIX standard: pipes (or unnamed pipes) and named pipes (also called FIFO files).

Pipes or unnamed pipes are IPC mechanism used between processes having parent and child relationship. The processes communicating via pipes not only have to reside on the same system but also must have a parent-child relationship or are connected via the dup() function! Unrelated processes cannot use (unnamed) pipes to communicate with each other.

When a parent process creates a pipe before it spawns a child, the pipe is inherited by its child. Since both of them have the same pipe, they can use it for their communication.

Just like water in a water pipe flowing in only one direction, information in a computer software pipe flows in only one direction too. One process can write information into one end of a pipe and the other process can read the information from the other end. Because of this, very often, processes create and use a pair of pipes in order to have a bidirectional information exchange.

We have demonstrated how to use pipes in parent-child process communication in section 7-5.

11-1-6 Named Pipes

Named pipes in Unix/Linux operating systems are special files. They are also referred to as FIFO (fist-in-first-out) files. As long as they know the pathname associated with a named pipe, processes can open a named pipe to write into or read from it and thus communicate with each other. Information is read from a named pipe in the exact order it's written into; that's why they are called FIFO files.

Named pipes allow unrelated processes to communicate with one another. The processes communicating via FIFOs must reside on the same system.

However, since any process with permission may read from or write into a named pipe, a named pipe communication channel is not private.

Note that both Unix/Linux systems and Microsoft Windows have "named pipes". Although they have the same name, they are not the same thing. Named pipes in Unix/Linux are unidirectional whereas named pipes in Windows are bidirectional and are more like Unix Domain sockets in Unix/Linux.

One thing with communication using name pipes is there is no message boundary if the writer just sends a bunch of text messages.

We will discuss named pipes in the next section in this chapter.

11-1-7 Message Queues

System V message queues are for sending and receiving messages between processes running on the same system. They work only within a single system. Again, this technology has existed in Unix operating systems since 1983.

System V message queues allow processes to send formatted data to arbitrary processes on the same system. Multiple senders can communicate with multiple receivers using the same message queue. A message type can be used to identify different receiver targets. The communicating processes do not have to be related. All is needed is they all know the id of the message queue (the values of the IPCKEYPATH and PROJID). What users have rights (read and/or write) to access the message queue is controlled by the permission bits set on the message queue.

Once created by a creator, a System V message queue exists in the operating system until it is explicitly removed. It lives beyond its creator or any single process. That is, until it is explicitly removed by someone or some program that has permission to do so, a System V message queue lives as long as the system stays up. We will discuss this in section 11-3.

11-1-8 Memory-mapped Files

Memory-mapped file is used to improve performance, especially for reading or writing large files. It simplifies application programs in that it makes file I/O becomes memory access. Once a file is mapped into a process' virtual memory, reading a file becomes reading from memory and writing a file becomes writing to memory.

Memory-mapped file can be used as an IPC mechanism when multiple processes all map and share the same file. The processes communicating using memory mapped file don't have to be related.

Note that many engineers wrongly call memory-mapped file as shared memory. As we explain below in section 11-4, it is not shared memory.

11-1-9 Summary

As you can see, there exists many different interprocess communication mechanisms. Each is designed to be used in a different situation and for its own purpose. As you design software, pick and choose the IPC mechanism(s) that best fits your application and construct your building blocks with it or them.

After giving a very brief overview and stating what each of the IPC mechanisms is used for, we will introduce some of these mechanisms that we have not talked about yet so far in further details in the subsequent sections. Socket will be introduced in chapter 12.

11-2 Named Pipes (FIFOs)

11-2-1 The mkfifo() Function

As we said it above, in Unix/Linux systems, a named pipe is a FIFO special file. Yes, FIFO is a file type.

To use a named pipe as an IPC mechanism, some process needs to invoke the mkfifo() function to create the named pipe first:

```
#include <sys/types.h>
#include <sys/stat.h>

int mkfifo(const char *path, mode_t mode);
```

The mkfifo() function creates a FIFO (First-In First-Out) special file in the file system. A FIFO special file is similar to a pipe. The difference is that a pipe is anonymous whereas a FIFO is named. Therefore, a FIFO is also called a named pipe.

Each named pipe has a pathname associated with it. The first parameter 'path' provides that. Since it's a file, it needs to have permission too. The second parameter 'mode' provides that. The owner of the FIFO file will be set to the calling process' effective user ID.
The FIFO file's group ID shall be set to the effective group ID of the calling process or the group ID of the parent directory.

Once a named pipe is created, it can be used like a normal file. Processes will be able to open it and write to it or read from it, hence using it to communicate with each other.

A pipe is an anonymous communication channel typically used in between a parent and a child processes or two processes connected through the use of the dup() function. In contrast, a FIFO can be used as a communication channel between two unrelated processes because it is named and exists in the file system and thus is accessible to any processes as long as they are given permission. Obviously, processes communicating via a FIFO must reside on the same system.

Note that, as demonstrated in the example programs in Figure 11-1 below, normally when the O_NONBLOCK flag is not specified in the open() call, that is, in the normal blocking I/O mode, a call to open a FIFO for write-only will block until some other process opens the FIFO for reading. Similarly, a call to open a FIFO for read-only will

```
block until some other process opens the FIFO for writing.
```

When a process calls mkfifo() to create a FIFO file, if it already exists, the call will fail and return error EEXIST, meaning the file already exists.

Figure 11-1 shows a pair of programs that illustrate how to use a FIFO as a pipe to communicate between two unrelated processes. The setup is such that you can start either program first. Each program first checks if the FIFO exists. If not, then create it. Therefore, whoever starts first will find the FIFO does not exist and create it. The programs use the file_exists() function to check if the FIFO already exists or not. If it already exists, the file_exists() function returns 0. If it does not exist, the file_exists() function returns ENOENT.

In addition, the example writer program sends a structure instead of just a simple text message, trying to create a message boundary. If you send just a simple text message each time, the reader may end up reading more than one message at a time.

When a named pipe is no longer needed, it must be closed and removed. The FIFO writer program does the cleanup and closes and removes the FIFO when it's done writing. This ensures that it's a clean start each time if you run the same programs multiple times.

Figure 11-1 Two unrelated processes communicating using a FIFO (fifowriter.c and fiforeader.c)

(a) fifowriter.c

```
/*
 * A FIFO writer
 * This program creates a FIFO and writes messages to it.
 * Copyright (c) 2013, 2014, 2019 Mr. Jin-Jwei Chen. All rights reserved.
 */

#include <stdio.h>
#include <errno.h>
#include <sys/types.h>
#include <sys/stat.h>
#include <fcntl.h>
#include <unistd.h>
#include <string.h>

#define  FIFO_PATH  "/tmp/myfifo1"
#define  MSGLEN  64
struct fifobuf
{
  int    pid;           /* pid of sender */
  char   msg[MSGLEN];   /* text message from sender */
};

int file_exists(char *pathname)
{
  int    ret;
  struct stat  finfo;       /* information about a file or directory */
```

```
  if (pathname == NULL)
    return(EINVAL);
  ret = stat(pathname, &finfo);
  if (ret == 0)   /* file exists */
    return(0);
  return(errno);   /* errno is ENOENT if the file doesn't exist */
}

int main(int argc, char *argv[])
{
  int    ret;
  int    fd;
  mode_t  mode=0644;
  struct fifobuf  buf;
  ssize_t  bytes;

  /* Check if the FIFO already exists */
  ret = file_exists(FIFO_PATH);

  /* Create the FIFO if it does not already exist */
  if (ret == ENOENT)
  {
    /* Create the FIFO */
    ret = mkfifo(FIFO_PATH, mode);
    if (ret == -1)
    {
      fprintf(stderr, "FIFO writer: mkfifo() failed, errno=%d\n", errno);
      return(-1);
    }
  }

  /* This is the writer process. It writes to the FIFO. */
  fd = open(FIFO_PATH, O_WRONLY, mode);
  if (fd == -1)
  {
    fprintf(stderr, "FIFO writer: open() for write failed, errno=%d\n", errno);
    return(errno);
  }

  /* Write some messages to the FIFO */
  sprintf(buf.msg, "%s", "This is a message 1 from writer.");
  buf.pid = (int) getpid();
  bytes = write(fd, &buf, sizeof(buf));
  fprintf(stdout, "FIFO writer: just wrote pid=%d msg='%s'\n", buf.pid, buf.msg);
  sprintf(buf.msg, "%s", "This is a message 2 from writer.");
  bytes = write(fd, &buf, sizeof(buf));
  fprintf(stdout, "FIFO writer: just wrote pid=%d msg='%s'\n", buf.pid, buf.msg);

  sprintf(buf.msg, "%s", "Bye!");
  bytes = write(fd, &buf, sizeof(buf));
  fprintf(stdout, "FIFO writer: just wrote pid=%d msg='%s'\n", buf.pid, buf.msg);

  close(fd);
  /* Remove the FIFO */
  unlink(FIFO_PATH);
```

```
  return(0);
}

    (b)  fiforeader.c

/*
 * A FIFO reader.
 * This program creates a FIFO and reads from it.
 * Copyright (c) 2013, 2014, 2019 Mr. Jin-Jwei Chen. All rights reserved.
 */

#include <stdio.h>
#include <errno.h>
#include <sys/types.h>
#include <sys/stat.h>
#include <fcntl.h>
#include <unistd.h>
#include <string.h>

#define   FIFO_PATH   "/tmp/myfifo1"
#define   MSGLEN   64
struct fifobuf
{
  int     pid;             /* pid of sender */
  char    msg[MSGLEN];     /* text message from sender */
};

int file_exists(char *pathname)
{
  int     ret;
  struct stat  finfo;         /* information about a file or directory */

  if (pathname == NULL)
    return(EINVAL);
  errno = 0;
  ret = stat(pathname, &finfo);
  if (ret == 0)   /* file exists */
    return(0);
  return(errno);   /* errno is ENOENT if the file doesn't exist */
}

int main(int argc, char *argv[])
{
  int    ret;
  int    fd;
  mode_t  mode=0644;
  struct fifobuf  buf;
  ssize_t  bytes;

  /* Check if the FIFO already exists */
  ret = file_exists(FIFO_PATH);

  /* Create the FIFO if it does not already exist */
  if (ret == ENOENT)
  {
    /* Create the FIFO */
```

```
    ret = mkfifo(FIFO_PATH, mode);
    if (ret == -1)
    {
      fprintf(stderr, "mkfifo() failed, errno=%d\n", errno);
      return(-1);
    }
}

/* This is the FIFO reader. It reads from the FIFO. */

/* Open the FIFO for read only */
fd = open(FIFO_PATH, O_RDONLY, 0644);
if (fd == -1)
{
    fprintf(stderr, "FIFO reader: open() for read failed, errno=%d\n", errno);
    return(errno);
}

/* Read from the FIFO until it's done */
do
{
    bytes = read(fd, (char *)&buf, sizeof(struct fifobuf));
    if (bytes < 0)
    {
      fprintf(stderr, "FIFO reader: read() failed, errno=%d\n", errno);
      close(fd);
      return(errno);
    }
    buf.msg[strlen(buf.msg)] = '\0';
    if (bytes > 0)
      fprintf(stdout, "FIFO reader: just read pid=%d msg='%s'\n", buf.pid,
          buf.msg);
} while (bytes > 0);

close(fd);
return(0);
}
```

Below is the output of the fifowriter and fiforeader programs:

```
$ ./fifowriter
FIFO writer: just wrote pid=3000 msg='This is a message 1 from writer.'
FIFO writer: just wrote pid=3000 msg='This is a message 2 from writer.'
FIFO writer: just wrote pid=3000 msg='Bye!'

$ ./fiforeader
FIFO reader: just read pid=3000 msg='This is a message 1 from writer.'
FIFO reader: just read pid=3000 msg='This is a message 2 from writer.'
FIFO reader: just read pid=3000 msg='Bye!'
```

Note that if a FIFO writer opens a FIFO with write-only and with the
O_NONBLOCK flag set, then since it is a non-blocking I/O mode, the writer
will not block anymore at its open if there is no reader opens the FIFO
for reading. In that case, the writer's open will fail with error ENXIO.

When there are multiple writers writing to the same named pipe at the same time, the maximum amount of information that can be atomically written to the FIFO is defined by the configurable parameter PIPE_BUF, which can be obtained by calling the pathconf() function as we discussed in section 5-6.

11-2-2 The mkfifoat() Function

The mkfifo() function has a variation, which is the mkfifoat() function:

```
int mkfifoat(int fd, const char *path, mode_t mode);
```

The mkfifoat() function is equivalent to the mkfifo() function except in the case where the path parameter specifies a relative path.
In this case the FIFO file is created relative to the directory associated with the file descriptor fd instead of the current working directory.

If the access mode of the open file description associated with the file descriptor is not O_SEARCH, the function will check whether directory search is permitted using the current permissions of the directory underlying the file descriptor. If the access mode is O_SEARCH, the function will not perform the check.

If the fd argument to mkfifoat() specifies the special value AT_FDCWD the current working directory will be used and the behavior should be identical to mkfifo().

11-3 System V Message Queues

Before processes can use a System V message queue, it has to exist.
So some process must first create it by calling the msgget() system call.

The process creating a message queue in the first place will become the creator and owner of the message queue. During the creation, permissions can be specified for the owner itself, the group members and others.

If necessary, the creator/owner of a message queue can relinquish ownership via the msgctl() function.

Notice that sending a message to a message queue is a synchronous, blocking. The sending process may block until the message being sent gets put on the message queue. Similarly, a process receiving a message from a message queue could be blocked until a message is available.

It's also worth noting that a once popular transaction processing software named Tuxedo developed by AT&T Bell Labs in 1980s was built on the System V message queues.

11-3-1 Create a Message Queue -- msgget()

A program invokes the msgget() function to create or get a message queue.

```
int msgget(key_t key, int msgqflags);
```

The msgget() function returns the message queue identifier of the message

queue associated with the key specified. If a message queue associated with
the given key already exists, the msgget() call just returns its identifier.
If the message queue does not already exist, a new message queue and the
data structure (of type "struct msqid_ds") associated with the queue will
be created if IPC_CREAT is specified in the msgqflags argument.

Note that if both IPC_CREAT and IPC_EXCL flags are specified in the msgqflags
argument and a message queue associated with the specified key already
exists, then msgget() will return an error with errno set to EEXIST.
The IPC_EXCL flag means you want to create it only if it does not exist.

The key parameter can have one of the two values:

1. IPC_PRIVATE

   If you specify IPC_PRIVATE as the key value, it means the message queue
   will be private and cannot be accessed by other processes.

   If the message queue flag specifies IPC_CREATE, then the operating system
   will create a new message queue with a private key (the key value shown
   in the output of the ipcs command will be 0).

2. A key value returned by the ftok() function. This means the message queue
   can be shared and accessed by other processes as long as they have the
   permission.

The maximum number of message queues the operating system can create
is limited by the tunable kernel parameter MSGMNI.

Figure 11-2 lists a program that creates a message queue.
Make sure you create the file pathname by running the following command
before you run the example program.

```
$ touch mymsgq
```

Figure 11-2 Create or attach to a message queue (msgget.c)

```c
/*
 * Create a System V message queue.
 * Create the unique file pathname (IPCKEYPATH) before running this program.
 * Authored by Mr. Jin-Jwei Chen
 * Copyright (c) 2019, Mr. Jin-Jwei Chen. All rights reserved.
 */

#include <stdio.h>
#include <errno.h>
#include <sys/types.h>
#include <sys/ipc.h>
#include <sys/msg.h>

#define   IPCKEYPATH   "./mymsgq"   /* pick an unique pathname */
#define   PROJID       'q'          /* project id to make the key */

int main (int argc, char *argv[])
{
    int       msgqid = 0;
```

```
int       key;
int       msgflags = (IPC_CREAT | 0660);

/* Compute the IPC key value from the pathname and project id */
/* ftok() got error 2 if the pathname (IPCKEYPATH) does not exist. */
if ((key = ftok(IPCKEYPATH, PROJID)) == (key_t)-1) {
  fprintf(stderr, "ftok() failed, errno=%d\n", errno);
  return(-errno);
}

/* Create or attach to a message queue using the derived key. */
msgqid = msgget(key, msgflags);
if (msgqid == (-1))
{
  fprintf(stderr, "msgget() failed, errno=%d\n", errno);
  return(-errno);
}
fprintf(stdout, "msgget() succeeded, msgqid=%d\n", msgqid);

return(0);
}
```

11-3-2 Send and Receive Messages -- msgsnd() and msgrcv()

Note that a message queue can be shared by many processes which send and receive different kinds of messages. Therefore, message queue send and receive operations go by message type.

Each message in a message queue has a message type associated with it.
A message sender sets the type of the message it sends and
a message receiver specifies which type of message it intends to receive.

A program calls the msgsnd() and msgrcv() functions to send and receive
a message, respectively.

```
    int msgsnd(int msgqid, const void *msgbufp, size_t msgsz, int msgflg);

    ssize_t  msgrcv(int msgqid, void *msgbufp, size_t msgsz, long msgtype,
        int msgflg);
```

The first argument msgqid specifies the message queue id returned by msgget().

The second argument msgbufp provides the address of the input or output
buffer holding the input or output message.

The third argument msgsz provides the maximum size of the message, which
is the size of the msgbuf.mtext field.

The msgflg argument specifies the flags for the operation.
It can be 0 or OR-ing together the following flags:

    IPC_NOWAIT - Return immediately if no message of the requested type is
        in the message queue. The function returns -1 with errno set to ENOMSG.

    MSG_EXCEPT - Used with msgtype greater than 0 to read the first message in the message queue with message type that differs from msgtype.

MSG_NOERROR - Truncate the message text if it's longer than msgsz bytes.

The msgrcv() function has one additional argument, msgtype. This indicates what type of messages the call is interested in receiving.
The msgtype argument is used to pick the first message of the particular type specified on the message queue to be received. We will discuss this a little more in just a moment.

Once a message is sent, it is copied into the message queue and stored there. You can always run the ipcs command to see how many messages are in a message queue and how many total bytes they are.

Once a message is received by a receiver, it is removed from the message queue.

Figure 11-3 lists a program that sends a couple of messages to a message queue. Figure 11-4 lists a program that receives messages of a particular type from a message queue. For demonstration purposes, we make the msgsnd example program send two messages of the same type and we put the msgrcv program in a loop of receiving.

Figure 11-3 Send messages to a message queue (msgsnd.c)

```c
/*
 * Create a System V message queue and send messages.
 * Create the unique file pathname (IPCKEYPATH) before running this program.
 * Authored by Mr. Jin-Jwei Chen
 * Copyright (c) 2019, 2020 Mr. Jin-Jwei Chen. All rights reserved.
 */

#include <stdio.h>
#include <errno.h>
#include <sys/types.h>
#include <sys/ipc.h>
#include <sys/msg.h>
#include <string.h>
#include <stdlib.h>

#define    IPCKEYPATH    "./mymsgq"    /* pick an unique pathname */
#define    PROJID        'q'           /* project id to make the key */
#define    MSGSZ         1024          /* size of messages */
#define    MSGTYPE1      1             /* first type of messages */
#define    MSGTYPE2      2             /* second type of messages */
#define    NMSGS         2             /* number of messages to send for each type */

/* General format of messages for System V message queue.
 * "struct msgbuf" is already defined in sys/msg.h in Solaris, AIX, HPUX
 * except Linux. Therefore, make sure to use a different name here.
 */
struct mymsgbuf {
  long mtype;            /* message type, must be > 0 */
  char mtext[MSGSZ];     /* message data */
};
```

```c
int main (int argc, char *argv[])
{
  int       msgqid = 0;
  int       key;
  int       msgflags = (IPC_CREAT | 0660);
  int       msgsndflg = 0;
  int       ret, i;
  int       msgtype = MSGTYPE1;
  struct    mymsgbuf    obuf;              /* buffer for outgoing message */

  /* Get the message type from user */
  if (argc > 1)
  {
    msgtype = atoi(argv[1]);
  }

  /* Compute the IPC key value from the pathname and project id */
  /* ftok() got error 2 if the pathname (IPCKEYPATH) does not exist. */
  if ((key = ftok(IPCKEYPATH, PROJID)) == (key_t)-1) {
    fprintf(stderr, "ftok() failed, errno=%d\n", errno);
    return(-errno);
  }

  /* Create or attach to a message queue using the derived key. */
  msgqid = msgget(key, msgflags);
  if (msgqid == (-1))
  {
    fprintf(stderr, "msgget() failed, errno=%d\n", errno);
    return(-errno);
  }
  fprintf(stdout, "msgget() succeeded, msgqid=%d\n", msgqid);

  /* Send  a couple of messages of the same type */
  obuf.mtype = (long)msgtype;
  for (i = 1; i <= NMSGS; i++)
  {
    sprintf(obuf.mtext, "This is message #%2d of type %2d from the message "
      "sender.", i, msgtype);
    ret = msgsnd(msgqid, (void *)&obuf, (size_t)strlen(obuf.mtext), msgsndflg);
    if (ret == (-1))
    {
      fprintf(stderr, "msgsnd() failed, errno=%d\n", errno);
      return(-errno);
    }
    fprintf(stdout, "A message of type %2d was successfully sent.\n", msgtype);
  }

  return(0);
}
```

Figure 11-4 Receive messages from a message queue (msgrcv.c)

```c
/*
 * Create a System V message queue and receive messages.
 * Create the unique file pathname (IPCKEYPATH) before running this program.
 * Authored by Mr. Jin-Jwei Chen
```

```c
 * Copyright (c) 2019, 2020 Mr. Jin-Jwei Chen. All rights reserved.
 */

#include <stdio.h>
#include <errno.h>
#include <sys/types.h>
#include <sys/ipc.h>
#include <sys/msg.h>
#include <string.h>
#include <stdlib.h>

#define   IPCKEYPATH  "./mymsgq"   /* pick an unique pathname */
#define   PROJID      'q'          /* project id to make the key */
#define   MSGSZ       1024         /* size of messages */
#define   MSGTYPE1    1            /* first type of message */

/* General format of messages for System V message queue.
 * "struct msgbuf" is already defined in sys/msg.h in Solaris, AIX, HPUX
 * except Linux.
 */
struct mymsgbuf {
  long mtype;              /* message type, must be > 0 */
  char mtext[MSGSZ];   /* message data */
};

int main (int argc, char *argv[])
{
  int      msgqid = 0;
  int      key;
  int      msgflags = (IPC_CREAT | 0660);
  int      msgrcvflg = 0;
  int      ret;
  int      msgtype = MSGTYPE1;
  struct   mymsgbuf    inbuf;              /* buffer for outgoing message */
  int      msgcnt = 0;                     /* number of messages received */

  /* Get the message type from the user */
  if (argc > 1)
    msgtype = atoi(argv[1]);

  /* Compute the IPC key value from the pathname and project id */
  /* ftok() got error 2 if the pathname (IPCKEYPATH) does not exist. */
  if ((key = ftok(IPCKEYPATH, PROJID)) == (key_t)-1) {
    fprintf(stderr, "ftok() failed, errno=%d\n", errno);
    return(-errno);
  }

  /* Create or attach to a message queue using the derived key. */
  msgqid = msgget(key, msgflags);
  if (msgqid == (-1))
  {
    fprintf(stderr, "msgget() failed, errno=%d\n", errno);
    return(-errno);
  }
  fprintf(stdout, "msgget() succeeded, msgqid=%d\n", msgqid);
```

654

```
/* Receive messages */
while (msgcnt < 2)
{
  ret = msgrcv(msgqid, (void *)&inbuf, (size_t)MSGSZ, (long)msgtype, msgrcvflg);
  if (ret == (-1))
  {
    fprintf(stderr, "msgrcv() failed, errno=%d\n", errno);
    return(-errno);
  }
  /* Remember to terminate the string */
  inbuf.mtext[ret] = '\0';
  fprintf(stdout, "The following message of %d bytes was received.\n", ret);
  fprintf(stdout, "msgtype=%ld\n", inbuf.mtype);
  fprintf(stdout, "%s\n", inbuf.mtext);
  msgcnt++;
}

  return(0);
}
```

Some Details on Return Code and Behavior

On success, the msgsnd() call returns 0 and the msgrcv() call returns the
number of bytes received into the msgbuf.mtext field.
On failure, both msgsnd() and msgrcv() calls return -1 with error set to
the real error.

A msgsnd() call will succeed and return immediately if sufficient space
is available in the message queue. If not, it will block until enough
space becomes available. In this situation, if IPC_NOWAIT flag is
specified in the msgflg argument, the call will fail and return -1
with errno set to EAGAIN.

A blocked msgsnd() will fail with errno set to EINTR if a signal is caught.
It may also fail with errno set to EIDRM if the message queue is removed
when the call is blocked.

Also notice that there is a message boundary concept in message queue.
A msgsnd() call sends a message, adding one more message to the queue.
And a msgrcv() call receives one message, not more, not less.

Other Receiving Options

So far what we have seen is how to use msgrcv() function to receive the
first message of a particular type in the message queue. And that is done
by specifying a positive message type number. The result is that the first
message of that particular type on the message queue is received.

Indeed, there are two other options in terms of which message in the queue
that a msgrcv() call would like to receive.

If a msgrcv() call specifies a value of 0 in the msgtype argument,
as opposed to a positive number, then the first message on the queue
is received. Alternatively, if a msgrcv() call specifies a msgtype value
that is less than zero, then the lowest message type that is less than
or equal to its absolute value is received.

For example, if there are three messages in the queue and their types are 5, 4 and 3. They were sent in the order 5, 4, and 3. Then a msgrcv() specifying a msgtype of -4 will receive the message of type 3 first even if the message is at the end of the queue because that is the lowest type that is less than or equals to 4 (absolute value of -4)!
And the next msgrcv() with -4 as the msgtype will receive the message of type 4 because that is the lowest less than or equal to 4 in the queue.
Figure 11-5 shows exactly this.

Figure 11-5 Receiving message of the lowest type

```
$ ./msgsnd 5
msgget() succeeded, msgqid=196614
A message of type  5 was successfully sent.
A message of type  5 was successfully sent.

$ ./msgsnd 4
msgget() succeeded, msgqid=196614
A message of type  4 was successfully sent.
A message of type  4 was successfully sent.

$ ./msgsnd 3
msgget() succeeded, msgqid=196614
A message of type  3 was successfully sent.
A message of type  3 was successfully sent.

$ ./msgrcv -4
msgget() succeeded, msgqid=196614
The following message of 55 bytes was received.
msgtype=3
This is message # 1 of type  3 from the message sender.
The following message of 55 bytes was received.
msgtype=3
This is message # 2 of type  3 from the message sender.
The following message of 55 bytes was received.
msgtype=4
This is message # 1 of type  4 from the message sender.
The following message of 55 bytes was received.
msgtype=4
This is message # 2 of type  4 from the message sender.
```

11-3-3 Perform Control Commands on Message Queue -- msgctl()

There are a small number of control commands that one can perform on a message queue. They are carried out by calling the msgctl() function.

```
int msgctl(int msgqid, int cmd, struct msqid_ds *buf);
```

Some operating systems have implemented their own commands. Please see each operating system's documentation for details (e.g. 'man msgctl').
But the POSIX Standard requires the following commands being implemented:

1. IPC_STAT

Getting a copy of the current statistics of a message queue.

This command will make a copy of the msqid_ds data structure associated with the specified message queue from the operating system kernel into the user buffer provided by the caller in the third argument of the call.

The msqid_ds data structure is defined in <sys/msg.h> as follows:

```
struct msqid_ds {
    struct ipc_perm msg_perm;      /* Ownership and permissions */
    time_t          msg_stime;     /* Time of last msgsnd() */
    time_t          msg_rtime;     /* Time of last msgrcv() */
    time_t          msg_ctime;     /* Time of last change */
    unsigned long   __msg_cbytes;  /* Current number of bytes in
                                      queue (non-standard) */
    msgqnum_t       msg_qnum;      /* Current number of messages
                                      in queue */
    msglen_t        msg_qbytes;    /* Maximum number of bytes
                                      allowed in queue */
    pid_t           msg_lspid;     /* PID of last msgsnd() */
    pid_t           msg_lrpid;     /* PID of last msgrcv() */
};
```

2. IPC_SET

   This command allows the caller to perform operations such as changing the ownership and permissions of a message queue.

   The caller must have an effective user ID equal to the value of msg_perm.cuid or msg_perm.uid in the msqid_ds data structure of the message queue, or it must be the super user.
   Essentially, the caller must be the creator or current owner of the message queue or the super user to execute this command.

   The following members of the msqid_ds data structure associated with the specified message queue can be set by this command:

   msg_perm.uid   - effective user id of owner of the message queue
   msg_perm.gid   - effective group id of owner of the message queue
   msg_perm.mode   - read/write permissions of the message queue
   msg_qbytes   - maximum # of bytes allowed in the message queue

   The entire ipc_perm structure is defined as below:

```
struct ipc_perm {
    key_t key;               /* Key supplied to msgget() */
    uid_t uid;               /* Effective UID of owner */
    gid_t gid;               /* Effective GID of owner */
    uid_t cuid;              /* Effective UID of creator */
    gid_t cgid;              /* Effective GID of creator */
    unsigned short mode;     /* Permissions */
    unsigned short seq;      /* Sequence number */
};
```

   This operation will cause the msg_ctime timestamp to be set to the current time.

3. IPC_RMID

   This command removes the message queue from the system whose identifier
   is specified by msgqid argument of the call.

   It destroys the message queue and msqid_ds data structure associated
   with it. IPC_RMD can only be executed by a process with appropriate
   privileges or one that has an effective user ID equal to the value
   of msg_perm.cuid or msg_perm.uid in the msqid_ds data structure of
   the message queue.

Upon success, msgctl() will return 0; otherwise, it will return -1 and
set errno to indicate the error.

Figure 11-6 lists a program which does an IPC_STAT command on a message queue.

   Figure 11-6 Print statistics of a message queue (msgstat.c)

```c
/*
 * Print current state (IPC_STAT) of a message queue.
 * Create the unique file pathname (IPCKEYPATH) before running this program.
 * Authored by Mr. Jin-Jwei Chen
 * Copyright (c) 2019, 2020 Mr. Jin-Jwei Chen. All rights reserved.
 */

#include <stdio.h>
#include <errno.h>
#include <sys/types.h>
#include <sys/ipc.h>
#include <sys/msg.h>
#include <string.h>

#define  IPCKEYPATH  "./mymsgq"  /* pick an unique pathname */
#define  PROJID      'q'         /* project id to make the key */

int main (int argc, char *argv[])
{
  int      msgqid = 0;
  int      key;
  int      msgflags = (IPC_CREAT | 0660);
  int      ret;
  struct msqid_ds  buf;       /* buffer for IPC_STAT operation */

  /* Compute the IPC key value from the pathname and project id */
  /* ftok() got error 2 if the pathname (IPCKEYPATH) does not exist. */
  if ((key = ftok(IPCKEYPATH, PROJID)) == (key_t)-1) {
    fprintf(stderr, "ftok() failed, errno=%d\n", errno);
    return(-errno);
  }

  /* Create or attach to a message queue using the derived key. */
  msgqid = msgget(key, msgflags);
  if (msgqid == (-1))
  {
    fprintf(stderr, "msgget() failed, errno=%d\n", errno);
```

```
     return(-errno);
   }
   fprintf(stdout, "msgget() succeeded, msgqid=%d\n", msgqid);

   /* Perform an IPC_STAT operation on the message queue */
   ret = msgctl(msgqid, IPC_STAT, &buf);
   if (ret == (-1))
   {
     fprintf(stderr, "msgctl() failed, errno=%d\n", errno);
     return(-errno);
   }
   fprintf(stdout, "Number of messages in queue = %lu\n", buf.msg_qnum);
   fprintf(stdout, "Max. # of bytes allowed in queue = %lu\n", buf.msg_qbytes);
   fprintf(stdout, "Pid of last msgsnd() = %u\n", buf.msg_lspid);
   fprintf(stdout, "Time of last msgsnd() = %lu\n", buf.msg_stime);
   fprintf(stdout, "Pid of last msgrcv() = %u\n", buf.msg_lrpid);
   fprintf(stdout, "Time of last msgrcv() = %lu\n", buf.msg_rtime);

   return(0);
}
```

11-3-4 Remove a Message Queue

Just like other System V IPC resources such as semaphores and shared memory,
a message queue must be explicitly removed when it is no longer in use.
Otherwise, it will continue to occupy and consume system resources.

A program invokes the msgctl() function with the IPC_RMID command as
described in the above section to destroy a System V message queue.

Figure 11-7 lists a program removing a message queue.

Figure 11-7 Remove a message queue (msgrm.c)

```
/*
 * Remove a System V message queue.
 * Create the unique file pathname (IPCKEYPATH) before running this program.
 * Authored by Mr. Jin-Jwei Chen
 * Copyright (c) 2019, Mr. Jin-Jwei Chen. All rights reserved.
 */

#include <stdio.h>
#include <errno.h>
#include <sys/types.h>
#include <sys/ipc.h>
#include <sys/msg.h>
#include <string.h>

#define  IPCKEYPATH  "./mymsgq"  /* pick an unique pathname */
#define  PROJID       'q'        /* project id to make the key */

int main (int argc, char *argv[])
{
  int     msgqid = 0;
  int     key;
```

```
int       msgflags = (IPC_CREAT | 0660);
int       ret;

/* Compute the IPC key value from the pathname and project id */
/* ftok() got error 2 if the pathname (IPCKEYPATH) does not exist. */
if ((key = ftok(IPCKEYPATH, PROJID)) == (key_t)-1) {
  fprintf(stderr, "ftok() failed, errno=%d\n", errno);
  return(-errno);
}

/* Create or attach to a message queue using the derived key. */
msgqid = msgget(key, msgflags);
if (msgqid == (-1))
{
  fprintf(stderr, "msgget() failed, errno=%d\n", errno);
  return(-errno);
}
fprintf(stdout, "msgget() succeeded, msgqid=%d\n", msgqid);

/* Remove the message queue */
ret = msgctl(msgqid, IPC_RMID, (struct msqid_ds *)NULL);
if (ret == (-1))
{
  fprintf(stderr, "msgctl(IPC_RMID) failed, errno=%d\n", errno);
  return(-errno);
}
fprintf(stdout, "The message queue (id=%d) was successfully removed.\n",
  msgqid);

return(0);
}
```

11-4 Memory-mapped Files

Using a memory-mapped file is mapping some portion of a file on disk or some
file-like resource into a process' virtual memory such that a byte-for-byte
mapping between the two is created and that accessing the file contents
is done via accessing memory. It allows an application to treat the mapped
portion of a file as if it were in memory. That is, reading the mapped
memory is directly reading from the portion of file and writing to the
mapped memory is directly writing to that portion of the file.
In other words, **memory-mapped file allows a program to do I/O without
using I/O functions such as read() or write()**.

11-4-1 The mmap() and munmap() Functions

The POSIX.1 Standard defines a couple of APIs for doing memory-mapped files.

```
#include <sys/mman.h>

void *mmap(void *addr, size_t len, int prot, int flags,
           int fd, off_t offs);

int munmap(void *addr, size_t len);
```

The mmap() function allows you to map a file or a device into memory such
that you can read/write memory instead of doing input/output operations
to read/write information to or from the file or device.
Reading or writing memory is easier to program than performing file
or device I/O operations.

The mmap() call establishes a mapping between the address space
of the calling process at an address pa for len bytes to the memory
object represented by the file descriptor fd at offset offs for len bytes.
The value of pa is an implementation-defined function of the parameter
addr and the values of flags, which we will further describe below.

When successful, the mmap() function returns pa as its result.

Specifically, the mmap() function allows you to map a certain number of bytes
(as specified by the len argument) starting at a certain offset
(as specified by the offs argument) from a file (specified by the
file descriptor argument fd) into memory at a starting address
specified (by the addr argument).

The addr parameter specifies the starting virtual address of where you want
the mapped region to start. If this value is 0, then the operating system
will choose the starting address. This is typically what people do.
The returned value of the mmap() function is the starting memory address
of the mapped region.

The third argument prot indicates the desired protection of the memory.
It can be PROT_NONE or bitwise OR of one or more of the other flags:

    PROT_NONE - Data in mapped memory pages may not be accessed.
    PROT_READ - Data in mapped memory pages are readable.
    PROT_WRITE - Data in mapped memory pages are writeable.
    PROT_EXEC - Data in mapped memory pages can be executed.

The protection cannot conflict with the open mode of the file.

The flags argument specifies some map options as described below:

    MAP_FIXED - Do not map to a different memory address than specified
      by the addr argument. Setting this flag may cause mmap() to
      return MAP_FAILED and set errno to EINVAL.
      If the memory region specified by the addr and len arguments
      overlaps some existing mapping, then the whole page(s) of any
      previous mapping(s) in the overlapped area will be removed as if
      a munmap() call is done.

      If MAP_FIXED is not specified, then the operating system may decide
      to map to a different address as appropriate. A value of zero in the
      addr argument gives the operating system complete freedom to choose
      the starting address for the mapping.

    MAP_SHARED - Share whatever I write to the mapped object with all other
      processes that also map the same object. With this flag, writing to
      the mapped memory region is equivalent to writing to the mapped file.
      That is, with this flag write operations actually change the underlying

object. The actual file may or may not be updated right away
due to file system cache effect. Some of the updated contents may
not actually be updated until a msync() or munmap() is called.

MAP_PRIVATE - Making my write references private, not seen by other
processes. That is, create a private copy-on-write mapping.
As soon as I modify the mapped object, make a private copy of it
just for me to use.

The behavior is unspecified whether or not changes made to the file
after the mmap() call are visible in the mapped region.

Either MAP_SHARED or MAP_PRIVATE can be specified, but not both.

The fd parameter is the file descriptor of the file that you like to map.
Your program has to open the file before it can map the file into the
program's address space.

If success, mmap() function returns the starting memory address of the
mapping. From that address, the next len bytes of address space of
the calling process is legitimate. Similarly, the range starting at the
offs byte and continuing for len bytes in the file or device mapped
should be legitimate too. A program will get the Segmentation Fault error
if it tries to access beyond the memory range of the mapped region.

On failure, mmap() returns MAP_FAILED, which is ((void *) -1) and
errno is set to indicate the error.

The system performs mapping operations over whole pages, although the
value of len parameter does not need to meet the constraint.

The munmap() function deletes the mapping for the specified address range.
This will result in any references to addresses within the range illegal.
The memory region is automatically unmapped when the process is terminated.

However, closing the file descriptor does not unmap the region.

On success, munmap() returns 0. On error it returns -1, and errno is set.

Figure 11-8 lists two example programs of using memory-mapped files.
The mmap_writer program writes to a memory-mapped file and the mmap_reader
reads from the file using mmap(). The mmap_reader program waits until
mmap_writer comes along to create the file just in case the reader program
starts before the writer.

Figure 11-8 Memory-mapped files -- mmap_reader.c and mmap_writer.c

(a) mmap_writer.c

```
/*
 * Create a file and write messages to it using mmap().
 * Authored by Mr. Jin-Jwei Chen
 * Copyright (c) 2019, 2020 Mr. Jin-Jwei Chen. All rights reserved.
 */

#include <stdio.h>
```

```c
#include <errno.h>
#include <sys/types.h>
#include <sys/stat.h>
#include <fcntl.h>                  /* open() */
#include <unistd.h>                 /* lseek(), write() */
#include <string.h>
#include <sys/mman.h>               /* mmap(), munmap() */
#include <stdlib.h>

#define DEFAULT_FNAME  "./mymmap_file1"  /* default file name */
#define DEFAULT_KBS    1024  /* default file size in KB */
#define NMSGS          2000  /* number of messages to write */

/* Create a file of the specified size and return the file descriptor */
int create_file(char *fname, unsigned int fsize, int flags, mode_t mode)
{
  int     fd;        /* file descriptor */
  int     ret;

  if (fname == NULL)
    return(EINVAL);

  /* Create the file */
  fd = open(fname, flags, mode);
  if (fd == -1)
  {
    fprintf(stderr, "create_file(): open() failed, errno=%d\n", errno);
    return(-1);
  }

  /* Stretch the file size to the size specified. */
  ret = lseek(fd, fsize, SEEK_SET);
  if (ret == -1)
  {
    fprintf(stderr, "create_file(): lseek() failed, errno=%d\n", errno);
    close(fd);
    return(-2);
  }

  /* Write a null byte at end of file */
  ret = write(fd, "", 1);
  if (ret == -1)
  {
    fprintf(stderr, "create_file(): write() failed, errno=%d\n", errno);
    close(fd);
    return(-3);
  }

  return(fd);
}

int main (int argc, char *argv[])
{
  int     ret;
  int     fd;                      /* file descriptor */
  char    *fname = DEFAULT_FNAME;  /* default file name */
```

```c
int     kbs = DEFAULT_KBS;            /* default file size in KBs */
int     fsize = (DEFAULT_KBS*1024);   /* default file size in bytes */
char    *mapstart;                    /* starting address of the mmap */
char    *curptr;                      /* current pointer to memory map */
int     bytes;                        /* number of bytes written */
int     i;                            /* loop counter */

/* Print usage */
if ((argc > 1) &&
    ((strcmp(argv[1], "-h") == 0) || (strcmp(argv[1], "-help") == 0)))
{
  fprintf(stdout, "Usage: %s [KBs] [fname]\n", argv[0]);
  return(-1);
}

/* Get file size and file name, if any */
if (argc > 1)
{
  kbs = atoi(argv[1]);
  if (kbs <= 0)
    kbs = DEFAULT_KBS;
}

if (argc > 2)
  fname = argv[2];

/* Create the file */
fsize = (kbs * 1024);
fd = create_file(fname, fsize, (O_RDWR|O_CREAT|O_TRUNC), (mode_t)0664);

/* Map the file into memory */
mapstart = mmap(0, fsize, (PROT_READ|PROT_WRITE), MAP_SHARED , fd, 0);
if (mapstart == MAP_FAILED)
{
  fprintf(stderr, "mmap() failed, errno=%d\n", errno);
  close(fd);
  return(errno);
}

/* Write to the file by writing to the mapped memory */
curptr = mapstart;
for (i = 0; i < NMSGS; i++)
{
  bytes = sprintf(curptr, "%s%u%s", "This is message #", i, " from sender.\n");
  curptr = curptr + bytes;
}

/* Unmap it */
ret = munmap(mapstart, fsize);
if (ret == -1)
{
  fprintf(stderr, "munmap() failed, errno=%d\n", errno);
  close(fd);
  return(errno);
}
```

```
  /* Close the file */
  close(fd);
  return(0);
}
```

(b) mmap_reader.c

```
/*
 * Read a file using mmap() and print its contents.
 * Authored by Mr. Jin-Jwei Chen
 * Copyright (c) 2019, 2020 Mr. Jin-Jwei Chen. All rights reserved.
 */

#include <stdio.h>
#include <errno.h>
#include <sys/types.h>
#include <sys/stat.h>
#include <fcntl.h>                /* open() */
#include <unistd.h>               /* lseek(), write() */
#include <string.h>
#include <sys/mman.h>             /* mmap(), munmap() */
#include <stdlib.h>

#define DEFAULT_FNAME   "./mymmap_file1"  /* default file name */
#define DEFAULT_KBS     1024   /* default file size in KB */
#define NMSGS           2000   /* number of messages to write */

int main (int argc, char *argv[])
{
  int     ret = 0;
  int     fd;                      /* file descriptor */
  char    *fname = DEFAULT_FNAME;  /* default file name */
  int     kbs = DEFAULT_KBS;       /* default file size in KBs */
  int     fsize = (DEFAULT_KBS*1024);  /* default file size in bytes */
  char    *mapstart;               /* starting address of the mmap */
  char    *curptr;                 /* current pointer to memory map */
  int     bytes;                   /* number of bytes written */
  int     i;                       /* loop counter */

  /* Print usage */
  if ((argc > 1) &&
      ((strcmp(argv[1], "-h") == 0) || (strcmp(argv[1], "-help") == 0)))
  {
    fprintf(stdout, "Usage: %s [KBs] [fname]\n", argv[0]);
    return(-1);
  }

  /* Get file size and file name, if any */
  if (argc > 1)
  {
    kbs = atoi(argv[1]);
    if (kbs <= 0)
      kbs = DEFAULT_KBS;
  }

  if (argc > 2)
```

```
    fname = argv[2];

    /* Open the file. Wait until the writer starts. */
    fd = -1;
    while (fd < 0)
    {
      fd = open(fname, O_RDONLY);
      if (fd == -1)
        fprintf(stderr, "open() failed, errno=%d\n", errno);
    }

    /* Map the file into memory */
    mapstart = mmap(0, fsize, (PROT_READ), MAP_SHARED , fd, 0);
    if (mapstart == MAP_FAILED)
    {
      fprintf(stderr, "mmap() failed, errno=%d\n", errno);
      close(fd);
      return(errno);
    }

    /* Read from the file and dump its contents on stdout */
    ret = write(1, mapstart, fsize);
    if (ret == -1)
      fprintf(stderr, "Reading mapped file failed, errno=%d\n", errno);
    else
      fprintf(stdout, "%d bytes were read and printed.\n", ret);

    /* Unmap it */
    ret = munmap(mapstart, fsize);
    if (ret == -1)
    {
      fprintf(stderr, "munmap() failed, errno=%d\n", errno);
      close(fd);
      return(errno);
    }

    /* Close the file */
    close(fd);
    return(ret);
}
```

Note that with memory-mapped file when a program reads from memory the
operating system actually reads the file data from disk. That is,
behind the scene, the operating system actually does disk I/O.
Similarly, when a program writes to the mapped memory, the written data
eventually gets written to disk by the operating system behind the scene.

IPC Between Parent and Child Processes

Note that a memory-mapped region is part of a process' address space.
When a process spawns a child process, the child inherits the parent's
address space. Thus, a child inherits its parent's memory-mapped file too.
Because of this, a memory-mapped file can be used as an IPC mechanism
between a parent process and its child.

Platform Support

Most operating systems support memory-mapped files as defined by the POSIX Standard.

Many programming languages, including Java, Perl, Python and Ruby also have run-time libraries that support some form of memory-mapped file access as well.

11-4-2 Pros and Cons of Using Memory-mapped Files

As we said, first advantage of using memory-mapped files is easier and simpler coding. Once the file-to-memory mapping is done, programs read and write memory instead of calling I/O functions to perform file I/O.

When doing memory-mapped I/O, the operating system kernel may do I/O directly to the mapped memory buffer. If implemented this way, the performance is faster because it saves a data copying operation. This is second advantage. In doing normal file I/O when your program uses read()/write() functions, the operating system kernel typically does I/O to kernel's buffers -- the file system cache. Consequently, there is an extra copy operation to copy the data between kernel buffers and application program's memory buffers.

Memory maps are always aligned to memory page size. This means although a program can access just a few bytes in the mapped memory, file contents are brought in from disk to the mapped memory in memory page size, which is typically 4KB and is bigger than normal disk sector size.

Memory-mapped file I/O may have a performance advantage when used with very large files whereas performance may suffer for small files. This is because actual disk I/O is done in disk sector size in normal file I/O but in memory page size in memory-mapped file I/O. Waste may exist for accessing just small amount of data.

Also, if an I/O device is mapped, some I/O errors might occur which typically don't during memory access.

Note that for files larger than the CPU architecture's maximum address space, only part of the file may be able to be mapped at a time.

11-4-3 Memory-mapped File Is Not Shared Memory

It's worth pointing out that memory-mapped file is not shared memory. Many software engineers working in the industry call it shared memory, which is wrong.

There are many differences between shared memory and memory-mapped files.

First, shared memory does not (no need to) involve any file whereas memory-mapped file must involve a file.

Second, they are designed for different purposes. Shared memory is for multiple processes to share data in memory while memory-mapped file is for a process to do file I/O without actually invoking I/O functions. It does not have to share with other processes. In fact, with memory-mapped file, a process can choose to map the file private so that no other processes can see its updates at all. This is completely against shared memory's purpose.

Third, shared memory is largely for concurrent, random updates of the shared data while memory-mapped file is mainly for sequentially reading or writing a large file.

Fourth, with shared memory, there is only a single copy of the shared data in the entire system and any update to a shared memory is immediately seen by all processes sharing it. It's conceivably not necessarily so in memory-mapped file. In fact, depending on actual implementation, file system cache might keep updates by one process not being immediately seen by others, although the Standard says this should not happen when multiple processes map the same file region.

Fifth, the ways a program accesses shared memory and memory-mapped file are very different. Contents of shared memory also have specific structure and layout.

Lastly, these two technologies are defined in POSIX Standard as two unrelated, separate features using different sets of APIs.

Questions

1. Briefly describe all of the IPC mechanisms you know about, what they are for, and what their scopes are.

2. What are the differences between anonymous pipes and named pipes?

3. Compare the System V message queues with sockets in exchanging messages between processes and discuss their strength and weakness.

4. Explain what a memory-mapped file is and how it works.

Exercises

1. Write a program to create a message queue and then change its owner (to a different user) and permissions using the IPC_SET control command.

2. Write a message sender program and two message receiver programs. The sender communicates with the receivers by sending messages via a message queue.

3. Write a program in which the parent process creates a child process and communicates with it using named pipes (FIFO).

4. Write a program using the mkfifoat() function.

5. Write a client program and a server program where both communicate via a pair of named pipes. The client sends requests to the server using one named pipe and the server sends replies back to the client via another.

6. Write a server program that communicates with two clients using named pipes.

7. Modify the fifowriter.c and add the O_NONBLOCK flag to its open() call:

   fd = open(FIFO_PATH, O_WRONLY|O_NONBLOCK, mode);

   Compile and run the program without starting fiforeader.
   Explain what you see.

8. Write a program to copy a file using memory-mapped file I/O.
   The program should map both source and destination files into memory.

9. Modify the example programs mmap_reader.c and mmap_writer.c such that they run forever as mmap_writer acts as a log file writer and mmap_reader acts as a log file reader. When the log file gets full or reaches the end, the mmap_writer and mmap_reader should wrap around.

   How do you synchronize the writer and reader so that contents that have not been read by the reader do not get overwritten?
   Can you use a special file area to store read and write byte offsets for this synchronization?

10. Expand the example programs mmap_reader.c and mmap_writer.c such that multiple writers use a single file to communicate with a reader.
    Do you have to do anything to prevent the multiple writers from over-writing one another?

References

1. The Open Group Base Specifications Issue 7, 2018 edition
   IEEE Std 1003.1™-2017 (Revision of IEEE Std 1003.1-2008)
   Copyright © 2001-2018 IEEE and The Open Group
   http://pubs.opengroup.org/onlinepubs/9699919799/

2. AT&T UNIX System V Release 4 Programmer's Guide: System Services
   Prentice-Hall, Inc. 1990

3. https://en.wikipedia.org/wiki/Memory-mapped_file

Appendix A   List of Example Programs

Example programs in this book. Please look it up in the index for the page number
where each program is on.

For information about how to get access to an online copy of the example programs,
please send email to jjchen8@comcast.net or jcnh888@gmail.com with the ISBN number(s),
the 14-character book ID number(s), and the printing date of the book(s)
on the last page inside the back cover of the book(s) you have.

Chapter 3

3-3 triplelt.c, echoMsg.c
3-4 libtst1.exp (AIX)
3-5 uselink.c
3-6 useload.c

Chapter 4

4-8 gendataf.c
4-9 read.c
4-10 copy.c
4-11 (a) writer.c (b) reader.c
4-12 randomwr.c
4-14 readv.c
4-15 writev.c
4-16 aiowrite.c
4-17 aioread.c
4-18 directiowr.c

Chapter 5

5-2a linkat.c
5-3 symlink.c
5-4 unlink.c
5-5 remove.c
5-6 rename.c
5-8 pathconf.c
5-9 chdir.c
5-10 fstat.c
5-11 readdir_r.c
5-12 chmod.c

Appendix A

Chapter 6

Chapter 7

Appendix A

Appendix A

Chapter 10

Chapter 11

Chapter 12

Appendix A

15-30 (a) tlsserver1.c (b) tlsclient1.c
15-31 (a) tlsserver2.c (b) tlsclient2.c
15-32 (a) tlsserver3.c (b) tlsclient3.c
15-34 (a) tlsserver4.c (b) tlsclient4.c
15-35 tlsserver5.c
15-37 (a) tlsserver6.c (b) tlsclient6.c
15-38 (a) netlib.h   (b) netlib.c
15-39 (a) myopenssl.h   (b) mycryptolib.c

(240606)

INDEX

Index

H

I

Index

N

O

T

X

Y

Z

Made in the USA
Middletown, DE
08 June 2024